MEDIA LITERACY

EDITION **6**

W. JAMES POTTER

MEDIA LITERACY

EDITION 6

Los Angeles | London | New Delhi
Singapore | Washington DC

Los Angeles | London | New Delhi
Singapore | Washington DC

FOR INFORMATION:

SAGE Publications, Inc.
2455 Teller Road
Thousand Oaks, California 91320
E-mail: order@sagepub.com

SAGE Publications Ltd.
1 Oliver's Yard
55 City Road
London EC1Y 1SP
United Kingdom

SAGE Publications India Pvt. Ltd.
B 1/I 1 Mohan Cooperative Industrial Area
Mathura Road, New Delhi 110 044
India

SAGE Publications Asia-Pacific Pte. Ltd.
33 Pekin Street #02-01
Far East Square
Singapore 048763

Acquisitions Editor: Matthew Byrnie
Associate Editor: Nathan Davidson
Assistant Editor: Theresa Accomazzo
Editorial Assistant: Stephanie Palermini
Production Editor: Catherine M. Chilton
Copy Editor: Gillian Dickens
Typesetter: C&M Digitals (P) Ltd.
Proofreader: Sally Jaskold
Indexer: Hyde Park Publishing Services
Cover Designer: Scott Van Atta
Marketing Manager: Liz Thornton
Permissions Editor: Karen Ehrmann

Printed in the United States of America

Library of Congress Cataloging-in-Publication Data

Potter, W. James.

Media literacy/W. James Potter. — 6th ed.

p. cm.
Includes bibliographical references and index.

ISBN 978-1-4522-0625-7 (pbk. : acid-free paper)

1. Media literacy. I. Title.

P96.M4P68 2013
302.23—dc23   2011041810

This book is printed on acid-free paper.

12 13 14 15 16 10 9 8 7 6 5 4 3 2 1

Brief Contents

Detailed Contents

PART 3
Industry   83

6. Development of the Mass Media Industries   85

7. The Economic Game   95

8. The Current Picture   121

PART 4
Content   139

9. Mass Media Content and Reality   141

10. News   155

PART 5
Effects   257

14. Proactive Perspective on Media Effects   259

15. Broadening Our Perspective on Media Effects   277

PART 6
Confronting the Issues   293

16. Who Owns and Controls the Mass Media?   295

PART 7
The Springboard   393

Preface

Most of us think we are fairly media literate. We know the names of a great many television shows, films, magazines, books, song titles, and websites. We recognize the faces of many celebrities and know many facts about their lives. We know how to read and text. We can easily follow plots in movies and television shows. We understand what flashbacks mean, and we know enough to get scared when the soft background music builds to a shattering crescendo as a character steps into danger. We might even be skilled at playing games on a computer, downloading songs, and uploading videos onto our own websites. Clearly, we know how to expose ourselves to the media, absorb information from them, and be entertained by them.

Are we media literate? Yes, of course. We have acquired a great deal of information and developed remarkable skills. The abilities to speak a language, read, understand photographs, and follow narratives are achievements that many people take for granted.

We should not overlook what we have accomplished. However, it is also important to acknowledge that we all can be *much more* media literate. In many ways, your overall level of media literacy now is probably about the same as it was when you first became a teenager. Since that time, your information base has grown enormously about some types of media messages, such as popular songs, Internet sites, movies, and TV shows. However, your information base is not likely to have grown much in other areas—about how messages are produced and programmed, who controls the media, the economics of the industry, and how the media exert their continual effects on you and society. Thus, your current level of media literacy allows you to do many things with the media. However, you could be exercising much more control and getting more out of your media exposures—if you grew your knowledge in other areas.

The more you are aware of how the media operate and how they affect you, the more you gain control over those effects, and the more you will separate yourself from typical media users who have turned over a great deal of their lives to the media without realizing it. By "turning over a great deal of their lives to the media," I mean more than time and money, although both of those are considerable. I also mean that most people *have allowed the mass media to program them*. The mass media are very sophisticated—and successful—at programming our exposure habits. The media have programmed the way we look at the world by setting our expectations for relationships, attractiveness, success, celebrity, health, newsworthy events, problems, and solutions. When we operate at a low level of media literacy, we know enough to get by—that is, we can find the messages we want and process them enough to enjoy them. But those messages then go to work on our minds by shaping our beliefs and expectations about life; if we remain at a low level of media literacy, we are not aware of this shaping process and we therefore have no chance at altering the way the mass media are programming us. Ascending to higher levels of media literacy gives us the ability to gradually undo the media definitions and erase those "lines of code" that the media have programmed into our minds and replace the media programming with ideas of our own. This book is written to show you what it means to operate at a higher level of media literacy and thereby gain more power to use the media to achieve your own goals rather than letting the media use you to achieve their goals.

This book is composed of 22 chapters that are organized into seven parts: Introduction, Audiences, Industry, Content, Effects, Confronting the Issues, and Springboard. The two chapters in the Introduction section ask you to confront the following questions: Why should I work on developing my media literacy? and How should I go about such a task? In Chapter 1, I show you why developing media literacy is such an important thing to do. Chapter 2 presents what I call the "media literacy approach."

Part 2 presents three chapters to help you build your knowledge structures about audiences. Chapter 3 focuses on the audience from the individual's perspective, while Chapter 4 focuses on the audience from the mass media industries' perspective. Chapter 5 examines children as a special audience.

The three chapters in Part 3 deal with important concepts that you can use to build your knowledge structures about the media industries. Chapter 6 helps you see the media industries from a historical perspective. Using a life cycle structure, it shows what is behind the innovation and development of the media industries. An economic perspective is used in Chapter 7 to show the business foundations of the industries. Chapter 8 profiles the current nature of the mass media industries. These three chapters do not present many details because their purpose is to keep your focus on the general patterns and big ideas about the mass media industries. For those who want more details, look in Appendix A to see a detailed profile of each of the nine mass media industries.

Part 4 contains five chapters that focus on media content. Chapter 9 introduces the idea of content and presents the major characteristic of all media content—what I call "one-step remove" reality. Then, Chapter 10 focuses on news content, Chapter 11 on entertainment content, Chapter 12 on advertising content, and Chapter 13 on interactive content, such as mass media games and social networking media.

The two chapters in Part 5 deal with the effects of the media. How the effects processes work on us is explored in Chapter 14. Those processes are hardly ever simple or direct. More often, the media work in concert with many other factors that each serve to increase the probability that an effect may occur. When we take a broader perspective on effects, we can more accurately assess the influence of the media in our lives. This also puts us in a much better position to manage the effects of the media. Chapter 15 will help you expand your vision about what constitutes a media effect. Effects are both long term as well as immediate. Although they can influence our behavior, they also have profound influences on us cognitively, affectively, emotionally, and physiologically. And they have positive as well as negative effects. To illustrate the big ideas presented in Chapters 14 and 15, I have presented many examples of mass media effects in Appendix B.

Part 6 presents five issues that are important to consider when thinking of the media. Chapter 16 deals with the issue of how the ownership of the media has become more concentrated. Chapter 17 examines the issue of privacy and how the new media environment is making it much more difficult for you to protect your privacy. Chapter 18 takes up the issue of piracy of media messages by individuals and companies. Chapter 19 examines the issue of violence in the media and how this type of message might be affecting you and society. This section concludes with Chapter 20, which analyzes how money is driving the development of sports.

Finally, Part 7 wraps up the book with two chapters. Chapter 21 focuses on personal strategies for improving one's level of media literacy. Chapter 22 provides you with strategies to help other people with their media literacy.

HOW TO GET THE MOST OUT OF THIS BOOK

When you read each of these chapters, think in terms of developing your knowledge structures. Begin with the "key idea," which is presented at the beginning of each chapter. Then look at the outline to see the list of the important topics covered in that chapter. Outlines will show you the major branches off that key idea and each branch's supporting ideas. Then read the text actively. By *actively*, I mean don't just scan the words and sentences; instead, start with an agenda of questions, and then as you scan through each section, look specifically for answers to your questions. After you have read through a chapter, close the book and see how much you can recall. Can you remember only a random mass of facts, or can you envision an organized set of knowledge structured by your questions?

This book has a self-help tone as it presents guidance and practical exercises to help you achieve higher levels of media literacy. Do not get caught in the trap of thinking that it is sufficient to memorize the facts in each chapter and then stop thinking about the material. Simply memorizing facts will not help you increase your media literacy much. Instead, you need to *internalize* the information by drawing it into your own experiences. Continually ask yourself, "How does this new information fit in with what I already know?" "Can I find an example of this in my own life?" and "How can I *apply* this when I deal with the media?" The exercises at the end of each chapter will help you get started with this. The more you think through the exercises and the more you develop new exercises for yourself, the more you will be internalizing the information and thus making it more a natural part of the way you think. For example, in the chapter on broadening your perspective on media effects, I present a four-dimensional scheme. If you simply memorize this scheme, it may help you a bit on a test, but memorization alone won't help you become a more acute observer of media effects. To develop such acuity, you need to *apply* the scheme to guide your observations of your own behaviors and the behaviors of others around you. Thus, the more you practice spotting and naming these effects, the more you will be internalizing the information and learning a useful skill that will help you the rest of your life.

If you want to do more reading on a particular topic, start with the books and other sources of information I recommend at the end of most chapters in the Further Reading lists. Also, you will notice that many chapters also have a Keeping Up to Date section with several sources of information. This book has gone through a complicated process of publication and marketing since I finished writing the manuscript. So by the time you read the book, some of the facts and figures may have gone out of date in this fast-changing topic of mass media. You can get more timely information by going to the websites I suggest in these Keeping Up to Date sections.

In summary, the purpose of this book is to help you develop strong, accurate knowledge structures about the media. Will the book provide you with *all* the information you need?

No. That would require too much information to fit into one book; you will need to continue reading. At the end of most chapters, I suggest several books for further reading on the topic of that chapter. Although some of those books are fairly technical, most of them are easy to read and very interesting.

ANCILLARIES

Media Literacy, Sixth Edition is accompanied by the following supplements, tailored to match the content of the book:

Student Study Site (www.sagepub.com/potter6e): The study site features a variety of resources, including chapter-specific Web quizzes, Internet resources and activities, and recommended readings. There are also discussion and writing questions, an updated precourse media literacy quiz, and a list of media literacy organization websites.

Instructor Teaching Site (www.sagepub.com/potter6e): The password-protected instructor teaching site includes a test bank, PowerPoint slides, and key points and ideas for every chapter. An updated precourse media literacy quiz (with answer key), sample syllabi, video links, activities, and discussion questions are also provided to aid in teaching your course. If you are a qualified adopter and have your e-mail address and password on file with SAGE, you may log in to the site and begin accessing the instructor materials immediately. If you are not yet a qualified adopter with SAGE, you will need to register on the site.

TO CONCLUDE

This book is an introduction. It is designed to show you the big picture so you can get started efficiently on increasing your own media literacy. It is important to get started now. The world is rapidly changing because of newer information technologies that allow people to not only access all kinds of information quickly but also create and share their own messages.

I hope you will have fun reading this book. And I hope it will expose you to new perspectives from which you can perceive much more about the media. If it does, you will be gaining new insights about your old habits and interpretations. If this happens, I hope you will share your new insights and "war stories" with me. Much of this book has been written to reflect some of the problems and insights my students have had in the media literacy courses I have taught. I have learned much from them. I'd like to learn even more from you. So let me know what you think and send me a message at wjpotter@comm.ucsb.edu.

See you on the journey!

Acknowledgments

This book project has traveled a very long distance from its initial conceptualization in the mid-1990s. Since then, I have had the privilege of using various versions of the book with hundreds of students at Florida State University, UCLA, Stanford University, and the University of California at Santa Barbara. These students helped me form the idea into a useful book for a broad range of undergraduates and refine the material through two subsequent editions. I thank them for every question, every puzzled look, and every smile of satisfaction from an insight gained. Over the years, *Media Literacy* has been translated from English into four other languages, which makes it accessible to readers in many parts of the world. Some of those readers have provided me with their reactions, and I thank them.

I thank the many reviewers whom SAGE called on to critique the text in each edition. Some contacted me directly; others chose to remain anonymous. In all cases, their comments were valuable. The reviewers include Angela Paradise, Stonehill College; Steven Middleton, Morehead State University; Clare Scully, Carlow College; Christofer Meissner, Lake Region State College; Stephanie Brommer, City University of Seattle; Tim Chandler, Hardin-Simmons University; Ted Satterfield, Northwestern Oklahoma State University; Narin Yegiyan, University of California Davis; Sharyn Obsatz, Santa Monica College; Sarah Stone Watt, Pepperdine University; Kevin Carragee, Suffolk University; and Faiz Hirji, McMaster University.

I am grateful for the support of SAGE with its many highly skilled staff members over the years. First, I need to thank Margaret Seawell, who initially signed this project and then shepherded it through three editions, then Todd Armstrong who took over for Margaret on the fourth and fifth editions, then Matt Byrnie who took over for Todd and gave me considerable help with this sixth edition. I also must thank Todd's assistant, Deya Saoud, as well as Matt's assistant, Nathan Davidson. In the Production Department, Astrid Virding skillfully took the first edition from manuscript to bound book, as did Claudia Hoffman on the second edition, Tracy Alpern on the third, Astrid Virding again on the fourth and fifth editions, and Catherine Chilton on the sixth edition. They made it look easy, although there must have been days when it was anything but. I also want to thank Carmel Withers in Marketing and SAGE salespeople for their enthusiastic support of the new edition. Finally, I must thank the many fine copy editors SAGE has assigned to this project over the years, especially Gillian Dickens, who did a great job on this sixth edition.

If you like this book, then I share the credit of success with all the people I mentioned above. If you find a mistake, a shortcoming, or a misinterpretation, then it is my fault for not fully assimilating all the high-quality help I have been privileged to experience.

Introduction

This introductory part of the book focuses your attention on the foundational issues of why media literacy is so important and what it means to be media literate. This first part of the book consists of two chapters. The first chapter shows you how the information problem has changed from one of gaining access to one of protecting oneself from drowning in the flood of detail. The second chapter presents a definition of media literacy and then explains the major advantages of media literacy.

As you read this introductory part of the book, keep the following questions active in your mind, and you will stay focused on the most important ideas in the two chapters.

- Why is information a problem in our current culture?
- What specifically does it mean to be more media literate?
- Why is it important for me to work on increasing my level of media literacy?

CHAPTER 1

Key Idea: To survive in our information-saturated culture, we put our minds on "automatic pilot" to protect ourselves from the flood of media messages we constantly encounter. The danger with this automatic processing of messages is that it allows the media to condition our thought processes.

Living in the Message-Saturated World

MESSAGE SATURATION

Our culture is saturated with information, and the amount of information available to each of us continues to grow at an ever increasing rate. For example, think about the one medium of books. Google estimated that by 2009, there had been 130 million published throughout the world in all of modern history (Mashable, 2011). That number is so huge, it is difficult to grasp its size. So let's say you wanted to read all these books; to do so, you would have to start at age 5 and read 70 books each and every second of every day until you were 65 to get through them all—if you took no breaks. Of course, by the time you finished those 130 million books, there would likely be a huge pile of new books for you to read. As of now, about 1,500 new books are published each day throughout the world, and the rate of book publishing is increasing each year (Fiore, 2011). In addition, radio stations send out 65.5 million hours of original programming each year, and television adds another 48 million hours. Add to this the massive amount of information produced by the other traditional media of newspapers, magazines, film, and recordings, and you can start to see the truly stunning size of the flood of information.

What is even more alarming is that the amount of information being produced and distributed by the traditional media mentioned in the previous paragraph is relatively small compared to the amount of information produced and made available by the newer media, especially by computers and the Internet. The size of the World Wide Web has grown to 35 billion indexed Web pages (WorldWideWebSize.com, 2011). Thus, for every one of the 130 million books in existence, there are now 270 Web pages. At this point, you may be thinking that if the average book is about 270 pages, then the total of Web pages would be no larger than the total of published book pages, and you would be right. However, people have been writing and publishing books for several millennia, but the contributions to the Web have all taken place within the span of your lifetime.

More information has been generated since you were born than the sum total of all information throughout all recorded history up until the time of your birth. Half of all the scientists who have ever lived are alive today and producing information. Also, the number of people in the United States who identify themselves as musicians has more than doubled in the past four decades, the number of artists has tripled, and the number of authors has increased fivefold (U.S. Bureau of the Census, 2011). But the largest portion of information generated each day is by ordinary people who send e-mails and update their Web pages and blogs. There are now 2 billion Internet users, and they send and receive 300 billion e-mail messages each day; Twitter has 70 million tweets per day; YouTube has more than 50,000 hours of video uploaded by users every day; and Facebook reports that 100 million photos are uploaded each and every day (Pingdom, 2011). In 2010, 500 billion images were captured in photos. YouTube was streaming more than a billion videos a day (Gleick, 2011, p. 397).

In 2010, the world produced 1 zettabyte, which is 1 trillion gigabytes, or the equivalent of 250 billion DVDs—that is more than 60 DVDs of information produced in that one year alone for every person alive. And this figure is expected to grow to 35 zettabytes by 2020 ("The Leaky Corporation," 2011).

The amount of information available to us is truly overwhelming. And it continues to grow at an ever accelerating rate. The challenge is no longer accessing information; instead, the challenge is organizing it so that we can make meaningful use of it rather than letting it drown us in chaos. For example, if you Google "information overload," you will get 7.3 million results in .07 seconds. There is even a clutter of different terms referring to this idea—data asphyxiation, data smog, information fatigue syndrome, cognitive overload, and time famine ("Too Much Information," 2011).

HIGH DEGREE OF EXPOSURE

People continue to spend more and more time with the media. Over the past three decades, every new survey of media use has shown that the average person is increasing exposure

every year. As the figures were reaching about 8 hours per day by 2000, researchers were finding that the increases in exposure were more and more due to multitasking, especially with the newer generations. For example, D. F. Roberts and Foehr (2008) found that the average child (ages 8–18) was exposed to 7:50 hours per day of daily electronic media but packed all that exposure into just over 5:48 hours of media use. This means that the amount of media exposure is not constrained to the limit of 24 hours in a day. With multitasking, a person can listen to recorded music, text friends, and watch video on a pop-up window all at the same time and thus get credit for 3 hours of media exposure for each hour of clock time.

As our exposure to the media increases each year, it comes now primarily from video games and computer usage, which is typically engaged at the same time as other media use, especially listening to music or watching television (D. F. Roberts & Foehr, 2008). The use of these newer technologies is so prominent among people ages 8 to 18 that a report generated by the Kaiser Family Foundation characterized them as the "M Generation" for their focus so strongly on media use. This report found that children and adolescents were spending 49 minutes per day with video games and another 1:02 with the computer (Kaiser Family Foundation, 2005).

Worldwide, there are more than 2 billion Internet users, which is about one third of the world's population (Pingdom, 2011). In the United States, four out of every five people 12 years old and older are Internet users (Project for Excellence in Journalism, 2006), and the average person now spends more than 2 hours per day with the computer.

It is clear that the media are an extremely important part of people's everyday lives. We are constantly connected to the media either directly or indirectly. Direct exposure is when we perceive a media message, such as listen to a recorded song, watch a video, or surf the Web. Indirect exposure occurs when we think about some element in a media message while we are not being exposed to it at the time; this includes talking about messages with friends, thinking about why you like certain kinds of songs, and making judgments about your friends by using standards for people (attractiveness, wittiness, trustworthiness, etc.) that the media have conditioned. In our information-saturated culture, we are constantly connected to our friends, our society, and the entire world through the media.

THE INFORMATION PROBLEM

Individual people and societies have always had a problem with information. For millennia, the information problem was one of generating enough information about important aspects of life and then providing people with access to that information. But with the rise of the mass media, especially over the past half century, the information problem has shifted from one of gaining access to one of protecting ourselves from too much information.

To illustrate this point, let's focus on just one medium—books. Until about two centuries ago, the majority of the population could not read, and even if it could, there were few books available. In the early 1300s, the Sorbonne Library in Paris contained only 1,338 books and yet was thought to be the largest library in Europe. Only elites had access to those books. Today, there are many libraries with more than 8 million books, and they lend out their books to millions of people every year. In 2004, Google embarked on a project to scan into a database all 130 million books that had been published worldwide up to that point and make all that information available to Google users. By the end of 2010, Google was about 10% through this task.

With literacy rates high, the ease of buying books from websites, and the availability of free public libraries in every town, especially with the Google book digitization project, *access* to books is no problem. Time, however, is a big problem. We are now well beyond the point where a person can keep up with the easily available messages from even only one medium. To illustrate, there are now about 31 million hours of original TV programming each year throughout the world. If you wanted to watch all the television programming broadcast in this year alone, it would take you about 35 centuries—if you took no breaks!

We live in an environment that is far different from any environment humans have ever experienced before. And the environment changes at an ever increasing pace. This is due to the accelerating generation of information and the sharing of that information through the increasing number of media channels and the heavy traffic of media vehicles traversing those channels. Messages are being delivered to everyone, everywhere, constantly. We are all saturated with information, and each year the media are more aggressive in seeking our attention. It is a hopeless expectation to keep up with all the information available. The most important challenge now lies in making good selections when the media are constantly offering us millions of messages on any given topic.

The Challenge of Selection

How do we meet the challenge of making selections from among the overwhelming number of messages in the constant and increasing flood of information? The answer to this question is that we encounter almost all media messages in a state of automaticity— that is, we put our minds on "automatic pilot," where our minds automatically filter out almost all message options. I realize that this might sound strange, but think about it. We cannot possibly consider every possible message and consciously decide whether to pay attention to it. There are too many messages to consider. So our minds have developed routines that guide this filtering process very quickly and efficiently so we don't have to spend much, if any, mental effort.

To illustrate this automatic processing, consider what you do when you go to the supermarket to buy food. Let's say you walk into the store with a list of 25 items you need to buy and 15 minutes later you walk out of the store with your 25 items. In this scenario, how many decisions have you made? The temptation is to say 25 decisions, because you needed to have made a decision to buy each of your 25 items. But what about all the items you *decided not to buy?* The average supermarket today has about 40,000 items on its shelves. So you actually made 40,000 decisions in the relatively short time you were in the supermarket—25 decisions to buy a product and 39,975 decisions not to buy a product.

Our culture is a grand supermarket of media messages. Those messages are everywhere whether we realize it or not, except that there are far more messages in our culture than there are products in any supermarket.

Automatic Routines

The human mind is wondrously complex. It can perform all kinds of creative tasks such as imagining the future, constructing fantasies, making up lies, and contemplating an infinitely wide range of if-then speculations. It also performs many mundane tasks with remarkable efficiency by using automatic routines, which are sequences of behaviors or thoughts that we learn from experience and then apply again and again with little effort. Once you have learned a sequence—such as tying your shoes, brushing your teeth, driving to school, or playing a song on the guitar—you can perform it over and over again with very little effort compared to the effort it took you to learn it in the first place. As we learn to do something, we are writing the instructions like a computer code in our minds. Once that code is written, it can later be loaded into our minds and run automatically to guide us through the task with very little thought.

To navigate our way efficiently day to day through our information-saturated culture, we rely on automatic processing. Psychologists refer to this automatic processing of information as *automaticity.* Automaticity is a state where our minds operate without any conscious effort from us. Thus, we can perform even complicated tasks routinely without even thinking about them. For example, typing is a relatively complicated task, but after we learn to type, we do it automatically. Think about your experience in first learning to type. You had to think of the individual letters in each word, think about which key controlled which letter, and then command a finger to press the correct key. It took you a long time to type out a word. But with practice, you are now able to type out paragraphs without thinking much about which finger needs to strike which key in which order. Now when you type, you enter the state of automaticity where well-developed habits guide your actions without requiring you to think about them.

In our everyday lives—like when we enter a supermarket—we load an automatic program into our mind that tells it what to look for and ignore the rest. Automatic processing guides most—but certainly not all—of our media exposures. With automatic processing, we experience a great deal of media messages without paying much attention to them; thus, we have the feeling that we are filtering them out because we are not paying conscious attention to them. Every once in a while, something in the message or in our environment triggers our conscious attention to a media message. To illustrate this, imagine yourself driving in your car, with music from your iPod playing through your car's sound system, but your attention is on the conversation you are having with your friend who is seated next to you. Then your favorite song starts playing, and your attention shifts from the conversation to the music. Or perhaps your conversation is interrupted when you friend notices that the radio is playing her favorite song, and she starts singing along with the music. In both scenarios, you are being exposed to a stream of media messages from your car sound system without paying conscious attention to them, but then something happens to trigger your conscious attention to the music from the radio.

Advantages and Disadvantages of Automatic Processing

The huge advantage of automatic processing of information in our environment is that it helps us get through a great many decisions with almost no effort. However, there are some serious disadvantages. With so many messages constantly available, we are overwhelmed and begin to think that the value of any one message is almost nothing, so we make poor exposure decisions and while we are exposing ourselves to more and more messages, we are paying less and less attention to them. With reduced concentration, our increased exposure does not translate into increased learning. In fact, the opposite is true; it is likely that the more time people spend with the media in general, the less likely they are to learn from any one message, especially with the multitasking further reducing attention to any one message. With so many messages and so many exposures, the value of any one message keeps getting reduced. In 1971, the Nobel Prize–winning economist Herbert Simon observed that "a wealth of information crates a poverty of attention" (Angwin, 2009, p. 239).

When our minds are on automatic pilot, we may be missing a lot of messages that might be helpful or enjoyable to us. We might not have programmed all the triggers we need to help us get out of automatic processing when a useful message comes our way. Returning to the supermarket example from above, let's say you are very health conscious. Had you been less concerned with efficiency when you went into the supermarket, you would have considered a wider range of products and read their labels for ingredients. Not all low-fat products have the same fat content; not all products with vitamins added have the same vitamins or the same proportions. Or perhaps you are very price conscious. Had you been less concerned with efficiency, you would have considered a wider variety of competing products and looked more carefully at the unit pricing, so you could get more value for your money. When we are *too* concerned with efficiency, we lose opportunities to expand our experience and to put ourselves in a position to make better decisions that can make us healthier, wealthier, and happier.

THE BIG QUESTION

Given that we live in a culture highly saturated with information and given that we protect ourselves from this flood of information with automatic routines programmed into our minds, the big question becomes the following: Who has programmed the computer code that governs these automatic routines?

For some of us, the answer to this question is that *we* have programmed the code that governs our automatic routines. When we are aware of our needs for certain kinds of messages, it is easy to program our triggers. Also, if we have an intensely enjoyable reaction to a media message, we consciously decide to look for that kind of message again and again. And if we have a strong negative reaction to a media message, we consciously decide to avoid that type of message every time in the future. When we consciously think through our decisions, we program our code.

For many of us, our automatic code has been programmed by the mass media and advertisers. When we are not consciously paying attention and carefully evaluating our

media exposures, the mass media continually reinforce certain behavioral patterns of exposure until they become automatic habits. For many of us, we turn on the radio every time we get in our cars, turn on the television as soon as we get home, and turn on our computers when we get up in the morning. Advertisers constantly program the way we think about ourselves. Advertisers program an uneasy self-consciousness into our minds so that we are on the lookout for products that will make us look, feel, and smell better. Advertisers have programmed many of us into a shopping habit. People in America spend more time shopping than people in any other country. Americans go to shopping centers about once a week, more often than they go to houses of worship, and Americans now have more shopping centers than high schools. A few years ago, 93% of teenage girls surveyed said that shopping was their favorite activity (B. Schwartz, 2004). Advertising works by programming our automatic routines so that we shop even when it would be in our best interest to do other things.

For most of us, our minds have been programmed by a combination of factors—our friends, our parents, the mass media, and advertisers. Some of these agents of programming truly know you and have your best interests in mind as they reinforce your special strengths and help you overcome your troublesome weaknesses; they are trying to make you happier and make your life better. Other agents of programming are trying to use you as a tool to achieve their goals, which are often very different from your own goals. When this occurs, the programming makes you less and less happy as they "help" you solve problems you don't have and make worse the problems you do have. When you allow others to dominate the programming of your mind, then when your mind runs on automatic pilot, you end up behaving in ways that achieve the goals of those programmers rather than behaving in ways that would make you happier. Therefore, it is important that you periodically examine the code that has been programmed into your mind.

The purpose of this book is to help you analyze the code that has been programmed into your mind by the constant flow of mass media messages up to this point in your life. To be able to conduct such an analysis, you need certain kinds of knowledge, particular skills, and the willingness to use that knowledge and skills. In short, you need to know how to increase your level of media literacy.

MEDIA LITERACY

Taking control is what media literacy is all about. Becoming more media literate gives you a much clearer perspective to see the border between your real world and the world manufactured by the media. When you are media literate, you have clear maps to help you navigate better in the media world so that you can get to those experiences and information you want without becoming distracted by those things that are harmful to you. You are able to build the life that *you* want rather than letting the media build the life *they* want for you.

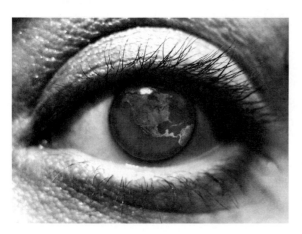

Those who slip into media illiteracy will get swept along in a tide of harmful messages. This condition of media illiteracy has been characterized as "potentially as damaging and poisonous to the human spirit as contaminated water and food is to our physical well-being" (Dennis, 1993, p. 4). The metaphor of pollution is an apt one. The media industries provide us with many products that we desire—products that are good for us—but these same media industries are also producing harmful by-products and dumping them into our culture. If we

are not literate, we don't know the difference, and we consume the bad with the good.

This book will show you how you can become more media literate. It will present you with many things to think about, and the more sensitive you are to these issues on a day-to-day basis, the more you will be able to increase the amount of code you are programming into your automatic routines and the less the media will be programming your code without your awareness or permission.

SUMMARY

We cannot physically avoid the glut of information that aggressively seeks our attention in our culture. Instead, we protect ourselves by psychologically avoiding almost all of the messages in the flood of information. We do this by keeping our minds on automatic pilot most of the time. This automaticity allows us to avoid almost all messages and to do so efficiently.

Automaticity, however, comes with a price. We allow the media to condition us while we are in this automatic state. The media condition us to habitual exposure patterns. They want to attract us to the messages they have planned for us, not necessarily the messages that are most useful for us. This increases the risk that we will miss many of the messages that might have higher value for us. The media also condition us to accept unchallenged the meaning they present in their messages. This increases the risk we will accept faulty meaning.

Chapter Resources: To test your knowledge and learn more about the topics discussed in this chapter, visit the Student Study Site at www.sagepub.com/potter6e.

FURTHER READING

Gleick, J. (2011). *The information: A history, a theory, a flood*. New York: Pantheon. (526 pages including index)

This is a rather long book that gets very technical in places with mathematical and engineering-type descriptions. But it is a worthwhile read if you really want to understand the nature of information and how it has changed forms over the years.

Schwartz, B. (2004). *The paradox of choice: Why more is less.* New York: HarperCollins. (265 pages including end notes and index)

Barry Schwartz writes about how much choice the average person is now confronted with everyday. He argues that increasing choice up to a point is a good thing but that beyond that point, increasing choice overwhelms people, and they cease to make good decisions.

Wright, A. (2007). *Glut: Mastering information through the ages.* Washington, DC: Joseph Henry Press. (252 pages with index)

The author, who characterizes himself as an information architect, takes a historical approach to showing how humans have evolved in the way they generate, organize, and use information. He argues that all information systems are either nondemocratic and top-down (a hierarchy) or peer to peer and open (a network). Tracing the development of human information, he uses perspectives from mythology, library science, biology, neurology, and culture. He uses this historical background to critique the nature of information on the Internet.

KEEPING UP TO DATE

For some chapters, the material I talk about is very fluid and quickly changes. Therefore, some of the facts and figures I present may be out of date by the time you read a particular chapter. To help you find more up-to-date figures, I have included some sources of information that you can check out to get the most recent figures available.

Infoniac.com (http://www.infoniac.com/hi-tech)

This site presents information about the growth of information in the world, and more generally, it provides information about new developments in technologies.

Pingdom (royal.pingdom.com)

This is a blog written by members of the Pingdom team on a wide variety of topics concerning the Internet and Web tech issues. Pingdom is a company that provides Internet services to companies around the world.

Statistical Abstract of the United States (http://www.census.gov/compendia/statab/)

The Department of Commerce releases a new statistical abstract every year. For updates on this material in this chapter, go to the section on Information and Communication.

WorldWideWebSize.com (http://www.worldwidewebsize.com/)

This site constantly updates the size of the Web from how many Web pages are indexed by the major search engines.

Media Literacy Approach

CHAPTER 2

*Key Idea: Media
literacy is a set of
perspectives that
we actively use to
expose ourselves to
the media and
interpret the
meaning of the
messages we
encounter. It is
multidimensional
and a continuum.*

As we learned in the first chapter, we are constantly flooded with a huge number of messages from the mass media. We must screen out all but a tiny percentage. To help us do this screening with the least amount of mental effort, we put our minds on automatic pilot, where our minds automatically screen out messages without thinking about the process until a particular message triggers our attention. This filtering out and triggering attention is governed by a kind of mental computer code. While this process of screening is largely automatic, we can exert greater control over it if we increase our media literacy by building strong knowledge structures that we can actively use as perspectives on the media.

WHAT IS MEDIA LITERACY?

Many people have written about media literacy (for an assortment of these ideas, see the list of Further Reading at the end of this chapter). One characteristic about all this thinking about media literacy is that authors will focus on different kinds of media. The most fundamental use of the term *literacy* applies to a person's ability to read the written word. With the advent of additional technologies to convey messages, people have also written about the need for visual literacy, story literacy, and computer literacy, to name a few areas of media focus. In this book, I take a broad perspective that is concerned with people's ability to access and process information from any form of transmission.

Another characteristic of most of the writings about media literacy is a focus on the mass media as being harmful. In this book, I agree that the mass media are capable of producing harmful effects on individuals and on society at large; however, I take a more balanced approach and acknowledge that the mass media also offer many positive effects. To illustrate this point, let's briefly consider the criticism that newer forms of technology have harmed people's ability to write well. On one side of this controversy are people like John Sutherland, an English professor at the University College of London, who argues that PowerPoint presentations have taken the place of well-reasoned essays, that Facebook reinforces narcissistic drivel, and that texting has reduced language into a "bleak, bald, sad shorthand" (quoted in Thompson, 2009). He says that today's technologies of communication that encourage or even require shorter messages like Twitter have shortened people's attention spans and therefore their ability to think in longer arcs, which is required for constructing well-reasoned essays. Arguing against this position are people like Andrea Lunsford, who is a professor of writing and rhetoric at Stanford University. Lunsford is convinced that the newer information technologies have actually increased literacy. She says, "I think we're in the midst of a literacy revolution the likes of which we haven't seen since Greek civilization" and further argues that these new technologies of communication are not killing our ability to write well but instead pushing it in new directions of being more personal, creative, and concise. She reached this conclusion after systematically analyzing more than 14,000 student writing samples over a 5-year period. She explains that young people today are adept at understanding the needs of their audiences and writing messages especially crafted to appeal to them. For today's youth, writing is about discovering themselves, organizing their thoughts concisely, managing impressions, and persuading their readers. The point of this illustration is that the mass media, with their forms of information and requirements for producing and processing that information, may be reducing some skills, but at the same time, the media are also offering opportunities to increase other skills. Thus, it is shortsighted to view the mass media as either all good or all bad. Instead, we need to view this as change—that is, some things deteriorate but other things get better. The key is to avoid looking only at the negative but to also consider the positive. When we take a more balanced approach, we are in a better position to adapt to our changing world in a way that not only avoids the negative but also embraces the positive.

Media literacy focuses on adapting to our changing world by being skilled at assessing the meaning in any kind of messages, organizing that meaning so that it is useful, and then constructing messages to convey that meaning to others. Thus, the idea of literacy incorporates many different skills. Some types of media foster the development of one set of skills, while other media help with the development of another set of skills. The key to becoming more literate lies not in arguing for the importance of one set of skills over another set but rather in developing a broad set of skills that can help with any type of message from any type of medium. Skills are the tools that help us gain control over our mental programming. Skills are essential, but we need more.

THE THREE BUILDING BLOCKS OF MEDIA LITERACY

The three building blocks of media literacy are personal locus, knowledge structures, and skills. These three are necessary to build a person's wider set of perspectives on the media. Your personal locus is the energy and your plan. The knowledge structures are the raw materials. The skills are the tools.

Personal Locus

Your personal locus is composed of goals and drives. The goals shape the information-processing tasks by determining what gets filtered in and what gets ignored. The more you are aware of your goals, the more you can direct the process of information seeking. And the stronger your drives for information are, the more effort you will expend to attain your goals. However, when your locus is weak (i.e., you are not aware of particular goals and your drive energy is low), you will default to media control where you allow the media to exercise a high degree of control over exposures and information processing.

The more you know about this locus and the more you make conscious decisions to shape it, the more you can control the process of media influence on you. The more you pay conscious attention to your locus, the more you control the process of information acquisition and usage. The more you engage your locus, the more you will be increasing your media literacy. Being media literate, however, does not mean that the locus is always fully engaged. This is an impossible task because no one can maintain that high a degree of concentration continuously. Media literacy is a process, not a product. Therefore, becoming more media literate means that a person uses the locus more (thus less time with mindless exposures) and uses it more actively.

The locus operates in two modes: conscious and unconscious. When the locus operates in the conscious mode, you are aware of options and can exercise your will in making decisions. In contrast, when the locus operates in the unconscious mode, the decisions are made outside of your awareness and control. In both modes, knowledge structures can get formed and elaborated. However, when you are consciously using your locus, you are in control of the information processing and meaning making, but when your locus is operating in the unconscious mode, the media exert their most powerful effect.

Knowledge Structures

Knowledge structures are sets of organized information in a person's memory. Knowledge structures do not occur spontaneously; they must be built with care and precision. They are not just a pile of facts; they are made by carefully crafting pieces of information into an overall design. The structure helps us see the patterns. We use these patterns as maps to tell us where to get more information and also where to go to retrieve information we have previously crafted into our knowledge structure.

Information is the essential ingredient in knowledge structures. But not all information is equally useful to building a knowledge structure. Some information is rather superficial, such as the names of television shows or the melodies of popular music. If all a person has is the recognition of surface information such as lyrics to television show theme songs, names of characters and actors, settings for shows, and the like, he or she is operating a low level of media literacy because this type of information addresses only the question of "what." The more useful information comes in the form of the answers to the questions of "how" and "why." But remember that you first need to know something about the "what" before you can delve deeper into the questions of how and why.

In everyday language, the terms *information* and *knowledge* are often used as synonyms, but in this book, they have meanings very different from one another. Information is piecemeal and transitory, whereas knowledge is structured, organized, and of more enduring significance. Information resides in the messages, whereas knowledge resides in a person's mind. Information gives something to the person to interpret, whereas knowledge reflects that which has already been interpreted by the person.

Information is composed of facts. Facts by themselves are not knowledge any more than a pile of lumber is a house. Knowledge requires structure to provide context and thereby exhibit meaning. Think of messages as the raw materials and skills as the tools you use to do something with the raw materials. That "something" is in the service of attaining the goal of pulling the information out of the messages and turning that information into knowledge—that is, to reconstruct the information so that it will contribute to our knowledge structures. A characteristic of higher media literacy is the ability and habit of transforming information into knowledge structures.

While I'm on the topic of distinguishing information from knowledge, I also need to define a few terms related to the idea of information: message, factual information, and social information. Messages are those instruments that deliver information to us. Information is the content of those messages. Messages can be delivered in many different media—computers, smartphones, television, radio, CDs, video games, books, newspapers, magazines, websites, conversations, lectures, concerts, signs along the streets, labels on the products we buy, and so on. They can be large (an entire Hollywood movie) or small (one utterance by one character in a movie).

Messages are composed of two kinds of information: factual and social. A fact is something raw, unprocessed, and context free. For example, when you watch the news and hear messages about terrorism, those messages are composed of facts, such as the following: *Barack Obama was elected to the office of president of the United States in the fall of 2008.* This statement contains facts. Facts are discrete bits of information, such as names (of people, places, characters, etc.), dates, titles, definitions of terms, formula, lists, and the like.

Social information is composed of accepted beliefs that cannot be verified by authorities in the same way factual information can be. This is not to say that social information is less valuable or less real to people. Social information is composed of techniques that people learn from observing social interactions. Examples of social information are guidelines we learn about how to dress, talk, and act to be considered attractive, smart, athletic, hip, and so forth.

With media literacy, we need strong knowledge structures in five areas: media effects, media content, media industries, the real world, and the self. With knowledge in these five areas, people are much more aware during the information-processing tasks and are therefore more able to make better decisions about seeking out information, working with that information, and constructing meaning from it that will be useful to serve their own goals. The information that makes these awarenesses possible resides in knowledge structures.

People who have had a wider range of experiences in the real world have a broader base from which to appreciate and analyze media messages. For example, those who have helped someone run for political office can understand and analyze press coverage of political campaigns to a greater depth than those who have not had any real-world experience with political campaigns. People who have played sports will be able to appreciate the athletic accomplishments they see on television to a greater depth than those who have not physically tested themselves on those challenges. People who have had a wide range of relationships and family experiences will have a higher degree of understanding and more in-depth emotional reactions to those portrayals in the media.

Knowledge structures provide the context we use when trying to make sense of new media messages. The more knowledge structures we have, the more confident we can be in making sense of a wide range of messages. For example, you may have a very large, well-developed knowledge structure about a particular television series. You may know the names of all the characters in that TV show. You may know everything that has happened to those characters in all the episodes. You may even know the names and histories of the actors who play the characters. If you have all of this information well organized so that you can recall any of it at a moment's notice, you have a well-developed knowledge structure about that television series. Are you media literate? Within the small corner of the media world where that one TV show resides, you are. But if this were the only knowledge structure you had developed, you would have little understanding of the content produced by the other media. You would have difficulty understanding trends about who owns and controls the media, how the media have developed over time, why certain kinds of content are never seen while other types are continually repeated, and what effects that content may be having on you. With many highly developed knowledge structures, you could understand the entire span of media issues and therefore be able to "see the big picture" about why the media are the way they are.

Skills

To construct knowledge structures, we rely on a set of skills. These skills are the tools. We use these tools to mine through the large piles of facts, so that we can uncover the particular facts we need and brush away the rest. Once we have selected the facts we need, we shape those facts into sets of information and carefully fit those pieces of information into their proper places in a structure.

Skills are like muscles; the more you exercise them, the stronger they get. Without practice, skills become weaker.

The skills crucial to media literacy are analysis, evaluation, grouping, induction, deduction, synthesis, and abstraction (see Figure 2.1). These skills are not exclusive to media literacy tasks; instead, we use these skills in all sorts of ways in our everyday lives. We all have some ability with each of these skills, so the media literacy challenge is not to acquire these skills; rather, our challenge is to get better at using each of these skills as we encounter media messages. In the remainder of this section, I will define each of these skills and show how they are applied in a media literacy context.

Analysis is the breaking down of a message into meaningful elements. As we encounter media messages, we can simply accept these messages on the surface or dig deeper into the messages themselves by breaking them down into their components and examining the composition of the elements that make up the messages. For example, with a news story, we can accept what a journalist tells us or analyze the story for completeness. That is, we can break the story down into its who, what, when, where, why, and how to determine if the story is complete or not.

Evaluation is making a judgment about the value of an element. This judgment is made by comparing a message element to some standard. When we encounter opinions expressed by experts in media messages, we could simply memorize those opinions and make them our own. Or we could take the information elements in the message and compare them to our standards. If those elements meet or exceed our standards, we

FIGURE 2.1 The Seven Skills of Media Literacy

1. Analysis: breaking down a message into meaningful elements

2. Evaluation: judging the value of an element; the judgment is made by comparing a message element to some standard

3. Grouping: determining which elements are alike in some way; determining how a group of elements are different from other groups of elements

4. Induction: inferring a pattern across a small set of elements, then generalizing the pattern to all elements in the set

5. Deduction: using general principles to explain particulars

6. Synthesis: assembling elements into a new structure

7. Abstracting: creating a brief, clear, and accurate description capturing the essence of a message in a smaller number of words than the message itself

conclude that the message—and the opinion expressed there—is good, but if the elements fall short of our standard, it is unacceptable.

There is a lot of evidence that people simply accept the opinions they hear in media messages without making their own evaluations. One example of this is the now widespread opinion that in the United States, the educational system is not very good and a big reason for this is that children now spend too much time with the media, especially TV. To illustrate, the National Center for Education Statistics (NCES) is an agency of the U.S. federal government

that uses standardized testing to assess the level of learning of America's youth in reading, mathematics, and science each year and then compares their levels of learning with youth in other countries. The 2009 Condition of Education report says that adolescents in the United States are ranked 8th out of 28 countries in reading, 24th out of 29 countries in mathematics, and 17th out of 29 countries in science (National Center for Education Statistics, 2009). Critiques of the U.S. educational system use information like this to argue that adolescents spend too much time with the media, and this makes their minds lazy, reduces their creativity, and turns them into lethargic entertainment junkies. If this happens, children will not value achievement and will not do well in school.

This belief is faulty because it blames the media, not the child or the parent, for poor academic performance. It also focuses only on the negative effect and gives the media no

credit for potentially positive effects. However, when we look carefully at the research evidence, we can see that the typically reported finding is wrong and that when we look more carefully, there are several effects happening simultaneously (see W. J. Potter, 1987a). For example, the typically reported finding is that television viewing is negatively related to academic achievement. And a fair amount of research reports this conclusion. What makes this faulty is that this relationship is explained better by something else—IQ. School achievement is overwhelmingly related to IQ. Also, children with lower IQs watch more television. So it is IQ that accounts for lower achievement and higher television viewing. Research analyses that take a child's IQ into account find that there is no overall negative relationship; instead, there is a much more interesting pattern. The negative relationship does not show up until the child's viewing has passed the threshold of 30 hours per week. Beyond that 30-hour point, the more television children watch, the lower their academic achievement, and that effect gets stronger with the more hours they watch beyond that threshold. This means that academic achievement goes down only after television viewing starts to cut into study time and sleep. But there is no negative effect for less than 30 hours of viewing per week. In fact, at the lowest levels of television viewing, there is actually a positive effect; that is, a child who watches none or only a few hours a week is likely to do less well academically than a child who watches a moderate amount (around 12–15 hours per week). Thus, the pattern is as follows: Children who are deprived of the source of information that television provides do less well in school than children who watch a moderate amount of television; however, when a child gets to the point where the amount of television viewing cuts into needed study time, academic performance goes down. We must realize that television—as well as the Internet and all other forms of the media—has potentially positive as well as negative effects. Television exposure can displace constructive behaviors such as studying, but television can expand our experience, teach us valuable social lessons, and stimulate our imaginations. Preventing children from using television can prevent a potentially negative effect, but it also prevents positive effects as well.

When we pose the question, "What effect does viewing television have on a child's academic performance?" we could give the simple, popular answer: There is a negative effect. But now you can see that this answer is too simple—it is simpleminded. It is also misleading because it reinforces the limited belief that media effects are negative and polarized and that the media are to blame.

The reason faulty beliefs are such a dangerous trap is because they are self-reinforcing. By this, I mean that as people are continually exposed to faulty information, they feel even more secure that their faulty beliefs are accurate. They feel less and less motivated to challenge them. When someone points out that the information on which their beliefs are based is faulty, they do not accept this criticism because they are so sure that they are correct. Thus, over time, they are not only less likely to examine their beliefs but also less tolerant of other beliefs having the possibility of being correct.

Grouping is determining which elements are alike in some way and then determining how a group of elements is different from other groups of elements. The key to doing this well is determining a classification rule. The media tell us what classification rules are, so if we accept their classification rules, we will end up with the groups they want us to use. But if we make the effort to determine which classification rules are the best ways for us to organize our perceptions of the world, we will end up with groups that have more meaning and more value for us.

Induction is inferring a pattern across a small number of elements, then generalizing the pattern to all elements in the larger set. When we examine the result of public opinion polls, we can see that many people are using elements in media stories to infer patterns about real life, and this creates faulty beliefs about real life. For example, when people are asked about health care in the United States, 90% of adults say that the health care system is in crisis; this is what many news stories and pundits tell the public. But when people are asked about their own health care, almost 90% feel that their health care is of good quality. About 63% of people think other people's doctors are too interested in making money, but only 20% think their own doctor is too interested in making money. People are using elements they have learned in media messages to dominate their perception of a pattern in real life. They accept a faulty belief because they do not take their own real-life experience into account when inferring a pattern; that is, they do not use induction well, instead preferring to use elements from mass media stories and not the elements from their own lives when inferring a pattern.

This faulty use of induction also shows up in other beliefs. For example, in public opinion polls about crime, typically only about one person in six thinks crime is a big problem in their own community, whereas five out of six say that crime is a big problem in society (Whitman & Loftus, 1996). People think this way because most do not experience crime in their own lives and therefore do not think it is a big problem where they live. However, they are convinced that it is a big problem in society. Where could the public get such an idea? From the media's fixation on deviance in the news. Also the news media prefer to present *sensationalized* events rather than *typical* events. So when a crime is reported, it is usually a violent crime, following the news ethic of "if it bleeds, it leads." Watching evening newscasts with their highlighting of crime and violence leads us to infer that there must be a high rate of crime and that most of it is violent assaults. But in reality, less than 20% of all crime is violent. More than 87% of all crime is property crime, with the victim not even present (U.S. Bureau of the Census, 2011). Furthermore, the rate for violent crime has been declining in this country since the mid-1980s, yet very few people are aware of this decline (Whitman & Loftus, 1996). Instead, most people believe that violent crime is increasing because they continually see crime stories and gory images in the media. They have fashioned their opinions on sensationalized events, and this type of information provides no useful basis to infer an accurate picture about crime. As for education, 64% give the nation's schools a grade of C or D, but at the same time, 66% give their public school a grade of A or B. As for religion, 65% say that religion is losing its influence on American life, whereas 62% say religion is becoming a stronger influence in own their lives. As for responsibility, almost 90% believe that a major problem with society is that people don't live up to their commitments, but more than 75% say they meet their commitments to families, kids, and employers. Nearly half of the population believes it is impossible for most families to achieve the American Dream, whereas 63% believe they have achieved or are close to the American Dream. And 40% to 50% think the nation is moving in the wrong direction, but 88% of Americans think their own lives and families are moving in the right direction (Whitman, 1996).

Deduction is using general principles to explain particulars, typically with the use of syllogistic reasoning. A well-known syllogism is (1) all men are mortal (general principle). (2) Socrates is a man (particular observation). (3) Therefore, Socrates is mortal (conclusion reached through logical reasoning).

When we have faulty general principles, we will explain particular occurrences in a faulty manner. One general principle that most people hold to be true is that the media, especially television, have a very strong negative effect on other people. They have an unrealistic opinion that the media cause other people to behave violently. Some believe that if you allow PSAs (public service announcements) on TV about using condoms, children will learn that it is permissible and even a good thing to have sex. This is clearly an overestimation. At the same time, people *under*estimate the influence the media have on them. When they are asked if they think the media have any effect on them personally, 88% say no. These people argue that the media are primarily channels of entertainment and diversion, so they have no negative effect on them. The people who believe this say that they have watched thousands of hours of crime shows and have never shot anyone or robbed a bank. Although this may be true, this argument does not fully support the claim that the media have no effect on them; this argument is based on the false premise that the media only trigger high-profile, negative, behavioral effects that are easy to recognize. But there are many more types of effects, such as giving people the false impression that crime is a more serious problem than it really is or that most crime is violent.

Synthesis is the assembling of elements into a new structure. This is the primary skill we use when building our knowledge structures. As we take in new information, we must analyze it or break it down into useful elements. Then we evaluate the elements to determine which are useful, credible, and interesting. The elements that are evaluated positively need to be grouped along with the elements already in our existing knowledge structures; this will often require us to create new groups and look for new patterns. Thus, the process of synthesis is using our new media messages to keep reformulating, refining, and updating our existing knowledge structures.

Abstracting is creating a brief, clear, and accurate description capturing the essence of a message in a significantly smaller number of words than the message itself. Thus, when we are describing a media message to someone else or reviewing the message in our own minds, we use the skill of abstracting. The key to using this skill well is to be able to capture the "big picture" or central idea of the media message in as few words as possible.

THE DEFINITION OF MEDIA LITERACY

Now that I have laid the foundation for media literacy by setting out its three major building blocks, it is time to present its formal definition. *Media literacy is a set of perspectives that we actively use to expose ourselves to the mass media to interpret the meaning of the messages we encounter.* We build our perspectives from knowledge structures. To build our knowledge structures, we need tools, raw material, and willingness. The tools are our skills. The raw material is information from the media and from the real world. The willingness comes from our personal locus.

What is a perspective? I'll illustrate this with an analogy. Let's say you wanted to learn about the Earth. You could build a 100-foot-tall tower, climb up to the top, and use that as your perspective to study the Earth. That would give you a good perspective that would not be blocked by trees so that you could see for perhaps several miles in any direction. If your tower were in a forest, you would conclude that Earth is covered with trees. But if your tower were in a suburban neighborhood, you would conclude that Earth is covered with houses, roads, and shopping centers. If your tower were inside the New Orleans Superdome stadium, you would conclude something quite different. Each of these perspectives would give you a very different idea about Earth. We could get into all kinds of arguments about which perspective delivers the most accurate or best set of ideas about Earth, but such arguments are rather useless. None of these perspectives is better than any other. The key to understanding Earth is to build lots of these towers so you have many different perspectives to enlarge your understanding about what the Earth is. And not all of these towers need to be 100 feet tall. Some should be very short so that you can better see what is happening between the blades of grass in a lawn. And others should be hundreds of miles away from the surface so that you can tell that Earth is a sphere and that there are large weather formations constantly churning around the globe.

To illuminate this idea of media literacy further, I need to describe two of its most important characteristics. First, media literacy is a multidimensional concept with many interesting facets. Therefore, we need to view it from many different perspectives to appreciate all it has to offer. Second, media literacy is a continuum, not a category.

Media Literacy Is Multidimensional

When we think of information, we typically think of sets of facts such as from a textbook, a newspaper, or a magazine article. But this is only one type of information—cognitive. Media literacy requires that we acquire information and build knowledge in more than just the cognitive dimension but also consider information from emotional, aesthetic, and moral dimensions. Each of these four dimensions focuses on a different domain of understanding. The cognitive domain refers to factual information—dates, names, definitions, and the like. Think of cognitive information as that which resides in the brain.

The emotional domain contains information about feelings, such as love, hate, anger, happiness, and frustration. Think of emotional information as that which lives in the heart—feelings of happy times, moments of fear, instances of embarrassment. Some people have very little ability to experience an emotion during exposure to the media, whereas others are very sensitive to cues that generate all sorts of feelings in them. For example, we all have the ability to perceive rage, fear, lust, hate, and other strong emotions. Producers use easy-to-recognize symbols to trigger these, so they do not require a high degree of literacy to perceive and understand. But some of us are much better than others at perceiving the more subtle emotions such as ambivalence, confusion, wariness, and so on. Crafting messages about these emotions requires more production skill from writers, directors, and actors. Perceiving these subtle emotions accurately requires a higher degree of literacy from the audience.

The aesthetic domain contains information about how to produce messages. This information gives us the basis for making judgments about who are great writers, photographers, actors, dancers, choreographers, singers, musicians, composers, directors, and other kinds of artists. It also helps us make judgments about other products of creative craftsmanship, such as editing, lighting, set designing, costuming, sound recording, graphic layout, and so forth. This appreciation skill is very important to some scholars (Messaris, 1994; Silverblatt, 2007; Wulff, 1997). For example, Messaris (1994) argues that viewers who are visually literate should have an awareness of artistry and visual manipulation. By this, he means an awareness about the processes by which meaning is created through the visual media. What is expected of sophisticated viewers is some degree of self-consciousness about their role as interpreters. This includes the ability to detect artifice (in staged behavior and editing) and to spot authorial presence (style of the producer/director).

Think of aesthetic information as that which resides in our eyes and ears. Some of us have a good ear for dialog or musical composition. Some of us have a good eye for lighting, photographic composition, or movement. The more information we have from this aesthetic domain, the finer discriminations we can make between a great actress and a very good one, between a great song that will endure and a currently popular "flash in the pan," between a film director's best and very best work, between art and artificiality.

The moral domain contains information about values. Think of moral information as that which resides in your conscience or your soul. This type of information provides us with the basis for making judgments about right and wrong. When we see characters make decisions in a story, we judge them on a moral dimension, that is, the characters' goodness or evilness. The more detailed and refined our moral information is, the more deeply we can perceive the values underlying messages in the media and the more sophisticated and reasoned are our judgments about those values. It takes a highly media-literate person to perceive moral themes well. You must be able to think past individual characters to focus your meaning making at the overall narrative level. You are able to separate characters from their actions—you might not like a particular character, but you like his or her actions in terms of fitting in with (or reinforcing) your values. You do not focus your viewing on only one character's point of view but try to empathize with many characters so you can vicariously experience the consequences of their actions throughout the course of the narrative.

Your media literacy perspective needs to include information from all four of these domains. For example, you may be able to be highly analytical when you watch a movie and quote lots of facts about the history of the genre, the director's point of view, and the underlying theme. But if you cannot evoke an emotional reaction, you are simply going through a dry, academic exercise.

Media Literacy Is a Continuum, Not a Category

Media literacy is not a category—like a box—where either you are in the category or you are not. For example, either you are a high school graduate or you are not; either you are an American citizen or you are not. In contrast, media literacy is best regarded as a continuum—like a thermometer—where there are degrees.

We all occupy some position on the media literacy continuum. There is no point below which we could say that someone has no literacy, and there is no point at the high end where we can say that someone is fully literate—there is always room for improvement. People are positioned along that continuum based on the strength of their overall perspective on the media. The strength of a person's perspective is based on the number and quality of knowledge structures. And the quality of knowledge structures is based on the level of a person's skills and experiences. Because people vary substantially on skills and experiences, they will vary on the number and quality of their knowledge structures. Hence, there will be a great variation of media literacy across people.

People operating at lower levels of media literacy have weak and limited perspectives on the media. They have smaller, more superficial, and less organized knowledge structures, which provide an inadequate perspective to use in interpreting the meaning of a media message. These people are also habitually reluctant or unwilling to use their skills, which remain underdeveloped and therefore more difficult to employ successfully.

THE DEVELOPMENT OF MEDIA LITERACY

Remember that media literacy is a continuum. People are positioned along that continuum based on the skills and knowledge they bring to bear (cognitively, emotionally, aesthetically, and morally) for the purpose of gaining control over the meaning process. Along that continuum, we can identify some key positions (see Figure 2.2). As people develop a higher level of skills and construct a broader range of perspectives on the media, they develop higher levels of media literacy.

The lowest three levels are stages we go through as young children. Acquiring fundamentals happens during the first year of life; language acquisition occurs during years 2 and 3; then narrative acquisition happens during years 3 to 5. These are stages that are left behind by children as they age into adolescence and adulthood.

The developing skepticism stage occurs from about ages 5 to 9, and the intensive development stage is shortly after. Many people stay in this stage the rest of their lives, because this stage is fully functional—that is, people in this stage feel they are getting exposure to the messages they want and getting the meaning out of those messages they want. They feel they are fully media literate and that there is nothing more they need to learn.

The next three stages can be regarded as advanced because they require the continual use of higher level skills and the active development of elaborate knowledge structures. People in the experiential exploring stage feel that their media exposure has been very narrow, and they seek exposure to a much wider range of messages. For example, people who have watched only primetime action/adventure and situation comedy programs will begin to watch news, PBS documentaries, travelogues, MTV, science fiction, offbeat sports, and so on. They will pick up niche magazines and books about unusual topics. The thrill for these people is to see something they have never seen before. This makes them think about the variety of human experience.

FIGURE 2.2	Development of Media Literacy
Stage	*Characteristics*
Acquiring fundamentals	• Learn that there are human beings and other physical things apart from oneself; these things look different and serve different functions • Learn the meaning of facial expressions and natural sounds • Recognize shapes, form, size, color, movement, and spatial relations • Rudimentary concept of time—regular patterns
Language acquisition	• Recognize speech sounds and attach meaning to them • Be able to reproduce speech sounds • Orient to visual and audio media • Make emotional and behavior responses to music and sounds • Recognize certain characters in visual media and follow their movement

Narrative acquisition	Develop understanding of differences:
	• Fiction versus nonfiction
	• Ads versus entertainment
	• Real versus make-believe
	• Understand how to connect plot elements
	  ○ By time sequencing
	  ○ By motive-action-consequence

Developing skepticism	• Discount claims made in ads • Sharpen differences between likes and dislikes for shows, characters, and actions • Make fun of certain characters even through those characters are not presented as foils in their shows
Intensive development	• Strong motivation to seek out information on certain topics • Developing a detailed set of information on particular topics (sports, politics, etc.) • High awareness of utility of information and quick facility in processing information judged to be useful
Experiential exploring	• Seek out different forms of content and narratives • Focus on searching for surprises and new emotional, moral, and aesthetic reactions
Critical appreciation	• Accept messages on their own terms, then evaluate them within that sphere • Develop very broad and detailed understanding of the historical, economic, political, and artistic contexts of message systems • Ability to make subtle comparisons and contrasts among many different message elements simultaneously • Ability to construct a summary judgment about the overall strengths and weaknesses of a message
Social responsibility	• Take a moral stand that certain messages are more constructive for society than others; this is a multidimensional perspective based on thorough analyses of the media landscape • Recognize that one's own individual decisions affect society—no matter how minutely • Recognize that an individual can take some actions to make a constructive impact on society

People in the critical appreciation stage see themselves as connoisseurs of the media. They seek out better (cognitively, emotionally, aesthetically, and morally) messages. They have strongly held opinions about who are the best writers, the best producers, the best news reporters, and so on, and they have lots of evidence to support their well-reasoned opinions. They can talk fluently and at length about what makes a good writer and how these elements are exhibited in a particular writer's body of work.

Social responsibility is characterized by people having critical appreciation of all kinds of media messages, but instead of having a primarily internal perspective (as with the previous stage), the perspective here is external. The person at this stage not only asks, "What is best from my point of view and why?" but also is concerned with questions such as, "What types of messages are best for others and for society?"

Be careful not to think of these positions as fixed, discrete stages. Rather, these are overlapping stages in a fluid process. They are offered more for purposes of illustration instead of being definitive, fixed positions. You have a typical position on the continuum, but that position is not static. You move up and down depending on what medium you are interacting with, depending on the message, and depending on your motive for the exposure. For example, when you are reading a book that is considered a classic novel for a college course, you may be able to reach the critical appreciation level. But when you flick on the television and watch MTV's *Pimp My Ride* or *The Hills* to relax, you might sink down to the intensive development level. There is nothing wrong with dropping down a level. There are times when we just want to "veg out" and don't want to spend the effort to stay at the highest stages. But remember there is a difference between people who stay at the lower stages because they are unable or unwilling to operate at higher stages and people who are able to operate at all stages but who choose to take it easier at lower stages occasionally.

We all have a stage at which we feel generally at home. This is where we are most comfortable interacting with the media. We are usually able to move up a stage or two from our home base. But moving up a stage requires a conscious effort where we must expend more energy to apply higher level skills. So we don't move up unless we are strongly motivated to do so.

ADVANTAGES OF DEVELOPING A HIGHER DEGREE OF MEDIA LITERACY

What are the advantages of developing a higher degree of media literacy? I will emphasize three. First, media literacy grows one's appetite for a wider variety of media messages.

Second, it gives people knowledge about how to program their own mental codes. And third, it provides people with more control over the media.

Appetite for Wider Variety of Media Messages

The media offer an incredible array of choices. The Internet contains websites on every topic that humans can conceive. Books are published each year on an extremely wide range of topics. Magazines with their 10,000 titles published each year offer a much wider range than any one person can consume. Cable television is a bit more narrow still, but with 500-plus channels from most cable TV providers, the choice is much wider than any one person can keep up with. However, the mass media continually try to direct our choices to a smaller set. For example, with magazines, although there are about 10,000 magazines published in the United States, even a large bookstore is likely to have only about 300 on its magazine shelves. You don't want to have to scan through all 300 magazines, so you rely on your automatic filtering to narrow your choice down to about a dozen magazines that you have found interesting in the past—that is, the media have conditioned you to like these magazines. Your choice is then to buy one or two from this smaller list of 12. Do you have a choice? Yes, of course. But see how the media—first through the bookstore buyer, then through media conditioning—have narrowed your choice down to 12; in other words, the decision you made was determined 99.88% by factors other than you. The media have programmed you to think that you have choices when in fact the degree of choice is greatly limited. It is rather like parents laying out two pairs of dress pants—one black and the other dark blue—for their 4-year-old son and giving him the total power to choose what he is to wear today. Whether you regard this as a real choice depends on how much you know about the real range of options. If the boy knows about jeans, cargo pants, skater shorts, bathing trunks, and football pants, then he will not think the two dress pants is much of a choice. But what if he only knows about dark dress pants? In this case, he believes he does have a big choice between black and dark blue.

The mass media continually try to constrain your choices so they can condition you into habitual exposure of a few types of media vehicles. This makes you more predictable from

a marketing point of view, and this predictability increases mass media companies' ability to reduce their business risk. However, the choices are still there for you to take advantage of, but most of us prefer our habitual patterns of exposure. Most of us do not explore much of the range in media messages.

The media literacy perspective asks you to be more adventurous and explore a wider range of messages. When you do so, you will likely find many of those messages are not interesting or useful to you. But you will also likely find a few types of messages that are highly useful, and this will expand your exposure repertoire.

More Self-Programming of Mental Codes

The purpose of media literacy is to empower individuals to control media programming.

When I use the term *programming* in this sense, I do not mean television programs; instead, I mean the way the mass media in general alter the way you think about things. An individual by himself or herself will not have much influence on altering how the mass media craft or schedule their messages. An individual will never be able to exercise much control over what gets offered to the public. However, a person can learn to exert a great deal of control over the way one's mind gets programmed. Thus, the purpose of media literacy is to show people how to shift control from the media to themselves. This is what I mean when I say that the purpose of media literacy is to help people control media programming.

The first step in shifting control away from the media to the individual is for individuals to understand how the media program them. This programming by the media continually takes place in a two-phase cycle that repeats over and over again. One of these phases of the cycle is the constraining of choices, and the second phase is the reinforcing of experience.

More Control Over Media

The mass media are composed of businesses that are very sophisticated in knowing how to attract your attention and condition you for repeat exposures. The media are very successful in using you to achieve their business goals. Often the media's business goals and your personal goals are the same, so it is a win-win situation. But there are also many times when your personal goals are different from the media's goals; when this occurs, you need to break away from your media-conditioned habits to follow your own goals. The media literacy perspective will help you recognize this divergence of goals and take alternative steps. Thus, you are more likely to treat media messages as tools to reach your own goals.

SUMMARY

The chapter presents a definition of media literacy as a perspective from which we expose ourselves to the media and interpret the meaning of the messages we encounter. It is not a category; there are degrees of media literacy. It is multidimensional, with development taking place cognitively, emotionally, aesthetically, and morally.

Media literacy is composed of three building blocks: personal locus, knowledge structures, and skills. The skills are the tools that we use to work on information in the media messages to build strong knowledge structures. The direction and drive to do this work lie in one's personal locus.

People who are highly media literate are able to see much more in a given message. They are more aware of the levels of meaning. This enhances understanding. They are more in charge of programming their own mental codes. This enhances control. They are much more likely to get what they want from the messages. This enhances appreciation. Thus, people operating at higher levels of media literacy fulfill the goals of higher understanding, control, and appreciation.

Chapter Resources: To test your knowledge and learn more about the topics discussed in this chapter, visit the Student Study Site at www.sagepub.com/potter6e.

FURTHER READING

Adams, D., & Hamm, M. (2001). *Literacy in a multimedia age.* Norwood, MA: Christopher-Gordon. (199 pages, including glossary and index)

Coming from an educational technology background, the authors argue that media literacy needs to include media analysis, multimedia production, collaborative inquiry, and networking technologies. They present many practical ideas to help teachers guide their students to learn how to get the most out of messages in all forms of media.

Buckingham, D. (2003). *Media education: Literacy, learning, and contemporary culture.* Cambridge, UK: Polity. (232 pages)

This is a survey of the field of media education. It focuses attention on key debates and controversies, then lays out some guidelines for the future.

Frechette, J. D. (2002). *Developing media literacy in cyberspace: Pedagogy and critical learning for the twenty-first–century classroom.* New York: Praeger. (185 pages)

This book offers a vision of learning that values social empowerment over technical skills. The author argues that media literacy offers the best long-term training for today's youth to become experienced practitioners of 21st-century technology. The author provides guidelines to help educators develop and provide concrete learning strategies that enable students to judge the validity and worth of what they see on the Internet as they strive to become critically autonomous in a technology-laden world.

Jenkins, H., Purushotma, R., Weigel, M., & Clinton, K. (2006). *Confronting the challenges of participatory culture: Media education for the 21st century.* Cambridge, MA: MIT Press. (128 pages)

Funded by the John D. and Catherine T. MacArthur Foundation, this book focuses on the skills that are most important for dealing with the new media culture, which is characterized by interactive media, making it possible for people to participate in society in ways not available before.

Kubey, R., & Ruben, B. (Eds.). (2001). *Media literacy in the information age: Current perspectives* (Information and Behavior, Vol. 6). New Brunswick, NJ: Transaction Publishers. (484 pages)

This is an edited volume of 22 chapters written by leading media educators from many countries around the world. The focus of most chapters is not just how to deal with technological change in the media but how to create an educational process that will help students become more media literate.

Macedo, D. P., & Steinberg, S. R. (Eds.). (2007). *Media literacy: A reader.* New York: Peter Lang. (710 pages)

> The editors say the purpose of this book is to help students develop the ability to interpret media as well as understand the ways they themselves consume and emotionally invest in media. The book is an extensive collection of essays written primarily for people who are not expert in media literacy and want more of an introduction to the topic rather than a scholarly treatment.

Mackey, M. (2007). *Literacies across media* (2nd ed.). New York: Routledge. (224 pages)

> This book describes an 18-month-long project that was designed to study how a group of boys and girls, ages from 10 to 14, made sense of narratives in a variety of formats, including print, electronic book, video, DVD, computer game, and CD-ROM. The author's analyses reveal how those children developed strategies for interpreting narratives through encounters with a diverse range of texts and media.

Masterman, L. (1985). *Teaching the media.* London: Comedia. (341 pages, including annotated bibliography and appendixes)

> Written for teachers of media, this book addresses the following questions: Why teach about the media? What are the best ways to teach about the media? Why are media texts the way they are? It seeks to present a set of general principles for teaching about any mass medium.

Messaris, P. (1994). *Visual "literacy": Image, mind, and reality.* Boulder, CO: Westview. (208 pages)

> Paul Messaris, a communications professor at the University of Pennsylvania, argues against some commonly held assumptions about visual literacy. For example, he rejects the popular notion among many scholars that there can be no objective standards to judge the reality of visual images. He says that there are generic cognitive skills that people apply when they experience the pictorial media. His notion of training people to be media literate focuses on helping viewers detect unrealistic visual manipulation.

Metallinos, N. (Ed.). (1994). *Verbo-visual literacy: Understanding and applying new educational communication media technologies.* Montreal, Canada: 3Dmt Research and Information Center. (276 pages)

> These 38 chapters are from a symposium of the International Visual Literacy Association. They focus on suggestions about how best to use the emerging new technologies to foster verbal and visual literacy.

Silverblatt, A. (2007). *Media literacy: Keys to interpreting media messages.* Westport, CT: Praeger. (340 pages, including index)

> This is a mass media book that presents some chapters with information about what is needed as far as knowledge about the media. It has the feel of a textbook for an introductory-level course with its use of photographs and exercises for students to undertake.

Tyner, K. (Ed.). (2010). *Media literacy: New agendas in communication.* New York: Routledge. (243 pages with index)

> The 10 chapters in this edited volume deal with how media literacy initiatives have taken place in the past and what they should emphasize going forward. These initiatives are organized into four contexts: community-based settings, K–12 classrooms, higher education, and virtual environments.

Part 2

Audience

In this part of the book, we focus attention on the audience. We can use two major perspectives to examine mass media audiences—from the perspective of the individual audience member (in Chapter 3) and from the perspective of the mass media (in Chapter 4). These are very different perspectives, but both are essential if you are to understand how audiences are constructed and how we as individuals experience media messages when we are in the audience. Then Chapter 5 explores the issue of why children are regarded as a special audience.

As you read this part of the book, keep the following questions active in your mind, and you will stay focused on the most important ideas in the three chapters:

- To which media audiences do you belong?
- How did you get attracted into those audiences?
- How do the media condition you for repeat exposures so that you will continue to be part of those audiences?

- Does your participation in those audiences do more to achieve your goals or the goals of the mass media organizations?
- Are you a member of any audiences that should be considered special?

Individual Perspective

Key Idea: In our information-saturated culture, individuals are constantly processing media messages as they make decisions either consciously or automatically about filtering, meaning matching, and meaning construction. They continually are making these decisions in one of four exposure states: automatic, attentional, transported, and self-reflexive.

CHAPTER 3

Harry and Ann are discussing their relationship over lunch on campus.

"Harry, you never pay attention to what I say!"

"How can you say that? We spend almost all day together every day and you are constantly talking," Harry replies. "I hear what you say."

"Maybe, but you don't understand what I say."

"Yes, I do. I know a lot about you. I know the names of all your brothers and sisters, and where you went to high school, and your favorite color and. . . ."

Ann interrupts, "Those are facts about me. They are not me! You don't seem to know me."

"I know the meaning of every word you say. I don't need a dictionary!"

"There is more to meaning than the definitions of the words I use!"

In interpersonal conversations, we often get ourselves into trouble if we are not careful to make a distinction between literal meaning—the dictionary-type meanings we all share for common words and phrases—and the deeper meaning that resides in how we say things. This difference is also important with understanding the meaning of media messages. In this chapter, we deal with this distinction as two—meaning matching and meaning construction—of the three information-processing tasks in which we are constantly engaged. The third of these tasks is message filtering. After I lay the foundation by defining these three information-processing tasks, we will analyze the idea of what it means to have exposure to media messages. Then I will introduce the idea of exposure states. When you finish reading this chapter, you should have a much stronger psychological perspective of how you experience media messages and how this understanding can empower you to get more out of your media exposures.

INFORMATION-PROCESSING TASKS

We are constantly engaged in a series of three information-processing tasks every waking minute of every day. These tasks are filtering, meaning matching, and meaning construction (see Table 3.1). First, we encounter a message and are faced with the task of deciding whether to filter the message out (ignore it) or filter it in (process it). If we decide to filter it in, then we must make sense of it, that is, recognize the symbols and match our learned definitions to the symbols. Next, we need to construct the meaning of the message.

Sometimes we engage in this sequence of tasks in a very conscious manner, such that we are aware and control our decisions. However, most of the time, we engage in this sequence of tasks unconsciously—that is, our minds are on automatic pilot where our mental code automatically makes filtering and meaning-matching decisions and short-circuits the meaning construction process. Let's examine each of these three information-processing tasks in more detail.

TABLE 3.1 Summary of Three Tasks of Information Processing	
Filtering Message	*Goal:* To access previously learned meanings efficiently
Task: To make decisions about which messages to filter out (ignore) and which to filter in (pay attention to)	Focus: Referents in messages
Goal: To attend to only those messages that have some kind of usefulness for the person and ignore all other messages	**Meaning Construction**
Focus: Messages in the environment	*Task:* To use skills in order to move beyond meaning matching and to construct meaning for one's self to personalize and get more out of a message
Meaning Matching	*Goal:* To interpret messages from more than one perspective as a means of identifying the range of meaning options, then choose one or synthesize across several
Task: To use basic competencies to recognize referents and locate previously learned definitions for each	*Focus:* One's own knowledge structures

Filtering

As we go through each day, we are constantly flooded with information. To protect ourselves from being overwhelmed, we continually filter that flood by ignoring most and paying attention to a small percentage that gets through our filtering. Recall from the previous chapter that most of this filtering is accomplished when our minds are on automatic pilot. During this automatic process of filtering, our attention is governed by a mental code that tells our senses to avoid paying attention to all messages (filtering them out) until an element in a particular message trips a trigger code in our mind and we begin paying attention to the message.

Once we have filtered in a message (start paying attention to it), we need to determine its meaning. This determination of meaning involves two—not one—tasks. First, we match meaning. Oftentimes, the information-processing sequence stops with this task. But sometimes we move into the next task of constructing meaning.

Meaning Matching

With meaning matching, meaning is assumed to reside outside the person in an authority, such as a teacher, an expert, a dictionary, a textbook, or the like. The task for the person is to find those meanings and memorize them. Parents and educational institutions are primarily responsible for housing the authoritative information and teaching it to each next generation. The media are also a major source of information, and for many people, the media have attained the status of an authoritative source, so people accept the meanings presented there and simply memorize those meanings.

Meaning matching is the process of recognizing elements (referents) in the message and accessing our memory to find the meanings we have memorized for those elements. This is a relatively automatic task. It may require a good deal of effort to learn to recognize symbols in media messages and to memorize their standard meanings, but once learned, this process becomes routine. To illustrate, think back to when you first learned to read. You had to learn how to recognize words printed on a page. Then you had to memorize the meaning of each word. The first time you saw the sentence "Dick threw the ball to Jane," it required a good deal of work to divide the sentence into words, to recall the meaning of each word, and to put it all together. With practice, you were able to perform this process more quickly and more easily. Learning to read in elementary school is essentially the process of being able to recognize a longer list of referents and to memorize their denoted meanings. Some referents in media messages were words, some were numbers, some were pictures, and some were sounds.

This type of learning develops competencies. By competency, I mean that either you are able to do something correctly or you are not. For example, when you see the phrase "2 + 2," you either recognize the "2" referents as particular quantities or you do not. You either recognize the " + " referent as addition or you do not. You can either perform this mathematical operation and arrive at 4 or you cannot. Working with these referents does not require—or allow for—individual interpretation and creative meaning construction. Competencies are our abilities to recognize standard referents and recall the memorized denoted meanings for those referents. If we did not have a common set of referents and shared meanings for each of these referents, communication would not be possible. Education at the elementary level is the training of the next generation to develop the basic competencies of recognizing these referents and memorizing the designated meaning for each one.

Meaning Construction

Meaning matching is essentially a task that can be accomplished well automatically once we have acquired some basic competencies. In contrast, meaning construction is a much more challenging task. It is not an automatic process but instead requires us to think about moving beyond the standard denoted meaning and to create meaning for ourselves by using the skills of induction, deduction, grouping, and synthesis. We engage in the meaning construction process either when we have no denoted meaning for a particular message in our memory banks or when the denoted meaning does not satisfy us and we want to arrive at a different meaning.

Many meanings can be constructed from any media message; furthermore, there are many ways to go about constructing that meaning. Thus, we cannot learn a complete set of rules to accomplish this task; instead, we need to be guided by our own information goals, and we need to use skills (rather than competencies) to creatively construct a path to reach our goals. For these reasons, meaning construction rarely takes place in an automatic fashion. Instead, we need to make conscious decisions when we are constructing meaning for ourselves. Also, every meaning construction task is different, so we cannot program our minds to follow the same one procedure automatically when we are confronted with a range of meaning construction tasks.

While meaning matching relies on competencies, meaning construction relies on skills. This is one of the fundamental differences between the two tasks of meaning matching and meaning construction. Competencies are categorical—that is, either you have a competency or you do not. However, skill ability is not categorical; on any given skill, there is a wide range of ability. That is, some people have little ability, whereas other people have enormous ability. Also, skills are like muscles. Without practice, skills become weaker. With practice and exercise, they grow stronger. When the personal locus has strong drive states for using skills, those skills have a much greater chance of developing to higher levels.

To illustrate this distinction between competency and skills, let's return to the example of "reading" as it is taught in elementary school. Children learn to recognize referents that are words. They learn how to vocalize those words and how to fit those words together into sentences. These are competencies. By the time people have completed elementary school, it is assumed that they have achieved a basic level of reading competency, yet they still practice reading. At these more advanced grades, however, reading is regarded less as a competency and more as a skill. Students focus on how to get more meaning out of paragraphs and stories. For example, when teachers ask students to read aloud in elementary school, it is to check students' competencies at word recognition and pronunciation. But when teachers ask students to read aloud in high school, it is to check students' skill at reading expression, which indicates how they are constructing their own meaning. Also, at higher grades, students are asked to write essays about a story they have read and express what that story meant to them.

The two processes of meaning matching and meaning construction are not discrete; they are intertwined. To construct meaning, we first have to recognize referents and understand the sense in which those referents are being used in the message. Thus, the meaning-matching process is more fundamental because the product of the meaning-matching process then is imported into the meaning construction process.

ANALYZING THE IDEA OF EXPOSURE TO MEDIA MESSAGES

When we examine the idea of audience from the individual perspective, we need to focus on several important concerns. First, we need to analyze what it means to be exposed to a media message and whether exposure is the same thing as attention. Second, we need to analyze the experience of exposure to sensitize ourselves to the different psychological states in which we experience media messages.

Exposure and Attention

In everyday language, exposure is a term that is often used synonymously with the term attention, but with media literacy, we must draw an important distinction between the two terms. Furthermore, there is a sequence of three types of exposure: physical exposure, perceptual exposure, and psychological exposure to media messages. Only when all three conditions of exposure are met can there be attention.

Physical Exposure

The most foundational criterion for exposure is physical presence. A person must experience some proximity to a message in order for exposure to take place. Physical exposure means that the message and the person occupy the same physical space for some period of time. Thus, space and time are regarded as barriers to exposure. If a magazine is lying face-up on a table in a room and Harry walks through that room, Harry is physically exposed to a message on the cover of the magazine but not to any of the messages inside the magazine unless Harry picks it up and flips through the pages. Also, if Harry does not walk through that room when the magazine is on the table, there is no physical exposure to the message on the cover of the magazine. Likewise, if a TV is turned on in the lunch room during the noon hour and then is turned off at 1 p.m., anyone who walks through that room after 1 p.m. is not physically exposed to TV messages.

Physical proximity is a necessary condition for media exposure, but it is not a sufficient condition. A second necessary condition is perceptual exposure.

Perceptual Exposure

The perceptual consideration refers to a human's sensory bandwidth or the ability to receive appropriate sensory input through the visual and auditory senses. There are limits to a human's sense organs. For example, human sensitivity to sound frequency extends from around 16 Hz to 20,000 Hz, but sounds are heard best when they are between 1,000 Hz and 4,000 Hz (Metallinos, 1996; Plack, 2005). A dog whistle is pitched at a frequency higher than 20,000 Hz, so humans cannot perceive that sound—that is, it is outside their range of human sensitivity to sounds. With the human eye, people can see light, which travels at a certain frequency, but not sound, which travels at another frequency. Any auditory or visual signal that occurs outside of a person's sense organ's ability to perceive it is nonexposure.

The perceptual criterion, however, has a feature beyond simple bandwidth; we must also consider the sensory-input/brain connection. There are instances when the sensory input gets to the brain, but the brain transforms the raw stimuli, such that we cannot perceive the raw stimuli and therefore do not realize we are being exposed to the raw stimuli; instead, we perceive the transformed stimuli. For example, when we watch a movie in a theater, we are exposed to individual static images projected at about 24 images per second. But humans cannot perceive 24 individual images in a given second, so our brains miss seeing the 24 individual static pictures and instead "see" motion. Also with film projection, there is a brief time between each of those 24 individual images every second when the screen is blank, but the eye-brain connection is not quick enough to process the blanks, so we do not "see" those blanks as blanks; instead, we only "see" smooth motion. If the projection rate of images were to slow down to under 10 images per second, we would begin to see a flutter—that is, our brains would begin to see the blanks because the replacement of still images is slow enough for the eye-brain connection to begin processing them.

Stimuli that are outside the boundaries of human perception are called subliminal. Subliminal messages can leave no psychological trace because they cannot be physically perceived—that is, humans lack the sensory organs to take in stimuli and/or the hardwiring in the brain to be sensitive to them.

There is a widespread misconception that the mass media put people at risk for "subliminal communication." This belief is based on confusing *sub-liminal* with *sub-conscious*. An important distinction needs to be made between subliminal and subconscious because they are two very different things and have two very different implications for exposure. *Subliminal* refers to being outside a human's ability to sense or perceive, and thus it is always regarded as nonexposure. However, once media stimuli cross over the subliminal line and are able to be sensed and perceived by humans, it is regarded as exposure. However, this does not mean that all exposure is conscious, and this brings us to the third criterion in our definition—psychological.

Psychological Exposure

For psychological exposure to occur, some trace element must be created in a person's mind. This element can be an image, a sound, an emotion, a pattern, and so on. It can last for a brief time (several seconds in short-term memory, then cleared out) or a lifetime (when cataloged into long-term memory). It can enter the mind consciously (often called the central route), where people are fully aware of the elements in the exposure, or unconsciously (often called the peripheral route), where people are unaware that elements are being entered into their minds (see Petty & Cacioppo, 1986). Thus, a great variety of elements potentially can meet this criterion for psychological exposure. The challenge then becomes organizing all these elements into meaningful sets and explaining how different kinds of elements are experienced by the individual and how they are processed as information.

Attention

For attention to occur, a person must first clear all three of the exposure hurdles described above—physical, perceptual, and psychological exposure. However, these three things alone do not guarantee attention; something else must also occur. That something else is conscious awareness of the media message. As you can now see, a lot of things have to happen in order for us to pay attention to a media message. For this reason, attention rarely occurs. And when we do pay attention to one media message, that attention can be quickly distracted to something else. Harold Pashler, who wrote *The Psychology of Attention* (1998), explains that at any given moment, awareness encompasses only a tiny proportion of the stimuli impinging on a person's sensory systems. Furthermore, while we are paying attention to one thing, our attention can be distracted away to another thing. He says there are times when "attention is directed or grabbed without any voluntary choice having taken place, even against strong wishes to the contrary" (p. 3). Thus, when we are paying attention to a conversation with our roommate, our attention can be grabbed by a sound or an image that pops up on our computer screen, and we shift our attention away from our roommate to the screen.

Exposure States

Thus far, I have made a distinction between automatic processing and paying attention to particular media messages. This suggests two exposure states, but there are four. These four exposure states are automatic, attentional, transported, and self-reflexive. Each of these states is a qualitatively different experience for the audience member. By this I mean that they are not distinguished simply by degree of attention. Instead, crossing the line from one state to another results in a qualitatively different experience with the message.

Automatic State

In the automatic state of exposure, people are in environments where they are exposed to media messages but are not aware of those messages—that is, their mind is on automatic pilot while they screen out all the messages from conscious exposure. There is no conscious goal or strategy for seeking out messages, but screening out messages still takes place. This screening out continues automatically with no effort until some element in a message breaks through people's default screen and captures their attention.

In the automatic processing state, message elements are physically perceived but processed automatically in an unconscious manner. This exposure state resides above the threshold of human sense perception but below the threshold of conscious awareness. The person is in a perceptual flow that continues until an interruption stops the exposure or "bumps" the person's perceptual processing into a different state of exposure or until the media message moves outside of a person's physical or perceptual ability to be exposed to it.

In the automatic state, people can look active to outside observers, but they are not thinking about what they are doing. People in the automatic state can be clicking through a series of websites without paying attention to the messages on those sites. While it may look to an observer that the person is actively searching the Web, the person may be just randomly clicking through Web pages while thinking about something totally different. Even when there is evidence of exposure behavior, this does not necessarily mean that people's minds are engaged and that they are "making" decisions. Rather, the decisions are happening to them automatically.

Exposure to much of the media is in the automatic state. People have no conscious awareness of the exposure when it is taking place, nor do they have a recollection of many details in the experience if they are asked about it later. This is especially the case when people are multitasking. Someone might be listening to music, surfing the Web, and talking to a friend on the phone; while the person may be paying attention to the phone conversation, he is in an automatic exposure state with regard to the music and the Web pages. If his attention suddenly shifts to an image on a Web page, then he slips into the automatic state with the phone conversation and no longer pays attention to what his friend is saying.

Attentional State

Attentional exposure refers to people being aware of the messages and actively interacting with the elements in the messages. This does not mean they must have a high level of concentration, although that is possible. The key is conscious awareness of the messages during exposures.

Within the attentional state, there is a range of attention depending on how much of a person's mental resources one devotes to the exposure. At minimum, the person must be aware of the message and consciously track it, but there is a fair degree of elasticity in the degree of concentration, which can range from partial to quite extensive processing depending on the number of elements handled and the depth of analysis employed.

Transported State

When people are in the attentional state but then are pulled into the message so strongly that they lose awareness of being apart from the message, they cross over into the transported state. In the transported state, audience members lose their sense of separateness from the message—that is, they are swept away with the message, enter the world of the message, and lose track of their own social world surroundings. For example, while watching a movie in a theater, people can get so caught up in the action that they feel they are involved with that action. They experience the same intense emotions as the characters do. They lose the sense that they are in a theater. Their concentration level is so high that they lose touch with their real-world environment. They lose track of real time; instead, they experience narrative time—that is, they feel time pass like the characters feel time pass. This transported state typically occurs when people are playing video and computer games.

The transported state is not simply the high end of the attentional state. Instead, the transported state is qualitatively different from the attentional state. While attention is very high in the transported state, the attention is also very narrow—that is, people have tunnel

vision and focus on the media message in a way that eliminates the barrier between them and the message. People are swept away and "enter" the message. In this sense, it is the opposite of the automatic state where people stay grounded in their social world and are unaware of the media messages in their perceptual environment; in the transported exposure state, people enter the media message and lose track of their social world.

Self-Reflexive State

In the self-reflexive state, people are hyperaware of the message *and of their processing of the message*. It is as if they are sitting on their shoulder and monitoring their own reactions as they experience the message. This represents the fullest degree of awareness—that is, people are aware of the media message, their own social world, and their position in the social world while they process the media message. In the self-reflexive exposure state, the viewer exercises the greatest control over perceptions by reflecting on questions such as, Why am I exposing myself to this message? What am I getting out of this exposure and why? and Why am I making these interpretations of meaning? Not only is there analysis, but there is also meta-analysis. This means that the person is analyzing the media message, as well as his or her analysis of the media message.

While the self-reflexive and transported states might appear similar in that they are characterized by high involvement by audience members, the two exposure states are very different. In the transported state, people are highly involved emotionally and lose themselves in the action. In contrast, the self-reflexive state is characterized by people who are highly involved cognitively and very much aware of themselves as they analytically process the exposure messages.

THE MEDIA LITERACY APPROACH

The ideas presented in this chapter can be used to increase one's media literacy, that is, to increase one's power over filtering decisions, meaning-matching decisions, and meaning construction decisions. Remember that increasing your media literacy means doing particular things while you are paying attention to messages so that you control the coding of your mental processes, such that when those mental processes run automatically, they are serving your needs rather than the needs of the mass media or of advertisers.

As for the filtering task, you should periodically examine your media exposure habits and ask yourself why you are spending time with particular media and particular messages while ignoring others. If you have good reasons for your habits, then it is likely that those filtering habits are helping you achieve your own goals. But if you are puzzled by some of your habits, it is time to think about changing those habits to see if your needs can be met better through exposure to different media and different kinds of messages.

As for meaning matching, you should periodically check some of the meanings you have memorized. Perhaps you have acquired some of those meanings by simply memorizing the opinions of so-called experts, such as newscasters, pundits, cultural critics, and so on. Perhaps the experts were later found to be wrong, yet you still hold onto a memorized opinion that is now faulty. Or perhaps you should not have memorized an expert's opinion but instead constructed your own opinion that fits better with your own personal beliefs and experiences. It is likely that your large set of memorized meanings contains elements that are out of date, are causing friction with what you believe, or are faulty in some way. If you don't identify them and clear them out of your "mental dictionary," you will continue to automatically use those meanings, and this can take you further away from your goals.

As for meaning construction, you should identify areas where decisions are most important in your life. As you use the media messages to pull in information, ask yourself if you are simply accepting that information as is or transforming it to fit into your needs and goals—that is, the more you are working on transforming that information as raw materials, the more you are constructing your own meanings. If we simply accept the surface meaning from the media messages and do not construct meaning for ourselves, we are in danger of negative effects. Some of these effects are relatively minor, but many are more profound and change the way we think about reality, truth, and ourselves. Ignoring the problem makes it worse because the messages will continue to aggressively invade our subconscious and shape our fundamental values as well as the way we think.

The meaning of media messages is not always the way it might seem on the surface. There are often many layers of meanings. The more you are aware of the layers of meaning in messages, the more you can control the selection of which meanings you want. The constant exposure to media messages influences the way we think about the world and ourselves. It influences our beliefs about crime, education, religion, families, and the world in general.

Some people perform these information-processing tasks better than others and are therefore more media literate than other people. Literacy begins with our personal locus. Some of us have no plan to our lives or for our media exposures; thus, we let the media fully program us. We need to be aware of our personal goals and needs, then exert the drive energy to take control of our meanings. We also need tools to execute our plans. Those tools are competencies and skills. Competencies are the tools people have acquired to help them interact with the media and to access information in the messages. Competencies are learned early in life, then applied automatically. Competencies are categorical; that is, either people are able to do something or they are not able. For example, either people know how to recognize a word and match its meaning to a memorized meaning or they do not. Having competencies does not make one media literate, but lacking these competencies prevents one from being media literate because this deficiency prevents a person from accessing particular kinds of information. For example, people who do not have a basic reading competency cannot access printed material. This will greatly limit what they can build into their knowledge structures. This will also suppress the drive states in the locus; people who cannot read will have very low motivation to expose themselves to printed information.

Media literacy is much more concerned with addressing improvement of skills rather than the attainment of competencies. Although competencies are relatively high, 14.5% of the adult population in this country cannot read at a functional level (National Center for Education Statistics, 2003). This is a large percentage when we think of the educational system failing to teach one in seven people the basic competency of reading; these people are having their exposure to media messages severely limited, and it is important that we have advocates for reading literacy to work on shrinking this percentage. However, the larger concern is with the other 85.5% of the adult population who has the basic competencies but may be lacking the level of skills needed to be media literate. Skills are the tools we use to construct our knowledge structures. Skill development is what really can make a large difference in a person moving from lower to higher levels of media literacy. People who have weak skills will not be able to do much with the information they encounter. They are likely to ignore good information and fixate on inaccurate or bad information because they are unable to tell the difference and therefore do not make good selections among all the available information. They will organize information poorly, thus creating weak and faulty knowledge structures. In the worst case, people with weak skills will try to avoid thinking about information altogether and become passive; the active information providers—such as advertisers and entertainers—will become the constructors of people's knowledge structures and will take control over of how people see the world by altering their beliefs and by giving people faulty standards that they then use to create their attitudes.

Skills and competencies work together in a continual cyclical process. With certain information-processing tasks, some skills or competencies may be more important than others. For example, with the task of filtering, the skills of analysis and evaluation are most important. With the task of meaning matching, the competencies are most important. And with the task of meaning construction, the skills of grouping, induction, deduction, synthesis, and abstracting are most important. However, the value of the individual skills and competencies varies by particular challenges presented by different types of messages.

SUMMARY

Recall from Chapter 2 that we spend a great deal of time in the automatic state of exposure to filter out almost all media messages efficiently. However, it is important to analyze our media habits periodically so that we can identify which habits are working to achieve our goals and which are diverting our time and attention away into wasteful or harmful practices. Once we can make this distinction clearly, we can reprogram our automatic codes so that when we return to the state of automaticity and our mind makes thousands of decisions while on automatic pilot, those decisions will make us more productive, smarter, and happier.

> **Chapter Resources:** To test your knowledge and learn more about the topics discussed in this chapter, visit the Student Study Site at www.sagepub.com/potter6e.

FURTHER READING

Potter, W. J. (2005). *Becoming a strategic thinker: Developing skills for success.* Upper Saddle River, NJ: Pearson Prentice-Hall. (183 pages with index)

In this book, I show that success in higher education is based on how well students have mastered eight skills. Seven of these skills are also key to developing higher levels of media literacy. This book presents lots of examples and exercises for each skill.

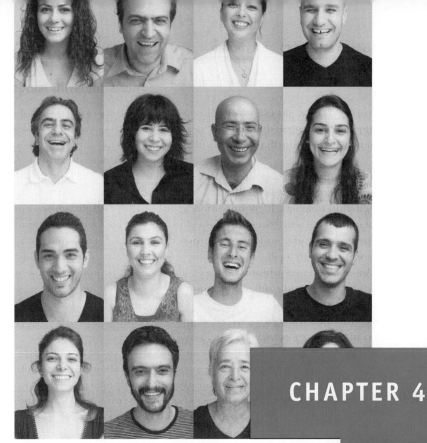

CHAPTER 4

Key Idea: The mass media segment the general population into marketing niches, then construct niche audiences by creating special content to attract people in each niche so those audiences can be rented to advertisers.

Industry Perspective on Audience

Alan and Jean were having coffee when Alan started to complain, "I'm starting to feel old these days."

"Oh Alan, don't be ridiculous. You're not old. You still have all your hair and it hasn't even started to turn gray. You don't even need to wear glasses yet."

"I know that, but I still am feeling old."

"Are you starting to have mysterious aches and pains?"

"No. I feel fine."

"Is it hard for you to wake up in the morning and have enough energy to get through the day?"

"No. I still have lots of energy."

Jean was frustrated. "I don't get it. Why are you feeling old?"

"Well, it's my favorite shows on television."

"Are they being canceled?"

"No it's not that. It's the ads in my shows. All the ads are for old people products like Geritol, denture cream, electric wheel chairs, retirement cruises, stuff like that!"

"Is that all that is bothering you?" Jean replied, feeling relieved. "That's no big deal. You can easily fix that. I had that same feeling last year and all I needed to do was watch other TV shows."

"What shows?"

"There are lots of shows with ads for cheap trucks, beer, and fast food."

"Watching those shows helped you feel young again?"

"Yes, it did. I no longer think about whether I have enough health insurance when I'm retired and whether I should strap on a diaper when I go to bed."

"Like that is so awesome, dude." Alan was already feeling younger.

"Of course there is one problem with this," said Jean. "The TV shows you have to watch seem so juvenile and silly."

The mass media construct audiences so they can rent those audiences out to advertisers. In constructing those audiences, the media focus on particular niches where they can provide content that serves a need not already being met. They attract particular kinds of people into those audiences and then condition them for repeat exposures. In this chapter, we will examine these strategies of audience attraction and conditioning. But first, we need to examine the more fundamental issue about how the mass media have changed their perspective on the audience as being a mass to being a wide range of smaller niche audiences.

SHIFT FROM MASS TO NICHE PERSPECTIVE ON AUDIENCE

Media programmers no longer think of the audience as a large mass of undifferentiated people. Now they think of audiences as many niches of people as defined by their special interests.

What Is a Mass Audience?

Until fairly recently, many media programmers and researchers believed there was something called a "mass" audience for the media. The term mass communication came into use about a century ago, when early social philosophers posited that newspapers, magazines, and books communicated their ideas to all audience members in roughly the same way. If a message affected one member a certain way, it would affect all audience members the same way. The term *mass* did not refer to a *large* audience as much as it referred to a certain *type* of audience. Sociologists in the early 20th century focused on the way people felt about themselves and others in social networks in industrialized societies. They felt that people in the modern mass society were becoming both isolated and alienated from other members of society because increasing technology was turning people into machines.

Scholars defined a "mass" with four characteristics. First, the audience composition is heterogeneous. This means that the audience is composed of people of all kinds, and no one is excluded. Second, the audience members are anonymous. The message designers don't know the names of anyone in the audience—nor do they care to—because the designers regard everyone to be the same and interchangeable. Third, there is no interaction among the members in the audience. People don't talk to each other about the media messages, so the messages do not get modified in conversations. Instead, those messages have a direct effect on each person in a uniform manner. And fourth, the mass audience has no social organization, no body of custom and tradition, no established set of rules or rituals, no organized group of sentiments, and no structure or status roles (Blumer, 1946).

Starting with the Industrial Revolution in the mid-1800s, the United States and Western European countries were regarded as having mass societies. Because these countries were heavily industrialized, it was believed that this technological progress had shaped the lives of people. Less industrialized countries did not have mass societies because people there were tightly integrated into social networks in which they interacted continually with others on a daily basis. So the United States was regarded as having a mass society and India was not, even though the population of India was much larger than that of the United States.

Because it was believed that communication did take place in a mass-like fashion, it was assumed that a message reached everyone in the same way and was processed by everyone in the same manner. It was also believed that the processing itself was very simple; that is, people were vulnerable and had no psychological defenses against messages because they did not discuss messages with other people.

As evidence for this position, social critics pointed to the way that Adolph Hitler used the mass medium of radio in the 1930s to mobilize the German population to support him. Kate Smith's radio telethons for war bonds, in which she raised millions of dollars, were also offered as evidence that people were highly susceptible to media messages. Another often-cited example of the public's seeming lack of defense against media messages is provided by the widespread reaction to Orson Welles's 1939 Mercury Theater presentation of *War of the Worlds*. Some listeners to the radio play believed what seemed to be news bulletins interrupting the show were real reports of Martians landing in New Jersey. These people panicked, and this reaction was frequently cited as evidence that the media exert a powerful effect.

Sociologists of the 1930s and 1940s were very vocal in their warnings about the dangers of mass communication. A more careful analysis of the three examples mentioned, however, revealed that most people were *not* affected by those messages (Cantril, 1947). Furthermore, it was later shown that the people who were affected were not all affected in the same manner, nor did they all react in the same way. Thus, the idea of mass audience and its supporting belief that all audience members reacted to the messages in the same way was breaking down.

Rejection of the Idea of Mass Audience

By the 1950s, it became apparent to many scholars that the assumption of the audience as a "mass" was incorrect. Friedson (1953) was the first to criticize this view of the audience. He felt that people attend movies, listen to the radio, and watch television within an interpersonal context. Discussions of media material frequently take place before, during, and after exposure.

He acknowledged that a well-developed web of organized social relationships existed among audience members. This social environment continually influenced what audience members exposed themselves to and how messages affected them. Media behavior was merely a part of their more general social behavior. Friedson (1953) warned that the concept of mass is not accurately applicable to the audience. Since Friedson made this point, many other researchers have supported this position (Bauer & Bauer, 1960).

Today, the term *mass communication* is still used. But rarely is there a time when everyone is exposed to the same message. Even with events such as the Super Bowl, only about 60% of people watch. And more important, those people who do watch the Super Bowl do not all experience the same thing. Some viewers are elated as their team is winning, others are depressed as their team is losing, some are happy that there is a reason to party, and others have no idea which teams are playing the game. There is little common experience. Also, during the viewing, people talk to each other and help each other interpret events.

There is no "mass" communication because there is no "mass" audience. Instead, there are many audiences, some with structures and leadership and others without these characteristics. Some audiences last for only a few hours (Super Bowl viewers), whereas others last for a whole season (diehard football fans). Some audiences are based on a need for immediate information (viewers of CNN) or in-depth information (readers of news magazines), a need for a religious experience, or a need for political stimulation, musical entertainment, romantic fantasy, and on and on.

The Idea of Niche Audience

Mass media programmers and product marketers know that there is no mass audience. Therefore, they almost never attempt to sell a product, service, or media message to everyone. Instead, media programmers construct particular kinds of messages to appeal to particular kinds of people—niche audiences. They send those messages out in their media channels, hoping to attract as many of those targeted people as possible. Once they have attracted them, they rent that audience's attention out to advertisers, who want to get their messages in front of those targets and persuade them to buy their products and services. Thus, media programmers are in the business of constructing niche audiences. For example, if a website designer wants to attract an upscale, highly educated, professional audience, the designer must identify an interest these people would have, for example, an interest in golf. The Web designer then would have to assemble content that would satisfy a need that these people have that is not already being met by other websites, cable TV networks, magazines, and books. The Web designers must then find out where this potential audience is spending its time with the media and put ads in those media messages to attract those people to the newly designed website on golf. Once the website starts attracting these people, a sales staff will sell access to this audience to certain advertisers, such as luxury car dealers, jewelers, travel agencies, and stores that sell golf equipment.

Each person is a member of multiple-niche audiences. You are a member of a local community that the local newspaper and cable TV franchise target. You are a member of virtual communities when you get on the Internet—communities that quickly form and may last for only one evening. You are a member of certain hobby groups that are targeted by certain websites and magazines, although other members of your audience are spread out all over the world and will never meet you in person.

IDENTIFYING NICHES

One of the key challenges for mass media programmers is to identify useful niches. To perform this task, they begin by trying to divide the total population into meaningful segments. Then they select the segments—niches—of interest to them and develop messages to try to attract people in those niches.

Over the years, audience segmentation schemes have become more complex in an effort to generate more precise groupings. This is illustrated by showing the development of thinking over five types of segmentation methods: geographic, demographic, social class, geodemographic, and psychographic segmentation.

Geographic Segmentation

This type of segmentation scheme is most important to newspapers, radio, and local television where there are geographical boundaries to their coverage areas. But it has also been useful to other media in thinking about getting their messages out to certain regions of the country.

This is the oldest form of segmentation, and it worked well when regions of the country were culturally diverse. A company would begin a business in a certain locale and produce products that the people in that locale wanted. Because of limits on distribution, that company would only do business and only advertise in that one area. If that company wanted to expand, it would move out from its home locale to other places in the region where the product met a need. If there was a nationwide need, then the company could expand into national distribution and advertising—but then there would be no need to do geographic segmentation. As many businesses took their products into the national market, regional differences eroded.

Geographic segmentation is becoming less useful as the country becomes more geographically homogenized. We are a mobile society. Each year, about 20% of the population moves to a new home. Therefore, regions are not as insulated as they once were. Also, regions are not as different from one another as they once were. Over time, there has been much more of a sharing of foods, music, clothing styles, and other cultural elements across regions.

Demographic Segmentation

Demographics focus on the relatively enduring characteristics about each person— such as gender, ethnic background, age, income, and education. These are fairly stable characteristics and have been quite useful in classifying us into meaningful audience segments. Although people can change their status on some of these (such as education and income), such change requires a great deal of effort and takes some time to evolve.

The usefulness of demographics as an audience segmentation device has been diminishing. Decades ago, when adult women typically stayed home and raised children, it made sense to market household and child care products to women only. Also, radio and television presented female-type programs during the daytime hours when women were home. But now that the percentage of women in the labor force is the same as that for men, gender is less useful as a segmenter. Also, with the mobile nature of the newer media, people can access the same media and messages whether they are home-bound, at work, or traveling.

Ethnicity also used to be a stronger demographic segmenter than it is today as the range of income, education, political views, and cultural needs is much greater within any ethnic group than it is across ethnic groups. With the tremendous growth of credit, household income has not been as useful a segmenter. Educational level is also less useful. Fifty years ago, having a college degree put you in an elite—the top 5% of the population. But now,

20% of American adults have at least one college degree, and another 20% have earned some college credit.

Social Class Segmentation

We could think of social class solely in terms of household income level, but then social class would mean the same thing as the demographic of income. Why would we need both types of segmentation schemes if they put the same people into the same groups? Instead, social class is a mix of characteristics. One of those characteristics is income, but psychological characteristics are also part of the mix. For example, being in the lower class, of course, means a low income. But you as a college student have a very low income. Do you consider yourself lower class? No, obviously there is more to the definition. Being in the lower class means taking the psychological perspective that what happens in life is not under your control. Lower-class people feel that they were born into a situation with not much opportunity and that they must struggle to maintain their existence. Because fate has put them in this situation, all they can do is to try to make the best of it when they can. Therefore, when they get a windfall of money, they want to have as much fun as they can before someone takes it away from them. There is no point in saving for a tomorrow that will never come.

Being middle class means holding the value that it is good to put off immediate pleasures for more important longer term goals. Thus, middle-class people have a strong work ethic, believing that work is good for them and for society in general. The fact that you are in college is a good indication that you hold a middle-class perspective. You believe that it is a good idea to make economic, time, and lifestyle sacrifices for 4 years now so that later you will receive much larger rewards for your efforts. You believe that your current actions influence your future. You believe that you control your fate—not the other way around.

Being upper class does not mean simply having more money; it means being able to control more resources—yours and those of others. It means the ability to raise large sums and wield a high degree of power.

Geodemographic Segmentation

A relatively recent innovation in consumer segmentation is geodemographic, which is a blend of geographic and demographic segmentation. It is based on the assumption that we choose to live in neighborhoods where other people are like us. So neighborhoods tend to be homogeneous on important characteristics, and these characteristics are very different across neighborhoods.

One example of geodemographic segmentation is the PRIZM scheme, which was developed by the Claritas Corporation in 1974. PRIZM is based on a complex analysis of the U.S. census data. It began with the 35,000 ZIP code neighborhoods and concluded that there were 40 different kinds of neighborhoods in the United States. It gave the clusters memorable (and trademarked) nicknames such as "sun belt singles" (which are southern suburban areas populated by young professionals), "Norma Rae–ville" (named after the movie of a working-class woman who unionized factory employees), "Marlboro country" (evoking a western rural

area with rugged men on horses), "furs and station wagons" (typified by new money living in expensive new neighborhoods), and "hardscrabble" (which represents areas in the Ozark mountains, Dakota badlands, and south Texas border).

Psychographic Segmentation

Psychographics is the current cutting edge of segmentation schemes. It is not limited to one or two characteristics of people but uses a wide variety of variables to create its segments. Typically, a psychographic segmentation scheme will use demographics, lifestyle, and product usage variables in segmenting consumers. There are many examples of psychographic segmentation. Two stand out as being very influential.

Twelve American Lifestyles

William Wells, director of advertising research at Needham, Harper & Steers in Chicago, developed the 12 American lifestyles that include Joe the factory worker and his wife Judy, Phyllis the career woman and her liberated husband Dale, Thelma the contented homemaker, and Harry the cigar-chomping middle-aged salesman. Each of these creations represents a different lifestyle. For example, Joe is a lower-middle-class male in his 30s who makes an hourly wage doing semiskilled work. He watches a lot of television, especially sports and action/adventure programs; he rarely reads. He drives a pickup truck and knows a lot about automotive parts and accessories. In contrast, Phyllis is a career woman in her 30s with a graduate degree. She reads a lot, and when she watches television, it is usually news or a good movie. She likes fine food, dining out, and travel.

VALS Typology

VALS was developed at SRI (Stanford Research Institute) by Arnold Mitchell. After monitoring social, economic, and political trends during the 1960s and 1970s, Mitchell constructed an 85-page measurement instrument that asked questions ranging from people's sexual habits to what brands of margarine they ate. He had 1,635 people fill out the questionnaire, and the answers became the database for his book *Nine American Lifestyles,* published in 1983. In the book, Mitchell argued that people's values strongly influence their spending patterns and media behaviors. So if we know which value group a person identifies with, we can predict a great deal about the products and services he or she will want. For example, one of the groups is called Experientials. The people in this value grouping like to try new and different things to see what they are like. They like to travel. They are early users of new types of products. And they are constantly looking for something different.

The VALS typology has made SRI very successful, with income more than $200 million per year. By the mid-1980s, SRI had 130 VALS clients, including the major TV networks, major ad agencies, major publishers such as Time, and major corporations such as AT&T, Avon, Coke, General Motors, P&G, RJ Reynolds, and Tupperware. For example, Timex, a giant corporation best known for its watches, wanted to move into the home health care market with a selection of new products, including digital thermometers and blood pressure monitors. It decided to focus on two VALS segments: Societally Conscious and the Achievers. Everything about the packaging and the advertisements was chosen with these two groups in mind. Models were upscale, mature in comfortable surroundings with plants and books. The tagline was "Technology where it does the most good." Within months, all Timex products were the leaders in this new and fast-growing industry.

Over the years, as the American culture has changed, VALS has changed its segments to keep up. Today, the VALS typology of segments looks very different than it did in the early 1980s. By keeping up with changes in people's lifestyles over the years, VALS has remained a valuable tool to mass media programmers and marketers.

ATTRACTING AUDIENCES

Attracting audience attention is critical for the thousands of advertisers who spend billions of dollars each year to get their messages out to their target audiences. But as more and more advertisers as well as media outlets compete for the attention of the public, attention has become the scarce resource of the information economy. In their fascinating book *The Attention Economy: Understanding the New Currency of Business,* Davenport and Beck (2001) argue, "In postindustrialized societies, attention has become a more valuable currency than the kind you store in bank accounts. . . . Understanding and managing attention is now the single most important determinant of business success" (p. 3).

After a media organization has selected a niche audience to target, it must develop content to attract people into that audience. The mass media employ two tactics to do this. First, they try to appeal to your existing needs and interests. Second, they use cross-media and cross-vehicle promotion to attract your attention.

Appeal to Existing Needs and Interests

The mass media do not develop vehicles and messages and then go looking for an audience; instead, they conduct research to try to identify the message needs of potential audiences, and then they develop that content. Not everyone has the same needs and interests, so the media can identify a range of different types of people as defined by those different needs. For example, some people are very interested in sports, but other people are more interested in news and public affairs. These are two important niches for the media. Each of these has subniches. Some sports fanatics might like baseball, whereas others cannot stand baseball but love football.

How do media companies know what the existing needs are? The easiest way to answer this question is to look at what messages are already being consumed. The messages that already are attracting the most attention within a niche audience demonstrate that there is a particular existing need. The new competitors then try to create their own messages to attract that same audience by appealing to that same need. This is why many new films, TV shows, and popular songs typically look and sound like last year's most popular films, TV shows, and songs.

Programmers know that we have a relatively narrow exposure repertoire—that is, a set of message types we attend to—so if the new competitors can make their messages very similar to what we are already attending to, we will likely pay attention to those new messages also. Messages that are too different than what we are already exposing ourselves to will not break through the automaticity. We typically stay in this state of automaticity until something triggers our attention, and then we pay attention to it. Therefore, media programmers look for what has triggered our attention in the past, and they construct their messages in a similar manner so their messages will also trigger our attention.

Although we have a wide variety of media and messages available to us, we usually select a small subset of them that tend to serve our needs best. This fact about a small set of message preferences—or media repertoire—was clearly established several decades ago when there were far fewer media choices than we have today. For example, Ferguson (1992) found that even in cable TV households with more than 100 choices of channels, TV viewers typically watched only 5 to 8 channels and ignored the rest. Also, having a remote control device to change TV channels or a device to record shows was not found to increase the size of a person's channel repertoire. Thus, when the media expand the number of messages offered, individuals do not increase the range of their exposures; instead, the expanded number of messages increases the number of niche audiences. With a larger range of messages available, individuals can find particular messages that better serve their needs. As the newer interactive media make it possible to have even greater choice in how we use the media, each of us still has a relatively narrow focus on the types of media and messages we like best.

Cross-Media and Cross-Vehicle Promotion

Media programmers must find potential members of their audience in other audiences so the programmers can promote their new messages and thus attract people to the audience they are trying to construct. Programmers therefore will engage in a great deal of cross-media promotion and cross-vehicle promotion.

Several decades ago, media programmers were most concerned about branding their particular vehicles and trying to build loyalty to those vehicles. For example, local television stations wanted you to watch only them. A newspaper wanted you to be loyal to that newspaper and get your news only there—not from magazines, television, or the radio. But with the rise of media consolidation, media programmers have shifted their focus to the message and away from the vehicle. So, for example, a conservative commentator on the radio might also be asked to post a column on a website and appear on a TV show where the company that owns the radio station also owns the website and the television station. That company might also own a magazine and book publishing firm, in which case the commentator would be encouraged to write a column for the magazine and publish a book. When this media conglomerate company brands its message—the commentator—the company then tries to market that message through as many media and vehicles that it owns so as to increase the number of revenue streams without adding much to the already existing expenses. Therefore, media companies think of audiences more in terms of messages that would attract them rather than as groups of people limited to one medium or one vehicle.

Differences across media are also blurring over time. Newspapers have become more like magazines in their editorial outlook, featuring more soft news and human interest pieces that are not time sensitive and that appeal more as entertainment than as information. Trade books are becoming shorter and less literary. And computers with their games, encyclopedias, and Web pages are becoming more like films, books, magazines, and newspapers. Given the focus on messages and the convergence of channels, the content is becoming much more of a focus than is the delivery system.

Several decades ago, some futurists argued that we are moving toward convergence where all the media will be one—"a single, high capacity, digital network of networks that will bridge what we now know as the separate domains of computing, telephony, broadcasting, motion pictures, and publishing" (Neuman, 1991, p. x). This convergence has been happening and continues to happen (Jenkins, 2006).

CONDITIONING AUDIENCES

Once a mass media organization has attracted you to a message, it immediately tries to condition you for repeated exposures. This drive toward audience conditioning is an essential strategy for all mass media. The costs of attracting members of an audience to their first exposure to a message are so high that media organizations must rely on repeated exposures to recoup their initial investment and eventually make a profit.

Before we begin this section, look at Exercise 4.1 and estimate how much you are exposed to the media in an average week. Make some quick estimates, and then return to this point in the chapter. The mass media have conditioned us to certain behavioral patterns of exposure. These are continually reinforced until they become habits, and then they are reinforced some more so that we do not change our habits.

Media exposures are inertial. This means that when we are paying attention to a particular message, we tend to keep paying attention to that message, and when we are in an automatic state, we tend to stay in that state and filter out all the messages around us. For example, let's say we turn on our television set at 8 p.m. to watch a show we like—one that is in our viewing repertoire, so we have developed the habit of watching it each time it is on television. Let's say the show is a 30-minute situation comedy. At 8:30, the show will be over. Television programmers know that if they present another situation comedy of the same type at 8:30, there is a high probability that you will continue to watch their channel. This is called audience flow-through. Television programmers try to attract you early in the evening and then present similar types of shows to keep you and your fellow audience members viewing their channels and flowing through all the way to the end of the night. It has been well known for some time that the best predictor for a program's rating is the rating of the lead-in program and the lead-out program (R. Cooper, 1993). For this reason, television programmers will put similar-type programs together (like four situation comedies back-to-back) to hold onto its audience. If they interrupted the block of situation comedies with a game show, they would lose all the viewers who did not have that type of program in their viewing repertoire. For the same reason, websites work to get a link to their site on other websites so that audiences of those other websites will flow through to their website.

SUMMARY

This is an exciting time to be a part of our culture. The media are constantly identifying our needs for information and entertainment. Once the media have identified a new need, they work quickly to develop all kinds of messages that will attract people with that need; in this way, they create audiences. Then once a media company has developed an audience, it works hard to condition that audience for repeat exposures. This accounts for why the mass media pump out an incredible assortment of messages each year.

When we are well aware of our needs, we can use the mass media as a rich resource to satisfy every conceivable need. But if we are not self-aware, the most aggressive of the mass media will herd us into audiences for their most profitable messages. Increasing media literacy gives you more control so you can use the mass media as a tool in achieving your needs, rather than allowing the mass media to use you as a tool to achieve their needs.

After reading through this chapter, you should be more sensitized to your media exposures, and you should be more aware of those exposures. Now do Exercise 4.2, which asks you to keep a diary of your media exposures. If you are like most people, your diary will reveal that you are exposed much more than you thought when you made your initial estimate. The reason for this is that the media have conditioned many exposure patterns so well that we don't think about them during the actual exposures, and we cannot remember them later when we try to recall them. Much of our exposure is automatic.

Chapter Resources: To test your knowledge and learn more about the topics discussed in this chapter, visit the Student Study Site at www.sagepub.com/potter6e.

FURTHER READING

Davenport, T. H., & Beck, J. C. (2001). *The attention economy: Understanding the new currency of business.* Boston: Harvard Business School Press. (253 pages with index)

This is a very readable book written by two business school professors who explain why attention deficit is such a serious problem in our economy. But they are not social critics who are interested in pointing out a problem and then exploring recommendations for ameliorating the problem. Instead, they write more as marketing consultants who provide suggestions to businesses about how to attract the public's attention.

Napoli, P. M. (2011). *Audience evolution: New technologies and the transformation of media audiences.* New York: Columbia University Press.

Written by a professor at Fordham University, this book shows how the conceptualization of audiences has changed over time, particularly with the development of the newer media technologies that serve to fragment society. The scholarly analysis of this phenomenon focuses on political, economic, and social perspectives.

Neuman, W. R. (1991). *The future of the mass audience.* New York: Cambridge University Press. (218 pages)

Neuman begins with a good, balanced discussion of the difficult idea of postindustrialism and with the conflict between fragmentation and homogenization. He argues that education contributes to fragmentation, with people able to peruse their specialized interests. Family has been changing since women entered the workforce in large percentage. He also shows that media use has fragmented. He argues that this is not a new issue but is a continuing and central problem of political communications. The key issue is that of balance: balance between the center and the periphery, between different interest factions, between competing elites, and between an efficient and effective central authority and the conflicting demands of the broader electorate (p. 167). This is the conflict between community and pluralism.

EXERCISE 4.1

Estimate Your Media Exposure

Try to estimate how many minutes and hours you spend with each of the following media during a typical week.

_____ Watching television (cable, broadcast, movies played on a VCR or DVD player, etc.)

_____ Watching films at a theater

_____ Listening to radio (at home, in your car, etc.)

_____ Listening to recordings (CDs and tapes)

_____ Reading newspapers

_____ Reading magazines of all kinds

_____ Reading books (texts for class, novels for pleasure, etc.)

_____ Computer usage (games, word processing, surfing the Internet, etc.)

_____ TOTAL *(Continued)*

EXERCISE 4.2

Track Your Media Exposures

Keep a *Media Exposure Diary* for 1 week. Get a small notebook—one you can carry with you wherever you go for 7 days. Every time you are exposed to a message from the media either directly or indirectly, make an entry of the time and what the message was.

Direct exposures are those where you come in contact with a medium and experience a message during that contact. For example, if you watch *The Simpsons,* then write, "Message: *The Simpsons;* Time: Monday 8–8:30." Listening to KXXX for 30 minutes in the car is also a direct exposure.

Indirect exposures are those where you see a reminder of a media message, such as seeing a title of a movie on the marquee or at a bus stop. You don't see the film itself (which would be a direct exposure), but you see something that reminds you of it. Also, listen to conversations. If people talk about something they heard from the media, then you have been exposed to that media message indirectly. For example, if you heard your friends talk about *The Simpsons,* then write, "Message: Talked with friends about *The Simpsons;* Time: Tuesday morning 10–11:30." If you happened to hear your roommate humming a popular song that is played often on the radio, then write, "Message: Roommate hummed X song; Time: Wednesday all day!"

At the end of the week, analyze the entries in your diary to answer the following questions:

1. How much total time were you exposed to media messages?

2. How many exposures did you experience in that 1 week?

3. What proportion of the exposures was direct and what proportion was indirect?

4. What proportion of media exposures were initiated by you (active) and what proportion just happened (passive)?

5. How do your diary data compare to your estimates from Exercise 4.1?

6. What kinds of messages were most prevalent?

EXERCISE 4.3

What Segments Are You In?

1. Pick three of your favorite television shows. Write the name of each on the column heading line below. Then watch each of these shows and list the products being advertised in each commercial on the lines in the column for that show.

Show 1:	Show 2:	Show 3:

2. Now look at the lists of products and try to imagine who the advertisers had in mind as a target audience when they decided to advertise in these shows.

   - Are those products oriented more toward males or females, or doesn't it matter?
   - What age group are the products aimed at?
   - What economic level are the products aimed at?
   - What educational level are the products aimed at?
   - What geographical location are the products aimed at, or doesn't it matter?
   - What values do the advertisers think you have?

3. Did you notice any ads for other TV shows? If so, what other shows where those ads trying to get you to watch? Do you watch those other shows? Why or why not?

4. Now try the same exercise using three websites that you like.

5. Monitor the e-mails you receive from companies trying to sell you something. Think about how these companies got your e-mail address.

CHAPTER 5

Key Idea: Children are treated as a special audience because of their lack of maturation and experience; however, maturation and experience alone do not make someone media literate.

Children as a Special Audience

Kyle sent his report on the battle of Gettysburg to the color printer attached to his family's computer. He had done his research on Wikipedia, then pasted some pictures of the battlefield he had taken with his digital camera during his family's vacation the previous summer. He looked proudly at the report and thought that Mrs. Hawthorne, his fourth-grade teacher, would surely give him another A. To reward himself, he clicked on his favorite social networking Internet site and began texting his growing list of friends when his brother Bobby interrupted him.

"Hey Kyle, let's play some online games. How about some poker!"

"Yeah, right. If Mom catches us playing poker again, she's gonna ban me from the computer for a month."

"Come on, she's not going to find out."

"No way."

"Then show me how to get on the poker site. I want to play."

"I already showed you a million times." Kyle tried changing the subject. "Did you do your homework, Bobby?"

"Boring. Besides I forgot how to get on that math site."

"I'll show you—again." Kyle was getting irritated with his brother. Kyle felt that Bobby, who was in the sixth grade, should be teaching things to Kyle, not the other way around.

Researchers, policy makers, and the public in general have treated children as a special audience, because they believe that children are especially vulnerable to negative effects from the mass media. It is true that younger children *in general* are more vulnerable to media manipulation and negative effects than older children *in general*. However, what many people fail to understand is that there is a wide variation in vulnerability at any given age because there is a wide variation of the degree of media literacy at any given age. For example, some fourth graders are more naturally media literate than other fourth graders, and some fourth graders may even be more naturally media literate than other children who are older than they are. Just because people have lived more years does not automatically mean that they are more media literate and therefore less vulnerable to media manipulation and negative effects. The key questions, then, are the following: Why are children in general regarded as especially vulnerable to media influence—that is, why are children treated as a special audience? and Why is it that some children are naturally more media literate than other children of the same age?

WHY TREAT CHILDREN AS A SPECIAL AUDIENCE?

There are two major reasons why children are regarded as a special group when it comes to the mass media. One reason is that certain reasoning abilities—cognitive, emotional, and moral—are at fairly low levels and take some time to develop to a point where those abilities can adequately protect a person from media manipulation. A second reason is that children lack the degree of real-world experience required to process media messages well. Real-world experience is a necessary context to help people determine when media messages are misleading them. Let's examine each of these two major reasons in more detail.

Maturation

Our abilities increase from when we are infants through adolescence. This is obvious physically; that is, as we age from infancy, we are able to run faster, jump higher, and lift heavier objects.

We also need cognitive development in addition to physical development. When we are very young, our minds are not developed enough to allow for an understanding of abstract thoughts, such as required by mathematical reasoning, for example. A task of reasoning (such as multiplying 4 times 5) is very difficult for us when we are 4 years old but very easy for us a few short years later. We also need emotional development (Goleman, 1995) and moral development (Kohlberg, 1981) to help us understand more things in our environment. As we reach higher levels of maturation cognitively, emotionally, and morally, we are able to perceive more elements in media messages and to understand them to a greater depth.

Think of maturation as a series of gates along the path to higher media literacy. When we encounter one of these gates, we must wait behind it until we mature to a certain level, and then the gate opens and we can proceed. There are a series cognitive gates, emotional gates, and moral gates. These gates occur every few years throughout childhood and hold us back in the early stages of media literacy. For example, most humans are not capable of acquiring the skill of reading until they are beyond the age of 4 or 5 because their minds have not matured to a point where such learning is possible. Trying to teach reading to 2-year-olds is very frustrating. No matter how hard you work as a teacher or how hard the children work to learn, they will not get much out of this effort because their minds have not matured enough to handle this task. But once a child's mind matures to the point where he or she can use those skills, the practice of reading begins to pay off.

Let's take a closer look at how people develop multidimensionally—cognitively, emotionally, and morally.

Cognitive Development

The most influential thinker on the topic of cognitive maturation during childhood has been the Swiss psychologist Jean Piaget. From years of research, Piaget has found that a child's mind matures from birth to about 12 years of age, during which time it goes through several identifiable stages (P. K. Smith & Cowie, 1988). Until age 2, children are in the sensorimotor stage and then advance to the preoperational stage from 2 to 7 years of age. Then they progress to the concrete operational stage, and by age 12, they move into the formal operational stage, where they are regarded as having matured cognitively into adulthood. In each of these stages, children's minds mature to a point where they can accomplish a new set of cognitive tasks. For example, in the concrete operational stage (ages 7–12), children are able to organize objects into series. If you try to teach this skill to a child of age 3, you will fail—no matter how organized and clear your lessons are. Another skill that is developed throughout childhood is conservation, which is the ability to realize that certain attributes of an object are constant, even though that object is transformed in appearance (Pulaski, 1980). For example, ask a child to make two balls of clay the same size. Then roll one of them out into a long, thin shape like a snake, and ask the child which of the two pieces of clay is bigger. Younger children will say the snake is bigger than the ball because the snake is longer. The child does not have the ability to understand that the same amount of clay has been conserved; only the shape (not the quantity) has been changed. Children's minds have matured enough to understand the idea of conservation by the time they reach about age 7.

Children begin paying attention to the TV screen as early as 6 months of age (Hollenbeck & Slaby, 1979), and by age 3, many children have developed regular patterns of viewing of about an hour or two per day (Huston et al., 1983). Their viewing is primarily exploratory. This means that they are looking for individual events that stand out because of certain motions, color, music, sound effects, or unusual voices. They look for action, not dialogue. They have great difficulty in understanding that individual events are ordered into plots, that characters have motives that influence the action, and that characters change as a result of what happens in the plot (Wartella, 1981). The reason for this is that young children have not developed a very sophisticated understanding of narratives. Until they learn more of the principles of narrative progression, they will have difficulty making sense out of stories longer than a minute or two (Meadowcroft & Reeves, 1989).

By about age 4, children are spending less time in the exploratory mode and more time in a search mode. This means that children begin developing an agenda of what to look for;

their attention does not simply bounce haphazardly around from one high-profile action to another. By kindergarten, a continuous storyline holds their attention. They focus their attention on formal features in making their decisions about what is important in the shows. For example, they interpret that a laugh track signals that a program is a comedy.

Also by age 4, children begin trying to distinguish between ads and programs. At first this is difficult, until they develop the skills of perceptual discrimination. During this trial-and-error learning, children either express confusion about the difference or use superficial perceptual or affective cues as the basis for the distinction. With practice, they become more skilled at separating ads from program content.

Children must also acquire the knowledge that ads are paid messages that are designed to get them to buy something—or make them ask their parents to buy something. Only 10% of children 5 to 7 years of age have a clear understanding of the profit-seeking motives of commercials; 55% are totally unaware of the nature of ads and believe commercials are purely for entertainment. For example, Wilson and Weiss (1992) found that compared to older children (ages 7–11), younger children (ages 4–6) were less able to recognize an ad for a particular toy and comprehend its intent when it was shown in a cartoon program, even when the product "spokesperson" was a character from a different cartoon program.

Disclaimers placed before ads to alert children to the fact that the program is being interrupted and that an ad is about to be shown do not generally work well with children younger than age 7 because they do not fully understand what an ad is. However, when disclaimers are in both the audio and video tracks, children are better able to perceive them. Also, when disclaimers are reworded into the language of children, their comprehension dramatically increases. By the second or third grade, most children have overcome their difficulty distinguishing between programs and commercials. With the combination of cognitive maturation, experience, and active application of critical skills, children no longer have any trouble understanding the purpose of ads and distinguishing ads from the program content.

As children develop an understanding of the purpose of advertising, they also develop an ability for critically evaluating ads. By the fourth grade, children have developed a critical and skeptical attitude toward advertising. They are also cynical about the credibility of commercials and begin feeling that they have been lied to in an effort by the advertiser to get them to buy products that are not as desirable as the commercials' portrayal. However, this skepticism is usually limited to their experience with products. For example, the skepticism is high with ads for familiar toys. Presumably, they have had real-world experiences with these toys and have learned that the ads contain exaggerated claims. However, children are much less skeptical of ads for medical or nutritional products; understandably, they have much less technical knowledge about these products and have less of a basis for skepticism.

By ages 8 to 10, most children have developed a good understanding of fictional plots. They understand how motives of characters influence plot points and how characters change as a result of what happens to them. Children of this age are not limited to understanding characters on only their physical traits but can also infer personality characteristics.

By ages 10 to 12, children have a rudimentary idea of the economic nature of TV. They recognize that different businesses produce media messages and that these businesses have a profit-making motive.

Emotional Development

Media messages can arouse emotions in people of all ages. Emotions do not need to be learned in the sense that we must learn to recognize words in order to read. Instead, emotions are hardwired into our brains (Goleman, 1995). Regardless of the culture in which we are raised, we all can recognize in ourselves and others the basic emotions of anger, sadness, fear, enjoyment, love, surprise, disgust, and shame.

We develop higher levels of emotional literacy by gaining experience with emotions and by paying close attention to our feelings when we interact with the media. As we gain greater experience with emotions, we are able to make finer discriminations. For example, we are all familiar with anger because that is one of the basic emotions. But it takes experience with this emotion to be able to tell the difference between hatred, outrage, fury, wrath, animosity, hostility, resentment, indignation, acrimony, annoyance, irritability, and exasperation.

A lack of cognitive development can be a barrier to appropriate emotional reactions to media messages. For example, very young children cannot follow the interconnected elements in a continuing plot; instead, they focus on individual elements. Therefore, they cannot understand suspense, and without such an understanding, they cannot become emotionally aroused as the suspense builds. So a child's ability to have an emotional reaction to the media messages is low not because of a lack of ability to feel emotions but because of a lack of ability to understand why certain things are happening at particular parts of a story.

By adolescence, children have reached cognitive maturity, and all the gates are open to a full understanding of all kinds of narratives. But some adolescents and adults still do not have much of an emotional reaction to media stories. Some people can be very highly developed cognitively but very undeveloped emotionally. Goleman (1995) argues that a person's emotional intelligence interacts with IQ when he says, "We have two brains, two minds—and two different kinds of intelligence: rational and emotional. How we do in life is determined by both—it is not just IQ, but emotional intelligence that matters. Indeed, intellect cannot work at its best without emotional intelligence" (p. 28).

In summary, emotional literacy is tied to cognitive development. Children who cannot read or follow visual narratives will have their emotional reactions limited to reactions of micro-elements in messages. As people mature emotionally, they are better able to "read" emotions in themselves and others by having a higher degree of empathy and a greater self-awareness. In contrast, people at lower levels of emotional development are less able to experience emotions vicariously through characters or they experience the wrong emotions.

Moral Development

We also develop along a moral dimension. We are not born with a moral code or a sensitivity to what is right and wrong. We must learn these as young children, and children learn these things in stages. Like Piaget, Lawrence Kohlberg has studied the development of children. While Piaget was concerned with cognitive development, Kohlberg focused on moral development. He suggested that there are three levels of moral development:

preconventional, conventional, and postconventional. The centerpiece is *conventional,* which stands for fair, honest, concerned, and well regarded—characteristics of the typically good person (Kohlberg, 1966, 1981).

The preconventional stage begins at about age 2 and runs to about age 7 or 8. This is when the child is dependent on authority, and inner controls are weak. Young children depend on their parents and other adults to tell them what is right and to filter the world for them. The child's conscience is external; that is, the children must be told by others what is right.

During the conventional stage, children develop a conscience for themselves as they internalize what is right and wrong. They distinguish between truth and lies. However, the threat of punishment is still a strong motivator.

The postconventional stage can begin as early as middle adolescence, when some people are able to transcend conventional notions of right and wrong. They tend to focus on fundamental principles. This requires the ability to think abstractly and therefore recognize the ideals behind society's laws. Thus, the stages in this level are characterized by a sense that being socially conscious is more important than adhering to rigid legal principles.

Kohlberg's stages are not fixed steps that everyone follows in the same sequence. People can move around among the steps, given particular problems and moods. However, each stage is very different, and those stages are hierarchically ordered such that the more evolved person is likely to operate most often at higher levels.

Gilligan (1993) has extended the ideas of Kohlberg by arguing that there is a gender difference in moral development. Men more typically base their moral judgments on rights and rules, whereas women tend to think in terms of care and cooperation. So in a conflict situation, women are likely to try to preserve relationships. In contrast, men are likely to search for a moral rule and try to apply it even if it hurts their relationship.

Let's examine these stages with a media example. Joey is a young child in a family that allows him to spend a lot of time playing highly competitive and aggressive video games and watch a great deal of television unsupervised. There is no parent or authority figure to help him process the messages or to show him alternatives to what is portrayed in the media world. Therefore, his moral development during the preconventional stages is shaped by the themes in the television messages, mainly cartoons, action/adventure shows, and situation comedies. From his steady exposure to these types of shows and values, Joey is likely to learn the following moral lessons: Aggression (both physical and verbal) is an acceptable and successful way to solve problems; with a little hard work, everyone can be successful, that is, be wealthy, powerful, and famous; family relationships are full of conflict and deceit, but everyone still loves each other; and romantic relationships are exciting but superficial and temporary.

As Joey moves into the conventional stages, much of his behavior will be governed by these moral lessons. He feels that the best way to get approval from others is to be funny, live dangerously, and have lots of peer relationships filled with conflict—that is the active, interesting life.

Finally, as Joey reaches late adolescence and confronts the postconventional stages, he should begin asking questions such as the following: How can I live my life so as to benefit society in general? How can I resolve moral dilemmas so that I don't decide on a purely selfish basis? Given Joey's moral development and the lessons learned, it is unlikely that he will be interested in these postconventional questions. It is probable that he will stay at the conventional stage and continue to make moral decisions based on the principles he learned while watching TV as a preschooler.

Experience

Children are regarded as having less worldly experience than older people. For example, Dorr (1986) uses this reasoning as the basis for her argument that "children may accept program content as accurate 'information' when other more knowledgeable viewers know it to be otherwise" (p. 13). Children have not had as much time as adolescents or adults to develop knowledge structures on most things. This is why a good elementary education is so important—so that children can acquire the basic ideas about science, history, civics, geography, and so on. Until children have developed many knowledge structures, they don't have many perspectives from which to view the world.

SPECIAL TREATMENT FROM REGULATORS

Advocates of protecting children and policy makers have focused their attention primarily on television because this medium comes into virtually every American household and children spend a great deal of time with it even when they are very young. This activity has been focused primarily on policies intended to protect children from negative effects of exposure to TV content as well as policies designed to protect children from unfair advertising practices (Kunkel & Wilcox, 2001).

Protecting Children From Negative TV Content

For more than 50 years, Congress has been periodically holding hearings on television violence and its possible effects on children. During that time, Congress passed no legislation regulating content, but it did pressure the television networks to adopt some changes. In 1975, the TV industry tried a self-regulatory policy called the "family hour" where programmers pushed violence and other material regarded as being harmful to children later into the evening, leaving the first hour of primetime solely for content appropriate for so-called family viewing. However, several stations filed suit, citing infringement of free speech, and won their suit in court. Then the omnibus Telecommunication Act of 1996 included an amendment mandating that all TV receivers sold in the United States after 1999 should have a V-Chip, which is a screening device that allows TV owners to program their sets to avoid programs with certain ratings for violence, sex, and language.

The Federal Communications Commission (FCC) has been more aggressive in regulating indecent material, such as sexual depictions as well as specific words deemed offensive. In one instance during the 1970s, the FCC took steps to fine a radio station that aired a George

Carlin skit entitled "Filthy Words," where he repeatedly said the seven words explicitly prohibited on the airwaves. The station appealed, but the FCC ruling was upheld by the Supreme Court that reasoned it was in the public's interest to protect radio listeners from hearing those words during parts of the day when children were likely to be in the audience. More recently, shock jock Howard Stern was fined, as was the company that controlled the radio stations that broadcasted his explicit sexual references.

Protecting Children From Unfair Advertising Practices

Kunkel and Wilcox (2001) point out that two types of regulations are aimed at protecting children from unfair practices in television advertising. One of these is to limit the amount of time devoted to advertising in programs aimed at children. The limits are 12 minutes per hour on weekdays and 10.5 minutes per hour on weekends. While compliance is relatively good, there are exceptions. For example, Viacom was cited for 600 violations in one year and fined $1 million. Viacom blamed the problem on human error (Shiver, 2004).

A second type of regulation aimed at protecting children is the policy to keep a clear separation between program content and commercial content. Young children are fuzzy about the difference between entertainment and advertising content. Thus, the FCC requires bumpers, which are 5-second segments before and after commercial breaks to alert young children about the switch in content. These bumpers typically take the form of "And now a word from our sponsor." The FCC also prohibits host selling, which is the use of a character from a TV show being the product spokesperson for products advertised in ads inserted into that program. This too has relatively high compliance, but again there are exceptions. Disney was found to air 31 half-hour episodes in which commercials for products associated with the children's program were aired. Disney was fined $500,000 and blamed the problem on human error (Shiver, 2004).

SPECIAL TREATMENT FROM PARENTS

Parents of young children have been found to use a variety of techniques to help their children process media messages and protect them from harmful ones. These techniques can be usefully grouped into three categories as follows: rules (or restrictive mediation), coviewing, and active mediation (Nathanson, 2001a; Valkenburg, Krcmar, Peeters, & Marseille, 1999).

Restrictive Mediation

Restrictive mediation involves setting rules about how much, when, and which types of television can be viewed. It appears that many households do not have any rules for TV viewing in general. For example, about half (49%) of all children have no rules for TV viewing in their households, and 42% of children say that TV is on most of the time in their house (Rideout, Foehr, Roberts, & Brodie, 1999). However, Jordan (2001) reports that about 61% of parents say they have rules for TV viewing.

What are the rules? Of those families who say they have rules, 92% say they prohibit certain programs, 76% say they require their children to finish homework or chores before viewing, and 69% say they limit the amount of hours their children are allowed to watch (Stanger, 1997).

Who uses the rules? The parents who have rules for TV use tend to be mothers who are educated and highly concerned about the negative effects of television (J. D. Brown, Childers, Bauman, & Koch, 1990; Valkenburg et al., 1999). The children who receive restrictive mediation tend to be younger, but there are no gender differences (Abelman, 1999; J. D. Brown et al., 1990). Among children age 8 and older, 61% say they have no rules for television viewing (Rideout et al., 1999).

Parents who have rules appear to be motivated not by a general concern about exposure but more by a fear that certain content will trigger negative effects. For example, Valkenburg et al. (1999) found in a Dutch survey that parents who have viewing rules are motivated by the concern that their children will watch something that will either scare them or teach them to behave aggressively. This concern was also found by Krcmar and Cantor (1996), who reported that 90% of parents in an American sample said they limit their children's viewing of violent content. Also, Jordan (2001) reports that more parents are concerned about what their children watch on TV (70%) than they are about the amount of TV they watch (19%).

Coviewing

Coviewing involves parents and children watching TV together. No conversation is required. There is a discrepancy in the research about how often coviewing occurs. Some surveys have found coviewing to be very common (Sang, Schmitz, & Tasche, 1992; Valkenburg et al., 1999), with as many as 93% of parents saying they watch TV with their children at least once in a while (Jordan, 2001). Other surveys have found coviewing to be rare (Dorr, Kovaric, & Doubleday, 1989; F. Lawrence & Wozniak, 1989), with as many as 95% of children 7 years of age and older saying that they never watch TV with their parents and 81% of children ages 2 to 7 saying they never watch with their parents (Rideout et al., 1999). Notice that the discrepancy in findings may be due to who the researchers ask. When researchers ask parents if they watch with their children, coviewing appears to be common. But when researchers ask children if parents view with them, coviewing appears to be rare.

Active Mediation

Active mediation consists of conversations that parents or other adults have with children about television. This talk need not be evaluative. An analysis of the literature on active mediation studies over the years has revealed four types of mediation approaches that parents use when viewing with the children (Austin, Bolls, Fujioka, & Engelbertson, 1999). These are nonmediators (parents who talk about television with their children infrequently), optimists (those whose discussion primarily reinforces television content), cynics (those whose discussion primarily counters television content), and selectives (those who use both positive and negative discussion techniques, depending on the situation). There is a difference between positive mediation, which is pointing out the good things in television messages as well as encouraging children to emulate those good things, and negative mediation, which is pointing out the bad behaviors of characters and being critical of what is portrayed.

Active mediation has been found to be rare over many decades of research. Several studies have found that there is generally no dialogue when a parent and child are viewing together (Austin, 1993; Himmelweit, Oppenheim, & Vince, 1958; Mohr, 1979). And a Gallup poll indicates that when parents and a child are viewing television and some offensive material comes on the screen, parents are seven times more likely to ignore it by quickly changing the channel than to discuss the offending content with their child (Austin, 1993).

Active mediation has also been found from caregivers at day care centers. Nathanson, Eveland, Park, and Paul (2002) conducted a survey of 265 nonparent caregivers of second through eighth graders. They found the caregivers provided more active mediation and censorship for violence than for sex on television. They found that when caregivers thought they had effective techniques of active mediation, they were more likely to use mediation when there were high-threat situations. But when the caregivers did not feel they could mediate effectively, they were more likely to use restrictive mediation.

Use of Program Ratings

Some tools are available to parents to help children monitor their exposure. One of these tools is the ratings of films provided by the MPAA (Motion Picture Association of America) for the past three decades. However, in repeated studies, about one third or fewer parents use the MPAA age-based ratings system (Abelman, 1999; Bash, 1997; Mifflin, 1997).

Then, in the mid-1990s, Congress mandated program ratings for television programs so that this information could be fed into the V-Chip. However, parents were slow to learn about the ratings. Six months after the introduction of the ratings, a survey found that children and adolescents seldom used the ratings (B. S. Greenberg, Rampoldi-Hnilo, & Hofschire, 2000). The survey was repeated a year later, and the findings were the same; it was found that about 30% of mothers were not aware of the ratings at all, and those who were aware of the ratings gave them below-average grades for clarity (Rampoldi-Hnilo & Greenberg, 2000). Similar results were found in a pair of studies funded by the Kaiser Family Foundation. In a Kaiser study, 82% said they were aware of the ratings, but among those who were aware, only half said they used the ratings (Foehr, Rideout, & Miller, 2000), and these figures remained largely unchanged a year later when the survey was repeated (Kaiser Family Foundation, 1999). It appears that parents who are most in need of the ratings are least likely to use them; the ratings are used most by parents who already carefully monitor their children's viewing (Abelman, 1999; B. S. Greenberg & Rampoldi-Hnilo, 2001). The development of the TV ratings has done little to stimulate other parents to become more involved in the monitoring of their children's viewing. Only 39% of parents say that they use the ratings on a regular basis (Jordan, 2001).

How Useful Are These Techniques?

This is a dreadful situation. Parents think they are doing much more than they are, if children's take on things can be believed. If parents are coviewing with children, laying down rules, and actively mediating their television exposures, this is not making an impression on many of those children.

For years, media advocates for children have been pressuring the industry to provide program ratings for parents to help them monitor their children's exposures. With the mandating of the V-Chip, advocates secured a victory, but the television ratings system that the television networks developed has been widely criticized as not being accurate or useful. For example, there is evidence that the V-Chip is not as helpful as hoped (Kunkel et al., 2002). Researchers found that although the age-based ratings (TV-G, TV-PG, TV-14, and TV-MA) were reasonably accurate, the content descriptors (V, S, D, and L) were not being used on the vast majority of programs that contained violence, sexual behavior or dialogue, and adult language. Furthermore, there is evidence that only a small minority of parents is even aware of the meanings of the labels (Kaiser Family Foundation, 1999; Schmitt, 2000). For a more detailed discussion of this topic, see W. J. Potter (2003).

The problem with parents and other adults providing so little help to children seems to be traceable to two characteristics. First, it appears that parents have little real motivation to help in this area. Of course, parents say they are concerned, and of course they care about the well-being of their children. But parents do not behave in a way that follows through on that concern. Most television viewing and other media exposures go unmonitored, which leads to a second criticism: Many parents do not know what to say to their children to help them become more media literate, nor do they have an educated rationale for viewing rules. Unless parents themselves are media literate, their help is likely to lead to negative effects rather than truly helping their children.

REEXAMINING THE CASE FOR SPECIAL TREATMENT

Clearly young children are at a disadvantage compared to adolescents and adults; young children have lower levels of maturation and experience. Therefore, it is understandable why children are treated as a special group that needs protection from risks of negative media effects. However, we must also realize that many adolescents and even adults are subject to significant deficiencies in maturation and experience. Let's examine these deficiencies in more detail and look at the implications of these deficiencies for media literacy.

Maturation

It is tempting to think that once we have completed childhood, we have matured to the point cognitively, emotionally, and morally that we can take care of ourselves during media exposures and that we do not need the help. Evidence for such a belief comes from Piaget and his stage theory of cognitive development. Most people think that because Piaget's stages end at age 12, we all become adults cognitively at age 13. However, this is a misinterpretation of Piaget's stage theory. While it is true that Piaget's theory does stop its explanation at adolescence, there is no evidence in his writing that he believed cognitive development stopped at age 12. He simply confined his investigation and explanations to children. However, over time, Piaget's lack of attention to older age levels has been used as an argument that humans plateau at age 12 and stay at this level of cognitive development—that is, their capacity stays the same. People at other age levels share the same stage cognitive ability, and their differences in learning are then attributable to other things such as IQ, experience, and persistence. For example, Eron, Huesmann, Lefkowitz, and Walder (1972) argue that once a child reaches adolescence, his or her behavioral dispositions and inhibitory controls have become crystallized. This appears to be a faulty belief.

A growing literature documents how adults continue to experience cognitive changes throughout their lives. For example, P. M. King (1986) conducted a review of the published literature that tested the formal reasoning abilities of adults and concluded that "a rather large proportion of adults do not evidence formal thinking, even among those who have been enrolled in college" (p. 6). This conclusion holds up over the 25 studies she analyzed, including a variety of tests of formal reasoning ability and a variety of samples of adults 18 to 79 years old. In one third of the samples, less than 30% of the respondents exhibited reasoning at the fully formal level, and in almost all samples, no more than 70% of the adults were found to be fully functioning at the formal level, yet Piaget's stage theory of cognitive development explains that children reach the stage of formal development at 12 years of age.

Ability to reason morally is not always shown to be more advanced with age. For example, van der Voort (1986) found no evidence that children judge violent behavior more critically in a moral sense as they age. He found no reduction in the approval of the good guys' behavior. And as children aged, they were even more likely to approve of the violent actions of the bad guys. So although children acquire additional cognitive abilities with age, they do not necessarily acquire additional moral insights. There is a range of moral development among people of any given age. Also, older children are not automatically more highly developed morally than are younger children.

In summary, there is ample evidence that people develop cognitively, emotionally, and morally over the course of childhood and that this development does not stop at adolescence but continues throughout one's entire life. Furthermore, it is important to note that not everyone at a given age is at the same level of development; there are significant differences across people at any particular age. It is likely that there are many adults who are not as highly developed cognitively, emotionally, or morally as many children.

Experience

It is obviously true that young children have spent less time on earth than have adults. However, it does not necessarily follow that experience is the same as age. Many adolescents and adults have the same experience over and over; their lives are so routinized that they do pretty much the same thing every day. In contrast, many children try very different things every day. This is especially true with new technologies; children are the eager users of all kinds of innovations while many adults lag behind in their willingness to try iPods, camera phones, and other new technologies. Also, younger people are much more willing to try different kinds of messages—more likely to go to movies, more likely to try video games, more likely to keep up with changes in popular music, and more likely to try a wider range of Internet sites.

Age is not the same thing as experience. People of whatever age who are eager to try new experiences, new media, and new kinds of messages are more likely to develop more perspectives on the media and on life. And recall from the definition of media literacy that the more perspectives a person has, the more media literate he or she is. Ask yourself about how broad your real-world experiences are. Do you have lots of friends, but they are all pretty much the same as far as background, values, political attitudes, personality, and so on? Do you spend your time pretty much the same every week—that is, stuck in habits? Do you shop at the same stores? Do you commute to school or work the same way every time? When you take trips, do you go to the same places?

Natural Abilities

In this section, I will show that some natural abilities vary greatly across people. People who have a high degree of these natural abilities will be more media literate and hence need less protection from the media. In contrast, people who have a low degree of these natural abilities will be much less able to protect themselves from potential harm from media exposures. Because these natural abilities are not related to age, we cannot rely on a person's age alone to decide whether that person is at risk for harmful effects.

Of the seven natural abilities that are most related to media literacy, four are cognitive abilities—field independency, crystalline intelligence, fluid intelligence, and conceptual differentiation. The remaining three are emotional abilities—emotional intelligence, tolerance for ambiguity, and nonimpulsiveness.

Field Independency

Perhaps the most important ability related to media literacy is field independency. Think of field independency as your natural ability to distinguish between the signal and the noise in any message. The noise is the chaos of symbols and images. The signal is the information that emerges from the chaos. People who are highly field independent are able to sort quickly through the field to identify the elements of importance and ignore the distracting elements. In contrast, people who are more field dependent get stuck in the field of chaos—seeing all the details but missing the patterns and the "big picture," which is the signal (Witkin & Goodenough, 1977). For example, when reading a news story on a website, field-independent people will be able to identify the key information of the who, what, when, where, and why of the story. They will quickly sort through what is said, the graphics, and the visuals to focus on the essence of the event being covered. People who are field dependent will perceive the same key elements in the story but will also pay an equal amount of attention to the background elements of pop-up pictures, ads, borders, and so on. To the field-dependent person, all of these elements are of fairly equal importance, so they are as likely to remember the trivial as they are to remember the main points of the story. This is not to say that field-dependent people retain more information because they pay attention to more; on the contrary, field-dependent people retain less information because the information is not organized well and is likely to contain as much noise (peripheral and tangential elements) as signal (elements about the main idea).

Let's try one more example of this concept. Have you ever had to read a long novel and gotten so lost about 100 pages into it that you had to quit in frustration? You may have felt that just when the author was getting the story going with one set of characters, he or she would switch to a different setting at a different time with a totally new set of characters. This may have been happening every few pages! There were too many characters talking about too many different things. You were overwhelmed by all the detail and could not make sense of the overall story. This indicates that the novelist was making demands on you to be much more field independent than you could be as you read his or her novel. If you had been more field independent, you would have been able to see through all the details and recognize a thematic pattern of some sort, then use that thematic pattern as a tool to sort through all the details about characters, settings, time, dialogue, and action to direct your attention efficiently to those elements that were most important.

We live in a culture that is highly saturated with media messages. Much of this is noise; that is, it does not provide us with the information or emotional reactions we want. The sheer bulk of all the information makes it more difficult to sort the important from the trivial, so many of us do not bother to sort. Instead, we default to a passive state as we float along in this stream of messages. The advantage of this automatic processing is that it screens out the noise, but the disadvantage is that it screens out much of the signal too. When we are more field independent, we can better program our attention triggers to maximize the filtering *in* of signal and at the same time maximize the filtering *out* of noise.

Crystalline Intelligence

It is helpful to make a distinction between two types of intelligence: crystalline and fluid. Both types of intelligence are important for media literacy. Crystalline intelligence is the ability to memorize facts. It is best measured by tests requiring knowledge of the cultural milieu in which one lives, for example, vocabulary and general information.

Highly developed crystalline intelligence gives us the facility to absorb the images, definitions, opinions, and agendas of others. With most adults, crystallized intelligence seems to increase throughout the life span, although at a decreasing rate in later years (Sternberg & Berg, 1987). This means that as adults get older, they do better on tests requiring factual knowledge of their world, such as vocabulary and general information. In general, older people can more easily add new information to existing knowledge structures and more easily retrieve that information from those knowledge structures they use most often. When you have a well-developed knowledge structure on a topic, it is easy to sort through new information as you are exposed to it, compare the new information to what you already have in your knowledge structure, and make a determination whether the new information is useful to remember. If the new information is worthwhile to remember, it is easy to catalog it in a way that it is easy to recall later. However, if you are exposed to a message on a brand-new topic (one for which you do not have a knowledge structure), it is difficult to process that new information. To test this, pick a topic that is of equal interest to you and your parents (your neighborhood, your family, politics, sports, etc.) and then see how much detail your parents remember compared to you.

People strong in crystalline intelligence are good at what is called vertical thinking. Vertical thinking is systematic, logical thinking that proceeds step by step in an orderly progression. This is the type of thinking we need to learn the introductory information on any topic. We need to be systematic when we are trying to learn basic arithmetic, spelling, and dates in history. People high in crystalline intelligence are likely to have a more extensive list of competencies because they have memorized a much larger set of symbols and their denoted meanings.

Fluid Intelligence

The other type of intelligence is fluid, which is the ability to be creative, make leaps of insight, and perceive things in a fresh and novel manner. Fluid intelligence is best measured by tests requiring mental manipulation of abstract symbols, for example, figural analogies and number series completions. Fluid intelligence increases in early adulthood but then decreases.

People strong in fluid intelligence are good at what is called lateral thinking. Lateral thinking, in contrast to vertical thinking, does not proceed step by step in a straight line. Instead, when confronted with a problem, the lateral thinker jumps to a new and quite arbitrary position, then works backwards and tries to construct a logical path between this new position and the starting point. Lateral thinkers tend to arrive at a solution to a problem that other thinkers, who are locked into a vertical form of thinking, would never arrive at. Lateral thinkers are more intuitive and creative. They reject the standard beginning points to solving problems and instead begin with an intuitive guess, a brainstorming of ideas, or a proposed solution "out of the blue."

Few people have a natural aptitude for lateral thinking. Those who have such aptitude use it often. Many inventors and scientists usually produce a string of new ideas, not just one. For example, Thomas Edison invented so many things that by the end of his life, he had more than 1,300 patents in the areas of the telegraph, telephone, phonograph, movie camera, and projectors. This suggests that there is a capacity for generating new ideas that is better developed in some people than in others. This capacity does not seem to be related to sheer intelligence but more to a particular way of thinking. There are smart and not so smart lateral thinkers, just like there are smart and not so smart vertical thinkers.

There are advantages and disadvantages to both forms of thinking. Vertical thinkers tend to do best at solving traditional problems for which the solutions can be learned. However, when their traditional methods of solving problems break down and they reach a dead-end, they are stuck and have nowhere to go. In contrast, lateral thinkers can often be flighty and may come up with many unique ideas; however, none of those ideas may work or be feasible ways of solving a problem. When others are stuck at a dead-end of thinking, it is the lateral thinkers who break through the barriers. People who are good at both and who know when to try each approach are, of course, the most successful problem solvers.

Being strong on both these abilities helps with increasing one's level of media literacy. Highly developed crystalline intelligence gives us the facility to absorb the images, definitions, opinions, and agendas of others. This helps us a great deal in the meaning-matching task because we are likely to have acquired a large set of accurate matches of symbols and meanings. Highly developed fluid intelligence gives us the facility to challenge what we see on the surface, to look deeper and broader, and to recognize new patterns. This helps us a great deal in the meaning construction task because we are able to move beyond the surface meaning and construct meanings that are more useful for our own purposes.

Conceptual Differentiation

This refers to how people group and classify things. People who classify objects into a large number of mutually exclusive categories exhibit a high degree of conceptual differentiation (Gardner, 1968). In contrast, people who use a small number of categories have a low degree of conceptual differentiation.

Related to the number of categories is category width (Bruner, Goodnow, & Austin, 1956). People who have few categories to classify something usually have broad categories so as to contain all types of messages. For example, if a person only has three categories for all media messages (news, ads, and entertainment), then each of these categories must contain a wide variety of things. In contrast, someone who has a great many categories would be dividing media messages into thinner slices (breaking news, feature news, documentary, commercial ads, public service announcements, action/adventure shows, sitcoms, game shows, talk shows, cartoons, and reality shows).

When we encounter a new message, we must categorize it by using either a leveling or a sharpening strategy. With the leveling strategy, we look for similarities between the new message and previous messages we have stored away as examples in our categories. We look for the best fit between the new message and one of remembered messages. We will never find a perfect fit; that is, the new message always has slightly different characteristics than our category calls for, but we tend to ignore those differences. In contrast, the sharpening strategy focuses on differences and tries to maintain a high degree of separation between the new message and older messages (Pritchard, 1975). To illustrate this, let's say two people are comparing this year's Super Bowl with last year's Super Bowl. A leveler would argue that the two games were similar and point out all the things the two had in common. The sharpener would disagree and point out all the differences between the two Super Bowls. Levelers tend to have fewer categories so that many things can fit into the same category, whereas sharpeners have many categories. In our example, the first person would likely have only one category for Super Bowls, feeling that all the Super Bowls are the same. A sharpener might have a different category for every Super Bowl, treating each one as unique. Increasing one's level of media literacy requires one to do more sharpening of categories for media messages, media companies, and media effects.

Emotional Intelligence

Our ability to understand and control our emotions is called emotional intelligence. Emotional intelligence is thought to be composed of several related abilities, such as the ability to read the emotions of other people (empathy), the ability to be aware of one's own emotions, the ability to harness and manage one's own emotions productively, and the ability to handle the emotional demands of relationships.

Those of us with stronger emotional intelligence have a well-developed sense of empathy; we are able to see the world from another person's perspective. The more perspectives we can access, the more emotional intelligence we have. When we are highly developed emotionally, we are more aware of our own emotions. We also better understand the factors that cause those emotions, so we are able to seek the kinds of messages to get us the emotional reactions we want. In addition, we are less impulsive and are able to exercise more self-control. We can concentrate on the task at hand rather than become distracted by peripheral emotions.

Tolerance for Ambiguity

Every day, we encounter people and situations that are unfamiliar to us. To prepare ourselves for such situations, we have developed sets of expectations. What do we do when our expectations are not met and we are surprised? That depends on our tolerance level for ambiguity. If we have a low tolerance for ambiguity, we will likely choose to ignore those messages that do not meet our expectations; we feel too confused or frustrated to work out the discrepancies.

In contrast, if we are willing to follow situations into unfamiliar territory that go beyond our preconceptions, then we have a high tolerance for ambiguity. Initial confusion does not stop us. Instead, this confusion motivates us to search harder for clarity. We do not feel an emotional barrier that prevents us from examining messages more closely. We are willing to break any message down into components and make comparisons and evaluations in a quest to understand the nature of the message and to examine why our initial expectations were wrong.

During media exposures, people with a low tolerance encounter messages on the surface. If the surface meaning fits their preconceptions, then it is filed away and becomes a confirmation (or reinforcement) of those preconceptions. If the surface meaning does not meet a person's preconceptions, the message is ignored. In short, there is no analysis.

People with a high tolerance for ambiguity do not have a barrier to analysis. They are willing to break any message down into components and make comparisons and evaluations in a quest to understand the nature of the message and why their own expectations were wrong. People who consistently attempt to verify their observations and judgments are called scanners because they are perpetually looking for more information (Gardner, 1968).

Nonimpulsiveness

This refers to how quickly people make decisions about messages (Kagan, Rosman, Day, Albert, & Phillips, 1964). People who rush to a decision are impulsive. In contrast, people who take a long time and consider things from many perspectives are reflective or nonimpulsive.

Typically, there is a trade-off between speed and accuracy. Impulsive people are most concerned with speed; they feel overwhelmed by decisions, so they want to have things resolved as soon as possible. For them, it is worth the risk to make a bad decision as long as they can quickly end the worry that comes with being faced with a decision-making task. Reflective people are most concerned with accuracy; they dread being wrong, so they think about all the options of a decision, even if it takes a long time.

How much time we take to make decisions is governed by our emotions. If we feel comfortable encountering new information and like to work through problems carefully, we are likely to act reflectively and take our time. However, if we feel a negative emotion (such as frustration), we tend to make decisions as quickly as possible to eliminate the negative emotional state.

SUMMARY

The public and policy makers regard children as a special audience that needs protection from potentially negative effects of mass media exposure. There has been a good deal of research to show that children are indeed vulnerable to certain types of messages. However, adolescents and adults have also been found to be vulnerable to certain types of messages.

The argument for protecting children is based on the idea that children are at lower levels of development—cognitive, emotional, and moral—as well as lower levels of experience. These deficiencies make them especially vulnerable to negative effects. However, the research shows that many adolescents and adults are also vulnerable.

Media literacy can help children, adolescents, and adults reduce negative effects and increase positive effects of exposure to media messages. Media literacy can be developed. That development is easier among people who keep improving on their natural abilities, searching for a wide range of experiences in both the media as well as the real world, and applying their skills actively to build more elaborate and useful knowledge structures.

Chapter Resources: To test your knowledge and learn more about the topics discussed in this chapter, visit the Student Study Site at www.sagepub.com/potter6e.

FURTHER READING

Goleman, D. (1995). *Emotional intelligence.* New York: Bantam. (352 pages with index)

In this very readable best seller, Goleman argues that there is an emotional IQ, not just an intellectual one. He challenges the long-held belief that a person's intelligence, as measured by a narrow IQ test, is an adequate predictor of success or ability. First he broadens the conception of intelligence, and then he shows how a person's emotional development interacts with a broad range of cognitive abilities. He cites data to show that emotions are strongly linked to the body's physiological reactions.

Kohlberg, L. (1981). *The philosophy of moral development: Moral stages and the idea of justice.* New York: Harper & Row. (428 pages, including references and index)

Kohlberg lays out his moral development scheme of three stages, each with two substages. There are many examples relating this structure to how people come to understand the concept of justice.

Pulaski, M. A. S. (1980). *Understanding Piaget: An introduction to children's cognitive development* (Revised and expanded edition). New York: Harper & Row. (248 pages with index)

This is a very clear, well-organized description of most of Piaget's thinking and research. Many drawings illustrate key concepts.

Singer, D. G., & Singer, J. L. (Eds.). (2001). *Handbook of children and the media.* Thousand Oaks, CA: Sage. (765 pages including index)

This is a definitive handbook on the topic of children and the media. It consists of 39 chapters, each written by an expert in the field. The chapters are clustered to address the following topics: children's uses of the media and the gratifications they obtain from them; cognitive functions and school-readiness skills; hazards of TV viewing; personality, social attitudes, and health; the media industry and its technology; and policy issues and advocacy.

KEEPING UP TO DATE

National Institute on Media and the Family (http://www.mediafamily.org/)

This website provides information on how children are affected by media exposures and how parents and others can help increase their coping with these influences.

Media Awareness Network (http://www.media-awareness.ca/english/issues/)

Like the website above, this is a good source of information about how children are affected by media exposures and how parents and others can help increase their coping with these influences.

Journal of Children and Media (http://www.tandf.co.uk/journals/titles/17482798.asp)

This is a scholarly journal that is published quarterly. It presents research articles in the areas of children as consumers of media, how children are portrayed in media messages, and how media organizations produce content for children.

Part 3

Industry

The three chapters in this part of the book focus your attention on the businesses that make up the mass media industries. Chapter 6 takes a historical perspective and shows you how each of the mass media industries has followed a fairly common pattern to get where it is today. Chapter 7 takes an economic approach and explores the resources used in the mass media industries and how exchanges of those resources take place. Chapter 8 examines the nature of each of the mass media industries as it exists today.

As you read this part of the book, keep the following questions active in your mind and you will stay focused on the most important ideas in the three chapters:

- What do the mass media do to attract and maintain all sorts of niche audiences?
- How has each of the mass media industries changed over time to make the most of its opportunities and to overcome its challenges from other mass media industries?
- How has each of the mass media industries maintained its economic power?

GPS

CHAPTER 6

Key Idea: The development of the media industries generally moves from the innovation stage through growth, peak, decline, and then adaptation.

Development of the Mass Media Industries

Heather was determined to do well and earn a high grade in a course entitled "Development of the Mass Media." She had bought the textbook, which included a dozen chapters, each one on a different type of mass medium. She had read each chapter carefully and highlighted the important facts in green. Now as she prepared to study for a major test, she noticed that almost every word on every page was green. She felt frustrated and thought, "How am I ever going to learn all this material? It's too much. There are a million tiny facts. There is no way I can memorize all these facts."

It is likely that many of you have felt like Heather when you were confronted with a subject that is composed of a great number of facts. The mass media industries is a topic composed of a great amount of detail—dates, names of inventors, historical occurrences, business practices, names of businesses, complicated charts of who owns what, and tons of financial data. When I first started writing about this topic, I too was overwhelmed. As a writer, I could have made it easy on myself and simply presented one fact after another in a long and boring historical sequence. But that way of presenting facts would not have made it easy on you—the learner. Learning is much easier when you start with a simple, clear map. Once you have a map, you can efficiently navigate through all the detail and not get lost.

In this chapter—as well as the next two chapters—I present you with maps of the most important ideas about the mass media industries. These maps will show you the overall shape of the important knowledge structures. Once you understand the overall structures of ideas, then you can fill in the details. Many of those details about the media industries are provided in Appendix A.

The map presented in this chapter is a life cycle pattern that focuses your attention on how mass media industries have developed over time. While each of the mass media industries has a unique history shaped by particular innovations, special needs for consumers, and distinct content, those media industries also follow some consistent patterns. When we focus our attention on those patterns that are common to all the media industries, we can develop a better appreciation for the nature of all mass media.

PATTERNS OF DEVELOPMENT

The life cycle pattern provides a useful framework for examining the media industries because it focuses your attention on how the industries have gone through changes and why. The life cycle pattern contains five stages: innovation (or birth), penetration (or growth), peak (maturity), decline, and adaptation.

Innovation Stage

Each of the mass media industries began as an innovation. The innovation stage of a medium's development is characterized by a technological innovation that makes a channel of transmission possible. For example, there would be no film industry if someone had not invented the motion picture camera and projector. However, technology by itself is not enough to create a mass medium. A mass medium is more than an invention; many technological innovations have failed or are still sitting on a shelf somewhere. So the innovation stage is also characterized by marketing innovations in addition to technological innovations. This means that someone had to create a business that would use the technology to deliver messages and thus build audiences.

A successful marketing innovation begins with an entrepreneur recognizing a need in the population, then using a new technology to satisfy that need in a way that people begin recognizing the value of the new medium and how it can help them. To do this, the entrepreneur must have a mass-like orientation; that is, he or she must exploit the channel's potential to attract particular audiences and then continue to use that channel to condition those audiences for repeat exposures. For example, in the early 1900s, after the motion picture camera and projector were invented, some entrepreneurs turned their living rooms into theaters and began charging people to watch movies. These entrepreneurs found that there was a market for this kind of entertainment, so they took steps to grow that market by renting out storefronts to accommodate larger audiences; then they rented concert theaters and then built their own theaters that were primarily for showing films. This demand from the theaters led other entrepreneurs to create film production companies to make and distribute films to the theaters. Without all these marketing entrepreneurs who recognized a public need and marketed their services to grow that need into a habit, the motion picture camera and projector would never have grown into more than a curious invention. When a business innovation was successful in marketing the technological innovation of distributing messages that audiences wanted, the channel of transmission started to grow into a major mass media industry.

Penetration Stage

Once an innovation has created a new mass media channel, that channel needs to appeal to a very large, heterogeneous population if it is to be effective as a mass medium. This is called penetration. The penetration stage of a medium's development is characterized by the public's growing acceptance of that medium. The public's reaction to a new medium is based on the medium's ability to satisfy existing needs or to create new needs.

Sometimes, the public has a need that is already being satisfied by existing media, but a new medium comes along that can satisfy those needs better in some way. For example, in the 1940s, people were satisfying their need for entertainment with radio and with films. But then broadcast television came along and was better than radio because it offered pictures in addition to sound. Thus, television provided more to audiences in return for the same attention. Television was better at satisfying many people's need for entertainment compared to film because television brought many hours of entertainment into a person's home each and every day, so there was no need to leave the house, get a babysitter, find a parking place, or buy a ticket. Television was much more convenient.

A new medium can be successful in the penetration stage by generating a new need or increase an existing need. Television is credited with increasing the American public's appetite for entertainment. The amount of viewing has steadily increased since television was first introduced; now, the average household has the set on for more than 50 hours per week, most of which is entertainment programming. As each medium grows, it is influenced by factors that shape its growth. These factors include the public's need and desire for the medium, additional innovations that change the appeal of other competing media, political and regulatory constraints, and the economic demands of the private enterprises that own and operate the mass media.

Peak Stage

The peak stage is reached when the medium commands the most attention from the public and generates the most revenue compared to other media. This usually happens when the medium has achieved maximum penetration; that is, a very high percentage of households has accepted a medium, and the medium cannot grow in penetration any more. Of course, it can continue to absorb a greater proportion of an audience member's time and money.

For example, broadcast television reached a peak in the 1960s after taking audiences away from radio and film. Broadcast television also had taken national advertisers away from magazines and radio. Until the middle to late 1990s, broadcast television remained at a peak as the most dominant mass medium, because people were spending more time with broadcast television every day compared to any other medium. Also, most people regarded broadcast television as their primary (and often only) source of entertainment and news.

Decline Stage

Eventually, a peak medium will be challenged by a newer one and go into a decline. In the decline stage, the medium is characterized by a loss of audience acceptance and therefore by a loss in revenues. A decline in audience size results not from a decline in need for a particular kind of message but by those message needs being satisfied better by a competing medium that is growing in penetration and moving toward its own peak.

Adaptation Stage

A medium enters the adaptation stage of development when it begins to redefine its position in the media marketplace. Repositioning is achieved by identifying a new set of needs that the medium can meet, because the old needs it used to fulfill are now met better by another medium. For example, after radio lost its audience to television, radio adapted by doing three things. First, it stopped competing directly with television by eliminating its general entertainment programs such as soap operas, situation comedies, and mystery dramas. Instead, radio shifted to music formats where disk jockeys would play popular songs one after another. Second, it abandoned its strategy of trying to appeal to a general audience and instead segmented the market according to musical tastes, and each station aimed its programming at the people in one of those niches. So now in each radio market, there is likely to be a top 40 station, a rhythm and blues station, a jazz station, an album-oriented rock station, a golden oldies station, a country and western station, a classical music station, and so forth—each appealing to a different set of listeners. Third, it realized that with the invention of the transistor radio in the 1950s, it could be portable, whereas television could not. So radio developed playlists that formed a kind of background mood-shaping experience as people drove in their cars, laid out on beaches, and talked on the phone.

COMPARISONS ACROSS MASS MEDIA

In this section, we'll look at the big picture *across* the media industries. We'll compare the development of the different mass media industries to get a sense of which are the newest and when each was the strongest.

Life Cycle Pattern

Take a minute to look at the life cycle patterns displayed in Figure 6.1. Notice that the print media of books, newspapers, and magazines are the oldest, with each of them moving out of their innovation stage more than a century ago. Computers are the newest mass medium, with its innovation stage finishing about the time you were born. Notice also that all of the mass media, with the exception of cable TV and computers, are currently in the adaptation stage. This means they are all trying to figure out how to coexist with the other up-and-coming media as well as with each other.

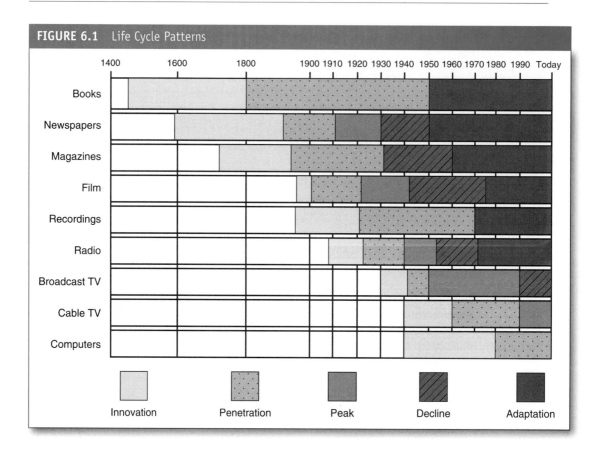

FIGURE 6.1 Life Cycle Patterns

Although the life cycle pattern is a good template for showing patterns, it is not perfect. For example, notice that several of the media (books, magazines, and recordings) never reached a peak. This does not mean that those media are not important or successful; it only means that those media never achieved dominance as the most important mass medium at a given time.

Indicators of Peak

We are at an interesting time in the development of the media industries. Broadcast television has left the peak stage, which lasted for about 40 years, during which time it accounted for almost all of the television audience. But cable channels have been eroding broadcast television's hold on the audience, and now broadcast television has slipped below 50% of the television-viewing audience, and its revenues are now lagging behind that of cable television. Cable has been at the peak for more than a decade but is threatened by the medium of computers (which includes receiving media messages on desktops, laptops, notebooks, mobile phones, and the like). The computer medium is showing that it can be the delivery system for books, newspapers, magazines, recordings, film, and video; it can deliver those messages anywhere through a wire or wireless; and it provides the additional feature of being interactive so that users can easily make copies of messages, transform them, and pass them along to others. For all of these reasons, the medium of computers is well on its way to a peak.

When a medium is at its peak, it is usually the dominant medium; that is, it is the most important medium to the greatest number of people. This can be seen in terms of how much money the industry generates and how much time people spend with that medium. Given these criteria, it appears that cable television (along with its satellite delivery services) is still the most dominant medium. Cable and satellite TV now has revenues greater than any other medium (see Table 6.1). Notice that radio is in second place with the amount of time that people spend with it per year. Does this mean that radio should be considered the second most dominant medium? The answer is no—for several reasons. First, although people spend a lot of time with their radios on, they are using the medium for background noise; that is, they are not really paying much attention to those messages. When radio was at its peak in the 1920s and 1930s, its programming commanded listeners' full attention. That programming included a wide range of genres that are now seen on television. People would listen to soap operas, detective shows, game shows, and comedies. But now, most of radio listening is background music. While listening to this music, people are typically exposing themselves to other media (such as reading books, magazines, and newspapers), or they are doing something else (such as talking on the phone, jogging, or working) that requires more attention. Even though the radio is on for so many hours in the lives of so many people, it does not hold people's full attention for very long.

Second, radio does not generate as much revenue as other media. Notice that in Table 6.1, both radio and broadcast TV have no figures listed in the dollars spent per year columns. Does this mean people do not spend money on these media? Of course not. It means that these media do not get any income *directly* from the consumer. People must buy receivers, but that money goes to Circuit City, Best Buy, or

	Hours:Minutes Per Day	Money (U.S.$)
TABLE 6.1 Time and Money Spent With Various Mass Media		
Mass Medium		
Cable and satellite TV	2:51	375.22
Radio	2:05	NA
Broadcast TV	1:50	NA
Internet services	0:30	58.90
Recorded music	0:28	44.92
Newspapers	0:26	47.33
Magazines	0:19	45.93
Books	0:18	105.83
Video games	0:15	44.64
Other	0:45	206.27
Total	9:47	929.04

SOURCE: U.S. Census Bureau (2009). *The 2009 Statistical Abstract: The National Data Book.* Washington DC: Department of Commerce, Table 1089.

NOTE: Time figures are hours per person per day on average. Money figures are dollars per person per year in 2009 paid directly to a business in that medium; these figures do not include advertising revenue. NA = not applicable; consumers did not make direct payments to broadcast TV or radio.

wherever people buy their sets. Broadcast radio and television get almost all of their revenue from advertising, which comes from consumers but only indirectly. Table 6.1 includes only direct revenues from consumers to the media businesses themselves.

We are currently in a very dynamic and interesting time with the development of the mass media. The newer technologies that can be grouped under the title of computer are changing the way audiences access media messages by giving them much more control and variety. Take film, for example. In 2010, Americans spent almost twice the money on home viewing of movies (on-demand videos, digital downloads, and DVDs) than going to theaters ("Unkind Unwind," 2011). When people are limited to theaters to view films, they have only about a dozen choices at any given time, and they must be at the theater when the film starts and sit there for the entire running of the film unless they want to miss some of it. However, when people watch a film through their cable provider or especially from a website, they have a virtually unlimited range of choices and can watch the film whenever they want and interrupt whenever they want. Access to news is much faster and up to date on websites than waiting for printed newspapers or magazines to be delivered. Access to books and recordings is faster when downloading them to handheld devices than driving to a brick-and-mortar store. The newer media are growing fast and moving quickly through the penetration stage. They are putting growing pressure on the older media, forcing them to continue adapting.

SUMMARY

The development of the media industries generally moves from the innovation stage to growth, peak, decline, and then adaptation. Remembering this will help you understand how the media industries start, how they grow, and where they are today.

There are nine major mass media industries: book, newspaper, magazine, film, recording, radio, broadcast television, cable television, and computer. Each of these industries was born out of a combination of technological and marketing innovations. Technological developments created the new channel of communication, but it took marketing entrepreneurs to figure out how to use the new channels to attract audiences and condition those audiences for repeat exposures.

After an innovation stage, each industry entered a stage of penetration, where it increased its appeal to more and more people. Acceptance of a medium is based on its ability to satisfy an existing need or to create a new, widespread need that it can then satisfy.

A peak stage is reached when the medium commands the most attention from the public and generates the most revenue compared to other media. This usually happens when the medium has achieved maximum penetration.

Eventually, a medium at its peak will be challenged by a newer one and go into a decline. In the decline stage, the medium is characterized by a loss of audience acceptance and therefore by a loss in revenues. A decline in audience support results not from an atrophied need but by the needs being satisfied better by a competing medium.

A medium enters the adaptation stage of development when it accepts the challenge of redefining its position in the media marketplace. Repositioning is achieved by identifying a new set of needs that the medium can meet because the old set of needs it used to fulfill is now met better by another medium.

Most of the mass media are currently in the adaptation stage, where they share audiences and advertisers by serving a different function from the other competing media. There is reason to believe that they will continue refining their messages and thereby continue to survive in a healthy manner.

This chapter has focused your attention on the big picture of how the media develop and change as industries. Now that you have a basic knowledge structure about the development of the media industries, you can add details to your barebones knowledge structure by reading the elaborated profiles of the media industries in Appendix A.

Chapter Resources: To test your knowledge and learn more about the topics discussed in this chapter, visit the Student Study Site at www.sagepub.com/potter6e.

FURTHER READING

Croteau, D., & Hoynes, W. (2001). *The business of media: Corporate media and the public interest.* Thousand Oaks, CA: Pine Forge Press. (302 pages, including appendix, endnotes, references, and index)

This book takes a critical perspective on how the media industries developed in the United States. The authors say, "We are concerned with the tension between the media industry's insatiable quest for profits and a democratic society's need for a media system that serves the public interest" (p. xiii). The book presents seven chapters organized into three sections: (1) Profits and the Public Interest: Theoretical and Historical Context, (2) Industry Structure and Corporate Strategy: Explaining the Rise of Media Conglomerates, and (3) Neglecting the Public Interest: Media Conglomerates and the Public Sphere.

Drapes, M. R., & Lichtenberg, N. R. (2008). *Vault guide to the top media & entertainment employers.* New York: Vault. Com, Inc. (326 pages)

This book provides profiles of 41 large companies covering all facets of the mass media. While there is practical information about how to go about getting a job in these companies, the profiles provide much more detail about the companies themselves—how they are organized and how they developed over time.

Greco, A. N. (Ed.). (2000). *The media and entertainment industries.* Needham Heights, MA: Allyn & Bacon. (279 pages, including index)

Each of the 10 chapters in this edited book illuminates one of the mass media industries. Authors describe how their industry is structured to gather all the resources they need to produce messages and get those messages out to all the target segments in their audiences. Most chapters present numerous tables of quantitative data to show how the numbers and names of the business in the industry have changed over time, as well as the amount of time and money people spend with the products produced by those businesses. Most of the chapter authors have expanded on their topic in a book published as part of the Allyn & Bacon Mass Communication Series.

Neuman, W. R. (Ed.). (2010). *Media, technology, and society: Theories of media evolution.* Ann Arbor: University of Michigan Press. (231 pages with index)

This edited volume consists of 10 chapters written by various scholars. Seven chapters trace the development of a different mass medium—newspapers, telephone, film, radio, television, cable, and the Internet. The remaining three chapters focus on theories of media evolution, privacy and security policy, and the future of ownership.

KEEPING UP TO DATE

Statistical Abstract of the United States (http://www.census.gov/compendia/statab/)

The Department of Commerce releases a new statistical abstract every year. For updates on the material in this chapter, go to the section on Information and Communication.

Zap 2 It (http://www.zap2it.com/)

This website provides ratings of television shows and figures about popularity of various Hollywood movies.

The Economic Game

CHAPTER 7

Key Idea: The businesses in the media industries are in strong competition with each other to acquire limited resources, play the high-risk game of appealing to audiences, and achieve a maximum profit.

The other day I was talking to my neighbor Blaine, who had just graduated from college with a degree in economics. He was telling me how important it was to maximize resources in one's personal life. "When it comes to the mass media, I try to keep my costs down. That is why I go to the library and borrow books rather than buy them," he told me. "I also read newspapers and magazines there for free."

"What if you want a book that someone else has checked out or what if someone else is reading the newspaper when you want to read it?"

"Then I wait." He switched the subject. "I check out movies and documentaries, then take them home and copy them for free."

"But don't you have to buy blank DVDs and flash drives to store your copies?"

"Okay, it's not completely free, but it's a lot less expensive than buying all that stuff. I also make copies of music for my MP3 player for free. I now have 10,000 songs in my music library."

"Doesn't that take a lot of time to make all those copies and keep organizing your library?"

"Yes, it takes some time, but it's a hobby."

"How much time do you spend watching all these DVDs?"

"That's the beauty of having a large film library. I have so many choices that if one doesn't grab my interest right away, I just start watching another one until I find one I like. There are so many bad movies these days that you need a large library to find one that's any good."

"And your music? How much time do you spend listening to all that music?"

"Not as much as I would like. There's just not enough time in the day!" He thought for a minute and then added, "Also, after a while all the new songs sound so derivative of other songs; they all begin to sound alike."

"Blaine, it sounds to me as if you are very careful about not spending much money on the media, but you do spend an awful lot of time. And it also seems that you don't get much in return for this investment of time."

"How can you say that? I have amassed a huge library of movies and songs."

"But what is the point of having acquired all those messages if you don't enjoy them much? The real payoff is personal enjoyment. It doesn't seem to me that your huge investment of time has much payoff."

The economic perspective focuses on resources. As a consumer of mass media messages, your key resources are money and time. The mass media are very successful each year at getting us to give them large amounts of our money and time in exchange

for our exposures to a wide range of media messages, now up to $970 billion in direct expenditures each year (U.S. Bureau of the Census, 2009). How much of this money came from you? Before you read on, take a few minutes to complete Exercise 7.1. Then consider how much time you spend with the mass media. Take a few more minutes and complete Exercise 7.2.

THE MEDIA GAME OF ECONOMICS

Economics is a huge game, with many players and lots of resources at stake. Each player brings particular resources to the game. Players trade away their resources to get other resources they want more. The overall strategy of good game players is to negotiate the exchanges well so that they give up relatively few of their personal resources to get relatively large resources from other players.

The Players

There are four types of players who vary in terms of their goals, resources, and abilities to play the game. The players are (a) you the consumer, (b) the advertisers, (c) the media companies, and (d) the employees of media companies.

We are the consumers, and our resources include not only our money but, even more important, our time. We seek to exchange our money and time for entertainment and information. We as consumers are the largest group with 310 million people in the United States and more than 6 billion people worldwide. We have the greatest amount of resources. If we pulled out of the game entirely, the game would collapse. However, our resources are dispersed over so many people that no one individual feels he or she has that much power in playing the game. This feeling is a mistake. While no one individual has a significant amount of power to change the game, each of us has in our power the ability to play the game well. If we don't play the game well, we will make poor economic exchanges and continually get shortchanged on our expenditures of time and money. Playing the game well requires us to keep track of our resources and our needs so that when we want to satisfy a need, we are able to get full value in return for the resources we give up.

The advertisers are a second group of players. Advertisers bring money to the game. They negotiate an exchange of their money for time and space in the media to present their ads to their target audiences. Advertisers want to get access to their target audiences for the lowest cost possible. So they look for media vehicles that have constructed the largest assemblages of the audience members they want without also including other kinds of audience members they do not want. For example, sellers of tennis rackets want to get their ad messages in front of as many people who play tennis as possible, but they do not want to pay a lot of money to get access to a large audience that might also include toddlers, invalids, and people who hate tennis. So they look for media vehicles (such as particular

sports TV shows, Internet sites, and magazines) that have constructed an audience of only tennis players and negotiate a good ad price to rent that smaller, niche audience.

The media companies are the third group of players. These businesses bring money, messages, and audiences to the game to compete in three different markets simultaneously. First, each media business competes in the talent market to try to get the best writers, journalists, actors, directors, website designers, and so on under contract to them. They try to keep these personnel costs low, but because talent is in short supply, their expenses escalate each year. Second, media businesses compete in the audience market; that is, they present the messages produced by their talented employees in such a way to attract the greatest number of people within certain types of audiences. In the media industries of magazines, newspapers, cable, and Internet, those companies sell subscriptions, so they want to maximize their revenue by attracting as many subscribers as possible. Media companies also sell messages in the form of books, recordings (music and movies), and theater tickets. Third, media companies compete in the advertising market. When media companies have constructed quality niche audiences, they have something valuable to offer advertisers who want to get their messages in front of certain types of consumers.

The media employees comprise the fourth group of players. Employees bring their time, skills, and talent to the game. Their goal is to increase the pay and benefits for each hour worked. In the media, we make a distinction between below-the-line employees and above-the-line employees. Below-the-line employees are typically the crafts and clerical people who need various skills to be able to perform their jobs well. These skills can be learned by many people and can be improved with practice. That is, with the proper training and motivation, most people could perform well in most below-the-line jobs, such as a lighting technician, sound boom operator, copy editor, ticket taker, cable installer, secretary, or receptionist. A very large number of people potentially could do these jobs, so the supply (people wanting these jobs) is much larger than the demand (number of these jobs available). Therefore, the pay for people in these positions is relatively low.

The above-the-line employees are the creative types, and this requires talent much more than training or effort, although training and effort are also important. These above-the-line people are the writers, producers, directors, photographers, actors, singers, Web designers, choreographers, and so on. We typically regard talent as being artistic ability, but for the mass media industries, talent is regarded more as the ability to attract large audiences than to make them want to return for repeated exposures. Sometimes, the two conceptualizations of talent are the same, but more often, the two are very different. For example, the singing ability of Lady Gaga, Miley Cyrus, and Justin Bieber, although good, cannot alone account for their huge popularity—that is, these recording artists have some inexplicable ability to attract large audiences that cannot be explained solely by the artistic quality of their singing ability. Also, many television stars are not particularly good actors, yet they are in high demand by television producers because these people can attract large audiences.

Above-the-line people are paid a lot more than below-the-line people (at least twice as much on average), and the difference in wages is growing. From 2003 to 2009, below-the-line salaries increased 12% on average, while the average salary of above-the-line people increased 25% (Hagel, Brown, Kulasooriya, & Elbert, 2010). Why are above-the-line people paid so much more? The reason is because this kind of talent is in short supply. For example, many people can sing and play musical instruments well, but very few musicians can attract enough fans who will buy their recordings in the millions. The celebrities who can attract the most attention are paid the most (see Table 7.1).

Another elite set of employees are the media company managers, who are often also partial owners of the companies. The talent of these managers is to oversee the construction of messages and their distribution so that those messages are experienced by the greatest number of targeted consumers. In essence, the talent of managers is to construct these audiences by attracting consumers with above-the-line talent and try to maintain those audiences by making the exposures continually rewarding and at low cognitive costs to the audience members. These media managers also have a talent that is in short supply, so they are also paid very well (see Table 7.2). While

TABLE 7.1	2010 Income of Highly Paid Media Celebrities	
Millionsª	Person	Profession
290	Oprah Winfrey	Personality
195	U2	Musicians
130	Tyler Perry	Director/producer
125	Bon Jovi	Musician
113	Jerry Bruckheimer	Producer/director
107	Steven Spielberg	Filmmaker
100	Elton John	Musician
90	Lady Gaga	Singer
90	Simon Cowell	Personality
84	James Patterson	Novelist
80	Dr. Phil McGraw	Personality
77	Leonardo DiCaprio	Actor
76	Howard Stern	Radio personality
70	James Cameron	Filmmaker
67	Paul McCartney	Musician
64	Rush Limbaugh	Radio personality
61	Ryan Seacrest	Radio and TV personality
61	Black Eyed Peas	Musicians
53	Justin Bieber	Singer
50	Johnny Depp	Actor
45	Taylor Swift	Singer
45	Ellen DeGeneres	TV personality
44	Katy Perry	Singer
40	Charlie Sheen	Actor
40	Glenn Beck	TV personality
30	Angelina Jolie	Actress

SOURCE: "World's Most Powerful Celebrities" (2011).

a. Figures in left column represent annual income in 2010 in millions of U.S. dollars.

you may recognize a few names on this list, most people who have created and run the large media companies are not known to the general public.

The Goal

For all four types of players, the general goal is to maximize the value of the exchange for themselves. But value is computed in very different ways for different players. For the media businesses, employees, and advertisers, value can be computed quantitatively—numbers of dollars. But for individuals, value is not a quantitative concept—it is satisfaction. Individuals rarely engage in the economic game with the media to increase their financial resources. Instead, the primary resource they seek in playing the media economic game is satisfaction from messages. However, people do not devote much effort in carefully analyzing the economic game and determining whether they are a **net winner** or **net loser** in their economic exchanges. As long as they feel some satisfaction, they will continue accessing the same types of messages.

One form of costs is financial. For example, people can reduce their financial costs by finding information on free Internet sites rather than paying magazine and newspaper subscriptions. Another form of cost is time. People can go to sources of information with which they are familiar, and this saves time over seeking out new sources. And another form of cost is cognitive energy. Making decisions and thinking through their implications requires cognitive effort; it is easier for people to stick with habits and not have to think about everything they do.

Another important thing to realize when understanding this economic game is that the game is ongoing. Because it does not end, there is no ultimate winner or loser. Instead, the goal is to maintain value throughout the process, so players continually

TABLE 7.2	Salaries of Media Moguls		
Name	*2010 Pay*	*Company*	*Company Revenue*
Philippe P. Dauman	84.5	Viacom	9.3
Leslie Moonves	57.7	CBS	14.1
Stephen B. Burke	34.7	NBC Universal	37.9
Michael D. White	32.9	DirecTV	24.1
Brian L. Roberts	31.1	Comcast	37.9
Robert A. Iger	29.6	Walt Disney	38.1
Jeffrey L. Bewkes	26.3	Time Warner	26.9
Chase Carey	26.0	News Corp.	32.8
Charles F. Dolan	13.8	Cablevision	7.2
Michael R. Burns	6.9	Lions Gate	1.6
Jeffrey Katzenberg	6.7	DreamWorks	0.8
Reed Hastings	5.5	Netflix	2.2

NOTE: Pay figures are in millions of U.S. dollars and include cash and stock options paid in 2010; company revenue figures are in the billions of U.S. dollars and indicate the companies' total revenue in 2010 (James, 2011).

assess their resource exchanges to see if they are getting the value they expect, so that they can be a net winner in each exchange. Media businesses are better at making this assessment than are individuals. They can do this by performing the simple calculation of adding up all their revenue and then subtracting out their expenses, thereby determining their profit. If they are able to make a profit, they are a net winner for that year because their revenues (resources they take in) exceed their expenses (resources they give up). And if the size of the profit continues to grow each year, those businesses become more powerful because they amass more resources. So you need to ask yourself, If most media businesses are net winners, who are the net losers? Are you a net loser—that is, do you give them more valuable resources than you are receiving back from them?

Notice that the goals of the four groups are very different from one another. Also, there are times when the goals are in direct conflict. For example, a film company will prefer to pay an actor little money to reduce its business expenses on the film and thus maximize its profit. In contrast, the actor in the negotiation wants to be paid a huge amount of money and be handsomely rewarded for his talent to attract a huge audience for the film company. Thus, the negotiations are more often competitive than cooperative. This means that often there is one player who benefits more than other players, given the outcome of a particular negotiation. This competitive stance leads certain players to approach the game with the attitude that they have to increase their wealth in the negotiations, even if it means that other players must reduce theirs.

The Rules

The most central rule of this economic game is that to play, you must have resources and a willingness to exchange them for other resources. If you lack either the resources or the willingness to exchange, you cannot play. All the other rules are made up by players as they negotiate. When rules are made up, it is done to maintain a sense of fairness in the exchange. Players who begin to perceive the game as unfair will cease to trust the other players and will stop playing, and this diminishes the game. For the game to remain exciting, it must attract huge numbers of players who willingly exchange their resources.

Although there are few rules, many characteristics guide the play of the game. These characteristics are illuminated in the next section.

CHARACTERISTICS OF THE GAME

To understand more about how the economic game is played with the mass media, you need to understand five characteristics of that game. These characteristics are as follows: the importance of valuing resources well, indirect as well as direct support, the complex interdependency among players, the nature of competition, and advertising as the engine. An understanding of this set of principles will help you comprehend how the negotiation for resources takes place.

Importance of Valuing Resources Well

The key to being successful in negotiations is to value resources accurately. If one player can do this and the second player cannot, the second player is at a real disadvantage. Two considerations go into resource valuation, and both of these require considerable skill to do well. One factor in valuing a resource is making an assessment about how well the resource will achieve a particular goal. A second factor that is important in valuing resources is to consider supply and demand.

The more skill people have in these areas, the better they will be able to make accurate assessments of the value of their resources, and the more valuable those people will be in a negotiation. For example, let's say you find something in your parents' attic that you think may be valuable. You take it to an antique dealer to sell it. The dealer gives you a price of $60 for it. Should you accept the $60 and sell it to the dealer? If you have no knowledge of antiques and no idea about how rare the piece is, you are operating in the dark. You might think you are savvy and ask for $100, then settle for $80, feeling good that you "got the dealer to raise her price" $20. But maybe the piece is worth $1,000. If you don't have a good operating knowledge about what your resources are worth, you will continually fall into one of two traps. One trap is to *over*value your resources, and no one will want to enter into exchanges with you. The other trap is to *under*value your resources, in which case you make lots of exchanges, but you continually are shortchanged. When you have little knowledge of the value of your resources, you can only play the game to lose.

Indirect as Well as Direct Support

Recall that this chapter began with the statement that the media industries generate about $970 billion revenue a year. To put this huge sum in perspective, look at Table 7.3, which shows that in 2010, the federal government spent a total of $958.7 on many very expensive and important services, yet these combined expenditures are less than the money we consumers spent directly on the media that year. This comparison should show you how important the mass media are to the average person in the United States.

This figure breaks down to about $3,125 for every man, woman, child, and infant in the United States. If you are an average person in your media spending habits, you spend this amount of money each year buying books, recordings, and movie admissions; subscriptions to magazines, newspapers, and Internet sites; and purchasing hardware, such as TVs, DVD players, MP3 players, video games, and other media products. However, this is an underestimation of how much money you spend each year supporting the mass media; you are spending about $1,000 more each year in indirect support of the media. This money is an invisible "surcharge" on advertised products that you buy. By paying more for products of all kinds—toothpaste, hamburgers, cereal, and so on—you subsidize the advertising industry, which turns its money over to the mass media. Thus, the mass media receive **direct support** from consumers in the form of payments to mass media organizations as well as **indirect support** from consumers who buy advertised products.

TABLE 7.3 Expenditures of the Federal Government in 2010	
Billions (U.S.$)	
372.3	Health (health care services, research, training, occupational safety)
142.5	Education, job training, and social services
124.7	Veterans benefits and services (education, housing, hospitalization, rehabilitation)
106.5	Transportation (highways, airports, trains, etc.)
55.0	Justice (federal law enforcement, courts, correctional facilities, etc.)
51.1	International affairs (embassies, foreign aid, and loans)
47.0	Natural resources and environment (recreational facilities, pollution control, etc.)
33.0	Science and technology
26.6	Agriculture

SOURCE: U.S. Bureau of the Census (2011, Table 471).

The media of books, films, and recordings are supported almost entirely by direct costs to the consumer. There are a few examples of ads being stuck in books and recordings and displayed before films, but this revenue from these ads is minor compared to direct costs. With magazines, newspapers, cable TV, and now the Internet, the costs are split between direct (subscriptions) and indirect (advertising). With broadcast television and radio, there is no direct cost for exposure to a program, but there is a high cost for purchasing the means to receive a program (radios and television sets), in addition to indirect costs in the guise of advertising.

The balance between direct and indirect support is shifting from direct to indirect payment. The reason for this is that the costs of some hardware such as TVs, radios, CD players, VCRs and DVD players, and computers are coming down each year while the revenues generated through advertising of all kinds increase each year.

Complex Interdependency Among Players

Some exchanges are relatively simple, such as when two people make an exchange and no one else is affected or concerned with that individual exchange. For example, a newspaper wants to minimize its costs. Let's say you are an employee of the newspaper, and you want a raise in pay and benefits. If you are a receptionist or a secretary, most of the negotiating power lies with the newspaper and not with you, because there is a very large supply of people with these skills relative to the demand. The newspaper will offer you a wage not much above the minimum wage. Either you take this offer or you look for work elsewhere.

There are, however, many times when the negotiations are more involved, and this illustrates the complex interdependence among the different players in the media economic game. For example, let's say a radio station wants to attract more advertisers, so it cuts the price of its ads by 20% in its highest rated show. Advertisers want to buy those ad times (called avails), so demand for the avails at this station increases. The station, which used to air 15 minutes of ads during an hour, decides to air 20 minutes of ads, thus increasing its supply of avails to meet the increasing demand. The station likes this because even though it has cut its income per ad by 20%, it is now selling 33% more avails, and thus the station has increased its total revenue. But the audience notices this change and becomes upset that there are so many ads and not nearly as much music. Most of the audience switches channels during the ads and never comes back. The station's ratings drop dramatically. Then advertisers become unhappy because it is no bargain to get a 20% discount on ads if the audience they expected is almost gone. Advertisers begin feeling they are wasting their money, so they stop buying those ads.

Three other characteristics make this interrelationship even more complex. First, the situation is highly dynamic and interrelated. When a person at one media company makes a decision, it can often have an impact on other companies in the same industry and perhaps other media industries. Returning to the radio station example above, when advertisers flocked to the station to get the discounted price for the avail, other radio stations (as well as television stations, newspapers, and local magazines) most likely lost advertising revenue. So when the revenues of one vehicle dramatically increase in the short term, the revenues of other competing vehicles are affected and usually go down. The same ripple effect can be seen with expenses of the media companies. For example, if several media companies started paying writers more money, then the better writers would be attracted to those companies, and the other companies would either have to pay more or make do with lesser talented writers, which would lower the quality of their shows and result in losing audience size and hence lower revenue. When something changes in a tightly linked industry, that change ripples outward and affects other players.

A second characteristic that contributes to the complexity is that sometimes decision makers are conflicted because they are experiencing cross-purposes. An example of this is when a decision maker might be a member of more than one group—each with a different economic goal. Let's say you work at a small newspaper and also own half of the newspaper company. As an employee, you might want a raise in salary, but this would increase overall personnel expenses and therefore reduce profits, making your investment less valuable. On a different scale, let's say you work for a large newspaper and own stock in the company that owns the newspaper. A raise in your wages will benefit you a great deal more than would a nonraise benefit shareholders. So your needs as an employee greatly outweigh your needs as an owner.

Third, media vehicles compete in different markets. A market is a segment of the audience to which you offer your product or service. Markets differ in size, with the largest market in the United States being the national one. Only a few vehicles, such as television network primetime broadcast programs, *USA Today* newspaper, *TV Guide* magazine, and major Hollywood movies, see themselves competing in a national market. More typically, vehicles carve out a special niche. One way of identifying a niche is geographically, such as the case with newspapers, radio stations, and broadcast television stations. Media vehicles in these industries have their own geographical locale, such as a city or a limited region. Another way of identifying a niche is by audience interest, which is common with magazines, books, and radio. For example, *Surfer* magazine appeals to a very different audience niche than does *Ladies' Home Journal.* College texts are marketed very differently than religious books. Country and western–formatted radio stations appeal to a very different audience than does a rap station.

Clearly, the economics of the mass media industries are complex. The complexity can be traced to the fact that there are many different components, each with its own needs that are most often in conflict with the needs of other components. This requires a constant negotiation process, and as decisions are made, effects ripple out and influence the decisions of others. All parties are profoundly interlinked.

Nature of Competition

Although this economic game involves many people and businesses, there is a limited amount of resources. Competition for those resources is strong—especially for the most valuable of those resources. However, because the game is ongoing, we must consider that certain companies and people get stronger and stronger at the game and, as a result, become more powerful. Some of these companies are attaining near-monopoly status within segments of the market. Thus, we have evolved into a situation referred to as monopolistic competition—*monopolistic* because each firm is large relative to the size of the market for its products (also, there are very high barriers to entry in most media industries) and *competition* because firms in an industry compete aggressively for resources.

Unusually high profits in an industry typically attract new firms, which results in greater competition. With greater competition, there are more firms and hence expanded output, lower prices, reduced profits, and greater benefits for consumers. But this trend is not apparent in most mass media industries where a few companies generate the majority of the revenue and make very high profits. Although these companies compete with each other, the industry does not attract other companies because the cost of entry into those industries has become so high.

Another characteristic of the competition is that within a market, all products are relatively indistinguishable; that is, the messages are not identical but very similar. For example, the website of CNN looks very similar to the website of MSNBC with pictures, headlines, and advertising; they cover the same stories and are continually updated at the same rate. A situation comedy on ABC is very similar to one on CBS; the characters have different names, but the stereotypes, settings, and plot points are very similar. With computer software, all spreadsheet application programs are pretty much the same; also, Web browsers are almost identical in user features. The key to competition is making consumers believe that your product is different from the others. Media businesses do not really compete on product features as much as they compete on product images. This is why advertising is so important. Advertising gets people to look beyond the product features to consider product images as well as psychological advantages of using the product.

Advertising as the Engine

Advertising is the engine that drives the growth of the media industries. The cost of doing business in the United States has greatly increased as advertising continually becomes a stronger economic force. In 1900, about $500 million was spent on all forms of advertising. By 1940, it was $2 billion, so it took 40 years to multiply four times. In 1980, it was $60 billion or a growth of 30 times in those 40 years. Now it is more than $316 billion (eMarketer, 2011a). Of this total, 32% will go to television (including cable and satellite), 15% to movies and video, 14% to magazines, 14% to newspapers, 13% to Internet, 8% to radio, and 4% to outdoor.

Why is advertising so important to our economy? Some dramatic changes of the economy of this and other Western countries over the past 100 years, especially over the past 50 years, have worked in combination with advertising to increase both the sale of goods and services as well as the importance of advertising. First, there has been a decline in the proportion of farmers and blue-collar workers and an increase in the proportion of white-collar professional workers. This means that people are not as self-sufficient and must buy their food and clothing. Second, there has been a high level of employment, which gives people the resources to buy goods and services. We have more discretionary income, which makes it possible for us to purchase things at a point well beyond the mere subsistence level. Over time, the standard of living has steadily increased as people's earning power increases and their expenditures for food, clothing, automobiles, housing, media, and luxuries have all increased.

Advertising has been the engine for this growth. Advertising makes it possible for new goods to enter markets and let us know immediately that they are available. With more product successes, more and more companies are willing to introduce an even wider range of new products. These companies fuel advertising agencies with money, which is passed through to the media. As the media grow, they offer more information and entertainment to us. More of us spend more time with the media, thus generating many more audiences, which the media rent out to advertisers. The money cycles from us to products, to the manufacturers of those products, to those companies' advertising agencies, to the media. Advertising drives this cycle faster and faster each year. If we stopped buying advertised products, the cycle would slow down and eventually stop.

MEDIA INDUSTRIES' STRATEGIES

The media industries have developed some general economic strategies over the years that make them successful at playing the economic game and achieving their goals. Three major strategies are illuminated in this section: maximizing profits, constructing audiences, and reducing risk.

Maximizing Profits

Almost all mass media are profit-oriented enterprises. As businesses, they are run to make as large a profit as possible. Remember that profit is the payoff or reward for doing business. This reward can be conceptualized in several different ways. First, it can be regarded as the difference between a company's revenue (total income) and expenses (total costs)—usually expressed as a percentage of revenues. For example, let's say you run a small magazine and at the end of the year, you total up everything and find that your revenues (all income through subscriptions and advertiser's fees) came to $100,000. Your expenses (paying writers, editors, photographers, printers, distribution, taxes, office supplies, utilities, etc.) sum to $90,000. That means you have $10,000 left over after having paid all your expenses for the year. This is your reward. You get to keep 10% of all your revenues; that is, your ROR (return on revenues) is $10,000 divided by $100,000.

A second way of computing your reward is to compare your profit to your assets, which is the money you have invested in the business. Let's extend the same example above where you had a $10,000 profit at the end of the year. If you had $50,000 invested in the business (office furniture, computers, printers, fax, and other equipment), then your ROA (return on assets) would be 20%, which is very good.

Both ROR and ROA are very important indicators of the reward of doing business, but they look at reward in different ways. For example, let's say you bought a radio station for $1 million and at the end of the year, you had generated a profit of $10,000 on revenues of $100,000. That 10% ROR is pretty good, but the ROA is only 1%, which is terrible! You could have invested the $1 million in a savings account at the bank and done better without taking any risk or doing any work. In another example, let's say you start a small weekly newspaper and your only assets are a computer and a few pieces of furniture totaling $4,000. Your newspaper generates revenue of $50,000, but your expenses are $49,000 so your profit is only $1,000. While your ROA is very high at 25% ($1,000 profit divided by assets of $4,000), your ROR is only 2% ($1,000 profit divided by revenues of $50,000).

While the ROA of American businesses in general fluctuates around 10% to 12% (Hagel et al., 2010), media businesses typically exhibit higher returns (see Table 7.4). Newspapers appear to be the best of the mass media industries because they have very high percentages on both ROR and ROA. Remember these are industry-wide averages; some newspapers do much better than these figures, and others have been losing money.

On the weaker end is the audio recording industry, with the lowest ROR. As for ROA, the cable television and film industries are the lowest, but both of these industries have huge asset bases, and this is what tends to make their ROA percentages appear smaller.

TABLE 7.4 Comparison of Profits Across Media Industries		
Industry	*ROR (%)*	*ROA (%)*
Television broadcasting	22	18
Radio	20	16
Newspapers	17	26
Cable and pay television	15	9
Magazines	11	24
Films	11	9
Books	10	14
Audio recordings	7	14

NOTE: Format adapted from Picard (1989, p. 89); data from Standard & Poor's (1996) *Index to Surveys* and *U.S. Statistical Abstract: 1999* (U.S. Bureau of the Census, 2000).

Increasing Revenue Streams

A major strategy employed by media businesses to maximize their overall revenue is to increase the number of revenue streams. Given the way audiences have been fragmenting into smaller and smaller slivers, the level of revenue that can be generated by any one audience has been decreasing. So to work around this problem of fragmenting audiences, media businesses have had to develop multiple revenue streams. One way is by trying to appeal to more than one audience. Another way is by trying to develop several ways to generate money from the same audience. For example, a film studio will develop an action adventure movie to attract a certain kind of audience to buy tickets at a theater when the movie is first released. Although movie studios typically spend $50 million advertising a film, they know that many films will not earn this much at the box office. So the studio sells the movie on DVDs. They also lease the movie to foreign distributors, and this adds another revenue stream. They lease the film to the airlines for showing during flights. They also market the music from the film on CDs. Often, they try to produce toys, clothing, or other artifacts from the film and sell those to the public. They sometimes hire writers to turn the movie into a book. Or they could hire someone to translate the movie into a comic book format. And they also sell product placements in the films. All these revenue streams increase the total revenue and thus give the film more of a chance to be profitable. This strategy is not limited to film but applies to all the media industries. Look at Table 7.5 to see how the cable television industry has developed multiple revenue streams.

This strategy is enhanced when one media company starts buying up other media companies. When a media company becomes a conglomerate, controlling the distribution of messages in many media channels, it can easily market a single message across many channels and thus quickly create multiple revenue streams for that one message.

Minimizing Expenses

One of the largest expenses across all the media industries is personnel. Recall from earlier in this chapter that I made a distinction between below-the-line and above-the-line employees. Because the talent of above-the-line employees is at a premium, media companies must pay huge sums to hire this talent. To compensate for this increasing cost of talent, companies are pressured to keep the below-the-line costs down. Most of the positions in the media industries are fairly low-level jobs that entail routine assignments that can be done by many different people with little training. These are the secretaries, receptionists, ticket

TABLE 7.5	Revenue and Expenses of Cable Distribution Industry

Millions (U.S.$)

42,918	Basic cable subscriptions
10,250	Premium cable subscriptions
3,072	Pay per view
13,156	Internet access
4,566	Selling air time (for advertisements and infomercials)
3,767	Telephone service
3,141	Renting equipment
729	Installation services
4,906	Other revenue
	Expenses
24,499	Production and programming costs
15,445	Personnel costs
14,918	Depreciation of buildings and equipment
1,923	Governmental taxes and licensing fees
2,189	Advertising and promotions
699	Repairs and maintenance
991	Supplies and materials
13,874	Other expenses for buildings and equipment

SOURCE: U.S. Bureau of the Census (2009, Table 1114).

takers, and low-level craftspeople. A bit higher than this are the assistant producers, camera operators, disk jockeys, and the like. Some of these people have special talent and quickly move up to the top of their industry, but most of them do not.

The media pay the people with a lot of talent a lot of money because these people are required for a company to generate large revenues. To counterbalance the large payments to talent, companies reduce expenses by paying clerical people as little as possible. Because the supply of potential workers for entry-level positions is so much larger than the demand, media companies can pay near minimum wage and get good workers.

The media reduce expenses through **economies of scale** and **economies of scope**. Economies of scale exist when marginal costs are lower than average costs, that is, when producing an extra unit of a good decreases as the scale of output expands. Large production runs are good because they spread out the startup expenses over many units; thus, with each additional unit manufactured, the per-unit cost continues to go down (Doyle, 2002). To illustrate, let's say you are a newspaper publisher and your cost of operation (cost of paying all your reporters, editors, salespeople, office staff, rent on building, depreciation of all your equipment, supplies, phones, other utilities, etc.) is $6,000 per day. This is your fixed cost. If you print only one copy of the newspaper each day, you will have to sell it for $6,000 just to cover your fixed costs. If you print two copies, you would have to sell each for $3,000 to cover all your costs; your average fixed cost per copy is cut in half. If you print 60,000 copies, your average fixed cost per copy is only 10 cents. Thus, your average fixed costs keep going down as these costs are spread over more and more copies.

However, when you print more copies, the cost of paper, ink, and distribution increases; these are your variable costs because they vary according to how many copies you print. The more copies you print, the more paper and ink you will need, and the price you pay for a roll of paper or a gallon of ink will go down because you can buy these materials in bulk and get big discounts. Although your total cost for ink and paper will go up when printing more copies, your *average* variable cost for these will go down. This is known as economies of scale. The bigger the scale of your business, the more likely your costs will go down either through the ability to demand greater discounts or because you are able to operate more efficiently beyond a certain point.

The more copies you print, the more your distribution costs will go up—both in total and on average. To illustrate this point, imagine that you publish only 1,000 copies of your newspaper. You could hire 10 youngsters each to deliver 100 papers after school and pay them a nickel for each paper delivered. Thus, your average distribution cost is 5 cents per newspaper. But let's say you wanted to publish 50,000 newspapers. You would need to hire 500 youngsters, and this would require you to develop a whole new layer of administration to recruit, train, and keep track of all these paper carriers. You would have to buy some trucks and hire drivers to get the newspapers out to these 500 carriers quickly every day. You would also have to hire some bookkeepers to keep track of all the subscriptions and billing. So the average variable cost might increase from 5 cents to 15 cents *per newspaper* delivered as you go from 1,000 to 50,000 in circulation.

The media companies, like any business, want to keep their expenses down, so they will find the point at which the combination of both their average fixed costs and their average variable costs are lowest. Beyond this point, distributing more copies only serves to increase unit costs and thus reduce profit. So newspapers, magazines, books, and recordings each seek the point where their average total costs (the sum of average fixed costs and average variable costs) are lowest.

With economies of scale, broadcast television, radio, and websites are different from the other media. They have no variable costs, only fixed costs. For example, with broadcast television, there is no cost to the station of adding an additional viewer to the audience. Viewers pay for their own television receivers, and they pay for the electricity to run them. The station has no distribution costs other than the electricity of the broadcast signal, and the power used to broadcast a station's signal is the same whether 100 or 100,000 sets are tuned in. It is fixed. With no variable costs and with a very high first-copy fixed cost, broadcast television stations keep dropping their average total costs with each additional audience member added. For this reason, the broadcast media (both radio and television) are strongly motivated, more than any other medium, to increase the size of their audiences. The same pattern holds with websites.

Economies of scope also serve to reduce a firm's expenses per unit. Economies of scope are achieved through multiproduct production; that is, there are variations on the product produced. Recall the example above about a movie company generating many revenue streams for a single movie. As the revenues increase for each new revenue stream, the expenses remain relatively low; that is, once you have produced the movie, it is relatively inexpensive to record it on videocassettes and DVDs. By increasing the scope of distributing the same product, very little additional costs are incurred, and yet the potential for revenues increasing is great.

Digitization has made economies of scope even more attractive because it creates little cost to retransmit a message in many different channels. Also, digitization allows for compression of greater amounts of data or more layers of content to be packed into a product. Now you can buy a DVD disk with an entire movie; it also can have interviews with the writer, director, and stars; outtakes; director's cut; alternative endings; and so on. Yet the DVD disk is much smaller than the videocassette, which holds much less information.

Constructing Audiences

Because advertising is the principal source of revenue for most of the commercial media throughout the world, media companies are in the business of constructing desirable audiences and renting them out to advertisers. A medium builds an audience by recognizing where there is a need for entertainment or information, then providing those products and services to satisfy those needs. This can be done generally in one of two ways. A media business can either (a) orient toward a **quantity audience goal** (i.e., attract as *large* an audience as possible) or (b) orient toward a **quality audience goal** (i.e., attract a certain *kind* of niche audience).

The dominant mass media in the past have typically followed a quantity goal. They tried to present whatever content they felt would attract the greatest number of consumers. This is what the commercial television networks have done in the past, especially for their primetime period (8–11 p.m. each night). A primetime show that generated a rating of 11 was regarded a failure. This means that only 11% of all households—"only" 19 million people—watched it. Even though this is more than all the people who saw the Broadway smash hit *A Chorus Line* in its extraordinarily long 10-year run, the television networks are not satisfied by such a small audience. A difference of 1 rating point for a show over the course of a single season could mean almost $100 million in advertising revenue to the network, so networks are strongly motivated to increase the size of their audiences as much as possible. But this quantitative goal is now unrealistic for broadcast television, and there are indications that this industry is going to a niche-oriented approach, as have all the other mass media industries.

Attracting People to Niche Audiences

The radio and magazine industries have been very successful for years in attracting people to a niche audience. For example, a radio station will develop a certain sound to appeal to one kind of listener, then try to attract as many of those kinds of listeners as possible. So one station will use rap music to attract urban youth, whereas another station will use golden oldies to attract the aging baby boomers. The audience for each of these stations is relatively small compared to an audience for broadcast television. But small, highly targeted audiences have great value to many advertisers. Special groups of people have special needs. Businesses that are marketing products for a special audience will pay a premium to the media vehicles that attract that special audience. For example, joggers as a group have a special need for information on running practices, equipment, and training techniques. They support several magazines that publish nothing but this type of information. Manufacturers of jogging equipment pay a premium to place ads in these magazines, knowing that the buying of advertising space in these magazines is a very efficient purchase because the ads placed there will be reaching their most likely customers.

Conditioning Audiences

Once a mass media business has constructed an audience, it needs to keep that audience, so it can continue to rent it out to advertisers. The mass media businesses are not especially interested in providing a message for a single exposure, like a rock concert promoter might. The mass media want to stay in business over the long term, and this requires that they maintain their audiences. Therefore, they must condition their audience members so that they develop a habit of exposure.

Reducing Risk

All businesses face risk. About 90% of new businesses fail shortly after being founded, and venture capitalist firms that finance new businesses for a living are happy when 20% of their investments are successful. Risk is especially high with new media businesses, like with Internet startup companies, and even with established companies that must continually develop new messages, like Hollywood films. Very few Hollywood films earn enough at the box office to cover their initial production costs, and less than 2% of films released each year in the United States account for 80% of box office returns (Schumpeter, 2011).

How do media companies reduce the risk that their messages will fail to attract a large enough audience to recover their initial costs of production? Media businesses have shifted their thinking toward something called the marketing concept. Instead of beginning with messages and then trying to find audiences for those messages, media businesses begin with audience needs and then construct messages to meet those needs. With the marketing concept, managers conduct research to identify particular niche audiences, then find out what the unmet needs are for those audiences. Then the media develop messages to meet those previously unmet needs. Beginning with research first and product development second reduces risk of message failure once the messages are released into the market.

This procedure is used frequently by the media industries. Researchers look at what works, then develop shows that are sequels or spinoffs of successful shows. Also, in the magazine industry, a large conglomerate will do market testing for unmet needs for magazines; once a need is found, the company will develop a magazine to reach that niche audience, then rent those consumers to a particular set of advertisers who need to expose that particular audience to their ad messages. Hollywood is fond of sequels because they reduce risk. This is why the number of sequels has increased each year, and in 2011, it reached an all-time high, with a sequel of a major Hollywood movie being released every other week (Lussier, 2011).

Even when message designers carefully conduct market research, follow the trends, and use talented people, they can still lose money—even a lot of money. This is especially true with Hollywood films. For example, the movie *Sahara* was based on a best-selling novel by Clive Cussler. It began filming in November 2003 and ran up production costs of $160 million plus other expenses for distribution (see Table 7.6). The film opened in April 2005 and earned only $79.5 million net at the box office. While the studio projected total revenues of $202.9 million over 10 years from all its expected revenue streams (home video sales, pay television, network television, and foreign distribution), it was still predicted to lose more than $78 million once all the expenses for not only production but also for promotion were paid off.

TABLE 7.6 Revenue Streams and Expenses for a Hollywood Movie: *Sahara*	
	US$
Total Production Costs	160 million
Sets and property (set construction, wardrobe, makeup)	24.1 million
Transportation and location costs (hotels, custom fees, airplanes, etc.)	20.1 million
Cast and extras	18.6 million
Matthew McConaughey	8 million
Steve Zahn	2.2 million
Penelope Cruz	1.6 million
William Macy	750,000
Rainn Wilson	45,000
Extras	402,569
Other	5.9 million
Writers (buying rights to novel on which film was based; screenplay)	14.1 million
Shooting units (marine unit, aerial unit, dive equipment)	13.6 million
Production units (support staff and accountants)	13.0 million
Post production	10.3 million
Special effects	7.3 million
General expenses (insurance, publicity, etc.)	24.4 million
Other production costs	14.3 million
Other Expenses	121.2 million
Prints and advertising	61.0 million
Home video	21.9 million
Distribution fees	20.1 million
Other expenses	18.2 million

SOURCE: Data from Bunting (2007).

CONSUMERS' STRATEGIES

We as consumers follow strategies just like the media industries do. However, our strategies are quite different from the profit-maximizing strategies of the mass media. We have two options for strategies. We can follow a default strategy or a media literacy strategy.

Default Strategy

The **default strategy** follows a goal of maintaining a minimal level of uninterrupted satisfaction. We continually expose ourselves to media messages in a habitual pattern and allow the media to condition us. If we did not read any novels last year, we avoid reading novels this year. If we usually watch the evening news during dinner, we continue to watch the evening news during dinner. If we like a half-dozen music groups, we follow their new releases and typically ignore the music of other groups and are completely unaware of the music in other genres. We watch a few favorite shows on television and download a few movies—usually the same kinds of movies with the same stars. We follow these habits because it is easy. These habits were developed in the past when we tried something new and felt it was a pleasant experience, so we continue with it without thinking much. We rarely search out the experience for a very different type of message, because we are not sure what other messages are out there or feel that searching out those messages will entail much more effort than it is worth; that is, we will not feel more rewarded by them. Although the messages we currently experience are not providing huge rewards, they have almost no costs to us because they are routine habits. Therefore, value is determined more by the low cost of the exposures than by the high return.

Media Literacy Strategy

People who follow a media literacy strategy understand the economic game and how to be a better player. This means they have higher expectations for a return on the resources they expend. They want more than minimal satisfaction from exposures. They think much more about the value of their own resources, and they want to negotiate a better exchange for those resources.

What separates the use of the default strategy and the media literacy strategy? The answer is the strength of one's personal locus. People with a weak personal locus will settle for little in the exchanges because it requires too much effort to become a better player in the economic game. In contrast, people with a strong personal locus find it essential that they become more of a winner at this game. Expending the greater effort of using skills better and building more elaborate knowledge structures (see Table 7.7) is fun because it pays them back with much more interesting experiences.

SUMMARY

When you add the economic information from this chapter to your knowledge structure about the media, you develop a deeper understanding about how decisions are made. Remember that the media industries are composed of businesses that are run to make as large a profit as they can. Each of the media industries does this well, and each earns a profit much higher than the average of almost all other industries in the United States.

The media businesses play the economic game very well because they follow three strategies. First, they maximize profits by increasing revenue and decreasing expenses. Second, they construct niche audiences, then condition audience members into habits of continual exposures. Third, they reduce their risks by using the marketing concept.

We as consumers have two strategies available to us. One strategy is the default strategy, where we follow habits conditioned by the media. By following this strategy, we exchange our resources of time and money for a continual state of satisfaction with our habitual exposures; our focus is on keeping our costs low by limiting our exposures to content we

TABLE 7.7 Types of Skills and Knowledge Structures Needed to Understand the Economic Nature of the Mass Media

	Skills	*Knowledge*
Cognitive	• Ability to analyze reports on media industries and companies to determine revenue, expenses, and profits • Ability to compare/contrast across industries and companies on economic indicators • Ability to evaluate the economic health of media industries and companies • Ability to generalize from particular companies to industry trends • Ability to synthesize a prediction for future trends in the media industries and companies • Ability to analyze media industries and companies to recognize the operation of the five economic characteristics	• Knowledge of revenue, expenses, and profits of media industries and specific companies
Emotional	• Ability to analyze your feelings in reaction to the economic practices of media	• Knowledge of your experiences in buying and using media products
Moral	• Ability to analyze the moral implications of economic decisions • Ability to compare/contrast the moral implications across different companies • Ability to evaluate the ethical responsibilities of the mass media to society	• Knowledge of values in the media • Knowledge of your ethical system

have liked in the past and avoiding the risk of trying new content that would require more effort to find and understand. The alternative is to follow a media literacy strategy, where we expend more effort to develop our skills and knowledge structures *so that we profit by using the media better to fulfill our own needs for entertainment and information.*

Chapter Resources: To test your knowledge and learn more about the topics discussed in this chapter, visit the Student Study Site at www.sagepub.com/potter6e.

FURTHER READING

Albarran, A. B. (2010). *The media economy.* New York: Taylor & Francis. (202 pages with index)

The author covers a lot of ground in this relatively short book. He includes chapters on theories, technologies, regulatory issues, globalization, and labor issues.

Alexander, A., Owers, J., & Carveth, R. (Eds.). (2003). *Media economics: Theory and practice.* Hillsdale, NJ: Lawrence Erlbaum. (312 pages with index)

There are 15 chapters in this edited volume, which contains a good deal of technical economic information but is presented in a readable manner. Also, a glossary defines the key terms presented throughout the book.

Doyle, G. (2002). *Understanding media economics.* London: Sage. (184 pages, including references and index)

This book was written for people who do not have a background in economics but want to learn about how the media industries operate along economic principles. Although the examples are primarily from Great Britain and Europe, they illustrate economic trends and principles that also operate in the United States.

Vogel, H. L. (2011). *Entertainment industry economics: A guide for financial analysis* (8th ed.). New York: Cambridge University Press. (655 pages including appendixes, glossary, and index)

This textbook presents a wealth of details about the economics of each of the media industries in 15 chapters. It presents a lot of facts and figures (rather than anecdotes and insider stories) about the economic history and current nature of the entertainment industries primarily in the United States.

KEEPING UP TO DATE

Advertising Age (http://adage.com/datacenter/article?article_id = 106352)

This website provides lots of information about the leading media companies.

Forbes.com (http://www.forbes.com/lists/2008/54/400list08_The-400-Richest-Americans_Rank.html)

This website provides stories on economics and rank-ordered lists of wealthy people.

Statistical Abstract of the United States (http://www.census.gov/compendia/statab/)

The Department of Commerce releases a new statistical abstract every year. For updates on this material in this chapter, go to the section on Information and Communication.

EXERCISE 7.1

Estimating Your Personal Expenditures of Money on the Media

1. Before you go any further, stop and make a general estimate about how much money you spent on all forms of the media over the past year. Write your estimate here: $ _____

2. Now, let's itemize those expenditures. Think back one year from today and try to remember how much money you spent on each of the following over the past 12 months. If you want to do this accurately, get out your checkbook register and credit card receipts.

    $_____ Cable subscription (take monthly bill and multiply by 12)

    $_____ Magazine subscriptions

    $_____ Buying individual issues of magazines

    $_____ Newspaper subscriptions

    $_____ Buying individual newspapers

    $_____ Buying textbooks

    $_____ Other books (pleasure reading, gifts, reference books, etc.)

    $_____ Movie theater admissions

    $_____ Rental and downloading costs of movies

    $_____ Buying radios, televisions, DVD players, MP3 players, etc.

    $_____ Repairs on media equipment

    $_____ Buying computer hardware and peripherals (printer, game controllers, etc.)

    $_____ Buying computer software and/or manuals

    $_____ Subscription to computer services (Internet service provider, website access, etc.)

    $_____ Buying musical recordings

    $_____ Buying video or computer games

    $_____ Playing video games at arcades

    $_____ **Total** (sum of all the figures down the column)

3. How close are your figures in #1 and #2?

4. Does the amount of money you spent surprise you? Why?

EXERCISE 7.2

Estimating Your Personal Expenditures of Time on the Media

1. Begin with a wild guess about how much time you spend with the media each year. Write your estimate here: _____ hours

2. Now, let's itemize those expenditures of time. To make this task manageable, think about an average week. In the spaces below, estimate how many hours and minutes you spend with each of the following activities. Remember that you can be doing more than one of these at the same time.

   _____ Reading magazines

   _____ Reading newspapers

   _____ Reading textbooks and other materials for classes

   _____ Reading for pleasure

   _____ Listening to the radio (in your car, portable players, at home, etc.)

   _____ Listening to recorded music (nonradio; MP3 player, stereo system at home, etc.)

   _____ Watching films at theaters

   _____ Watching television (messages of all kinds on your television)

   _____ Working on a computer (word processing, doing research, etc.)

   _____ Communicating on a computer (e-mailing, texting, social networking, etc.)

   _____ Playing on a computer (games, visiting websites for entertainment, etc.)

   _____ **Total** (sum of all the figures down the column)

3. How close are your figures in #1 and #2?

4. Does the amount of time you spent surprise you? Why?

EXERCISE 7.3

Financial Analysis

1. Go to the library and get a list of media companies. Try the *Hoover's Guide to Media Companies* or get your reference librarian to help you. Find two media companies that look interesting to you.

2. For each company, do a brief financial analysis by answering the following questions:

   a. How much revenue did the company have last year?

   b. What were the major sources of that income?

   c. Given the sources of income, would you say that the company is primarily concerned with media businesses, or are media businesses really a sideline to other more important businesses?

   d. What were the company's expenses for the year?

   e. What was the company's profit margin? (Can you get both ROR and ROA?)

   f. What did the company do with its profits? Did it disperse all or part to the shareholders who invested in the company? Or did the company keep all or most of the profits for investing in additional media properties or other businesses?

3. Given your two analyses of the companies, in which would you rather invest your money? Why?

The Current Picture

CHAPTER 8

Key Idea: Media businesses are currently struggling to adapt to the most important force that is now shaping all mass media. That force is convergence.

"Mom, stop bothering me!" Henry was upset that his mother was interrupting his concentration.

"I told you to stop watching television. Turn it off."

"But I'm not watching television."

Henry's mom put her hand on the big 52-inch high-definition screen sitting on the family's home entertainment center and said, "This, young man, is a television set. And you are spending too much time watching it. Now turn it off."

"But Mom, I'm not watching television. I'm playing a video game." He walked over to the high-definition screen, placed his hand on it, and said, "I use this to play games and to watch movies. I never use this to watch television. I only watch television on my computer or my cell phone. Don't you know anything?"

This chapter presents the big picture of where the media industries are today by highlighting three topics. First, the chapter shows you that the mass media industries are currently undergoing major changes as a result of something called convergence. Second, the chapter examines how the news industry is struggling as traditional media businesses adapt to challenges from the Internet. Third, the chapter provides an employment profile across the various media industries.

THE POWERFUL FORCE OF CONVERGENCE

The key to understanding the nature of the mass media industries today is to realize how powerful a force convergence has been over the past decade and will continue to be well into the future. In the most general sense, convergence simply means the moving together over time of things that were previously separated. With the media, convergence means the moving together of previously distinct channels of communication such that the barriers that separated those channels and made them unique have broken down. In this section, we'll examine this force of convergence in three contexts—technological, marketing, and psychological.

Technological Convergence

The key technological innovation that has been driving convergence is not the computer per se but the software code that runs computers. This software code is digital—that is, it is written, stored, and read as discrete, individual numbers that are arranged in sequences to communicate patterns. While computers and digital code have been around for more than half a century, it was not until about two decades ago that the media began moving away from analog coding and began using digital coding instead. Analog coding is the recording, storage, and retrieval of information that relies on the physical properties of a medium. For example, from the early days of sound recording, engineers used an analog method of storing the information of sound recordings. The primary medium of transmitting recordings was the vinyl disk. The recording was pressed into the disk in the form of a groove that was composed of tiny fluctuations in the depth and width of the groove. A needle moved through the groove as the vinyl disk revolved on a turntable. The needle picked up the tiny fluctuations in the groove and translated them into electrical impulses that were sent to an amplifier and then to a speaker, where those impulses were translated into movements in the speaker, which sent out waves of compressed air to human ears. In the 1970s, recording companies began shifting from vinyl disks to magnetic tapes, but the analog system of coding was still used. Both the vinyl disks and tapes were subject to wear and tear—that is, the messages degraded with use. Then in the 1990s, recording companies began translating music into digital code and storing that code on compact disks (CDs), which could be read with a laser, and this greatly reduced the wear and tear on the recording. It also had several other major advantages. One of these advantages is that the digital code is compressed so that all the music on an album can be put on a CD, which is much smaller than the old vinyl disks. Advances in compression technologies have now made it possible to store thousands of albums on a device the size of your thumb. An even more important advantage than compression is ease of copying. Digitized musical recordings can be played with ease on many different platforms—your computer, iPod, smartphone, and so on.

All of the mass media have been switching over from analog to digital means of recording, storing, and retrieving their messages. Digital refers to using a sequence of symbols or bytes (usually numbers) that are not dependent on the physical characteristics of any one medium. With analog, sounds are stored and retrieved in a very different manner than are photographic images, so it is not possible to store both on the same device or to copy one into the other. However, when messages are translated into the digital format, they all share

the same fundamental coding system, so they can be moved seamlessly across all kinds of media. Thus, the computer is not simply a channel that allows you to access messages on the Internet. It also allows you to access messages previously available only on paper (newspapers, magazines, books, and photographs) as well as recordings, video, and films. Thus, the barriers that have traditionally separated the different media into distinct channels of distribution have broken down.

While digitization of messages has been the major technological development leading to convergence, several other important technological developments also have helped this trend. One of these is the switching from copper wire to fiber-optics in sending signals to televisions and computers. With the combination of compression of digitized information and fiber-optics, both the amount of information and its speed have been increased thousands of times over the past few decades. This has led to the availability of two-way communication. Now computer users can both upload and download enormous files—such as huge software programs and videos—in a matter of seconds. People can engage in texting, instant messaging, and video conferences in real time.

Marketing Convergence

How have the media businesses responded to the advances in technological convergence of information? They have moved away from distinctions by channel of distribution and focused much more on the messages and the audiences.

In the past, media companies used to define themselves by channels. For example, movie studios produced movies only, magazine companies created magazines only, and recording companies produced and sold recordings only. With a focus on channel, companies within a medium competed with one another to get their share of the audience. For example, a television network such as ABC saw itself as competing against other major television networks, such as CBS, NBC, and perhaps PBS. The television viewing public made up a big pie of viewers, and each network would try to grow the size of its slice of the pie each year by taking away viewers from the other networks. Over time, as other broadcast networks and then cable networks came into the market, competition was growing fast while the size of the pie was growing slowly. Television networks began looking for other ways to make money without growing their share of the pie. If they could take their share of the audience for a particular TV show and sell those people musical recordings from the show, magazines about the stars of the show, and perhaps produce a movie based on the characters in the show, then that TV company could make money in four ways rather than one. Thus, the company thought of itself less in terms of a TV company and more in terms of particular messages.

Technological convergence has given media businesses more options in the adaptation phase of their development. In the past, when a new medium had grown through the penetration and reached a peak, it forced the other existing media to adapt by developing different types of messages to satisfy audience needs that were not being satisfied by the newer medium. For example, when television came along in the 1940s and took away radio's traditional audience for entertainment programming (soap operas, comedies, mystery series, etc.), radio had to change its content to music and became more mobile so it could serve a function that TV could not.

With technological convergence, channels are much less important than they used to be, and now the message is of central importance. Therefore, media businesses do not have to think about developing a different type of message for each medium; instead, they focus on developing messages that would serve the unmet needs of their audience, then market this message to that audience across all platforms. This marketing convergence has motivated media businesses to acquire other media businesses with access to other platforms (see Chapter 16).

Now mass media companies think first about the needs of different niche audiences, then develop messages to satisfy those audience needs. They translate that message into as many forms as possible to attract and hold that audience—film, TV, websites accessed through computers, notebooks, cell phones, and so on. This procedure has two major advantages. One advantage is that a single message can generate many streams of revenue, so once the media company pays to have the message produced, it can collect revenues several times (recall the idea of economies of scale from the previous chapter). The second advantage is that when the message appears in one channel, it stimulates audience members to expose themselves to the message in other channels. For example, people who read the Harry Potter books are stimulated to see those characters, settings, and events depicted in a movie. They want to read about the actors in those movies in magazines, newspapers, and fan websites.

This trend toward convergence also has changed the way media companies view audiences. The big media companies used to try to program to the largest audiences possible. To do this, they would make sure their messages could appeal to everyone without offending anyone with language or with certain themes that a part of the general audience might find distasteful. Thus, they adopted the programming principle of LCD—lowest common denominator. Programming has now shifted to what is called long tail marketing. To understand what a long tail is, think of the bell curve, which is referred to as a normal distribution by statisticians and college professors who "grade on the curve." On any characteristic—height, weight, IQ, scores on tests, and so on—people form a distribution. Let's take height, for instance. Most adult men are between 5 foot 7 inches and 6 feet; this majority forms the fat part of the curve. On either side of this fat part are fewer people who are either shorter than the majority or taller; these small areas on either side of the fat part are the tails. With height, the tails are rather small. For example, very few adult men are taller than 7 feet or shorter than 4 foot 7 inches. However, when it comes to personal interests, such as preferences for music or magazine content, the tails can be very long to account for all the niche interests—each with a relatively small number of people holding those interests. Thus, long tail marketing refers to finding out what the special needs are for each of the many small niche audiences that form the long tail.

Media companies used to focus only on the fat part of the distribution because that is where most people are. But now, savvy media companies know that they can make a lot of money by identifying several niche audiences and developing products that are highly attractive to only them. And once the media company has attracted a niche audience, it can sell access to that audience to advertisers for a premium.

Long tail marketing is now a viable marketing strategy given the trends discussed above. Huge media conglomerates have deep pockets and can afford to pay for the research necessary to discover these new niche interests and then accept the risk of developing new messages. Also, media companies can digitize their messages and send them to their niche audiences in all sorts of newer technological channels. While the large media are recognizing that marketing to a very large audience is a thing of the past and are trying to market to smaller niche audiences, there is a limit to how small a viable audience is for them. But with long tail marketing, there is no limit in small size. For example, Netflix with its huge warehouse can offer movies to all kinds of small niche audiences that a local video rental store cannot. The Web allows for more experimentation and creativity because it is not so risk adverse. Also, Amazon.com markets to the long tail very well by providing so many media products that the needs of even the smallest audience are satisfied; more than half of Amazon's sale of books is to audiences ranked lower than 130,000 (Bollier, 2008). This means that Amazon does not need to focus only on bestselling books for its revenue if it can satisfy the needs of enough niche audiences. Newer artists (musicians, videographers, poets, etc.) are willing to work for very little money to get known and build an audience.

Psychological Convergence

Convergence is not just a technological or marketing force; it also has profoundly changed the psychology of the audience (Jenkins, 2006). Psychological convergence refers to changes in people's perceptions about barriers that previously existed that are now breaking down or totally eliminated due to recent changes in the media. These changes have served to help people see things in a different way and have provided them with tools to act on those changes in perception. One of these changes in perception concerns geography—that is, geographical barriers are no longer important. With e-mail, instant messaging, social networking websites, and mobile phones, people can stay in close contact psychologically with friends and colleagues, even when those people are not physically present. There has also been the breaking down of sociological barriers of social class and social distinctions of status as defined by occupation or generational difference. With newer media platforms, a person can cross all those barriers to make contact with anyone. With the removal of these geographical and sociological barriers, people have redefined their social spheres.

Convergence has changed the way people think about the media and use them. That is, digitization has allowed people to access messages from various platforms and merge those into their own messages. The interactive features of many platforms have allowed users to bring together all kinds of previously unacquainted people into a single network of friends or professional colleagues. Thus, there is a convergence of people's individual needs with the available ways to satisfy those needs. People are more active now and do not have to wait for media companies to recognize their needs and develop messages; instead, they can assemble their own messages as their needs arise. People think of themselves not only as consumers of the media but also as essential contributors.

Current Picture

Now the computer medium is moving into dominance. This industry is very dynamic as it grows and changes each year. The media businesses in this industry can be organized into three categories. One category includes those businesses that have been primarily the developers of hardware and software that they have sold to relatively large audiences; for profiles of several of these companies, see Table 8.1. A second group includes conglomerates that have acquired many media companies over the years and now market messages across many different channels. This segment includes huge media conglomerates such as The Walt Disney Company and Time Warner. These are examined in more detail in Chapter 16. The third group includes companies that provide Internet-based services (see Table 8.2).

TRANSFORMATION OF NEWS

The forces of convergence are profoundly affecting the news. The traditional business model for news that has been so successful for more than a century is being forced to change due to challenges from the Internet (Standage, 2011). There are three major reasons for this: loss of readers, loss of advertisers, and social participation in newsgathering. American newspapers have been losing readers for the past 70 years, especially in the past 25 years. At its peak, 40% of adults subscribed to a newspaper, and now that is down to 10%, with little sign that the decline is over. Viewership for broadcast and cable television news programs has also been in decline for a decade. The highest rated television news source is Fox News, which now attracts only 1.8 million viewers a day (Easley, 2010). A big reason for the decline in the size of audiences for the traditional news media has been the lack of immediacy and control compared to the Internet news outlets. People who want immediate information about a news story are now more likely to go to a website, which can show text and photographs along with real-time video any time of the night or day.

TABLE 8.1 Profiles of Major Hardware and Software Companies

IBM ("1100100 and Counting," 2011)

1886	Founded by Herman Hollerith, a statistician who invented a computing machine for the U.S. census
1915	Thomas Watson Sr. took over the company and, using his experience as head of National Cash Register, built it from 400 employees into a global force with tens of thousands of employees.
1924	The company changed its name from CTR (Computing Tabulating Recording Company) to IBM (International Business Machines). Watson built a highly trained sales force to help companies with their business productivity needs.
1940	The company redefined itself when electronic calculating machines and magnetic tapes came along. Its first big platform was the electronic age, and the company spent $5 billion of 1960s money (more than the cost of the Manhattan project that developed the atomic bomb) to develop the System/360 mainframe computer that was launched in 1964.
1969	IBM became the first IT company and had a 70% share of the computer market.
1980s	IBM was shifting away from mainframe computers to more distributed computing with desktop PCs.
1993	Lou Gerstner, then CEO, shifted IBM's focus from machines and onto providing technological services to businesses as a way of increasing their productivity.
Around 2000	IBM began emphasizing the use of vast data centers that delivered services over networks, thus an early forerunner of the idea of the cloud.
Since 2005	IBM spent $14 billion to buy two dozen firms offering all kinds of gear for business analysis. One such acquisition was Skype, an Internet phone and video calling service for $8.5 billion.
Present	IBM's huge sales force works along with its research department of more than 3,000 employees, and IBM works with businesses to develop custom products to help them with their individual challenges.

Sony (Gardiner, 2010)

1946	Sony was founded as a radio repair shop.
1968	Introduced Trinitron color TV, which was twice as bright as other TVs at the time
1970	First Japanese company listed on the NYSE
1975	Introduced the first Betamax VCR
1979	Launched the age of personal, portable music with the Walkman
1982	Introduced the first CD player, ushering in the era of digital music playback
1994	Launched PlayStation, which overtakes Nintendo as the most popular video game platform
2008	Introduced Blu-ray disc format for video with five times the storage capacity of a regular DVD
2010	Introduced Bravia 3-D TV

Microsoft ("Middle-Aged Blues," 2011)

1975	Founded by Bill Gates. Quickly rose to dominate the world of personal computing with its Windows operating system and office software for word processing, spreadsheets, and presentations.

2000	Bill Gates turned over the leadership to Steve Ballmer, and Microsoft since has lost its reputation as a tech trendsetter to what is called the gang of four: Google, Apple, Amazon, and Facebook, which are all fast-growing, consumer-oriented businesses.	selling it at a premium price—PCs, music players, smartphones, and table computers. Apple went through a tough time in the 1990s when Jobs left the company to others to run, but when he returned in 1997, Apple again became enormously successful in the development and marketing of cutting-edge products. The future of Apple came into question in the fall of 2011 as the company shifted its focus into cloud computing services and Steve Jobs died. ("The Test of Time," 2011).

Apple was founded in 1976 by Steve Jobs with the idea of taking the latest technology, packaging it in a simple, elegant form, and

When news organizations lose viewers for their messages, they also lose advertisers. Thus, newspapers have been especially affected by this loss of subscribers because until recently, newspapers generated 87% of their revenue through advertising. Much of this advertising has been from classified ads, but this revenue has dropped dramatically in the past 5 years because of Craigslist, which has become the ninth most popular website on the Internet. People can post their classified ads on Craigslist immediately for free, read the ads for free, and respond to those ads through e-mail for free. Commercial advertisers have also moved from traditional print newspapers to the Internet, so newspapers have been creating websites to attract those advertisers back. Those newspaper websites typically offer some teaser news stories for free on a homepage but keep most of their content behind what is called a paywall, which prevents all visitors except subscribers from having access. This paywall structure has not generated much in the way of subscription revenue, so newspapers have tried a metered paywall that allows visitors access to a relatively large number of stories (such as 25) or a certain number of days of free access as a way of attracting them and conditioning them to habitual exposure, at which point the newspaper starts charging them a subscription fee. While this has brought in some revenue to the newspapers, they still rely on advertising support, which has failed to increase to levels they expected. Advertisers who use the Web are resisting traditional display advertising rates, which are based on a number of visitors to a site, and instead prefer advertising rates to follow a Google model, which is based on the number of times users click on an ad to get more information about the advertised product. Banner ads on websites used to be a good advertising vehicle, but by 2011, for every 1,000 displays ads that popped up, less than two were clicked on, and prices have slumped. Now they are not viable as a support; some media firms such as News Corporation have concluded that online ads will never bring in enough money to support a newspaper. Search advertising has taken the place of banner ads; in 2000, it accounted for only 1% of American online ad spending but by 2011 had accounted for half. It is responsible for turning Google into a $172 billion company ("Mad Men," 2011). The advantage of search ads is that they are highly targeted—that is, ads pop up only when an Internet surfer has expressed a particular interest.

As for participation, nonjournalists have increased access as informants and reporters. Now anyone with a cell phone camera can record events as they happen and immediately

TABLE 8.2   Profiles of Major Internet Companies Providing Services

MySpace (Angwin, 2009; Chmielewski, 2011b; Khouri, 2011)

- Began in the summer of 2003 on a shoestring budget as a social networking site by an Internet company called eUniverse. It allotted each user a profile page with pictures and interests along with the ability to link to friends. It also provided games, blogging (called journals early on), and even horoscopes.
- Early adopters were teenage girls who used it to keep in touch with their friends around the clock by posting photos and actively blogging. MySpace allowed them to customize their profiles, which had strong appeal for the early users. They also downloaded songs and "mashed up" songs in remixes. MySpace also allowed Fakesters by allowing users to be whoever they wanted to be—themselves, a celebrity, a pet animal, or a wholly made-up person with a created identity. The major activity was "friending," which is getting people to add you to their friends list and agreeing to be on your friends list; many users felt it was a competition to have the largest friends list.
- Until April 2004, only MySpace members could view the profiles of other MySpace members, but because of the shifting focus to advertising support, MySpace was opened up to the outside world. MySpace needed viewers more than it needed members.
- In July 2005, News Corp bought Intermix, an Internet company with several entertainment-type websites, including MySpace, for $580 million and added it to its new and struggling Interactive Media division within News Corp. Not until December 2006 did this division start making a profit, and within 2 years, it was making more than $1 billion a year, primarily through advertising.
- MySpace made some changes to increase its appeal. It created its own content to attract audiences and then rent those audiences out to advertisers. For example, in 2006, MySpace created Secret Shows, which is a program of free concerts for MySpace members. It costs MySpace $20,000 a month to host the shows, and Chili's restaurants pay MySpace $3 million a year for sponsorship rights.
- MySpace spent $19 million to acquire ILike, a music recommendation service similar to a service used by its rival Facebook. This shows continued evolution from a teen hangout to a broad-based entertainment service. ILike allows users to post playlists of the songs they like most and indicate when they plan to attend a concert. ILike then takes this information and shares it with online retailers, who then pay ILike for referring purchases of songs and concert tickets.
- In July 2008, Web surfers viewed 41.1 billion pages of MySpace, making it the most trafficked in terms of page views in the United States by a wide margin. Yahoo was second with about 32 billion page views. MySpace was by far the market leader in social networking with 75 million unique visitors, nearly twice the monthly visitors of Facebook, which was second.
- All kinds of people were using MySpace. Individuals used it to connect with their friends in the same room or in some far-away foreign land with text, pictures, video, and music; dig out information on long-lost friends; meet strangers to make them friends, romantic partners, or even a spouse; make business contacts and advertise services for sale, legal and illegal; create an entirely new person; and even organize political campaigns at all levels, including president of the United States.
- Many different kinds of people have used MySpace as a platform for their own needs.
- In May 2006, Buena Vista Pictures, a subsidiary of Disney, held a contest on MySpace inviting dancers to submit videos for a chance to appear in the credits of an upcoming low-budget movie called *Step Up*. Despite the short 2-week duration of the contest, Disney received several hundred submissions and accumulated more than 120,000 friends on its MySpace profile. Some of the dancers were cast in the movie, and some of the videos were run after the ending credits of the movie. Disney also used MySpace to market the movie and ended up doubling the expected box office gross during the opening weekend of the movie's release. Since then, other movie studios have used MySpace for promoting their movies.

- Advertisers used MySpace to build a profile for their brands by creating a MySpace presence and tracking who is attracted to their profile, asking them questions, and then altering their product image accordingly. This was done by Adidas in its sponsorship of the World Cup soccer tournament; Honda did it to profile Element, its compact sports utility vehicle; and Jack in the Box used it to build a profile for Jack, its mascot (Angwin, 2009, p. 240). Fans of celebrities have created profiles for their celebrities. People aspiring to a career in pornography will post suggestive photos (MySpace does not allow nudity) and information about themselves, hoping to catch the attention of people in the industry.
- MySpace peaked around 2008 to 2009 and has been in a downward trend ever since as Facebook surpassed it as the dominant social networking site. In 2008, it had 75 million unique visitors a month, which was nearly twice the monthly visitors of Facebook, which was second. MySpace had 41.1 billion pages, making it the most trafficked in terms of page views in the United States by a wide margin.
- At its height, MySpace was the world's dominant social network and was the fifth most visited site on the entire Internet. It attracted 3 million bands, 8,000 comedians, and countless others. Rupert Murdoch bought it in 2005 for $580 million when it was valued at $65 billion. In 2006, Google agree to pay $900 million for the exclusive right to provide a search function on MySpace and sell advertising. By 2007, it had nearly 100 million monthly users worldwide. But it failed to keep pace with its chief competitor, Facebook, in terms of innovations and started losing visitors until the summer of 2011, when it was sold for $35 million (Chmielewski & Guynn, 2011).
- By 2009, there were many racy pictures of females on MySpace, the most famous of which is of Tila Tequila and porn star Jenna Jameson. In fact, it has been estimated that 95% of porn stars have MySpace pages.
- By 2010, MySpace was falling behind Facebook in terms of innovating and providing services. Observers felt it lost its vision; it inundated users with too many ads and failed to keep up with offering users exciting new services.
- In January 2011, MySpace was in rapid decline. It had peaked in October 2008 with 76.3 million users but then fell to 35 million in May 2011. In 2009, its ad revenue was $470 million, and that dropped to $184 million. MySpace had 1,000 employees at the beginning of 2011 but laid off 500 people in January 2011, with 250 more expected to be laid off in the summer.
- In summer 2011, News Corp sold MySpace for $35 million to Specific Media, which vowed to make MySpace "cool again" by attracting popular artists and attracting users who wanted contact with those artists. It also created a partnership with Justin Timberlake.

Facebook (Angwin, 2009; Olivarez-Giles, 2011)

- Facebook was launched in 2004 by Mark Zuckerberg while he was a computer science undergraduate at Harvard University. The website's membership was initially limited to Harvard students but was expanded to other colleges in the Boston area, the Ivy League, and Stanford University. It later expanded further to include any university student, then high school students, and, finally, anyone age 13 and older.
- Facebook in October 2005 was a much smaller website than MySpace, with just 10 million monthly visitors compared with 24 million for MySpace, but it was growing quickly. Up until that time, it had been restricted to college students, but then it started letting high school students join. By November, Facebook was narrowing the gap with visitors by introducing several new features. One was "News Feed," which provided members with updates about their friends' activities. Second, it allowed anyone to join.
- In May 2007, Facebook released a guidebook that enabled software developers to write programs called widgets (small slide shows) that could run on Facebook's website. This allowed widget developers to use Facebook as a platform to make money through selling advertising on their own Facebook pages.

(Continued)

(Continued)

MySpace prohibited third parties from advertising, thus controlling all the advertising themselves. By July, developers had built more than 2,000 widgets for Facebook.

- By 2009, the website currently had more than 250 million active users worldwide. It now employs 700 people and generates more than $300 million a year (Facebook, n.d.).
- Facebook is valued at $76 billion ("The New Tech Bubble," 2011).
- Facebook grew enormously from its beginning to around the summer of 2011, where, at its growth peak, it was adding 20 million new users a month until it reached about 700 million users worldwide and stabilized at about 150 million users in the United States. Also, 50% of those Facebook users were found to log in every day.

YouTube (Chmielewski, 2011a; Pingdom, 2011; YouTube, n.d.)

- In February 2005, three former PayPal employees created YouTube as a video-sharing website on which users can upload and share videos. Unregistered users can watch the videos, while registered users are permitted to upload an unlimited number of videos.
- The first YouTube video was uploaded in April. Entitled "Me at the Zoo," it shows one of the founders, Jawed Karim, at San Diego Zoo.
- The site was opened to the public in November 2005, and it grew rapidly. The company, which is based in San Bruno, California, uses Adobe Flash Video technology to display a wide variety of user-generated video content, including movie clips, TV clips, and music videos, as well as amateur content such as video blogging and short original videos. Most of the content on YouTube has been uploaded by individuals, although media corporations, including CBS, the BBC, UMG, and other organizations, offer some of their material via the site, as part of the YouTube partnership program.

- By July 2006, the company announced that more than 65,000 new videos were being uploaded every day and that the site was receiving 100 million video views per day.
- In November 2006, YouTube, LLC was bought by Google, Inc. for $1.65 billion and is now operated as a subsidiary of Google.
- In 2007, YouTube consumed as much bandwidth as the entire Internet in 2000. In March 2008, YouTube's bandwidth costs were estimated at approximately $1 million a day.
- In June 2008, a *Forbes* magazine article projected the 2008 revenue at U.S.$200 million, noting progress in advertising sales. In November 2008, YouTube reached an agreement with MGM, Lions Gate Entertainment, and CBS, which will allow the companies to post full-length films and television shows on the site, accompanied by advertisements. The move is intended to create competition with websites such as Hulu, which features material from NBC, Fox, and Disney.
- By January 2009, YouTube was the dominant provider of online video in the United States, with a market share of around 43% and more than 6 billion videos viewed in January 2009. It is estimated that 20 hours of new videos are uploaded to the site every minute and that around three quarters of the material comes from outside the United States. Internet surfers view more than 2 billion videos on YouTube per day.
- By spring 2011, YouTube was the world's largest video platform with 500 million monthly viewers; users upload 48 hours of videos every minute; every day, more than 3 billion videos are viewed; and more video is uploaded to YouTube in 60 days than the three major U.S. networks created in 60 years. The site sells advertising and will cross the $1 billion mark in 2011; it also is now in the movie rental business and competes with Netflix.

stream them to all kinds of news organizations, including their own blogs. This broadens the idea of news beyond the narrow confines of traditional media organizations. Standage (2011) explains, "Thanks to the rise of social media, news is no longer gathered exclusively by reporters and turned into a story but emerges form an ecosystem in which journalists, sources, readers and viewers exchange information. The change began around 1999, when blogging tools first became widely available" (p. 10). At first traditional news organizations denigrated bloggers, regarding them as crackpots sitting in their pajamas writing only their opinions about things they knew little about and using questionable sources when they used sources at all. While there are likely to be bloggers who fit this disparaging description, many bloggers are deeply concerned about social, economic, and political issues and spend a lot of effort researching and writing about their cause. With WikiLeaks, bloggers can get information that reporters at any traditional news organization can get. Founded in 2006, WikiLeaks is an organization that publishes leaked documents supplied to it anonymously. In its first few years, its big successes were the publication of documents about the church of Scientology, Sarah Palin's e-mails, and corruption in Kenya. Then in 2010, it published a set of 75,000 documents relating to the war in Afghanistan and another 400,000 documents about the war in Iraq.

There are many examples where a blogger has done a better job of uncovering a news story or writing about an issue in more depth than can be found in traditional news media. The most high-profile example of this took place in 2004, when CBS News ran a report on *60 Minutes* that President George Bush, Jr. had used his family connections to receive favorable treatment in the Air National Guard when he was a young man and eligible for the draft during the Vietnam War. Bloggers questioned the authenticity of the memos that CBS had used as the basis for its story. The bloggers were correct that the source memos were faulty, and CBS had to retract the story. Furthermore, Dan Rather, who was the news anchor at CBS, resigned in disgrace.

Some people see the current trend in the news industry as not something new but instead as a return to how news was gathered and presented before big news organizations took over the industry. They point out that in the early 1800s in the United States, there were many news outlets, each of which had a small, partisan niche audience where readers frequently contributed to the stories. Now traditional media have been changing their focus on news to one that is more partisan. For example, Fox News unapologetically appeals to conservative viewers, and in response to this, MSNBC has been positioning itself to appeal to more liberal viewers. As the news audience continues to fragment into smaller audiences, it is likely that the traditional news organizations will be forced to identify a set of niches and craft different news products to appeal to each niche.

GENERAL EMPLOYMENT TRENDS

The media employ a wide variety of people in many different businesses and occupations. However, you may be surprised to learn that the media employ only a very small percentage of the workforce—less than 2 million people, which is less than 1% of the adult population in the United States. While the general rate of growth in employment is expected to be about 8% across all industries in this country in this decade (2008–2018), the media are expected to grow about 10% (Bureau of Labor Statistics, 2011). Let's take a look at where these people work. There are two ways to examine this. One way is to examine the relative size of the workforce and businesses across the different media (see Table 8.3). Another way is to examine how people identify with occupations (see Table 8.4).

The largest employer within the media industries has been newspapers, along with film and video production (Table 8.3). Software publishing has recently grown rather large in terms of employees, especially in terms of establishments (unique businesses). On the other end of the range is cable TV and sound recording.

It is also important to look at employment from an additional perspective to get a more accurate picture because many people who work in the media occupations do so only part-time, as with actors or musicians. Also, people contribute a great deal to various media industries without being employees of any of those businesses. For example, 70% of authors and writers are self-employed, which means that they get paid when they sell their work to a book publisher or producer of a movie or video project without ever being considered an employee of a media company. Table 8.4 shows us that many people consider themselves developers of computer applications, and many of them are self-employed. This segment of the media is growing very well and projected to increase by 21% in this decade (2008–2018). The segment that includes people with occupations in public relations and advertising is also expected to grow very well. In contrast, the demand for journalists (broadcast and print) is expected to decline. As for salaries, the figures need

TABLE 8.3   Number of Employees and Number of Establishments Across Media Industries

Mass Medium	Number of Employees	Number of Establishments	Average Number of Employees Per Establishment
Newspapers	380,100	14,376	26.4
Software publishing	327,600	33,983	9.6
Film/video production	292,100	12,404	23.6
Periodicals	158,800	9,940	16.0
TV broadcasting	124,200	7,064	17.6
Radio	124,100	6,136	20.2
Book publishing	83,600	4,656	18.0
Internet service providers	72,700	7,588	9.6
Cable TV	38,800	4,154	9.3
Sound recording	22,300	1,636	13.6

SOURCE: U.S. Bureau of the Census (2009, Table 1086).

TABLE 8.4   Media-Related Occupations, Growth Rates, and Media Salaries

Occupation	Number of People	Growth Rate (%)	Median Salary (US$)
Computer application development	514,800	21	85,430
Producers and directors	98,600	11	64,430
Public relations and advertising	275,200	24	51,280
Editors (film and video)	25,500	11	50,560
Editors (print)	129,600	12	49,990
Camera operators	26,300	11	41,670
Sound engineers	114,600	8	38,050
Authors and writers	151,700	8	35,010
Journalists	138,600	−6	34,850
Photographers	152,000	12	29,440
Musicians and singers	186,400	8	21.24/hour
Actors	56,500	11	16.59/hour

SOURCE: Bureau of Labor Statistics (2011).

to be regarded with some skepticism because the salary range for each occupation is quite large. However, I present the median salaries (point at which half the people are paid more and half are paid less per year) to give you a rough idea of the pay rank ordering across the variety of media occupations. The two occupations at the bottom of that table are reported as hourly pay rates rather than yearly salaries because actors, musicians, and singers vary so widely in terms of how often they work.

Demographic Patterns

When looking at the total labor force in this country, we can see a trend toward more and more women becoming employed outside the home. Now, about 45% of the labor force is female. With the mass media industries, there has been a growth in the number of women employed, but there are still many more men working in the mass media than there are women.

The media industries that have the highest percentage of women employed are magazines and books, where women make up more than 50% of the labor force. The most growth in terms of the percentage of women has been in the newspaper industry. In 1960, only 20% of all people working on newspapers were women, but this percentage has been growing slightly each year. A major reason for this increase has been that newspapers have been moving away from the traditionally male-oriented press jobs and into more clerical and technologically oriented jobs. In broadcasting, 23% of all employees were women in 1960. This remained fairly static until 1972, when the federal government began monitoring hiring practices in businesses. Since that time, there has been a gradual increase to the current figure of about 30%.

In motion pictures, about 40% of all employees are women, but this varies depending on the sector of the industry. In the large exhibition sector (ticket takers, concession clerks, projectionists, etc.), about 45% of all employees are women. But in the production sector (actors, directors, producers, and writers), 95% are men.

Journalism

A popular profession within the media industries is journalism. In this journalistic community, there are about 67,000 reporters and correspondents, 23,000 writers and editors, and 67,000 radio and television announcers and newscasters. Most are male, White, and young. About one third of working journalists are women, which is an unusually low percentage given that about two thirds of students in journalism schools over the past decade have been women. Only about 8% are minorities (3.7% African American, 2.2% Hispanic, 1% Asian American, and 0.6% Native American). More than half of U.S. journalists are younger than 35, and only 10% are 55 or older. Almost all have a college degree, either with a major in the skill of journalism or another content-based area, such as English, American studies, and political science. In the United States, there are more than 300 universities with journalism/ mass communication programs, and each year, about 20,000 bachelor degrees are granted by those journalism programs.

Writers

In the television and film industries, most writers are men, and most of these men are young. Bielby and Bielby (2001) collected data on the careers of 8,990 television and film writers and found that writers are getting younger. The researchers explained this trend by saying that marketing strategies in television and film have been shifting to target younger audiences more, so these industries are hiring younger writers to tell stories that would attract that target market.

The Writers Guild of America has a membership of about 3,000 employed TV writers, and among these people, only 10% are minorities and 27% are women. Film is worse. Among the 1,770 employed film writers, 6% are minorities and 18% are women (Verrier, 2005).

Advertising

According to the American Association of Advertising Agencies, about 160,000 people are currently employed in advertising agencies in the United States: about 24% in creative, 15% in account management, 10% in media, 10% in financial, 8% in special support services, and the rest in secretarial and clerical areas (i.e., about 33%). Women account for 55% (Bureau of Labor Statistics, 2011).

Status

Women who are employed in the media industries are usually in positions of lower status, earn less money, and have less education. For example, in newspapers, women hold about 120 managing editorships at 1,700 newspapers in the United States. As far as policy-making positions on newspapers, women hold about 361 (11%), whereas men hold 3,057 (89%). With book publishing, about 64% of editors, vice presidents, and professionals are men; however, there is better representation in the smaller publishing houses.

SUMMARY

The media industries employ fewer workers than most people would guess. And those workers do not reflect the demographics of the population of the country. Although the media have been trying to hire a larger proportion of women and minorities, those groups are still very much underrepresented in the media workforce.

Chapter Resources: To test your knowledge and learn more about the topics discussed in this chapter, visit the Student Study Site at www.sagepub.com/potter6e.

FURTHER READING

Drapes, M. (2009). *Vault guide to the top media & entertainment employers.* New York: Vault, Inc. (137 pages, including appendixes)

This guidebook gives practical advice about getting hired in the media industries, particularly film, magazines, and book publishing. There is also a section that describes in detail what industry people do in their day-to-day jobs, whether it be on the business or creative side of the industries.

Mogel, L. (2000). *Careers in communications and entertainment.* New York: Simon & Schuster. (374 pages)

This is an exceptionally detailed book about the mass media industries with chapters on books, magazine, newspaper, television, radio, movies, special effects, advertising, public relations, new media, and sage advice. Each chapter describes the organization of its industry, the jobs, and the types of people who work there. It is filled with a great deal of practice advice for people who want to seek jobs in any of these communication industries.

KEEPING UP TO DATE

Bureau of Labor Statistics (www.bls.gov/ces/home.htm)

This is a website run by an agency of the federal government that reports information on all kinds of occupations in the United States, including salaries, duties, and required educational training.

Vault.com (http://www.vault.com/wps/portal/usa)

This website provides lots of useful information about various industries; particularly relevant to media literacy are the industries of publishing, newspapers, Internet and new media, music, broadcast and cable, advertising, and public relations.

Part 4

Content

This part deals with five issues of content. Chapter 9 provides a foundation for thinking about media content by examining the issue of reality; that is, media content is always a mixture of real elements and fantasy elements. The next three chapters each focus on a traditional type of media content: news, entertainment, and advertising. The final chapter in this part of the book focuses on the newest type of media content—interactive messages.

As you read this part of the book, keep the following questions active in your mind and you will stay focused on the most important ideas in the five chapters:

- How do all kinds of media messages conform to standard formulas that capture our attention and condition us for repeat exposures?
- What is it about those formulas that makes it possible for us to process them easily?
- What kinds of rewards do different kinds of media messages deliver to us?

Mass Media Content and Reality

Key Idea: The media spin reality to make it appear more exciting and thus attract people away from their real lives.

"This is a great idea for a show I call *Act Real,*" said Cosmo as he started his pitch for a reality television show to Sylvia, a television network vice president of reality programming. "So Sylv, my idea is to get about 8 to 10 aspiring young actors and stick them in a house in downtown New York City. Every few days they audition for a part in a major Broadway show or TV show. After each round of auditions, only one gets hired and that person moves out of the house. The rest of them stay in the house and we hear them complain and get all depressed. Each week the number of actors in the house goes down and we are left with the actors who feel more and more like losers."

"Well, then where's the payoff?" asked Sylvia.

"Get this, Sylv, the payoff is that the last guy ends up getting the best acting job of all of them. But he doesn't know that until the last episode when he is the most depressed and the most pissed off because all the other actors who he thinks are not as good as him are all given jobs. It's beautiful!"

"What kind of support do you need from the network?"

"First, I want you to put out a casting call for actors for a new show on your network. We should get thousands of applications. We choose the most unstable actors, the real drama queens. Then we need to hire some writers to give the actors cool nicknames and back stories. Also, the writers should write some lines here and there for the actors so we get some feuds going. We need your best editors to cut down all our footage because we will have cameras in every room in that house and end up with about 3,000 hours of footage."

"Sounds like a lot of production. What makes this a 'reality' show?"

"We don't pay the actors!"

"I don't know about that. The actors' union will not allow that."

"Yes they will, Sylv. These guys are actors in real life, but on our show, they are just ordinary people who want to be hired as actors. We don't have to pay ordinary people to be on a reality show. It's beautiful!"

We all live in two worlds: the real world and the media world. Attaining higher levels of media literacy does not mean avoiding the media world. Instead, it means being able to tell the two worlds apart as the two merge together under pressures from newer message formats and newer technologies that seem to make the boundary lines between the two worlds very fuzzy.

Most of us feel that the real world is too limited; that is, we cannot get all the experiences and information we want in the real world. To get those experiences and information, we journey into the media world. For example, you might feel that your life is too boring and you want to experience some exciting romance. You could read a novel, go to a movie, or watch a television program to get this kind of experience. Or you might be curious about what happened in your city today, so you watch the evening news, where reporters take you to all the places of the day's actions—crime scenes, fire locations, courthouses, sporting arenas. Although these are all real-world locations, you are not visiting them in the real world. Instead, you enter the media world to visit them.

We are continually entering the media world to get experiences and information we cannot get very well in our real lives. We enter the media world to expand our real-world experience and to help us understand the real world better. But those experiences we have in the media world are different than if we had experienced them directly in the real world. We often forget this as we bring media-world experiences back into our real world. As we constantly cross the border between the real world and the media world, the border sometimes gets blurred, and over time we tend to forget which memories are from experiences in the real world and which were originally experienced in the media world.

This blurring of the line and the interlacing of memories makes it important that we spend some mental energy considering the nature of reality and how the reality of the two worlds is different.

WHAT IS REALITY?

Reality is one of the most difficult concepts to define in any context. Philosophers have been trying to define it for millennia, and ever since the field of psychology was founded more than a dozen decades ago, psychologists have been focused on the fundamental problem of how the human mind encounters the world and seeks to make sense of what is real.

With media studies, it would seem as if the task of delineating reality would be easier by simply drawing the line of reality between the media world and the real world. The real world is real, and the media world is fantasy. But this is far too easy a distinction, and drawing the line in this way will be highly inaccurate and misleading. Still, we do have to make a distinction because developing a sophisticated understanding of the nature of reality is very important when trying to gain control over media effects. Let's begin by examining how scholars have analyzed how people make this distinction.

Magic Window

Media scholars have encountered the issue of determining reality primarily as a concern in dealing with children. The assumption has been that children see the media, especially television, as a magic window on the world. Psychologists believe that young children perceive television as the simple, unvarnished truth of what is happening in the real world. Media researchers have found that very young children (younger than 3 years of age) do regard television as a magic window, but as children's minds mature cognitively (as you saw in Chapter 5), they develop a skepticism about the literal reality of media messages and are better able to distinguish reality from fantasy (Taylor & Howell, 1973). By age 5, children can distinguish between fictional programs and news or documentaries. At this point, children clearly know what fiction is but continue to develop a better understanding about nonfiction as they grow older and as their experience grows with news shows (Wright, Huston, Reitz, & Piemyat, 1994).

Researchers have labeled this shift away from a magic window belief in the literal reality of media messages as "adult discount," where children begin thinking like adults and are more skeptical of the reality of the messages (Hawkins, 1977). Most researchers seem to believe that children have fully incorporated an adult discount into their thinking by age 12.

There is evidence, however, that not all people apply an adult discount by the time they reach age 12. For example, van der Voort (1986) found that although children's perceptions of reality decreased from ages 9 to 12 for fantasy programs, there was no change in their perceptions of the reality of so-called reality programs. It appears that children base their perceptions of reality not on the *accuracy* of portrayals or information but on the *probability* that something could occur in their lives. By age 12, they have not developed an understanding that, in many ways, news is a construction by journalists, just as fiction programming is a creation of writers.

As we age, we do not automatically acquire the ability to make accurate differentiations between reality and fantasy. Believing that we do may be the strongest evidence that our belief in what we think is the reality of the situation is actually a fantasy. Misperceptions of reality are not limited to children. *If we are to understand how people make decisions about what is real in the media, we need to look at more dimensions than the magic window one.*

Multiple Dimensions of Reality

Frequently, the judgment of reality is multidimensional; that is, we consider multiple characteristics in making judgments of reality. For example, it is possible to judge some science fiction movies (such as *Aliens* or *Star Wars*) as being more realistic than many situation comedies on television. A science fiction movie may take place in a fantasy world where no human has ever gone, contain characters that exist only in the imagination, and have laws of physics that are unlike anything on earth; however, the plots, dialogue, and themes could be judged as very realistic. In contrast, although a situation comedy may take place in a house very much like the viewers' own and have characters that dress like everyday people and engage in everyday problems, many viewers may roll their eyes and feel that those comedies have nothing to do with real life. Real people do not act like situation comedy characters act, and problems in the real world never get neatly resolved

in 30 minutes like they do in situation comedies.

The beginning point of judging reality is usually with an assessment of whether a portrayal actually happened. But viewers rarely stop at this judgment. There is more to judging reality. Viewers—especially with fictional content—make assessments about whether something *could* happen as portrayed. That which could never happen is fantasy. So the judgment must move beyond the *actualities* of occurrence and consider the *possibilities* that different characters could be people encountered in real life and that particular situations could actually occur.

Researchers have found that people will go beyond magic window considerations and also judge the reality of media messages along the dimensions of social utility and identity (Dorr, 1981; Hawkins, 1977; W. J. Potter, 1986). The social utility judgment is based on whether viewers believe they can use the information in the portrayal in their own lives. The more fantastic the characters and actions, the less viewers believe they can translate that information into something they can use in their day-to-day interactions with people. The identity judgment is based on a feeling of parasocial involvement with particular characters. The closer a viewer feels to a character, the more real that character is to that viewer.

Viewers make judgments on these three dimensions in an independent manner; that is, if a program is perceived as highly realistic on one dimension, the person may or may not perceive the show as being realistic on the other two dimensions. For example, *Star Wars* is likely to be regarded as fantasy when considering it along the magic window dimension, but it could be regarded as highly realistic by many on the identity and social utility dimensions.

Some scholars have claimed that there are even more than three dimensions underlying the concept of reality. For example, Hall (2003) conducted a series of focus groups in which she asked participants to conceptualize media realism. She found complex definitions that varied by **genre** and were based on six ideas: factuality, plausibility, typicality, emotional involvement, narrative consistency, and perceptual persuasiveness. *Factuality* is what actually happened. *Plausibility* is what could happen. *Typicality* is what usually happens. *Emotional involvement* is the degree to which a person's feelings and sense of identity are pulled into a message. *Narrative consistency* refers to the plot of a story and how well it makes people feel that sequence actions are believable. *Perceptual persuasiveness* refers to how real the images look. Of all these six dimensions, it appears that plausibility is the most often used conceptualization employed by people to determine the degree of reality in a media message.

Differences Across Individuals

As you have seen with the arguments laid out above, reality is a complex idea. There are many dimensions. There are also considerable differences across individuals in how they make their judgments of reality of media portrayals. These judgments of reality can vary widely even among people of the same age and experience. Not every child of the same age is making the same judgments about reality. For example, van der Voort (1986) reports that perceptions of reality and the degree of identification with characters vary substantially at any given age. In his research, he found that some children became absorbed in watching the violent videos and judged the violence to be realistic, which led to a stronger emotional reaction, which led to a belief that the violence was terrible, which did *not* lead to aggressive behavior in real life. In contrast, other children who were also absorbed in viewing violence and believed it to be realistic had an uncritical attitude toward program violence, which led to them being more jaded and less emotionally involved, which led to more aggressive behavior in real life.

To further illustrate the idea of a range of perceptions of reality, consider the situation as described in Box 9.1. The people who wrote to the Coast Guard, begging them to rescue Gilligan and his friends from the island, appear silly. You might be thinking that such a problem with reality is rare, and you would probably be right because this is such an extreme situation. But consider how much variation there is on perceptions of reality across people on shows such as the *World Wrestling Federation, Jersey Shore, The Hills,* and *COPS.* Think about how people watch docudramas and go about making judgments about which elements in those shows are real and which are made up. Think about people listening to a political debate where each candidate presents a very different set of evidence; how do people make judgments about which elements of evidence are real and which are made up?

Box 9.1

In 1964, Sherwood Schwartz produced a show called *Gilligan's Island.* This was a farcical comedy where seven characters who had been on a pleasure cruise encountered a storm that left them shipwrecked on an island somewhere in the Pacific Ocean. After about six episodes had aired, Schwartz was contacted by the Coast Guard and told that it had received several dozen telegrams from people who were complaining that the military should send a ship to rescue these seven people. Those telegrams were serious. Schwartz was dumfounded, calling this the "most extreme case of suspension of belief I ever heard of." He wondered, "Who did these viewers think was filming the castaways on that island? There was even a laugh track on the show. Who was laughing at the survivors of the wreck of the *S. S. Minnow?* It boggled the mind" (S. Schwartz, 1984, p. 2).

For the past decade, one of the most popular and enduring shows on television has been *Survivor,* which bills itself as reality television. This show takes 16 real people and puts them in a wilderness setting where the individuals depend on each other for survival (food, shelter, fire). At the same time, they are competing against one another for $1 million. In what sense is this show real? The players were selected from thousands of applicants not

because they were ordinary people; instead, they were selected on the basis of their potential attractiveness to audiences and their ability to generate conflict. The situation is artificial in the sense that none of these people lives their typical life in the wilderness, and none (with the exception of the all-star season) has played this game before—or any game for $1 million. Although the setting looks like a deserted wilderness, the players are not really alone. There are dozens of production people (including camera crews, sound engineers, crews to design and build sets for the challenges and tribal councils) and the host, Jeff Probst. Where do these production people live? How do they get to the survivors' camps to record their actions? Are there helicopter and boat crews? How do all these production people eat—are there cooks? How does their food get to the island? The show is not scripted in the sense that dialogue has been written by a member of the Writers Guild of America. But each contestant carefully writes his or her own lines, in the sense that the contestant's interactions are highly calculated to put himself or herself in the best position to win the game. Also, the show is carefully edited to present to the viewing public the most dramatic version of what takes place. The 960 hours over the course of the 40 days of the game are edited down to about 20 hours that are shown to the public. That is less than 2% of what happened, so the editors of all that recorded material exercise considerable control over which stories to tell. The editors and producers of "reality" media messages never tell the audience the full story; they edit out what they think is boring and assemble the pieces they think will be the most dramatic. This example makes us confront the issue of where we draw the line between reality and fantasy when something appears in the media. Reality and fantasy are not two mutually exclusive categories where we can make simple classification decisions. Instead, it is better to think of fantasy as one end of a continuum and reality at the other far end of that continuum; many degrees of difference separate the two ends.

Up to this point in the chapter, I have shown you how complex the idea of reality can be. We must consider multiple dimensions that are independent from one another. We must consider that children are less capable than adults in making certain kinds of judgments about reality but become more sophisticated on certain dimensions as they age. We must consider that there is a wide range of sophistication in making reality judgments across adults. And we must consider that many adults overestimate the degree of reality on so-called reality programs as well as news.

How can we simplify this complex array of ideas so that we can focus attention on why all this should matter to media literacy? What do people really need to know about the nature of the reality of media messages to be literate and protect themselves from harmful effects?

ORGANIZING PRINCIPLE: NEXT-STEP REALITY

Much of the complexity in the research about perceptions of reality can be explained simply by the idea of what I call next-step reality. When we think about what audiences really want from media messages, we can see that many of their exposure decisions are guided by a desire for next-step reality. Also, when we look at decisions from a programmer's perspective, we can again see the emergence of next-step reality. This idea is embedded in how media messages get produced and why certain messages attract large audiences, whereas other messages do not. In this section, I bring this idea to the surface and show you how it serves as a useful organizing principle for thinking about all kinds of media content.

Audience's Perspective

Why do people expose themselves to media messages? At the most fundamental level, they expose themselves to the media to find messages that they cannot get in real life. If people were getting all the messages they needed in real life, they would have no motivation to go to the expense (money and time) to search through the media for these messages. There are two reasons why people are motivated to get certain messages but go to the media rather than get those messages in real life. One is that it is impossible for them to get those messages in real life. For example, for most people, it is impossible to know what the Earth looks like from outer space or what the surface of other planets looks like. It is impossible to know what it was like to live on a farm during the American Civil War, to be a knight of the Round Table in medieval England, or to watch Jesus Christ preach. To get access to these images, sounds, and emotions, people must access messages from the media.

A second reason that motivates people to get messages from the media instead of real life is that the costs of getting those messages in the media are far lower than the costs required in real life. For example, it is easier to watch a one-hour travelogue on France than to pay the money to travel there for a week. It is far easier to watch a presidential news conference on television than it is to go to journalism school, get a job on a major newspaper or television service, get credentialed as a White House reporter, and attend the press conference in person. And it is less costly emotionally to watch characters in a movie try to meet each other, establish relationships, break up, and learn from their mistakes than it is to go through all of that in real life to learn the same thing.

Audiences therefore have a strong, continuing motivation to seek out messages in the media. They search for messages that have two general characteristics. First, those messages must appear real. They must have many elements that signal viewers that they are real; that is, they are close enough to resonate strongly with a viewer's experience of everyday reality, and thus those messages are accurate representations or at least plausible and probable. If they do not appear real, then audiences will not trust that the information is useful enough to bring it back into their everyday lives. Second, those messages must present a little more than everyday reality. Without this something extra, there is no reason to search out the media message because the person is already getting the message in his or her real life. This is what I mean by next-step reality—the message is presented as reality to resonate with the audience's experience and make it have the potential to be useful in everyday situations, but the message is "sweetened" by an extra added ingredient that takes it one step outside of the audience's everyday existence.

Therefore, people want media messages that are not so real that they are the same as their everyday lives. But neither do they want media messages that are so far removed from their experiences and needs that the messages have no immediate relevance. So people want messages that are one step removed from real life; they want messages that show what is easily possible and make it seem probable and even actual.

Programmers' Perspective

Programmers intuitively know that to attract audiences, they must take their audience's sense of reality and tweak it a bit to make it seem more interesting. Thus, the producers of media messages typically keep the elements of their messages anchored in the real world as much as possible so that they can accurately resonate with the audience's experiences in real life. But producers of media messages also know they cannot simply reproduce those messages; there would be no point to this because it would be easier for people to stay with their own real-world messages.

Producers of fiction know that their art is in telling stories that are "bigger" than life in some way. Producers can take an ordinary setting and a typical plot (boy meets girl) but change the characters so that they are a little more attractive or a little more interesting than people in real life. Or producers can take ordinary characters and put them in a plot that is a bit more dramatic in events and consequences than what happens to most people in real life. Skilled producers can take the audience on a journey by removing the audience one step at a time until they have taken them willingly to an absurd place. This is the formula with farce. The story begins with what looks like an ordinary everyday situation; then, step by step, the producer takes the audience far away from that reality but does it in a way that the audience is not lost but willingly awaits each new step. Thus, producers depend on viewers' willing suspension of disbelief. To make people willing, producers must take it one step at a time.

The next-step reality is also easy to understand with persuasive messages. For example, the typical problem-solution advertising message shows ordinary people with an ordinary problem, such as bad breath, a headache, dirty laundry, hunger for a good lunch, and so on. The advertiser invites the audience to take the step of faith into a solution, that is, to buy and use the advertised product on the promise that it will solve the problem better than any other solution—that is, more quickly, more completely, more cheaply, or more satisfying emotionally.

The next-step reality is a bit more difficult to understand with information-type messages. For example, if the purpose of news organizations is to report the events of the day, how can the next-step reality apply to journalists? The answer is that when journalists select what gets reported, they are not as interested in the typical events as they are in the anomalous events. Recall the old saying that if a dog bites a man, it is not news, but if a man bites a dog, that is news. The twist in the event makes it news. Crimes are news because they are aberrant behaviors. Violent crimes are more newsworthy than are property crimes because they are more aberrant and more rare.

All kinds of messages—entertainment, persuasion, and information—are crafted to retain the appearance of a high degree of reality, but all are really one step removed from reality. The more skillful this one-step remove transforms the reality, the more interesting the message will be and the more likely it will attract and hold people's attention.

Because we spend so much time with the media world in addition to the real world, and because the boundary between the two is often obscured, we can often get confused. This is especially the case after thousands of hours of automatic processing of both the mundane real-world messages and the massive flow of media-world messages. In all of that continuous flow, there is a constant intermingling of perceptions.

Reality Programming as a Genre

A new genre of the reality series began appearing in 2000. This type of show was popular with programmers because they are less expensive to produce (Einstein, 2004). The public also liked these new series, and audiences quickly grew.

The most popular of the reality series has been *Survivor*. Even before airing the first episode, CBS received 6,000 applicants who wanted to be marooned on a small island in the South China Sea and compete for $1 million (Bauder, 2000b). The popularity of *Survivor* quickly generated a slew of other entries into this genre of reality programming. What these shows have in common is that each takes a handful of real people and puts them in a competitive situation. As the participants compete and reveal their personalities, audience members begin to identify with (or at least root for) certain players. For example, on *The Bachelor*, a young man who is looking for a wife is introduced to 25 beautiful women. Each week, he eliminates some of the women until he gets it down to 1 woman and proposes marriage to her. Another example is *The Apprentice*, where 16 men and women compete in the business world to get hired as an apprentice to entrepreneur Donald Trump. The reality series is a relatively new genre, but already there are dozens of reality type shows where ordinary people (not professional actors) find love, friendship, treasure, a job, a new family, or financial backing for inventions; get their houses rebuilt, their wardrobes upgraded, their vehicles tricked out, and their bodily appearance reshaped; and compete with others to attain the honor of being the best singer, dancer, entertainer, chef, or human punching bag.

THE IMPORTANCE OF MEDIA LITERACY

Increasingly, the border between our real world and the media world is becoming harder to discern. More and more often, the media do not wait for us to cross over into their world; they bring their messages into our world. Because much of our exposure to media messages is not planned by us, we don't realize how much we are exposed to the media. Consider the exposure you have to media messages every day in your real world without you being aware of them. For example, there are radio messages coming out of other people's cars as you walk down the street in your real world; you pass messages on kiosks, billboards, newspapers lying on tables, and people talking about the media messages they have experienced. As the media pump messages into our world at an ever increasing rate, the borderline becomes blurred. We take almost all of this for granted.

There are many places where the border between the real world and the media world is not so clear. Think about what makes the following programs real, as the media claim: *COPS, Big Brother, Extreme Makeover, American Idol, The Hills, Pimp My Ride,* and *Monday Night Football.* To what extent do these shows fit into your real world and resonate with your real experiences?

As genres change and the line between reality and fantasy programming becomes even more blurred, we must avoid falling into the trap of debating which shows are real and which are fantasy. This is why the next-step reality is so fundamental to media literacy because it shifts the question and hence the focus of our attention. The question should *not* be, "How real are media messages?" The next-step reality organizing principle shows us that every media message is a mix of reality and fantasy. Instead, the question should be, "Which elements in this message reflect reality and which elements are removed from reality in some way?" When you are guided by the organizing principle of next-step reality, you need to analyze media messages to answer these more appropriate questions. This analysis will help you develop a sensitivity to how big of a step you usually tolerate in the one-step remove messages. Some people will tolerate a very small step and limit themselves to messages that very closely match their own experiences and knowledge. On the other end of that spectrum are people who insist on radical departures from what their everyday lives provide them.

The key to becoming media literate is not in how close we move to the reality end of the spectrum; that would only limit our range of information and emotional reactions. Instead, the key to media literacy is to be flexible and aware. Being flexible means being willing to traverse the entire spectrum of messages and enjoy the full range of messages. Being aware means thinking about where you are in the spectrum and knowing the different standards of appreciation to apply to different places on the spectrum of reality. By being both flexible and aware, you can much better enjoy the enormous variety of messages in the media and, at the same time, control the effects of those messages so that you avoid the negative ones that usually come from automatic exposure and instead more intensely enjoy the positive effects that can result from any media message.

All of us must continually decide how closely media messages reflect real life and what the implications of those differences are on our beliefs about reality. Sometimes, these decisions about what is real are relatively easy; it is simple for most of us to understand that there is nothing in real life anything like *Gilligan's Island.* But some of the decisions are harder to make accurately—especially when they are subtly shaped over a long period of time by the accumulation of thousands of journeys into the media world. Over time, we have come to accept much of the media world as the real world. For example, who is the president of the United States? Are you sure? Have you ever met him? If you have not met him, how do you know he really exists? If you have met him, how do you know he is who he says he is? I am not trying to make you paranoid. I am only asking you to consider the degree to which you trust the information and experiences you bring back from the media world into your real world. When encountering some of that information, you should have a high degree of skepticism, but other information should be accepted by you with a feeling of trust. Do you know which is which?

This is why being media literate is so important. Media messages are not always the way they seem. There are often many layers of meanings. Some of those layers are highly unrealistic (never happened in actuality, never will happen, and never could happen), but they are interlaced among layers of realistic elements that could transform the overall message in your perception from "fantasy" to "it might happen" to "it is likely to happen" to "I need to try this." The more you are aware of the layers of meaning in messages, the more you can control the selection of which meanings you want. Being more analytical is the first step toward controlling how the media affect you. If you are unaware of the meanings, then the media stay in control of how you perceive the world.

When you understand this organizing principle of next-step reality, you can better appreciate media content. You can focus your analysis on how different media, different vehicles, and different artists achieve the resonance of reality and then take that one step to remove their message from that reality. This is where the artistic talent comes into play. So a good understanding of this concept can help you develop a keener aesthetic sense as you experience individual messages. Also important, this concept should motivate you to ask questions about patterns in the one-step remove. There are patterns of life in the real world, and there are patterns of stories in the media world. The two patterns are not the same. The more you recognize the story patterns and how they are different from real-world life patterns, the less trouble you will have in recognizing the border between reality and fantasy. The next three chapters focus on those media-world patterns and the ways they deviate from real-world patterns.

SUMMARY

Clearly, the issue of reality entails more than making a simple decision about whether something actually happened. People are able to think in terms of degrees of reality, and when they are assessing the degree of reality, they consider more than one dimension. It is also important to understand that there is not a huge gap between children's ability to perceive reality accurately and adults' ability. This is a trap that adults frequently fall into. Being in this trap gives those adults a false sense of security that they do not need to think carefully about the reality of media messages because they are no longer children and therefore are protected by the adult discount. Because the degree of belief in reality is associated with higher negative effects, adults are vulnerable, as are children (W. J. Potter, 1986; Rubin, Perse, & Taylor, 1988).

The most useful way to think about reality is with the "next-step reality" organizing principle. This focuses your attention on the degree to which media messages are both real and fantasy. This then sets up more important questions: Which elements in the message do I regard as real, and how did I arrive at that perception? Which elements in the message do I regard as fantasy? To what extent am I attracted to the fantasy and willing to try to make it my reality? Keep these questions in mind as you read through the next four chapters on different types of media content.

Chapter Resources: To test your knowledge and learn more about the topics discussed in this chapter, visit the Student Study Site at www.sagepub.com/potter6e.

FURTHER READING

Essany, M. (2008). *Reality check: The business and art of producing reality TV.* Burlington, MA: Focal Press. (260 pages with index and glossary of TV production terms)

This is an easy to read book with a self-help tone. The author is an industry insider who produced and starred in his own reality television series telecast on E! The book presents a lot of practical information about what goes on during the planning and production of a reality series for American television.

Ouellette, L., & Murray, S. (Eds.). (2009). *Reality TV: Remaking television culture.* New York: New York University Press. (377 pages with index)

This edited volume consists of 17 chapters written by critical and cultural scholars. The chapters are organized into four groups: genre, industry, culture/power, and interactivity.

Pozner, J. L. (2010). *Reality bites back: The troubling truth about guilty pleasure TV.* New York: Seal Press.

The author is a journalist, social critic, and founder of Women In Media & News (WIMN), a media justice group that amplifies women's presence and power in the public debate through media analysis, education, and advocacy. This book presents an extended criticism of so-called reality television programs.

KEEPING UP TO DATE

JobMonkey.com

This general website posts information about lots of different kinds of job opportunities. Click on http://www.jobmonkey.com/realitytv/reality-tv-statistics.html to access the page that presents a lot of information about productions and casting opportunities for a wide range of reality programs.

EXERCISE 9.1

Delineating the Elusive Line Between Reality and Fantasy

1. *Analyze Television Programs:* For each of the genres of programs listed below, pick one particular program and analyze it.

   - Situation comedy
   - Drama (police drama or family drama)
   - "Reality" program (such as *Survivor, The Bachelor, Extreme Makeover, The Apprentice,* and *COPS*)
   - News program

(Continued)

(Continued)

For each program, take a sheet of paper and write the name of the program at the top. Then draw a vertical line down the middle of the page. Label the left column as "Reality Indicators" and list in the column all the things about the program that you think would lead someone to believe that the program content is real, that is, depicts reality. Then label the right column "Nonreal World" and list in that column all the things about the program that you think would lead someone to believe that the program was not real.

2. *Tabulate Lists:* Count all the items you have listed in the Reality Indicators column and write that number at the bottom of that column. Then count all the items you have listed in the Nonreal World column and write that number at the bottom of that column. Do the same for all sheets, so that you have two totals at the bottom of the page for each program you have analyzed for reality. Turn totals into percentages. For example, if on one sheet you listed five things in the left column (reality items) and five things in the right column (nonreality items), then this would compute to 50% reality and 50% nonreality. If instead you had one item in the reality column and four items in the unreality column, this would compute to 20% and 80%.

3. *Check for Patterns:* If you were a perceptive television viewer, you are likely to have at least a handful of items in each column. No program is purely reality—there are all kinds of production decisions (about characters, plot, settings, customs, makeup, dialog, camera placement, editing, etc.) that take messages out of the pure reality realm. Also, no program is purely fantasy—there are character types, situations, language, settings, and so forth that are very much like the real world.

Look at the pairs of percentages at the bottom of each page. Are the splits in percentages favoring the first types of shows, which are the more fantasy shows? Or are they favoring the more reality types of shows, which are the second two genres? Or is there no difference? Now try this exercise again

- With movies
- With stories in magazines
- With newspaper stories
- With Internet sites
- With video games

Do reality proportions vary across the medium?

News

Key Idea: News is
not a reflection of
actual events; it is
a construction by
news workers who
are subjected to
many influences
and constraints.

**Traditional Issues About
News**
    Is News a Reflection or
      a Construction?
    Can Journalists Be
      Objective?
Emerging Issues About News
    Who Qualifies as a
      Journalist?
    What Qualifies as News?
    What Should Be the
      Standard of Quality?
**Becoming Literate With
News Content**
    Analyze the News
      Perspective

Search for Context
Develop Alternative
    Sources of
    Information
Be Skeptical About
    Public Opinion
Expose Yourself to
    More News, Not Less

Summary
Further Reading
Keeping Up to Date
Exercises

Kristen was shopping at the mall when a person came up to her holding a clipboard and said, "I'm taking a survey. Could you answer a few questions for me?"

"Okay, what are they about?"

"This is a survey about news. My first question is: What newspapers do you read?"

"I don't read any newspapers," said Kristen.

The interviewer made a mark on her form and then asked, "What news magazines do you read?"

"None."

"Do you listen to newscasts on the radio?"

"No."

"How about the evening news on television?"

"No."

The interviewer glanced over her form and then looked up at Kristen. "So you avoid all news?"

"No. I love news and watch about 2 hours of it every night on TV. I always watch the *Daily Show with John Stewart* and the *Colbert Report*. Then I watch *The Late Show with David Letterman*."

"But those aren't news shows. They're comedy shows."

"They present lots of news. I always learn a lot more about what is going on in the world by watching those shows than when I used to watch the evening news programs. And they're fun to watch."

"Those shows make stuff up to be funny!"

"Yes they do. But I can always tell when they are making something up. With the so-called real news shows, I am never sure what they are making up."

In America, we appear to have a love-hate relationship with journalism. On one hand, we love to be stimulated by information and want to keep up with the important occurrences around us every day. On the other hand, we are skeptical that journalists are misleading us or flooding us with information that is of no value. This love-hate relationship is not new; it goes back as far as the founding of our country. For example, we often quote Thomas Jefferson, who said in 1787, "Were it left to me to decide whether we should have a government without newspapers or newspapers without a government, I should not hesitate a moment to prefer the latter" (quoted in C. Jensen, 1997, p. 11). However, Thomas Jefferson also delivered one of the most strident criticisms of the press after he became president and had to deal with it on a daily basis. In 1807, he said, "The man who never looks into a newspaper is better informed than he who reads them." Jefferson took the position that "he who knows nothing is nearer to truth than he whose mind is filled with falsehoods and errors" (quoted in C. Jensen, 1997, p. 11). Thus, Jefferson was arguing that nothing printed in a newspaper could be believed.

Why do we have this love-hate relationship with news and journalism? The reason is that most of us expect journalists to present us with the most important ideas and events each day in an objective and useful manner. But journalists often fail at this task, presenting instead inaccurate facts in misleading stories with little context. People expect news stories to be accurate reflections of real-world events. But this has never been the case, and it never will be.

This chapter is organized into three sections. The first section deals with the most important traditional issues concerning news, and this forms the foundation for the second section, which outlines the emerging issues about news now that we are in a new media environment that forces us to reexamine our assumptions about many things we have previously taken for granted. The third and final section in this chapter translates what we know about these traditional and emerging issues into a set of procedures to help you become more media literate with respect to the idea of news.

TRADITIONAL ISSUES ABOUT NEWS

The two most debated issues about the nature of news are examined in this section. The first of these issues shows you how important it is to get beyond the idea that news is a simple reflection of the most important happenings each day and instead realize that news is a construction. The second issue is a challenge to the widespread belief in the public that news is—or should be—objective.

Is News a Reflection or a Construction?

If you were to ask someone how the news differs from entertainment programming, most people would say that entertainment is fiction and therefore made up by writers, whereas news presents actual events that happened. We think of news as a reflection of the events of the day; that is, the media are merely holding a mirror up to reality.

But when we take a closer look at the news, it becomes clear that news does not *reflect* reality. Instead, it is a construction by journalists. News coverage is triggered, of course, by actual occurrences. But what we see presented as news by the media are not the events themselves. Instead, the media present us with stories *about* the events, and those stories are constructed by journalists who are influenced by constraints, news-framing influences, and something called the "news perspective." Let's examine each of these factors that prevent news from being a simple reflection of the day's events.

Constraints

Three basic constraints limit what is presented in news stories. These constraints are usually regarded as being outside the ability of journalists to control them, although this is changing. Those three constraints are deadlines, resource limitations, and geographical focus.

Deadlines. Sometimes an event will begin before a deadline but continue beyond the deadline, so the journalist cannot get all the information on the ongoing event. In this case, the journalist must file a partial story. What is left out of the story may eventually prove to be more important than what is put into the partial story.

Deadlines often prevent journalists from gathering all the facts and presenting a complete and accurate story about the event. For example, daily newspapers have a deadline every single day. Morning newspapers usually have a deadline about 11 p.m. the night before. Let's say a fire breaks out in a well-known building 2 a.m. on a Wednesday morning and firefighters battle the blaze until 4 a.m., when the fire is out and the building is gone. People reading their Wednesday morning newspaper over breakfast would want to learn about the fire, but no report of it will be in the Wednesday morning paper. The editor of the newspaper must then decide whether to print a story of the fire in the Thursday morning edition, which would make the story old news. The deadline constraint has prevented the newspaper from reporting the fire as "news." Deadlines are even more troublesome for weekly newspapers and news magazines; by the time their readers get their stories, the stories seem less like news because much time has elapsed between the event occurring and the "news" story being made available to the audience.

Some media channels, such as radio, television, and the Internet, are not constrained much by deadlines because journalists working in these media can continue to file updates of stories as new information becomes available. However, these journalists are still subject to other constraints and influences.

Resource Limitations. Although the newsgathering departments of the major media organizations—especially broadcast networks and the major daily newspapers—are very large and have considerable resources, there are still limits to those resources. There are never enough resources to be able to cover all the events that happen in a given day, and assignment editors must decide which stories will get covered and which will not.

This used to be an especially difficult problem for local television stations. To cover a story, a local TV station would have to send more than just a reporter; it would also have to send a crew of camera and sound people in a relatively large van to hold the people and equipment. But with new technological developments, this constraint is not as limiting as it once was. For example, E. Slater (2004) points out that "reporters from every television network and cable outlet now carry miniature broadcast-quality digital video cameras. In addition to at least one cell-phone, many journalists carry a digital voice recorder, at least one hand-held e-mail device and a wireless modem" (p. A11). This allows many more stories to be covered. Of course, other resource constraints, such as a limit on the column inches a newspaper devotes to news, are not changing to allow for more stories to be printed, so these technological enhancements are putting more pressure on other constraints to hold the status quo.

The argument that resource constraints are responsible for limiting what we see as news is often faulty. This is revealed in the way a lot of the news organizations duplicate their efforts, thus making for inefficient use of limited resources. For example, the Associated Press news service has more than 100 reporters in Washington, DC alone, and many of them are trying to develop the same contacts at the White House. Every 4 years, the two major political parties hold nominating conventions to select their party's candidate for president. News organizations send about 16,000 journalists to these nonevents; I call this a nonevent because the person who is nominated is usually known months in advance of the "nominating" conventions, so the news value of the convention is very small. If those journalistic resources that were assigned to the convention were instead directed to other locations, the news audiences would likely receive a much wider and richer span of news from those same limited resources. This same principle applies every day on smaller scales in every town of the United States, with several newspapers, magazines, radio stations, and TV stations all sending reporters to the same police stations, city halls, and athletic contests.

The budgets of all the major news organizations have been expanding over the past few decades without a corresponding expansion in the amount of news covered. For example, the annual budget of the ABC network news department grew from about $1 million in the

early 1960s to more than $300 million in the late 1980s, but with that enormous growth in resources, the amount and/or quality of news did not increase 300 times during that period.

Also, CNN and all-news radio shows have significant budgets and a very large news hole. But the number of stories they cover is very small compared to the space they have. Their news perspective has not allowed them to provide a greatly expanded breadth of stories. Instead, CNN maintains a narrow vision of what is important and continually presents a small set of stories over and over all day. The reason is that it is much less expensive to cover a few stories and to update them all day than to cover fresh stories every hour.

Geographical Focus. Each news organization is focused on covering the events in its own locale so it can report those stories to its local audiences. With few exceptions in the United States, newspapers each have their own geographical territory and focus their coverage within the bounds of that territory.

Another form of geographical constraint refers to the condition that, even outside of a news organization's local area, there appears to be a belief that certain parts of the world are more important (more newsworthy) than others. For example, Larson (1983) examined international news coverage on television and found that events in the Third World (the poorer, less industrialized countries) were covered less than events in industrialized countries and that what coverage there was about the Third World was crisis oriented. The same pattern was found by W. J. Potter (1987b) in newspapers. Kim and Barnett (1996) show clearly that the news flow of information around the world is dominated by the Western industrialized countries at the center. This power is associated with the degree of economic development. So, for example, if a dozen people are killed by a bomb in a London department store, this is likely to get far more coverage in the United States than if 100 people are killed in an earthquake in Guatemala.

Even within this country, the news coverage is not balanced geographically. In the United States, events occurring in the Northeast and on the Pacific Coast are covered the most, whereas events happening in the rest of the country are covered less in the national news services (Graber, 1994).

News-Framing Influences

News-framing influences are like constraints in the sense that they can be seen as forces that shape what gets selected and presented as news. However, these news-framing influences are different from constraints because they are purely constructions of journalists to help them do their jobs more easily and to fulfill the goals of the businesses that employ them.

Commercialism. Arguably, the strongest influence on the construction of news is its commercial nature (Altheide, 1976). News organizations are in the business of constructing large audiences so they can rent those audiences to advertisers. The larger the audience, the higher the rent and the more revenue the news organization generates. Therefore, the ultimate goal of news is a commercial one, and journalists are driven to construct stories that will attract large audiences. Therefore, news organizations must be careful not to run hard-hitting stories that would offend audiences. Also, news organizations must be careful not to offend their advertisers (M. Lee & Solomon, 1990). For example, the harmfulness of tobacco has been greatly underreported because tobacco advertising is so important to the survival of many magazines and newspapers. Television has also been affected, even though no tobacco products have been advertised on television for more than three decades. The tobacco companies are large conglomerates that sell and advertise many nontobacco products. A television news show that offends a tobacco company is in danger of losing advertising of other brands controlled by the large tobacco conglomerates.

Also, journalists will write stories that are not strictly news but that instead have the value of promoting other commercial products being marketed by the organization that owns the news organization. For example, Kaniss (1996) criticized news shows in the Philadelphia area by pointing out that during the November 1996 sweeps month, the local CBS affiliate on its evening news show ran nine stories on the *Titanic,* a ship that sank 84 years prior to those "news" stories but was the subject of a CBS mini-series. The Philadelphia ABC affiliate was cited as frequently running "news" stories about Mickey Mouse because the ABC network is owned by Disney. Local affiliates in many TV markets are also found to frequently run news stories about stars on their network series and often run soft news stories on topics of made-for-TV movies appearing that night on the network.

Marketing Perspective. One of the core debates in newsrooms has been whether to give news audiences what journalists think they need or to give audiences what they want—that is, entertainment that is sensationalized and personalized. The pressures of commercialism set up a conflict between two perspectives on news. One of these is the professional responsibility perspective. This is where journalists regard themselves as having a responsibility to inform the public about the most important and significant events of the day so that people can use the information to make better decisions as citizens of that society. For example, journalists operating within this perspective would strive to provide in-depth information on candidates and issues during a campaign so that voters can make a more informed decision. These journalists would also try to present clear explanations about economic conditions, implications of government policies, the patterns of changes in society, and other broad-scale issues so the public is exposed to the context behind individual issues. But there is a danger of providing such in-depth coverage of complicated issues; that is, such coverage is likely to bore most audience members.

In contrast, there is the marketing perspective. This is where news workers pay careful attention to what kinds of stories and presentation formats generate the largest audience. For example, journalists operating under the marketing perspective are more likely to present stories that grab the attention of large audiences by highlighting the unusual so as to shock people. This marketing perspective has led news workers to believe that the public wants more soft news items than stories about the government, the economy, and political matters. In a content analysis of 13,000 items in 12 daily newspapers, it was found that newspapers with a strong market orientation publish fewer items about government and public affairs and more items about lifestyle and sports than do newspapers with a weak market orientation. "Today, the newsrooms of hundreds of U.S. newspapers, magazines, and television stations have embraced, to greater or lesser extents, this approach to making news. Typically a market-driven organization selects target markets for its product, identifies the wants and needs of potential customers in its target markets, and seeks to satisfy those wants and needs as efficiently as possible" (R. A. Beam, 2003, p. 368). Also, Schudson (2003) reports that soft news increased from 35% in 1980 to 50% in 1998 in television networks, major news magazines, and leading national newspapers.

People like deviance, so the news media are interested in presenting things that deviate from the normal (Shoemaker, Danielian, & Brendlinger, 1991). Deviance covers those things that are out of the ordinary, and the more they differ from reality, the more they are considered newsworthy.

With news coverage, there are two types of deviance (Shoemaker & Reese, 1996). There is statistical deviance, which "causes things that are unusual (either good or bad) to be considered more newsworthy than commonplace events" (p. 47). For example, if a woman gives birth to four children over a decade, that is not news. But if a woman gives birth to quadruplets, that is unusual and therefore is newsworthy. The statistical probability of giving birth to four children at once is very low, so this gets covered.

The other type of deviance is normative, which refers to ideas or events that break norms or laws. For example, if a person goes to a bank and puts money in his account, that is normal and will not get covered. But if a person goes to a bank and withdraws money from other people's accounts at gunpoint, that breaks the law and gets covered. Thus, the media like to focus on crime because it occurs outside the norm. Within crime news, there is a preference for violent action (Windhauser, Seiter, & Winfree, 1990) and crimes against people (Ammons, Dimmick, & Pilotta, 1982; Fedler & Jordan, 1982), which are rarer and more deviant than property crimes. Also, deaths due to violence are more likely to be reported than deaths due to disease (Combs & Slovic, 1979). This overreporting of crime is also found in other countries, such as England (Roshier, 1981).

The irony is that we depend on the news to tell us what the norm is. To be well informed, we need to know how things typically work, what is likely to happen tomorrow, and what the relative risks of harm are. But the news media focus our attention on the deviant. Because we see so many portrayals of the deviant, we come to believe that the deviant is the norm.

The influence of commercialism has moved the news away from the professional responsibility perspective and placed it squarely under the marketing perspective. As a result, the news has attempted to be more entertaining. The stories are shorter. There is more focus on personalities than on genuine leaders. There is more focus on celebrities than on people of substance. And there is more focus on gossip than on news.

This ambivalence between social responsibility and entertainment is evident in public opinion polls. For example, when Americans were asked whether television stations should broadcast live coverage of a hostage being held at gunpoint, only 22% said yes. But when those same people were asked whether they would watch such coverage, 59% said yes (Luntz, 2000). Most of us know that it is irresponsible for media to broadcast certain events. However, we are attracted to such events and would watch if we could.

There is growing evidence that this choice to use the marketing perspective over the responsibility perspective may not be working well. News organizations are having a hard time attracting the next generation to their messages. For example, one research study reports that people 25 years of age and younger spend an average of only 31 minutes a day with news messages, while 65 years of age and older spend 81 minutes a day exposed to the news (C. Jones, 2005).

Organizational Structures. Organizational structures vary. Small companies are more flexible and entrepreneurial. They search out new needs and quickly adapt. In contrast, large companies are compartmentalized, with each division having a special function and its own staff of technical people. Large bureaucracies are more resistant to change.

Ownership. Ownership patterns can also influence the content. For example, the *New York Times* remained in the hands of one family for more than 100 years. There was very high potential for the members of that family to have a strong influence on that newspaper. In contrast, other newspapers might be owned by a large media conglomerate with thousands of shareholders, each with a very low potential for influence.

Although there are some examples of newspapers changing their editorial stance because of pressure from an owner, these are rare. What is more typical is strong pressure from owners that the newspaper make a larger profit. This reinforces the marketing perspective.

Use of Sources. News is shaped by the sources that journalists use to gather information. The dominant sources of news are public information officers in businesses and governmental units. Most companies and institutions have public relations departments whose sole job is to establish themselves as experts and feed information to journalists. Once a person is established as an expert source, he or she is called by journalists when they want an expert opinion on that particular issue.

How do journalists know who is an expert? Most journalists don't. They lack the experience or education to evaluate the credentials of many people who could serve as experts in news stories, so they choose people not on the basis of knowledge but on their *appearance* of expertise and their willingness to tell a good story. This point is illustrated by Steele (1995), who examined how television news organizations selected and used expert sources to interpret the news. She found that news organizations chose expert sources that reflected journalists' understanding of expertise. Experts were selected according to how well their specialized knowledge conformed to television's "operational bias," which places its emphasis on players, policies, and predictions of what will happen next. Steele concluded that these processes undermine the ideals of balance and objectivity as well as severely limit how news is framed.

The major news organizations all use the same sources, many of whom are unnamed, so the same types of stories always get covered. This is a clear conclusion of two journalists—M. Lee and Solomon (1990)—who wrote a book titled *Unreliable Sources: A Guide to Detecting Bias in News Media,* in which they expressed strong criticism of American journalistic practices. These journalists observed that over time, reporters become close friends with their sources and stop looking for other points of view. This makes their jobs easier, because these reporters do not have to continually develop new and better sources of information. But the problem with this practice is that the sources have their own agendas. Frequently, the sources are public relations people for various governmental agencies, businesses, or political action groups. Thus, these sources are not trying to provide unbiased expertise to help journalists understand the issue better; instead, these people are paid to present only their one side of the issue and to make their side appear as the only valid position on the issue. For example, the military establishment has always had a sophisticated public relations operation that works to maintain strong public support for its goals and its need for increasing funding. In the 1960s, when the Soviet Union had 100 long-range missiles and the United States had 2,000, the Pentagon convinced the American people that the United States lagged far behind Russia in weapons, and the public ended up supporting greater defense budgets. During the Reagan administration, the Pentagon had an annual public relations budget of $100 million and employed 3,000 staff people.

Sources often have an incestuous relationship with journalists. Many journalists go into government and serve as press secretaries or public information officers. Also, press secretaries go into journalism. Over time, the two professions converge, and this revolving door homogenizes the coverage. Schudson (2003) observes, "Political institutions and media institutions are so deeply intertwined, so thoroughly engaged in a complex dance with each other, that is not easy to distinguish where one begins and the other leaves off" (p. 154). W. L. Bennett (2003) argues that this close relationship leads to what he calls indexing. By this, he means that journalists take their direction from the government when deciding the range of public opinion. What the government recognizes as the range of public opinion, journalists accept and limit their reporting to that range.

Branding. News shows brand their reporters. Notice that at the beginning and end of news reports, the reporters will often mention their names, and sometimes their names will be in graphics superimposed over the visuals. Local TV stations do this so that audience members will follow the reporters in addition to the stories. If the stories are not particularly good one evening, audience members will still tune in to see their favorite reporters. This has the effect of turning news reporters into celebrities. When these news celebrities become really well known, they begin commanding very large fees for speaking at private functions. For example, Cokie Roberts of ABC commands a fee of $35,000 per appearance, and Ted Koppel gets $50,000 (Schudson, 2003).

Some journalists get involved in making the news events themselves. For example, *Newsweek* columnist George Will helped Ronald Reagan prepare for the televised debates during the 1980 presidential election. Also, former CBS news anchor Dan Rather made a speech at a Democratic fund-raiser in 2001 (Schudson, 2003).

Values. Journalists believe that Americans hold certain core values, so they try to tell stories that resonate with these values. This becomes one of the important characteristics in telling a good story and holding the audience's attention. What are these values? Shoemaker and Reese (1996) say there are eight of them (see Table 10.1).

These values of journalists and news organizations show up in the way they tell their stories. For example, consider how wars are covered in the news. A content analysis of 1,822 images from U.S. mainstream media—network and cable television news outlets, news websites, newspapers, and news magazines—revealed that the visual framing of the U.S.-led invasion of Iraq in 2003 shifted from a focus on conflict to human interest. During the campaign's first 5 weeks, journalists framed their stories as conflict that supported a government-promoted patriotic perspective. But as the war dragged on, journalists became more critical and shifted the way they told their stories to focus on the individual human beings fighting and the sacrifices they were making (Schwalbe, Silcock, & Keith, 2008). Which set of values (patriotism vs. personal sacrifice) is more accurate? They both are, but each type of value provides only a partial context. If you watch news stories with a patriotic

---

TABLE 10.1 Core American Values

- *Individualism*—Audiences like to hear about people who do things their own way, even against powerful odds.
- *Moderatism*—Fanaticism of any kind arouses skepticism.
- *Social order*—Peace and order are valued; people who deviate from this are labeled as wrongdoers.
- *Leadership*—There are high expectations for leaders; those who are found to be weak, dishonest, or immoral are investigated.
- *Ethnocentrism*—Other countries are judged against American standards.
- *Altruistic democracy*—There is a democratic ideal of efficient government and participation by all citizens; deviations from this are news.
- *Responsible capitalism*—There should be fair competition without unreasonable profits or exploiting workers.
- *Small-town pastoralism*—Small towns and rural areas are the font of virtue.

underlying value, you are likely to support the war and feel pride in America's strength. If in contrast you watch news stories with a human sacrifice underlying value, you are likely be critical of the aggression of the American government.

Hyperlocalism. As the audience for news fragments, news vehicles are getting more and more specialized, which is known as hyperlocalism. The news watchdog group The Project for Excellence in Journalism says that the mass media are having a very hard time holding onto their audiences for news, with the overall audience shrinking for newspapers, TV news, and even Internet news. Also, the smaller and smaller number of people who care about exposing themselves to news messages has more and more options, beyond newspapers and network news programs (Rainey, 2007). Cable news is pulling away a lot of viewers who like personality-driven news shows (such as Bill O'Reilly), comedy news shows (such as the *Daily Show* or the *Colbert Report*), sports-focused news shows (such as *SportsCenter*), or celebrity-focused news (such as *E!*). These news seekers are less interested in global or national issues than they are interested in more local or hobby-type things that interest them personally. News organizations realize this, so they are developing more and more specialized vehicles to appeal to all these many niche audiences.

Story Formula. Journalists are very busy people. Their days are filled with an incredible amount of detail that must be processed on short deadlines. A reporter at a daily newspaper may have to write several dozen stories every day. Do reporters spend hours thinking about the best way to communicate the essence of each story, then several more hours polishing draft after draft? No. Rarely do they have this kind of time. Instead, they must assemble the facts of a story in a matter of minutes, then move on to the next story. How do they do this? They use story formulas.

Formulas are the procedures that journalists learn as shortcuts to help them quickly select and write stories. The most popular information-gathering formula is the series of questions: Who? What? When? Where? Why? and How? Journalists confronted with a new story begin by asking these questions, then structure their story to answer each of these questions.

One popular news-writing formula is the inverted pyramid. This formula tells the journalist to put the most important information at the beginning of the story, then add the next most important set of information. Journalists move down their list of information, ranked according to importance, until all the information is in the story. This formula was developed in the early days of the telegraph, when journalists in the field would send their stories to their newspapers over telegraph lines. They needed to send the most important information first in case the telegraph line went dead before they were done transmitting the entire story. We are way past the days of dependence on telegraph lines, but the formula still has value because editors will cut stories if they run too long. For example, a newspaper editor might want to use a reporter's 20-inch story but only has room for 16 inches, so the editor will typically cut off the last 4 inches.

Another popular formula is to use a narrative to tell a story in an entertainment format. Journalists who use this formula will begin the story with a heated conflict, a gruesome description, or an unusual quote—all designed to grab the reader's attention in an emotional manner. Then the writer moves through the plot, much like a fictional storyteller would.

Perhaps the most popular formula for telling stories in the news is what I call simplified extended conflict (SEC). When covering a story, journalists look for some angle of conflict that appears very simple. They believe that a story that has no conflict will not *grab* the audience's attention, but if the conflict is complex, the story will not *hold* the audience's attention. Furthermore, if the story can be played out over several days—or longer—so much the better. Political elections offer lots of good examples of the SEC. Campaigns always involve conflict between the candidates, and this can usually be reduced to two people. Also, the campaign, which goes on for weeks or months, can be portrayed as a race, with one candidate ahead and the other candidate running hard to catch up. If the conflict is focused on the finer points of complex issues, the story will not appeal to a large audience. Therefore, journalists look for a simple form of conflict, and that is best seen in the "horse race" metaphor. Political coverage is much more about who is winning and whether the challenger can come from behind and close the gap than it is about issues. Other examples of SEC are O. J. Simpson against the court system, the United States against Iraq, various crusaders against Congress, the little guy against city hall, and the forces of pro-life against the forces of pro-choice. The press can present the conflict in these situations in a very simple manner and keep the conflict going for a long time. It does this by polarizing the people or issues in the conflict, inviting the audience to identify with one side, and then playing out the fight with lots of drama.

When the press has a big story that will consume news space for several weeks or months, it has an opportunity to more fully develop the nuances of the parties in the conflict. With political issues, the press could choose to tell the story of how competing interests have some common ground and how compromise is crafted. With criminal trials, the press could choose to tell the story of how humans can go astray and what justice means in each situation. Instead, the press rarely digs deep into a story—illuminating its complexity and educating the public about the underlying nature of the problem. The press stays with the surface information—polishing it to a more glitzy finish to make it more attractive to passive viewers.

News Perspective

All of the constraints and news-framing influences shape how journalists select which events to cover and how they construct their stories. When we take all these influences and constraints together, we call this the news perspective. This news perspective is not something that is consciously imposed by the owners of the media. Instead, it grows naturally out of the practices of the status quo and leads us to ask, How could the news be any other way?

People who are hired as journalists become socialized by this news perspective as they learn their jobs. The news perspective is so pervasive and common among journalists that it is taken for granted. It is also generally shared by journalists in all kinds of vehicles and all media, as evidenced in several research studies. One of these studies found that there is a considerable overlap in news stories at local television stations in the same market. Davie and Lee (1993) found that 56% of stories were the same, with network sources having more similarity. The nonoverlapping stories were more likely to be from local sources. In another study, Davie and Lee (1995) analyzed local television newscasts and found that there is a distinct preference for sensational stories that feature acts of sex and violence and are easy to explain. There was little differentiation among the stations, leading to the conclusion that the news sense of all local producers is almost the same. Hudson (1992) also arrived at the same conclusion as a result of an experiment on more than 100 news directors and executive producers from all size markets all over the country. He showed them a violent incident and asked them how much of the incident they would show in a newscast. Editors exhibited the same news judgment in all size markets and across all kinds of stations.

To illustrate the idea of news perspective, let's consider the topic of health and how that is covered in the news. First, let's examine what is covered. In a content analysis of 14,849 local television news stories from across the United States, Haberkorn (2009) kept track of how often the major causes of death (heart disease, lung cancer, and diabetes) were covered. She found that of all news stories, only 5.9% deal with a health issue of any kind. And among that small number of health stories, only 5.8% focused on the top three causes of death. She concluded that there is a poverty of information on local television news programs concerning serious health risks that affect most people. Another content analysis of news (local and national newspapers, television, and magazines) found that news coverage underrepresented the contribution of lung cancer; furthermore, news presented almost no information concerning the prevention and detection of cancers (M. D. Slater, Long, & Bettinghaus, 2008). However, while the news media underreport serious illnesses common throughout the population, they are increasing their coverage of elective plastic surgeries (Cho, 2007).

Advantage. The advantage of the news perspective is that it helps journalists simplify and organize the overwhelming amount of material they must sift through on a daily basis. It makes it possible for journalists to do their jobs efficiently.

Disadvantage. The disadvantage of the news perspective is that its limited vision results in a very narrow view of what is news. It also leads journalists to treat those selected stories superficially, thus distorting reality. Altheide (1976) argues that "the organizational, practical, and other mundane features of news work promote a way of looking at events which fundamentally distorts them. . . . In order to make events news, news reporting decontextualizes and thereby changes them" (pp. 24–25).

Changes. The news perspective has changed over time from social responsibility to marketing because of the business constraints as mentioned above. The news perspective used to be guided by the criteria of significance, proximity, and timeliness. The more an occurrence had these characteristics, the more likely it would be covered. But the criteria have changed to focus more on conflict, appeal to emotions, and visualization. For an event to be covered today, it must meet these newer criteria. To illustrate this change, Slattery and Hakanen (1994) compared local television newscasts from 1976 and 1992. They found that hard news coverage of the government declined dramatically from 64% to 19%, whereas coverage of human interest stories and sensationalism climbed from 10% to 41%. During the same time, there was shrinkage in the news hole of the late-evening newscasts from 13 minutes to 11.8 minutes, thus allowing more time for advertising. This is the classic pattern of the marketing perspective.

Can Journalists Be Objective?

In 1922, the American Society of Newspaper Editors (ASNE) adopted a Statement of Principles that contains six articles: responsibility, freedom of the press, independence, truth and accuracy, impartiality, and fair play. The document was revised and renamed "Statement of Principles" in 1975. The idea of objectivity appears nowhere in the document, but the general public still thinks of this as the fundamental criterion of journalism.

There is a strong ethic of objectivity in journalism (Parenti, 1986). But what does this mean? Editors may be objective in the sense that they don't want to publish a "slanted" story. However, they have no choice but to use their personal judgment in deciding which stories get assigned, which stories get written by the best reporters, which stories get edited down, and which stories get printed on the front page.

The idea of objectivity has many layers of meaning. Let's "peel the onion" and work our way through some of these layers to develop an appreciation for this most important of all journalistic standards.

Layer One: Fabrication

The most surface layer of meaning for objectivity is making up news stories that have no basis in fact. Everyone would agree that it is a serious violation of objectivity if journalists make up facts and sources. Fabrication is always a threat because sometimes journalists do not have enough time or are too lazy to get all the facts they need, so they make some up or accept some facts without checking them out fully. Also, Jamieson and Waldman (2003) point out that sometimes journalists are tempted to tell a good story and ignore facts that get in the way of telling that story.

Fortunately, there are not many examples of fabrication, but the few major instances that have been revealed have really damaged journalism's credibility. In an article published in the *American Journalism Review*, Lori Robertson (2001) highlighted almost two dozen high-profile acts of ethical violations that resulted in the firing of journalists. The problem seems to be in all kinds of print vehicles, including well-known magazines (*Time, New Republic, Business Week*), large newspapers (*Wall Street Journal, New York Times, Boston Globe*), and small newspapers (*Myrtle Beach SC Sun News, Bloomsburg, PA Press Enterprise, Owensboro, KY Messenger-Inquirer*), and cuts across all kinds of reporters, including sports, business, general news, columnists, and arts critics.

Perhaps the most publicized ethical problems were perpetrated by Jayson Blair, a 27-year-old reporter on the fast track at the *New York Times*. To enhance his career, he tried to write stories that would be so interesting that they would be selected for publication in the most prominent places in the newspaper. However, to write such stories, he liberally embellished the facts, even going so far as to make up whole stories. When *Times* editors finally began checking his stories, they found many fabrications and quickly fired Blair. But the damage to the credibility of the *Times* was done, and the editors felt compelled to publish a 14,000-word apologia on its front page (Wolff, 2003).

Layer Two: Bias

When we dig a little deeper beyond fabrication, we find the idea of bias. Uncovering bias requires interpretation, and this makes it a more difficult violation of objectivity to spot.

Assessing whether a fact was fabricated requires relatively little interpretation, but with bias, we must infer whether the story has essential elements that the journalist failed to report because those elements supported a side of the issue that the journalist did not want supported. Therefore, bias—like fabrication—is a willful distortion on the part of a journalist, but it is difficult for audiences to recognize when this is occurring. If you agree with the journalist, you conclude that there has been no bias; in contrast, if you are a critic of the journalist, you argue that bias exists. Let's examine two ways bias can influence journalists' decisions: bias in ignoring stories and bias in the writing of a story, particularly political stories.

Bias in Ignoring Important Stories. News organizations cover only a tiny fraction of the occurrences on any given day. Does bias influence how they decide what to cover? Some people make a strong case that bias is a major influence. For example, let's look at the findings of Project Censored, a yearly analysis that compares happenings in the real world with events covered by the news organizations (C. Jensen, 1997). This project began in 1976 to monitor news coverage in the mass media and determine if major events or issues were not being covered. C. Jensen (1997) says, "The essential issue raised by the Project is the failure of the mass media to provide people with all the information they need to make informed decisions concerning their own lives. Only an informed electorate can achieve a fair and just society. The public has a right to know about issues that affect it and the press has a responsibility to keep the public well-informed about those issues" (p. 10). Jensen argues that the media are biased in the way they select which events they choose to cover. He says,

> The media are more concerned with their next quarterly profit than with the unique opportunity given them by the First Amendment. And most journalists are more concerned with keeping their jobs and increasing their income than with fighting for the public's right to know. . . . America's mainstream mass media basically serve three segments of society today—the wealthy, politicians, and the sports-minded. The news media have done an exceptional job providing full and, on the whole, reliable information to those who are involved in or follow the stock market and to those who are involved in or follow politics and to those who are involved in or follow sports. (p. 12)

Jensen says that there is no conscious conspiracy among journalists to censor the news.

> News is too diverse, fast-breaking, and unpredictable to be controlled by some sinister conservative eastern establishment media cabal. However, there is a congruence of attitudes and interests on the part of the owners and managers of mass media organizations. That non-conspiracy conspiracy, when combined with a variety of other factors, leads to the systematic failure of the news media to inform the public. While it is not an overt form of censorship, such as the kind we observe in some other societies, it is nonetheless real and often equally as dangerous to the public's well being. (pp. 14–15)

In his book *Censored: The News That Didn't Make the News—And Why,* C. Jensen (1995) describes many seemingly important stories that did not receive much, if any, coverage by the news media. For example, in 1985, the National Institute for Occupational Safety and Health (NIOSH) found that more than 240,000 people were in danger in 258 work sites around the United States. It is the purpose of NIOSH to monitor safety in the workplace and to inform workers when they are in serious danger of contracting life-threatening diseases from exposure to chemicals and other hazardous materials in the workplace. By 1995, NIOSH had informed less than 30% of the people whom it had found to be in daily danger a decade earlier. Thus, NIOSH knew that 170,000 people were working in highly risky environments every day and let 10 years go by without telling them. The news media ignored this governmental negligence for more than a decade.

A more recent example is the lack of adequate news coverage in the lead-up to the Iraq War. News organizations simply accepted the Bush administration's claim that Iraq had weapons of mass destruction that threatened the security of the United States and the world—a claim that was later found to be groundless.

Bias Toward Particular Political Views. Those who follow the media closely often complain about a liberal or a conservative news bias, or they say that there is too much negativism. An analysis of Gallup public opinion data found that more than half of Americans felt that the media were influenced by advertisers, business corporations, Democrats, the federal government, liberals, the military, and Republicans (Becker, Kosicki, & Jones, 1992). The newspaper industry itself has found the same thing in its own surveys. For example, a survey by the American Society of Newspaper Editors found that most people believe the media have political leanings (Jeffres, 1994).

What is interesting is that conservatives feel that the media have a generally liberal leaning, whereas liberals feel that the media are conservative. Conservatives complain that most news reporters are liberal in their own views, and these liberal journalists show their bias when they present their stories. In contrast, liberals feel that conservative commentators have too much power and have redefined the American agenda to stigmatize liberals.

In the early days of the United States, most newspapers were founded by men who had a clear political viewpoint that they wanted to promote. Towns had multiple newspapers, each one appealing to a different niche of political thinking. Newspapers were biased politically, and the bias was clearly labeled. But by the late 1800s, newspapers had shifted from a political focus to a business focus, with the goal of building the largest circulation. To do this, newspapers lost their political edge so as to avoid offending any potential readers. This business focus still underlies the mass media. Decisions are made to build audiences, not to espouse a political point of view. Sometimes, arguing for a particular political point of view can be used as a tool to build an audience, but these instances are usually found within those media with a niche orientation. Instead, the large national news organizations such as the television networks and the large newspapers try to present both sides of any political issue so as to appear objective and balanced because they want to appeal to all kinds of people across the political spectrum. This conclusion has been supported by D'Alessio and Allen (2000), who conducted a meta-analysis of 59 quantitative studies of news bias in presidential campaigns since 1948. They found no evidence of bias with newspapers or magazines and only an "insubstantial" bias in network television news.

It is important to be sensitive to whether particular news vehicles present either a liberal or a conservative bias. But it is far more important to be sensitive to the broader bias underlying all news vehicles—that is, the bias of commercialism, entertainment, and superficiality. If all we do is debate the liberal-conservative issue when it comes to news bias, we are in danger of missing the larger picture that the news media are providing us with a worldview that determines not only what we think about (as in agenda setting) but also what we think, how we think, and who we are.

Layer Three: Partial Story

At an even deeper level of analysis is the idea that journalists are not objective because they are telling us only part of the story. This type of distortion is not usually regarded as bias because there does not seem to be an intention by the journalist to mislead the audience. Instead, the journalist has run out of time or does not have enough sources or ability to tell the entire story. Even though the journalist is not trying to mislead the audience, people exposed to a partial story are still shown a distorted picture of the occurrence, and therefore the story cannot be regarded as being objective.

One form of partial story is when a major story stops getting covered, even though important events continue to occur. An example of this is the $21 billion settlement by the tobacco industry that was covered during negotiations. But then the press stopped covering the story as the tobacco companies began paying billions of dollars to state governments between 2000 and 2002. Why would it be important to cover how the money was used? The settlement specified that states should spend the money for health care and to educate people, especially children, about the health risks of smoking. But only 5% of this total payout went toward antismoking efforts as it was intended. Instead, it got funneled to all sorts of pork barrel projects across the 50 states, and in North Carolina, much of it went to subsidize tobacco farmers. These subsidies did not go to help tobacco farmers transition to other crops; instead, much of it went to modernize their tobacco farms (Mnookin, 2002). Also, the press did a poor job of educating the public about where the money for the payout was coming from. Most people know that it is from the major tobacco companies, but most people do not know where the tobacco companies get much of their revenue that they use to make their payments to states in the tobacco settlement. Each of the major tobacco companies now controls hundreds of brands of all kinds of food products in supermarkets. So the payout was likely financed by a rise in prices of crackers, cereals, peanut butter, dog food, soups, and so on.

Another type of partial story is when a journalist tells a story from a single point of view. American journalists typically tell their stories from the point of view that America is always justified in its military actions, and those we aggress against are not justified. For example, Fishman and Marvin (2003) analyzed 21 years of photographs appearing on the front pages of the *New York Times*. They focused on violence and found that non-U.S. agents were represented as more explicitly violent than were U.S. agents and that the latter are associated with disguised modes of violence more often than the former. The recurring image of non-U.S. violence is that of order brutally ruptured or enforced. By contrast, images of U.S. violence are less alarming and suggest order without cruelty. Thus, violence is associated more with out-group status than with in-group status.

Layer Four: Context

Perhaps the deepest level of analysis of the idea of objectivity occurs when we consider the nature of context. This is the concern over how much background-type information to present to help readers make sense of the event. Without context, the story has ambiguous meaning. For example, a story could report that Mr. Jones was arrested for murder this morning. That fact can convey very different meanings if we vary the context. Let's say that the journalist put in some historical context that Mr. Jones had murdered several people a decade ago, was caught and convicted, served time in prison, but was recently let go because of a ruling of an inexperienced and liberal judge. In contrast, let's say that Mr. Jones, one of the candidates running for mayor, was arrested despite the fact that police had in custody another man who possessed the probable murder weapon and who had confessed. The fact of the arrest takes on a very different meaning within different contexts.

Bagdikian (1992) argues that the most significant form of bias in journalism appears when a story is reported with a lack of context. The fear is that context is only the journalist's opinion, and opinion must be avoided in "objective reporting." Bagdikian continues, "But there is a difference between partisanship and placing facts in a reasonably informed context of history and social circumstance. American journalism has not made a workable distinction between them" (p. 214). He says that "there are powerful commercial pressures to remove social significance from standard American news. Informed social-economic context has unavoidable political implications which may disturb some in the audience whose world view differs" (p. 214). So the media report undisputed facts about things but ignore the meaning behind the facts and, in so doing, severely limit our ability to see that underlying meaning.

Although contextual material is very important, many stories present very little context (Parenti, 1986). For example, the many stories about crimes that we see reported every day are each limited to the facts of that one crime. Rarely is there any context about crime rates or how the particular crime reported in the story matches some kind of a pattern—historical, social, economic, and so forth. Crime stories are like popcorn for the mind. Each story is small, simple, and relatively the same. They give our mind the sense that it is consuming information, but those stories have little nutritional value. After years of munching on this information, we have come to believe that most crime is violent street crime and that it is increasing all around us. But the real-world figures indicate that most crime is white collar (embezzlement, fraud, forgery, identity theft, etc.) and property crimes (larceny, shoplifting, etc.) rather than violent crime (murder, rape, armed robbery, etc.). But it is the more rare violent crime that gets reported because it is more deviant and thus more likely to capture the attention of the news audience.

Asking journalists to build more context into their stories presents two problems. First, journalists vary widely in talent, and it takes a very talented and experienced journalist to be able to dig out a great deal of relevant contextual information on deadline. Second, when journalists have the responsibility of constructing the context, they may be manifesting a lot of power to define the meaning of the event for the readers. Journalists can substantially change the meaning if they leave out (whether intentionally or through an oversight) an important contextual element.

Let's examine an example of a story reporting facts that are accurate but that leads readers to a wrong conclusion because the reporter does not provide an adequate context for those facts. In 2004, *Los Angeles Times* reporter Larry Stewart wrote a story from a report by a group calling itself the Institute for Diversity and Ethics in Sport. In his newspaper story, Stewart indicated that the report said that it found six of the schools in the 2004 National Collegiate Athletic Association (NCAA) basketball tournament sweet 16 had graduation rates no higher than 50%. This leaves the reader with the impression that universities (at least six) were exploiting their athletes. But what the reporter did not put in the story is that, nationwide, only about 50% of students who enter a 4-year program as freshmen end up graduating with a bachelor's degree. Therefore, the problem is not with basketball teams having unusually low graduation rates, which is what the story implied. The real issue is the relatively large dropout rate of all college students. Also, the reporter said that the report complained that only 3 of the 16 teams had an African American head coach. Why is this number bad? What should the number be? If the number should be proportional to the number of African Americans in the United States, then we should expect 12% of coaches to be African American, and that would make it two coaches. Or instead, should the number of African American coaches be proportional to the number of African American players on NCAA basketball teams? This would be a much larger percentage, but then this begs the question that perhaps African Americans are overrepresented on these basketball teams and that the problem is that there needs to be better representation from non–African Americans on NCAA basketball teams—why are there not many more Hispanic or Asian American players? The determination of adequate representation is a complex issue. If newspapers see themselves as having the function of informing their readers so those readers can make good decisions, then journalists must provide more detailed contexts. If, instead, a journalist writes a superficial story that features only a controversy, then this serves to stir up negative emotions instead of educating readers.

In summary, you can see that objectivity is a complex concept, with many layers of meaning. This makes it difficult to understand what people really mean when they use the term. Thus, it is useful to move past objectivity and focus on something else, such as balance, as a reasonable criterion for quality news coverage.

Layer Five: Balance

As we have seen from earlier sections of this chapter, all journalists must make many decisions about news coverage, and although they use a news perspective to make these decisions, this perspective does not contain a formal list of steps to follow. Each journalist interprets the news perspective through his or her personal perspective. So the idea of objectivity is an unattainable goal. If we hold the work of journalists up to the criterion of objectivity, we will always be finding serious fault. Therefore, we need to shift to a more reasonable and useful criterion—such as balance.

Many journalists prefer the criterion of balance, which is the recognition that when an event has more than one side to it, journalists should present those viewpoints. With some stories, there are many sides. In stories of simple conflicts, there are usually two sharply differing sides. To be fair, journalists present both sides and try to do so with equal weight.

Are news stories balanced? Fico and Soffin (1995) looked at balance in newspaper coverage of controversial issues such as abortion, condoms in schools, and various governmental bills. Balance was assessed by examining whether both sides of an issue were illuminated in terms of sources interviewed for both sides and whether assertions for both sides were in the headline, first paragraph, and graphics. They found that 48% of stories analyzed were one-sided; that is, a second side was not covered at all. They counted the number of story elements that illuminated the different sides of each issue and found that, on average, one side received three more elements compared to the other side—therefore, the average story was imbalanced. Only 7% of stories were completely balanced. The authors concluded that professional capability and/or ethical self-consciousness are lacking in many journalists.

Although balance is a simpler criterion than is objectivity, it still presents some problems. One problem is determining how many sides there are to an issue. As I pointed out above, journalists using the simplified extended conflict formula will characterize issues by having two sides only. However, complex issues may have more than two sides, so balance requires covering all sides—not just two. Another problem with balance lies with the selection of sources of information. Some sources are more credible than others.

EMERGING ISSUES ABOUT NEWS

While the traditional issues examined in the section above are still important to consider, more pressing issues are emerging as media platforms shift from one-way to interactive. These issues include the following: Who qualifies as a journalist, what qualifies as news, and what should be the standard for quality?

Who Qualifies as a Journalist?

The new media environment forces us to consider what it means to be a journalist. In the United States, there is no professional certification for journalists like there is for physicians, lawyers, accountants, and even massage therapists. There are no educational or degree requirements. In the past, being a journalist simply meant being a reporter or an editor employed in a newspaper. But today, anyone can create a **blog.** Blogs (short for Web logs) are comments posted online that range from an individual's personal diary entries to Web pages that look a lot like newspapers with headlines and pictures. As of the summer of 2011, there were already 152 million blogs in existence (Pingdom, 2011).

Some of these blogs have readerships as large or larger than well-established print newspapers. For example, the Huffington Post had grown to more than 35 million readers a day by May 2011, which made it read by more people than the *New York Times* (Romenesko, 2011). The articles posted on the Huffington blog are written by well-respected traditional journalists. But many blogs have postings written by people who are unknown, so it raises a serious question about who should be given the status of a journalist. This is not an insignificant title, because journalists are protected from being forced to reveal the sources of their news stories. Also, journalists are given access to events

where the public is prohibited so that journalists can report those events to the public. What would happen if 50 million bloggers each asked for a press pass to the next presidential nominating convention or to the press box at a sporting event? How can we draw the line between "real journalists" and bloggers? At the present time, no one has an answer that is not arbitrary. Perhaps the construction of a good answer lies in first answering a more fundamental question of, "What is news?"

What Qualifies as News?

Traditional definitions of news typically emphasize that it is the reporting of events that are significant, timely, and proximate to the readers. But what if your best friend tweets you that she cannot meet you for lunch? This is significant, timely, and proximate to you. This may be news to you but not to anyone else. So does news need to be significant to people beyond yourself? If so, how many people? You can see that this is a very slippery slope, especially considering how the audience is fragmenting and the focus of one's life may be shifting from global to local; that is, to many people, who they meet for lunch is much more significant, timely, and proximate than an earthquake in Chile, a political scandal in New York, or a news conference in the White House. The Kaiser Family Foundation (2010) conducted a survey of young Americans ages 8 to 18 years and found that from 2005 to 2010, time spent reading magazines and newspapers dropped (from 14 to 9 minutes for magazines and from 6 to 3 minutes for newspapers). The proportion of young people who read a newspaper in a typical day dropped from 42% in 1999 to 23% in 2009. On the other hand, young people now spend an average of 2 minutes a day reading magazines or newspapers online. In contrast, 7th to 12th graders report spending an average of 1 hour,

35 minutes a day sending or receiving texts. This means that the average teenager spends 19 times as much time texting each day than reading newspapers (in print and online). This tells us that while the next generation has a strong interest in other people and the world outside themselves, that interest is not being addressed by newspapers or magazines. And taking this reasoning one step further, we need to confront the idea that news being used by editors at newspapers and magazines is not the same as news being used by the next generation.

What Should Be the Standard of Quality?

As you saw in the first part of this chapter, objectivity has been an unattainable criterion for news in the past, and this continues to hold with the new media environment. What criterion is a reasonable one to guide our evaluation of news messages, especially in the new media environment? Let's examine three criteria (usefulness, accuracy, and credibility) and illustrate their value through an example. Let's say the town council in your city is trying to pass a budget for next year and the Democrats who control the town council claim that the new budget will be balanced—that is, expected revenues from all fees and taxes next year will cover all the expenditures. However, the Republicans claim that the budget as proposed will result in a deficit of $100 million, and therefore expenditures must be cut back. Journalists (including reporters for the local newspapers, television, and radio stations as well as political bloggers) report the controversy. You are satisfied with this initial reporting because the city budget is a significant issue that is both timely and proximate to you. Let's say the controversy drags on for a week or two, and now you need something more from the news besides reporting that there is a controversy because you already know that and it is no longer news. You need something more. Let's consider the utility criterion and say you need information that you can use to formulate your own opinion on this budget controversy—that is, you need journalists to help you resolve this controversy in your own mind. Let's say you are a lifelong Democrat, in which case you need journalists to present you with information to support the Democrat's position. Here utility does not mean that you need information useful to construct a better informed opinion; instead, utility means that you need information to reinforce your existing beliefs.

Now let's consider an alternative criterion of accuracy. Perhaps the Democrat's figures are inaccurate, so if you reinforce your existing belief using faulty information, you could suffer later. Accuracy is important, and journalists need to check their facts. With some stories, it is relatively easy for journalists to check facts, such as the name of a person arrested for a crime, the date of the arrest, the charges files, and the like. But with a budget proposal that is likely to be hundreds of pages of spreadsheets, the task of accuracy is much more involved. To apply this criterion of accuracy, you would have to check every line on the proposed budget yourself so you could establish a standard for the truth, and then you would need to compare the stories of all journalists to see who reported the truth most closely. This is far too involved a task for news audiences, so accuracy is not a workable standard for many stories.

That leaves us with the criterion of credibility, which is the most practical of the three standards. Credibility is what you believe about the accuracy of each journalist. A judgment of credibility is much easier to achieve than a judgment about the actual accuracy of each journalist's reporting. With credibility, you could analyze stories for the amount of evidence presented to support each conclusion and the way the evidence is presented in a logical fashion to arrive at those conclusions. And even better, you could monitor the development of news stories over time and determine which journalists presented stories that were better able to describe the unfolding events. In our example, perhaps one journalist has been reporting on budget controversies over the years and has been able to show which proposals have been faulty and why. Credibility then is keyed to the journalist, not to the news outlet. Perhaps in our example, a blogger has a better history of presenting key facts and ignoring misleading ones because she is a certified public accountant; she has carefully analyzed each proposed budget over the years and has demonstrated the ability to write in a way to expose inaccuracies that the public can understand. In contrast, perhaps the respected newspaper in town has a new reporter covering the budget controversy and does not understand accounting or public financing. Across journalists of all kinds, there is a wide range of analytical ability, work ethic, and motives. To increase our media literacy, we need to ferret out the most credible journalists.

BECOMING LITERATE WITH NEWS CONTENT

For many people, watching 30 minutes of news each night provides them with a feeling that they are staying informed of all the important issues of the day. About half the adult population also reads a newspaper every day, and this exposure serves to further reinforce in them the feeling that they are informed. Many people feel that because they are marinating in so much information every day, they are well informed.

Becoming well informed requires more than following a habit of exposure to news. News stories are typically commercialized messages designed to attract audience attention with easy treatments of flashy topics; they are not usually well-balanced, in-depth analyses of important issues. To be well informed, you need to do more than float in the flood of information; you need to pay attention to messages and really think about them. Thus, you need to get out of the automatic processing state and devote some conscious attention to the content of certain media messages.

How can we protect ourselves from the illusion that we are being informed about the important events of the day when we faithfully expose ourselves to news messages in the media? The key is to develop higher media literacy with more elaborated knowledge structures, more well-developed skills, and a stronger personal locus that drives us to analyze news and hold it to a higher standard than we have in the past.

Now that you have more information about news as a construction, the news perspective, the myth of objectivity, and the importance of balance, you have a stronger knowledge structure about media content. And now that you have confronted some important issues raised by the news media environment, you should have a broader conception of news. When you use this broader knowledge structure with advanced skills, you will be able to see much more in messages of news and information. Table 10.2 shows the cognitive, emotional, aesthetic, and moral skills you will need. It also provides some examples of knowledge across these four domains. These lists are not exhaustive. You could use other examples of skills and knowledge to increase your media literacy during exposures to media messages.

Keep this template in mind as you watch the news. Think about how useful your knowledge structures are. Seek to elaborate your existing knowledge structures by using five strategies: (a) analyze the news perspective, (b) search for context, (c) develop alternative sources of information, (d) be skeptical of public opinion, and (e) expose yourself to more news, not less.

TABLE 10.2	Types of Skills and Knowledge Needed to Deal With News and Information Messages in a Media-Literate Manner	
	Skills	*Knowledge*
Cognitive	Ability to analyze a news story to identify key points of information	
	Ability to compare and contrast key points of information in the news story with facts in your knowledge structure	Knowledge on topic from many sources (media and real world)
	Ability to evaluate veracity of information in story	
	Ability to evaluate if story presents a balanced presentation of the news event/issue	
Emotional	Ability to analyze the feelings of people in the news story	
	Ability to put one's self into the position of different people in the story	Recall from personal experiences how it would feel to be in the situation in the story
	Ability to extend empathy to other people contiguous to the news story	
Aesthetic	Ability to analyze the craft and artistic elements in the story	Knowledge of writing, graphics, photography, and so on
	Ability to compare and contrast the artistry used to tell this story with that used to tell other stories	Knowledge of good and bad stories and the elements that contributed to those qualities
Moral	Ability to analyze the moral elements in a story	Knowledge of criticism of news and knowledge of the meaning of bias, objectivity, balance, and fairness
	Ability to compare and contrast this story with other stories	Knowledge of other stories on this topic and how those journalists achieved balance and fairness
	Ability to evaluate the ethical responsibilities of the journalists on this story	Highly developed moral code for journalism

Analyze the News Perspective

Remember, news is a construction by news workers. Journalists make their selections and decisions based on their news perspective. So when we watch a news program on TV or read a newspaper, we are seeing as much (or more) about those news organizations as we are seeing the events in the story—if we know what to look for. By keeping this in mind, we will be learning a great deal about news values while at the same time protecting ourselves from accepting the false belief that news is a complete, accurate, and balanced picture of our world. Getting a more accurate picture should be our goal. But to achieve that goal, we must seek out many sources and be actively critical of their information.

Search for Context

Often, we hear the term *news and information* and read this as a single concept rather than as two. But it is important to make a distinction between news and information. News is that which is "new" in some sense. If it is something we already know, it is not news. Therefore, it must be out of the ordinary—that is, deviant. It must make us think, "Gee whiz, I never knew that! Isn't that strange?" It must entertain or excite us in some way. In contrast, information tells us something of value about our world. It makes us think, "That is something I should know; that is something I can use."

Of course, this is not a neat, categorical distinction; something can be both news and information. For example, a news story might begin with the announcement that J. J. Jones was arrested for jumping out of a tree and mugging an old woman as she walked through the city park. This is highly unusual and deviant, so it would get covered as news. People watching this story would say, "Gee whiz. What is the world coming to?" If the story ends at this point, it is merely news. But if the story continues by putting the arrest in context, then it most likely would contain information, such as changes in the rate of crime in the park, reasons for the changes, the police department's success rate of solving those crimes, and the like. This context provides readers with something they can use—not just a fleeting emotional reaction. At higher levels of media literacy, people can more clearly see this distinction between news and information—and demand more information. If all your exposure to news is sensationalized events presented in a superficial manner, you will eventually construct beliefs about the world that are highly misleading.

Develop Alternative Sources of Information

In their book *How to Watch TV News,* Postman and Powers (1992) say that for people to prepare themselves to watch television news, they need to prepare their minds through extensive reading about the world. In short, if individual messages in the media do not provide much context, then you need to search that context out for yourself. With important social, political, and economic issues, this usually means reading books and magazines. But when you do this, make sure you read a variety of viewpoints. Context is more than getting exposure to one perspective on a problem—no matter how in-depth. A fully developed knowledge structure requires in-depth exposure to the issue from as many different points of view as possible. So if you find a detailed article on a topic in a conservative magazine, try to find the same topic treated in liberal, middle-of-the-road, and nonpolitical magazines. Following this strategy will result in your knowledge structure on this topic being much more elaborate, and your resulting opinion will be much sounder.

This is especially important with news from the Internet where there are so many news services, bulletin boards, and blogs on current events. Often it is not possible to tell who has constructed the stories, how balanced the coverage is, and how accurate the "facts" are. It is essential to access information from a wide variety of websites to develop a sense of where the most accurate information and credible contexts are being presented.

Be Skeptical About Public Opinion

The problem with public opinion is not with measuring it accurately. Good measurement technology can accurately capture public opinion—when opinions exist. The problem is that often people don't have an opinion about something, or they are not sure what their opinion is—they are ambivalent. To illustrate this, take your own informal opinion poll. Ask several of your friends for their opinions on the deficit, health care reform, campaign finance reform, capital punishment, and some local issues of concern to you. Notice that most respondents will feel that they should have an opinion, and they will give you one. Then ask them why they hold those opinions. Do they quote many facts in a logical, well-reasoned argument that provides a strong foundation for their opinions? Or do they act kind of embarrassed and defensive? Are those opinions deeply held and of strong value to them? Or are those opinions superficial and based on a few random facts? How do you feel about national policy being formulated on the basis of these opinions?

When we do these things, we will attain a higher level of media literacy with the news. This requires an interplay between our knowledge structures and our skills (see Table 10.2). Stronger skills translate into stronger knowledge structures.

Expose Yourself to More News, Not Less

Americans have developed a high degree of skepticism about the press. Typically, only about half the population has a favorable opinion about the press (Luntz, 2000), and only about a third of the public believes the media get the facts straight (Rainey, 2005). Given such high skepticism about journalism, it is not surprising that news exposure is declining, especially among younger people.

Why are younger people more likely to avoid seeking out news? The answer seems to lie in the larger trend of people feeling overwhelmed by information. We cannot process it all. We feel fatigued and look for ways to reduce the exposure. With news, people do not want to seek out information unless it is relevant to them. For example, Chew and Palmer (1994) conducted a survey and found that people's need for information varies according to how relevant the issue is to them. With low-relevance issues, people are primarily concerned about information about how that issue would affect them. With high-relevance issues, people are more interested in gathering information that will help them form a good opinion, so they want information covering different viewpoints and want to hear from experts.

Also, many people feel fatigued with bad news. For a long time, people have been complaining about the amount of bad or negative news and ask for more good news

(Galician, 1986). They say that bad news is not necessarily more interesting. But the news organizations continue to predominantly feature bad news (such as crime, scandal, and controversy).

The reasons cited above—too much news is irrelevant and bad—are understandable explanations for why people are increasing their avoidance of news. But avoiding news limits one's experience, and this is a mistake. Instead, people need to expose themselves to a wider range of news from a wider range of news organizations. In this way, people can find the positive as well as the negative and find the coverage that is relevant to their needs. With more information, people can make better decisions about which facts are more accurate. And with more information, people have more options in filtering in certain facts and constructing knowledge structures that are more useful to them.

SUMMARY

News is not a reflection of actual events; it is a construction by news workers who are subjected to many influences and constraints. Each day, journalists must select from all of human activity those things that they feel should be reported to the public. For each event selected, journalists must then decide what the focus of the story should be so that it will hook an audience. Finally, journalists must assemble the news elements into some structure to tell the story. When performing all these tasks, news workers cannot be objective, so they try for the goal of being balanced. However, careful analyses of the news indicate that most stories are not balanced.

Formulas guide the construction process. The purpose of these formulas is to help news workers do their jobs efficiently. The formulas are part of the news perspective, which is shaped by many influences and constraints. This news perspective shifts the goal of news workers from informing the public to entertaining as many people as possible, thereby generating the maximum revenue for the news organization. This has led to a focus on the sensational and the superficial. News now asks only for our eyeballs, not our gray matter.

Many of us feel we have a good understanding of current events because we read newspapers and magazines and keep up with news on radio and television. But without a complete knowledge of the day's events themselves, we cannot tell if the news coverage is complete, balanced, or accurate.

Being media literate requires us to search out a wide range of sources and build stronger knowledge structures that provide us with the context that mainstream news programs do not provide. We need to be careful about analyzing the news perspective, search for context, develop alternative sources of information, and be skeptical. In short, we need to be more active and conscious in using more well-developed skills to process news messages.

Chapter Resources: To test your knowledge and learn more about the topics discussed in this chapter, visit the Student Study Site at www.sagepub.com/potter6e.

FURTHER READING

Henry, N. (2007). *American carnival: Journalism under siege in an age of new media.* Berkeley: University of California Press. (326 pages with index)

This book is written by a journalist who is concerned about how traditional journalism can survive in the new media environment.

Jensen, C. (1995). *Censored: The news that didn't make the news—and why.* New York: Four Walls Eight Windows. (332 pages with index)

Begun by the author in 1976, Project Censored invites journalists, scholars, librarians, and the general public to nominate stories that they feel were not reported adequately during that year. From the hundreds of submissions, the list is reduced to 25 based on "the amount of coverage the story received, the national or international importance of the issue, the reliability of the source, and the potential impact the story may have" (p. 15). A blue-ribbon panel of judges then selects the top 10 censored stories for the year.

Mindich, T. Z. (2005). *Tuned out: Why Americans under 40 don't follow the news.* New York: Oxford University Press. (172 pages with index)

The author clearly documents that the last two generations of Americans have exhibited drastic declines in attention to news in the traditional media. Furthermore, only 11% of young people even attend to the news on the Internet. He develops some explanations for why news has become so irrelevant to the younger generations, then speculates about how this will affect the political system and society in general.

Paul, R. P., & Elder, L. (2006). *How to detect media bias & propaganda* (3rd ed.). Dillon, Beach, CA: Foundation for Critical Thinking. (46 pages with glossary)

This is a short book focusing on critical thinking and the news. It presents a lot of practical advice about how to think about news stories critically and thereby protect one's self from bias, especially from novelty and sensationalism.

Postman, N., & Powers, S. (1992). *How to watch TV news.* New York: Penguin. (178 pages with index)

These authors argue that what television news says it is presenting and what it actually presents are two different things. The authors say that TV presents the important happenings of the day that all citizens should know. But what it really presents is superficial constructions designed to create large audiences for advertisers. The authors say that for people to prepare themselves to watch television news, they need to prepare their minds through extensive reading about the world.

Schudson, M. (2003). *The sociology of news.* New York: Norton. (261 pages including end notes and index)

Schudson sharpens and clarifies many points in the argument that journalists "not only report reality but create it" (p. 2). He digs deep into the issue and offers explanations about how the news construction occurs and the effect those constructions have on the public. After providing a brief history of journalism, he identifies two criticisms as being especially salient today. The first is that news coverage of politics is critical and this promotes cynicism in the public. Second, news itself has gone soft; that is, it is a mix of information with entertainment rather than a legitimate effort to explain complex situations.

Shoemaker, P. J., & Reese, S. D. (1996). *Mediating the message: Theories of influences on mass media content* (2nd ed.). White Plains, NY: Longman. (313 pages)

In this book, the authors review research on media content and build toward a theory with assumptions, propositions, and hypotheses. The strength of this book is its broad look at research on news. It includes much empirical social science work, many industry examples and anecdotes, and an entire chapter on a cultural approach to ideology. It has two shortcomings. First, its span purports to be all media content, but it focuses almost exclusively on news. Once we get to Chapter 5, there is almost nothing on entertainment content. And nowhere is there anything on ad content. Also, the focus is limited to the media of television and newspapers. A second limitation is that there is really nothing new here. Their "theory" is really several lists.

KEEPING UP TO DATE

Journal of Broadcasting & Electronic Media and *Journalism & Mass Communication Quarterly*

These scholarly journals publish research that examines how news is presented in the content of the mass media, particularly newspapers and television.

WikiLeaks (www.wikileaks.ch)

Founded in 2007, WikiLeaks is a not-for-profit media organization that provides a secure and anonymous way for sources to leak information to the public. It relies on a network of volunteers from around the world. Leakers are typically whistleblowers who work in private businesses and government agencies where they feel their organization is doing something harmful to the public so they steal the private information of that organization and make it available for the public to view.

News Blogs

There are thousands of news blogs. Many are owned by major news organizations such as CNN (news.blogs.cnn.com) and the New York Times (http://www.nytimes.com/interactive/blogs/directory.html). The most popular news blog is the Huffington Post (http://www.huffingtonpost.com), which was started by Arianna Huffington independent of any news organization but was bought by AOL in 2011.

Technorati (http://technorati.com/blogs/directory)

Technorati is an Internet search engine for searching blogs. The name Technorati is a blend of the words *technology* and *literati,* which invokes the notion of technological intelligence or intellectualism. Technorati uses and contributes to open-source software. It has an active software developer community, many of them from open-source culture.

EXERCISE 10.1

Practicing Analyzing the News

1. Take a blank sheet of paper and draw the structure of Table 10.2 on it. That is, create two columns: Label one column "Skills" and the other column "Knowledge." Now create four rows, labeling them "Cognitive," "Emotional," "Aesthetic," and "Moral." Your table should have eight blocks. Make a copy of this table so that you have two of them.

2. Watch a news story on television. Videotape the story so that you can watch it more than once.

3. After a single viewing, write down the skills and knowledge you needed to achieve a basic minimal understanding of what the story says. Think in terms of your everyday viewing of news, where you just want to monitor the surface facts to keep up with the day's major events.

4. Think about the skills and knowledge you would need to achieve a much more complete understanding about the meaning of the event in the news story. Think in terms of what it would take for you to be an expert on the event. This may require you to view the tape several times.

5. Look at what you have written in response to Question 4. Does it differ much from what you have written in response to Question 3? How much detail do you have in each of the eight blocks? With which blocks did you struggle the most? Why do you think you struggled there?

6. Compare the results of your tables with those of a friend. Did your friend have more details in certain blocks compared to yours? If so, did that additional detail extend your thinking? The more people's work you compare, the more you can see a range of differences.

EXERCISE 10.2

Inferring News Workers' Decisions

Gather together three or four newspapers for the same day—the more the better.

1. Look at the composition of the first page across those newspapers, and think about the differences and similarities of news perspective.

   a. What are the major stories in terms of placement and size?

   b. What pictures and graphics are used? Are they used to present substance, or are they used merely to make the page more appealing to the eye?

   c. How much of the front pages is composed of non-news matter?

2. Read the major news stories.

   a. What criteria must have been used to select them?

   b. What types of elements are emphasized in the stories? What are the facts that make this story news? What facts provide background context?

   c. Is the story balanced, or are obvious viewpoints ignored?

3. Look at the sections of the newspapers.

   a. Which sections are there? (such as sports, women, business, etc.)

   b. Look at how the space is allocated. How much space is given to ads? How much to hard news? How much to soft, entertainment-type news?

4. What happened within the last 24 hours that did not get covered?

5. In summary, which of these newspapers do you think is the best and why?

6. Later today, listen to some news on the radio and watch some on television. How is the news different in these media compared to newspapers?

EXERCISE 10.3

Exercising Your Skills

Think of some current event of interest to you. Now pretend you are an editor of a newspaper. What elements would you want to have in the story?

1. What sources would you want to interview?

2. What facts and figures would you want to gather?

3. What historical contextual factors would you want?

4. Would you want visuals—graphics or photographs?

CHAPTER 11

Entertainment

Key Idea:
*Entertainment
messages from the
media follow
formulas that are
designed to attract
our attention and
condition us for
repeat exposures.*

Katherine, a freelance scriptwriter, had waited 3 weeks to get an appointment with the vice president of Prestige Films & Entertainment Company so she could pitch her idea for a TV movie. If the vice president liked her idea, he would green-light the project, which would mean she would get paid to write the script and Prestige would likely produce the 2-hour movie that could turn into a pilot for a television series.

Katherine was very nervous as she began her pitch. "This story is about family values as seen through the eyes of a brother and sister who are suddenly orphaned. Chloe is 10 years old and Tony is her 14-year-old brother. The story opens with Chloe, Tony, and their parents on the run from some evil corporation thugs who are trying to track down the father for being a whistleblower and exposing some illegal practices of the company where the father worked. The children narrowly escape the thugs, who find their parents and kill them. Now orphans with no family or friends, the children have to keep moving around so that the thugs don't find them. Most of the movie is about how the brother and sister form a strong bond as they take care of each other, as they have to quickly grow up. There is a series of scenes showing how they struggle to find transportation, shelter, and food to eat while they evade the thugs chasing them. There are also some tender scenes with Chloe and Tony talking about their grief and fear. Finally, in the climax, the kids figure out a way to trick the thugs into an ambush where they are able to kill the thugs. They take the thugs' car and discover its trunk is full of cash. So the movie ends on a high note."

The vice president smiled broadly. "I love your idea. It's got so many great story elements. It's got tragedy. It's got action and suspense. It's got kids fighting to survive. It's got family values. It's got violence and retribution. I love it!"

"So you'll green-light the project?" Katherine couldn't believe that after 2 years of pitching various film projects, she finally had a winner.

"Yes. Definitely yes! But I'd like to see one change—one small, tiny change. If you agree to that, it's a go."

"What kind of change?"

"Could you make Tony a porpoise?

"A porpoise—a fish?"

"Yes, let's make Tony a fish. TV viewers love animals!"

Entertainment messages, like news and information-type messages, follow particular formulas. Producers of entertainment messages must follow these formulas so as to grab the attention of audiences and hold their attention throughout their stories. The more completely producers understand these formulas and the more skillfully they can use them to construct their stories, the more successful their messages will be. As consumers of media messages, we too can benefit from greater understanding of these formulas.

ENTERTAINMENT FORMULA

On the surface, it appears that the media present a wide variety of entertainment messages. But when we analyze those messages, we can see that they follow standard patterns. For example, a wide variety of songs have been presented as popular music in recordings, cassettes, and CDs and on the radio over many decades. Each of those songs follows certain formulas. None of those songs is a purely random sequence of notes. Musical formulas tell musicians which notes are played in sequence (melody progressions) and which notes are to be played together (chords). There are a small number of standard rhythms. All of the songs are creative variations on the standard formula. The same can be said for any media message.

General Story Formula

There are formulas for telling stories. Screenwriter Sue Clayton analyzed successful and unsuccessful Hollywood films to try to figure out which elements are most associated with success. From this analysis, she discovered a formula, which she calls the genetic blueprint for a successful movie. This blueprint calls for 30% action, 17% comedy, 13% good versus evil, 12% love/sex/romance, 10% special effects, 10% plot, and 8% music. This formula shows that *Titanic* and *Toy Story 2* were perfect movies (Baker, 2003). While it is doubtful that we could ever reduce the formula for a successful movie or story to a precise mathematical formula, all stories must have certain characteristics to appeal to audiences. Thus, we can identify a general entertainment story formula. All stories begin with a conflict or a problem. The conflict is heightened throughout the story, and the main characters try to solve the problem. Finally, during the climactic scene, the problem is solved, and the conflict is eliminated or at least significantly reduced.

This general formula is used not only by the creators of media messages but also by us—the audience—to help us easily recognize the good and bad characters and to quickly find where we are in the story. Stories that follow the formulas the closest usually have the largest audiences because they are the easiest to follow. The more experience we have with entertainment messages, the more we learn the story formula. We are conditioned to expect certain plot points, certain pacing, certain types of characters, and certain themes.

Genres

The overall entertainment story formula is elaborated in different ways across different genres of entertainment. Let's examine the story formula in the genres of drama, comedy, romance, and reality programming.

Drama

The drama genre has three basic subgenres that illuminate three types of drama entertainment: tragedy, mystery, and action/horror (Sayre & King, 2003). Tragedy must have characters that are perceived by the audience as noble and good. However, bad things happen to these characters either because they have a fatal flaw they cannot get around (as is the case in Shakespearean tragedies) or because fate has conspired to do them in, such as what happens in the movie *Titanic*).What audiences enjoy about tragedies is the opportunity to compare themselves with the tragic characters and feel better off than those unfortunate characters.

With the mystery formula, an important element of the plot is missing. For example, in a "whodunit" mystery, the *who* is missing. A serious crime usually triggers the story, and someone must use the information available to figure out who committed the crime. The suspense is in solving the puzzle. Audiences are drawn into the story as they try to solve the mystery for themselves.

The action/horror formula is primarily plot driven as good and evil fight it out in ever deepening conflict. Characters are stereotypes or comic book types. Within several seconds after being introduced to a character, we know whether that character is a hero or a villain. Characters are static and don't change. The plot relies on fast-paced action that maximizes arousal in the audience. The primary emotions evoked are fear, suspense, and vengeance. Violence is a staple in almost all of these stories. The formula of violence tells us that it is okay for criminals to behave violently throughout a program as long as they are caught at the end of the show. This restores a sense of peace—at least until the commercials are over and the next show begins. Also, we feel that it is permissible for police officers, private eyes, and good guy vigilantes to break the law and use violence as long as it is used successfully against the bad guys.

Comedy

With the comedy formula, minor conflict situations flare up and set the action in motion. The conflict is heightened verbally, usually through deceit or insults. Characters are developed through their unusual foibles and quick wit. The action is neatly resolved at the end of the show, and all the main characters end up happy because their problems have been eliminated.

One subgenre of comedy is the character comedy or comedy of manners. Here the humor arises out of character quirks that illuminate the craziness of everyday situations. Characters find themselves in difficult situations that we all encounter everyday. As characters try to work their way through these situations, the absurdity of certain social conventions is illustrated, and this makes us laugh. Examples include *Seinfeld* and *Everybody Loves Raymond*. Another subgenre of comedy is the put-down comedy, where certain characters have power over other characters and exercise that power in humorous ways. Examples include *Two and a Half Men* and *The Office*. The situation comedy formula is so well known by viewers that Nickelodeon has created some 60-second sitcoms. Because viewers have no trouble recognizing typical plots and stereotypical characters, we have no trouble following the action.

Romance

A romance story begins with a person experiencing either loneliness from a lack of a relationship or a relationship that is bad due to betrayal, jealousy, or fear. As audience members, we are made to identify with the main character and feel her pain. But she is full of hope for what seems like an unattainable goal. Through hard work and virtue, she gets closer and closer to her goal—even though she experiences frequent heart-rendering setbacks—until the story climaxes with the fulfillment of the goal, which transmits intense emotions to the audience.

Writers who have mastered this formula are very successful. For example, among all paperbacks sold in the United States, about half are in the genre of the romance novel. One romance novelist who has really understood the formula is Nora Roberts. She has published 127 romance novels, all following the same basic romance formula. In one year, she had 11 titles on the *New York Times* best-seller list. In total, she has 85 million books in print, and her work has been translated into 25 languages (Riggs, 1999). Has she produced a body of great literature that will be read for centuries? No, of course not. Has she recognized a market for a particular kind of story and manufactured many products to meet that need? There is no doubt of this.

The most dominant two genres in primetime television from the 1970s through the 1990s were dramas and situation comedies. The type of drama shifted from action/adventure and westerns in the 1960s to crime/detective dramas in the 1970s. However, the comedy genre is king with audiences; comedies account for half of the top 100 television shows and top 100 movies of all time (Sayre & King, 2003).

After years of watching stories on television and in the movies, we have become adept at following the formulas about characters, plots, and themes. We know these formulas so well that many of us think we can write and produce our own shows. Perhaps some of us can, but producing a successful show is a very difficult undertaking. While the formulas are deceptively simple, making them work well is very difficult.

Constraints

Although these formulas are relatively simple for audiences to understand, they are exceedingly difficult for producers to follow well when creating television series. The reasons for this are that producers must work around so many constraints. Some of these constraints are introduced by the media, and other constraints are introduced by society's norms.

Constraints by Medium

Telling an entertaining story presents a different challenge as you move from one medium to another. If you plan to tell a story in print, you have only one perceptual channel (eyes), and you need to use words to trigger vivid images in the minds of the readers. If you plan to tell a story in song, you again need to trigger vivid images and strong emotions, but you must do this through the audience's ears, not their eyes. With a song, you also need to use words that sound good; that is, they must have a certain cadence that goes along with the rhythm of the music, and often there is a rhyming pattern. Also, the words must tell their story in 2 or 3 minutes.

Television is by far the most challenging medium for telling stories. At first, it might seem the least challenging because it appears to have few perceptual constraints; that is, you can use audio as well as video elements. Also, you are not dependent on the reading abilities of audience members. But there are two significant challenges with the television medium. First, stories must be enormously compelling. When people watch a show on television, it is extremely easy for them to switch away from the show to many other competing channels. Also, television stories are frequently interrupted by breaks for commercials, and some of these breaks have a dozen or more ads and last for 4 or more minutes. Viewers can forget about the story or lose their motivation to stay tuned unless that story has really intrigued them. Therefore, storytellers on television must do things to catch the audience's interest right from the beginning; they must build the action to a high point before each commercial break so that the audience will want to stay tuned throughout the commercial pod and find out what happens when the show returns, and they must keep the action interesting every minute so that people who are flipping through channels will want to stop and watch the show.

Second, television stories must be fairly simple. This is why formulas are so standard. People might tune into a story in the middle. If the story follows a simple formula, people can easily understand where the story is when they start watching. Audiences must instantly be able to know who the characters are. Also, unlike print, people can't control the pacing of the story or turn back a few chapters and reread an earlier part. Of course, people can now record video and play back the action to catch things they did not understand on first viewing, but they rarely do this. As a result of this constraint, television stories must be simple and very easy to follow; people must get the gist of the story, even if they are not paying much attention to it.

With television programs, producers not only must use the well-known formulas but also be creative enough to break with the story formula to keep their stories fresh to viewers who have seen the same plot hundreds of times. These two tasks seem impossible to attain at the same time, and this is why the percentage of television series that have lasted more than several dozen episodes is small.

Entertainment messages on the Web (such as videos on YouTube and Hulu) do not have the constraints of timing (they can be any length and accessed at any time) that videos on traditional television channels have. However, Web messages face a great deal more competition. Every month, 20 million videos are uploaded to Facebook, and if you wanted to view the videos uploaded on YouTube last year, it would take you 21 centuries (Pingdom, 2011). So if you want your uploaded video to attract a significant audience, you have a huge challenge of breaking through the clutter of all the competition.

Societal Constraints

The public has certain expectations about what it will and will not tolerate in entertainment. We can see where this line of acceptability is when the public gets offended and complains—particularly in the areas of bad language, sexual portrayals, and violence. Television programmers are essentially conservative and fearful of offending viewers, so they present content that they believe reflects mainstream American values.

This line of acceptability, however, changes over time as people get over their shock at a new kind of portrayal, then eventually get used to it. For example, writing in the late 1980s, George Comstock (1989) pointed out that "much of what is on television today would not have been considered acceptable by broadcasters or the public 20 or even 10 years ago. Public tastes and social standards have changed, and television has made some contribution to these changes by probing the borders of convention accompanying each season. . . . These conventions of popular entertainment provide television, as they do other media, with rules that minimize the possibility of public offense" (p. 182). Since Comstock wrote that, television has continued to push the line of public acceptance, and what offended viewers in the 1980s hardly gets their attention today.

The same evolution of a formula has been occurring with popular music. The basic formula of popular songs is a story about love or sex. For example, in one content analysis of themes in popular music over the past 60 years, it was found that 70 % of all songs have dealt with the topics of sex and love (Christianson & Roberts, 1998). What has changed in the formula is the way this theme is treated. Love used to be treated as an emotion, and the lyrics were symbolic; that is, the words suggested actions but left it up to the listeners to imagine the sex. Now love is treated as a physical act, and the lyrics are much more explicit in describing those acts, so listeners do not need to use their imaginations as much.

Storytelling formulas evolve as public tastes change over time. People get bored with too much repetition and look for something slightly different. Producers need to know how far they can push the line of acceptability at any given time without offending people and hence losing audience members. The media have become much more sensitive to these changes in taste because they know if they can push the line and not offend audiences, they will be the first to present a new twist in the old familiar formula, and this will attract large audiences.

The Fox television network is especially known for pushing the line of television programming. It aired shows such as *When Good Pets Go Bad* and *World's Scariest Police Shootouts*. When these shows came under harsh criticism, Sandy Grushow, director of programming for Fox, made public apologies. And in the late 1990s, Grushow spent a lot of time apologizing. Then, in February 2000, Grushow made the decision to air *Who Wants to Marry a Multimillionaire?* The show was a sensation, drawing 23 million viewers, but it again was an embarrassment when it was revealed that the selected bride, Darva Conger, had not really intended to get married on the program but went through with it only to get an annulment several weeks later. Grushow apologized again but this time offered an explanation for continuing to program these types of shows: "It's like someone who goes to their boss and says, 'We can make something at half the cost that will make twice as much money.' The boss would say, 'Go do it, but don't embarrass us.' This has turned into an embarrassing situation and now they have to fix it" (Bauder, 2000a, p. 3E).

CHARACTER PATTERNS

The population of characters on television is very different from the population of people in the real world. This is not to say that there are not types of people in real life like almost every character on television. Instead, in the aggregate, the pattern in the population of TV characters is different from the pattern of people in the real world. These differences can be seen most clearly in two ways. First, when we look at patterns in the aggregate, we see that the demographic balance is very different in the television world compared to the real world. Second, we see that the characters are presented as stereotypes.

Demographic Patterns

When we look past the individual characters and focus instead on patterns across the entire population of television characters, we can see that the television world has been portrayed very differently from the real world (see Table 11.1). The patterns of gender, ethnicity, age, marital status, socioeconomic status (SES), and occupations have been very different in the television world compared to the real world over the years. If we notice these demographic patterns in the television world and assume that they are the same in the real world, we will be creating faulty information for ourselves. For example, look at Table 11.2 to see the differences by occupation between the TV and real worlds.

The entertainment stories in the mass media also have a fairly standard set of characters, and this set of character types does not change much across media or vehicles. For example, one study of characters appearing in shows across 32 channels on a typical cable system found the same patterns of gender, race, and age across all channels (Kubey, Shifflet, Weerakkody, & Ukeiley, 1996).

On almost all of the demographic indicators, the television world has displayed very different patterns from the real world. However, it is interesting to note that one minority— African Americans—has fought for better representation on television programs and is now proportionally more likely to be represented in the television world (16%) than in the real world (12%). This group continues to fight successfully for representation. For example, during the fall 1999 television season, African American leaders severely criticized the big four television networks that premiered 26 new series; in all of those series, the lead characters and nearly all the cast regulars were White, even those on shows where the action takes place in urban high schools and New York City nightspots (Lowry, Jensen, & Braxton, 1999).

What can account for this dominance of males, Whites, and youthful adults? Perhaps it is due to the demographics of the people who are television writers. Turow (1992) pointed out that according to the Writers Guild of America, White males account for more than three quarters of the writers employed in film and TV. Minorities accounted for 2% of all writers. And it appears that the demographics of the writers are not getting more diverse. In a survey of the age, gender, and ethnicity of writers working in Hollywood's television and film industries in 1985, it was reported that it was dominated by White males. In 2002, the same pattern was found as far as gender and ethnicity (Bielby & Bielby, 2002), and Glascock (2001) reported that males outnumber females 3.6 to 1 among creative personnel, which includes producers, directors, and writers.

Stereotypical Portrayals

There is a positive as well as negative side to stereotypes. Stereotypes are positive from the point of view that they are easy for viewers to recognize. But stereotypes can also have a

TABLE 11.1 Demographic Patterns

Gender: Males used to outnumber females three to one in the television world. The gender difference has been moving more toward a balance over the years but very gradually. Now on primetime TV, 60% of characters are men and 40% women.

Men are more likely to be shown as working and in a wider variety of jobs than are women. However, the percentage of women in professional status jobs is the same as men in those types of jobs. Also, compared to the U.S. labor force, TV professionals and law enforcement agents are overrepresented, while managerial jobs, laborers, and service workers are underrepresented.

This gender imbalance varies by type of program. In soap operas, there is a balance among the genders. Also, in situation comedies and family dramas, there is almost a balance, but in police/detective shows, males outnumber females five to one.

Ethnicity: Eighty percent of all characters are White Americans. African Americans comprised only 2% of television characters until the late 1960s, when they jumped to about 10% of all characters. Now, African Americans account for about 16% of the main and minor roles, which is larger than their percentage (12%) in the real-world population of the United States. Hispanics, however, have not fared as well. Although Hispanics make up about 9% of the U.S. population, only about 2% of all television characters are Hispanic. Asian Americans and Native Americans combined account for about 1% of all television characters.

Age: Three quarters of all television characters are between the ages of 20 and 50, but in the real world, only one third of the population is between these ages. Young children and the elderly are underrepresented on television. Fictional characters younger than age 19 make up only 10% of the total television population, even though they make up one third of the U.S. population. Also, characters older than age 50 account for about 15% of all television characters. The most dramatic imbalance is in the over-65 age group. Barely more than 2% of television characters are at least 65 years old, but 11% of the real-life population is in this age bracket.

Marital status: Marital status is obvious with about 80% of the women and 45% of the men. Of those for whom you can tell their marital status, more than 50% of the women are married, whereas less than one third of the men are married.

Socioeconomic status (SES): Almost half the characters on television are wealthy or ultra-wealthy, and very few (less than 10%) are lower class.

Occupations: The higher prestige occupations are overrepresented on fictional television. Nearly one third of the television labor force is professional and managerial, whereas in real life, the figure is only 11%. Working-class people are greatly underrepresented, except for a few television world professions. For example, prostitutes outnumber machinists by 12 to 1, and there are twice as many doctors as welfare workers, 8 times more butlers than miners, and 12 times more private detectives than production line workers. But the world of work may be changing a bit. Vande Berg and Streckfuss (1992) analyzed occupations in primetime television and found that there was a slight increase in the representation of women and in the variety of their occupational portrayals. Still, women remain underrepresented and limited in their depictions in organizational settings. Males outnumbered females 2 to 1 in the workplace.

SOURCES: Comstock, Chaffee, Katzman, McCombs, and Roberts (1978); B. Davis (1990); Glascock (2001); B. S. Greenberg, Edison, Korzenny, Fernandez-Collado, and Atkin (1980); Mastro and Greenberg (2000); Signorielli and Kahlenberg (2001).

TABLE 11.2	Comparison of Occupation Prevalence in TV World and Real World	
Occupation	*TV World (%)*	*Real World (%)*
Medical workers	12.1	0.9
Police	11.4	0.9
Lawyers	8.3	0.7
Executives/managers	6.4	31.0
Media people	8.3	0.3
Space travelers	5.9	0.0001
Salespeople	2.6	11.8
Forensic specialists	4.5	0.01

SOURCE: Medich (2002, p. 16).

negative effect because they are often inadequate as well as biased, often serve as obstacles to rational assessment, and are resistant to social change.

We use stereotypes in dealing with real-world information, not just media portrayals. For example, when we meet a new person, we try to "type" that person based on the characteristics we can immediately see, such as age, gender, appearance, how he or she talks, and so on. Once we have typed someone, we have a set of expectations for that person. For example, if we see a 5-year-old girl in a fancy dress playing with a doll on the steps of a church, we would immediately call up a specific set of expectations. In contrast, if we see a middle-aged man with a beer belly straining through his dirty T-shirt, chewing tobacco, and cleaning a rifle, we would call up a very different set of expectations. Stereotypes provide us with a set of expectations that we can access quickly as we encounter people and events. They are a necessary mode of processing characters, especially when thousands of messages come at us quickly every day and we need to create order out of "the great blooming, buzzing confusion of reality" (Lippmann, 1922, p. 96).

Characters in the television world are developed as stereotypes according to certain formulas, which make the characters easily and quickly recognizable to viewers. Look at the examples of stereotypes in Table 11.3. For each of these stereotypes, a clear image likely comes into your mind. You have seen each of these characters many times. When one of them appears in a story, it only takes a few seconds for you to recognize who that character is.

TABLE 11.3	Examples of Prevalent Stereotypes

- The strong, self-reliant police detective who uses unconventional methods to deal with the scum on the street. He is irritated by his authoritarian bosses but always gets the job done using his own unorthodox methods.
- The nurturing mother who has kooky kids and an idiot husband
- The sexy young female actress/model/nurse/secretary who becomes a romantic interest of a male hero

- The dumb blonde who is superficial, cares only about physical appearance and dress styles, and has no common sense
- The young street punk who commits petty and violent crimes, usually for drugs. He is tough and sassy until police intimidate him into making a plea bargain.
- The nerdy male adolescent who displays hilariously dysfunctional social skills. Although he is very sensitive, he never learns from his social mistakes.

Stereotypes, however, can be harmful when they lead audiences to believe that all people of a given type share certain negative characteristics. This is why two groups— African Americans and women—are vocal in their complaints about how their demographic groups are stereotypically portrayed in television stories. Stereotypes in some other areas, such as occupations, families, the elderly, and body images, can also be harmful.

African Americans

It appears that the stereotype of African Americans on television has changed. In a review of the literature on ethnicity on television, Busselle and Crandall (2002) drew three conclusions. First, the world of situation comedy is one in which African Americans are approximately as prevalent as they are in the real world. But unlike the real world, discrimination, poverty, and crime do not exist. Second, drama programs about Black families are rare. And as argued by several researchers, when Black families are portrayed, their lives are consistent with the beliefs that opportunities abound and that hard work begets economic comfort. Third, we know relatively little about the roles of African American characters in programs with predominantly White casts. From the extant evidence, it appears that Black and White characters most often interact in the workplace, and Blacks most often occupy positions of superiority over Whites rather than positions of subservience or equality (Entman & Rojecki, 2001). Finally, when African American characters are not members of the middle or upper class, they are portrayed as social undesirables rather than as the working poor.

Gender

There is a good deal of gender stereotyping. Females are more likely to complain about these gender stereotypes because there are more negative female stereotypes compared to male stereotypes. Males are usually portrayed with positive personality characteristics such as competency, leadership, and bravery. As for females, there are two primary stereotypes. If a woman is single, she is often portrayed as a sex object. There is a strong emphasis on the female body being attractive, desirable, and youthful. If a woman is a mother, she is usually portrayed as wise and nurturing. The profile of women on primetime television has not changed much in 50 years (Elasmar, Hasegawa, & Brain, 1999).

Gender stereotyping is also in educational programming. Barner (1999) examined sex role stereotyping within children's educational programming mandated by the Federal Communications Commission (FCC). A content analysis revealed that males had a greater representation than females, and both male and female characters exhibited sex role stereotypical behavior. Also, males were more likely to evoke some consequence for their actions, whereas female actions tended to be ignored altogether.

Occupations

Research has consistently found that the world of work is dominated by male characters and that more women than men cannot be categorized by occupation (Signorielli, 1990; Signorielli & Bacue, 1999; Vande Berg & Streckfuss, 1992). In the 1990s, for example, Signorielli and Bacue (1999) found that 4 of 10 female characters did not work (20.3%) or their occupation was unknown (19.2%). By comparison, fewer than 1 of 4 male characters could not be classified in an occupation (12.4%) or were seen as not working (12.3%). These images may ultimately suggest that working outside of the home is not as important for women as it is for men.

In the world of work, female characters usually have less status than do males, but this does reflect the real world. As Farley (1998) notes, on average, males still make more than females, and male participation (or lack thereof) in household tasks is often related to the discrepancy in earnings between spouses.

Interestingly, marital status is an important predictor of employment for women. Content analyses of programming in the 1970s and 1980s indicated that married women were less likely to be employed outside the home, whereas single women and women who were divorced or widowed were more likely to be portrayed as working outside the home. By comparison, the marital status of male characters did not restrict their employment. Most male characters were portrayed as working, with single men the smallest group of male characters who did not work (Signorielli, 1982, 1990; Signorielli & Kahlenberg, 2001).

Ethnicity also plays a pivotal role in the depiction of occupations on television. Fewer non-Whites than Whites are professionals, but proportionally, more non-Whites have law enforcement jobs. Compared to the U.S. labor force, professionals and law enforcement agents are overrepresented, whereas managerial jobs, laborers, and service workers are underrepresented (Signorielli & Kahlenberg, 2001).

Governmental employees do not fare well in television stereotyping. An analysis of 1,234 primetime series episodes from 1955 to 1998 reveals that governmental employees are often portrayed in negative roles. With politicians, 51% were in negative roles—either as corrupt or scatterbrained (Aversa, 1999).

Families

There have been some changes in the way families are portrayed on television. In a study comparing families in TV situation comedies from the 1950s through the 1980s, Scharrer (2001) found that fathers in the more recent seasons were portrayed as fools compared to fathers in earlier seasons. On domestic comedies, the adult members of families are now more likely to interact more openly, and there is more expression of feelings in spousal relationships (Douglas & Olson, 1995). But the adults are also shown as having more conflicts with children. As a result, the relational environment has become more conflictual and less cohesive in modern TV families than in families from earlier decades. Also, modern families are less able to manage day-to-day life and less able to socialize children effectively (Douglas & Olson, 1996).

Elderly Characters

Older characters are typically not revered or treated with respect in television entertainment. They are typically portrayed as being eccentric, infirm, stubborn, and foolish.

Body Image

A content analysis of three magazines from 1967 to 1997 found that male bodies were portrayed as more lean, muscular, and V-shaped. This fits with the male body image ideal of thin and athletic. "Sociocultural standards of beauty for males emphasize strength and muscularity" (Law & Labre, 2002, p. 697).

Hollywood movies are also a target of critics of the media's obsession with a certain type of body image. Alexandra Kuczynski wrote *Beauty Junkies: Inside Our $15 Billion Obsession With Cosmetic Surgery,* in which she argued that Hollywood has created a standard of beauty that does not exist in nature. "This standard is pert, symmetrical features atop a skinny body with large breasts (also called 'tits on sticks')" (Kantrowitz, 2006, p. 54). She says that Hollywood creates celebrities with perfect bodies and then floods the media with these images, making them the standard to which everyone tries to meet. When people cannot meet this standard, they undergo surgeries or get depressed. Also, Himes and Thompson (2007) conducted a study to examine how overweight characters were presented in movies and television shows. They found that fat characters were typically stigmatized— that is, nonoverweight characters used humor to put down overweight characters often directly to their face. They also found that male characters were three times more likely to engage in fat stigmatization commentary or fat humor than female characters.

CONTROVERSIAL CONTENT ELEMENTS

In the world of media entertainment, everything can be forgiven except dullness. When TV was being criticized for having so much violence, then–CBS president Howard Stringer was arguing against standards to clean up television by saying, "We don't want to turn the vast wasteland into a dull wasteland" (*USA Today,* July 1, 1993, p. 2A). And that is the key—TV and all the entertainment media must avoid being dull.

Recall from an earlier section in this chapter that it is very difficult for producers to apply the story formula in a way to attract and hold audiences. It takes a very talented writer to create a story that is not dull. Less talented writers can rely on three staples to avoid dullness. These are sex, violence, and "bad" language. Each of these three is controversial because if writers and producers go too far, many viewers will complain. Still, producers frequently use these elements to arouse their audiences and keep otherwise uncreative plots and uninteresting characters from appearing dull.

Sex

A large number of people in the American culture are offended by sexual portrayals and nudity on television. The FCC is sensitive to this and acts as a watchdog. For example, the FCC fined CBS $550,000 for the breast-baring incident at the 2004 Super Bowl to placate the large number of people who complained (G. Fabrikant, 2004b). However, producers continually push the line to test the public's tolerance of sexual portrayals.

Frequency

Sexual activity on television has been prevalent since the 1970s (Buerkel-Rothfuss, 1993; Cassata & Skill, 1983). If we limit our definition of sex to visual depictions of intercourse, the rate fluctuates around one (B. S. Greenberg et al., 1993) or two (Fernandez-Collado, Greenberg, Korzenny, & Atkin, 1978) acts per hour of primetime. In soap operas, the rate is even higher.

If we expand the definition to include all visual depictions of sexual activity, such as kissing, petting, homosexuality, prostitution, and rape, the hourly rates go up to about 3 acts on primetime and 3.7 acts per hour on soap operas (B. S. Greenberg et al., 1993). And when the definition is further expanded to include talk about sex as well as sexual imagery, the rate climbs to 16 instances per hour on primetime (Sapolsky & Tabarlet, 1990). Most of this talk about sex is on situation comedies in the early evening, when it is presented in a humorous context.

The most recent major set of studies, conducted from 1997 to 2002, analyzed 2,817 programs across 10 channels and found that about two thirds of all shows (64%) contain some sexual content and 14% have sexual intercourse. Among the 20 top-rated shows among teens, 83% contained sexual portrayals. The overall rate was about three scenes per hour. Two thirds (67%) of all network primetime shows contain either talk about sex or sexual behavior, averaging more than five scenes per hour. And the rates of sexual portrayal continue to increase. Over that 5-year time span, the percentage of shows portraying sexual intercourse doubled from 7% to 14% (Kaiser Family Foundation, 2003; Kunkel, Eyal, & Donnerstein, 2007). However, when we take a longer time span, the opposite pattern is revealed. To illustrate, Hetsroni (2007) conducted a meta-analysis of the findings from content analysis about sexual portrayals on television. After examining the findings derived from 2,588 hours of broadcasts from 18 seasons, Hetsroni concluded that the frequency per hour of most sexual content had decreased over the years. This is particularly notable for dialogues about sex and normative heterosexual conduct, but it is also true for illegal sexual interactions and messages about risks and responsibilities in sexual behavior.

Which conclusion should we believe? Are sexual portrayals increasing or decreasing on television? It appears the best way to answer these questions is to acknowledge that the rates of sexual portrayals change over time and that these changes go in cycles. Across some time periods, there appears to be an increase in portrayals as producers push the line of acceptability, while across other time periods, there appears to be a decrease in portrayals as producers cut back in response to public complaints. The bottom line here is that sexual portrayals will always be a part of media entertainment messages because humans have always been—and will always be—interested in sex.

Consequences

Most depictions of sexual behavior are not presented responsibly from a health point of view. Schrag (1990) reports that American children and teens view an average of more than 14,000 sexual references and innuendos on television each year. Of these, fewer than 150 refer to the use of birth control, so the rate of unprotected sex is very high, yet there is a very low incidence of sexually transmitted diseases (STDs) or pregnancies depicted in these stories. This situation may be changing. For example, by the 1997–1998 television season, about 9% of shows dealing with sex presented safe-sex messages, and this had increased to 15% of shows in the 2001–2002 television season (Kaiser Family Foundation, 2003). Although sexual portrayals are improving in their depiction of safe practices, fewer than one in every six shows that present sexual content will have any mention of the possible risks or responsibilities of sexual activity or any reference to contraception, protection, or safer sex. Kunkel et al. (2007) found that topics related to sexual risks or responsibilities (e.g., condom use, abstinence) are increasingly included on television but nonetheless remain infrequent overall. Such safe-sex messages occur most frequently in program environments where they are most relevant (i.e., when sexual intercourse is included in the story).

Homosexuality

The U.S. television industry has a long history of ignoring, stereotyping, and marginalizing homosexuality (Harrington, 2003). Gay and lesbian issues or characters were virtually invisible on television in the 1950s and early 1960s. Then, in the 1970s, gay characters began to appear, but they were limited to two treatments. One treatment was the coming-out story, and the other was the "queer monster" story. Furthermore, although the 1970s ushered in primetime shows about gay characters, they were typically played by straight actors and marketed to a straight audience.

In the 1980s, depictions of homosexuality declined dramatically due to the conservatism of the Reagan years and the growing concern about HIV/AIDS (and its association with gay male sexuality) (Gross, 2001). Gay characters began to appear in greater frequency throughout the 1990s in part due to a growing stigma attached to antigay prejudice and a growing recognition of a gay consumer market (Gross, 2001). By the late 1990s, about 50 network series had lesbian, gay, or bisexual recurring characters, more than twice the total of all previous decades of television. In 1997, primetime viewers witnessed the first lesbian lead actress/character on network television, which was the comedienne Ellen DeGeneres, who played Ellen Morgan on ABC's *Ellen*. The following year, NBC featured the first network gay male lead in its hit show *Will*

& Grace. During the fall 1999 television season, the big four television networks premiered 26 new series. There were 17 gay characters on the four major networks—about the same number of Black, Asian, and Latino characters combined. A big reason for this is that there are many gays in Hollywood and not many minorities (Brownfield, 1999).

In many respects, the 1990s seemed to transcend the longstanding "rules" for representing homosexuality on television: (a) Gay or lesbian characters must be restricted to one-time appearances in television series or one-shot television movies; (b) gay and lesbian characters can never be "incidentally" gay—instead, their sexuality must be the "problem" to be "solved"; (c) their problem should be explored in terms of its effects on heterosexuals; and (d) gay and lesbian erotic desire must be completely absent (Dow, 2001, pp. 129–130; see also Gross, 2001).

Although there are more representations of homosexuality than ever before, scholars caution against the presumption that these are necessarily more progressive representations.

As throughout television history, gays and lesbians are still more likely to appear in comedies than in dramas, where the line between "laughing with" and "laughing at" remains strategically ambiguous. Also, gay and lesbian characters are still typically portrayed by straight (or not "out") actors and marketed to straight audiences (Battles & Hilton-Morrow, 2002; Dow, 2001; Gross, 2001).

The most recent analysis of sexual portrayals on television programs found portrayals of nonheterosexuals in about 15% of programs overall. Of 14 genres, only movies and variety/comedy shows had substantial percentages of programs that contained nonheterosexual content. Programs on commercial broadcast networks were less likely to have nonheterosexual content than those on cable networks, especially those on premium cable movie networks (Fisher, Hill, Grube, & Gruber, 2007). Also, in his meta-analysis of the findings from content analysis about sexual portrayals on television over 18 seasons, Hetsroni (2007) reports that the frequency of portrayals of homosexuality has increased considerably.

Violence

Violence was the most studied form of content in all of the mass media, from the advent of television as a mass medium around 1950 to the turn of the century. Scholars continually monitored the amount of violence on television, producing at least 60 major content analyses (see W. J. Potter, 1999), and then interest waned.

Depending on the definition used, violence has been found in 57% to 80% of all entertainment programs (Columbia Broadcasting System, 1980; Greenberg, Edison, Korzenny, Fernandez-Collado, & Atkin, 1980; Lichter & Lichter, 1983; "NCTV Says," 1983; W. J. Potter & Ware, 1987; Schramm, Lyle, & Parker, 1961; Signorielli, 1990; Smythe, 1954; Williams, Zabrack, & Joy, 1982).

The most consistent examination of television violence has been conducted by Gerbner and his associates (e.g., see Gerbner, Gross, Morgan, & Signorielli, 1980). Since the late 1960s, they have documented the frequency of violent acts that fit the definition: the overt expression of physical force (with or without a weapon) against self or other, compelling action against one's will on pain of being hurt or killed, or actually hurting or killing. Signorielli (1990) reports that from 1967 to 1985, the hourly rate fluctuated from about four to seven violent acts, with peaks occurring about every 4 years.

The most comprehensive analysis of violence on television has been conducted with the National Television Violence Study (NTVS, 1996), which analyzed the content of a total of 3,185 programs across 23 television channels for all day parts from 6 a.m. to 11 p.m., 7 days a week, over the course of a television season. NTVS researchers report that 57% of all programs analyzed had some violence and that one third of programs presented nine or more violent interactions.

The numbers in the above paragraphs are limited to physical forms of violence and do not include verbal violence. Verbal violence is even more prevalent on television than is physical violence. For example, Williams et al. (1982) reported finding a rate of 9.5 acts of verbal violence as well as 9 acts of physical violence per hour on North American (United States and Canada) television. W. J. Potter and Ware (1987) found about 8 acts per hour of physical violence and an additional 12 acts of verbal violence on American television. Also, B. S. Greenberg and his colleagues (1980) reported that an average primetime hour of television contains 22 acts of verbal aggression and 12 acts of physical aggression. In a comparison of rates of violence on television from the mid-1970s to the mid-1990s, W. J. Potter and Vaughan (1997) found that the rates of physical violence remained stable but that the rates of verbal violence had increased dramatically. They reasoned that programmers were wary of increasing physical violence because such an increase would trigger a public outcry, but the substantial increase in verbal violence was tolerated by the public, so the increase continued.

There have also been some scientific studies of the amount of violence in films. For example, the top-grossing 50 films of 1998 contained a total of 2,300 acts of violence, according to the Center for Media and Public Affairs, based in Washington, D.C. "Violence was not only a staple of popular entertainment, it was often portrayed as laudable, necessary or relatively harmless activity," said S. Robert Lichter, the center's president (Goldstein, 1999, p. B1). In another analysis of violent films, Sapolsky, Molitor, and Luque (2003) content analyzed popular slasher films in the 1990s and found more acts of violence in them than in similar films from the 1980s. One change was that recent slasher films rarely mixed scenes of sex and violence. The researchers also posed the question about whether females were more victimized than males and concluded that in all slasher films, there were more male victims than there were female victims. But they did not stop with this conclusion; they also found that the ratio of female victims was higher in slasher films than in commercially successful action/adventure films of the 1990s. This means that when a female is shown in a slasher film, she has a greater chance of being victimized. Also, females are shown in fear longer than males.

Movie previews also present a high degree of violence. In one study of video rentals, it was found that the majority of previews on rental tapes contained violence, and these portrayals were common across MPAA ratings (G/PG, PG-13, and R) (Oliver & Kalyanaraman, 2002). Rates of aggression in previews were positively associated with increased marketing and distribution costs for the previewed films.

Violence on television has been examined not only for its frequency but also for its context—that is, the way it is presented. For example, W. J. Potter and Ware (1987) found that with much of the violence, the perpetrator is rewarded and the victims are rarely shown with much pain and suffering. This was also the case in the NTVS studies, where violent acts were rarely punished, and rarely were victims shown as suffering any harmful consequences. Also, 37% of the perpetrators of violence were portrayed as being attractive, and 44% of the acts were shown as being justified. These patterns led the researchers to conclude that violence not only was prevalent throughout the entire television landscape but was also typically shown as sanitized and glamorized (see W. J. Potter & Smith, 2000).

This level of violence in the media is far higher than the real-world levels of violence and crime. This was demonstrated by Oliver (1994), who analyzed pseudo-reality-based police shows, such as *COPS*. She found that the Federal Bureau of Investigation (FBI) figures for murder, rape, robbery, and aggregated assault were 13.2% of all crimes, but in the television world, these four violent crimes accounted for 87% of all crimes. Also, the FBI reports that 18.0% of crimes are cleared, but on television, 61.5% are cleared—that is, the perpetrator is arrested, is killed, or commits suicide. Again, television focuses on the most arousing crimes rather than the dull ones. Also, there is a more satisfying resolution to crimes than there is in the real world.

Language

It appears as if "bad" language has broken the barrier on television and is here to stay. For example, Kaye and Sapolsky (2001) examined primetime network programs to ascertain whether usage of offensive language increased throughout the 1990s when a content-based rating system was implemented. The per-hour rate of objectionable words increased between 1990 and 1994 but decreased in 1997 to a level slightly below that found in 1990. Although the FCC deemed the "seven dirty words" as too offensive for television, five of these words had made their way onto the primetime airwaves.

People continue to complain about bad language on television, and the FCC monitors television programs to determine whether they are obscene. In making their determination, the FCC takes context into consideration. For example, many people complained about indecency in the movie *Saving Private Ryan*, but the FCC ruled that it did not contain indecency, although there was considerable profanity and violence. The FCC reasoned that the language was appropriate for soldiers fighting in a war ("FCC Finds No Indecency," 2005).

In addition to obscenity, bad language also includes racial and gender slurs. In the spring of 2007, radio shock jock Don Imus referred to the Rutgers University women's basketball team as "nappy headed ho's" in an offhanded comment during one of his radio broadcasts. Many listeners were greatly offended and criticized his language. This triggered the attention of the media, which made it a prominent controversial story. African American and feminist leaders harshly criticized Imus's comments. Although Imus met with Rutgers officials and formally apologized, and even though his apology was accepted by the members of the women's basketball team, Imus was fired from his job. Imus had found that after three decades as a popular shock jock where he insulted a wide range of politicians and public figures, his language in this instance had crossed a line where the consequences were severe and immediate.

HEALTH

The television world is a generally healthy one when we look at patterns across all kinds of shows. While some of this pattern of health portrayals is very responsible in presenting healthy messages to viewers, other parts of this pattern are deceptive—that is, some portrayals present a very misleading message about health.

Deceptive Health Patterns

Although there are many indicators of deceptive health, I'll present only five in this section. First, although most characters are not shown having particularly healthy habits (eating responsibly, regularly exercising, and getting medical checkups to prevent illnesses), most characters appear healthy, fit, and thin. It has been estimated that 64.5% of the American population is overweight or obese (American Obesity Association, 2004), but on television, only 6% of the males and 2% of the females are. Furthermore, characters do not gain weight from their high-calorie diets, although eating and drinking are frequent activities on entertainment programs. About 75% of all shows display this activity, but the eating is usually unhealthy. The traditional meals of breakfast, lunch, and dinner combined account for only about half of the eating; snacking accounts for the rest. Fruit is the snack in only 4% to 5% of the episodes.

Second, although there is a high degree of violence on many shows, few characters are portrayed as suffering any harm. In fact, most characters are portrayed as being healthy and active. Only 6% to 7% of major characters are portrayed as having had injuries or illnesses that require treatment. Pain, suffering, or medical help rarely follows violent activity. In children's programs, despite greater mayhem, only 3% of characters are shown receiving medical treatment. Primetime characters are not only healthy but also relatively safe from accidents, even though they rarely wear seat belts when they drive. And they are rarely portrayed as suffering from impairments of any kinds as a result of an accident.

A third indicator of deceptive health is that the everyday normal health maladies are rarely shown. Most health problems that are portrayed are serious and life threatening. When help for medical problems is portrayed, it is not in a preventative or therapeutic manner but in a dramatic and social way. Hardly anyone dies a natural death on television.

Primetime characters are not shown with any kind of physical impairments. Rarely does a character even wear glasses; even in old age, only one out of four characters wears them. Only 2% of characters on primetime shows are physically disabled. When they do appear, they tend to be older, less positively presented, and more likely to be victimized. Almost none appear on children's shows.

Fourth, mental health is portrayed in a dangerously stereotypical manner. In real life, mentally ill people are usually passive and withdrawn, frightened, and avoidant. But on television, mentally ill characters were found to be 10 times more likely to be a violent criminal than non–mentally ill television characters (Diefenbach & West, 2007). In television stories, mentally ill characters are typically shown to be active, confused, aggressive, dangerous, and unpredictable.

Fifth, doctors are greatly overrepresented on television compared to their numbers in real life. Health care professionals dominate the ranks of professionals, despite the paucity of sick characters on television. They are five times their numbers in real life proportionally. Only criminals or law enforcers are more numerous. Also, many of these doctors are shown making house calls and devoting far more time to individual patients than real-life doctors are able to do.

Responsible Health Patterns

The depiction of alcohol, tobacco, and illegal drug use has dramatically declined over the years. Smoking was a frequent activity until the mid-1980s, until it almost completely disappeared except for reruns of old movies.

Alcohol use has also substantially declined. When it is presented now, it is frequently shown with negative consequences. Until the mid-1980s, alcohol consumption was common on television. Drinking alcohol was shown twice as often as drinking coffee and tea, 14 times that of soft drinks, and 15 times that of water. It was shown as sociable, happy, and problem free. Also, alcohol use was rarely portrayed with any negative consequences. When negative consequences were shown, they were usually very slight, such as a temporary hangover. Despite high rates of consumption across many characters, only 1% of television drinkers are portrayed as having a drinking problem.

Although television is showing more responsible portrayals of drug and alcohol use, the movies do not fare so well. An analysis of the 200 most popular movies of 1996 and 1997 reveals that characters frequently abuse drugs and alcohol. Moreover, these characters are not portrayed as worrying about the consequences (Hartman, 1999).

VALUES

Examining the arts within a culture is a way to determine the values of that culture. For example, the ancient Greek and Roman cultures exhibited the values of perfection, harmony, and beauty in their art. During the European Middle Ages, the art reflected the dominance of the Catholic Church, with its focus on the life of Christ, especially his birth, miracles, crucifixion, and resurrection. Earthly existence was mundane and painful, whereas the afterlife was glorious. During the Renaissance, the art reflected the values of a scientific approach to understanding the world. During the European Romantic era, the focus shifted from the logical and intellectual concerns that were dominant during the Renaissance to the emotions of humans. During the Modern era, the arts were decoupled from the church and political institutions. Art glorified the individual and his or her unique way of looking at the world and constructing meaning (Metallinos, 1996).

Today, we can examine the broad span of messages from the mass media and ask, "What do our stories tell us about our current culture?" Some researchers and social critics have attempted to answer this question. Table 11.4 shows what two media scholars have observed to be the themes in television entertainment. Notice that the first of Comstock's (1989) themes deals with material consumption. Comstock is not referring to the ads in the stories but to the values in the stories themselves. He says, "It is not solely that so many stories revolve around the rich, but that in so many instances dwellings and their furnishings are beyond the means of those portrayed as occupying them" (p. 172). For example, the popular situation comedy *Friends* featured Monica, a part-time cook, and Rachel, a waitress in a coffeehouse, who are shown supporting themselves in a well-furnished two-bedroom apartment in downtown Manhattan.

Notice also how the lists of Comstock (1989) and Walsh (1994) overlap. For example, Walsh is also concerned with the value of materialism, which he argues is at odds with a healthy society. Walsh also argues that the values of the marketplace are as follows: Happiness equals wealth, instant gratification, and me first. In contrast, the values of a healthy society are the following: self-esteem comes from within, moderation, tolerance, understanding, and social responsibility.

In complaining about the direction of programming on TV aimed at young people, *U.S. News & World Report* columnist John Leo (1999) said, "These shows are also carriers of heavy cultural messages, the most obvious being that parents are fools. In the teen soap

TABLE 11.4   Values Underlying Entertainment Messages

Comstock's (1989) List

1. Material consumption is very satisfying.

2. The world is a mean and risky place. There is a great deal of crime and violence throughout the television world.

3. The TV world has turned the social pyramid upside down by showing most characters as wealthy and powerful and very few of them as working class.

4. Males are more powerful than females in terms of income, job status, and decision making. This is slowly changing, but we are still far from a balance of power.

5. Occupational status is highly valued. Professional occupations are depicted as worthwhile, whereas manual work is uninteresting. People attain the status of a worthwhile profession through upward mobility from the middle class. This upward mobility is accomplished through self-confidence and toughness; goodness of character alone is not enough. The movement upward is usually quick and painless.

6. There are a few privileged professions in which the people are almost always shown as doing good and helping others. However, most businesspeople are shady. Businesses are frequently portrayed as taking advantage of the gullible public and abusing their power.

7. Law enforcers are overrepresented as being successful, strong, and justified. Private eyes are almost always shown as better than the police.

8. There is a belief in the occult, life on other planets, life after death, and hidden, malevolent purposes behind the inexplicable.

9. A person's self-interest is very important. People are motivated to get what they want regardless of the feelings of others. Examples include extramarital affairs, crime, hard-driving businesspeople, and police who disregard the rights of others to achieve their goals.

10. There are often truly heroic acts portrayed where there are daring rescues, selflessness, loyalty to others, and the struggle against difficult odds to do the right thing.

Walsh's (1994) List

1. Happiness is found in having things.

2. Get all you can for yourself.

3. Get it all as quickly as you can.

4. Win at all costs.

5. Violence is entertaining.

6. Always seek pleasure and avoid boredom.

operas, parents are absent, stupid, irrelevant, zanily adulterous, on the lam, or in jail. The unmistakable message is that kids are on their own, with no need to listen to parents, who know little or nothing anyway. This helps the TV industry certify teenagers as an autonomous culture with its own set of ethics and consumption patterns" (p. 15).

Young people are a very important target for many Hollywood films, and a particular kind of film is believed to be the best draw for them. For example, in a profile of a literary manager, Warren Zide, *L.A. Times* reporter Claudia Eller (1999) examines the values operating in Hollywood. She said, "When it came to getting the script for *American Pie* in shape to be sold, Zide said he and his colleagues advised [the writer] 'to write the raunchiest script possible without worrying about the rating.' Apparently it was good advice. The

R-rated comedy about four high-school buddies who make a pact to lose their virginity before graduation piqued the interest of several studios before it was sold to Universal Pictures for $650,000" (p. C5). Eller also quotes Zide on his reaction to a script about teenagers on a spring break: "I hated when I was growing up and you go to see some R-rated movie and there's no nudity in it, and you're like, 'Oh, man, I was gypped.'" So, now as a literary agent, Zide asks, "Do we have enough T&A in it?" (p. C5).

CONTENT ANALYSIS METHOD

Many of the facts about content patterns reported in this chapter were generated by media researchers using a method known as content analysis. Content analysis is a scientific technique of counting occurrences of various things, such as the gender of characters, that relies on analyzing samples that are representative of the total population. For example, when researchers analyze entertainment programming for the prevalence of male and female characters, they do not analyze all television programming; instead, they take a sample of entertainment programs and analyze the gender of characters in only those programs in their sample and then generalize their findings to all entertainment programming, which is their population of interest. Therefore, in order for this generalizing to be meaningful, the samples that researchers use must be representative of the population.

Deriving representative samples of television programming in the past has been relatively easy because there were few channels, but with the growth of cable channels in the 1980s and now with the easy availability of so many video platforms (such as Hulu and YouTube), the population of video offerings is so large and varied, it has become enormously difficult to derive a representative sample. Therefore, the use of content analysis to document broad patterns of character portrayals across the television landscape has been dwindling in the past decade and will likely continue to dwindle as television entertainment fragments into a wide variety of platforms, each with its own patterns of characters and types of stories. Content analysis will continue to have value as a research method in documenting patterns of entertainment content, but its value will be limited to smaller and more specialized segments of the overall media environment. For example, it will be more rare to see content analyses that document the gender or economic status of all characters in the television world. However, content analysis will retain its value as a useful research technique for recording the frequency of different types of program elements within limited segments of media entertainment, such as the gender and age of standup comedians on Comedy Central, sexual portrayals in music videos on MTV, or utterances of "bad" language in primetime situation comedies.

BECOMING MEDIA LITERATE WITH ENTERTAINMENT MESSAGES

Recall from the previous chapter that media messages contain many elements to make them appear like the real world, but those messages must also contain elements that remove them from the mundane real world. In this chapter, you have seen how the entertainment messages depart from the real world when it comes to character portrayals, controversial content, health, and values. The more you know about these discrepancies, the more you can separate your media-world knowledge from your real-world knowledge and thus prevent the media-world distortions to influence your expectations for the real world.

Television and film ignore things that are not visually interesting, such as thinking by ourselves, reading, walking, and other quiet activities that make up much of our lives. Activities such as housework, running errands, and small talk with neighbors are vastly underrepresented. Instead of ennobling our ordinary experiences, television suggests that they are not of sufficient interest to document.

Producers, however, are under no obligation to present an accurate account of the mundane world. Their task is to build as large an audience as possible. To do this, they must rely on all their creative powers to achieve a dramatic effect, so they deliberately distort the world to surprise and startle us. Some creative people produce fantasy that, by definition, is totally unlike real life—they do this to allow us to escape our lives and to see imaginative occurrences. Other producers who try to capture real life must do so in an intriguing manner. That is, they avoid presenting the mundane mainstream of real life and instead highlight the occurrences at the margins where there are particularly interesting people or events. This is real life in the sense that it could happen or even did happen. For example, family dramas appear to be very realistic in their settings, characters, and types of problems encountered. But they are unrealistic in their pacing, with most problems solved in 60 minutes.

The purpose of storytellers who use the mass media is simply to tell a good story so as to attract people and keep them coming back. The writers are not psychologists or sociologists; they are not usually trying to tell us much about how the human mind works or about how society works, but they still do present us with elements that we use to generalize our own conclusions about how the human mind works and how society works.

The danger to us as viewers of these stories is that we gradually absorb the individual fantasy elements. Over time, we start to confuse the "one-step remove" elements from the more realistic elements. Eventually, we come to believe that the patterns of fantasy that we continually see in media stories should be how we live our real lives.

The way to deal with the unrealistic picture presented by television entertainment is *not* to pressure producers to make their world of fiction more realistic. That would be silly. Instead, the best way to deal with this situation is to educate yourself about the content patterns in the media world and to become more sensitive, recognizing where those patterns diverge from real-world patterns. Learn to appreciate the divergences as fantasy and limit yourself to being entertained by their unreality. And avoid being guided by unrealistic expectations based on what media characters look like and how they act.

Now that you have more information about patterns of characters, plots, and values of entertainment stories in the media, you have a stronger knowledge structure about media content. When you use this knowledge structure to guide yourself through your exposures to media stories in the future, you will be able to see much more in those messages. Table 11.5 shows the cognitive, emotional, aesthetic, and moral skills you will need to do this in a conscious, active manner. But do not restrict yourself to the specifics in Table 11.5; instead, use the information presented there to stimulate your thinking about other skills and knowledge. Then, during your exposures to media entertainment, recall the knowledge you will need and consciously apply the skills in all four domains.

During exposure to the media, remember that entertainment messages follow a formula. The people who create this world must be creative within a rigid formula. Viewers want formulaic characters and plots so that the entertainment messages are easy to follow. Look at how closely stories follow formulas. Also, notice how stories deviate from a formula and try to assess the magnitude of those deviations. How much can a story deviate before you become confused and lose sense of what is happening? Look at the stories that are most popular, that is, highest-rated television programs and movies with the largest box office.

TABLE 11.5	Types of Skills and Knowledge Structures Needed to Deal With Entertainment Messages in a Media-Literate Manner	
	Skills	*Knowledge*
Cognitive	Ability to analyze entertainment content to identify key plot points, types of characters, and themes	Knowledge of elements in entertainment formula
	Ability to see entertainment formulas	
	Ability to compare/contrast plot points, characters, and themes across vehicles and media	
Emotional	Ability to analyze the portrayed feelings of characters	
	Ability to put one's self into the position of different characters in the story	Recall from personal experiences how it would feel to be in the situation depicted in the story
	Ability to control emotions elicited by the plot and themes	
Aesthetic	Ability to analyze the craft and artistic elements in the story	Knowledge of writing, directing, acting, editing, sound mixing, and so on
	Ability to compare and contrast the artistry used to tell this story with that used to tell other stories	Knowledge of good and bad stories and the elements that contributed to those qualities
Moral	Ability to analyze the moral elements as evidenced by decisions made by characters, implications of those decisions revealed by the plot, and underlying theme	Knowledge of what moral systems say about different decisions as well as knowledge of the moral implications of your decisions
	Ability to compare and contrast ethical decisions presented in this story with other stories	Knowledge of other stories that have portrayed this topic, both good and bad
	Ability to evaluate the ethical responsibilities of the producers and programmers	Knowledge of values of people in the media industries

How closely do they follow a formula? Examine the actors and actresses in those popular stories. What do they do that would make them so popular?

Keep asking questions about these stories. Be skeptical. Take nothing for granted. If you stay active during your exposures, you will be increasing your media literacy and thus gain more control over setting expectations for life that are both realistic and special to you.

> **Chapter Resources:** To test your knowledge and learn more about the topics discussed in this chapter, visit the Student Study Site at www.sagepub.com/potter6e.

FURTHER READING

Cantor, M. G. (1980). *Prime-time television*. Beverly Hills, CA: Sage. (143 pages, including index)

Written by a sociologist who spent 10 years interviewing actors, writers, and producers, this book explains how decisions about content are made in the television industry. She develops a model to show that many forces shape the development of any television program. The examples in the book are dated, but the principles still apply.

Medved, M. (1992). *Hollywood vs. America: Popular culture and the war on traditional values*. New York: HarperCollins.

This film critic argues that Hollywood has a value system that is very different from that of mainstream America. Hollywood glorifies the perverse, ridicules all forms of mainstream religion, tears down the image of the family, and glorifies ugliness with violence, bad language, and America bashing. Then the industry is puzzled why attendance is dropping and criticism is increasing.

Metallinos, N. (1996). *Television aesthetics: Perceptual, cognitive, and compositional bases*. Mahwah, NJ: Lawrence Erlbaum. (305 pages with index)

This book lays out many principles of aesthetics from both a social science as well as an artistic perspective. He demonstrates that humans are bound by their perceptual capabilities and the functioning processes of their brains. However, people also create culture through their art. A person who is visually literate needs to have information in the areas of perception, cognition, and artistic composition.

Postman, N. (1984). *Amusing ourselves to death: Public discourse in the age of show business*. New York: Penguin. (184 pages with index)

This is a strong, well-written argument about how the media, especially television, have conditioned us to expect entertainment. Because our perceptions of ideas are shaped by the form of their expression, we are now image oriented. We respond to pleasure, not thought and reflection.

Sayre, S., & King, C. (2003). *Entertainment & society: Audiences, trends, and impacts*. Thousand Oaks, CA: Sage. (422 pages, including end notes and index)

This book spans the entire gamut of media-provided entertainment in 16 chapters. It provides some history of thinking about entertainment, a theory of entertainment content and effects, conceptions of audiences, medium comparisons, and even predictions for the future of entertainment.

KEEPING UP TO DATE

Critical Studies in Media Communication, Discourse & Society, Film Quarterly, and *Sight & Sound*

These journals publish scholarship from a humanistic perspective and therefore provide analyses of media content, especially film and television, from a cultural or critical perspective.

Journal of Broadcasting & Electronic Media and *Journalism & Mass Communication Quarterly*

These scholarly journals publish research studies that examine entertainment-type messages in the mass media, particularly television, primarily using scientific-type methods, such as content analysis. The reported findings typically focus attention on broad patterns.

EXERCISE 11.1

Practicing Media Literacy Skills on Entertainment Programming

Watch a television program, then think about the following tasks:

1. *Analysis:* Break down the program by

    a. Listing the main characters

    b. Listing the main plot points

    c. Were there violent elements? If so, list them.

    d. Were there sexual elements? Is so, list them.

    e. Were their health-related elements? If so, list them.

2. *Grouping:* Select the two main characters.

    a. How are they the same/different demographically?

    b. How are they the same/different by personality characteristics?

    c. How are they the same/different in the way they move the plot forward?

3. *Evaluation:* Think about all the characters and make the following judgments.

    a. In your judgment, which character was the most humorous? Why?

    b. In your judgment, which character was the most ethical in his or her behavior? Why?

    c. In your judgment, which actor or actress displayed the best acting skills? Why?

d. In your judgment, which of the plot points were the strongest? Which were the weakest?

e. In your judgment, what is the theme of this show?

4. *Abstracting:* Describe your show (characters and plot) in 50 words or less.

5. *Generalizing:* Start with particular characters and particular happenings in your show, then infer general patterns of people and events in general.

a. Think about the demographics of the characters in your show. Do those demographics in your show match the patterns of demographics in the real world?

b. Think about the plot elements (sex, violence, health) in your show. Do these elements in your show match the patterns of these elements in the real world?

6. *Appreciating*

a. Emotional: Was the show able to evoke emotions in you? If so, list those emotions and explain how the show triggered those particular emotions.

b. Aesthetic: Is there something about the writing, directing, editing, lighting, set design, costuming, or music/sound effects that you found of particular high quality? If so, explain what led you to appreciate that element so much.

c. Moral: Did the show raise ethical considerations (either explicitly or implicitly)? If so, did you appreciate how the show dealt with those ethical considerations?

EXERCISE 11.2

Analyzing the Content of Television Entertainment

1. Write a definition for sexual behavior. This is not as easy as it might seem. You must consider issues such as the following: What must the characters do, what are their intentions (a kiss or a hug is not always sexual), and what do they talk about (if a character talks about what he or she wants to do, does that count)?

2. Watch two different situation comedies and count how many acts occur that meet your definition. Note the gender, age, and ethnic background of the characters.

3. Discuss your results with others in class who did their own content analyses of sex.

   a. What is the range in the numbers of acts found? Can this range be attributed to differences in definitions or differences in shows?

   b. Profile the types of characters who were most often involved in sexual activity.

   c. Are there any noticeable differences in character profiles across types of situation comedies?

4. Now try using your definition to analyze the content on soap operas, music videos, and action/adventure dramas.

   a. Do you see any big differences in the number of sexual acts across different types of shows?

   b. Do you see any big differences in the profiles of characters involved in sexual activity across shows?

5. Now think about how sex is portrayed in the television world.

   a. What types of activity are the most prevalent?

   b. How responsibly is sex portrayed in the television world—that is, are the physical and emotional risks often discussed or considered? Is sex portrayed as a normal part of a loving, stable relationship, or is it portrayed more as a game of conquest or a source of silliness?

   c. Did you find anything in the patterns that surprised you?

6. What do you need to know about how sex is portrayed in the media and the role of sex in the real world for you to construct a strong knowledge structure on this subject?

Advertising

Key Idea: We live in a culture saturated with advertising messages. Some popular criticisms of advertising form the public discourse, but the issues that should concern us more lie at a deeper level.

"I hate ads. They are so annoying the way they interrupt TV shows, and all those pop-ups and banner ads on websites. I refuse to pay attention to any of them. I don't contribute much to advertisers. They must hate me."

"Not necessarily. Do you buy advertised products?"

"Like what?"

"Like when you go to the grocery store, you probably buy cereals, snacks, toothpaste. Do you buy well-known brands or the generic house brands?"

"I buy the well-known brands, but not because they are well known or because they are so heavily advertised."

"Then why do you buy them?"

"They have higher quality."

"How do you know that?"

"Everybody knows that."

"If you read the labels carefully, you would see that the ingredients in the house brands are identical to the advertised brands. Also, the same governmental regulations that apply to advertised brands also apply to house brands, so house brands do not have impurities or harmful ingredients. And the house brands are almost always made in the same manufacturing plants as make the advertised brands. Yet you pay a lot more for the advertised brands, because you are not just buying the product. You are also buying the advertising."

"I still think the well-known brands are better."

"Then I think that advertisers must love you!"

Let's begin with the question: What are the products of advertising? Some of you might interpret this to mean the things we buy in stores—cars, clothes, soft drinks, hamburgers, and so on. Others might think that the products are the ads we see—after all, that is what the people in the industry create and show to us constantly. While both of these interpretations have some truth to them on the surface, both miss the point of the real nature of advertising. The most important product of advertising is *you*.

Advertisers have trained you and all members of the public to give them your time, attention, and money. Advertisers have spent hundreds of billions of dollars over your lifetime to craft special messages that have put hundreds of thousands of images, jingles, ideas, and desires into your memory banks. They have done this with your permission and even your blessing. And they have even convinced you to pay them for conditioning you.

ADVERTISING IS PERVASIVE

Our country is saturated with advertising. With about 8% of the world's population, the United States absorbs almost half of the world's advertising expenditures. We are literally surrounded by ads constantly (see Table 12.1). Estimates range from 247 to more than 5,000 for the number of ads the average person is exposed to per day ("American Advertising," 2011). Even if we take the low end of this range, that is more than 15 ad exposures for every waking hour each day.

Each year, the amount of money spent on advertising grows dramatically. In 1900, about $500 million was spent on all forms of advertising in the United States. By 1940, it was $2 billion, so it took 40 years to multiply four times. In 1980, it was $60 billion, or a growth of 30 times in those 40 years. By 2010, it had grown to more than $260 billion per year. These numbers are so large that they are difficult to comprehend. Let's break down the expenditures by number of people in the population. In 1940, the industry spent $16 on each person in this country; by 1980, it was $260; and now it is more than $1,160 per person per year.

An advertiser who wants to introduce a new product and break through the existing clutter to get consumers to realize that there is a new product on the market must spend about a $50-million minimum to introduce a new product in grocery or drug stores nationally. Of course, the new advertisements add to the clutter, making it even more expensive for the next product introduction. All of this behavior serves to increase the clutter exponentially. And we are still in a growth cycle.

Why can we expect continued growth? Because we—the public—do not mind all this advertising. Of course, we sometimes criticize certain ads that we don't like, and sometimes we get upset when we watch television and have our shows repeatedly interrupted by commercial breaks. However, few Americans have a negative attitude about advertising. About 45% say they have a generally favorable attitude toward advertising, whereas only 15% have an unfavorable attitude. The rest are neutral. Thus, advertisers have done a good job conditioning us to accept the flood of advertising messages with few complaints.

Our criticisms are minor compared to our unthinking support of advertising. By "unthinking" support, I mean that most of us do not realize how much advertising exposure we experience every day and how it has shaped our attitudes and behaviors. We accept the saturation, and we allow our behavior to be shaped by it. I'll present two examples of this point to help you understand how much you have been influenced by advertising.

The first example deals with how much money we spend on advertised products when we have a choice of buying brands that are unadvertised and sell for much less money. For example, J. P. Jones (2004) points out that Cheerios, which is the leading brand in cold cereals, has a unit price of $5.10 per pound, but most stores sell a very similar cereal as a house brand for about $2.66 per pound. "The taste of the store brand is quite satisfactory, although most people would slightly prefer the taste of Cheerios. But Cheerios is 92 percent

TABLE 12.1　Pervasiveness of Advertising in America

Newspapers

- Sixty percent of the typical newspaper is advertising. Newspapers are now primarily vehicles for ads more so than for news. For example, the *New York Times* Sunday edition contains 350 pages of ads.
- Despite the growth in the size of most newspapers, the space given to the news (the news hole) has remained the same. Newspapers have given about the same amount of space to news content since 1910, but because the overall size of newspapers doubled during that time, the percentage of the newspaper that contains news has shrunk by half.

Film

- Movie theaters bombard viewers with ads. A series of ads is projected on their screens while the audience waits for the show to begin. When the film begins, there are usually ads for the theater's concession stand. The ticket a person buys usually has an ad on it.
- Films themselves are full of ads in the form of paid product placements. There are more than 30 companies operating in Hollywood to place products within movies and TV shows. Over the years, Ford, Apple, and Coca-Cola have each paid for product placement in more than 100 top-grossing films. Some films, like *Just Go With It,* which was released in the winter of 2011, contain more than 50 examples of paid product placement (Brand Channel, 2011).

Radio

- For years, the industry standard for maximum number of ad minutes per hour has been 18, but this is not a legally imposed limit but rather a guideline. Many radio stations exceed this guideline of up to 40 minutes of ads per hour during particular times of the day.

Television

- The percentage of programming on television given to commercial messages has been increasing over the years. By 2009, it had climbed to 41% during primetime, with unscripted reality programming having the highest percentage of ads at 49% (MC Marketing Charts, 2009).
- TV advertising is now in airports, in elevators in high-end hotels, and in doctors' waiting rooms—all beaming messages to captive audiences (Croteau & Hoynes, 2001).

Books

- Advertisers are paying for product placement in novels. Cover Girl cosmetics got writer Sean Stewart to mention a particular kind of makeup in his novel about adolescent girls, and the publisher increased the book run from 30,000 to 100,000 copies based on the promotional strength of the deal (Smiley, 2006).

Computers

- The Internet Advertising Bureau says that in 1998, advertising on the Internet was less than $2 billion. This figure continues to grow dramatically each year. By 2011, the figure had grown to over $29 billion (Internet Advertising Bureau, 2011).

Nonmedia

- Ads are on the sides of buildings, on taxis and buses, and even on the clothing of people walking the streets.
- There are now talking billboards that are fitted with a low-power radio transmitter that tells motorists where to tune for more information on the product advertised on the billboard (Horowitz, 1996).
- Ads have even moved into public toilets. Chicago's United Center sports arena charges advertisers $1,000 a year for an 8-by-11-inch space on its bathroom walls.
- Ads have been appearing on police cars in Oxnard, California, where the city council approved a money-raising plan to sell advertising space on police cruisers ("Police Cars," 1995).

- Pepsi-Cola has produced the first TV commercial in space by paying Russia to have its cosmonauts aboard its space station, *Mir,* deploying a can of Pepsi into space (Horowitz, 1996). PepsiCo, owner of Pizza Hut, has also sponsored the Russian space program in another way. In November 1999, the Russians launched a Proton rocket that had a 30-foot logo of Pizza Hut painted on it.
- Sporting events are themselves vehicles for ads.
- Ads are in public schools. Whittle Communications gives to all participating public schools the equipment needed to receive satellite programming and provides them with a 12-minute news program daily. Inserted in those programs are 2 minutes of ads paid for by companies interested in getting their ad messages in front of youngsters. About 65% of the public in national polls objected to this, but Whittle went ahead in the schools that did not object (Turow, 1992). Also, by the late 1990s, Channel One was in more than 12,000 schools in the United States and commanded a daily audience of more than 8 million children. The schools get television sets for each classroom, VCRs, and a satellite link along with the programming. Channel One rents this captive audience out to advertisers (Croteau & Hoynes, 2001).

- Even the pope has been commercialized. The Vatican acknowledges that the pope's visits are costly, so they have agreed to sponsorship. The pope's 4-day visit to Mexico in the winter of 1999 was sponsored by Frito-Lay and PepsiCo. Some Catholics criticized this practice. But the church defends it.
- In Sweden, advertisers have tried interrupting personal phone calls with ads.
- Ads are everywhere: stickers on fresh fruit, walls of toilet stalls, gas pumps, backs of store receipts, tickets to theaters and sporting events, and church bulletins (Croteau & Hoynes, 2001).
- Ads get stamped on the back of patrons' hands as they go into bars or concerts. HBO premiered its show *Entourage* with bouncers at nightclubs stamping the back of patrons' hands at nightclubs with the show's logo and name (D. Greenberg, 2006).
- People are now getting ad logos tattooed on their skin. Examples include Chanel, Gucci, Windows, and PlayStation (Teslik, 2006). One even had the Polo pony tattooed on his chest. Many do it for free, but some get paid. For example, one man sold ad space on his forehead, and pregnant women have sold space on their bellies. One woman had fake tattoos put on her pregnant belly for an Internet casino for $8,800 (Dickerson, 2005).

more expensive. Consumers are perfectly aware of the prices of the two brands because the cereals are displayed alongside one another, yet Cheerios outsells the store brand by about four to one" (p. 25). The minor difference in taste alone does not account for the fact that 80% of consumers spend the extra money to buy the advertised brand. It appears that Cheerios advertising has made most consumers believe that something special about Cheerios warrants the very high price relative to the same cereal in the house brand box.

A second example is how much you voluntarily participate as an advertiser. Look at the clothing you have on now. How many clothing logos are you displaying on your shirt, pants, shoes, hat, book bag, and so on? You are advertising those products everywhere you go. How much are those companies paying you to advertise for them? They pay you nothing, right? In fact, you are paying them. Had you bought the same piece of clothing without the prized logo, it would have cost you less money. Therefore, you have chosen to pay more for the privilege of wearing a particular brand and displaying its logo. This is a good deal for those manufacturers who have you working for them *and* having *you* pay *them!*

POPULAR SURFACE CRITICISMS

Over the years, there has been public criticism of advertising for all sorts of reasons. Six of these reasons are analyzed in this chapter. With each of these issues, we will start with the surface criticism on which the public generally fixates. Then we will analyze each in more depth. Through this analysis, you should learn two types of things. First, you should learn more about the nature of advertising and its potential power over you. Second, you will learn more about your own opinions and behaviors concerning advertising.

Advertising Manipulates Us Into Buying Things We Don't Need

This is a popular surface criticism. Parents say this to their children who pester them for the toys, candy, and cereals the children see advertised on television. The key to analyzing this criticism lies in addressing how we define a need. If we stick to basic survival needs, then, yes, advertisers ask us to buy many things beyond our absolute basic needs for survival. At base, we really only need a set of clothes, a shelter, and some daily food.

The psychologist Abraham Maslow has pointed out that humans have a hierarchy of needs—that is, our needs are arranged by levels such that when our needs at a lower level are met, we move to needs at a higher level, so that we are always striving to satisfy some kind of need. Humans' most basic level of needs are those required for survival (food, water, shelter). The next level includes the safety needs (freedom from attack from predators and disease). Next is the social level of needs (friendship, family, and belonging to groups). Then there is the self-esteem level of needs (achievement, confidence, respect from others). And the highest level of need is self-actualization (fulfilling one's self through creativity and morality). For example, when our survival and safety needs are met, the drive to satisfy our needs shifts up to the social level in the hierarchy, and we become focused on friendship or family problems. For these social needs, we need many different outfits of clothes to help us feel comfortable in a variety of social situations. We need a certain type of car. We need to live in a certain kind of home. We need certain kinds of foods and beverages to go along with our lifestyles. We use all these products to define ourselves in social situations. Are these products luxuries or necessities? Each person must define what is a necessity for himself or herself.

Advertising Makes Us Too Materialistic

Some critics claim that advertising makes us too materialistic. However, when we analyze this criticism, we are faced with the question, How much is *too* much? Some people believe we should conserve natural resources and live at a lower level of consumption. Other people believe that we should always strive for more of everything; if it looks like we might run short of resources, we will be able to figure out a way to solve the problem. With less than 8% of the world's population, the United States consumes nearly 30% of the planet's resources. Americans can choose from more than 40,000 supermarket items, including 200 kinds of cereal. Do we really need all these material products?

Americans say they are dissatisfied with materialism despite all the abundance. In surveys, more than 80% of Americans typically agree that most of us buy and consume far more than we need. And about two thirds agree that Americans cause many of the world's environmental problems because we consume more resources and produce more waste than anyone else in the world (Koenenn, 1997). Yet we continue to consume at a greater rate each year. Thus, the public is schizophrenic about consumption. We believe we are too materialistic but keep asking for more products.

Advertising Is Deceptive

In everyday language, we think of deception as lying. Do ads lie? The answer is no in the sense that lying is presenting a blatant falsehood. Advertisers know that if they present a factual claim they cannot support with evidence, they can be fined, so they avoid making explicit claims that can be checked for truth. Also, major advertisers know that their products differ from their competitors' products in very minor ways, so there is no point in making claims that their product is clearly superior in some way. Instead, advertisers are fond of using what is called "puffery," which is the making of implicit claims that cannot be tested for truth. For example, advertisers will claim that their product is the best in their class without specifying what that class is. Advertisers puff up their products with exaggerations that are expressions of opinion rather than claims of some objective quality or characteristic of the product. Puffery gives the illusion to viewers that they are being given important information about the product, but this illusion evaporates when we look more closely at the ad. For example, have you ever seen an ad where any of the following claims were made: "the best of its kind," "the most beautiful," or "the finest"? These slogans at first seem to be telling us something, but upon closer examination, they are empty claims because they cannot be tested.

Also, some ads present implied superiority claims, such as "Nothing beats a great pair of L'eggs" (pantyhose), "The ones to beat" (Chrysler K cars), and "Nobody does it better" (Winston Lights cigarettes). On the surface, these slogans imply that their products are superior, but when we examine them more closely, we realize that they are not really making a clear comparison with another product.

Another element of puffery is when an ad tells the truth—but not the whole truth. For example, many brands that are labeled as a fruit juice drink contain only 10% fruit juice; the ad contains an element of truth, but it is misleading. Also, ads for many cereals show a brand as "part of this complete breakfast," which features several nutritious foods such as fruit, bread, and milk. This statement is literally truthful, but almost none of the nutrition in the claim comes from the cereal that is being advertised.

How do advertisers use puffery to suppress the truth? Jamieson and Campbell (1988) list the following tactics:

- *Pseudo-claims:* An example of this is "X fights cavities," but we are not told how. Is it a chemical in the toothpaste, the movement of the brush on the teeth, or the habit of brushing?
- *Comparison with an unidentified other:* "X has better cleaning action." Better than what? Better than another brand? Better than not cleaning? There is an implied comparison that makes the product sound superior, but it really is a meaningless claim.
- *Comparison of the product to its earlier form:* "X is new and improved!" Again, on the surface, this seems like a good thing—until we start thinking about it. What was wrong with the old version? And what is wrong with this current version that will end up being new and improved again next year?
- *Irrelevant comparisons:* "X is the best-selling product of its kind." What kind? Maybe *kind* is defined so narrowly that there is only one brand of its kind. Also, maybe it is the best-seller because it is the cheapest or because it wears out so fast.
- *Pseudo-survey:* "Four out of five dentists surveyed said they recommend X." Who are these five? Maybe they were paid to recommend it.
- *Juxtaposition:* A smiling person holds a product so that viewers associate happiness with the product.

Thus, advertising messages are designed to use puffery to trick us into believing there is more to the product than there really is. They give us the illusion of making a strong claim when in fact the claims are weak or even nonexistent.

This leaves us stuck in the place between truth and a lie. Although most advertising is not technically false, it cannot be considered true. When ads use puffery, they are making claims that sound good, but those claims cannot be tested. Without good tests, the claims cannot be proven false. For example, if you are marketing a brand of trucks and claim that "our trucks last longer than the trucks of any other company," this can be tested, and if someone finds a competitor's truck that is older or in better shape than your trucks, your claim is proven false. So advertisers stay away from claims like that and instead say something like, "Our trucks are built tough," which cannot be satisfactorily proven false.

Companies Manipulate Us Through Subliminal Advertising

Is there such a thing as subliminal advertising—that is, are there subliminal messages that have a powerful effect on us? To answer this question, we first need to be clear about what *subliminal* means. The popularized version of subliminal persuasion reflects a conscious effort on the part of the sender to deceive viewers by adding something to a message that is not consciously perceivable by the audience—but the person's unconscious mind sees that "extra message." For example, in the 1950s, James Vicary inserted messages of "Eat Popcorn" and "Drink Coke" into a theatrical film and claimed that the theater audience bought much more popcorn and Coke, even though no one reported seeing the ads because they were projected too quickly. Later, it was found that Vicary's results were a hoax. But this story has entered our folklore, and many people believe that unscrupulous advertisers are exposing us to subliminal messages all the time.

The idea of subliminal advertising having an effect on us is also a hoax. The word *subliminal* means below our threshold to perceive. For example, the human eye cannot see an image if it is shown for less than about one sixteenth of a second—that is below our line of ability to perceive an image. This is why we perceive movies as a smooth flow of moving images when, in actuality, what is being projected on the screen is a series of still shots. If those shots are projected at about 12 per second, we see flicker in between shots, but we still perceive motion. Once those individual images are projected at 16 per second, the flicker disappears; that is, it happens too fast to register an impression on us. The flicker between the individual images is still there, but we can no longer perceive it. Hollywood films are projected at 24 or more frames per second. At this speed, there is no chance for any individual frame to register a unique impression on us. So even if an advertiser placed an ad in 1 frame every second, each of those exposures would be too brief to cross the line of our ability to perceive them. If our sense organs cannot perceive an image, then it can have no effect on us. I'll further clarify this point with an audio example. You can train a dog to come to you when you blow a dog whistle, which emits a very high-pitched sound that the dog can hear but you cannot. The pitch of the sound is outside of the hearing range of humans; that is, the sound does not cross the line into our perceptual ability to hear it. Can you train a person to come to you every time you blow a dog whistle? If people cannot hear the whistle, they cannot know when you are blowing it and, therefore, cannot respond to a stimulus that they cannot perceive. Thus, subliminal stimuli—because they are outside a human's ability to perceive them—can have no effect on humans.

When some people use the term *subliminal advertising effects,* what they really mean is "unconscious effects of advertising." This unconscious influence *is* a powerful effect with which we should be concerned. Here is a difference between subliminal and unconscious. With subliminal, we do not perceive the message, but with unconscious, we do perceive the message but do not think about it; thus, the message gets put into our subconscious without us knowing it. Advertising alters reality by creating worlds that do not exist and makes us want to be a part of those worlds. Advertising does this by showing us that we can change our attractiveness, body image, smell, whiteness of smile, relationships, self-image, and degree of happiness by using certain products.

Also, by using technology, advertisers can make the world look different. They can electronically morph people's appearance. They can insert their products into old movies. They can insert their products into real locations; for example, at sporting events, they can electronically paint the field with their product's logo so the television viewing audience can see it even though the logo does not exist at the stadium.

Advertisers can alter our perceptions of what is real. For example, until about the 1970s, advertisers used White actors almost exclusively, thus making audiences believe that minorities did not exist or, if they did, that they were unimportant. Then in the 1970s, African Americans began appearing on TV and eventually grew to about 10 % of the actors in ads and in television shows; however, other ethnic minorities are still almost invisible in ads (Mastro & Stern, 2003). Because television commercials not only promote consumption but also shape images and "sustain group boundaries that come to be taken for granted" (Coltrane & Messineo, 2000), it is important to consider how such representations might influence racial/ethnic minority viewers.

Because advertisers continually present the same kinds of messages, over the years, we also learn many general lessons about consumption and how to solve problems. Although each ad is trying to get you to buy a particular product, at a deeper level, all ads are teaching you lessons about who you should be and how you can get there. To illustrate, let's consider an example of an ad for toothpaste, which on the surface is only an ad for a particular toothpaste. But it comes with several layers of deeper meaning embedded in the message. At a deeper level, the ad is a message about the importance of health. At an even deeper level, it conveys a message about consumerism—that is, the ad tells you that you need to buy something to clean your teeth; you cannot simply use water to brush your teeth. Also at a deeper level is implied permission to eat foods that might contribute to decay because as long as you use the product to brush your teeth, you need not feel guilty about eating things that promote tooth decay. You can see that a "simple" ad for a toothpaste carries with it several layers of meaning, some of which may be consciously processed (the surface claims made in the particular ad) and some of which are unconsciously processed (how to solve problems, the nature of health, etc.).

Advertising Is Excessive

As you saw earlier in this chapter, our culture is saturated with advertising. Whether this is excessive requires an evaluative judgment. This means you must have an awareness of what is an acceptable amount. This amount then becomes your standard for excessiveness. If you have a high standard for excessiveness, then you will likely conclude that the amount of advertising has not yet reached that level, and therefore advertising is not excessive.

In public opinion polls, when people are asked, "Do you think there is too much advertising on television?" about 70% of people say yes. But if they are asked, "Do you

think that your being shown all this advertising is a fair price for you to pay to be able to see 'free' television?" again 70% will say yes. But television is hardly free; it just seems free. Now a large part of the cost of many products is advertising. For example, when you buy soap or toothpaste, about 35% of the cost goes for advertising. Also, most households now have cable television; these households pay for television, and they also pay more when they buy advertised products.

Let's examine this criticism more closely. Take direct mail or junk mail as an example. The average household receives

848 pieces of junk mail each year. This weighs 40 pounds and eats up 100 million trees each year. It is estimated that more than 40% of this junk mail ends up unopened in landfills each year. Consumer and environmental groups have gotten 19 states to consider legislation for a do-not-mail list, but none of these states has passed any legislation, primarily because junk mailers lobby strongly for their right to send out this material. So from an environmental point of view, this form of advertising does seem excessive and should be cut back drastically. However, the junk mail industry claims that the advertising it sends out generates $646 billion in sales each year (Caplan, 2008). If we were to cut back this form of advertising drastically, wouldn't sales also drop drastically? If sales drop, companies who advertise their products would make less money, so they would pay less in taxes to support social services and have to lay off employees, which would increase unemployment and hurt the overall economy. Viewed from this perspective, is direct mail advertising excessive?

You must decide for yourself whether you think advertising is excessive. When you are making this decision, consider the issue from as many perspectives as you can, so that your eventual opinion will be a fully informed one.

Advertising Perpetuates Stereotypes

Almost all advertisers must use stereotypes. A 15-second television commercial cannot develop a character in all the rich detail needed to make us feel that the character is not a two-dimensional stereotype. Advertisers must present their messages very quickly. This requires simplifying everything, including characters.

When we analyze this criticism, we can see that the problem has less to do with stereotyping than with whether portrayals are negative or positive. If an entire class of people (such as all women or all African Americans) is portrayed with negative characteristics, then it is reasonable to argue that this is bad. If all young blonde women are portrayed as dumb, this is a negative stereotype and is offensive to many people. However, if an entire class of people is portrayed as being attractive, smart, and successful, it is not likely that people would be offended by this, although this too is a stereotype.

SOCIAL RESPONSIBILITY VERSUS ECONOMIC RESPONSIBILITY

Sometimes, advertisers are criticized for not being responsible. What this criticism really means is that they are not *socially* responsible. And advertisers often do things to warrant such criticism. For example, for 50 years, liquor manufacturers had not used television to advertise their products because of a sense of social responsibility, in a voluntary attempt to protect children and teenagers from seeing liquor ads. This was an admirable display of social responsibility. But during the fall of 1996, Joseph E. Seagram & Sons began airing spots for two whisky brands on independent TV stations around the country. The company was motivated by the desire to increase sales and felt it was bad business to continue avoiding the use of the powerful advertising medium of television. In defense of his company's move, Tod Rodriguez, general sales manager, said, "There are a lot worse things than alcohol ads on TV" (Gellene, 1996, p. D2). Many people found this incident very upsetting and the Seagram Company's reasoning very self-serving. Incidents such as this illustrate the shift away from social responsibility toward marketing.

Anheuser-Busch—the number one brewer—found beer sales flat in 1998. Its typical target audience was young men, who are typically reached in sporting shows. To increase sales, Anheuser-Busch decided to increase beer drinking among women, who accounted for only about 17% of its sales. So Anheuser-Busch decided to break its self-imposed barrier of not targeting women in the television audience and began advertising in daytime TV. A consultant to the company said, "It should be done. For the beer people not to be selling full-bore ahead on one gender is absurd" (Arndorfer, 1998, p. 8).

Until the 1980s, pharmaceutical companies marketed their drugs only to physicians. Then in the 1980s, they began marketing to the general population to get people to request certain drugs from their doctors. What this does is extend the belief that people should live a perfect life, free of all physical and psychological barriers. This is especially the case with ads for antidepressants, in which people are told they never need to feel depressed (Critser, 2004). Pharmaceutical companies knew they could increase sales of prescription drugs if they went directly to people and bypassed physicians. In this way, people would imagine symptoms and put pressure on their doctors to prescribe the advertised drugs.

Psychologists, parents, and social critics are concerned about protecting children from a barrage of advertising. Recall from Chapter 5 that young children have not developed to a point where they can understand certain elements about ads and therefore cannot protect themselves. Also, children have had less experience with products than have adults, and therefore children are not as sophisticated in making decisions about how to spend their money. However, from an advertiser's point of view, children are regarded as an important market. Children are regarded as a highly desirable target market for many advertisers who are spending more money each year to convince children to consume their products. For example, tobacco companies have been targeting young people (ages 14–24) for decades as a prime market. In 1991, the Joe Camel campaign was launched to appeal to teens by focusing many ads around high schools and colleges. In 5 years, the sale of Camels to teens went from $6 million to $476 million (Holland, 1998). Teenagers are three times as likely as adults to respond to cigarette ads; 79% smoke brands depicted as fun, sexy, and popular ("Study Links Teen Smoking," 1996).

The problem of a lack of social responsibility is not limited to how some advertisers aggressively target women or children. The problem is much broader and extends to the very nature of all advertising. For example, Harvard economist and social critic John Kenneth Galbraith (Arens, 1999) argues that advertising is fundamentally a negative force on society because it serves to shift a society's resources from benefitting the public to benefitting only individuals, and this leads to a great deal of waste. When we sell large cars and SUVs to individuals who rarely travel with many passengers, there is a waste of fuel, and we need to build more and more expensive highways and parking lots. But if that money were put into public transportation, the resources would be used much more efficiently, and everyone in the public would benefit more. Advertising is what drives private demand. If it weren't for advertising, consumers would buy much less, and some of the resources that currently go into satisfying private demand could be reallocated for the common good, such as public education, public parks, and public transportation.

In contrast to Galbraith, historian David Potter (Arens, 1999) regards advertising as a positive force on society. He sees advertising as a social institution comparable to the school and the church in its power to convey information and to teach values. An important value in America is transforming natural resources into abundance. Advertising supports this value and reinforces our inherent need to consume and enjoy it.

Potter, however, does express some concern that advertising has no overriding responsibility to society. Other institutions (such as the family, education, religion, etc.) are altruistic; they try to improve the individual and society. Advertising is very different. Advertising is selfish; its only responsibility is to serve the marketing objectives of the company that pays for it.

BECOMING MORE LITERATE

With entertainment and news-type messages, we are typically more active in searching for exposures and processing the information in those messages compared to advertising messages. In contrast, we encounter almost all advertising messages in a state of automaticity, where we are unaware of how much exposure we are experiencing. For example, we plan our exposures to the morning newspaper, our favorite TV shows, films, books, and magazine stories. We rarely plan to expose ourselves to an ad; however, exposures to ads still occur at a rapid pace as we are searching for entertainment and news messages.

To protect ourselves from all this unplanned advertising exposure, we remain in a state of automatic processing so we don't have to pay attention to all of the ads. However, exposure to the ads continues even though we are not paying attention to them, and this makes our exposure unconscious, which is what most advertisers want. During unconscious exposure, advertisers can plant their messages into our subconscious, where they gradually shape our definitions for attractiveness, sex appeal, relationships, cleanliness, health, success, hunger, body shape, problems, and happiness. For example, we might have the radio on in the car as we concentrate on driving, and when ads come on, we do not pay much attention. Then later, we find ourselves humming a jingle, or a word phrase occurs to us, or we pass by a store and "remember" that there is a sale going on there. These flashes of sounds, words, and ideas emerge from our subconscious, where they had been put by ads that we did not pay attention to. Over time, all those images, sounds, and ideas build patterns in our subconscious and profoundly shape the way we think about ourselves and the world.

Almost all exposure to advertising is unconscious, yet it still works. Advertising works because it gets into the audience's unconscious without the audience attending to those messages and analyzing them. A very sophisticated marketing research industry earns more than $8 billion each year selling information about how to shape people's needs and behaviors.

To increase your media literacy about advertising, you need to have elaborate knowledge structures about advertising and about your own needs (see Table 12.2). To build a stronger knowledge structure about ads, do the exercises at the end of this chapter. Exercise 12.1 will help you notice more of the advertising in your environment. Exercise 12.2 will help strengthen your skills and thereby make you more in control of how advertising influences you. Exercise 12.2 will also help you become more aware of your needs. As you work through the exercises, think about what ads are really selling, what the intended effect of the ad is, and what your needs really are.

What Are Ads Really Selling?

Ads are designed to present a single product claim. This claim is presented as the reason you should buy the advertised product—that is, the product will do something of value for you. That something of value can be in the form of a physical feature, a functional feature, or a characterizational feature. Physical features focus attention on the product itself and its ingredients (e.g., Buy our toothpaste because it contains X#7, which is the strongest decay-fighting chemical ever!). Functional features focus attention on how the product is used (e.g., Buy our toothpaste because it comes in an easy-to-use pump!). Characterizational features

TABLE 12.2 Types of Skills and Knowledge Structures Needed to Deal With Advertising Messages in a Media-Literate Manner		
	Skills	*Knowledge*
Cognitive	Ability to analyze an advertisement to identify key elements of persuasion	
	Ability to compare and contrast key elements of persuasion in the ad with facts in your real-world knowledge structure	Knowledge on topic from many sources (media and real world)
	Ability to evaluate veracity of claims in the ad	
Emotional	Ability to analyze the feelings of people in the ad	
	Ability to put one's self into the position of different people in the ad	Recall from personal experiences how it feels to have a need for the advertised product
Aesthetic	Ability to analyze the craft and artistic elements of the ad	Knowledge of writing, graphics, photography and so on
	Ability to compare and contrast the artistry used to craft this ad with that used to craft other types of ads	Knowledge of successful and unsuccessful ads and the elements that contributed to those qualities
Moral	Ability to analyze the moral elements of an ad	Knowledge of criticism of advertising and knowledge of how ads can manipulate our attitudes and behaviors
	Ability to evaluate the ethical responsibilities of advertisers	Highly developed moral code

focus attention on the psychological consequences of the consumption (e.g., Buy our toothpaste because it will make you feel safe from tooth decay—no matter what you eat!).

Ads usually present one simple claim and emphasize that over and over. If the claim focuses on a physical or functional feature, it is very easy to spot. Characterizational ads are more ambiguous. They are usually designed to make you feel something, then link that feeling with the product.

What Is the Intended Effect of the Ad?

Most people think that ads are designed to convince people to buy the product. Very little of the advertising we see has this intention. Many ads, especially those for new products, are intending only to establish our awareness that the product exists. Some ads are designed to create an emotion in us and link that emotion with the product. Some ads are designed to inoculate us against the claims of competitors so that when we see an ad for one of their competitors, we will not come under its influence. But the most prevalent intention of ads is reinforcement. Most ads are aimed at target groups of people who already use the product. Thus, the advertisement is designed to remind those customers that the product still exists and that it is a good one. People usually remember ads for products they already buy, so most of the effect of advertising is one of reinforcement of existing attitudes and behaviors. Thus, reinforcement is the powerful effect of advertising. Most ads are designed to make people feel good about the products they already have bought so that they will buy them again.

What Are Your Needs?

The more you are aware of your needs, the more you can use advertising to control your life. If you are not aware of your needs, the constant flood of advertising messages will create and shape your needs—often without you knowing it. Stop reading this chapter now and go to Exercise 12.3.

How did you do on Part I? Were you able to come up with a long list of needs, or could you think only of one or two? Was it easy or hard to rank order your needs? Then in Part II, were you surprised by how many products you have brought into your home? Were you surprised about how many were well-advertised brands?

Now ask yourself, How aware am I of my needs? Make a comparison of your rank-ordered list from Part I with how you spend your money and time as indicated in the inventories in Part II. Is your primary need (from Part I) reflected in the inventories of your possessions and time (from Part II)? For example, let's say your number one–ranked need was health. Did the inventory of your closet reveal more clothes for workouts than any other type of clothes? Did your inventory of your kitchen reveal an absence of highly advertised high-caloric, high-fat, high-sugar, high-salt snacks? Did your inventory of your bathroom reveal more products for sore muscles or more for beauty? Is your toothpaste a decay preventer or a tooth whitener? Did the inventory of your time reveal that you are very active or mostly passive?

If your self-reported needs (from Part I) matched closely your inventories (from Part II), then congratulations! You are aware of your needs and know how to spend your resources to satisfy them. But if there are discrepancies between your self-reported needs and where you spend your money and time, then you have a faulty sense of your needs. You might be telling yourself that your needs are A, B, and C, but your real needs are X, Y, and Z. You are satisfying your real needs even though you are not aware of what they really are. More typically, discrepancies exist because you are not able to satisfy your needs; that is, you are very aware of what your needs are. But when you go to the store, you end up buying many things that really do not address those needs, but you hope they will because you want to believe the puffery in the ads. However, the will to believe is not enough. As time goes by, you become frustrated that you cannot fulfill your major needs, although it seems like you are doing what society (as channeled by advertisements) is telling you to do.

One of the biggest dangers concerning the manipulation of our natural needs is with prescription drugs. The number of ads for prescription drugs on television has grown each year, and in 2008, the average person was exposed to 16 hours of ads for prescription drugs, which is more time than people spent with their primary care doctors. These ads mislead the public by inflating their claims and by burying their risks in "a sea of unintelligible tiny print" (Foreman, 2009, p. E5). A content analysis of these ads found that while most ads (82%) made some factual claims and some rational arguments (86%) for product use, almost all of these ads (95%) used an emotional appeal. Many of the ads urged people to use their drug to achieve social approval (78%) and to regain control over some aspect of their lives (85%) (Frosch, Krueger, Hornik, Cronholm, & Barg, 2007). These ads lead people to diagnose themselves and then pressure their physicians to prescribe the drugs they see advertised, so they can achieve the wonderful life the drugs depict.

SUMMARY

Some people regard advertisers as unscrupulous manipulators who will do or say anything to get you to give them your money. They think advertising has changed the culture for the worse by making us too materialistic—creating a throwaway society of products, ideas, and people.

Other people regard advertisers as American heroes who are responsible for keeping the economy fired up by creatively encouraging more and more consumption. This has produced the richest society ever—one with the highest standard of living and the most variety in everything. They see advertising as a glamorous profession for creative people—a fast track to a rewarding career.

Who is right? Is advertising good or bad? What is the myth, and what is the truth? You must decide for yourself. In making such a decision, it is risky to base your decision on a few intuitive impressions. Instead, it is much better to base your decision on a strong knowledge structure. Building such a knowledge structure requires you to be sensitive to the issues of how advertising influences businesses, the economy, critics, the public, and individual consumers—especially children. On almost all of these issues, there is a range of opinion. When you understand that range and the philosophies underlying different positions, you are better able to construct a well-reasoned opinion for yourself.

> **Chapter Resources:** To test your knowledge and learn more about the topics discussed in this chapter, visit the Student Study Site at www.sagepub.com/potter6e.

FURTHER READING

Jones, J. P. (2004). *Fables, fashions, and facts about advertising: A study of 28 enduring myths.* Thousand Oaks, CA: Sage. (305 pages, including glossary and index)

This author is a college professor with 25 years' experience working in a major advertising agency. In this book, Jones confronts more than two dozen beliefs that the public holds about advertising and shows how each of these is faulty.

Kirkpatrick, J. (2007). *In defense of advertising: Arguments from reason, ethical egoism, and laissez-faire capitalism.* Westport, CT: Greenwood. (200 pages with index)

Written by a professor of international business and marketing, the book analyzes much of the economic and philosophical bases used to criticize advertising and then argues that these criticisms are based on a faulty view of the world. The author concludes that advertising is good because it supports the rational self-interest of consumers.

KEEPING UP TO DATE

Advertising Industry Periodicals

Advertising Age (http://adage.com)

Ad Week (http://www.adweek.com)

Professional Organizations

American Association of Advertising Agencies (http://www.aaaa.org/Pages/default.aspx)

Cable Television Advertising Bureau (http://www.thecab.tv)

Internet Advertising Bureau (http://www.iab.net)

Magazine Publishers of America (http://www.magazine.org)

Newspaper Association of America (http://www.naa.org)

Radio Advertising Bureau (http://www.rab.com)

Television Bureau of Advertising (http://www.tvb.org)

Consumer and Educational Associations Concerned With Advertising

Ad Council (http://www.adcouncil.org)

American Advertising Federation (http://www.aaf.org)

Better Business Bureau (http://www.bbb.org)

Scholarly journals that publish research examining the content and effects of advertising messages presented in the mass media, particularly newspapers, magazines, television, and on websites

Journal of Advertising

Journal of Advertising Research

Journal of Broadcasting & Electronic Media

Journalism & Mass Communication Quarterly

EXERCISE 12.1

Becoming Sensitized to Advertising

1. How much advertising are you exposed to on a daily basis? For one day, carry around a sheet of paper in your pocket and write down every time you are exposed to an advertising message. Record the time, the product advertised, and the channel. Remember channels can be media (newspapers, television, radio, etc.) or other types such as posters (on walls, cars, kiosks, sidewalks, etc.) and ads on clothing (sweatshirts, hats, footwear, etc.). How many ads were you exposed to in one day? How many different channels were used? How many of these exposures did you seek out?

2. Watch 1 hour of television and write down each ad. Remember that a promo for a station or a television show counts as an advertisement. How many did you record? Were you surprised at the number?

3. Go through your local newspaper page by page and count the ads. Are you surprised about how many ads there are? Does this amount bother you—if so, would you be willing to pay more for the newspaper if all ads were eliminated? About 80% of a newspaper's revenue comes from advertising. So if your newspaper currently costs 50 cents, that cost would increase to about $4.00 per issue if subscribers like you had to contribute all the revenue to your newspaper.

4. Get a piece of paper and make two lists. For one, list all the breakfast cereals you can remember. Then turn the paper over and list all the shampoos you can remember. Go to a supermarket and count how many different cereals and shampoos are on those shelves. Were you able to name them all? What percentage were you able to name? Of those you did not have on your list, can you recall anything about their advertising campaigns? If so, why do you think you could not remember them when you made your list?

5. Next time you go to the drug store or the supermarket to shop, try buying as many nonadvertised products in place of the advertised brands you usually buy. How much money did you save? Are the savings worth it, or do you feel that you have made a big mistake?

6. Run a taste test for your friends. Buy several brands of advertised cola and some obscure brands. Pour different brands into their own cups. Ask your friends to taste each and tell you which cola is in which cup. Could your friends guess the right brands? Were they sure of their choices, or were they making wild guesses?

EXERCISE 12.2

Practicing Media Literacy Skills With Advertising Messages

Look at several print ads from magazines and newspapers. Also, watch several ads on television. Use this set of ads in the following tasks.

1. Analysis:
   a. What is the main product claim (reason for buying the product) of the ad?
   b. Is the claim presented explicitly or implicitly (you have to infer it)?
   c. Do any of the ads use puffery?
   d. What is the intention of the ad (awareness, positive emotion, change attitude, inoculation, reinforcement, buying product)?
   e. Look beyond the surface of the ad and the particular product, and then list some values that these ads are teaching.

2. Compare/Contrast:
   a. How are product claims the same and different across the ads?
   b. Which product claims show up most often?
   c. How are intentions the same or different across ads?
   d. Which intention do you find most often?

3. Evaluation:
   a. In your judgment, which of the claims works best? Why?
   b. In your judgment, which of the claims does not work? Why?

4. Deduction: Can you see any patterns in these ads that exemplify any of the criticisms of advertising?

5. Appreciation:
   a. *Emotional:* Were any of the ads able to evoke strong emotions in you? If so, list those emotions and explain how the ad triggered those particular emotions.
   b. *Aesthetic:* Is there something about the writing, directing, editing, lighting, set design, costuming, or music/sound effects that you found of particular high quality? If so, explain what led you to appreciate that element so much.
   c. *Moral:* Did any of the ads raise ethical considerations (either explicitly or implicitly)?

EXERCISE 12.3

Needs Inventory

Part I

Take out a sheet of paper and write down your needs.

1. Begin by simply listing all your needs as they pop into your head.

2. Once you have a list, organize the elements into categories. Group all like needs together. For example, you might have several social needs (e.g., make more friends, become more popular), health needs (lose weight, exercise more, etc.), career needs, family needs, school needs, and so forth.

3. After you have your categories, rank order your groups. Which set of needs is most important to you? What set is second, and so on? Now put this paper aside and go on to Part II.

Part II

1. Go through your clothes closet. How many changes of clothes (outfits) do you have? How many pairs of shoes? If you have one or two changes of clothes, you are operating at a functional level; that is, you are satisfied to protect your body from the elements and for the sake of being modest. If you have many sets of clothes, group them according to your needs; that is, which are your social clothes, your business clothes, your exercise clothes, and so on? Which set of clothes contains the greatest number of outfits? Why? Do you have the most clothes in an area that is the same as what you designated as your highest ranked need area in Part I?

2. Go through your kitchen cabinets and pantry. How many prepared foods (in boxes, cans, and bags) do you have compared to natural foods (milk, fresh fruit, fresh vegetables, etc.)? What proportion of those products are advertised brands, and what proportion are unadvertised or generic?

3. Check your bathroom. How many "health and beauty" aids do you have? How many of those products are for basic health needs, and how many are image enhancers? What proportion of those products are advertised brands, and what proportion are unadvertised or generic?

4. Think about how you spend your time. How much time do you take getting washed, groomed, and dressed each day? How much time do you spend eating and snacking (how many times)? What do you do with your leisure time—are you active in satisfying your needs, or are you passively sitting in front of the TV or listening to music, where you are being told by others what your needs should be?

Interactive Media

Key Idea:
Interactive mass media are businesses that attract audiences to their websites, where those audience members create the content.

The topic of interactive media is included in this section on content rather than in the industry section because it is the content that is most characteristic of interactive media. The content presented by noninteractive media is created by professional writers and producers who are highly skilled at applying message formulas that will attract particular kinds of audiences and then condition them for repeat exposures. In contrast, the interactive media allow—actually require—their audiences to create the content, either by themselves, in interaction with other audience members, or in interaction with employees of mass media organizations. Audience members are not paid for creating any of this content; to the contrary, audience members not only create the content for free but also often pay the interactive mass media companies for access to the content either through subscription fees (as with many games) or by agreeing to be exposed to advertising.

With the interactive mass media especially, it is important to make a distinction between content and the businesses. In this chapter, the focus is on the types of interactive content, especially digital games and the various forms of social networking. But first, I need to lay out some basic ideas in the development of interactive services that allow users to create the content.

DEVELOPMENT OF INTERACTIVE MEDIA

Four forces have shaped the development of the interactive mass media and hence their content. These forces are convergence, the importance of a creative commons, the need for social contact and social networking, and the attraction of advertising support.

Convergence

Convergence has been a powerful force over the past two decades and continues to get even more powerful. This convergence is both technological and psychological.

Technological convergence refers to the way that recent technological developments, particularly digitization of messages, have made it possible for content to move seamlessly across channels of communication, such that all channels have converged in their ability to present the same content. This technological convergence has led to a change in the role of audiences from being passive receivers of fully formed messages produced by the media and into active receivers who interact with messages in an interactive fashion like being in a two-way conversation with the media and with other audience members. This audience change suggests a psychological convergence where audience members can break down the previous barriers between them and the mass media organizations and also between themselves and other audience members who were separated from them by geography or societal constraints. These ideas of convergence first arose in 1995 when Nicholas Negroponte published a best-selling book *Being Digital,* in which he characterized the media up until that time as forcing the audience into a passive role—that is, people had to accept the messages as they were presented. While audiences could reinterpret the meaning of the messages, they could not change the messages themselves or interact with those messages. But gradually with the digitization of information, the old media were being replaced by interactive new media. Negroponte took his argument in a technological direction, showing how the interactive features of the newer media would attract audiences away from the older media and force those media organizations to adapt because audience members could respond to messages much like in a conversation, and this made audiences much more active; this required the rethinking of audience composition and audience motives. Also, people could take bits from many different messages and mash them together to form their own messages; this required the rethinking of the creative process, the nature of messages, and the ownership of those messages.

Convergence also has a profound psychological impact. For example, Jenkins (2006) argues that convergence "occurs within the brains of individual consumers and through their social interactions with others" (p. 3), and therefore it should be examined as a cultural shift rather than as merely a technological one. Thus, technological convergence forces people to think about themselves, their needs, and their place in society in a different way. With social networks, it is now much easier for people to converge with others and build networks that were not possible before.

Creative Commons

In *Viral Spiral: How the Commoners Built a Digital Republic of Their Own,* David Bollier (2008) explains that the Internet was initially designed as a creative commons where there is a great deal of sharing of resources for the common good. With free software in the 1980s and the rise of the World Wide Web in the 1990s, the Internet was created and is still maintained as an open-source network that allows all people to interact freely in a wide variety of ways.

The term **viral spiral** means that the Internet provides for an upward spiral of innovation because of its open networking structure. By giving all people free access to ideas, the creators of those ideas can easily disseminate them widely and allow others to build on those ideas and extend them in creative ways. Threads of thinking radiate dynamically through countless nodes and influence all kinds of people in all kinds of ways to work collaboratively. Thus, the Internet has been able to avoid the costly overhead that comes with centralized production and marketing and replaced it with a wide dispersion of vitality throughout the social commons. Therefore, change is not planned, ordered, or mechanical; rather, change is messy and serendipitous.

When the Internet is preserved as a "commons," it allows all kinds of people to gather around an incredibly wide range of interests. People who cluster around a particular topic create a virtual community that is created and maintained by the collective of people with special regard for equitable access, use, and sustainability. The commons "is a means by which individuals can band together with like-minded souls and express a sovereignty of their own" (Bollier, 2008, p. 4).

This idea of a shared commons is more evident in the so-called Web 2.0 companies. Coined in 2004 by technology industry veteran Tim O'Reilly, the term Web 2.0 has a complicated meaning. At one level, it is a catchall phrase for a generation of Internet companies such as Google, MS, and YouTube to distinguish them from older Internet companies (Web 1.0) such as Yahoo, AOL, and Netscape. Web 2.0 also refers to companies that use the Web as a platform—that is, they built technology to run on the Web the way that software companies built programs to run on operating systems such as Microsoft Windows (Angwin, 2009, p. 214). But for many, the key idea of Web 2.0 is a perspective about the Internet that fosters a social dynamic where people have the freedom to share their work through all sorts of open websites. People are free to access all these sites, use what they want, create their own messages, and make their messages available to anyone. The easy availability of these collective resources celebrates open participation, resulting in an enormous increase in creative activity.

Need for Social Networking

There is a strong need among humans for social networking so they can experience social contact with other humans. This is why humans have created families, groups, organizations, and social institutions. Now with the widespread availability of the Internet, humans have a new tool to establish human contact and build ever larger networks.

Anthropologists who have studied all sorts of groups of people typically have found that as groups grow in size up to about 150 people, they can remain stable because the members can still achieve an acceptable degree of contact with one another, but above this size, the group becomes unstable. However, with the Internet and social networking sites, users can create networks of almost unlimited size. While many users of Internet sites create very large social networks, the average user builds a core network of only about 7 to 10 friends (Wolk, 2009).

The Internet allows people not only to maintain their strong ties with important people but also to create a large network of weak social ties. Strong ties are the close relationships we have with the friends and family members who are the most important to us. Weak ties are the acquaintances we make. These weak ties are also highly valuable because they open users up to new information and connect them with people who can give them expanded opportunities for jobs, hobbies, and so on.

Attraction of Advertising Support

Many of these interactive sites do not charge users a fee to use them, so they must support themselves through the selling of advertising. The largest of these sites have been very successful in attracting advertisers who want to appeal to their particular audiences. Over the past decade, advertising money has been shifting from the older media into the Internet.

From 2002 to 2006, U.S. advertisers increased Internet advertising from $6 billion to almost $16 billion (Angwin, 2009, p. 238) and increased to $30 billion in 2011 (eMarketer, 2011b).

ELECTRONIC GAMES

The earliest form of interactive media was the electronic game. Of course, all games are interactive. Board games such as checkers and chess require a player to interact with one opponent, and other games such as Monopoly allow a player to interact with several opponents. With the advent of electronic games, players could also interact with a computer (when they could not find an opponent) and were given the opportunity to interact with many other players around the world, so geography was not a limitation. Also, time was not a limitation because players could turn on a game at any time and play for as long as they liked on many different platforms—video, computer, arcade, consoles, and mobile. What all of these games have in common are digital game codes that govern game appearance and play, visual and audio features that attract users into the game, and input devices that the player uses to communicate with the digital code in playing the game (Kerr, 2006a, 2006b). Also, from a mass media point of view (recall media strategies from Chapter 4), the games are created in a manner to be highly attractive to particular niche audiences, and the games themselves are constructed so as to condition habitual use of them.

Arguably, the most salient characteristic that distinguishes these electronic games from other forms of entertainment offered by the media is that games do not take players through a story in the conventional narrative sense (Friedman, 1995). Instead, games offer the potential for players to construct their own stories as they move through the game. These games force the player to pay a heightened level of attention to the message stimuli, not to absorb its meaning passively but to make active decisions about those stimuli so as to enter into interactions with the game rules, characters, and environments. These decisions by the game player tend to change the arc and nature of the game. These changes give players a sense of power and wonder as they explore how far they can go into building a new story.

As you will see in the following sections, electronic games are commercial products that are marketed by media companies (Giddings & Kennedy, 2006) that design the games in a way to attract particular kinds of audience members and then condition them for repeat exposure. The nature of electronic games allows them to provide immediate feedback to players on their performance so they are continually rewarded for each step of success, and this serves to reinforce their playing.

History of Electronic Games

The innovation stage for interactive media games began in the 1950s with use of early mainframe computers being programmed for simple games such as tennis and tic-tac-toe. Electronic media games shifted into the penetration stage in the early 1970s when game consoles were marketed to the broad consumer market. The first commercial home video game systems were launched in 1972 by Magnavox with its Odyssey game and by Atari with its game of Pong. Both of these were console systems where consumers had to buy a piece of hardware with controls. Players hooked up the console to their television sets and manipulated handheld controls to play the game that appeared on their television screens. Throughout the 1970s, these companies marketed other games in the form of software that could be plugged into their consoles. The most popular among these games were Space Invaders, Zork, Pacman, Asteroids, and Battlezone. These companies also created arcade versions of their games to grow the interest in their games. By 1981, arcade video games were bringing in $5 billion in the United States, and another billion was spent on home video gaming systems (Kirriemuir, 2006).

When IBM introduced the first desktop personal computer in 1981, video gaming took off with games such as Flight Simulator. People who bought a computer could use it as a console to play games on their screens when they bought the game software. Gaming consoles and their games also continued to sell well, attracting new gaming companies such as Nintendo with games such as Super Mario Brothers.

Electronic gaming has shown steady growth for the past several decades and has evolved into an industry with three components that are distinguished by their delivery systems. The three components of digital gaming are TV console, handheld devices, and personal computers.

The TV console market is dominated by three companies: Sony, Microsoft, and Nintendo. Sony markets its PlayStation console. Sony's most popular games are *Grand Theft Auto, Madden Football,* and *Gran Turismo.* Microsoft has its Xbox consoles and markets games such as *Halo.* Nintendo sells its GameCube consoles that play its Mario and Zelda games along with its *Resident Evil* series of games. The state of the art now is Nintendo's Wii, which was introduced in November 2006. As a seventh-generation console, the Wii primarily competes with Microsoft's Xbox 360 and Sony's PlayStation 3. A distinguishing feature of the console is its wireless controller, the Wii Remote, which can be used as a handheld pointing device and detects movement in three dimensions. Another distinctive feature of the console is WiiConnect24, which enables it to receive messages and updates over the Internet while in standby mode. In 2011, Nintendo introduced Wii U, which has a controller with an embedded touch screen and produces 1080p high-definition graphics.

Electronic games continued throughout the penetration stage as companies developed more platforms and games to attract more and more audiences. Now cell phones also offer games that people can play by themselves or connect to other players and compete with them (Kirriemuir, 2006). This may grow into yet a fourth platform on par with TV consoles, handhelds, and computer games.

As electronic games have penetrated the culture, critics have speculated about their negative effects, especially on children. In response to this criticism, the video game industry established the Entertainment Software Ratings Board (ESRB) in 1994 to rate all games. The ESRB created an age-based system consisting of five levels of ratings: EC for Early Childhood (ages 3 and up), E for everyone (ages 6 and up), T for Teen (ages 13 and up), M for Mature (ages 17 and up), and AO for Adults Only (ages 18 and up). However, researchers have found that the ratings have been poorly enforced. One study showed that

69% of children younger than age 17 were able to buy M-rated games (Meehan, 2004). Furthermore, 87% of boys and 46% of girls played M-rated games.

Business of Electronic Games

For the past 25 years, growth of digital games has been about 7% in a typical year. However, when a company introduces a new innovation, such as a new platform, growth can spike up 20% in that one year. By 2006, the digital gaming industry generated about $18 billion per year in software sales and another $9 billion in hardware sales (Kerr, 2006a, 2006b). This 2006 revenue for electronic games is about three times the box office revenue for the film industry. Electronic games have truly grown into a healthy media industry, and while their sales have leveled off in recent years, it is still a $25 billion a year industry (Poulin, 2011).

Like all the other media, electronic game companies increase their overall income by developing multiple revenue streams. For example, Blizzard Software, the maker of *World of Warcraft,* has made more than $300 million thus far from its multiple revenue streams, which include selling software, monthly access fees, merchandising (T-shirts, jackets, hats, an a nondigital board game), seven novels based on their games, and now a movie deal (Levy, 2006d).

There is a good deal of vertical integration in the digital game industry. That means a company that owns the platform also develops the games and distributes them. The industry is controlled by Sony, Nintendo, and Microsoft with about 20 independent publishers of games. Small independents are usually bought up by the larger companies, thus increasing vertical integration (Kerr, 2006a, 2006b). Most publishers of games own their own distribution channels. When you buy a game at a retail store, about 30% of price goes to the retailer, 40% to the game developer/publisher, and 20% to the hardware company on which the game is played (Kerr, 2006a, 2006b). Some firms are producers of the games; some are publishers that manufacture the disks and distribute them through stores; some are operators of the games (control the servers and maintain the play). But the large companies perform all these functions (Sony, Electronic Arts, Mythic Entertainment, Disney).

Game Development

The cost of developing a new game and getting the world up and running is $5 million minimum with an investment of $30 million being spent by the larger companies. The big expenses are licensing (*Star Wars*) and providing the continuing live service. The key to success lies in understanding the consumer and having the talent at designing the game itself. The development of digital games is highly risky. Only about 3% of all games make a profit. Like with film, they use tried-and-true formulas, spin off new games from previously successful games, and engage in a lot of promotion of new games (Kerr, 2006a, 2006b).

The United States, United Kingdom, and Japan are the main centers of digital game development and production The United States and Japan employ about 30,000 people each, and the United Kingdom employs another 20,000 in digital gaming. Teams of about 12 to 20 people work on developing each game, which takes about 15 to 18 months to create and test.

The process of designing a game is a complicated endeavor involving many people and many tasks that can be organized into nine steps (Castronova, 2001). First, an idea is conceived and sketched out in a demo. Second, a team of designers determines what a player will do while playing the game. Third, artists render the environments and characters. Fourth, programmers take the instructions from the designers and artists and write the digital code. Fifth, when enough code is written, an alpha version is tested. Sixth, where the alpha test reveals design flaws, corrections are made. Seventh, a beta version is made available for wider testing. The goal of the beta test is to get a community of insiders hooked on the game so they make it available on downloads for free during a trial period. Eighth, when management is satisfied with the beta testing, the game "goes gold" and is released to the publisher. And ninth, the publisher designs the box, reproduces the game disks, and distributes them to wholesale and retail outlets.

Sykes (2006) elaborates the game design process by pointing out that game developers must make three fundamental decisions about the game they want to design. These decisions concern category of play, formality of play, and the affective tone. He says that there are six categories of play as determined by the objective of the game: Agon (competition is the primary focus; enjoyment derives from competing), Alea (games of chance), Mimicry (play involving make-believe; players take on a new identity), Ilinx (players seek vertigo, which is the temporary destabilization of the perceptual system, such as fairground rides), Exploration (fun experienced exploring new places and discovering new things), and Social play (contact with others by joining special clans with secret languages, nicknames, initiation rites, etc.). While there is a different niche audience for each of these six, the popular games usually combine two or more of these features in a single game to appeal to a broader base of players.

As for formality of play, Sykes (2006) says there is a range in the number of rules that a game can have. At the informal end of this range are games with very few rules or rituals; players experience the spontaneous expression of the animalistic impulse to play. At the formal end of the range of formality are games with many rules and rituals that require discipline to follow; players who learn the rules best and who are capable of using those rules to their advantage succeed the most.

As for affective tone, Sykes (2006) again points out that there is a range open to game designers. These designers must think about what they want their players to feel as they interact with the game. One feeling is aggression as players fight a series of stronger and stronger opponents; as they conquer these opponents, players themselves feel stronger and more confident in their abilities. Another popular feeling is mystery or suspense where players must figure out what is happening before something bad happens to them or others.

In addition to the design decisions outlined in the above paragraph, designers also follow some generic type rules to ensure that their games are able to attract players and then condition them for repeat playing. Six design rules apply to all successful digital games. Game developers carefully follow these rules to reduce the risk that players will reject their games. First, there must be some reward to the player, and the rewards must only go to the good players. Bad players should be punished, but the punishment should never be for something that happened outside a player's control. Second, the game should be relatively easy to learn. Of course, some games are very complex, but the complexity is not revealed to a player in the beginning. Instead, the complexity is gradually revealed step-by-step as the player moves through the game. Third, the game should be predictable. The game should follow logical rules so that players can predict the outcome of their actions. Fourth, the game should be consistent. The outcome of a particular action must always be the same. Fifth, there should be a fair degree of familiarity. This means that designers should consider what players bring to the game and use it. And sixth, the game should be challenging. If it is too simple, players will quickly lose interest. Instead, designers must build in layers where players advance to greater and greater challenges to keep them playing.

Marketing

Like with almost all media messages, digital games are marketed to niche audiences. Marketers of digital games typically see four types of audiences: explorers, socializers, achievers, and controllers. Each of these four niches is characterized by a different kind of player. Explorers are players who are curious and want to see what is in the game. They want to discover things and are happy when the world inside the game is very big and can only be found by persistence and creativity. Socializers are players who like to interact with other players. They want the game to present challenges that require forming groups so that players have an opportunity to work together in accomplishing shared objectives. They like games where there are towns and other clusters of people. They want social interaction in the games, so they want opportunities to join clubs and engage in cultural activities with others, such as weddings, parties, and other social rituals. Achievers are players who come to the games to build something, like a city, an empire, great personal wealth, or the like. These players want games that allow for the accumulation of resources that are visible and engender respect from other players. Finally, controllers are players who want to dominate others. They want games with a high degree of competition so they can figure out ways to defeat and dominate worthy opponents.

While games are typically marketed to players, game developers are also starting to market their game code to other game developers. This is called the middleware market. There are would-be designers of games who lack a depth of programming skills required to design a game from scratch; these developers are in the market to buy game engines, which is the basic programming needed to support a game. Buyers of a game engine then build the specifics of their games from the basic code (Castronova, 2001).

The traditional marketing of online games is on disks that come shrink-wrapped in plastic boxes that you buy in large retail stores such as Best Buy and Target. This segment is still healthy, but its sales fell 11 % in 2010. Game markets are looking for other ways to market their games, including downloading games on your phone for 99 cents, Internet subscriptions, and even downloading for free and then selling game items such as weapons and costumes. As the cost of developing a top-quality game is now more than $20 million, marketers are shifting from retailing games on disk to instead reducing initial costs to players, then selling them services as they play (Fritz & Pham, 2011).

Experience of Playing Electronic Games

When a digital game has been designed well, it delivers an experience to players that has been called "flow" or "telescoping." *Flow* is a term coined by a social psychologist with the almost unpronounceable name of Csikszentmihalyi (1988). He observed people getting lost in tasks and called this experience flow. To achieve this state of flow, people must deeply immerse themselves in a task so that they lose all track of time and place. With digital games, players often get so involved in playing the game that it is as if they enter the world presented by the screen and lose the sense that they are in the real world. Players become so focused on the pleasure of the game that other needs (such as thirst, sleep, hunger, etc.) become secondary—that is, satisfying those secondary needs gets put off in the interest of satisfying the primary need of achieving the next objective in the game. The expectation of completing the next game objective is so pleasurable that everything else is forgotten while in the flow state.

Telescoping is a term used by another social psychologist with a much more pronounceable name of Johnson (2006). He used this term to refer to the way electronic game players focus on the steps within the process of moving through a game. At any given point in an electronic game, the player must focus on an immediate objective that follows from previous objectives that were successfully achieved and lead to upcoming objectives that take the player to the end of the game. This focusing on the immediate objective is viewed as the foreground, and all the other objectives are the background context. Thus, game players must keep the big picture in mind as context while they focus on the immediate objectives they face at a given part of the game. When they meet their immediate objective, they do not stop playing; instead, they feel immediately propelled onward to meeting their next objective. Johnson says, "Talented gamers have mastered the ability to keep all these varied objectives alive in their heads simultaneously" (p. 54). Telescoping is not the same as multitasking. Multitasking is handling a chaotic stream of unrelated objectives, such as talking on the phone, instant messaging friends, listing to music on an iPod, and Googling topics. Telescoping focuses more on structure, that is, ordering objectives in a hierarchy of priority and then moving through them in the correct sequence.

Experiencing flow and telescoping can be very intense and rewarding. It can be like a narcotic that draws players back to gaming for a repeat of the experience. And once players feel the experience, they want it to continue uninterrupted. When it is interrupted, they want to get back to it as quickly as possible.

Castronova (2005) argues that another attraction of games is to escape the Sisyphus nature of many people's lives. Sisyphus, a character in Greek mythology, was doomed to push a heavy boulder up a hill, and each time he neared the top, he would weaken from the exertion and the boulder would roll back down the hill. Sisyphus would have to start all over again. Castronova says that many people feel like some burdens of their everyday life are too onerous to push over the top of a hill, so they play digital games where they can be successful—metaphorically, get that boulder all the way to the peak so it will roll down the other side. This gives game players a sense of elation over having met the challenge and motivates them to undertake the next challenge in the game. This movement through progressively stronger challenges along with the success of meeting each challenge is a powerful draw.

SOCIAL NETWORKING

Social networking websites are designed to give all kinds of people the means to connect with others for all sorts of reasons. In an interesting ethnographic study, Ito and his colleagues (2009) hung out with American children and teenagers over a 3-year period to study why they spent so much time with the interactive media. The researchers made two major observations. First, they observed that interactive media offer two strong attractions for today's youth—friendship-driven participation and interest-driven participation. Second, the researchers observed that interactions with media vary by degree of involvement. The least engaging degree of involvement is "hanging out" with friends and extending social networks. As users get more involved with the interactive media, they are required to develop new skills or a different kind of media literacy. This new media literacy is characterized by "deliberately casual forms of online speech, nuanced social norms for how to engage in social network activities, and new genres of media representation, such as machinima, mashups, remix, video blogs, Web comics, and fansubs" (p. 25).

Building from the ideas of Ito and colleagues (2009), I will organize this section by what I see as three broad functions provided by the interactive media. These functions are social contact, acquiring, and competition.

Social Contact

A major reason for using social networking sites is to achieve contact with other people. Nielsen data from April 2010 show that the average Internet visitor spends 22% of his or her time on social networks (Webpronews, 2011). Social networking sites have grown extremely popular over the past decade. Twitter has more than 175 million users and Facebook has more than 600 million users (Pingdom, 2011).

Social contact can take several forms. Some users want friendship, others want dating experiences, some want to live in a different world, and others want to share their opinions and values. It is likely the case that many of us want several of these or all four at times. Let's examine each of these in more detail below.

Friendship

Some sites are designed to help users make new friends and more efficiently maintain their existing relationships with friends. The two most popular social networking websites for friendship have been MySpace, which started in 2003, and Facebook, which started a year later.

MySpace started in the summer of 2003 by offering users a profile page with pictures and interests along with the ability to link to friends. It also provided games, blogging (called journals early on), and even horoscopes. The early adopters were teenage girls who used it to keep in touch with their friends around the clock by posting photos and actively blogging. MySpace allowed them to customize their profiles, and this had strong appeal for the early users. They also downloaded songs and "mashed up" songs in remixes. MySpace also allowed Fakesters by allowing users to be whoever they wanted to be—themselves, a celebrity, a pet animal, or a wholly made up person with a created identity. The major activity was "friending," which is getting people to add you to their friends list and agreeing to be on your friends list; many users felt it was a competition to have the largest friends list (Angwin, 2009, pp. 59–62).

Until April 2004, only MySpace members could view the profiles of other MySpace members, but because of the shifting focus to advertising support, MySpace was opened up to the outside world, and by 2008, it was by far the dominant social networking site but then went into a decline as its chief competitor, Facebook, provided people with superior technology and served their needs better, thus taking away most of MySpace's users and advertisers.

Facebook, a competitor with MySpace, was launched in 2004 by Mark Zuckerberg while he was a computer science undergraduate at Harvard University. The website's membership was initially limited to Harvard students but was expanded to other colleges in the Boston area, the Ivy League, and Stanford University. It later expanded further to include any university student, then high school students, and, finally, to anyone age 13 and older.

Facebook in October 2005 was a much smaller website than MySpace, with just 10 million monthly visitors compared with 24 million for MySpace, but it was growing quickly. Up until that time, it had been restricted to college students, but then it started letting high school students join (Angwin, 2009, p. 177). By November, Facebook was narrowing the gap with visitors by introducing several new features. One was "News Feed," which provided members with updates about their friends' activities. Second, it allowed anyone to join. By the summer of 2011, Facebook had 600 million users worldwide ("The New Tech Bubble," 2011).

Dating

While people frequently use the friendship networks from Facebook and MySpace to move beyond friendships and into dating, other forms of social networking also enhance dating. For example, smartphones have apps that use GPS to help singles find dates in the vicinity. With your phone, you can search online for photos and profiles of singles in your vicinity, then send instant messages to those people. This helps people meet up in sporting events, shopping malls, and other public places. This app is called Skout and, at 5 million users, is the largest with an average age of users about 26 (Li, 2011).

Living

For people who prefer to keep their contact with friends virtual and not interact in real life, there are virtual friendship sites. One of these is called Second Life, whose home page describes it as "A place to connect. A place to shop. A place to work. A place to love. A place to explore. A place to be different. A place to be yourself" (Second Life, n.d.). Second Life is an online virtual world developed by Linden Lab, which was launched in 2003. Anyone 13 years of age and older can join and create an avatar. These avatars, called residents, can explore the world (known as the grid), meet other residents, socialize, participate in individual and group activities, and create and trade virtual property and services with one another. As of 2011, Second Life had more than 20 million registered user accounts.

Opinion Sharing

Blogs are Web logs where people create a website and then post their thoughts so that others can access them. As of the summer of 2011, there were more than 150 million publicly accessible blogs. While a few of these blogs are very popular and get more than a million unique visitors each month, the overwhelming majority are run by single individuals who post their personal opinions about every conceivable topic.

Included in this blogosphere is Twitter, which restricts people to messages of 140 characters. In 2010, 175 million people on Twitter had sent 25 billion tweets (Pingdom, 2011). Tweets are typically impulse messages containing mundane information about their everyday lives (such as what they ate for breakfast) and their opinions about whatever they care about.

While most blogs feature the personal ramblings of opinionated individuals and receive only a few hundred visitors at most, other blogs do qualify as examples of the mass media. These are highly organized sites usually focused on a particular topic with many postings designed to attract large numbers of a particular kind of audience; they are also supported by advertising messages. For example, the Drudge Report, with 1.6 million unique monthly visitors, and the Huffington Post, with 773,000 visitors, are political blogs but have postings on entertainment, business, media, lifestyle, and other topics. Both in the range and quality of their messages as well as their reach among readers, they rival major newspapers.

Acquiring

People use social networks to acquire things such as information and physical goods. Of course, people can acquire information and physical goods from brick-and-mortar places. But this section of the book focuses on how people use social networks to acquire these things.

Acquiring Information

Many informational and educational websites are available. Some simply present their own information. Others provide search engines that direct users to other websites where specific information exists, such as Google, which gets more than 1 billion search queries a day globally (Guynn, 2011a). And some websites are truly interactive—that is, they allow users to contribute. The software technology that allows people to interact with these sites is called a wiki. A wiki is a website that allows any user to add material and to edit as well as delete what previous users have done. The term comes from the Hawaiian word *wikiwiki,* which means fast or speedy. In 1994, a computer programmer named Ward Cunningham developed an initial wiki server designed to be the simplest possible online database. He designed it so that information could be added and edited as easily as possible. Thus, this database is essentially democratic, where every user has equal access and equal ability to contribute.

The most well-known wiki so far is Wikipedia, which is a free Web-based encyclopedia that does not hire experts to write the content but allows anyone access to add, delete, and edit content. Wikipedia began in 2001. Initially, its greatest challenge was generating interest among the general public to volunteer to create articles for the encyclopedia without being paid. It met this challenge and by 2008 had generated close to 2.3 million articles and was growing by about 600,000 articles each year in the English edition (Lih, 2009). Now its challenge is to check the article writing and editing for accuracy. Also, there is a continuing challenge to ensure that people with certain political or religious orientations do not distort entries for their own purposes. For example, in 2006, Wikipedians noticed that unmet campaign promises of congressional representatives were being deleted from articles on those congressional representatives. It was discovered that these deletions were coming from Web addresses of congressional aides for those congressional representatives.

Also, it was found that the justice department was removing references to certain groups they felt were involved in terrorist activities. And they noticed that supporters of the Church of Scientology were entering a pro-Scientology viewpoint while critics were editing that out in favor of a critical viewpoint. In all of these (and many more instances), Wikipedia had to lock out those people from the editing function (Linthicum, 2010).

Anyone can create a new article, and anyone can edit an existing article. This open editing model is guided by the values of good writing, neutrality, reliable sources, and verifiability. People who create and edit the content are unpaid, and access to the site is free to everyone. The content is created by users for free and belongs to the community, not to the creators of Wikipedia.

What makes it work is that a large number of knowledgeable people are willing to participate. Whatever errors they make usually receive rapid correction, simply because so many minds are involved. This ensures a much more comprehensive resource than a small group of experts could produce. Also, the great number of people involved contributes to the elaboration of each topic—thus, more detail can be provided because it is coming from many different people. At first, accuracy might seem to be a problem, but the editing function allows errors to be quickly corrected by others. (For more on how the collective knowledge of groups is superior, see *Infotopia* by Cass Sunstein, 2006.)

Acquiring Music

People have been acquiring music by creating social networks since software by the name of Napster became available in 1999. A computer hacker named Shawn Fanning created Napster as a file-sharing software program while he was a student at Northeastern University in Boston. It was released in June 1999, and within a year, the software had been downloaded by 70 million users who used it primarily to allow other users to make copies of audio recordings they had stored in their computer memory. Napster used centralized file directories on the Internet to connect users to music files on thousands of individual computers, thus enabling any user to download virtually any recorded music in existence for free.

In December 1999, the Recording Industry Association of America (RIAA) sued Napster on the grounds that this music-sharing service allowed piracy of copyrighted music. The RIAA eventually succeeded in shutting Napster down in July 2001. Since then, many other P2P services (Grokster, Lime Wire, KaZaA, Gnutella, BitTorrent) have taken Napster's place in helping people facilitate online sharing and collaboration.

Acquiring Video

There are many sites where users can access and download videos. Some of these are interactive and allow users to upload videos. The most popular interactive video site is YouTube, which was created in February 2005. The first YouTube video was uploaded in April. Entitled "Me at the Zoo," it shows one of the founders, Jawed Karim, at the San Diego Zoo. The site was opened to the public in November 2005, and it grew rapidly. By July 2006, the company announced that more than 65,000 new videos were being uploaded every day and that the site was receiving 100 million video views per day. By 2007, YouTube consumed as much bandwidth as the entire Internet consumed in 2000 (YouTube, n.d.). And by 2011, Internet surfers were viewing more than 2 billion videos on YouTube per day (Pingdom, 2011).

Physical Goods

Perhaps the most successful social networking site for acquiring physical goods is eBay, which was founded in September 1995 by Pierre Omidyar as an online auction website where anyone who wanted to sell household items could post pictures and descriptions of their items online and allow viewers to bid on those items. When sellers accept a bid, they arrange for the sale of the item through eBay and then mail the item to the buyer.

Within 2 years, eBay had accounted for more than 1 million items sold. In 1998, the company went public, selling stock as a public corporation. By 2007, it had a quarter of a billion registered users worldwide with 100 million items on sale at any given time ranging from items selling for a few dollars to a Gulfstream II business jet that sold for $4.9 million in 2001 ("The Basics of Selling," 2007). By 2008, it had grown to 15,500 employees and generated $1.8 billion. (eBay, n.d.)

Competition

Many people are attracted to social networks for the purpose of competition. Many computer games take you out on the Internet where you play the game with others who could be anywhere in the world. Some of these games pit you against one other player, such as in a game of chess, while others pit you against a small number of players, such as poker, which grew quickly into a huge Internet industry. By 2003, about 1,800 gambling cites on the Internet had generated $4.2 billion; PokerStars was the largest of the online poker sites, with more than 200,000 people playing during peak times (Malcolm, 2005). But then in the winter of 2011, the U.S. government banned poker site gambling activity by freezing the accounts of its players. For example, players at PokerStars had $120 million in their accounts. This money was eventually returned to its players when the site shut down (Popper, 2011).

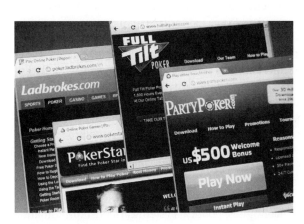

Another example is what is known as massively multiplayer online role-playing games or MMORPGs. These games are designed to attract a certain kind of audience and then massively condition that audience into continual play, even to the point of making the cyberworlds of the games more important to players than their real worlds. Although these games are relatively new, there is evidence of major effects.

One of the most popular and elaborate MMOPRPs is the *World of Warcraft* (*WOW*). Players of *WOW* "live" in a medieval-type world called Azeroth and aspire to venture into a dungeon to slay of group of villains known as the Four Horsemen. Beginners spend months building up their characters while avoiding being killed (called "ganked" in *WOW*) by more experienced players. After months of play, the good players get to level 60, where they join with other players in guilds and undertake intricately planned raids on dungeons and engage in massive rumbles against other guilds.

To play *WOW,* players must purchase the computer software for $50 and then pay a monthly fee of $15 to play online and another $30 to $50 a month for a high-speed Internet connection (Levy, 2006d). As of the summer of 2009, *WOW* had 11.5 million players worldwide, making it the most successful online video game in the world (Fritz, 2009).

Another popular MMORPG is is *EverQuest,* which is played by several hundred thousand people. It has generated a real-world economy comparable to that of a medium-sized country (Lichtarowicz, 2002). About one third of the adult players of *EverQuest* spend more time in a typical week in the virtual world than in paid employment (Castronova, 2001).

Key to MMORPGs is the creation of a cyberworld. Cyberworlds are growing. By 2004, there were already 15 cyberworlds, each with more than 10,000 subscribers. Castronova (2001) estimates that worldwide, there were at least 10 million regular players and perhaps

as many as 30 million (p. 55). Looking at video games in general, more than 50% of the population older than age 6 play video or computer games. While many people may think of game players as teenage boys, the average age of a player is 29, and 43% of all players are women (p. 57).

Amazingly, there are as yet no cyberworlds that have gone out of business. While it is very risky and expensive to get a game introduced and successful, 95% of all titles will fail and disappear from the shelves within 6 weeks. But once a game gets established, the players take over, and the game takes on a life of its own. Castronova (2001) says, "All of the oldest games have amazingly robust population counts. Synthetic worlds, it seems, almost never die" (p. 56). It should be noted here that a decade is considered very old for such games.

The effects of MMORPGs are profound. There is evidence of addiction. Yee (2002) found that many players of *EverQuest* considered themselves addicted to playing the game. There is also anecdotal evidence of other harmful effects, such as a Korean player who died of exhaustion after spending 80 continuous hours in *Lineage* without a break. An *EverQuest* user who committed suicide was said to have done so out of desperation at events within the game world (Castronova, 2005, p. 64).

To say that many players become addicted to playing and spend a large proportion of their waking hours playing—while true—underestimates the profound effect of these games on many players. The most profound effect of these games is that they create a cyberworld that often takes the place of a player's real world. For many players, the cyberworlds offer experiences they cannot get in their real world, so players move into the cyberworld and live their lives there, where they create economies, political systems, friendships, romantic attachments, and careers. In his book *Synthetic Worlds*, Edward Castronova (2005) argued the thesis that

> the synthetic worlds now emerging from the computer game industry . . . are becoming an important host of ordinary human affairs. There is much more than gaming going on there; conflict, governance, trade, love. The number of people who could be said to "live" out there in cyberspace is already numbering in the millions; it is growing and we are already beginning to see subtle and not-so-subtle effects of this behavior at the societal level in real Earth countries. (p. 2)

He says that the games are a virtual reality different from what scientists have been experimenting with. Scientists are interested in developing hardware (e.g., glasses, gloves, and chairs) that manipulate senses in a way to make people believe they are in a place or doing something they are not in the real world. Castronova (2005) says that gamers are instead developing software that engages players mentally and emotionally so strongly in a synthetic world that people stop paying attention to the fact that they are in a synthetic, nonreal, world. He says that gamers have been much more successful than scientists, such that virtual reality is thought of as a software paradigm rather than a hardware paradigm.

Castronova (2005) says,

> The fading of boundaries between our world and the synthetic worlds of cyberspace is what justifies serious inquiry, in my view. As the lines disappear, we move toward a state in which there is really no barrier to a complete translation of every interpersonal human phenomenon on Earth in the digital space. (p. 48)

Castronova (2005) conducted a study of users of these games and found that about 57% said they would quit their real-world job and work in the cyberworld if they could make enough money there to support themselves, and three quarters of players wish they could spend all of their time in the cyberworld of the game (p. 59).

All of these MMORPG cyberworlds have an internal economy where players are given opportunities to perform a range of work-like tasks ranging from simple receptive tasks to highly complex challenges. Players earn some type of "coin of the realm" for this work. Players can then enter into exchanges with other players. In this way, players can satisfy their game-playing needs and gradually amass wealth.

Players in many of these games have also created an economy external to the games where they pull resources out of the game and exchange them in real-world markets, then move resources back into the game. For example, many players of *EverQuest* will work at menial tasks in that particular cyberworld where they are paid around 300 platinum pieces an hour on average. The platinum piece is the coin of the *EverQuest* cyberworld. These players can then go to online markets such as eBay and sell their platinum pieces to other *EverQuest* game players for U.S. dollars. The exchange rate is about U.S.$3.50 for 300 *EverQuest* platinum pieces. Thus, a person can go to work in *EverQuest* and make $3.50 per hour (Castronova, 2005). Of course, $3.50 an hour is far below the minimum wage in America, but in other countries, it is a good income. So ambitious people in poor Third World countries can enter the *EverQuest* cyberworld and perform a task like hammering metal into suits of armor by clicking a mouse all day, then sell these suits of armor to other *EverQuest* game players on eBay.

As of 2004, eBay was hosting about $30 million of annual trade for goods that only exist in synthetic worlds. Much of this trade was for real currencies, meaning that eBay was in the foreign currency exchange market (Castronova, 2005, p. 149). There are now Internet sites that have been created especially for resource exchanges that cross the boundaries between the real and the cyberworlds.

This raises a serious concern for real-world economies. What if a lot of people choose to work in cyberworlds, producing digital goods and services rather than working in the real world? This would reduce the workforce in the real world. What if, then, these cyberworkers sold their cyber pay units in the real world for real-world currencies? This would shift resources out of the real world and into the cyberworld. Thus, the gross domestic product (GDP) of real-world economies would shrink while the cyberworld GDP would grow.

In addition to economic effects, there are also political effects of playing these games. These games give powerless people the chance to band together in groups or guilds that exercise considerable power against other groups or guilds in the cyberworld. Thus, players have the chance to compete for leadership positions and move up the ladder of power within the game. Most of this power is exercised within the playing of the game and directed at other players, but there are times when players will band together and attempt to exercise power against the creators of the games themselves with the goal of getting them to change some aspects of the game, that is, to rewrite the rules of the game.

MEDIA LITERACY

What are the implications of digital games for media literacy? To answer this question, I will highlight the difference between opportunity and addiction. Opportunities are good. If digital games are used by people as opportunities to expand their experience, challenge the limits of their lives, and give people a deeper understanding of who they are, then games are useful tools. People can use games to practice a wide variety of skills in relatively low-threat environments. Failures are easily forgiven, and it is easy to start a task over again.

In contrast, addictions are harmful. With addictions, people become slaves to the games and cannot exercise self-discipline. They are playing not to lose certain experiences rather than to gain more experiences. At this point, the games control the player, and the player has no power.

Therefore, if people are aware of their own goals and use the games as tools to achieve those personal goals, they are acting in a media-literate manner. However, media literacy is reduced to the extent that the games take over the person's personal goals and the person slavishly works to achieve the game's goals beyond the point where the game is bringing excitement or pleasure to the player.

One final concern relates to whether players' goals are prosocial or antisocial. Prosocial goals help the person function better and more successfully with other people and in society. Thus, players who spend time with games that teach business principles, leadership, interpersonal interaction, and the like are learning the value of prosocial behaviors and are developing their prosocial skills. However, many games are available that teach the techniques of fighting, stealing, deception, and even killing people with guns. The players who spend time with these games will learn that antisocial behaviors are successful in resolving conflicts, and they will build their confidence that they can be successful with such actions. Thus, these games have great potential for teaching behaviors, attitudes, emotions, and knowledge. If we use them as tools to help us live a better life for ourselves and other people, society can get stronger.

SUMMARY

Interactive mass media content has been made possible by three factors: the development of the Internet as a shared commons, audiences' need for social networking, and the ability of interactive sites to attract advertising support. Interactive content can be arranged in three broad categories of informational/educational, social networking, and games. Each of these forms of content is relatively new and fast growing in terms of attracting users.

> **Chapter Resources:** To test your knowledge and learn more about the topics discussed in this chapter, visit the Student Study Site at www.sagepub.com/potter6e.

FURTHER READING

Angwin, J. (2009). *Stealing MySpace: The battle to control the most popular website in America.* New York: Random House. (371 pages with index)

This is a detailed history of MySpace, from its launch in the summer of 2003. It also includes some background on the website's founders (Chris DeWolfe and Tom Anderson) along with the companies that owned the website (eUniverse, Intermix, and News Corp.). It is written in a journalistic style by a reporter for the *Wall Street Journal*. The author also deals with some larger issues such as the development of advertising on the Internet and personal privacy.

Bollier, D. (2008). *Viral spiral: How the commoners built a digital republic of their own.* New York: The New Press. (344 pages with index)

The thesis of this book is that the Internet was created as a creative commons where there is a great deal of sharing of resources for the common good. With free software in the 1980s and the rise of the World Wide Web in the 1990s, the Internet was created and is still maintained as an open-source network that allows all people to interact freely in a wide variety of ways. By viral spiral, Bollier argues that this open networking structure feeds an upward spiral of innovation. The Internet's transformative power comes from allowing people free access to the ideas of other people so they can build on and alter those ideas. Therefore, change is not planned, ordered, or mechanical; rather, change is messy and serendipitous. Threads of thinking radiate dynamically through countless nodes and influence all kinds of people in all kinds of ways to work collaboratively. Thus, the Internet has been able to avoid the costly overhead that comes with centralized production and marketing and replaced it with a wide dispersion of vitality throughout the social commons.

Castronova, E. (2005). *Synthetic worlds*. Chicago: University of Chicago Press. (332 pages including index, appendix, and end notes)

Professor and economist Edward Castronova says that the computer industry is not only producing synthetic worlds in which their games are played but also is stimulating the creation of other synthetic worlds by its players. People who use the games are not simply players; they often try to live the games and perform other human activities there, such as looking for friendships, love, employment, social connectedness, power, and prestige. There is much more than gaming going on: conflict, governance, trade, love. The number of people who could be said to "live" out there in cyberspace is already numbering in the millions; this number is growing, and we are already beginning to see subtle and not-so-subtle effects of this behavior at the societal level in real Earth countries. He focuses primarily on massive multiplayer online role playing games (MMORPG), treating the phenomenon from an economic point of view by showing economies within the game-playing worlds extend out of cyberspace and into the real world.

Ito, M., Horst, H. A., Bittanti, M., boyd, d., Herr-Stephenson, B., Lange, P. G., et al. (2009). *Living and learning with new media: Summary of findings from the Digital Youth Project*. Cambridge, MA: The MIT Press. (98 pages; no index)

This book presents the results of a 3-year ethnographic study that examined how young people use the new media and how they learn from those exposures. The authors also wanted to find out how the newer digital media were changing "the dynamics of youth-adult negotiations over literacy, learning, and authoritative knowledge" (p. xiv). They focus their attention on four ideas of new media ecology, networked publics, peer-based learning, and new media literacy.

Jenkins, H. (2006). *Convergence culture: Where old and new media collide.* New York: New York University Press. (308 pages including index and glossary)

In this widely cited book, Jenkins argues that there has been a massive shift in media practices and content toward convergence, and that this change should be considered much more a cultural rather than a technological phenomenon.

Lih, A. (2009). *The Wikipedia revolution: How a bunch of nobodies created the world's greatest encyclopedia*. New York: Hyperion. (246 pages with index)

This book tells the story about how the idea for Wikipedia was first conceived in 1995 and then went online in 2001. Within 8 years, it had stimulated people to write 10 million articles across 200 languages for free. How was this made possible? Read the book!

KEEPING UP TO DATE

Wikipedia (http://en.wikipedia.org/wiki/Main_Page)

This is the Wikipedia website's main page. Articles are constantly being added to this Web-based encyclopedia. If you have not already done so, check out this amazing resource. Also, you can use this to get more up-to-date information on almost all concepts presented in this book.

Yahoo videogames (http://videogames.yahoo.com/)

This website allows you to try demonstrations of many of the most popular video games.

Part 5

Effects

The effects from exposure to mass media messages are at the heart of media literacy. This part presents two chapters to help you understand the nature and range of those effects. Chapter 14 outlines a pro-active perspective on media effects that illustrates how the mass media are constantly exerting an influence on you, whether you can observe that influence or not. Then Chapter 15 uses a four-dimensional approach to broaden your perspective on the range of mass media effects.

As you read this part of the book, keep the following questions active in your mind and you will stay focused on the most important ideas in the two chapters:

- What mass media effects can you easily observe in your life?
- What mass media effects are probably happening to you every day without your noticing them?
- Which of those effects (from your answers to the previous two questions) are negative and which are positive?
- What can you do to increase the probability that the positive effects will occur more often and that the negative effects will occur less often?

Proactive Perspective on Media Effects

Key Idea: We need to be proactive—rather than reactive—in understanding how the media affect us. We also need to realize that there are many factors interacting in the effects process. When we understand these two ideas, we can achieve greater control over the process of effects.

Two boys watch the movie *The Deer Hunter,* a film in which American prisoners during the Vietnam War are forced by their captors to play the game of Russian roulette. Russian roulette is a game where one chamber in a revolver contains a bullet while the other chambers are empty. Each player in the game takes a turn pointing the gun at his head and pulling the trigger. If he is lucky and the chamber is empty, the gun does not fire and the player is saved. If he is unlucky, the chamber contains the bullet, which is then fired into his brain, killing him instantly.

Several days after watching this movie, the boys are playing in their parents' bedroom and find a revolver under the bed. They decide to play Russian roulette. Eventually, the gun fires, killing one of the boys.

The tragic incident described above actually happened, and when it was well covered by the press, it stimulated debate about who was to blame. There was a great deal of public criticism directed toward movies and television programs that were blamed for causing children to behave in violent ways. What this illustrates is that the public typically takes a reactive perspective—that is, when something happens that generates concern, the public likes to react to the event and debate where blame should be placed. While this reactive perspective is better than no perspective, still better would be a proactive one where the public gets concerned about risks—in this case, risks of harmful actions triggered by media portrayals—and educates people so that the probability of a tragedy occurring is greatly reduced.

When it comes to media effects, the media literacy perspective is much more oriented toward proactively dealing with potential risks through education rather than waiting until negative effects occur and then assessing blame when it is too late to take steps to prevent the problem from getting to a bad point. Learning how to be proactive will give you greater control over the process leading up to a negative effect. Also, it will allow you to position yourself better to achieve positive effects while you are avoiding negative ones.

To help you develop a more proactive perspective on mass media effects, this chapter will emphasize four ideas. First, it will show that media effects are constantly occurring. Second, it will illuminate the nature of factors that shape those effects. Third, it will help you develop a broader perspective on blame. And fourth, it will show you that you can control the effects process in your own life. We will then continue this discussion of media effects in the next chapter when we use the concepts presented in this chapter to explore the broad variety of media effects that are occurring in your lives every day.

MEDIA EFFECTS ARE CONSTANTLY OCCURRING

Many people think of media effects categorically—that is, either an effect occurs or it does not. The problem with this type of thinking is that it is reactive. If an effect occurs and it is negative, then all we can do is feel bad about it and try to assess blame. Or if an effect occurs and it is positive, then all we can do is be thankful that it occurred and hope it occurs again. This perspective does not give you much control over the effects because it is reactive. In contrast, media literacy helps you to develop a more proactive perspective, so that you can exercise some control over media effects. The more you understand about how the media exert their effects, the better you can help yourself avoid the negative effects and also increase the occurrence of positive effects. So in this section, I will show you the big picture about how the media exert their influence on all of us.

Manifested Effects and Process Effects

There are media effects that we can easily observe; these are the manifested effects. But there are also other things going on in our minds due to media influence. The media are constantly in a process of influencing how we think, feel, and act, whether we manifest these things or not. Let's call these other effects process effects because we are always in a process of being influenced by mass media messages. If we focus attention on only the manifested effects, we will greatly underestimate the degree of influence the media exert on us. Just because we do not see an outward manifestation of these things does not mean that the media are without influence. We also need to consider process effects.

To illustrate this distinction between manifested and process effects, let's return to the example at the beginning of this chapter. While the boys watched the *Deer Hunter* movie, they were being influenced by the messages presented there. They felt excitement over the danger of the characters playing Russian roulette. Their attitudes were shaped that this game was a cool thing to play. There may have been no outward manifestation of these changes in emotions and attitudes, but this does not mean that the boys were not influenced by the media message. It was not until the boys discovered a revolver and started playing the game was there a manifestation. If a parent had realized there were process effects occurring and did something to reduce those process effects, the boys would not have moved on to such a horrible manifested effect.

The public and media critics are fixated on manifested effects. However, if we are to regard media influence from a media literacy perspective, we need to think more in terms of process effects. The more we understand about process effects, the more we can control media influence. Let's examine this in more detail by moving on to consider two kinds of process effects: baseline and fluctuation.

Baseline Effects and Fluctuation Effects

To illustrate the important difference between baseline effects and fluctuation effects, look at Figure 14.1. In those figures, the horizontal lines represent time and the vertical lines represent degree of risk of experiencing an effect. Our **baseline** is our typical degree of risk that continues over time (see Figure 14.1a). Every once in a while, something will happen to dramatically change that risk level (Figure 14.1b). Notice how there is a sudden spike from the normal baseline; this is a fluctuation effect. The fluctuation is usually temporary; after a brief period, the risk level returns to the base level.

Now, let's add in the idea of a manifestation level. Think of the manifestation level as kind of a water level. Imagine yourself watching the surface of a lake, when suddenly a fish breaks through the surface, then dives back underwater. Until you see that fish break

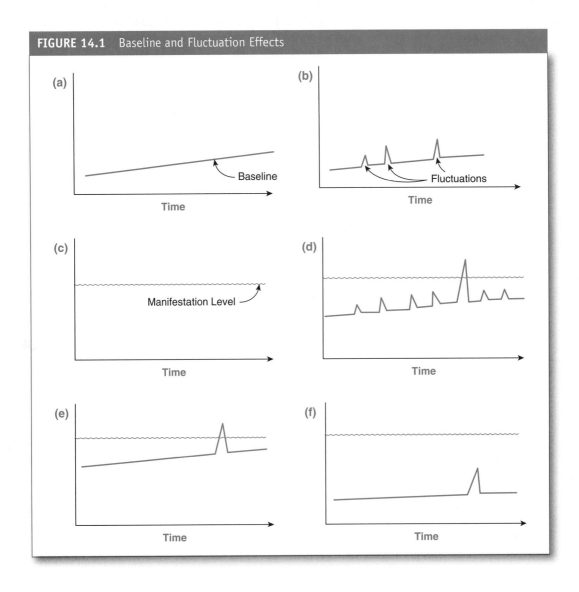

FIGURE 14.1 Baseline and Fluctuation Effects

through the surface, you are not sure if there are any fish in the lake. Just because you do not see them, does not mean there are not fish—as well as turtles, eels, plankton, and even a Loch Ness monster—swimming around underwater. Observing what happens occasionally above water level does not tell you much about all the processes that we cannot see under the water. The same is true with media effects. There could be many effects (baseline effects and fluctuation effects) occurring under the manifestation level, and rarely will a fluctuation effect be strong enough to break through the manifestation level (see Figure 14.1d).

When we talk about media effects, we typically mean only fluctuation effects that break through the manifestation level, that is, those changes in behavior or knowledge that we can observe. For example, while watching television, we notice that we are going to the kitchen to get that bag of potato chips to eat after watching a commercial for that product. Or we watch a news program covering a campaign and notice that our attitude toward one of the candidates has changed. These examples are of effects we can observe; they have clearly manifested themselves. But if we limit ourselves to considering only fluctuations that have broken above the manifestation level, we lose the opportunity to learn about a great deal of effects activity that take places underneath the manifestation level—these are the process effects.

When considering process effects, it is important to think in terms of baselines. As I said above, the baseline is the typical level of risk for an effect. It is fairly stable over time, but it can gradually increase or gradually decrease. Baselines are shaped by long-term conditioning. Some people are conditioned in a way that their baseline is very close to the manifestation level (see Figure 14.1e), so it does not take much in a media exposure to result in an effect being manifested. In contrast, other people have been conditioned in a way that their baseline is very far from the manifestation level, so it is unlikely that any one media exposure will result in an observable effect (see Figure 14.1f).

FACTORS INFLUENCING MEDIA EFFECTS

Every day, our baseline is being shaped by factors from the media and factors in our own lives. Some of those factors increase risk—that is, they serve to move our risk upward off the baseline perhaps even up to or beyond the manifestation level. Other factors also serve to move our risk downward and away from the manifestation level. All of these movements are process effects. Thus, effects are constantly occurring as a result of our unfolding experiences with the media. Some influences serve to reduce our risk level, while others serve to increase that level (see arrows in Figure 14.2). Notice that in Figure 14.2, there are more upward arrows than downward arrows; this indicates that more influences serve to increase risk compared to the influences that push the risk lower; as a result over time, the baseline gradually increases.

Many factors interact in the media effects process. In the following sections, I point out many of the more influential types of factors that are responsible for gradually changing a person's baseline and for triggering fluctuations off that baseline.

FIGURE 14.2   Factors Influencing the Baseline

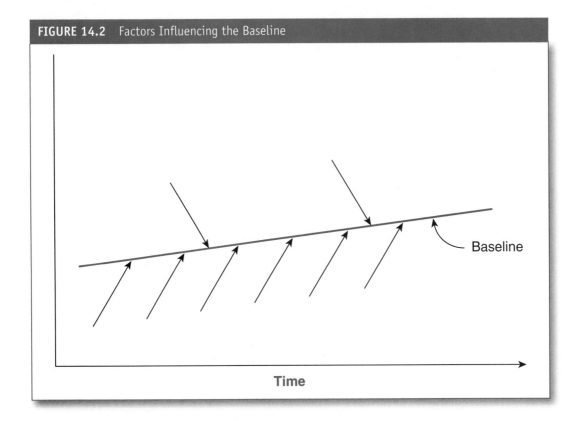

Baseline

Time

Baseline Factors

What are the general factors that are most influential on a person's baseline? I discuss seven of them in this section. Each of these seven types of factors exerts a subtle but continuing influence on a person, and this serves to make a person's baseline relatively fixed and enduring.

Developmental Maturities

We mature cognitively, emotionally, and morally as we age. Recall from Chapter 5 that when we are very young, our minds, emotions, and moral reasoning are beginning to develop and thus have a lower ceiling of capacity than when these are more fully developed. As we mature in these areas, we are able to process more information and to apply more sophisticated skills well. This gives us the capacity to move our baselines closer to the manifestation level for the effects we want to experience and away from the manifestation level for effects we want to avoid.

As children mature, they expand their cognitive abilities. That is, they are less influenced by a central, salient feature of a message and can process many more elements in a message, which allows them to understand context more fully; they are not limited to concrete thinking but get better at making inferences accurately; they are more sophisticated in making distinctions between fantasy and reality; and, perhaps most important, they can think about thinking itself—that is, engage in meta-thinking—which helps them monitor their media exposures and the potential effects of those exposures on them (Strasburger & Wilson, 2002). Thus, as children age, they are more capable of staying in a self-reflexive exposure state where they can process media messages and learn from them. This makes it possible for them to exert greater control over the shape of their baselines as well as over fluctuations from those baselines.

As for emotional reactions, people at lower levels of maturity are limited in their capacity to control their emotions and behavior. S. L. Smith and Wilson (2002) found that fear reactions from news are affected by age. Older children are more likely to comprehend news stories, and this leads them to be more frightened by the happenings reported. Also, emotional reactions to violent action/adventure films are influenced by humor, but there is a gender difference. For example, research has found that females find that wisecracking heroes add to their emotional distress, whereas male viewers find that wisecracking heroes reduce their distress a bit (C. M. King, 2000).

Recall from Chapter 5 that we must be careful not to fall into the trap of believing that everyone of the same age has reached the same level of development cognitively, emotionally, and morally. Yes, children are highly susceptible to certain influences. But there is reason to believe that adolescents and adults can also be susceptible to these same influences.

Cognitive Abilities

The developmental maturities suggest potentialities; that is, at a given age, there are limits to what people can understand and how they go about reasoning. But developmental potentialities are not the same as actual abilities; that is, not everyone who has the same potential exhibits the same level of cognitive abilities.

Four cognitive abilities—field dependency, type of intelligence, type of thinking, and conceptual differentiation—are most relevant to media literacy. Each of these has an influence on establishing a person's baseline for media effects. For example, people who are more field independent, higher on both fluid and crystalline intelligence, and more likely to differentiate information conceptually into categories will be more likely to control their baseline levels.

Knowledge Structures

People with the largest amount of knowledge learn most from media (Comstock, Chaffee, Katzman, McCombs, & Roberts, 1978). When people have a great deal of knowledge on a particular topic, they have a strong, well-developed knowledge structure. They are usually motivated to acquire more information on various topics and thus seek out media that will provide them with this information. When they see a new message on the topic, they are able to integrate that new information quickly and efficiently into their existing knowledge structure.

If a person's knowledge structure is composed primarily of information only from the media, then this structure may be dominated by media-stimulated generalizations. With many topics, we have no choice but to rely primarily on media information. This is what makes the media so powerful as a socializing influence—we cannot check out the media information by comparing it to information from other sources, such as real-life experiences. For example, almost no one knows what it feels like to be a professional athlete. We are given some insights about what the life of a professional athlete might be like, but very few people have an opportunity to check those insights out for themselves. This is true for almost all content of news; viewers have no real-world experience about being a political leader, a celebrity coming out of rehab, a professional athlete, or a mass murderer. The same is true for so-called reality programming; viewers have no real-world experience about being a Beverly Hills housewife, 16 and pregnant, or singing their way to becoming an American idol. And this is certainly true for fictional programming; viewers have no real-world experience about being a surgeon or a vampire or solving crimes in a forensics laboratory. Because viewers do not have an opportunity to check out these things in their real lives, it is impossible for them to make valid judgments about how accurate these media portrayals are. When people are asked if TV entertainment is credible and a reasonable representation of the way people live, most people say yes. As you increase your amount of viewing, your perceptions of the reality of TV entertainment programs increase. That is, you are more likely to believe the real world is like the TV world. This is especially true among children and those who have the least amount of variety of real-world experiences.

Sociological Factors

The degree of socialization is related to the amount of influence the media will have. People who have been consistently socialized with particular values for a long period will have a relatively weighty baseline—that is, the baseline will be very resistant to change. It is unlikely that the media will be able to exert a strong enough influence to cause a fluctuation, especially one big enough to break through the manifestation level. For example, if a person is a senior citizen and has been exposed consistently to anti-aggression values all her life from parents, friends, educational institutions, church, and so on, she has a baseline far away from a behavioral fluctuation of aggression. She could watch an entire evening of highly aggressive media messages and not move anywhere near the level of manifesting aggressive behavior herself. If, on the other hand, another person has been taught to fight back by his father, been taught that only the strong survive in a tough school, and been shown by his friends that the only way to get respect is to fight, he has a baseline fairly close to a manifestation level for aggression, and it would take very little media influence to push him above that manifestation level.

We learn norms by observing other people in real life and through the media. The media present many characters who communicate a great deal of social information to viewers. These messages are especially influential on the socialization of children because young people have less experience in real life to counterbalance the media portrayals. In addition, many adults have very limited real-world information to counterbalance media portrayals, so they too are susceptible to media influence. For example, people who have never served in government, never become active in a political party, and never attended a political rally depend on the media to provide them with all their information about how the political system works and the qualities of the candidates running for office. These people with highly limited political experience have no way to check the media portrayals against the real world, so they must accept the stories the media present as accurate.

We are all influenced by institutions, parents, friends, and other social forces. For example, with children, parental involvement in media exposure serves to influence learning. Children increase their understanding and recall of both central and incidental program content when adults provide comments to guide their children's attention and understanding during viewing. The more a person identifies with a peer group and the more cohesive is the group, the more the person will be influenced by the group and the less effect the media will have by themselves. Parental support for aggression as a means of problem solving has been found to have a greater influence on attitudes favorable to the use of aggression than the viewing of TV violence (Comstock, 1980; Hawkins & Pingree, 1982; McLeod, Fitzpatrick, Glynn, & Fallis, 1982). People have a shared schema they have learned about violence from years of viewing violent narratives in the media (W. J. Potter, Pashupati, Pekurny, Hoffman, & Davis, 2002). This learned schema forms their baseline as people use the schema to interpret all the violent messages they experience in the media.

Lifestyle

People who have active lifestyles where they interact with many people and institutions are generally less affected by the media. In contrast, people who have fewer real-life experiences because of lack of money, education, or vitality are more likely to have much higher

exposure to media that is not counterbalanced by other experiences. This is why the poor, low socioeconomic status (SES) individuals, ethnic minorities, and the elderly are particularly susceptible to the influence of the media, especially television, because they expose themselves to a great deal of TV due to their sociological and psychological isolation. TV becomes their window on the world and their primary source of information.

Personal Locus

Recall from Chapter 2 that the personal locus is the combination of an individual's goals and drives for media exposures. This may be the most important factor so far because it reflects the five factors above and, more important, activates the power of those five factors. Furthermore, it determines the seventh factor, which is a person's media exposure habits. When a personal locus is strong, the person has the drive energy to make the most of his or her maturities, skills, knowledge structures, sociological factors, and lifestyle.

People who have a strong personal locus have more awareness of the effects process, so they have constructed their baselines to conform to their personal goals. This means that they want to achieve particular effects with the help of the media; for these effects, they have constructed a baseline fairly close to the manifestation level so that a single exposure to the proper media message can achieve the effect. People with a strong personal locus are also aware that they do not want to manifest some effects themselves, so they construct baselines for those effects far from the manifestation level. To illustrate, let's say Jane and Phyllis both have a strong need to make friends. Jane is acutely aware of this need and uses the media to satisfy her need for friendship. She joins Facebook and actively searches out friends. She texts her new friends to find out more about their interests and consciously gravitates to those people with whom she shares the most interests. Over time, Jane has used the media to grow her circle of friends, and with her continual interactions, she builds more meaningful friendships both on Facebook and into the real world. In contrast, Phyllis feels lonely so she gravitates to television series where she can identify with certain kinds of characters. Over time, she gets pulled more into the world of those fictional characters where she feels part of their lives. However, since these media experiences are not interactive, Phyllis is only observing others and not building her friendship skills, so when she meets a person in real life, it is very difficult for her to interact in a friendly manner, and friendships are not manifested.

Media Exposure Habits

Each of us has a set of media exposure habits that focuses our attention on certain media and certain types of messages presented by those media. For example, some people like to surf the Internet and go to all kinds of sites indiscriminately. In this case, they are exposed to a very wide range of messages, and no single type of message is likely to have much effect on their baseline. In contrast, other people might spend all their time playing violent video games and watching action/adventure movies. These people are likely to have a baseline very close to the manifestation level for aggressive behavior (W. J. Potter, 1991).

Fluctuation Factors

While understanding where your baselines are in the processes of influence, it is also important to monitor the factors that will move you off your baseline and create a fluctuation effect. In this section, I present six types of factors about the media as well as three types of factors about you that are important in assessing whether fluctuations will occur.

Content of the Messages

It matters what you expose yourself to in a particular exposure session. Let's say you have a habitual exposure pattern of horror and action/adventure shows, and your baseline is very high for an aggressive effect. If you watch another hour of television, will that be enough to push you above the manifestation level? It depends on what content you watch. If you watch a comedy program in which the characters help each other and the themes are prosocial, then you are likely to move away from the manifestation level. But if you watch a highly violent program, then you will be more likely to move toward the manifestation level.

Context of Portrayals

The meaning of the messages arises from the way they are portrayed, especially social lessons. When the characters in a story are portrayed as being highly attractive, when their actions are portrayed as being justified, and when they are rewarded for those actions, then audiences will likely identify with those attractive characters, experience the action from their point of view, and learn from this vicarious experience. Audiences will accept the meaning of the experience that was portrayed by those characters.

This is why the portrayal of violence in the media is so dangerous. The "good guys" are as likely as the "bad guys" to commit acts of violence. The good guys' violent acts are almost always portrayed as being justified, and they are rarely punished. The meaning of violence, then, is that if you are a good guy, violence is an essential and successful means of resolving conflict. Because each viewer regards himself or herself as a good guy, viewers learn that it is okay for them to use violence.

Cognitive Complexity of Content

When the message makes few cognitive demands on viewers, people can process its meaning easier (Lang, Potter, & Bolls, 1999). The more demands the narrative makes on the working memory, the less well will facts be comprehended and remembered (Fisch, 2000). For example, children remember news better from TV than from print, regardless of their reading proficiency. This is because TV news can provide information in several channels at once (pictures, words, and sound), and when the information is semantically redundant—that is, it complements and reinforces each other—learning is achieved better (Gunter, Furnham, & Griffiths, 2000). Children's comprehension of educational content from media messages is dependent on the degree to which the information is central to the narrative. Facts that are tangential to the main flow of a message are learned less well than facts that are central to the message. Also, people remember information better when emotional cues are also used (Bucy & Newhagen, 1999).

Motivations

When people have a conscious need for a particular kind of information, they will actively seek out this type of information in the media, and the chance of them learning from this experience is high. When people are passive, learning can still occur, but it is not as likely. Also, people who have a higher education and higher intelligence are more motivated to seek out information from the media. These people select the information that has the greatest utility to them.

One reason why television violence is so popular is because many viewers are sensation seekers. These people are bored and want to feel arousal, and watching television violence is very arousing (Krcmar & Greene, 1999).

States

A state is a drive or emotional reaction that occurs in response to some temporary stimuli. It is relatively short lived. Oftentimes, something will happen in our lives that will cause us to feel angry or frustrated. This state can interact with media content and lead to certain effects. For example, someone who is frustrated and then views violence will be much more likely to behave aggressively than if only one of these conditions is present.

The media frequently alter our psychological states. Perhaps the most important of these states is arousal. When viewers are aroused, their attention is more concentrated, and the experience is more vivid for them. They will remember the portrayals more and will be more likely to act while aroused (Comstock et al., 1978; Zillmann, 1991). When viewers are aroused, their attention is more concentrated, and the experience is more vivid for them. They will remember the portrayals more and will be more likely to act while aroused (Comstock et al., 1978; Zillmann, 1991).

Certain production techniques tend to arouse viewers. These techniques include fast cuts, quick motion within a frame, loud music, and sound effects. Also, certain narrative conventions (such as suspense, fear, life-threatening violence, and erotica) can lead to arousal.

Although most states are regarded as physiological or emotional ones, there are cognitive states also, and these are especially important with media literacy. If you find yourself confronting information about a topic where you have no context or background information, you will likely find yourself in a state of ignorance. This cognitive state of ignorance is usually associated with emotional states of frustration or despair. But the cognitive part of this state is keyed to a lack of informational context. Like all states, cognitive states are short lived because people will typically avoid the message or search out more information on the topic. Either response is sufficient to end the experience of ignorance on that topic.

Degree of Identification

Identification with particular characters is also a key factor in the effects process because people will pay more attention to those characters with whom they identify. We become involved in media-depicted events through a psychological relationship with the characters in a two-step process. First, we make a judgment about how much we are attracted to the character and how much the character is like us—or how we would like to be. Second, we engage in an "as if" experience in which we imagine ourselves in the role of the character. Viewers form strong attachments to certain characters, depending on what those characters do and say (Hoffner & Cantor, 1991). The stronger the attachment, the stronger the probability of an effect (Bandura, 1986, 1994) that will show up as a fluctuation.

People identify with characters who have similarities to them but who also have qualities that they would like to possess but do not. We have known for a long time that in general, people like characters who are more similar to them in age, gender, ethnicity, and interests (Himmelweit, 1966). Although most people tend to select the same-gender character, girls often choose male characters as role models; boys rarely choose female characters. Girls look for physical attractiveness in their selections for role models; boys look for physical aggressiveness. Usually, identification is with a positive object, but it can also be induced through negative sentiment.

MEDIA LITERACY AND BLAME

Let's return once again to the Russian roulette situation from the beginning of this chapter and readdress the following question: Should the media be blamed for the death of the boy who shot himself? This question is continually asked when we hear about a killing that is modeled after a portrayal in a movie, television show, or a video game. Although a death resulting from someone imitating something he or she saw in the media is cause for public attention, the public discourse about this problem is very weak. People will typically blame the media, the gun, or the parents of the killed boy. There is little understanding that these three and many other factors are all contributing influences. If we are to blame one, we should blame them all, because all are contributing factors.

We need to understand that in our complex society, seldom does a single element cause an effect. There are always many influences, and they work in combination. This is not hard for us to understand when it comes to knowing what causes a fire, for example. A fire requires fuel, oxygen, and heat. All three must be present to have a fire. With media effects, many factors about the media portrayal, factors in the life of the people involved, and factors about the real-world situation all contribute to a probability that an effect will break through the manifestation level. No one of these factors is responsible by itself.

Who is to blame? It depends on how you ask the question. If the question is, "Should the gun manufacturers be held solely responsible for crimes committed using their guns?" the answer is no, of course not, because there are other influences involved. If the question instead is, "Are the gun manufacturers blameless?" the answer again is no because their guns have been essential ingredients in certain violent crimes. The key here is to recognize multiple influences and *not allow* any one of the influences to be absolved simply because it was not the *only* influence.

MEDIA LITERACY: CONTROLLING THE MEDIA EFFECTS PROCESS

The effects process is a complex one. That is why it requires a person of relatively high media literacy to appreciate the process. People who are at low levels of literacy will believe there is no effect because they do not know what to look for, or they will focus on artifacts that might not be attributable to the media. Either way, low-level media literacy misleads people into a false sense of awareness.

The key to controlling effects is an understanding of how they work and what factors most influence those workings. We need to think beyond those fluctuations that break through the manifestation level and also consider process effects. We also need to understand that baselines are even more important than fluctuations. This helps us take a proactive approach to media effects. When we understand where baselines are in relation to manifestation levels, we can help condition the direction of our baselines to bring them closer to the manifestation level for those effects we want to experience in our lives— effects such as high levels of learning, use of informed opinions, and the practice of behaviors that make us most happy and productive. At the same time, we need to condition our baselines for negative effects so that they move further and further away from the manifestation levels.

SUMMARY

Media effects are constantly occurring in a complex process. Perhaps it would be useful to think of this in a metaphorical way (see Box 14.1) to make these ideas more accessible. We are all familiar with the idea that there is always weather, but its effect on us is constantly changing.

Box 14.1 The Weather as an Analogy for Media Effects

Media effects are like the weather in many ways. Weather is always there, but it can take many forms. Sometimes it makes you shiver, sometimes it makes you wet, and sometimes it gives you a painful sunburn—but it is all weather. Weather is very difficult to predict with any precision because the factors that explain the weather are large in number, and their interaction is very complex. Supercomputers are used to try to handle all those factors in highly complex models. They help increase the predictive accuracy on the broad level; that is, they can tell us how much rainfall and how many sunny days a particular locale will have this year. But they cannot tell us with accuracy who will get wet on which days. Although the Weather Bureau cannot control the weather, we as individuals can control the weather's effect on us. We can carry an umbrella, use sunscreen, or close ourselves off from elements we don't like. And we can run out to embrace a beautiful day.

Like the weather, the media are pervasive and always around us. Also, like the weather, media influences are difficult to predict because the factors that explain such effects are large in number, and their interaction is very complex. We use powerful computers to examine large sets of variables in trying to make such predictions, and we have learned much about media effects. We know that certain types of messages will lead to certain kinds of opinions and behaviors in general, but we cannot predict with precision whose opinion or behavior will be changed. And as individuals, we do not have much power to control the media, but we have a great deal of power (if we will use it) to control the media's effects on us. To know how to use this power, we must be sufficiently literate about media effects.

There is an important difference between the weather and the influence of the media on us. With the weather, we all recognize its different forms and know when they are happening. It is fairly easy to tell the difference between rain, fog, and snow because there is much tangible evidence whenever these occur. But with media influence, the

> effects are often difficult to perceive until someone points them out. Then they become easier to spot. We need to train ourselves to be able to spot manifestations of media effects—positive as well as negative. And we need to be sensitive to the fact that there are also process effects in addition to manifested effects.

With media influence, it is important to keep in mind three ideas. First, media effects are constantly occurring because we are constantly being influenced directly and indirectly by media messages. Second, the media work with other factors in our lives in exerting their influence. And third, you can control the effects process in your own life—if you understand how the process works.

By now you should have a basic knowledge structure about how the effects process works. This will give you a much better perspective on controlling the process and thereby achieving the effects you want. However, this chapter cannot give you much detail about all the different factors that change the probabilities of all the media effects that could occur. I have alerted you to the different types of factors that have been found to influence many effects. But for you to elaborate this basic knowledge structure, you will need to take additional media effects courses and do additional reading of the relatively large literatures of media effects research studies.

This chapter focused on the nature of media effects and how they occur. However, it did not examine what those media effects were; that is the purpose of the next chapter.

> **Chapter Resources:** To test your knowledge and learn more about the topics discussed in this chapter, visit the Student Study Site at www.sagepub.com/potter6e.

FURTHER READING

Potter, W. J. (2011). *Media effects*. Thousand Oaks, CA: Sage.

I elaborate on the ideas in this chapter and the next chapter. I also present many more examples of media effects than I am able to present in the two effects chapters in this book.

Strasburger, V. C., & Wilson, B. J. (2002). *Children, adolescents, & the media*. Thousand Oaks, CA: Sage. (539 pages, including appendixes, references, and indexes)

This is a very readable book with lots of cartoons, pictures, and graphics. The content deals with how both children and adolescents are influenced by the media, particularly the content of advertising, violence, sexuality, drug use, music, and portrayals of food. It also has special chapters on the media of electronic games and the Internet. The authors take a public health perspective in showing the risks of different kinds of media content on individuals and society. The book concludes with chapters on recommendations to help individuals protect themselves as well as recommendations to others, such as programmers, advertisers, policy makers, educators, parents, and researchers.

EXERCISE 14.1

Profiling the Probability of an Effect

1. Analyze a particular media effect along with its pattern of factors that would influence the probability of the effect actually occurring. For example, choose the viewing of a violent movie and its potential effect on you behaving aggressively immediately after the viewing the film.

   a. Look at the list of 13 factors (7 set point factors and 6 factors special to a type of effect) in this chapter and use them to write a profile of the characteristics that would need to be present in the film and that would increase the probability of you behaving aggressively. For example, with context of portrayals, what contextual characteristics would need to be in the film to increase the probability of an aggressive effect?

   b. Now using the same 13 factors as a guide, write a profile that would keep the probability of an aggressive effect as low as possible.

   c. Look at the two profiles. Which one is closer to what you experience in your life? Are there factors about you personally that put you at risk for this type of effect? Are there characteristics about the films you typically see that increase your risk?

2. Do the same exercise above with another effect. Refer to Appendix B for choices.

3. Think about the possible effects of the media in your life and try to apply the following ideas:

   a. *Thresholds:* Have you noticed no effect in some area until you passed a certain level of exposure? What was the effect and level of threshold exposure?

   b. *Direct and indirect:* Can you think of any effects the media have had on you indirectly? For example, have your friends formed an opinion from media messages and then persuaded you to adopt that opinion without you ever being exposed to the original media messages?

EXERCISE 14.2

Diagnosing Risk

Each of the five following scenarios features a person interacting with some media message(s). For each of the five scenarios, think about the following five things:

a. Pick an effect that the person is at risk of fluctuating.

b. Think about where the person's baseline is for that effect. What factors went into positioning that baseline where it is?

c. What factors about a media exposure are likely to push the person toward the manifestation level?

d. What factors about the person's exposure experience or the person himself or herself are likely to push the person toward the manifestation level?

e. What could this person do to avoid being pushed toward the manifestation level?

Scenario 1: Bobby

Bobby is a 5-year-old who loves to watch action/adventure cartoons on Saturday morning television. His mother is happy that the television serves as a babysitter for Bobby, freeing time up for her to work in another part of the house.

Scenario 2: Jennifer

Jennifer is disgusted by watching political ads on television. She thinks all ads are negative and will not watch them. Also, she thinks all politicians are crooks and refuses to vote or pay attention to any news coverage of campaigns.

Scenario 3: Cool Dude

Cool Dude is a sophomore in college. For the past 4 years, he has been closely following heavy metal and rap music. He also watches a good deal of MTV. He stays up partying all night every night and sees himself as the center of social life at the school because of his dress, his talk, and his style.

Scenario 4: Alison

Four-year-old Alison has just watched Bambi's mother die in the movie. She is so grief stricken that she cannot take her nap.

Scenario 5: Percy

Percy is a teenager who has seen every horror film made. But now the thrill is gone. Recently, he has lost the ability to be scared while at the movies. Still, he continues to go to every new horror film—hoping that there will be some awesome special effect or super gruesome scene that can excite him.

Broadening Our Perspective on Media Effects

Key Idea: When we take a four-dimensional perspective—timing, type, valence, and intentionality—of effects, we can better appreciate the broad range of effects the media are constantly exerting on us.

Suzanne is babysitting her two younger brothers, ages 7 and 10. She is reading a magazine while they are watching Spiderman on television. She sees an ad for a new shampoo and tears out the coupon in the magazine ad, making a mental note to buy some of this brand when she is out shopping later today.

Her brothers are starting to shout at the television screen. Suzanne yells at her brothers to be quiet, then turns on her iPod to listen to some new music she has downloaded. As a new song starts playing, she starts to pay more attention to the lyrics and puts down her magazine. She begins to really like the song and wonders, "Who is singing this? I've never heard it before."

She begins to daydream about her date tonight. "I hope Tim takes me like to another like horror flick. It's like so much fun to like scream my lungs out and to attack him like during the bad parts."

When the song on the iPod finishes, she is in a happy mood, which is then shattered as her brothers begin yelling at each other and then wrestling around on the floor. Suzanne runs into the TV room and breaks up the fight. "You guys better behave yourselves or I won't let you watch your video of Spiderman anymore! Get back in your own chairs now."

Peace restored, Suzanne picks up a newspaper and notices a story about a drive-by shooting where a gang of youths imitated some action in a recent movie. She thinks, "The media have such a bad effect on young kids. My brothers are going to end up in jail if they keep watching those shows. Thank goodness the media don't have any effect on me!"

Many of us have a narrow view of media effects. We look for high-profile tragedies as evidence of a media effect and use those isolated incidents to conclude that there are media effects. Although these high-profile tragedies are indications of media effects, they are rare in number, and this leads many people to think that media effects do not happen often and that when effects do occur, they happen to *other* people. This is faulty thinking. Media effects are happening all around us every day. And those effects are not just happening to other people; they are happening to *all* people, including Suzanne and us. For example, in the scenario above, Suzanne was persuaded to buy a new shampoo, changed her mood by listening to the downloaded music to try to calm herself down, had fantasies triggered when she looked forward to a movie later that day, and learned about a crime by reading the newspaper, then generalized from that one story to an unreasonable fear about her brothers ending up as convicts.

If we have a narrow perspective on what media effects are, then we will not be able to perceive the many effects that are constantly occurring all around us. Such a narrow perspective does not eliminate the effects; those effects still happen, but they influence you without your awareness and, more important, occur outside your control. A key to media literacy is an awareness of the variety of media effects. When you have this knowledge, you can decide which effects you want to experience and which you want to avoid. You can gain control.

The purpose of this chapter is to help you become more aware of the variety of media effects by expanding your perspective. Many, many effects can occur from media exposures. For a description of many of the more important of these effects, see Appendix B. But before you look at a list of individual effects, focus on the big picture; that is, read through this chapter and build a better knowledge structure by learning to think about media effects in four dimensions. These dimensions are time, type, valence, and intentionality.

TIMING OF EFFECTS

Media effects can either be immediate or long term. The timing of effects distinction focuses your attention on *when the effect occurs,* not on *how long it lasts.*

An immediate effect is one that happens during exposure to the media message. If the effect does happen, it might last only for a short period (such as becoming afraid during a movie) or might last forever (such as learning the outcome of a presidential election), but it is still an immediate effect because it changed something in you during the exposure. For example, when you visit your friends' Facebook pages, you learn what's new in their lives. Or while reading a website on sports, you immediately feel happy when you learn that your favorite sports team won an important game. And when you watch an action/adventure film, you might begin jumping around in your seat and wrestling with your friends. These are all immediate effects, because something happened to you during the exposure.

Long-term effects show up only after many exposures. No single exposure or no single message is responsible for the effect. Instead, it is the *pattern* of repeated exposures that sets up the conditions for a long-term effect. For example, after watching years of crime programs and news reports, you might come to believe that your neighborhood is a high-crime environment. No single exposure or event "caused" this belief; the belief is slowly and gradually constructed over years of exposures until one day it occurs to you that you better buy another set of locks for your doors.

Immediate effects are much easier to notice than are long-term effects. There are two reasons for this. First, immediate effects are fluctuations that often break through the manifestation level. Recall from the previous chapter that fluctuation effects are sudden deviations from a person's baseline level. When these fluctuation effects are clearly manifested, you notice that a change in your behavior or a particular emotion—such as anger or lust—flares up all of a sudden. Long-term effects also take the form of changes, but those changes happen so gradually and take so long to build that it is very difficult to notice any one of those tiny slivers of changes.

A second reason immediate effects are easier to notice is because they occur during an exposure to a particular message, and this makes it easy to link the effect to the media message as a cause and conclude there was a media effect. By the time people notice a long-term effect, it is well after many media exposures and many other things happening in their lives, so it is more difficult to link the effect to media exposures.

TYPE OF EFFECTS

Most of the concern about the media focuses on the *behavior* of individuals. For example, there is a belief that watching violence will lead people to behave aggressively, that watching portrayals of sexual activity will make people promiscuous, and that watching crime will make people go out and commit the crimes they witness in media messages. However, we need to expand our focus beyond behavioral effects and also consider cognitive, attitudinal, emotional, and physiological effects. Also, we need to think beyond effects on individuals and also consider effects on more macro things, such as society and institutions.

Cognitive-Type Effect

Perhaps the most pervasive yet overlooked media-influenced effect is the cognitive-type effect. Media can affect what we know by planting ideas and information into our minds. This happens all the time and may be the most prevalent media effect. We are constantly acquiring information during every exposure to the media. But rarely do people credit the media with this type of effect when they are thinking about media effects. Think about all

the information you now possess that got into your mind from your exposures to textbooks, magazines, and newspapers.

This cognitive learning is not limited to factual information; we also learn a great deal of social information from the media. As children, we learn a great deal about our world by observing role models—parents, older siblings, friends, and so on. Observation of social models accounts for almost all of the information communicated to children up until the time they begin school. The mass media provide an enormous number of models and actions from which children might learn. Given the large amount of time children spend with the media, pictorially mediated models (especially television and movies) exert a strong influence on children's learning about social situations.

Even as adults, we continue to pay careful attention to social models. When we do not have the social models we need in our real lives, we can usually find them in the media. Some of us want to learn most from social models who are powerful, extremely witty, physically attractive, or very successful in a particular career or sport. We develop a vicarious relationship with a professional athlete, famous actor, powerful politician, or wealthy role model. By observing these role models in the media, we gather lots of social information about what it takes to be successful and happy. Think of all the information you have in your memory about characters in television shows and movies you have seen; think about all those names, faces, behaviors, witty lines, and emotions they portrayed.

Attitudinal-Type Effect

The media can create and shape our opinions, beliefs, and values. This is the attitudinal-type effect. Attitudes can also be learned immediately. We could hear a new song on our iPod and immediately decide that it is one of the best songs we have ever heard, that is, create a positive attitude about the song. Or we could read the discussion of a political candidate on some blog and immediately decide that she would be a good leader.

The media also exert long-term attitudinal effects. One long-term attitudinal effect is cultivation. Over years of watching criminals hurt people and steal their possessions, we come to form the attitude that the world is a mean and violent place. We come to believe that the crime rate is rising dramatically each year when in fact it is going down. Another long-term attitudinal effect is reinforcement. Most advertising messages are aimed at existing customers of particular products; the advertisers want to give their current customers additional reasons to keep buying those products and to continue feeling good doing so. Advertisers want to reinforce our brand-loyal habits and prevent us from trying competitors' products. As long as those advertisers can keep reinforcing our positive attitudes about their brands, those attitudes will become stronger and stronger over time and thus less likely to change.

Emotional-Type Effect

The media exert an emotional-type effect by making us feel things. They can trigger strong emotions such as fear, rage, and lust. They can also evoke weaker emotions such as sadness, peevishness, and boredom. Emotional reactions are related to physiological changes. In fact, some psychological theoreticians posit that emotions are nothing more than physiological arousal that we label (Zillmann, 1991). If a character on a YouTube video triggers a very high level of arousal, we might label this feeling love or hate; it depends on whether we are positive or negative about the character.

We have all experienced emotional changes while exposing ourselves to media messages. Horror movies trigger extreme fear, newspaper editorials can make us feel outrage, magazine pictures can make us feel lust, and calm music can help us feel more peaceful.

The media also exert long-term emotional effects. One long-term emotional effect is desensitization. Over years of watching violence in the media, which rarely show victims suffering and instead focus on the perpetrators of the violence and how attractive they are, we gradually come to lose the ability to feel sympathy for victims both in media portrayals and in real life. We might regard the homeless as people who are victims of their own bad judgment and don't deserve much sympathy from us.

Physiological-Type Effect

Media can influence our automatic bodily systems, which are physiological-type effects. These are usually beyond our conscious control, such as the contraction of the pupil of the eye when we look at a bright light. We cannot control the degree to which the pupil dilates, but we can look away from bright lights and thus prevent the iris from contracting.

With the media, there are many physiological effects that usually serve to arouse us. A suspenseful mystery serves to elevate our blood pressure and heart rate. A horror film triggers rapid breathing and sweaty palms. Hearing a patriotic song might raise goose bumps on our skin. Viewing erotic pictures can lead to vaginal lubrication, penile tumescence, and increased heart rate (Malamuth & Check, 1980). A farce might make us laugh so hard that we are unable to stop, even when laughing becomes painful. Or listening to music can calm and relax us by reducing our heartbeat and bringing our rate of breathing down to a regular, slow rate.

Over time, our physiological responses to particular media messages can change. For example, when we see our first horror movie, our heart rate might go through the roof. But if we keep watching horror movies, we might find that it takes more and more gore to trigger any increase in heart rate. Gradually, over many exposures to horror films, our physiological responses wear down.

Behavioral-Type Effect

Media can trigger actions. This is the behavioral-type effect. For example, after seeing an ad for a product, we might get on a website and order the product. Or we read about some disturbing event on a news site on the Internet and call a friend to talk about it.

There are also long-term effects to our behavior. For example, we might buy a computer and get on the Internet. For the first several weeks, our Internet sessions are relatively brief, perhaps 15 minutes or so. But over several years, the time we spend per day on the Internet might grow to several hours. The Internet behavioral habit is displacing other activities, such as watching television, exercising, or going to class.

Macro-Type Effects

The five types of effects presented above are all effects on individuals. The media also exert macro-type effects on larger units such as organizations, institutions, and society. Some institutions, such as politics, have fundamentally changed due to the direct influence of the media, especially television and now the Internet. Other institutions—such as the family, society, and religion—have changed because of many different social pressures, and the media have served to heighten these pressures.

To illustrate this point, let's consider the institution of family. In the span of a few generations, the makeup of the American family has changed radically. The number of traditional two-parent families has shrunk, eclipsed by childless couples, single parents, and people living alone (Perkins, 1996). From the early 1970s to 2009, the percentage of American households made up of married couples with children dropped from 45% to 25%. Marriage has also dropped from 75% of all adults in 1972 as being married to 57% in 2009 (U.S. Bureau of the Census, 2011).

One argument for the cause in the decline of the traditional family is that the rates of divorce are very high in the United States, and they have been climbing since television first penetrated our culture. In 1960, 16% of first marriages ended in divorce, and by 1996, the figure had climbed to 40% (Whitman, 1996). Critics claim that the rise in the divorce rate and the portrayals of broken families on television are not a mere coincidence; they claim that the television portrayals have socialized people to believe that divorce and having children out of wedlock are acceptable. Critics point out that television too frequently portrays divorce, single-parent households, and alternative lifestyles. These portrayals, presented over many different kinds of shows and over many years, tend to be internalized by viewers. Over time, people become dissatisfied with their own marriages and seek adventure with other partners. Also, popular television series, such as *Desperate Housewives,* portray married life in a negative manner, thus giving young people the idea that marriage is an unattractive lifestyle.

Television, as well as other media, has the potential to bring the family together to share a common experience. Families can build a bonding ritual around television by agreeing to watch a particular movie or series and then spend time talking about it after the exposure. In the 1970s, many households had only one television, and viewing was a common family activity (Medrich, Roizen, Rubin, & Buckley, 1982). However, few families now use television or other media in this way. Family members rarely share viewing time. Instead, family members are likely to watch very different shows at different times on different platforms, like laptops, smartphones, and iPods.

Also, parents have reduced the time they spend with their children—40% less time from the 1950s to the 1990s (Pipher, 1996). Pipher argues (1996), "Rapidly our technology is creating a new kind of human being, one who is plugged into machines instead of relationships, one who lives in a virtual reality rather than a family" (p. 92). "When people communicate by e-mail and fax, the nature of human interaction changes" (p. 88). The conveniences of technology serve to cut us off from others. We depend less and less on others (at least face-to-face). People are things or services, not human beings. Pipher says that 72% of Americans don't know their neighbors, and the number of people who say they have never spent time with the people next door has doubled in the past 20 years.

Even if we accept the argument that television has influenced the trend toward the breakdown of the traditional family, we must realize that there are also other influences, such as economic ones. For example, it takes more money to support a family. The median household income is now more than $58,400. So both adults are likely to work, and this makes it harder for them to have children and raise them at home. The percentage of women in the labor force has been steadily climbing, and women now comprise 47% of all employed people in the United States (U.S. Bureau of the Census, 2009).

Another reason that family structure and family interaction have changed is that careers have become more important to many people than their families. Wage earners work longer hours, and this takes them away from the home for a higher proportion of their waking hours. The strong stressors of time, money, and lifestyle make people regard the home as a place to recover from the workplace, not a place where they have high energy. No longer is family of paramount importance in most people's lives (Pipher, 1996). The irony is that perhaps people are working longer hours so they can afford more of the things advertised on television and thereby achieve a happier life as promised by advertisers, but by spending less time with our loved ones, we are steadily becoming less happy.

Clearly, family structures and interaction patterns have been changing over the past four decades. There are many reasons for this. Television is a key element, but not the only one, in this change. The additional elements of economic demands, the rise in the importance of careers, and changes in lifestyle preferences have all contributed to the probability of change in the institution of family.

Many other examples of changes in institutions can be attributed to media influence. Some of these macro-type effects are presented in more detail later in this book in Part VI when I deal with the topics of violence (Chapter 19) and sports (Chapter 20).

VALENCE OF EFFECTS

The effect can be in a positive or negative direction. These terms are value laden. Who is to decide what is positive and negative? The answer can be approached in two ways: the individual and society.

From the individual perspective, a positive direction is one where the effects help you achieve your personal goals. In this situation, you are usually aware of your goals and use the media strategically to achieve those goals. For example, if your goal is to get some information to satisfy your curiosity, then finding facts in a book, in a newspaper, or on the Internet is a positive cognitive effect. This can move you toward a goal of having more information and achieving a higher level of knowledge. In contrast, a negative effect occurs when the media use you as their tool to achieve their goals, if their goals are in conflict with your goals. For example, advertisers want you to spend more and more of your money on their products. If you do this, you may be going bankrupt trying to solve problems you really don't have.

We can also look at the valence of effects from a broad societal point of view. If the media teach people how to commit crimes and trigger that behavior, then the media are exerting a negative influence. However, the media also make a great deal of information available, which can serve to make the public more informed and therefore choose better leaders and support the best solutions for social problems. When this happens, society is stronger, and therefore this is a positive effect.

INTENTIONALITY OF EFFECTS

Oftentimes, we intend for an effect to happen, so we consciously seek out particular messages in the media to get that effect. For example, we may be bored and want to feel high excitement. To satisfy this conscious need, we go to a movie that presents a great deal of action and/or horror. During the movie, our blood pressure and heart rate go way up, and we are on the edge of our seat with fear. We have satisfied our need. Also, when we seek out factual knowledge in the media, we are consciously trying to achieve a positive cognitive effect. For example, you visit a sports site on the Internet to learn about which teams won their games yesterday, you watch a cooking show to copy down a new recipe, or you access an app on your smartphone that tells you which groups will be appearing in concert in your area. The information does not need to be extremely important, and it need not be remembered for more than a few minutes for an effect to have occurred. Every day, there are dozens of examples where you intentionally use the media to pick up a fact that you can use or trigger a feeling you want to experience.

Many times, we expose ourselves to the media for one reason, but other effects that we were not seeking also occur. To illustrate, most of our viewing of primetime television is purely for purposes of entertainment. We are looking for funny portrayals so we can laugh, or we watch dramatic programs to see what happens to our favorite characters. During these exposures, we will usually have our intended effects occur; that is, we will laugh and get some information on the travails of our favorite characters. But other effects are also occurring—effects we did not seek out and perhaps effects that we are not even aware of until someone later points them out. For example, our TV program may be interrupted by a series of advertisements, and some of those jingles or sayings stay with us. Or perhaps we begin snacking after seeing so many food products advertised. Our body did not tell us we were hungry—the media did. Also, we listen to popular songs primarily to be entertained, but we also unconsciously pick up the attitudes of the rappers. Thus, we frequently experience effects different from our intentions.

Unintentional effects are not limited to immediate learning. They can be long term as well, and they can be attitudinal, emotional, physiological, and behavioral. For example, after years of watching exciting movies, you develop a belief that the real world should be much more exciting. Also, your emotional and physiological reactions may have become desensitized; that is, it takes more excitement to make you happy. You did not intend for this to happen, but it happened anyway.

Even when you are experiencing an intentional effect, you may be subjected to unintended effects at the same time. For example, you watch a violent movie solely for the excitement, and the movie does deliver the excitement you wanted. However, the movie may also be delivering other effects with the excitement. You may be experiencing an emotional desensitization effect. Also, you have the elements forming to generalize to a belief that the world is a mean and dangerous place, which is a long-term cognitive effect.

Unintentional effects frequently occur when you are in the state of automaticity because your defenses are not engaged. You are not aware that any learning is taking place, and hence you are not actively evaluating and processing the information. However, even when you are trying to be an active viewer, unintended effects can occur. For example, let's say you watch a news program such as *Crossfire* or *Meet the Press*. You understand that the people on that program are spinning the story in a way to reach their own particular goals. They are not there to inform you about the complexity of the situation; they do not want to reach a compromise or a synthesis of a higher realization on the issue. Instead, they dumb down the issue and present their polarized position so the general public does not get lost, and they make their position look as attractive as possible so that most of the public will agree with them. Now, if you are actively watching this and processing this information, you can protect yourself from the influence of either message by acting media literate and trying to synthesize the two positions and construct a more common ground on the issue. This is much better than simply accepting one of the polarized positions. By analyzing and evaluating the messages actively, you gain control over your opinion formation, and this is good. But a negative effect may still occur as you develop a mistrust of political figures.

SUMMARY

A key step in increasing your media literacy is to expand your perspective about what is a media effect. Don't get trapped into thinking of the media only as kind of a candy store (see Box 15.1). Don't think that the media only affect others, such as young children who don't know any better or the criminal types who claim they copy what they see in the media.

Box 15.1 Candy as an Analogy for Media Effects

Many people think of media effects as if they were candy. As we walk down the street, there are people passing out all kinds of candy for free. They want us to taste their sweets, then come into the store and buy something. We are tempted. When we take a piece, it tastes good and makes us want another piece. Often we sneak another piece or two, thinking it can't hurt. But then a few minutes later, we experience a sugar rush followed by a crash of energy. Also, there is this lingering sweet taste in our mouths that becomes unpleasant as time goes by. We envision the sugar eating holes in our teeth. If we have kids with us, we find they are rambunctious and whine for more candy. And now we have to act like the bad guy and tell them no; it will spoil their dinner.

A lot of people think of the media as a candy store. Their messages are tempting, and we let ourselves sample and often like the experience. But afterwards, we feel guilty. We feel we should have been doing something more substantial or productive with our time. We feel that those messages are now eating holes in our brains as we can't get a jingle, a song, or a stupid joke out of our minds. If we have kids with us, we fear that they are soon going to imitate the bad language, bad attitudes, or bad behavior they have seen in the messages.

Yes, the media do offer lots of "candy" messages. If we indulge ourselves with a steady diet of candy over the years, we will clog up our arteries with fat and experience all sorts of negative health effects. But the media offer many other kinds of messages. If we can resist the initial temptation of candy and instead find the more nutritious messages in other parts of the media cafeteria, we can consume a more balanced and full range of vitamins and minerals. To live a more healthy life, we need to know what to consume and we need to exercise some self-discipline.

We live in a media-saturated environment, and the effects are constantly happening to us as they shape our knowledge patterns, attitudes, emotions, and behaviors. They even trigger physiological reactions, such as our heart rate, blood pressure, and other bodily functions. And we don't even need to experience a change in order to see that the media have had an effect on us because a prevalent effect is reinforcement—that is, solidifying our existing beliefs and behaviors.

In our everyday lives, the immediate and long-term processes work together. The immediate process gives us a new fact that either extends our learning or adds weight to our already existing structure. In the long term, we look for patterns across these facts and infer conclusions about how the world operates. These generalized conclusions then become part of our knowledge structures. If we are not aware that we are making generalizations, then we cannot control that process and ensure that those generalizations are reasonable and accurate. Thus, faulty principles will get into our knowledge structures and lead us to make more defective conclusions and guide our search for facts in a faulty manner.

Being media literate requires that we understand the full range of media effects. We need to recognize when those effects are having a negative influence on us so we can protect ourselves. And we need to recognize when the effects are having a positive influence on us so we can appreciate and enhance their power.

Now that you have a broader appreciation for media effects, take a look at the list of effects in Appendix B. This list is not exhaustive. Instead, the list provides illustrations of all kinds of effects. Look for these media effects in your own lives, and let this selection of effects sensitize you to look for many other media effects.

Chapter Resources: To test your knowledge and learn more about the topics discussed in this chapter, visit the Student Study Site at www.sagepub.com/potter6e.

FURTHER READING

Bryant, J., & Oliver, M. B. (Eds.). (2009). *Media effects: Advances in theory and research* (3rd ed.). New York: Routledge. (640 pages, including index)

Now in its third edition, this classic academic book presents a set of 27 chapters written by experts on a wide range of mass media effects. Each chapter provides an in-depth review of the research literature on a different effects theory (e.g., agenda setting, cultivation, social cognitive theory), type of effect (e.g., social perception, eating disorders, attitude change), or influence of type of content (e.g., sex, violence, educational television).

Johnson, S. (2006). *Everything bad is good for you.* New York: Riverhead Books. (250 pages, including end notes)

Steven Johnson, who is not an academic but a bestselling author, argues that the popular opinion that the media are harmful to us is wrong. Instead, he says that exposure to media, especially television and video games, produces more net good than harm. He says that media messages are getting more complex, not more simple, over time. This makes exposure more challenging and hence more rewarding. The storylines of TV shows are much more complex and involved now than they were several decades ago. And today's video games are far more challenging than early video games. He says the culture is getting more intellectually demanding, not less.

Nabi, R. L., & Oliver, M. B. (Eds.). (2009). *Media processes and effects.* Thousand Oaks, CA: Sage. (643 pages with index)

This edited volume includes 37 chapters that focus on a wide variety of media effects topics. It is organized into six sections: conceptual and methodological issues; society, politics, and culture; message selection and processing; persuasion and learning; content and audiences; and medium issues.

KEEPING UP TO DATE

Journal of Advertising

Journal of Advertising Research

Journal of Broadcasting & Electronic Media

Journal of Communication

Journal of Communication Research

Journalism & Mass Communication Quarterly

Media Psychology

There are perhaps several hundred scholarly journals that publish research examining how media messages affect individuals and institutions. The seven journals listed above are the ones that account for most of that type of research published each year.

EXERCISE 15.1

Thinking About Media Effects

1. Pick some child with whom you have spent a fair amount of time. Can you think of any effects that child exhibited that could be regarded as a media effect? (List them below.)

_____

_____

_____

2. Pick some adult with whom you have spent a fair amount of time—perhaps a parent or a neighbor. Can you think of any effects that adult exhibited that could be regarded as a media effect? (List them below.)

_____

_____

_____

3. Pick a friend about your own age. Can you think of any effects that friend exhibited that could be regarded as a media effect? (List them below.)

_____

_____

_____

4. Now think about yourself. Can you think of any effects that you exhibited that could be regarded as a media effect? (List them below.)

_____

_____

_____

EXERCISE 15.2

Recognizing Immediate Effects

Think about the differences among cognitive, attitudinal, emotional, behavioral, and physiological effects. Then think about what has happened to you in your life after particular media exposures.

On a blank sheet of paper, divide the page into five rows, labeling them cognitive, attitudinal, emotional, behavioral, and physiological effects.

For each row, see if you can list at least two effects that have happened to you immediately after being exposed to the media. Name the immediate effect, and then describe a specific example of how the media have affected you or someone you know.

Use the list below to guide your thinking.

a. *Cognitive:* Media can immediately plant ideas and information.

b. *Attitudinal:* Media can influence attitudes and feelings about things.

c. *Emotional:* Media can trigger an immediate emotional reaction, such as fear, attraction, sadness, and laughter.

d. *Behavioral:* Media can trigger behavior.

e. *Physiological:* Media can arouse or calm you.

EXERCISE 15.3

Recognizing Long-Term Effects

Think about how the media may have exercised a subtle effect on you over the long term.

On a blank sheet of paper, divide the page into five rows, labeling them cognitive, attitudinal, emotional, behavioral, and physiological effects.

For each row, see if you can list two long-term effects. Next to each effect, describe specifically how long-term exposure to media has led to that effect on you.

Use the following list to guide your thinking.

Long-term effects: Slow accumulation of information, attitudes, and images leads to beliefs about the real world.

a. *Cognitive:* Oftentimes, people will not expose themselves to the media with the purpose of learning anything. Rather, they will be interested in seeking escape or entertainment. This is especially true with television, radio, and film. However, acquisition of information and attitude change do take place. This type of learning is called *incidental learning.*

b. *Attitudes:* Erosion or building up of certain attitudes.

c. *Emotional:* People can build up a tolerance against emotional reactions over time and thus become desensitized.

d. *Behavioral:* New behaviors can be learned in the short term but not performed until much later.

e. *Physiological:* Increased tolerance for certain content; physiological dependency on a medium or certain content.

EXERCISE 15.4

What Have You Internalized From the Media Culture?

1. When you are driving and listening to your car radio, do you switch the channel, looking for something else, even when you are satisfied with the song you are currently hearing—thinking maybe a better song is on another station now? Do you flip through the channels on the television set looking for something better?

2. In romantic relationships, which is more important to you: commitment or perfection? When you are in a romantic relationship, are you happy when you make a lasting, strong commitment to the other person? Or do you worry that this person may not be the absolute best one for you and perhaps there is someone a little better out there?

3. In college, do you value learning or efficiency more? Do you make a commitment to each course, attend every session, and try to get all you can from them? Do you take a wide range of courses (some you know nothing about) to expand your experience?

   Or do you look for ways to spend your time better during class, such as going on a job interview, finishing a term paper for another course, or catching up on sleep? Do you look for courses on the basis of which ones require the least amount of work for the highest grades?

4. In your career, which will be more important to you: loyalty or success? Will you find a job and build your entire career there to pay back your employer for your first big opportunity? Or will you take the first job as a stepping stone to something better and leave as soon as you have learned all you can in that job?

5. When you have a major problem, are you upset when you cannot solve it in a short period of time?

Part 6

Confronting the Issues

This part of the book highlights the controversies surrounding five issues about the media:

- Ownership and Control of the Mass Media
- Privacy From the Mass Media
- Piracy of Mass Media Messages
- Violence
- Sports

Each of these is a very important issue for media literacy because there continues to be a high degree of public concern and debate over each of these issues. However, rarely does that debate move beyond a superficial level, and that is what makes these issues so much of a problem. The more you analyze these issues, the more you will understand how they are affecting your life—for both the good and the bad.

In each of these five chapters, I will present you with enough information so you can see the issue in more depth and understand more fully why each is a controversy. However, I do not present arguments to lead you to think a certain way. Instead, I give you the raw material to think for yourself. You need to evaluate the information on both sides of each controversy and develop your own informed opinion.

CHAPTER 16

Key Idea:
Ownership patterns show a strong movement toward concentration and away from localism.

Who Owns and Controls the Mass Media?

The issue of who should control the mass media has been an important one for as long as there have been mass media. It has its roots in a concern over how powerful an individual person or a single business should be allowed to become in American society. This concern was addressed during the founding of this country when some framers of the American Constitution wanted to limit the power of government and tried to spread power out over as many people as possible. Other framers of the Constitution wanted a strong federal government so that decisions could be made quickly and so that a single entity could be held accountable for those decisions. In a compromise, the Constitution created a strong federal government that was assigned certain powers, but it also reserved other powers for state and local governments.

This issue of concentration versus localism has also been debated in the business realm. Many people regard business monopolies as bad because consumers are better served by competition among businesses; they believe monopolies concentrate too much power in the hands of one business, which is then free to raise prices and degrade service because there are no competitors. Other people regard concentration of power in an industry as a good thing because it leads to economic efficiencies that are then passed on to customers in the form of lower prices. For example, huge companies such as Walmart and McDonald's can consistently offer lower prices because they are so big and efficient.

The issue of concentration of power is especially important with the mass media because the mass media control information. For example, critics worry that if one company controlled all the news outlets, then that one company could present only the news that it liked and ignore all the rest of the daily occurrences and political positions.

In this chapter, I will show you that the debate—at its most fundamental level—rests on the enduring conflict over two competing values in American culture. One of these values is localism, and the other is efficiency. Then I will show how the value of efficiency has been growing stronger as media companies have been growing larger. With this information as context, we turn our attention to the specific issues debated today concerning concentration in the media industries. It is important for you to realize that there are two sides to this issue—that is, both sides have advantages and disadvantages. When you understand the arguments on each side of an issue, you are in a better position to create your own opinion in an informed manner.

TWO COMPETING VALUES

In American culture, there have been two strong values competing with one another when addressing the issue of concentration of power—localism and efficiency. Localism values the sharing of power among as many people as possible. In contrast, efficiency values the concentration of power in the hands of a few people who can make decisions well and quickly. This essential tension between dispersion of power and concentration of power can be seen clearly in the development of the media industries. At times, consumers favor localism; they want a marketplace with as many voices as possible so they have lots of choices about how to satisfy their various needs for information and entertainment. But at other times, consumers favor concentration; they want a marketplace with easily available standard products for as low a price as possible, so they support concentrated retailers such as large restaurant chains and large department store chains. In the section below, let's examine how these two forces have been competing.

Localism

Localism is a populist value. It is exhibited by the belief that control of important institutions should be spread out as much as possible so that many people share the power. Thus, a considerable amount of power should exist at the local level, which is closest to individuals. It is based on the ideal that each person is a rational being, so each person should have an equal say in the political and economic arenas. This maximizes the freedom of each person. It also empowers all people by keeping them involved in as many important decisions as possible.

The founding fathers of America followed this value when creating a democratic form of government rather than a more efficient totalitarian one (such as a monarchy) at the national level. They also dispersed power by restricting the federal government from some areas and left decisions in these areas up to state and local governments. Thus, political power was structured so that it was spread out over many layers. America now has 18,000 municipalities and 17,000 townships. Within these, 500,000 local governmental units are directly elected by local residents, and 170,000 of them have the power to impose taxes.

Localism is a part of the American tradition. This country was founded on the belief that the individual is more important than are institutions or governments. When government is necessary, it should be decentralized so as to be closer to the people's needs and more accountable to them. Over time, the American public has retained its value for dispersion of power and has continued to support the overlapping, multilayered structure of government, even if it often seems inefficient.

Concerning the mass media, there is also a strong feeling by many that the media voices should be kept local if they are to serve best the needs of individuals and society. The media started as innovations at the local level. When a government was called upon to regulate them, the governmental agencies often favored this localism ethic in their policy making. A good example of this is how the federal government handled the development of the broadcasting industries. If you wanted to broadcast a radio or television signal, you would have to send your signal out on a frequency. If you and I wanted to use the same frequency to broadcast our different signals, then our signals would interfere with each other, and consumers would receive a garbled signal. A limited number of frequencies were set aside for broadcasting on what is called the electromagnetic spectrum. Someone had to decide who gets to use which frequencies, then enforce these decisions so that others don't come along later and interfere with your assigned frequency. The federal government decided that it was the one to make the decisions, reasoning that the electromagnetic spectrum belonged to all Americans much like a national park or any other resource that should be shared by all citizens.

In the early days of radio broadcasting, the federal government decided to require individuals to apply for a broadcast frequency with the Federal Communications Commission (FCC). The FCC was immediately flooded with applications for AM radio frequencies. But the AM band on the electromagnetic spectrum allowed for only about 117 frequencies. The FCC could have chosen 117 applicants and awarded each of them their own frequency. This would have led to 117 AM radio stations, with each using its frequency to broadcast its signal to the entire country. But that is not what the FCC did. Instead, the FCC divided the country into many local market areas and awarded some frequencies to each market. Also, each radio station was limited in the amount of power it could use to broadcast its signal so that the signals would not go beyond their local markets. This allowed the FCC to assign the same frequency to many different markets without having to worry about signals interfering with one another. The FCC chose this alternative because it wanted to spread the limited resource of broadcast frequencies around to as many different people as possible.

By keeping ownership of radio licenses at the local level, the FCC believed it was setting up a system whereby the stations would be operated in the best interests of their local communities. Private businesses were allowed to broadcast on these frequencies, provided they operate "in the public interest, convenience, and necessity." Therefore, the rationale for regulation in broadcasting was based on the following points: spectrum scarcity, localism, public interest, promoting diversity of content, and the prevention of monopolies.

Now the country has grown to about 215 broadcasting markets, with more than 13,000 radio stations. When television came along in the 1940s, the FCC used the same

procedure of allocating broadcasting licenses to local stations in the local markets. Now we have more than 6,800 broadcast television stations.

For decades, the FCC prevented broadcasting monopolies from developing by limiting the number of stations any one company could own to 7 AM, 7 FM, and 7 TV stations in total, with no two being in the same market. In the 1980s, the rules were relaxed to 12 AM, 12 FM, and 12 TV stations. Then the Telecommunications Act of 1996 further relaxed the limits to a significant extent in the guise of opening up competition. Also, the ban was lifted prohibiting a company from owning a TV and radio station in the same market. This deregulation triggered many mergers among media companies. During the 1990s, there was more than a total of $300 billion worth of major media deals in which companies bought multiple television and radio stations (Croteau & Hoynes, 2001). Since that time, the FCC periodically has held public hearings and has created more complex ownership rules that continue to allow for more concentration of ownership. Now a single company can own as many television stations as it wants as long at the coverage of that set of stations does not exceed 39.5% of viewers; it can also own more than one television station in a TV market. As for radio, a company can own as many stations as it wants, including 3 to 8 stations within a single radio market depending on the size of that market. Now one company—Clear Channel—owns more than 1,200 radio stations in the United States without violating the current "restrictions" on ownership.

Why does the FCC continually deregulate the broadcasting industry? The answer is that broadcasters put a great deal of pressure on the federal government to deregulate. Broadcasters have argued successfully that they were being unfairly limited in their rights to own multiple businesses. They pointed out that there were no ownership limits for magazines, book publishers, newspapers, and Internet sites; also, the previous limits on film studios had been relaxed. Consumer groups, who argued against relaxing the ownership rules, could present no convincing evidence that multiple ownership of broadcasting businesses caused harm to the public. In contrast, broadcasters showed that when businesses are consolidated, they are more efficient, and this efficiency is a benefit to consumers.

Cable operators have also been fighting to have limits relaxed so that they can expand. In 2009, the FCC had limited cable systems from servicing more than 30% of the U.S. population. Comcast, the nation's largest cable company at the time, with almost 25% of the nation's cable homes as subscribers, sued the FCC to raise its limit and won in a federal court of appeals, which reasoned that the restriction must be lifted to reflect the changing realities of the dynamic video marketplace where consumers have lots of alternatives to cable and therefore cable should not be regarded as a monopoly (Flint, 2009b).

Efficiency

Straining against this ethic of localism is a very strong trend toward concentration, consolidation, and centralization. Although almost every media company began as a small, local operation, they take on the characteristics of big business as they grow. Big businesses are complex organizations that market many different products and services but do so under a strong centralized system to achieve a more efficient operation. Big businesses grow by claiming a larger share of the markets in which they compete. They accomplish this by acquiring control of more resources, and this often leads to buying—or at least investing in—other companies.

General industry-wide trends show that fewer and fewer people control more and more of the media. And this trend will probably continue as the cost of buying and operating a media voice keeps going up and as entry into the industry becomes more difficult. Today, a person needs a great deal of money and expertise to attempt to buy a business in one of the established media industries. Because of this, only companies that already own media businesses are successful in acquiring new businesses. Entrepreneurs can still start a media business in the magazine, book publishing, and Internet industries, but those businesses begin as very small enterprises. Either those small companies go out of business quickly, or they grow successful and are usually bought by one of the big media conglomerates.

As media companies grow larger and more centralized, there is a danger that they will narrow the range of voices that will get heard. For example, if you send a letter to the editor of a newspaper with a circulation of 1,000, there is a good chance that your letter will get published. But if you send the same letter to a newspaper with a circulation of 1 million, your chance of being published is much smaller. Thus, the larger and more powerful the media company is, the less access you have for making a contribution to its messages or influencing the way it makes decisions. Larger companies must filter out more requests, and in this filtering-out process, there is a danger that some types of voices will not get heard at all.

With all the recent mergers and acquisitions in the media industries, ownership patterns have changed rapidly, but the one constant is the trend toward even greater concentration. For example, Bagdikian conducted an analysis of media ownership patterns in 1983 and found that the control of the media was essentially in the hands of 50 people—these were the CEOs of the largest media companies that, in combination, controlled more than half of the revenues and audiences in their media markets. Less than a decade later, Bagdikian (1992) found that the number had shrunk to 23 CEOs of corporations that control most of the business in the country's 25,000 media businesses. Eleven companies controlled most of the daily newspaper circulation. In magazine publishing, a majority of the total annual industry revenues went to two firms. Five firms controlled more than half of all book sales. Five media conglomerates shared 95% of the recordings market, with Warner and CBS alone controlling 65% of that market. Eight Hollywood studios accounted for 89% of U.S. feature film rentals. Three television networks earned more than two thirds of the total U.S. television revenues (Bagdikian, 1992). Then in 2000, Bagdikian published an updated version of his analysis and concluded that "six firms dominate all American mass media" (p. x). Each of these six companies (Bertelsmann, Disney, General Electric, News Corp., Time Warner, and Viacom) owned media vehicles in almost all of the mass media. All six own subsidiaries in many countries and market their messages all over the world.

CROSS-OWNERSHIP AND CONTROL

Types of Concentration

There are three different trends toward concentration. First, there is the horizontal merger. This is when one media company buys another media company of the same type. An example is a newspaper chain buying another newspaper. This pattern was very popular during the 1980s, when newspapers were being gobbled up by chains at the rate of 50 to 60 per year.

Second, there is the vertical merger. This is when one media company buys suppliers and/or distributors to create integration in the production and distribution of messages. An example is a book publisher buying a printing plant and some bookstores. Another example is Viacom, which owned television stations in Philadelphia, Boston, Dallas, Detroit, Pittsburgh, and Miami. It added significant vertical integration through its ownership of Paramount Pictures, thus allowing Viacom to control the production and distribution of television programs to the television networks (CBS or UPN) and through the Blockbuster stores that it owned. In addition, it could promote those shows' soundtracks on MTV and VH1 and do book tie-ins through Simon & Schuster—all of which were also owned by Viacom.

Third, there is the conglomerate merger. This is when a media company buys a combination of other media companies and/or companies in a nonmedia business. An example is a film studio that buys a newspaper, several radio stations, a talent agency, and a string of restaurants.

From the business point of view, cross-media ownership is attractive. Not only is it very profitable, but the arrangement also allows for cross-promotion of products. For example, when Paramount released its movie *The Brady Bunch,* Viacom aired several weeks of *Brady Bunch* TV reruns on its Nickelodeon cable channel as a way of promoting the movie.

Megamergers

During the 1980s, there were 2,308 mergers and acquisitions involving media companies for a total of $214 billion (Ozanich & Wirth, 1993). This activity served to consolidate resources in fewer companies. Thus, the CEOs of these newer, larger companies hold a greater concentration of power as they manage those resources. During the 1990s, mergers became more and more popular (see Table 16.1) because they are so profitable. For example, Westinghouse Electric Corporation, which began as a manufacturer of railroad air brakes in Pittsburgh in 1886, decided to change its line of business. By 1995, it had bought one of the major television networks—CBS—for $5.4 billion, then spent another $9 billion buying cable channels and radio stations over the next 2 years. In 1997, it moved its headquarters to New York City and took the name CBS ("CBS Headquarters," 1997). Then CBS was acquired by Viacom and folded into that conglomerate for a few years, but then Viacom spun CBS Corporation off into a separate company that was still owned by Viacom.

Phone companies keep looking for entertainment companies to buy. For example, GTE has 17 million phone lines and $20 billion revenue annually. BellSouth is the biggest regional phone company with 19 million phone lines, which bring in a total of $16 billion per year. With all their cash, the phone companies are looking to invest in profitable businesses, especially those that would give them access to customers who want to buy information and entertainment. In March 2011, AT&T bid $39 billion to buy T-Mobile from Germany's Deutsche Telekom, thus adding 34 million customers to its existing base of 96 million and making it even larger than Verizon Wireless. The combined share of the market of AT&T and Verizon is now 58%, but this will increase to 70% if the transaction goes through, but it has to get past governmental regulators. AT&T says that the deal will not be anti-competitive, citing the fact that wireless services in the United States fell by 50% from 1999 to 2009 ("An Audacious Merger," 2011).

TABLE 16.1 Media Megamergers and Acquisitions

- *January 1986:* Capital Cities Communications, Inc. purchases American Broadcasting Company for $3.5 billion to create Capital Cities/ABC, Inc.
- *June 1986:* General Electric Co. buys RCA Corp., parent company of National Broadcasting Co. and the NBC television network, for $6.4 billion. At the time, the deal was the largest non-oil acquisition in U.S. history. In the same year, Capital Cities bought ABC.
- *November 1989:* Sony Corp. buys film and television producer Columbia Pictures Entertainment, Inc. for $3.4 billion.
- *January 1990:* Warner Communications, Inc. and Time, Inc. complete a $14.1 billion merger, creating the world's biggest media conglomerate at the time.
- *January 1991:* Matsushita Electric Industrial Co. of Japan buys MCA, Inc. for $6.9 billion.
- *September 1993:* The New York Times Co. buys Affiliated Publications, Inc., parent company of *The Boston Globe,* for $1.1 billion, the biggest takeover in U.S. newspaper history.
- *July 1994:* Viacom, Inc. buys Paramount Communications, Inc. for $10 billion after winning a bidding war against QVC, Inc. to buy the movie, publishing, and sports company.
- *August 1994:* Viacom, Inc. buys video rental chain Blockbuster Entertainment Corp. for $8 billion.
- *August 1995:* Walt Disney Co. acquires Capital Cities/ABC, Inc. for $19 billion, making it the largest media company at the time.
- *November 1995:* Westinghouse Electric Corp. buys CBS, Inc. for $5.4 billion, giving the new company 15 TV stations and 39 radio stations that, combined, give it direct access to one third of the nation's households.
- *October 1996:* Time Warner and Turner Broadcasting System complete a $7.6 billion merger. This becomes the world's biggest media company, with annual revenues of more than $20 billion.
- *November 1996:* Penguin Group, the international publisher, buys Putnam Berkley Group, a U.S. subsidiary of MCA (owned by Seagram Co.) for $336 million. Penguin is strong with backlist books (Arthur Miller, Gabriel García Márquez, Toni Morrison, E. L. Doctorow, Joyce Carol Oates), and Putnam has a strong front list (Stephen King, Terry McMillan, Tom Clancy, Patricia Cornwell).
- *February 1997:* A merger of two radio companies created Chancellor Media Corp., which took control over 103 radio stations that generate more than $700 million annually in revenue. The top-ranked radio group is Infinity Broadcasting ($1.1 billion in revenue annually), which is owned by Westinghouse Electric Corp.
- *January 1998:* Compaq Computer Corp. buys Digital Equipment Corp. for $9.6 billion. This made Compaq one of the three largest computer companies in the world in terms of sales. This was the biggest buyout in the history of the computer industry to that point.
- *September 1999:* Viacom announces a merger with CBS Television Network for $38 billion, making it the biggest deal between any two media companies. The merger combines film, television, radio, Internet sites, book publishing, and many other businesses.
- *October 1999:* Clear Channel Communications, Inc. agrees to buy AMFM, Inc. for $16.6 billion in stock, creating the nation's largest radio company.
- *January 2000:* America Online, Inc. agrees to buy Time Warner, Inc. in a $164 billion merger agreement, the largest ever combination in the media industry.
- *January 2000:* Time Warner, Inc. (record labels of Atlantic, Elektra, and Warner Brothers) and Britain's EMI Group (record labels of Virgin, Priority, and Capitol) agreed to merge their music businesses, thus creating the world's biggest music company, with combined annual revenues of $8 billion. The new firm would represent 2,500 musicians.
- *December 2005:* Paramount Pictures agrees to buy independent film studio DreamWorks SKG, Inc. for $1.6 billion. The agreement does not include DreamWorks Animation SKG, Inc.

- *January 2006:* Walt Disney announces that it will buy Pixar, the successful animation studio majority owned by Apple's Steve Jobs, for $7.4 billion.
- *September 2006:* Vivendi's Universal Music agrees to acquire BMG Music Publishing in a $2 billion deal. The acquisition makes Universal's music publishing holdings the largest in the world.
- *October 2006:* Google, the Internet's leading search engine, announced that it is buying popular online video site YouTube for $1.65 billion.
- *April 2007:* Google buys DoubleClick, Inc. for $3.1 billion, thus creating the largest repository of details about people's behavior online.
- *October 2007:* NBC Universal pays $925 million to buy cable network Oxygen, which was started by Oprah Winfrey and others in 1998.
- *September 2009:* Walt Disney acquires Marvel comics for $4 billion.
- *January 2011:* Comcast buys controlling interest (51%) in NBC Universal for $30 billion.
- *March 2011:* AT&T bids $39 billion to buy T-Mobile from Germany's Deutsche Telekom, thus adding 34 million customers to its existing base of 96 million and making it even larger than Verizon Wireless.
- *May 2011:* Microsoft buys Skype (developed software that allows users to make voice and video calls over the Internet) for $8.5 billion.

SOURCE: Compiled from AP Online (2000); Arnold (2011); Chmielewski and Fritz (2009); Common Cause (n.d.); A. S. Fabrikant (1995); Greimel (2000); Hofmeister (1997a, 1997b); Holstein (1999); Lorimer (1994); Lyall (1996); McDonald (2000); Menn (2007).

International Perspective

It is not uncommon for foreign companies to buy or invest in American media companies. In one year, companies from the United Kingdom made 188 deals totaling $23.6 billion to buy U.S. media companies, Japanese companies made 45 transactions for $11.9 billion, Canadian companies made 46 deals for $9.7 billion, French companies made 26 deals for $3.0 billion, and German companies made 27 transactions for $1.2 billion. Also, through the decade of the 1990s, foreign companies were buying American media properties, especially film studios. For example, Pathé, a French-Italian firm, bought MGM and United Artists. Sony, a Japanese electronics manufacturer, bought Columbia Pictures from Coca-Cola. Also, about 13% of all American newspapers are owned by non-American companies (Albarran & Chan-Olmsted, 1998). An example of how American companies attract foreign investors is Rupert Murdoch, an Australian who owns newspapers in most of the major cities in Australia along with the country's only national daily, television stations, publishing houses, record companies, and a major airline. He went to Great Britain and bought the *London Times,* two sex and scandal sheets with a combined circulation of more than 8 million, a string of magazines, a string of provincial newspapers, and companies for manufacturing paper, printing, and distributing newsprint. He came to the United States and bought the *New York Post, New York Magazine, Village Voice, Chicago-Sun Times,* two other daily newspapers, and 17 suburban weeklies. He has also bought Metromedia's seven television stations in New York, Boston, and other major cities, giving him access to 21% of the total television audience. Recently, Murdoch's Australian firm, News Corp., bought the remaining 18% of its U.S. Fox Entertainment Group, Inc. unit, giving it full ownership of 20th Century Fox film studios and the Fox network and channels. His empire now generates $33 billion a year.

Globalization works both ways. American companies market their entertainment services worldwide. For example, by 1993, MTV was in cable systems in more than 71 countries, reaching more than 500 million people (Barber, 1995). By 1995, ESPN was offering programming to 150 countries in 18 languages. Media economist Alan Albarran (2002) explains that markets for media messages have been saturated in the United States, so for American media companies to open up even more revenue streams and to increase the flow of income even more, they need to market their messages in other countries.

Concentration Among Advertising Agencies

As the media become more concentrated, so too does the advertising industry. The large, national agencies are becoming larger so that they can deal better with the larger media companies. As ad agencies grow bigger, they become much less interested in local retailers and local markets, instead favoring the much larger national market where they can make bigger deals and more money. Thus, most of the advertising today is for national brands. For example, when most people think of hamburgers, they think of McDonald's, Burger King, and Wendy's—not the local restaurant run as a family business. So the trend toward concentration is not just within the media industries; it is also with retail stores and with advertising agencies.

Half of all the advertising placed in the United States each year is handled by one of the world's top 20 advertising agencies. This means there is an enormous amount of concentration, with many instances of an agency handling the accounts of direct competitors.

Concentration Among Advertisers

Manufacturers are buying each other up in an effort to get bigger and bigger. This gives them more power in the marketplace, helps them increase profits by diversifying into several businesses, and gives them more power as advertisers. For example, Proctor & Gamble usually has been the number one advertiser in the world since 1913. It sells its products in 140 countries and advertises heavily in all. It will spend more than $3 billion on advertising this year. On TV alone, it will buy more than 28,000 ads, which would take you 10 days of solid viewing (24 hours per day continuously) to watch them all. Therefore, Proctor & Gamble exerts an enormous amount of power. Other examples include McDonald's, which has 17,000 franchise restaurants in 90 different countries, including 760 in Japan; their largest restaurant is in Beijing. Coca-Cola is in 160 countries, and two thirds of Coke's revenue comes from outside the United States.

Some very large companies have so many products that we as consumers do not realize that many of the products that appear very different are marketed by the same company. For example, PepsiCo, Inc. markets beverages (Pepsi, Slice, Mountain Dew, and root beer), but it also owns and controls the largest restaurant system in the world, which includes Kentucky Fried Chicken, Pizza Hut, and Taco Bell. How about cigarettes? Are you trying to be socially responsible and not buy products that would support companies that market harmful products? You recognize the name of Phillip Morris as a cigarette company—it manufactures and sells Marlboro, Merit, Virginia Slims, and Benson & Hedges. Did you know that Phillip Morris Co. owns General Foods and Miller Brewing? General Foods includes Maxwell House coffee (Maxwell House, Sanka, International Coffees, Brim, and Yuban), Birds Eye frozen foods, Post cereals (Raisin Bran, Grape-Nuts, Honeycombs, Fruit & Fibre,

40% Bran Flakes, Crispy Critters, Pebbles, Super Golden Crisp, Alpha Bits), Tang, Country Time, Kool-Aid, Minute Rice, Stove Top Stuffing, Dream Whip, Jell-O, Crystal Light, Ronzoni, Shake 'n Bake, Log Cabin syrup, Oscar Meyer meats, Louis Rich, and many, many others. Miller, of course, makes Miller High-Life, Miller Lite, and Miller Genuine Draft, but it also makes Henry Weinhard's, Hamm's, and Milwaukee's Best.

ISSUES OF CONCERN

All this merger activity has raised many issues of concern. I will present four of them in this section: the fallout from deregulation, the reduced level of competition, the lack of access by the public to media voices, and how to deal with the Internet.

Deregulation

The common wisdom is that American business needs to be regulated to control for vertical integration, which is a company owning or controlling companies that produce the raw materials and services they need to produce their product and also to own and control the means of distribution and sale of their products. The belief is that companies that are strongly integrated vertically, while more efficient, are so powerful that they drive away competition and exploit the consumer. The same fear is applied even more strongly to media companies because they control information. There was a time when AT&T made electronic components, produced telecommunications equipment, and sold phone service, so the federal government took steps to break up the company to allow for more competition (Samuelson, 2006). Also, in the early days of the film industry, a few film studios were so strongly integrated vertically that they controlled film distribution, production, and exhibition. The federal government required these companies to divest themselves of some of their businesses, so the film studios sold off their theaters, which removed them from the exhibition sector, thus allowing theaters to compete for films. The Federal Communications Commission continually monitors ownership of radio and television broadcasting stations to try to preserve competition in those industries.

In recent decades, the business trend to consolidation has grown stronger than the government's impulse to regulate. For example, in 1996, Congress passed the Telecommunications Act and largely removed the last remaining limitations to consolidation. In that year alone, there were $25 billion in merger activity in the broadcasting industry and another $23 billion in the cable industry (C. Jensen, 1997). Since 1996, the FCC has been less concerned with preventing monopolies within the United States and more concerned with allowing American companies to grow significantly stronger to compete and dominate in the world market (Albarran & Chan-Olmsted, 1998). FCC Chairman William Kennard said that he is merely recognizing the realities of globalization and new technologies.

One feature of the 1996 deregulation eliminated the longstanding restriction of allowing one company to own two television stations in the same market. It had long been believed that broadcast television stations were far too precious a local resource to allow one company to own more than one in a given television market. Almost all local markets had very few broadcast stations (typically three to five broadcast television stations), so it was important to have as many owners as possible to ensure a diversity of voices within that small number of stations in a market. However, over time, as greater numbers of people subscribed to cable television services, regulators came to believe that people in all local communities had access to many different voices, and therefore the limits on broadcast station ownership were no longer important.

The media industries have been moving steadily toward greater concentration both within each industry and especially across media industries. Critics fear that this trend has already put too much power into the hands of a very few people. For example, Table 16.2 shows that the top eight firms in the recording and motion picture industries account for virtually all the revenue in those industries. Even in the book industry, which is fairly unconcentrated relative to the other media industries, the top eight companies account for half of all book revenue. Furthermore, the figures in Table 16.2, which reveal a high degree of concentration, are likely to underestimate the degree of concentration in the media industries because they do not take into consideration cross-ownership patterns; that is, they do not account for a firm owning and controlling revenue in several mass media industries at once. To see how much cross-ownership there is, look at what the top seven media conglomerates each control (see Table 16.3).

Change in Content

Critics argue that as competition among media companies decreases, the content of messages changes in a negative way. They argue that as companies grow larger, their content decreases in quality and that the messages are more likely to harm the public.

TABLE 16.2 Indicators of Concentration in Segments of the Mass Media

CR4	CR8	Mass Medium
98	99	Recording industry
78	99	Motion pictures
77	91	Magazine
77	88	Radio
53	80	Cable and satellite television
48	69	Daily newspapers
30	50	Book
NA	NA	Broadcast television
NA	NA	Internet

SOURCE: Compiled from Albarran (2002).

NOTE: CR4 = concentration ratio of top four firms: percent of total revenues of the major four players in the industry; CR8 = concentration ratio of top eight firms: percent of total revenues of the major eight players in the industry; NA = not applicable.

Has the quality of the media products declined? There is no evidence that it has. For example, research has not found that when a radio station is bought by a conglomerate, the content degrades. Lacy and Riffe (1994) looked at the news content of radio stations and compared group ownership effects. They found that group ownership had no impact on the financial commitment or the local and staff emphasis of news coverage. Also, a study done on newspaper content could find no change in content after a newspaper was bought by a chain (e.g., see Picard, Winter, McCombs, & Lacy, 1988). No evidence of change was found with the stories, the range of opinions on the editorial page, or the proportion of the newspaper displaying news.

Has the trend toward concentration of ownership led to an increase in harmful content? This has not yet been tested directly, but there is indirect evidence that concentration of ownership in the radio industry is associated with an increase in negative speech and obscenity. One research study found that as big broadcasters buy more radio stations, shock-jock programming often replaces local content. From 2000 to 2003, the nation's four largest radio companies racked up 96% of the fines handed out by the FCC, although their stations accounted for only about half the country's listening audience (Hofmeister, 2005).

This criticism that concentration of ownership reduces competition in a market seems valid on the surface, but it breaks down when analyzed. To illustrate, let's say a city has two newspapers. A chain buys one of those newspapers. The chain-owned newspaper cuts subscription costs and ad rates. Readers and advertisers switch to the chain newspaper because it is less expensive. Eventually, the other newspaper goes out of business. The degree of concentration in that market goes up. But this does not mean that the newspaper has no competition simply because it is the only newspaper in the market. The newspaper must compete for audiences and advertisers along with the radio, television, and cable stations in the market. Thus, if the newspaper degrades its news product, people will drop their subscriptions and turn to other sources of news. With lower circulation rates, the newspaper will need to drop the rate it charges advertisers, and this will produce less revenue. With less revenue, the newspaper will need to lay off reporters, and the news product further degrades. This downward cycle continues until the newspaper is out of business. But this almost never happens because chain-owned newspapers are driven by making large profits, and to do that, they must do everything they can to expand their circulations and hence their appeal to advertisers.

Newspapers, as well as all the other media, expand their revenues only by providing more and better services to consumers. How do they know what consumers want? They are constantly doing market research to test out new ideas. Also, they carefully monitor the

TABLE 16.3   Most Powerful Media Companies Operating in the United States

Bertlesmann ($16.3 billion)

- Founded 1835; home office in Gütersloh, Germany; 103,000 employees
- Books: world's largest publisher of books; sells over a million books a day in the United States alone through Random House, Knopf, Doubleday, and other publishing houses; owns book clubs across Europe, North America, and South America, including Book-of-the-Month Club and Literary Guild
- Recordings: BMG (Bertlesmann Music Group) operates in 54 countries; has 200 labels in the United States
- Broadcasting: owns the most radio and television stations in Europe

Comcast ($31 billion)

- Founded 1963; home office in Philadelphia, Pennsylvania; 100,000 employees
- Cable: nation's leading cable television operator; serves 24.6 million cable customers, including 16.3 million digital cable customers; SportsNet, E! Networks, the Golf Channel
- New media: high-speed Internet access; serves 14.4 million high-speed Internet customers and 5.6 million voice customers
- Sports: Philadelphia 76s (basketball) and Philadelphia Flyers (hockey)
- NBC Universal: Comcast owns controlling interest at 51%; GE owns other 49%
- Television: NBC television network and 10 broadcast stations in major markets
- Cable: 40 cable TV stations, including MSNBC, CNBC, Bravo, USA Network, and SyFy
- Film: Universal Studios
- Internet: Hulu, Fandango, and others
- Telemundo: 16 Spanish-speaking broadcast stations in major markets
- Other: Universal Theme Parks and Resorts

News Corporation ($33 billion)

- Founded in 1979; home office New York City; 64,000 employees

- Broadcast television: Fox network; 27 stations in the United States plus many broadcast stations around the world
- Film: 20th Century Fox, Fox 2000, Fox Studios, Fox Searchlight, Fox Animation Studios Studio
- Radio: Fox Sports Radio Network
- Cable: FX network, Fox Sports Net, Fox News Channel, Golf Channel, National Geographic
- Magazine: several dozen magazines mostly published in Australia
- Newspapers: 175 newspapers internationally, including the *Wall Street Journal* and *New York Post*
- Books: HarperCollins, William Morris Books, Avon Books, Regan Books
- Internet: owns AmericanIdol.com, AskMen, Fox.com, and other sites
- New media: DirectTV, Sky Network TV
- Sports: part owner of Colorado Rockies (baseball); part owner of Staples Center

Sony ($79 billion)

- Founded in 1946; home office in Tokyo, Japan; 180,500 employees, including nonmedia people
- Television: Columbia TriStar Television; HBO, Cinemax
- Film: Sony Pictures Entertainment, Columbia TriStar Motion Picture Group, Columbia TriStar Home Video, Columbia TriStar Television Group (*Spiderman, Men in Black*)
- Recordings: owns more than 50 recording labels, including Sony Music Entertainment, CBS Records, Columbia Records, Epic, Legacy, Tri-Star Music, and RCA Records
- New media: Sony PlayStation video games
- Other: Sony Electronics, Sony Ericsson Mobile Communications

The Walt Disney Company ($37.8 billion)

- Founded in 1923 by Walt Disney; home office in Burbank, California; 150,000 employees

- Film: Walt Disney Studios; Touchstone Films, Miramax Films, Hollywood Pictures, Buena Vista Filmed Entertainment, Walt Disney Feature Animation, Buena Vista International, Pixar, and a partnership with DreamWorks
- Broadcast television: 10 TV stations; ABC Television Network
- Cable: ESPN, Fox Family, Toon Disney, and Disney Channel; also holdings in Lifetime, A&E, History Channel, and Biography
- Radio: 59 radio stations; ABC Radio Network
- Magazines: *Discover, Los Angeles Magazine*
- Books: Hyperion books, ESPN Books, Disney Publishing Worldwide
- Recordings: Walt Disney Records, Buena Vista Records, Hollywood Records, Mammoth Records, Lyric Street Records, Wonderland Music Company
- Sports: Anaheim Angels (baseball); Mighty Ducks of Anaheim (hockey)
- Other: 11 theme parks; Marvel Comics (5,000 characters, including Spiderman, X-Men, Iron Man, Hulk, and Fantastic Four); consumer products; The Disney Store; cruise line, petroleum and natural gas production interests

Time Warner ($47 billion annual revenue)

- Founded 1990; home office in New York City; 86,400 employees
- Broadcast television: CW network; Kids' WB!
- Cable: Time Warner Cable (11 million subscribers); pay cable channels (HBO and Cinemax); 9 local news cable channels; Turner Broadcasting System (CNN, Headline News, TBS, TNT, Turner Classic Movies, The Cartoon Network)
- Film: TV production and film production (Warner Brothers Pictures, New Line Cinema, Fine Line Features, New Line International, New Line Television, Castle Rock Entertainment, and Telepictures Productions); library of more than 6,000 films, 25,000 TV programs, and thousands of animated shows (such as Looney Tunes and Hanna-Barbera); Warner Brothers International Cinemas (123 screens in the United States and 650 screens in other countries)

- Recordings: Warner Brothers Music Group, Atlantic, Elektra, and numerous smaller labels
- Magazines: largest publisher of magazines in the United States, with over 140 magazines reaching more than 300 million people worldwide, including *Time, Life, People, Fortune, Money, Mad* magazine, *Sports Illustrated, Entertainment Weekly, In Style, Sunset, Parenting, Southern Living,* and *Teen People*
- Internet: America Online (30 million subscribers); CompuServe; McAfee Virus Scan, Mapquest, Netscape, Winamp
- Newspapers: 7 dailies
- Books: Little, Brown; Book of the Month Club; DC Comics (Superman, Batman, *Mad* magazine, and 60 other titles)
- New media: AOL, with its 20 million Internet subscribers
- Sports: Atlanta Braves (baseball), Atlanta Hawks (basketball), Atlanta Thrashers (hockey)
- Other: Warner Brothers Studio Stores (more than 150 worldwide); MovieFone
- Was bought by AOL in 2000 for $164 billion; in 2009, AOL was spun off into a separate company, which is owned by Time Warner

Viacom ($14.6 billion)

- Founded 1971; home office in New York City; 11,500 employees
- Broadcast television: CBS and UPN television networks; Paramount Television Studio (*JAG, Entertainment Tonight*), Spelling Television, and King World Productions (*Jeopardy, Wheel of Fortune*); Viacom Stations Group (39 TV stations)
- Cable: Comedy Central, Nickelodeon, MTV, VH1, TV Land, TNN (now Spike TV), CMT (Country Music Television), Showtime, BET (Black Entertainment Television)
- Radio: Infinity Broadcasting chain of 183 radio stations; CBS radio network; Westwood One; Metro Networks
- Books: Simon & Schuster, Scribner, Pocket Books, Anne Schwartz Books, Archway Paperbacks, Lisa Drew Books, Fireside, Free Press, MTV Books, Nickelodeon Books, Pocket Books, Star Trek Books, Washington Square Press

(Continued)

(Continued)

- Film production: Paramount Pictures (including a library of more than 2,500 titles), Nickelodeon Movies, MTV Films, Nickelodeon Studios, United International Pictures (33%), Spelling Films, Republic Entertainment, Worldvision Enterprises
- Film theaters: Paramount Theaters, Famous Players Theaters (1,700 screens in 13 countries), United Cinemas International
- Recordings: Famous Music (copyright holders of more than 100,000 songs)
- New media: MTV Networks On Line and Marketwatch.com, CBS.com, CBSSportsLine.com, CBSMarketWatch.com, and Country.com
- Other: Blockbuster Video; five amusement parks; TDI Worldwide and Outdoor Systems, which sell ad space on 210,000 billboards nationwide; *Star Trek* franchise
- In 2006, the old Viacom spun off CBS television into its own company; home office in New York City; 25,920 employees and $14 billion in annual revenue. CBS Corporation was given Viacom's "slow-growth businesses"—namely, CBS, CBS Radio, Simon & Schuster, CBS Outdoor, Showtime, CBS Records, CBS Television Studios, and most television production assets. The new Viacom kept the high-growth businesses (MTV Networks and BET Networks in particular) so it could generate sufficient revenue to allow for future acquisitions and expansion.

SOURCE: Compiled from Albarran (2002); Bettig and Hall (2003); CBS Corporation (n.d.); Chmielewski and Fritz (2009); Comcast (n.d.); Croteau and Hoynes (2001); Flanigan (2003); NBC Universal (n.d.); News Corporation (n.d.); Polman (2003); Sony Corporation (n.d.); The Walt Disney Company (n.d.); Time Warner (n.d.); Verrier and James (2003); Viacom (n.d.).

public reactions, verbal as well as monetary, to their messages. When the public's tastes or wants change, the media know this, and they offer new types of products and messages.

Although the businesspeople in media organizations generally leave the creative people alone to do what they do best and attract large audiences, the business side can spill over onto the editorial side at newspapers in some cases. This was clearly illustrated in the fall of 1999, when the *Los Angeles Times Magazine* devoted coverage of the Staples Center, a new sports arena. The publisher, Kathryn M. Downing, had entered into a partnership agreement on the issue with the Staples Center, agreeing to have the Staples Center promote the magazine in return for sharing profits. Downing did not tell her reporters or editors about the business partnership. When the journalists found out, they complained about not knowing the magazine had been turned into a public relations device for the Staples Center. Downing, whose background was as a business manager and not as a journalist, apologized, saying that she did not realize that her actions would damage the journalistic integrity of the newspaper ("*L.A. Times* Publisher Errs, Apologizes," 1999).

The danger presented by so much consolidation is not in lost quality in the production of messages. The media companies have a huge stake in attracting and holding audiences, whether they have competition or not. The danger instead is that the messages are too slick and too commercial; this would greatly limit the scope of possible messages available to the public.

Lack of Access

Critics argue that as concentration increases, the individual's access to the media is reduced. *Access* here can mean two different things. One meaning is ownership; that is, how much access does an individual have to own a media property? Because most media companies are public corporations, any individual can buy a share of any company. But can a person own a media property fully? The answer still is yes. There are comparatively low barriers to entry in the magazine, book publishing, weekly newspaper, and computer industries. With several thousand dollars, a desktop computer, and a strong initiative, most people could begin a business in one of these media industries. Of course, he or she should be prepared to face very stiff competition to gain the attention of an audience and the confidence of advertisers. But it is possible to create one's own media voice in those industries. In contrast, barriers to entry are much higher in the radio, television, cable, and film industries, and the conglomerate mergers over the past several decades have raised those barriers much higher, almost to the point of being prohibitive for anyone except the wealthiest individuals and the biggest companies.

Access can also mean the ability to get your particular point of view heard through someone else's media property. This is still relatively easy to do at the local level, such as with newspapers and small-circulation magazines. Most still print letters to the editors, and most buy articles from people with little journalistic experience. Also, most markets have call-in radio programs where you can get your voice heard. In contrast, national media properties, such as *Newsweek* magazine or a TV or cable network, require a great deal of skill and good connections to get your voice heard because the competition to use those channels is so strong.

Many critics argue that the media industries lose diversity of voices when the industries become more concentrated. Fewer voices should mean fewer opinions getting aired. However, Einstein (2004) points out that "in study after study, scholars have determined that there is no proven causality between media ownership and programming content" (p. vii). Einstein argues that the reduction in the number of program choices is not due to consolidation but to television's reliance on advertising as its primary source of revenue. Because of this reliance, there are severe limits on content, which include timelines for length of program, the "lowest common denominator" mentality, and an avoidance of controversy. In an analysis of the TV industry over the past four decades, Einstein reveals that as the industry became more concentrated, programming became more diverse. She said that diversity was at its peak in the late 1960s and then declined when the FCC imposed regulations about sharing programs through syndication. Then, when those syndication rules were relaxed and broadcasters could keep the programs they produced to themselves, diversity increased sharply.

Internet

Although the Internet is still very new, there are signs that it is becoming concentrated. For example, estimates indicate that the top 100 visited websites account for half of all websites visited. Also, between March 1999 and March 2001, the total number of companies controlling half of U.S. user minutes online shrank from 11 to 4 (Bettig & Hall, 2003). This is indeed powerful evidence that the Internet is also becoming highly concentrated despite its newness and the wide variety of websites available. While the number of websites available to all users is truly staggering in its range, most of the Internet exposure is concentrated in a small number of those websites, and those heavily visited websites are likely to be owned by a media conglomerate.

One tool that has helped this concentration occur so quickly is the search engine. People use search engines—such as Google and Yahoo—to tell them which sites they should visit to get information on various topics. Users type in a keyword describing the topic, and the search engine provides the user with a list of sites. For example, as I write this, I get on Google and do a search for the keyword *news*. Google searches for 0.16 seconds, then tells me that it has found more than 12 billion websites concerning the topic of "news." Google then shows me the addresses of the first 10 of those 12 billion websites, so that I can click on one of those addresses and go to that website. The sites listed first are CNN.com, Google news, Foxnews.com, and msnbc. These sites are presumably the most popular. But let's think about how they got to be the most popular. They show up at the top of Google's list because they are the most popular, and because they are the most popular, they are presented first by Google. Kind of a circular process, isn't it? Then how does a website break into this cycle? The answer is to pay for placement on Google. This is why Google makes so much money as a company—it sells placement on its searches. You can buy popularity. If you buy a high enough placement in a Google search, then the most people will see your address and likely visit your website. When you get the most visits among all your competitors, you are the most popular and will continue to place high on the Google searches. The companies with the most money can buy the highest placements. Thus, the Internet becomes more and more concentrated in terms of a few websites on each topic area consuming the most visits.

At the same time as we see concentration of usage of websites, there is little evidence of vertical integration among companies providing computer services and hardware. "The computer industry is hugely splintered. Some firms sell components (Intel, AMD); some, software (Microsoft, SAP); some, services (IBM, EDS); some, hardware (Dell, Apple). There's overlap, but not much" (Samuelson, 2006, p. 45). Also, the Internet is dominated by newer companies, such as Google, Facebook, and eBay, not the older established companies.

This, however, could change as people and companies attempt to consolidate the existing Internet and new tech companies. For example, Barry Diller is a media mogul who ran Paramount Pictures and then Fox TV in the 1970s to the 1980s, and then in the mid-1990s, he began spending more than $20 billion in assembling a broad portfolio of diverse Web companies. Then he spent $1.7 billion to buy the fourth-place search firm (Ask.com) and used it to tie together services from his other companies such as Citysearch, Ticketmaster, Evite, ServiceMagic.com (booking local services such as plumbers), and ReserveAmerica.com (campground reservations). So the 40 million monthly users of Ask .com will be referred to other Diller companies when they search for particular services (Stone, 2006).

SUMMARY

Media critics are wary of the degree of concentration in the media industries. Their concern is focused on the central issue of which is more important: efficiency (brought about by industry integration and economics of scale) *or* localism (diversity of content and easier entry into the market, thus allowing alternative voices).

You likely have an opinion about this issue. But to synthesize a good opinion, you need to build it from an analysis of the situation. This chapter provides such an analysis to begin your thinking. You should continue your thinking on this topic by considering which value you think should dominate more in the formulation of the media industries. Do you favor localism, with its focus on having power distributed throughout society—through citizen activism and government regulations—to make the media be responsive to the different needs of the broad spectrum of people in the society? Or do you find more favor with concentration as a goal of businesses driven to operate more effectively and efficiently and thus generate larger profits that they can use to generate a wider range of products to satisfy more of our needs at low cost to us?

Once you get interested in this issue and begin formulating your opinion, you need to monitor changes in this dynamic situation and continually update your knowledge structures. Over time, the government has been relaxing regulations, and as a result, businesses have been moving strongly toward concentration. But there is still a great deal of competition among the media industries as they try to claim more of our attention and more of a share of the advertiser's dollar.

Chapter Resources: To test your knowledge and learn more about the topics discussed in this chapter, visit the Student Study Site at www.sagepub.com/potter6e.

FURTHER READING

Bagdikian, B. H. (2000). *The media monopoly* (6th ed.). Boston: Beacon. (288 pages with endnotes and index)

Since 1983, Bagdikian has been conducting an economic analysis of the media industries to track the degree of concentration. With each new edition, the number of powerful companies shrinks as their media (as well as nonmedia) holdings dramatically grow. This book is a must-read for anyone concerned about how much power is being concentrated in the hands of a few CEOs of media holding companies.

Bettig, R. V., & Hall, J. L. (2003). *Big media, big money: Cultural texts and political economies.* Lanham, MD: Rowman & Littlefield. (181 pages with bibliography and references)

In this book, two professors at Penn State University argue that the media have been unfettered in their drive for greater profits and control over constructing meaning in our culture. They present a great deal of detail in support of this thesis in their six chapters. The authors demonstrate that the result of this media consolidation is that a few very powerful companies are becoming even more invasive in our lives and are successfully supplanting family, friends, religion, and education as the controlling source of constructing meaning.

Einstein, M. (2004). *Media diversity: Economics, ownership, and the FCC.* Mahwah, NJ: Lawrence Erlbaum. (249 pages, including references, appendixes, and indexes)

The author examines the issue of whether the consolidation in the media industries has led to a lessening of diversity. This book offers strong historical and economic perspectives on the issue. She concludes that despite a clear consolidation of ownership of media properties and the narrowing in the number of people making decisions about media content, there is even more diversity in messages now than there was four decades ago.

Maney, K. (1995). *Megamedia shakeout: The inside story of the leaders and the losers in the exploding communications industry.* New York: John Wiley. (358 pages, including index)

This is a well-written description of the major players in the technologies landscape in the mid-1990s. There are lots of anecdotes and stories about what has been happening in the telephone, cable, computer, wireless, and entertainment industries. The book is full of facts and personal descriptions of the personalities involved. However, things are happening so fast in these industries with new rollouts and buyouts that the book is likely out of date.

McChesney, R. W., Newman, R., & Scott, B. (Eds.). (2005). *The future of media: Resistance and reform in the 21st century.* New York: Seven Stories Press. (376 pages with index)

This edited volume of 19 chapters plus an introduction was written by scholars who have been very concerned about the conglomeration of American media and the role of the Federal Communications Commission (FCC), which is not only allowing it to occur but also actually encouraging it. The authors document the increasing level of concentration in ownership of media properties by fewer and fewer companies and argue that this trend is harmful for consumers and citizens.

KEEPING UP TO DATE

Columbia Journalism Review (http://www.cjr.org/resources/)

This website allows you to check all the media holdings of many major conglomerates.

Vault.com (http://www.vault.com/wps/portal/usa)

This website provides lots of useful information about various industries; particularly relevant to media literacy are the industries of publishing, newspapers, Internet and new media, music, broadcast and cable, advertising, and public relations.

EXERCISE 16.1

What Is the Concentration of Media Ownership in Your Local Market?

This exercise asks you to be a detective to search out information in your local media market. See how creative you can be in coming up with strategies to get the answers to the following questions.

1. How many movie screens are in your market?

   a. How many theaters control those screens?

   b. Are the theaters owned by chains? If so, how many chains control the total set of screens?

2. How many radio stations are in your market?

   a. How many are group owned?

   b. How many of the stations are owned by companies that also own other media businesses in your market?

3. How many broadcast television stations are in your market?

   a. How many are group owned?

   b. How many of the stations are owned by companies that also own other media businesses in your market?

4. Is your local newspaper owned by a chain? If so, does it own other media businesses in your market?

5. Are there any magazines published in your market and distributed only in your market? If so, does the controlling company also own other media businesses?

6. What is the name of the company that provides your market with cable TV service? Is that cable company a multiple-system operator?

7. In total, how many different media outlets (voices) are in your market? How many individuals or companies control these voices?

8. If you wanted to express yourself through the media in your market, how hard do you think it would be to gain access to one of these outlets?

   a. For example, assume that you wanted to criticize some new governmental regulation or tax policy in your local area. Which outlet would be most likely to give you space or time to speak out?

   b. Which outlet(s) do you think would be the hardest or impossible?

9. Given your answers to the questions above, how concentrated do you think your market is—that is, do you think the outlets are in the control of too few individuals?

Privacy

"Hey, dude, check this out." Luke pointed to his computer screen, which showed his profile page of his social networking site.

"Woooo, awesome party. Is that you in the tie-dyed jock strap doing a beer bong?" Matt leaned toward the screen to get a better look. "You look totally wasted."

"Check this out." Luke brought up another page that showed a collage of photos of him draped over a variety of different women.

"How many chicks were you with?"

"At least six—if you count that blow-up doll from the porno store. She's the red head."

"Very lifelike. What's your girlfriend going to say when she sees this?"

"No worries. Heather will never see this. She's too busy studying for a test."

Privacy is not something we usually think about until it is too late to protect it. Once some information about you gets out, especially out on the Internet, you lose control over it, and your ability to pull that information back into the private realm is forever gone.

As the Internet continues to grow with its number of services, we spend more time and money on the Web, leaving an electronic trail behind us. Businesses and hackers grow more sophisticated each year in accessing the data in those electronic trails. Thus, it becomes very important that you understand how the media may be invading your privacy and how you can protect yourself.

DEFINING PRIVACY

Privacy is the secluding of personal information by individuals about themselves. It is based on four ideas. First, it suggests that certain things are private rather than public—that is, they belong to the individual. Second, it also suggests that the individual should have control over sharing this information and that if another person or an organization takes control of an individual's personal information without the individual's permission, that is an invasion of his or her privacy. Third, privacy is not a uniform condition—that is, there is an interaction between type of information and its boundaries as individuals make differential decisions about who can have access to which information. For example, we want our friends to have our phone numbers, address, and e-mail, but we want to keep this contact information away from telemarketers and other advertisers who might inundate them with unwanted messages. We want our medical doctor to have a complete history of our medical conditions, but we may have medical problems that we do not want to share with our friends.

Fourth, when we share some private information with another person, we expect that person to respect our boundaries. For example, when we give information about ourselves to our close friends, we expect them to follow a fundamental principle of fairness that they not share that information with a third party unless they first ask our permission or, at least, tell us that they have passed that information along to a third party. Many of us expect the same treatment when we interact with businesses—that is, when we buy something at a store or on the Internet, we expect this transaction to stay between us and the business and not to be shared with other businesses not involved in the transaction. But this is not the case. Businesses frequently collect all kinds of information on you, and once collected, they sell this information to other businesses—all without your explicit permission and knowledge. With computers, Internet marketers, e-mail, and telephones, our privacy is continually being invaded.

INVASIONS OF YOUR PRIVACY

This section outlines four families of media threats to your privacy. These four are spamming, commercial mining, theft of private information, and maliciousness. Each of these threats is relatively new. And each of these threats is growing more serious each year as we rely on digitized information and increase our use of the Internet to store our personal information and connect to other people. Because these threats are so new and evolve so fast, regulators are just beginning to experiment with various restrictions and laws to help us protect us without violating the rights of legitimate businesses. In the meantime, you need to understand these threats so you can take steps now to protect your privacy.

Spamming

Spamming is the using of media to invade your privacy with unsolicited and unwanted messages. It is especially focused on e-mail accounts but also applies to text messages sent to your phone and all kinds of attention-getting devices (pop-ups, banners, etc.) that clutter Web pages as we surf the Web. For most of us, we want to control our Internet sessions, so when someone interjects messages to deflect our attention or tries to direct us to unwanted sites, we feel manipulated and irritated. While spam typically is a minor nuisance as an invasion of our privacy, it can become a major irritant if it dominates our e-mails, destroys our surfing experiences, and even crashes the services on which we rely, such as our ISP (Internet service provider and e-mail accounts).

Each year, the amount of spam increases. In 2004, it was estimated that more than 15 billion pieces of spam were sent every day and that more than 60% of all e-mail messages were spam ("Can Spam," 2004). By 2009, the Internet security company McAfee reported that of the 200 billion e-mails sent each day on the Internet, 93% were from spammers (Lazarus, 2009). Now Pingdom (2011) estimates that 300 billion e-mails are sent each day and 89.1% are spam. That means the average e-mail account receives about 100 spam messages every day. If you have a good e-mail account provider, most of these messages are caught in their spam filters and never delivered to your mailbox.

Businesses that rely on e-mail have to develop ways of screening out the spam to prevent their mail systems from crashing. By 2004, American companies were spending more than $800 million a year to block spam ("Can Spam," 2004), and it has been estimated that spam now costs $10 billion a year in lost time dealing with spam.

Marketers who use e-mail to get their messages out to a wide variety of people see the Internet as a great tool to inform people of their products and services. They are not concerned with the additional costs to recipients of their messages. Instead, they are driven purely by e-mailing as many people as possible. While we welcome some of these commercial messages (such as announcements of sales at our favorite stores and restaurants), many of these messages are a growing nuisance. Skilled spammers can each send out 30 million e-mails a day, thus putting them on equal footing with a major advertiser such as a *Fortune* 500 company, which spends millions of dollars in television advertising a week to get its messages in front of that many people. Spammers are concerned with only one thing—maximizing their coverage, because spammers operate on a hit rate of 25 sales per 1 million e-mails. Therefore, they are motivated to increase the number of messages they send.

In their quest for reaching large numbers of people, spammers will buy long lists of e-mail addresses either legally or illegally. Spammers can buy CDs with 100 million e-mail addresses on them for as little as $2,000. Or they might hack into a company's private e-mail directory and steal those e-mail addresses. Sometimes, an employee of an ISP will sell the company's addresses. For example, in the summer of 2004, AOL, after fighting a daily battle with spammers who were clogging their service with unwanted e-mails, found out that one of its employees had sold AOL's list of 92 million e-mail addresses to a spammer for $100,000. The spammer used the addresses to promote his online gambling business, then sold those addresses to other spammers for tens of thousands of dollars himself (Gaither, 2004b).

ISPs are especially wary of spammers because a sudden inundation of hundreds of thousands of messages can slow their systems down, and a flood of a million messages can crash their systems. Slow service and crashed systems anger customers and cause ISPs with many of these problems to lose customers, so ISPs must hire technical people to filter out the spammers. A war between spammers and Internet companies has developed. The Internet companies have technicians set up spam traps—called honey pots—to collect spam e-mail and analyze it to figure out what spammers are doing; then they devise antispam software to screen it out. In response, spammers buy the antispam software to figure out how to get around it. Each week, the sophistication increases as the ISPs war with the spammers. As of now, it appears that the spammers are winning the war as the number of spam e-mails continues to increase each week.

One example of a huge spammer group calls itself the Alabama Spammers. This group dialed into Earthlink's high-powered servers and established several dozen connections simultaneously. Earthlink's spam abuse team spotted the attack within minutes, but it usually takes an hour to identify the accounts and manually terminate all the connections; meanwhile, the Alabama Spammers were able to send out thousands of messages. Earthlink filed civil lawsuits against 100 companies accusing them of hijacking Earthlink customer accounts to send spam under the RICO Act (Racketeer Influenced and Corrupt Organizations Act), which has been used to attack Mafia operations (Gaither, 2004a). The suit contended that in 2003, spam cost U.S. businesses $10 billion. One of the companies named in the suit is OptInRealBig.com and its owner, Scott Richter. This company uses contests and promotions to gather information on Internet users, then sells those addresses to other spammers. Richter's promotions include selling a diet pill named Inferno, a copy of Jennifer Lopez's engagement ring, Iraq's most-wanted playing cards, and an herbal supplement for "penile fitness." He sends out several hundred million e-mails each day, making his company one of the largest spammers. Richter does not like the term *spammer* and says, "We're a powerhouse in the e-mail marketing world. I stand up for what I do" (Jerome & Bane, 2004, pp. 125–126).

Some antispam services have been targeted by spammers. For example, for a year and half, Ron Guilmette published blacklists of spammers on his Monkeys.com website until September 2003, when he was inundated by a mass spam e-mail assault for 10 days until he had to shut down his website. Guilmette said, "I underestimated both the enemy's level of sophistication, and also the enemy's level of brute malevolence" (Gaither, 2004a, p. C1).

Spammers are not limited to e-mail; they have invaded Amazon with a proliferation of messages in the form of e-books. Users of Amazon's Kindle get on Amazon to buy e-books and download them to their Kindle. But the offerings for books are being clogged with spam in the form of PLR (Private Label Rights) content, which typically sell for about 99 cents each. Why are these PLR e-books regarded as spam? The answer is that most of these books are written by people who simply take an already published book that is selling well and make a few minor changes to target it better to a different demographic, and they do this multiple times to achieve a high volume of sales. Aspiring spammers can even buy a DVD called *Autopilot Kindle Cash* that promises to teach them how to publish 10 to 20 new Kindle books a day without writing a word. These books are then listed on Amazon along with more legitimate books, and the list of offerings gets enormously clogged with bogus e-books. How bad is the problem? In 2002, there were 215,000 traditional books published in the United States; people could buy a paper copy from a traditional publisher or bookstore. In the same year, 33,000 nontraditional books were published (these are typically self-published by individual authors without the use of a book publisher). So, the number of nontraditional books published in 2002 was only 15% of the number of traditional books published in that one year. By 2010, the number of traditional books had grown to 316,000, while the number of nontraditional books grew to 2.8 million or 886% the size of traditional book publishing ("Spam Clogging," 2011).

Another form of spamming is with the use of adware, which is advertising-supported software. When you access some commercial sites, that site sends a small program to your computer, and this software package automatically plays, displays, or downloads advertisements to a computer. These advertisements can be in the form of a pop-up. They may also be in the user interface of the software or on a screen presented to the user during the installation process. The object of the adware is to generate revenue for its author.

Commercial Mining

Another threat to your media privacy is what I call commercial mining, which refers to the ways businesses monitor your Internet activity and then sell that information to all kinds of other companies. Let's examine these two functions (monitoring and selling) in more detail.

Monitoring

When you buy products from an Internet store, all of your browsing and purchasing activity is recorded along with your name, address, credit card number, and so on. Amazon.com developed this model to enhance users' shopping experiences—that is, Amazon records visitors' browsing activities to note which books and products they click on and which they buy. Then next time each user gets on the site, Amazon displays a page of purchasing suggestions based on that particular user's browsing/purchasing history. This practice has now been adopted by many Internet stores, all of which appear to be providing you with a better, more personalized shopping experience. But underlying this "enhanced shopping experience" is a business practice of taking the information they have collected on your browsing and purchasing history and selling it to other marketers.

Facebook is another example of an Internet service that has grown very sophisticated in monitoring you. Facebook makes a copy of everything all users post through its service; this includes photos, text, audio, video, links, personal information, and even every e-mail. In addition, Facebook also monitors every opinion expressed, and in 2011, it added a facial recognition feature. This feature was presented to users as an added bonus of using the site—that is, users could pass a cursor over a photo of a picture of a person they do not recognize, and the person's name pops up. Many people do not want to be identified, so they have to search for a way to opt out of this feature, which means that identity is automatic unless people opt out (Guynn, 2011b). With these innovations, Facebook is "becoming in effect, the repository of identity for much of the Internet. If governments did that, the result would be outrage" ("Trolling for Your Soul," 2011, p. 58).

Clearly, Facebook collects a great deal of information about each user, and Facebook founder Mark Zuckerberg explained that Facebook not only owns the right to use this material but also retains the right in perpetuity, even after users quit the site (Sarno, 2009a). Since Facebook owns all this information, it has the right to sell it to other sites.

Your Web browser keeps a list of the websites you visit during an Internet session. You can set your browser defaults so that your browsing history will be erased after each time you close your browser. But while you are still browsing, many browsers allow third parties to access your browsing files and download the list of websites you have visited. This is called history stealing ("Anonymous No More," 2011). There is so much information available on the Internet that it makes monitoring the activities of other people easy. Everything you do online is recorded, put into all kinds of databases, and distributed to all kinds of services. Every time you post a picture, a video, or any text thought on any website, it is copied and stored by other people (Chmielewski & Semuels, 2006).

How do these sites monitor your Internet activity? The answer is that they use cookies, which are tiny computer files that are planted on your hard drive when you access many

websites. Cookies are what make monitoring of your Internet activities possible. Most people only have a fuzzy idea about what a cookie is or they have no idea at all.

Netscape created the innovation of cookies in 1994 as a special browser feature to make life easier for people browsing the Web. Netscape thought cookies would be especially useful in enabling "shopping cart" services on websites, such as Amazon.com. The idea was to allow consumers to click from page to page, choosing items to buy, while a virtual clerk kept track of the items by listing them in a small file called a cookie. Then the customer checks out of the virtual store by typing in credit card and address information so the company receives payment and knows where to send the purchases. But this information about the customer does not evaporate when he or she turns off the computer; instead, the information is preserved in a cookie that can be accessed during the customer's next shopping session. The advantage to the customers is that they will not have to reenter their addresses and credit card numbers, thus making subsequent trips to the online store more convenient for the customer. However, these cookies are accessed by the online store, which uses the information about past purchases to guide the customer to future purchases. For example, if you buy a book about dinosaurs from Amazon.com in one visit to its online store, in subsequent visits, you will miraculously be presented with ads about other dinosaur books, toys, and games. Virtual stores access the information stored in the cookies on people's hard drives to tailor how they present their products on the screen.

While online stores tell you they use cookies to make your shopping more efficient for you, they also use the information stored in cookies for their own purposes. They use this information to track which sites in their virtual stores attract the consumers' attention the most. They can also use this information to e-mail customers about sales and new products, and thus they can try to generate sales even when customers do not visit their online stores. They can also pull the information from cookies and create mailing lists along with customer profiles to sell to other stores.

Cookies are now used by other companies in addition to ISPs and online stores. There are now "third-party advertising networks," which use cookie files to track a user's activities all across the Web and trigger advertisements according to each user's apparent interests and needs. One of these third-party advertising networks is Doubleclick, which sprang up to oversee banner ads on websites.

When Netscape first developed cookies, it did not tell consumers how they worked. As the use of cookies grew in frequency, there were few complaints from consumers. But eventually, some consumers figured out that there was this clandestine activity taking place on their hard drives. Then the media reported on the cookie technology in January 1996, and a firestorm of criticism erupted when people began realizing how their privacy was being invaded without their knowledge. Officials at Netscape were surprised by the criticism and dismissed it. For example, Alex Edelstein, Netscape's product manager for Navigator 2.0, declared that cookie technology was an insignificant issue and would "blow over" (Pew Internet & American Life Project, 2000). But it didn't blow over. In subsequent public opinion polls, many people who understand what cookies are continued to criticize their use. In a 2000 poll, more than half (54%) of Internet users said they believed that websites' tracking of users is harmful because it invaded their privacy. Just 27% said tracking is helpful because it allows the sites to provide information tailored to specific consumers, and 54% of Internet users have chosen to provide personal information to use a website. An additional 10% say they would be willing to provide it under the right circumstances, and 27% are hard-core privacy protectionists and would never provide personal information (Pew Internet & American Life Project, 2000).

Under pressure, Netscape added a tool to disable cookies for the next version of their Web-browsing software. But it was not very easy to do the disabling. Web site users had cookies implanted on their machines unless they took affirmative steps to reject cookies—a classic "opt-out" scheme. Opt-out means that the consumer has to take steps to avoid cookies, and when they don't take these steps, companies are allowed to continue using cookies. With Netscape, a user had to dig two menu screens down in the browser to find the place to opt out of cookies.

Microsoft built in cookie controls in its more recent versions of Internet Explorer. Internet users are now alerted when a site tries to place a third-party cookie—that is, one that could help track their activities all across the Web. But even with these new tools provided by Internet browsers, only about 10% of people set their browsers to block cookies because many people still do not know what cookies are or how to prevent them (Pew Internet & American Life Project, 2000).

Some shocking uses of cookies have come to light. These examples show how powerful cookies are in monitoring activity on one's computer. The federal Office of National Drug Control Policy (the so-called drug czar's office) was found to be using cookies to track Web surfers' drug-related information requests. After a storm of criticism that this might allow the drug czar's office to clandestinely record citizens' online activities, the federal Office of Management and Budget banned the use of cookies on federal government websites.

Cookies are a relatively passive and limited form of monitoring. A specific website that you visit creates a cookie and stores information in that cookie about your interaction with that one website. Later when you visit that website, it can access your history from the cookie stored on your computer's hard drive. There are other more active and aggressive ways of monitoring your Internet activity. For example, the Federal Bureau of Investigation (FBI) developed and began using "Carnivore," a device that silently intercepts all traffic to and from a suspect's e-mail account without the person's knowledge or permission. It is similar to a wiretap without a court order. In the private sector, many businesses routinely monitor the e-mail and Internet activity of their employees. For example, Dow Chemical Company monitors its employees and recently fired 50 employees after a search of their e-mail revealed pornography or violent images. Also, some companies monitor who visits different websites and sell that information to other companies. For example, Pharmatrak, Inc., a Boston technology firm, acknowledged tracking consumers' activities on health-related sites without informing the public (Pew Internet & American Life Project, 2000).

A great deal of your activities are being monitored without your explicit knowledge. The federal government listens to phone conversations. ISPs collect information on which websites you visit and for how long. Search companies such as Google and Yahoo collect data on all your searches (Levy, 2006c). There are satellites that take pictures of your house in enough detail to show what is in your backyard; anyone can get access to these pictures for free at Zillow.com. When you buy a property, that information is recorded in the courthouse of the county where the property is located. That governmental information is available online for many cities. You can find out who owns which properties and how much they bought them for by getting on BlockShopper.com (Sarno, 2009b). If your employer provides you with a phone, a computer, or an Internet account, all of that activity is being monitored. A recent survey found that more than 75% of employers say they monitor how their employees use their computers (checking websites and using e-mail) and also monitor their phone calls (Levy, 2006c).

Retailing companies are becoming more sophisticated at marketing their products by assembling more detailed pictures of their customers than ever before. For example, Williams-Sonoma uses information about their 60 million customers' income and value of their houses to produce different versions of its catalog. Amazon.com uses customers' past buying behavior to drive its "recommendation engine," which is now responsible for stimulating 30% of its sales ("Building With Big Data," 2011).

Other companies are developing new technologies to gather even more information on consumers. For example, Placecast uses GPS tracking data on people's smartphones to track potential consumers and send them enticing offers when they get within a few yards of a Starbucks. Now Google and Microsoft HealthVault provide services to allow consumers to track their health and record their treatments. Manufacturers are embedding sensors into their products to allow them to monitor the use of their products. With cars, insurance companies can now monitor the driving styles of their customers and offer them rates based on their competence (or recklessness) rather than their age and sex ("Building With Big Data," 2011).

In his fascinating book, *The Filter Bubble: What the Internet Is Hiding From You,* Eli Pariser (2011) says that if you do a Google search and ask your friend to do a Google search for the same term at the same time, the results of the two searches will be different because Google adjusts its search algorithm across individuals based on the individual's personal interests as determined by their browsing and purchasing histories. Google claims this is an innovation designed to tailor searches to individuals and thus make searches more useful to each user. However, Pariser is very concerned about large powerful Internet companies gathering all this personal information for commercial purposes. Also, Pariser argues that the effect of this tailoring of searches tends to narrow our exposure to a range of information rather than opening us up to find genuinely new information on the Internet.

There is a great deal of data about you that you likely want to be kept very private, especially about your finances and health. However, every time you go to a doctor, your insurance company adds to your record of illnesses, the tests run and their results, and the prescriptions written and filled. Also, every time you use a credit card or check to pay for something or scan a store card for discounts, those purchases are added to a database. Some companies have a record of every time you have made a purchase, the brand name, and how much you paid. The collection of these financial data is getting easier for companies as our economy moves away from cash and checks to digital forms of payment, like credit cards, debit cards, and electronic transfers. In 2010, Americans used debit and credit cards for $3.7 trillion of purchases. Now smartphone apps let you buy merchandise on your way to a store so that you just walk in and pick up your purchase and have your bank account automatically debited for the purchase price. This is a big move toward paperless transactions ("Money?" 2011). Each of these transactions has an electronic record that goes into a huge database that can be sliced and diced and sold to all kinds of clients. Thus, there is a concern about privacy.

Selling Information

Many Internet companies mine data on all sorts of topics and sell this information to anyone willing to pay, such as advertisers, future employers, prospective romantic partners, identity thieves, and predators. While access to some of these information sites is free (e.g., check out Google.123people.com, PeekYou.com, and Snitch.name), it is more likely that companies will sell the information. For example, MySpace collects personal information from users to build profiles for advertisers. They were so serious about this that in February 2007, they spent $100 million to acquire Strategic Data Corp, which is a sophisticated data mining and analysis company. To illustrate, MySpace knows that people who list cars as a hobby are likely to click on car ads, so MySpace makes a list of all users with a car hobby and sells access to those users to car dealerships. Toyota has used MySpace to build a social network of more than 15,000 enthusiasts for hybrid cars (Angwin, 2009, p. 244). Of course, if you love cars, you may like the idea that all kinds of car dealers are suddenly sending you information. However, the decision to sell information about you to car dealerships was made outside your control and knowledge.

Companies are required to tell people when they will be collecting data on them and selling it, but they usually make such disclosures deep in the small print of user agreements that users are required to accept when they want access to websites. But some companies fail to disclose this information. For example, Toysrus.com was feeding shoppers' personal information to a data analysis firm without revealing this transaction to consumers. In response to complaints, Toysrus.com was forced to add information to its privacy policy about how customer data were treated.

Some companies that collect information from their customers promise not to sell it but then are later forced to do so. For example, in 2000, Toysmart.com filed for bankruptcy, and the Federal Trade Commission forced the company to sell off customer data to the highest bidder. The firm had promised site users that it would not divulge information gleaned from tracking users' activities on the site, but a court-appointed overseer believed the customer list was a valuable asset that could be sold to help pay off the firm's creditors. In this case, the court ruled that it was more important for a bankrupt company to partially pay back some of its creditors than it was to protect the privacy of its customers.

Many companies regard the selling of customer data as just another lucrative revenue stream. In early 2000, Internet advertiser Doubleclick decided it would combine two databases and sell the information. One database was an offline database that included people's geographical addresses and other private information. The other was the anonymous Web-surfing habits of millions of people that were gathered through cookies.

Theft of Private Information

The practices in the previous section are legal—even though you often do not know that when you hit the agree button as you create an account on an Internet site, you are giving that site permission to collect and share your data. In this section, we examine the threats to your privacy when people and organizations have no rights of any kind to your information but invade your privacy using illegal means to get that information. These techniques include spyware, phishing, hacking, identity theft, and hijacking.

Spyware is a small program that is inadvertently downloaded by a computer user and installs itself on that person's computer. Once installed, it collects pieces of information about users without their knowledge. The spyware then records keystrokes, sites visited,

and even personal information such as credit card numbers, e-mail address, passwords, and so on. The presence of spyware is typically hidden from the user and can be difficult to detect.

Phishing is a technique used to acquire sensitive information from innocent users by seemingly trustworthy message senders. Phishing is typically carried out by e-mail or instant messaging, and it often directs users to enter details at a fake website whose look and feel are almost identical to the legitimate one. For example, you might get an e-mail from someone who says she is a security officer at your bank and wants to help you increase the security on your accounts at no extra charge to you. To help her perform this "security procedure," you are asked to send her your name, address, phone number, and Social Security number to confirm that it is really you. After you provide this information, she says you have passed the security check and is satisfied it is really you. Then she asks you to list your bank account numbers so she can increase the security on them. The irony is that while you believe you are increasing the security on your private accounts, you are actually destroying the security and allowing a stranger to breach your accounts, clean out all your money, and steal your identity.

Breaching Secure Databases

There are individuals who break into supposedly secure databases and download all the information so that they can later sell it or use it for their own financial gain. This is not an

---

TABLE 17.1   Some Recent Security Breaches of Consumer Information

- In 2003, hackers got into San Diego State University's computer network and accessed the financial aid system where 200,000 Social Security numbers were stored.

- In June 2004, an employee at AOL stole 92 million e-mail addresses and sold them to a spammer for more than $100,000. This opened an investigation of the company that revealed to AOL subscribers that AOL regularly collects information on its subscribers' search requests. While the company identifies subscribers by number and not name, the search requests contain personal information such as their names, addresses, credit card numbers, medical conditions, and so on. Several subscribers filed a class action suit in the summer of 2006. AOL fired a few people and hired a chief privacy officer.

- In February 2005, an employee of Bank of America lost computer tapes containing 1.2 million records consisting of personal information for credit cards used by federal employees.

- In June 2005, hackers got into the database of CardSystems Solutions, Inc. and obtained access to 40 million Discover, Visa, MasterCard, and American Express numbers along with the secret code numbers printed on the actual cards.

- In June 2005, 3.9 million records were compromised when United Parcel Service lost computer tapes containing account and payment history data of Citigroup.

- In December 2006, UCLA admitted that one or more hackers had gained access to a UCLA database containing personal information on about 800,000 of the university's current and former students, faculty, and staff members.

- In June 2006, a data analyst from the Department of Veterans Affairs had downloaded a database containing more than 26 million personal records, taken it home with him, and then had his laptop stolen—exposing all the information necessary to swipe the identity of virtually every person released from military service since 1975.

- In April 2006, the Ohio secretary of state distributed 20 copies of registered voter lists that accidently included Social Security numbers of "millions" of voters in the state.

- In May 2009, hackers broke into a Virginia state website used by pharmacists to track prescription drug abuse. They deleted records on more than 8 million patients and replaced the site's homepage with a ransom note demanding $10 million for the return of the records (HIPAA-HiTech Security and Privacy, 2009).

- In April 2011, hackers accessed the names, addresses, passwords, and credit card details of 77 million accounts in a Sony network used to run their online gaming systems (such as PlayStation) as well as Qriocity, a service offering music, films, and television shows.

- In May 2011, hackers operating out of China broke through Google's firewall and accessed the gmail account information of senior U.S. government officials, Chinese political activists, officials from Asian countries, journalists, and military personnel.

SOURCE: "AOL Is Sued" (2006); Gaither (2004c); Levy (2006b); "Online Reputations" (2011); Rodriguez and Pierson (2011); Trounson (2006).

uncommon occurrence; see Table 17.1 for a few high-profile examples. The Privacy Rights Clearinghouse reports that since 2005, more than 530 million consumer accounts have been compromised in 2,520 known data breaches (Lazarus, 2011).

While a huge industry has grown to protect data on computers and on the Internet from being accessed by hackers, the problem of Internet security is likely to grow much worse as users and corporations shift the storage of private information into services that are marketed under the name of "cloud." The cloud is a way to store e-mails, calendars, photos, music, and other documents online and access them with PCs, smartphones, and other wireless devices. For example, with Apple, you can buy music from iTunes and store it on the cloud and access it with no additional cost. These cloud services are being heavily marketed by companies such as Apple, Amazon, and Microsoft, which are trying to convince companies to move their databases from their own in-house computers, which require expensive purchases of hardware and software as well as large staffs of experts to maintain them. Cloud services offer businesses considerable savings in costs and a reduction in the hassles of running in-house computer servers.

Cloud services are already a huge business and are growing rapidly. In 2010, cloud services generated $41 billion, and this figure is expected to grow to a quarter of a trillion dollars by 2020 ("Online Reputations," 2011). Cloud services are likely to grow exponentially in the coming years as businesses create ever larger databases and need to achieve efficiencies in accessing that information. Even the federal government is encouraging digitization of information. In April 2011, the Obama administration passed laws that gave the health care industry $28 billion in subsidies to encourage doctors and hospitals to digitize their records. The idea is that this will make sharing of patient data more efficient. But this also comes with risks; having all your illnesses listed in a file somewhere in the cloud puts everyone at risk for invasions of their privacy by hackers or anyone interested in buying the data, such as insurance companies and prospective employers. Anyone working for a doctor could access your full health records with a smartphone ("Heads in the Cloud," 2011).

But cloud services also present some problems. Because the cloud is really a conglomeration of networked computers worldwide, there are often problems when different parts of these networks communicate with one another. In April 2011, Amazon Web Services crashed, leaving users stranded without access to their service. But an even larger problem is with security. With many databases containing highly sensitive and personal information all on the same network, this becomes an enormously attractive target for hackers. And given the fact that cloud security is entrusted to thousands of technicians scattered around the world, the potential for hackers to find flaws in all the various interacting security systems is great.

Identity Theft

With the rise of the Internet comes the risk of identity theft. This crime feeds on the inability of consumers to control who has access to sensitive information and how it is safeguarded. As you saw in the previous section, hackers have been able to breach "secure" databases and get access to enough information on you to steal your identity. Also, scam artists have developed many ways to get you to give up key bits of information about you, then take over your identity. The key elements of your identity are your name, birth date, and Social Security number. When scam artists get these three pieces of information about you, they can apply for credit cards in your name and have them mailed to their own post office box. Then they go on a buying spree. The bills come to their post office box where they are ignored. Eventually, your creditors find you and demand payment; at this point,

when your credit is ruined and you are thousands of dollars in debt, you finally find out that your identity has been stolen.

A common scam of identity thieves is to set up an electronic auction site where people bid on items (K. Lee & Light, 2003). The person who wins is told to send his or her name and address so the merchandise can be mailed. The recipient is told to wait until the merchandise arrives and check it out before paying for it, so it sounds like a good deal from a reputable company to the recipient. But what the recipient does not know is that the thief uses the information to obtain a credit card in the recipient's name and charges the purchase on it.

Approximately 85% of victims of identity theft found out about the crime due to an adverse situation—denied credit or employment, notification by police or collection agencies, receipt of credit cards or bills never ordered, and so on. Only 15% found out through a positive action taken by a business group that verified a submitted application or a reported change of address.

There is so much theft of personal information and it is so easily available that criminals can now buy verified credit card numbers for as little as $1. Also, the cost of buying a complete identity (which includes a person's date of birth, number of a U.S. bank account, credit card number, and government-issued identification number, such as a Social Security number or driver's license number) is only $14 ("U.S. Is No. 1 Source," 2007).

Victims now spend an average of 600 hours recovering from this crime, often over a period of years. Based on 600 hours times the indicated victim's hourly wages, this equals nearly $16,000 in lost potential or realized income. Also, victims spend an average of $1,400 in out-of-pocket expenses. Although victims are finding out about the crime more quickly, it is taking far longer than ever before to clear their records and recover from the situation.

Even after the thief stops using the information, victims struggle with the impact of identity theft, which often includes increased insurance or credit card fees, inability to find a job, higher interest rates and battling collection agencies, and issuers who refuse to clear records despite substantiating evidence of the crime. This negative fallout may continue for more than 10 years after the crime was first discovered. The emotional impact on victims is likened to that felt by victims of more violent crime, including rape, violent assault, and repeated battering. Some victims feel dirty, defiled, ashamed and embarrassed, and undeserving of assistance. Others report a split with a significant other or spouse and being unsupported by family members.

Each year in the United States, 10 million people become victims of identity theft, and now about 1 in every 10 U.S. consumers has already been victimized by identity theft. Less than half of all victims discover their identity has been stolen within 3 months, and about one in six victims do not find out for 4 years or more. After suffering identity theft, 46% of victims installed antivirus software, anti-spyware, or a firewall on their computer; 23% switched their primary bank or credit union; and 22% switched credit card companies. The average victim spends 330 hours repairing the damage. On average, victims lose between $851 and $1,378 out of pocket trying to resolve identity theft. In total, this problem totals over $30 billion in the United States and more than $220 billion worldwide. To help protect themselves, 50.2 million Americans use a credit monitoring service, 44% of consumers view their credit reports using AnnualCreditReport.com, and 25.9 million Americans carry identity theft insurance (Official Identity Theft Statistics, 2011).

Identity theft creates significant costs to law enforcement agencies. The Government Auditing Office (GAO) conducted a study (GAO-02–363, issued March 2002) of the impact of the crime of identity theft on various federal agencies. The executive office for U.S. Attorneys estimates that the cost of prosecuting a white-collar crime case is $11,443. The Secret Service estimates that the average cost per financial crime investigation is $15,000. The FBI estimates that the average cost per financial crime investigation is $20,000. And the average arrest rate (according to law enforcement) is less than 5% of all reported cases by victims.

Hijacking

Another invasion of privacy is when your computer is hijacked and used by hackers without your permission and often without your knowledge. This can take several forms. One form is when someone takes control of your computer and links it up with others in what is called **bot network activity** to allow spammers to use the network as a server to send out millions of messages under your IP address, thus hiding his or her own IP address. A **botnet** is a network of infected computers (bots) that is remotely controlled by hackers who put these computers into round-the-clock service sending spam, fishing for credit card numbers, spying on Internet traffic, or logging users' keystrokes. Some of these botnets have been found to send out 30 billion spam e-mails per day. Almost all of this is done without the knowledge of the individuals who own the PCs in the botnet (Sarno, 2011).

Another form of **hijacking,** which is done by advertisers, is to take over your homepage with a browser or to implant a search engine in your computer. This appears innocent enough, but this browser or search engine is designed to direct you only to certain advertised websites. One is SearchCoolWeb, which provides a page of all kinds of interesting topics that you can click on to play games or go shopping. Although this page looks like a service helping you in your Internet surfing, what really is taking place is that your browser has been hijacked and your Internet browsing is being controlled by the hijacker.

Maliciousness

Some people invade your privacy without being motivated to benefit themselves by using your personal information. Instead, these people are motivated by maliciousness—that is, they want to harm you in some way. Two of these techniques are discussed below: infecting with viruses and trolling.

Infecting With Viruses

Some hackers create computer viruses for the sole purpose of corrupting computer files. Unlike the people who invade your privacy using any of the methods above, these virus disseminators are not motivated by stealing information from you or by directing your attention to certain sites so they can benefit financially. Instead, these people are motivated by purely destructive goals.

A virus is a hidden element of computer code that lurks unobserved in the computer until it is activated. The most common computer virus acts as a string of code that attaches itself to a normal software program, often affixing itself to file extensions that end in .COM or .EXE. All computer programs are made up of thousands of lines of software code, the actual language that creates the program. The string of viral code hides itself among the normal code. Once infected, software programs frequently change in size as the virus adds code to the beginning or end of the program. The most common computer viruses range in size between 2,000 and 4,000 bytes of code.

Computer viruses are highly contagious. Every time a user saves an infected program to a file, the virus gets saved too. Whenever that file is loaded onto a new computer, the virus gets loaded too. When that computer connects to a network server, the virus connects too. Because most viruses remain hidden, most users have no idea they are passing around the virus until it is too late. The viral code replicates itself and spreads quickly, infecting more and more computers as it grows.

With a single user, a virus can make dozens of perfect, identical copies of itself within minutes of infection. Once a computer is hooked up to a computer network system, that same virus can infect every other computer in an office environment in a very short period. Networks themselves do not necessarily become infected; instead, they may act as carriers of the virus, infecting all computers currently hooked up to the network system, as well as those that eventually log on. All computer systems can be exposed to viruses. Computer viruses can infect any form of writeable storage medium—including hard disks, floppy disks, tapes, CD-ROMs, optical media, and all forms of memory.

When a virus attack occurs, the most common setbacks to your system are that data files are lost or corrupted, program files are corrupted, hard drives are reformatted, and file addresses can be lost, making it impossible to retrieve files that still exist.

Computer viruses can be extremely damaging both to businesses and to individual users. A survey showed that in North American corporations with more than 400 PCs, more than 50% of companies had experienced a virus attack. The study also found that corporate PCs are infected with viruses at an increasingly alarming rate, with 26% of all sites discovering an infection in a single month. In another study, more than 9% of companies interviewed said they had experienced "disastrous" data losses due to a computer virus. In 2003, computer viruses cost at least $82 billion worldwide, and this does not include the emotional distress of crashing computers and lost files (Winik, 2004). Computer viruses have been reported in well over 100 countries around the world, reaching every continent on the globe.

The number of viruses has grown dramatically in less than two decades. In 1986, the National Computer Security Association estimated that there were only 4 known computer viruses. By 1990, that number had grown to 500, and by 2000, it was estimated that there were more than 50,000 identified viruses. In 2011, Symantec Corporation, which markets Norton Utilities computer software, estimated that there are more than 1 million viruses ("Number of Viruses," 2011).

Trolling is the "posting of willfully inflammatory, off-topic or simply stupid remarks" ("Trolling for Your Soul," 2011, p. 58). It is a side effect of online anonymity. Trolls mask their true identity with pseudonyms and post their comments usually to stimulate reactions for their entertainment value to the trollers. To combat trolling, Facebook and other sites are insisting that people use their real names, and these are posted with their comments.

PUBLIC OPINION AND REGULATIONS

Public opinion is strongly in favor of personal privacy. However, it is difficult for regulators to establish laws that draw a clear line distinguishing what is private and what is public. Although there are a few laws in existence, it is exceedingly difficult to prosecute and punish offenders.

Public Opinion

Privacy has become a much more important issue to the American public in the past few decades. A Lou Harris poll found that the percentage of Americans concerned about their privacy rights grew from 34% in 1970 to 90% in 1998 (Identity Theft Center, 2002). A lot of this concern is directed at the Internet. The Pew Internet & American Life Project (2000) reports two strong conclusions from its survey of Americans and their Internet habits. The first conclusion is that American Internet users overwhelmingly want the presumption of privacy when they go online. The second conclusion is that a great many Internet users do not know the basics of how their online activities are observed, and they do not use available tools to protect themselves.

The Pew Internet & American Life Project (2000) reported that 84% of Americans were "very concerned" or "somewhat concerned" about people accessing their personal information. Internet privacy has emerged as a central policy concern about the Internet as more Americans go online every day and as the news media continually report on new allegations about privacy violations by Internet companies.

A majority of Internet users (54%) are against online tracking because it invades their privacy. Advocates of cookies make the case that consumers will eventually come to appreciate cookies because cookies allow sites to provide information that is important and relevant to an individual Web user. In the case of advertising and marketing, cookie advocates argue that there is a great deal of waste that everyone hates in mass marketing through the mail (junk mail) and the media. These advocates argue that the ideal world created by cookies and tracking is one where the clutter of information and advertisements is cut to a minimum, and only useful material is put in users' and consumers' hands. However, what these cookie advocates fail to understand is that many Internet users want to make their own decisions about which messages show up on their computer screens; that is, they do not want any advertisers aggressively invading their screens. Only 27% of

Internet users feel that advertisers' use of cookies is helpful in tailoring information exposure to their particular needs. Almost three quarters of Internet users would prefer to make their own decisions about which messages to access (Pew Internet & American Life Project, 2000).

Internet users overwhelmingly call for strict enforcement of their privacy; 94% of Internet users want privacy violators to be disciplined. If an Internet company violated its stated privacy policy and used personal information in ways that it said it wouldn't, 11% of Internet users say the company's owners should be sent to prison, 27% say the owners should be fined, 26% say the site should be shut down, and 30% say the site should be placed on a list of fraudulent websites (Pew Internet & American Life Project, 2000).

Public opinion is very much against spam, with 77% of the public saying that spam had made their online experiences unpleasant and annoying. Also, 29% said spam had caused them to use e-mail less. The public is taking steps to protect itself but at great cost. It has been estimated that the public spent almost $1 billion in antispam software and services in 2004, which is an increase of 50% in 1 year (Gaither, 2004a).

Regulations

Governments have been slow to catch on to the problem of spamming, but there is a growing realization of how spam can involve criminal activity. In the spring of 2004, the New York State Attorney General and Microsoft Corporation filed a suit against a handful of spammers that had sent billions of illegal and deceptive e-mail messages. The e-mails were illegal because the spammers used forged sender names, false subject lines, and fake sender addresses (Jerome & Bane, 2004).

There are laws preventing the use of a person's name and address in a postal mailing list without his or her consent. "Although courts have yet to apply such statutes to list of e-mail addresses, given the rise of unsolicited e-mail advertisements, the time is ripe" (K. Lee & Light, 2003, p. 307). Part of the reason why such laws have such lax enforcement is that it is costly to track down violators, and when those lawbreakers are identified, they simply move out of the country and thus avoid punishment. For example, the first financial penalties to a spammer were handed down in California in October 2003 when PW Marketing and its owners, Paul Willis and Claudia Griffin, were fined $2 million for sending unsolicited or misleading e-mails. The spammers fled the country to avoid the judgment (Healey, 2003). Also, on January 1, 2004, a new law took effect outlawing many of the tricks spammers use. In response, many spammers have moved their operations outside the United States to avoid prosecution. Therefore, it appears useless for U.S. legislators to pass laws against spammers, identity thieves, and virus disseminators when those people can easily continue their practices in other countries where these actions are not illegal. The virtual geography of the Internet does not lend itself to the traditional ways of thinking about laws and enforcement.

The first felony prosecution of spam distributors was in the fall of 2004 with two spammers convicted of sending unsolicited junk mail to AOL customers. A brother and sister were convicted of sending e-mails with fraudulent and untraceable routing information; one was sentenced to a 9-year prison term, and the other was fined $7,500. These people were actually convicted of fraud and not spamming ("2 Convicted," 2004).

In the fall of 2004, California passed a law against spyware—the placing of software on a personal computer to collect information about the computer's owner (S. Lawrence, 2004). Other states are following suit. However, at this point, the problem of increasing threats to an individual's privacy is growing faster than is government regulation to protect individuals.

In 2003, the U.S. Federal Trade Commission (FTC) instituted some regulations that it called the CAN-SPAM Act (Controlling the Assault of Non-Solicited Pornography and Marketing Act) and then tightened its regulations in 2008. This act essentially requires senders of e-mail messages to more clearly identify themselves and to allow receivers of the messages to opt out of receiving any future messages from the senders.

WHAT CAN WE DO TO PROTECT OUR PRIVACY?

It is likely that regulators will never catch up with the technology that keeps developing new ways to invade our privacy. We cannot depend on other people to have our best interests at heart and protect us. The responsibility rests with each of us to protect our own privacy. But what can we do? There are seven major things you can do to take a big step toward protecting yourself (Table 17.2). These seven strategies require a fair degree of sophistication and work from us. But if we do not do the work to protect ourselves, we will likely have very little privacy left.

1. Search for information about yourself. Find out what information is already publically available on you. Go to websites such as Google. 123people.com, PeekYou.com, and Snitch. name. Type in your name and see what information others can easily get about you.

If you have your own Web pages, such as on a social networking website or a blog, access those pages and look at them like someone else would. For example, view those sites as your parents or another family member would. Imagine yourself at your wedding and this information is flashed on the walls as you exchange vows. Imagine you are interviewing for your dream professional job several years from now and the interviewer is looking at those websites. Remember that anything you post online is available forever.

Go to the websites of your banks, credit card companies, and health insurance companies. Look for the information those companies have in their records about you.

TABLE 17.2 Strategies to Protect Oneself From Invasions of Privacy	
1. Search for information about yourself.	5. Always study privacy policies.
2. Correct inaccuracies.	6. Download software to protect your computer from threats to your privacy.
3. Be careful what you post about yourself online.	7. Set up your Internet browsers to disallow cookies as the default.
4. Be skeptical about requests for information.	

Monitor your credit history to make sure the purchases that are charged to you are purchases you have made. Now all 50 states give residents three free credit checks each year from the three major credit reporting bureaus. Go to annualcreditreport.com to check on your credit. See who has been accessing your credit information. Do you recognize those people and businesses, such as your bank, places where you have applied for employment, and the like? If not, then there may be attempts to steal your identity.

2. *Correct inaccuracies.* As you go through all the sites in the previous step, make a note of any inaccuracies. Then contact those companies and try to get those inaccuracies corrected. But remember that what you have posted yourself is your responsibility. For example, if you posted a compromising picture of yourself in full party mode on your Facebook page last year and now you think it is "inaccurate" because that is really not you now, you can remove those images, but Facebook will retain a copy, and there may also be many other copies that visitors to your site have made over the past year.

3. *Be careful what you post about yourself online.* Think about what you post on websites that can be accessed by people you do not know. Things you post today can be copied to other sites where they can be copied to still other sites. These ideas and images can be altered and distorted as they spread to all kinds of places beyond your control and can remain in those places indefinitely.

4. *Be skeptical about requests for information.* On social networks, be very careful about accepting requests from strangers. Those requests may come from advertisers, spammers, or even predators. Never give out information you want kept private unless you know who is asking for it and what their privacy policy is.

5. *Always study privacy policies.* Many times when you first try to access a website, the company asks you to register, where you are asked for some private information about yourself, and then you are asked to read the privacy policy that goes on and on for many screens. Most of us simply click on the "I Agree" button without taking the time to read all the dense language. This is a mistake, because what you typically are agreeing to is giving away many of your rights to privacy.

Most websites have an opt-out rather than an opt-in policy as a default. With opt-in, the default is privacy, and consumers have to do something to grant advertisers permission to send them a message or to record information in a cookie; that is, advertisers cannot send e-mail to consumers or record information in cookies on consumers' computers unless they first ask those consumers and are explicitly granted permission. In contrast with opt-out, the default is that businesses have the right to send any information and to create cookies until consumers tell them to stop.

Businesses overwhelmingly prefer the opt-out option, because they can do whatever they want until a person tells them to stop, and few people tell businesses to stop, because most people are not aware of how those businesses are invading their privacy. When this is explained to people, 86% of Internet users say they prefer "opt-in" privacy policies.

Most regulations, however, are being crafted to favor businesses. For example, the policy negotiated by the Clinton administration, the FTC, and a consortium of Web advertisers gave websites the right to track Internet users unless the users take steps to "opt out" of being monitored. These privacy standards were regarded as being so favorable for online advertisers that shares in Doubleclick rose 13% in one day (Pew Internet & American Life Project, 2000). So far, this law has not been viewed as a success for consumers because fewer than 3% of consumers opt out (Stern, 2002). A primary reason why this figure is so low is that so few consumers know (a) that they have this option, (b) the consequences of not opting out, and (c) how to opt out.

To protect their privacy, a relatively small number of savvy users are devising their own "opt-in" policies and deciding that some websites are not worthy of getting their personal information. Also, 24% of Internet users said that they have provided a fake name or personal information to avoid giving a website real information, 9% of Internet users have used encryption to scramble their e-mail, and 5% of Internet users have used "anonymizing" software that hides their computer identity from websites they visit. But most people do not know how to protect themselves, and 56% of Internet users do not know what cookies are, much less know how to avoid them. Only 10% of Internet users have set their browsers to reject cookies (Pew Internet & American Life Project, 2000).

Always familiarize yourself with the privacy policy of every site that asks for information about you. Some sites give you options; if you have options, begin with the tightest security and loosen that security only when you feel comfortable. The standard privacy agreement now is that all your information can be used by the site and sold to others unless you opt out.

This is especially important when you buy products or donate to political campaigns online. You need to be careful about sharing your credit card or checking account information, as well as consider who might find out how you spend your money.

6. Download software to protect your computer from threats to your privacy. While major Internet service providers, such as Google's g-mail, Microsoft's hotmail, and your own university that provides you with an e-mail account have large staffs who work every day to identify threats and filter them out, it is still a good idea to download software to protect your own computer. Several companies (such as Norton and McAffee) sell software that you download onto your computer's hard drive that creates a firewall to screen out all kinds of threats, especially spam, spyware, and adware. Or you could go online and find software that you can download for free. This is called freeware, and there are many services available for download, but these are usually targeted to one threat such as spyware only or adware only. If you decide to try freeware, make sure you go to a reputable site that includes product reviews, so that you know you are downloading something that will help you. If you do not check out the software first, you may end up downloading a program that appears to offer protection but is really an adware or spyware program rather than a program that protects you.

7. Set up your Internet browsers to disallow cookies as the default. Allow cookies only from sites you trust, such as your online bank, which will require cookies for you to log onto your account and access your money.

Cookies themselves are not inherently bad or necessarily invasive to one's privacy. But they open the door for widespread abuse. In the most comprehensive and extreme cases, a Web company could build a profile of an Internet user that combines information about her purchases, her taste in music, the investment information she seeks, the health issues that concern her most, and the kind of news stories that seize her interest (Pew Internet & American Life Project, 2000).

When you allow cookies to exist in your hard drive, a hacker could get into your computer and, by reading the information in your cookies, infer a great deal about your interests, finances, health, personality, and lifestyle.

SUMMARY

Industry groups are working hard right now to protect their business practices that give them access to all kinds of information about you. If they get their way, they will continue to have the right to send advertising to your e-mail address, plant cookies on your hard drive, sell your e-mail unrestricted, and sell information they collect about you to other advertisers. When these businesses offer you options to restrict their use of your information, they place the burden on you to tell them no (opt-out) rather than accept the burden themselves to ask for your consent.

Given the technological devices that are now in common use, the area of a person's private life has been greatly reduced. There are so many businesses collecting information about you and selling that information with other businesses that it is virtually impossible to avoid being a part of hundreds of databases that are used by marketers to send you messages about thousands of products. Also, virtually any of your actions can be recorded and shared almost instantly. One chilling example of this is Michael Richards, who was delivering a comedy routine at a Los Angeles club when he veered into a racist outburst. This was recorded by a patron on his cell phone camera and uploaded to the Internet, where it got instant television, newspaper, and magazine coverage (Levy, 2006f). Michael Richards was a public figure before this incident, so he did not lose his privacy in this situation. However, this incident illustrates the potential that any one of us could have our speech and actions recorded and widely disseminated, transforming us instantly into a public figure.

With this issue of privacy, it is essential that you become informed about the risks to your privacy. If you remain ignorant about these risks, you will continue to lose much of your privacy and possibly even your identity.

Chapter Resources: To test your knowledge and learn more about the topics discussed in this chapter, visit the Student Study Site at www.sagepub.com/potter6e.

FURTHER READING

Calvert, C. (2004). *Voyeur nation: Media, privacy, and peering in modern culture.* New York: Basic Books. (274 pages)

This book clearly shows how our culture has become obsessed with voyeurism, which has been made possible by technological advances in surveillance along with a governmental Big Brother mentality. Also, the legal system has not kept pace with this phenomenon, so our privacy is being severely limited. The author is a professor at Pennsylvania State University and an expert in media law, privacy, and their interrelation.

Pariser, E. (2011). *The filter bubble: What the Internet is hiding from you.* New York: Penguin. (294 pages)

The author is an Internet activist who criticizes how certain Web services (particularly Google, Netflix, Amazon, Facebook, and Pandora) are recording your browsing information and using it for commercial marketing purposes.

Solove, D. J., Rotenberg, M., & Schwartz, P. M. (2010). *Privacy, information and technology* (2nd ed.). New York: Aspen Publishers. (320 pages with index)

Written by three law school professors, this book takes a strong legalistic approach to the problem of protecting people's privacy when they access media messages.

KEEPING UP TO DATE

Electronic Frontier Foundation (https://www.eff.org/)

This nonprofit organization bills itself as the "first line of defense" when the public's freedoms in the networked world come under attack. Founded in 1990, it champions the public interest by defending free speech, privacy, and consumer rights. Get on the official website and click on the Privacy tab to get updated information on litigation and news stories, resources, and research papers.

Electronic Privacy Information Center (http://epic.org/)

Established in 1994 in Washington, D.C., EPIC is a public interest research center with the mission of focusing public attention on emerging civil liberties issues and protecting privacy, the First Amendment, and constitutional values.

National Cyber Security (http://nationalcybersecurity.com/)

This website offers a range of news stories updated every 60 seconds. The stories focus on the activities of hackers and the law enforcement efforts to stop them. It also monitors government actions and offers tips to help readers protect themselves from invasions of their privacy on Internet platforms.

Spend on Life (http://www.spendonlife.com/guide/identity-theft-statistics)

This website collects figures on identity theft from a variety of sources. Its purpose is to educate consumers about the dangers of identity theft and how people can protect themselves from this fast-growing crime.

EXERCISE 17.1

If you have never checked your computer for cookies, make sure you do this exercise as soon as possible. Instructions are provided below for the two most popular Web browsers of Microsoft Explorer and Mozilla Firefox.

Microsoft Explorer

1. Look at the top right of your browser's page and click on the Tools tab. This will give you a drop-down menu.

2. At the bottom of the drop-down menu is "Internet Options." Click on Internet options.

3. You will see a box with seven tabs across the top. Click on the Privacy tab.

4. At the left of the box, you will see a settings bar. If you move the bar up, it will increase your security; if you move the bar down, it will decrease your security. As you move the bar, you can see a description on the right that indicates how you are changing the settings on cookies.

Mozilla Firefox

1. Look at the top of your browser's page and click on the Tools tab. This will give you a drop-down menu.

2. At the bottom of the drop-down menu is "Options." Click on Options.

3. You will see a box with eight icons across the top. Click on the Privacy icon.

4. You will see some functions with boxes to their left. One of those options says "Accept Cookies from Sites." This box is likely to be checked on your screen. This means that you have been granting all sites to insert their cookies into your computer.

5. If you want to see what cookies have been inserted into your computer, click on a button on the right that says "Show Cookies."

6. If you want to get rid of a cookie, highlight it and click on "Remove Cookies." If you want to get rid of all the cookies, click on "Remove All Cookies."

7. If you want to prevent anyone from putting cookies on your computer, click on the checked box next to "Accept Cookies from Sites," then at the bottom of the box, click "OK."

Piracy

CHAPTER 18

Key Idea: The fundamental issue with piracy is ownership—that is, who owns a media message—and the key to addressing ownership is determining what constitutes a unique media message.

Jane took a break from studying to look over at her roommate, now on her third straight hour on a computer file-sharing website. "Ruthie, are you downloading more songs? How many will be enough?"

"There's always new music," replied Ruthie. "I must be getting close to 5,000 songs."

"Don't you feel guilty that you download all that music without paying for it?"

"No, I never feel guilty. I look at it like I am providing a service to the recording companies because I tell all my friends about the best songs and post my reviews on my blog. I'm an advertiser for them. They should thank me."

"But you let all your friends and blog readers copy your music files."

"So?"

"So how does that help the recording companies? They make no money off any of the people you tell about their songs."

Ruthie paused a few second to think about that. "Yes, you're right, they don't. But that's not my problem."

The topics about **piracy** and privacy (which is treated in Chapter 17) are closely related. As with privacy, the issue of piracy is about drawing lines. One line is the separation of ownership and nonownership of a message. Another line is the perimeter of a message—that is, how much does a media message need to be changed in order for it to be considered a different message?

Whether something indicates piracy or privacy depends on your perspective. For example, let's say you pay to download a song to your iPod. You paid your money and you feel you have the right to use that song, so that if you want to share the song with your friends, that is your private business. If the record company tracks your sharing, you feel the company is invading your privacy. However, the record company wants to monitor the use of its music to track acts of piracy. When you bought the song, you gave the record company information about yourself—your e-mail address, your musical interests, your credit card number, and so on. The record company likely assembled that information into a file with other users and sold it to advertisers. When you find out the record company sold your personal information to other companies, you feel that it invaded your privacy and acted like pirates by taking something from you and selling it for its own benefit without compensating you or even explicitly asking for your permission.

Digitization of messages and high-speed transmission of information have made the issue of piracy an extremely serious one to mass media businesses. Computers and the Internet have made it easy for you to make copies and distribute any form of information, regardless of who is protected by **copyright.** These technologies raise fundamental questions about what rights of ownership are attached to various messages.

In this chapter, we first need to examine what piracy means. Then we need to get a sense of how big the problem of piracy is and how regulatory bodies are trying to deal with it. What you should notice in this chapter is that the idea of piracy is a highly volatile issue that sets up a debate between two very different value systems. On one side of this debate are media businesses and the creators of commercial media messages (rock stars, movie producers, novelists, and the like) who work hard to produce messages that will appeal to the public and want to be paid for their talent and efforts. They believe they own the product of their work and should benefit financially when others want to enjoy their work. Their argument is based on the traditional concept of copyright, which is the establishing of the creator's rights to his or her work. The public needs to pay for access to those copyrighted messages and thus compensate the copyright holder. These people believe that copyrights must be enforced so as to stimulate creative people to continually generate new media products.

On the other side of the debate are members of the public and some businesses who believe in the common sharing of information, so that ownership is not limited to any one individual or company. Their argument is encapsulated in the newer concept of copyleft, which is the removing of restrictions so that the messages are free and all users have the right to distribute copies and modified versions of a work. Furthermore, those who avail themselves of these free messages and reassemble them in new forms also should allow their reassembled messages to be distributed freely. Copyleft is a form of licensing and can be used to maintain copyright conditions for works such as computer software, documents, and art. In general, copyleft is about openness and common ownership, while copyright is about restricting access and personal ownership. These people believe that copyrights are barriers to widespread creativity.

WHAT IS PIRACY?

Piracy, in its simplest form, is the unauthorized use of copyrighted material. Protecting the rights of creators to benefit from their work has been a serious issue ever since the earliest mass media were made possible by the printing press. The mass media are both an essential tool and a threat to authors. As a tool, the mass media make authors' work widely available to audiences who pay for their work, which allows them to support themselves and continue producing creative work. At the same time, the mass media are a threat to creators because when their work is digitized and put out in mass media channels, it not only gets disseminated to people who will pay for it but also gets copied by people who do not pay for those unauthorized copies of their creations. Piracy is an umbrella idea that takes three forms: bootlegging, counterfeiting, and sharing copyrighted messages without paying for access. Bootlegging is the unauthorized recording of a live delivery of a message (such as recording songs during a concert or recording a movie in a theater), then the subsequent distribution of that recording. Counterfeiting refers to the duplication of a copyrighted message along with its packaging and selling it as the real product. Sharing messages typically takes place when individuals make the media messages they own available to others on the Internet by using peer-to-peer (P2P) downloading software.

Making sense of this issue requires the consideration of two factors. First, we must decide what a creative unit is. Second, we need to determine what a person owns when one buys a message. Before reading any further in this chapter, take a few minutes now and do Exercises 18.1 and 18.2 to find out what your position on piracy is. Then read through the chapter and see if your position changes or not.

Copyright

Foundational to piracy is the idea of ownership. You cannot steal something if ownership is shared among many people, including you. With media content, copyright is the legal establishment of ownership. But copyright has always been a fuzzy concept, and it is getting more ambiguous with the digitization of messages and the free exchange made possible through computers and the Internet.

Think of this book you are reading. The publisher copyrighted this book so that no other publisher can make copies of it and sell it; thus, my publisher owns the rights to distribute this book. However, if at the end of the semester, you sell your copy of the book to a used book dealer, that is okay given current copyright law. The used book dealer sells it to a bookstore, who then sells it to the next student. That is all okay. The used book dealer and the bookstore each make more money off their sales than the publisher did originally. And the used book buyer as well as the bookstore can buy and sell this copy of the book as many times as they want, each time making more money.

Now think of Web pages and computer software. Who owns the rights to those? Much of these are viewed as in the public domain—that is, they are available for anyone to access. Many of these Web pages are available for users to post their own content, such as Facebook, MySpace, YouTube, and all sorts of blogs. There is also freeware where users download all kinds of computer applications for free. And there is open-source software where users can not only download computer applications for free but also read the code and make changes to that code. Some of this code is copyrighted and some is what is called copylefted, which is based on sharing. Copyleft licensing was invented by Richard Stallman of the Free Software Foundation in 1985. So if you take a copylefted program, make some revisions, and sell it to other users, you must allow those other users to have access to your computer code and make their own improvements (Sunstein, 2006). Thus, each step in the dissemination and alteration of an application is open so that follow-on users each have the same opportunity to alter the code to improve it and expand the application's utility. With copyright, the creation is static once created, and its creator owns the rights and sells access to users in return for a royalty fee. In contrast with copyleft, the creation keeps evolving as each subsequent creator tinkers with it; no one person owns the creation, so it is shared openly with everyone.

With the digitization of messages and the rise of the Internet to widely disseminate messages of all kinds in all kinds of ways, the idea of a creation has changed. Eric Raymond uses the metaphors of cathedrals and bazaars to illustrate this change (Sunstein, 2006). According to Raymond, the cathedral approach relied on an expert who had a clear vision for the computer program and designed its architecture to exhibit that vision as elegantly as possible. In contrast is the bazaar, where lots of individuals with many different agendas and approaches work independently as they design bits and pieces to the computer program to fulfill their own special purposes. The bazaar process is what open-source software allows, and it has been surprisingly successful in creating a wide variety of applications. Raymond explains that computer hackers exist in a "gift culture" where social status is determined not by what they control but by what they give away. By making the products of their creativity freely available to others, hackers get known and admired by others. As with privacy, the issue of piracy is about drawing lines.

Some History

Piracy has been a problem for the music industry for decades. As early as the 1950s, people used tape recorders to pirate music by recording it off the radio. People could also make a copy of a record or tape on a tape cassette using home-recording equipment, but to do so, they had to already have a copy of the recording and could make only one copy at a time.

In 1992, Congress passed the Audio Home Recording Act (AHRA), an amendment to the federal copyright law. Under the AHRA, all digital recording devices were required to incorporate a Serial Copy Management System (SCMS), which allowed digital recorders to make a first-generation copy of a digitally recorded work. However, the technology prevented people from making a second-generation copy to be made from the first copy, but users could still make as many first-generation copies as they wanted. The AHRA also provided for a royalty tax of up to $8 per new digital recording machine and 3% of the price of all digital audiotapes or disks. This tax is paid by the manufacturers of digital media devices and distributed to the copyright owners whose music is presumably being copied. In consideration of this tax, copyright owners agree to forever waive the right to claim copyright infringement against consumers using audio-recording devices in their homes. This is commensurate with the fair use exception to copyright law, which allows consumers to make copies of copyrighted music for noncommercial purposes. The SCMS and its royalty requirements, however, only apply to digital audio-recording devices. Because computers are not digital audio-recording devices, they are not required to comply with SCMS ("Music Piracy and the Audio Home Recording Act," 2002).

In the 1990s, Internet users discovered MP3 files for music. These digital music files can be compressed to less than 10% of their original size and therefore be downloaded from the Internet relatively fast. By 1999, users were downloading 17 million MP3 files per day (Peraino, 1999). One of the most popular ways of sharing music was for downloaders to go to the Napster website, where they could get access to thousands of other users who were willing to share their music libraries.

The recording industry had been experiencing a steady growth in sales throughout the 1990s, reaching a high of almost 1 billion units (CDs, cassette tapes, and records of all kinds) sold per year. But then in 2000, there was a drop in sales. The recording industry immediately concluded that this drop in sales was due to the widespread sharing of music on the Internet, especially through the Napster website. The music industry fought back through the RIAA (Recording Industry Association of America), which represents the world's largest recording producers. First, they went after Napster and got its existing service suspended in 2001. Then the RIAA went after MP3.com, which was providing a database of 80,000 albums of copyrighted material. A federal judge ruled in the RIAA's favor, and MP3.com was required to pay $100 million to the record companies for the right to distribute their music legally. Other companies came along to take the place of Napster. These companies (such as Gnutella, Freenet, KaZaA, Morpheus, and iMesh) use P2P software, which allows one person to share his or her personal files with another person. Also, other companies have set up stores on the Internet to sell music. Apple launched the iTunes Music Store in 2003. Shortly afterwards, Windows versions were launched—buymusic.com and Listen.com's Rapsody. These Internet stores become immediately successful, so much so that it led to the closing of more than 600 brick-and-mortar music stores in 2003 (Kava, 2003).

HOW BIG IS THE PROBLEM?

In 1999, a debate flared up concerning how big the problem of music piracy really was. The recording industry claimed the problem was huge and growing. The industry was releasing figures such as that an estimated 3.6 billion songs were illegally downloaded each month in the United States. In 1999, the music industry estimated that one in four compact disks of new music was actually an unauthorized copy. By the end of 2001, the industry estimated that as many CDs were burned and copied as were bought ("Music Piracy and the Audio Home Recording Act," 2002). The music industry used these figures to claim that illegal file trading was responsible for reducing legitimate music sales (Newscientist.com, 2004).

In 1999, about 2% of Internet users said they shared music; 2 years later, more than 30% said they downloaded music (Moody, 2002). Also, in a *USA Weekend* poll of teenagers conducted in May 2002, 54% responded that they saw nothing wrong with downloading music off the Internet; only 10% thought it should not be done. Also, 45% said they frequently or occasionally downloaded music from the Internet ("Tunes & 'tudes," 2002).

The RIAA points to several studies suggesting a link between declining record sales and the growth of illegal file trading. RIAA spokeswoman Amy Weiss said that countless well-respected groups and analysts have all determined that illegal file sharing has adversely affected the sales of CDs. Lewin (2008) estimates that the average iPod or digital music player contains 842 illegally copied songs, with 14- to 17-year-olds having song libraries with an average of 61% of all songs illegally downloaded. The RIAA Web homepage cites a study that says that music piracy annually results in a loss of $12.5 billion to the U.S. economy as well as more than 70,000 lost jobs and $2 billion in lost wages to American workers. Also, the RIAA claims that by 2008, 95% of all music downloads were pirated, which made critics question their estimate as being wildly high. For example, Mahoney (2009) pointed out that the music industry had 2008 revenues of $3.7 billion, so if all this alleged downloaded music was paid for, the music industry revenues would have been $74 billion, which is more than five times the revenue of its best year. Also, a series of surveys conducted by a Houston-based company, Voter Consumer Research, reported that those people who download more songs illegally are less likely to buy music from legitimate retailers. Also, Felix Oberholzer-Gee at the Harvard Business School and Koleman Strumpf at the University of North Carolina tracked millions of music files downloaded through the OpenNap file-trading network and compared them with CD sales of the same music and concluded that, "at most, file sharing can explain a tiny fraction of this decline." Oberholzer-Gee and Strumpf monitored 680 albums, chosen from a range of musical genres, downloaded over 17 weeks in the second half of 2002. They used computer programs to automatically monitor downloads and compared these data to changes in album sales over the same period to see if a link could be established. The most heavily downloaded songs showed no decrease in CD sales as a result of increasing downloads. In fact, albums that sold more than 600,000 copies during this period appeared to sell better when downloaded more heavily. The study showed only a slight decline in sales as a result of online trading for the least popular music. "From a statistical point of view, what this means is that there is no effect between downloading and sales," say Oberholzer-Gee and Strumpf (Newscientist.com, 2004).

Although the debate over the extent of music piracy within the United States rages on, there is little debate that music piracy is a serious problem internationally. For example, the IFPI (International Federation of the Phonographic Industry) is an organization representing the international recording industry and has a membership of 1,500 record producers and distributors in 76 countries. The IFPI says that music piracy is an international problem, with worldwide sales of pressed pirate CDs of 500 million units a year, accounting for lost revenue of well over $4 billion in U.S. dollars. In territories with high piracy levels, such as China or Russia, it is exceptionally difficult to develop a legitimate market for recorded music.

Film

Piracy is also a problem with films. The U.S. film industry says it lost $6.1 billion to piracy in 2005. Furthermore, college students were blamed for half this loss in revenue because college students shifted their film access away from theater attendances and video rentals to downloading shared files online (Powers, 2006).

Piracy has become a big problem within the pornographic segment of the film industry. When YouTube launched in 2005, within a year, several similar sites also launched to provide users with access to pornographic content they could upload and share (PornoTube, RedTub, and YouPorn to name a few). These were flooded with free content that was licensed from legitimate companies and also a lot of material pirated from pay sites. These sites made their money by providing content for free to surfers and exposing them to banner ads. The audience shifted dramatically from pay sites to these free sites where they could watch movies, some of which were 30 minutes long. Within a few years, the revenue of pay sites that provided pornography dropped off 50 % to 80 % (Wallace, 2011).

Print

The Internet provides so much information—an 8-billion–page cut-and-pastable encyclopedia—that there is a big temptation for students to plagiarize. Software developers are now writing software to detect plagiarizing, and typically studies find that about 30 % of papers in college are plagiarized either partially or in full (T. Y. Jones, 2006).

CRACKDOWN ON PIRACY

In contrast to the issue of privacy where consumers are relatively ignorant of the problem, media organizations are highly sensitive to the issue of piracy, so they have been active in confronting the issue. They have taken a three-pronged approach of developing antipiracy technology, pressuring regulators to pass antipiracy laws, and taking legal action against pirates.

Antipiracy Technology

The largest record companies are developing antipiracy technology to protect their copyrighted music against the information technology industry's movement toward increasingly user-friendly digital hardware and software. A few of the "big five" major music labels are currently experimenting with antipiracy technologies designed to combat the online file sharing of their products through peer-to-peer networks, such as Napster. These copy protection programs encode electronic impediments onto commercial CDs, which prevent the disks from being played on any device that is not a simple CD player.

Sony has developed its own antipiracy technology, called "key2audio." The music label announced in January 2002 that it had produced a total of 10 million disks for 500 different albums that could not be played on personal computers by using its key2audio program, which prevents consumers from listening to CDs on any type of CD-ROM or DVD player. A second version of the software, key2audio4PC, is a bit more lenient than key2audio in that it does permit listeners to play copy-protected CDs on their personal computer. However, the disks are encrypted to limit usage to a single PC. For example, once the CD is played on the consumer's home computer, that person would not be able to play the same CD on his or her DVD player in the next room or on his or her computer at the office. Downloaded music files may be copied from the PC hard drive to a blank CD, but that CD would likewise be playable only in the specific PC on which the copy was made from an authorized download.

Another music label is licensing antipiracy technology from outside developers. BMG Entertainment began using the Cactus Data Shield antipiracy program, developed by Midbar Technology. Cactus is designed to prevent consumers from reformatting songs into MP3 files and burning copies or making them available on file-sharing systems. The software prevents listeners from playing the disks on CD-ROM drives, which means that the music will not play on the Sony PlayStation 2, a number of car stereos and DVD players, or PCs. The Cactus patent application states that the resulting playback distortion on an unauthorized copy would not only distort the sound but would also be "potentially damaging" to amplifiers and speakers. The Cactus system also disables stand-alone CD burners.

Digital rights management companies are also developing and marketing solutions for entertainment companies. Macrovision, in collaboration with TTR Technologies, developed multiple versions of an antipiracy technology called SafeAudio, a 100% software-based audio copy protection technology for music CDs. SafeAudio Version 2 allows CDs to operate in CD players and PC-based CD-ROMs but spoils any copy made to the hard drive or a CD burner by adding background noise to the playback sound. SafeAudio Version 3 allows CDs to be played in simple CD players but not in a CD-ROM or copied onto a hard disk drive. Products such as SafeAudio are proving to be a difficult sell to record labels in the United States, which are concerned about negative consumer backlash. Perhaps in response to this concern, Macrovision recently released its SafeAuthenticate product, which permits CDs that are authenticated by the product's software to be a genuine pressing to be played from the computer's CD-ROM drive or copied onto the hard drive for playback through Microsoft's Windows Media Player.

New Legislation

It is clear from the language of the AHRA, as well as subsequent judicial interpretations of the statute, that Congress did not anticipate 10 years ago that the SCMS would be inadequate to contain the impending home digital recording explosion that was made possible by the Internet. Responding to pressure from music copyright owners, the U.S. Senate began considering legislation that would require manufacturers of information technologies to implement safeguards against unauthorized copying of music. In March 2002, Senator Ernest Hollings (D-S.C.), chairman of the Senate Commerce Committee, introduced the Consumer Broadband and Digital Television Promotion Act (CBDTPA). This proposed legislation, which is heavily supported by music industry lobbies such as the Recording Industry Association of America, would require all new digital media devices to be encoded with security technology to prevent unauthorized copying of copyrighted works.

Critics of this legislation think that it goes too far. For example, members of the information technologies industry believe that the charge to make them responsible for inhibiting unauthorized copying is an impossible task because it is not technologically feasible to protect a digital work once it is in the public domain. Consumer groups such as DigitalConsumer.org feel that the bill violates individuals' rights to post-purchase flexible use of copyrighted materials. Media critics declare that as a cure, the CBDTPA would be far worse than the disease of digital content piracy. They say that making it more difficult to play a copy-protected CD on more than one digital media device would be only a speed bump for pirates who might easily circumvent antipiracy technology, but it could turn out to be a roadblock for the average music buyer.

Legal Action

Using the old antipiracy legislation, some law enforcement agencies have been going ahead with crackdowns on pirates. In April 2004, the U.S. Justice Department completed its largest investigation of the piracy of intellectual property over the Internet. This included an investigation of more than 100 people in 27 states and abroad who were involved in the theft of more than $50 million in music, movies, games, and computer software ("100 People Identified in Piracy Raid," 2004).

In the fall of 2006, music and movie studios were given an unmitigated victory in their 2001 suit against StreamCast and other companies that were providing file-sharing software that encouraged millions of users to improperly exchange songs, films, and other copyrighted material without permission. The ruling said that these companies engaged in massive copyright infringement because they developed a business model that relied on users who violated the law and did not attempt to block trading of copyrighted materials. The companies could be liable for as much as $150,000 for each copyrighted work shared illegally through a program called Morpheus. StreamCast argued that it did not encourage users to infringe on copyrighted works. But the music and record companies responded that the purpose of StreamCast's software was to give users the ability to scan one another's hard drives for songs, video clips, and games that they could then transfer to their own computers (Duhigg, Gaither, & Chmielewski, 2006).

Perhaps the highest profile conviction of a pirate was in December 2006. Johnny Ray Gasca—known as the Prince of Piracy—was sentenced to 7 years in federal prison for illegally taping Hollywood movies in theaters and selling bootlegged copies of the films. He was the first person to be sentenced to federal prison for this type of crime of piracy. Gasca said he made as much as $4,500 a week selling movies (Munoz, 2006).

Within the United States, the RIAA monitored the use of these P2P software services, many of them by college students who were using their university's computers. The RIAA then filed more than 21,000 lawsuits from September 2003 to September 2007 against people who allegedly downloaded music illegally. In response, the Electronic Freedom Foundation complained that the RIAA was going after ordinary people who download music for their own personal libraries rather than the big businesses that profit from their counterfeiting and bootlegging (Turow, 2010).

In the summer of 2011, some media companies formed a coalition to take more aggressive action against individuals who they thought were pirating their media products. The coalition was composed of movie and television studios, cable and phone companies, and record labels. It planned to monitor the Internet activity of households and identify those individuals who they believed were uploading and downloading copyrighted material illegally, then get ISP (Internet Service Providers) to cut off their Internet access (Flint, 2011b).

SUMMARY

Industry groups are working hard right now to shape up practices to protect their business interests by thwarting piracy. They have been successful in developing antipiracy technologies, getting laws passed, and taking legal action against pirates.

This issue, however, rests on a shaky definitional foundation. It is unclear what a creative unit is, and this will become even more problematic as more Web 2.0 services make it possible for individuals to share media messages and transform them interactively to serve their own needs better. If someone copies an entire copyrighted film, song recording, or book, that is clearly piracy. But if someone takes film clips and edits them together with home movie scenes, is that piracy? Or if someone takes a song but changes the lyrics and records it, is that piracy?

The issue of piracy has recently become very important as large media conglomerates fail to meet their revenue projections and reason that large numbers of people are copying the products they are trying to sell, particularly music and films. And this issue will continue to grow in importance as the conflict deepens as media businesses try to preserve the old idea of copyright while many individuals interact with the media using the newer idea of copyleft, where sharing and open creativity are stronger values.

Chapter Resources: To test your knowledge and learn more about the topics discussed in this chapter, visit the Student Study Site at www.sagepub.com/potter6e.

FURTHER READING

Bently, L., Davis, J., & Ginsburg, J. C. (Eds.). (2010). Copyright and piracy: An interdisciplinary critique. New York: Cambridge University Press. (471 pages with index)

This is an edited volume of 21 chapters organized into 11 sections: introduction, history, comparative law, economics, linguistics, computer software, information studies, literature, art, sociology/music, and criminology.

Strangelove, M. (2005). The empire of mind: Digital piracy and the anti-capitalist movement. Toronto: University of Toronto Press. (337 pages with index)

The author, a Canadian, argues that the mass media have established an empire by using capitalism and that this empire is now being challenged by the newer interactive media. Ordinary people can use the newer media platforms to transform old content and create their own in what the established media regard as acts of piracy.

KEEPING UP TO DATE

Association for Progressive Communications (http://www.apc.org)

Founded in 1990, the APC is an international network and nonprofit organization that works for open access to the Internet and media messages for everyone.

Motion Picture Association of America (http://www.mpaa.org/)

The MPAA is the professional association of the movie industry in the United States. Get on its website and click on the Content Protection tab.

Recording Industry Association of America (http://www.riaa.com/)

The RIAA is the professional organization of music producers in the United States. Get on its website and click on the Piracy tab to get information on its official position, its view of the problem, and updates on piracy law as it relates to music.

EXERCISE 18.1

Where Do You Draw the Line?

1. Let's say you buy a CD of songs by your favorite musical group. What do you really own? How much control do you have over using that music? Read each item in the list below and consider your rights of ownership. Put a checkmark next to each item you feel comfortable doing. For each item you think is wrong or illegal, do not put a checkmark.

_____ Listen to the CD alone in the privacy of your room

_____ Listen to the CD in your room with friends

_____ Take your CD to your friends' room and listen to it there

_____ Play your CD in your car with all the windows down so everyone on the street can hear it

_____ Make a backup copy of your CD

_____ Make a copy of your CD and rearrange the songs in the order you prefer

_____ Make a compilation CD with songs from several CDs you own

_____ Lend a CD that you own to one of your friends so he or she can make a copy for his or her own personal use

_____ Lend a CD that you own to a dozen of your friends so they can make a copy for their own personal use

_____ Copy the songs on a CD you own onto your computer so you can listen to them while you are on your computer

_____ Copy the songs on a CD you own onto your computer and then send an e-mail to a friend and arrange for one of those songs to play in the background as your friend reads your e-mail

_____ Copy the songs on a CD you own onto your computer and then send a song to your friend to let him or her check it out

_____ Copy the songs on a CD you own onto your computer and then send all those songs to your friend

_____ Copy the songs on a CD you own onto your computer and then make those songs available to anyone in cyberspace to make a copy

_____ Take your CD to a secondhand store and sell it to the store

_____ Sell your CD to another person on eBay

_____ Make copies of your CD and sell those copies to other people

2. Now go back over the list above, and every time you see something such as "a CD you own" or a "CD you bought," substitute it with "a CD you borrowed from the public library." Read each item in the list above and consider your rights of usage of borrowed material. Put a plus sign (+) next to each item you feel comfortable doing. For each item you think is wrong or illegal, do not put a plus sign.

3. Now compare the pattern of checked statements to the pattern of statements with plus signs. Look at the statements that have checkmarks but no plus signs; these are the special rights you feel you have as an owner of a CD compared to a user of someone else's CD.

EXERCISE 18.2

How Big Is a Creative Unit?

1. Now think about the size of the unit that is copyrighted. Where would you draw the line between what is protected by copyright and what is too small to be protected by copyright? Check those elements in the list below that you think should be protected by copyright.

   _____ An artist's entire body of work

   _____ An album

   _____ A song

   _____ A chorus in a song

   _____ A chord progression or a lyrical phrase

   _____ One note or word

2. Now think about how big a unit of information you would feel comfortable copying. At what point does the resulting CD stop being the work of other artists and become your artistic product? From the list below, check those products that you believe would be primarily your own creation.

   _____ Make a compilation CD of songs of one artist from several different CDs

   _____ Make a compilation CD of songs of different artists from different CDs

   _____ Make a compilation CD of songs of different artists along with recordings of your own original music

   _____ Make a compilation of CDs of songs of another artist—some performed by that artist and some performed by you

   _____ Record a song from a CD that you own as a soundtrack on a home movie that you made and will give to your parents on their anniversary

   _____ Record a song from a CD that you own as a soundtrack on a movie that you make for a grade in a film production course

   _____ Record a song from a CD that you own as a soundtrack on a movie you that make and enter into a contest to win a scholarship to college

   _____ Record a song from a CD that you own as a soundtrack on a movie that you make to show on a public-access cable TV program

3. Now that you have considered the options in #1 and #2 above, what is the key criterion that defines a creative unit?

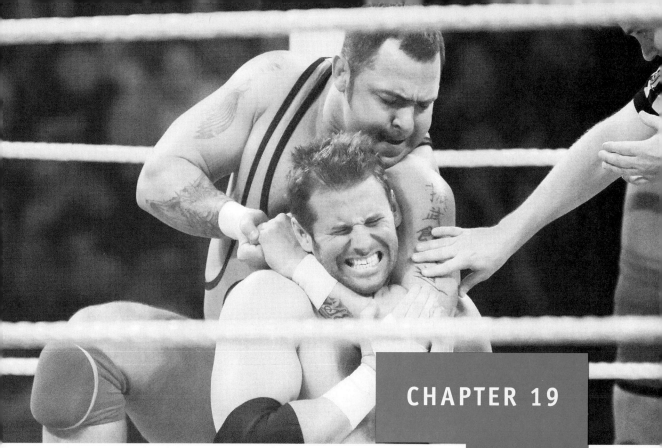

Violence

Key Idea: Many people complain about the amount of violence in the media, but those complaints are based on such a narrow definition of violence that they greatly underestimate the amount of violence and the effect it is having on audiences.

"I wish you would stop complaining about violence on television shows all the time. Just shut up already." Charlie was tired of hearing his brother Alan constantly complain about television.

"There is just so much! I worry that all the freaks in our society are watching all this violence and letting it affect them. You should be worried too, Charlie."

"How so?"

"All those unstable people who watch this violence end up wanting to behave violently themselves. These crime shows teach people how to commit crimes. Then TV viewers go out and commit those crimes in the real world. Where do you think all this violent crime comes from?"

"We have always had violent crime."

"Not like today." Alan was shaking his finger at Charlie to emphasize his point. "Not like the freaky violent crime we have today!"

"Okay, but if what you say is true—that watching crime shows makes people go out and commit violent crimes—why are you not behaving like that?"

Alan was getting exasperated. "I understand what's going on. I will not let those TV portrayals affect me."

"Oh no? You are obsessed with complaining all the time. And you change the locks on our doors so I keep getting locked out. And you won't go out for a walk in our neighborhood after dark even though there has not been a violent crime in our neighborhood in decades."

"See, being careful works."

People seem to have been complaining about violence in the media ever since storytellers have used the media. Criticism increases and decreases in cycles, and currently we are in a quiet part of the cycle after a lot of criticism during the 1990s (see Table 19.1). But this topic could heat up quickly again at any time. When it does heat up, will you be ready with an informed opinion, or will you be swept away with all the emotional rhetoric?

In this chapter, we will address the issue of media violence by focusing on the two fundamental topics underlying this issue. First, we will analyze the topic of effects, and then we will analyze the topic of the nature of violence in the media. The public has a very narrow conception of both of these topics. When people are limited by a narrow perspective on a problem, they are prevented from seeing many of the problem's key facets, and this limitation will distort their perceptions and prevent their criticism from being useful. The purpose of this chapter is to get you to expand your perspective on media violence and help you see the problem in a more complete and realistic manner. Thus, you will be able to construct a better informed opinion about media violence.

EFFECTS

If you ask the typical person, "Does violence on television and the movies have any effect?" most people will say yes—recalling a horrible instance when someone copied a violent

TABLE 19.1   Public Opinion About the Amount of Violence in the Media

- A 1975 Gallup poll found that two thirds of Americans found the present level of violent programming unacceptable (C. A. Cooper, 1996).
- In a 1993 poll, 70% of Americans felt that entertainment TV has too much violence, and 57% thought that TV news gives too much attention to stories about violent crime (Galloway, 1993).
- A 1994 *Parents* magazine poll found that an overwhelming majority of Americans—87% of those questioned—said that the media "contains too much violence" (Diamant, 1994).
- In a 1995 Time/CNN survey, 52% of adult Americans said they are very concerned about the amount of violence depicted in movies, television shows, and popular music; another 25% said they were fairly concerned; only 9% said they were not concerned at all (Lacayo, 1995).

- A 1997 nationwide poll by the *Los Angeles Times* found that two thirds of people think that television programming has gotten worse over the past decade, with 90% believing that television now has more violence and sex than it did 10 years ago (Lowry, 1997).
- A 1997 *USA Weekend* write-in poll generated 21,600 responses, with 92% of those respondents saying they regarded television content more offensive than ever, especially with violence, sexual content, and vulgarity.
- In a 1999 Gallup poll, 75% of the public said they think there is a relationship between violence on television and the crime rate in the United States (Navarro & Riddle, n.d.).
- In a 2003 ICM poll, 73% of the public said they believed that on-screen violence (in the form of films, television, and computer games) encourages violence in society (Navarro & Riddle, n.d.).

criminal act that was in a movie or in the news. However, if you were to ask those same people if violence on television and movies has had an effect on them, most would say no. Thus, most people believe that other people are at risk but think they are free from risk. This difference in perception between one's self and others has been labeled the *third-person effect*.

The reason for this third-person effect with media violence is that few people believe they behave aggressively after watching violence, but they have ample evidence that others are influenced to behave aggressively. There are frequent examples of copycat crimes and of kids going on shooting sprees at school, imitating movie and video game violence. Also, many adults notice their children imitating violent television characters they see on action/ adventure shows or on the *World Wrestling Federation*. We all remember children (or even ourselves as children) racing around the house, chasing siblings and pets while imitating sounds and movements from violent portrayals. But we recognize we do not behave that way now, so there is no effect on us. What makes this opinion possible is a narrow conception of what effects are possible from exposure to media violence. Recall from Chapter 15 that I showed you how to broaden your perspective on media effects. Let's work on broadening your perspective again, this time in the specific area of media violence.

Narrow Perspective

The public largely limits its view of effects of exposure to media violence as aggressive behavior. The public rarely considers that there may be physiological, emotional, attitudinal, and cognitive effects. Furthermore, they are limiting their concern to three groups as being susceptible to these aggressive behaviors: children, criminals, and young boys who play video games. Are these three groups at risk for negative effects? Yes, of course. To illustrate, let's examine video games more closely. Video games are very popular, with marketing surveys revealing that 92% of all children and adolescents ages 2 to 17 play video games. The average child spends 20 to 33 minutes a day playing these games. The most popular types of games are combat (42%), sports (41%), and adventure (36%). About 89% of the top-selling games contained violence, and 17% featured violence as the primary focus of the game (Kaiser Family Foundation, 2002). And a recent poll of children and adolescents ages 8 to 18 concluded that 8% of video game players are addicted to video game playing (Gentile, 2009).

Even if we do not play video games and even if we are not a child or a criminal, we are all susceptible to a wide range of negative effects from our constant exposure to media violence. Look at the list of effects displayed in Table 19.2. Each of these has been well documented by research. Notice that some are immediate effects (meaning that they occur during exposure to the media violence), whereas others are long-term effects (which take many exposures over a long period to build up to a manifestation). Notice also that although there are behavioral effects, there are also effects that are more physiological, attitudinal, emotional, and cognitive. When we don't take into consideration the full range of effects, it is easy to overlook what may be the most widespread effect of exposure to media violence.

The Overlooked Effect

Perhaps the most prevalent effect of constant exposure to violence is so subtle that most people overlook it. This is the effect of a cultivated belief that the world is violent and a related fear of being victimized. Of course, real-world violence and crime do exist, but they do not exist to the levels that the general public has been conditioned to believe. The crime rate in the United States increased from 1960 to 1990 and then began falling. Now the crime rate is the lowest in 40 years and the murder rate the lowest in 50 years ("Good News," 2011). While the crime rate was falling throughout the 1990s, a poll taken in 1996 found that only 7% of Americans believed that violent crime had declined in the previous 5-year period (Whitman & Loftus, 1996). Also, from March 1992 to August 1994, public perceptions of crime as the most important problem in the United States jumped from 5% to 52% (Lowry, Nio, & Leitner, 2003).

Where do people get the idea that crime is a problem when they don't experience any in real life? From the media. The media constantly present stories about crime. There are

TABLE 19.2 Immediate and Long-Term Effects From Exposure to Media Violence

The Immediate Effects

Behavioral Effect

1. *Imitation/copying behavior:* This is the effect that the public focuses on most when thinking about protecting people from the influence of media violence. This is understandable because copying behavior is very easy to spot and to see the link back to the media content. This type of effect is much more prevalent with children than with adults.

2. *Triggering novel behavior:* Triggering refers to a behavior that is neither imitated (mimicking a just-seen behavior in the media) nor activated (putting in motion a previously learned behavior). Triggering refers to the media stimulating a person to act in a violent manner but that person acts out in a novel way.

3. *Disinhibition:* Exposure to media violence can reduce viewers' normal inhibitions that prevent them from behaving in a violent manner. This effect has the largest research base.

4. *Attraction:* Many people are attracted to violence, maybe not all the time, but there come times when people want to see a violent show. If it were not for this effect, violent CDs would not sell, and horror movies would have no audiences. When you add up all the time and money spent by millions of people each year in seeking out this kind of content, this must be regarded as a major effect.

Physiological Effect

5. *Fight/flight:* Exposure to violence can temporarily arouse people physiologically. During exposure, a person's heart rate and blood pressure increase. These physiological changes are the body's way of getting ready to respond to the violence as if it were a real threat to the viewer. This type of arousal dissipates usually within an hour after exposure.

6. *Excitation transfer:* Violence presented in the media tends to arouse viewers and hence is an energizer. People do not necessarily need to use that energy in an aggressive manner—they can transfer that energy to other outlets. For example, people who are exposed to a strongly violent portrayal can become highly aroused (heightened heart rate) and are ready for action. If there are sexual reminders in their environment, they will be likely to stay highly aroused but shift into a sexual mode. The arousal needs direction because arousal by itself is not guided. If the viewer guides the energy into positive directions, then the exposure to violence will have a prosocial value. Whatever the direction, the energy from the arousal is short-lived and usually dissipates within several minutes after exposure.

Emotional Effect

7. *Temporary fear:* Violence in films and on television can produce intense fright reactions. Fright as an immediate emotional response is typically of relatively short duration, but it may endure on occasion for several hours, days, or even longer. It is composed of anxiety, distress, and increased physiological arousal that are frequently engendered in viewers as a result of exposure to specific types of media productions.

Attitudinal Effect

8. *Immediate creation/change of attitudes:* A person's attitude can be created or changed with as little as a single exposure. For example, researchers have shown that when people are exposed to a violent television program, they will show an immediate drop in sympathetic attitude.

Cognitive Effect

9. *Learning specific acts and lessons:* People can learn behavior patterns by watching

(Continued)

(Continued)

characters perform in the media. For example, children might watch a cartoon where characters beat each other over the head with rubber hammers and show no harm. The children do not imitate the behavior patterns they see because there are no rubber hammers available to them. But this does not mean they have not learned how to perform a certain aggressive behavioral sequence. Also, they have learned that such behavior is funny and not really harmful to the person who is hit in the head.

Long-Term Effects

Behavioral Effect

10. *Training behavior:* Violent video games train players to kill. When children watch graphic violence in movies and on TV shows and also play realistic, violent video games, it breaks down their natural resistance to killing. This training follows the same principles used by the U.S. military to transform peaceful young men into soldiers who must kill their enemies. The game playing has a physical component of training; that is, players are trained in eye-hand coordination, thus practicing the ability to fire at and kill moving targets. It also has an emotional component, whereby players overcome their natural resistance to killing, are rewarded for such behavior, and can experience intense pleasant emotions when they are highly successful at killing.

Physiological Effect

11. *Physiological habituation:* This is building or increasing physiological tolerance over the long term. With repeated fight-or-flight responses, the human body gradually builds resistance to the exposure to media violence. For example, the first time people see a horror film, their bodies respond with a fight-or-flight reaction that substantially increases heart rate and blood pressure. As they

continue to view horror films over the years, the body's reaction is not as substantial to this stimulus; the heart rate and blood pressure still increase but not as much. With repeated exposures, people build a higher tolerance to this type of message physiologically. In the extreme case, with massive exposure to this type of message, people might even extinguish all physiological reactions to horror.

12. *Narcotizing:* Not only does habitual viewing of violence over time dull our reactions, but some people also continue to crave the strong "arousal jag" they used to get from violent exposures. But to experience the same degree of arousal, they search out more graphic and stronger forms of violence. Thus, violence acts like a drug in the sense that people grow a stronger dependence on it over time while the drug loses its strength. In its extreme case, this narcotic of violence can lead to addiction.

Emotional Effect

13. *Desensitization:* Some portrayals are presented so often that we can no longer treat them with wonder or awe. Our tolerance has been increased so that those things that used to horrify or even upset us no longer do. This is especially important with the issue of violence. Viewing TV violence leads to lowered sensitivity to aggression and violence. And when people are exposed to violence continuously for a long period, this lowering of sensitivity is reinforced.

14. *Cultivation of fear:* There is a good deal of research support for the hypothesis that heavy exposure to the world of television, which is saturated with violent portrayals, leads people to construct unrealistically high estimates of risk of victimization and a corresponding belief that the world is a mean and violent place.

Attitudinal Effect

15. *Long-term reinforcement of attitudes/beliefs:*
Because the media provide so many messages
of violence and because those messages are
usually presented with the same cluster of
contextual factors, viewers' existing attitudes
about violence are reinforced over time. This
makes the attitudes stronger and therefore
harder to change as time goes by.

Cognitive Effect

16. *Learning social norms:* The learning of social
norms is a special case of generalizing
patterns. People can generalize patterns from
individual media exposures without that
pattern being a social norm. For example,
through repeated exposure to media violence,
a person overestimates the rate of crime and
the percentage of crimes that are cleared by
an arrest. Although these are generalizations,
they are not social norms. Social norms are
generalized patterns from social information
rather than factual information. Social norms
deal more with the rules of behavior in social
situations rather than society's factual
parameters, such as the numbers of lawyers,
crimes, trials, and executions—all of which
have a real factual indicator. But social norms
have no factual basis.

Effects on Society

17. *Changing institutions:* When violence
permeates the media year after year in all
kinds of programming, it puts pressure on
institutions to change. For example:

The *criminal justice system*—when the public
believes crime is one of the most important
social problems, candidates for elective office
run on a platform of getting tough on crime.
Municipalities hire more police officers,
arrests for certain crimes escalate, people are

asked to give up certain rights, courts are
under pressure to give stiffer sentences to
criminals, the prison population increases,
and states must build more prisons so they
raise taxes.

The *educational system*—because of some
high-profile shootings in public schools,
many schools now have metal detectors at
their doors; there are searches of lockers
and restrictions on who can walk into a
school building. Teachers are wary of
aggressive students, making it harder to
concentrate on the higher goals of
education, and focus instead on survival in
many school districts.

Religion may be changing as people turn to
that institution more out of a generalized
fear or out of a rejection of the changing
norms of society. Also, religions may be more
aggressive at drawing the line of acceptable
behaviors to stop the shift of society in an
antisocial direction. Thus, religion becomes
more concerned with moral issues than
spiritual ones. The focus may be shifting
more toward prescribing everyday behaviors
and away from focusing on the awe and
mystery of creation and humans' place in the
universe and eternity.

The institution of *family* may also be changing
as a result of these forces brought about by
media violence. Perhaps the generalized fear
makes parents less trusting of their children.
Perhaps couples are less willing to deal with
their arguments by looking for peaceful
solutions and being willing to compromise.
Instead, couples may be looking for more
fights to act on their aggressive impulses, feel
more justified in those confrontations, and
thus want to dominate the other in their
resolutions. Such adversarial behaviors are
likely to lead to more breakups and more
people choosing to live alone.

cable TV channels, such as Court TV, that present one high-profile crime after another. Also, the media, through the news, present a constant stream of crime news that reinforces this impression that there is a great deal of terrible crime. Researchers have found a link between exposure to local television news, which is saturated with coverage of crime and fear of crime (Romer, Jamieson, & Aday, 2003).

CONCEPTION OF VIOLENCE

When the public criticizes media violence, what is the public really criticizing? And when the public calls for less violence, what is the public really asking to be reduced? These are extremely important questions, and they are often overlooked. But if we are to get to the heart of the topic of media violence, we must find answers for them.

Public's Definition

The research evidence on this point indicates that the public is focused only on a particular kind of violence—that which is graphic. For example, W. J. Potter et al. (2002) reported that graphicness and explicitness are two of the important predictors of their participants' judgments of the degree of violence. Thus, audiences' judgments about the degree of violence are related much less to the number of violent acts than to the degree of graphicness. For example, people might not think an action/adventure movie with wall-to-wall car chases and gunfire is more violent than a drama in which one character is unexpectedly shot and we see the bullet tearing through flesh and bone. One highly graphic scene can earn a movie a perception of being more violent than another movie with repeated acts of sanitized violence.

Closely related to graphicness is the characteristic of offensiveness. If portrayals are not offensive—that is, evoking a negative reaction—then viewers do not pay much attention to violence compared to other program features (British Broadcasting Corporation, 1972), or when they do pay attention, it is not an important element that takes away from their enjoyment of programs (Diener & De Four, 1978; Diener & Woody, 1981). But when a violent portrayal is unusually graphic, it interrupts viewers' flow of enjoyment, and viewers experience strong negative emotions.

Another key element in the public's definition of violence is that humor is a camouflage. It appears that when humor blankets violence, the public does not see the violence. This is taken for granted by all kinds of people. An anecdote will illustrate this. In the winter of 1996, I was meeting with the staff of the Viacom Standards and Practices Department in New York City. These seven women were charged with previewing the content to be aired on Viacom's cable channels of MTV, VH1, and Nickelodeon. I was watching a music video while the seven women in the room explained how they screened music videos to determine if those videos met their standards or, if in their judgment, there were things in the portrayals that would offend viewers. For an hour, the women showed parts of music videos and explained how they asked the various music groups to remove or tone down certain images that they felt were demeaning to women. Finally, when I was given a chance to ask a question, I said, "What about violence in the videos?" Several women were eager to answer that they were sensitive to that issue and that the videos did not have any direct scenes of violence, although violence was implied in certain lyrics. Then I asked about violence on Nickelodeon. There was a rather long pause as the women looked at me as if I were a third grader who had just claimed that two plus two equals seven. One of the women looked very puzzled and said, "But there is no violence on Nickelodeon." I returned the puzzled look and replied, "What about your Saturday morning shows such as *Bugs Bunny* and *Ninja Turtles?*" Her puzzled look turned into a big smile as she said, "But those are not violent. Those are cartoons!" Were these women naive? No, they had a highly sophisticated understanding of violence—as defined by the general viewing public. These women knew that the public was not concerned by the actions—even the most brutal—portrayed in cartoons.

What is the reason for humor camouflaging the violence? It appears that humor tends to remove the threat of violence. For viewers to consider something violent, they need to feel a degree of personal threat. This insight can be found in the work of Barrie Gunter in Great Britain. He reported that viewers' ratings of the seriousness of violent acts were higher as the fictional settings were closer to everyday reality in terms of time and location. In contrast, "Violence depicted in clearly fantastic settings such as cartoons or science-fiction were perceived as essentially non-violent, non-frightening and nondisturbing" (Gunter, 1985, p. 245). Other researchers also report that people were much more concerned with acts that had a higher probability of occurrence, meaning the likelihood of the act happening to them in everyday life (Forgas, Brown, & Menyhart, 1980).

In summary, the public uses a conception of violence that is keyed to three factors. First there is graphicness. The more blood and gore shown in a portrayal, the more the portrayal risks offending viewers, and the more viewers will object to the act as being violent. Second, the seriousness of the action itself and the way the act is portrayed are more influential in the decision of violence than is the portrayal of harm to the victim. Third, people allow humor to camouflage violence. Humor reduces the feeling of personal threat to viewers and thereby eliminates the sense of violence.

Ironies

The way the public defines violence creates an irony. The kind of violence that upsets people the most is precisely the type of violence that they need to be exposed to more. In contrast, it is the violence that most people do not complain about—or even perceive—that is doing them the most harm.

If a show presents a highly graphic act of serious violence, people will be offended and complain that this type of portrayal is too violent and has no place in media messages. Their intention is to pressure the programmers to eliminate this type of content. The implication is that if the graphicness were reduced or if it were shown in a humorous context, the action would not be offensive to them.

The irony is that when people are shown violence, they *should* be offended, and they *should* complain. Such a reaction is the appropriate one to violent actions; it shows that they are sensitive to the violence. When they do not complain, this is a clear indication that they have been desensitized to the violence. There is a great deal of violence portrayed in the media, and the overwhelming majority of it is *not* met with complaints; thus, most people are desensitized to almost all of the violence they continually witness on TV.

When television programmers hear complaints about too much violence, the inclination of many creative types is not to reduce the amount of violent acts; instead, their typical response is to sanitize those acts. This means making the violence less graphic by showing less harm to the victims or to mask the harm with humor. Sanitized violence leads viewers to believe that violent acts are not such a big deal. So the less harm shown to the victims in television stories, the less chance that audiences will be offended, but at the same time, this sanitized violence is desensitizing viewers, so people are losing sympathy for victims in real life.

Another irony is that when people complain about the amount of violence, they are basing their complaints on only the graphic instances. This means that they are missing more than 90% of the violence presented—that is, violence that is formulaic and therefore coming into their subconscious, underneath their radar, which is only attuned to that which is highly graphic and therefore offensive.

Developing a Broader Sensitivity

Being media literate requires a broader sensitivity to media violence. This means getting beyond defining violence purely in terms of high graphicness. To begin this task, stop reading this chapter at this point and get a pencil and a piece of paper. Attempt to write your definition of violence in one sentence. When you finish, think about the violent portrayals you have seen in movies and on TV. Does your definition work well? Does it identify what would be violent in news shows? In an episode of *The Three Stooges?* In Saturday morning cartoons? With video or computer games?

The task of defining violence appears to be an easy one at first. But it turns out to be very difficult to write a definition that would provide adequate guidance to judge whether something is violent across all the nuances of portrayals across all media. Most people become frustrated with this task as they realize how complex it is to articulate precisely what they had previously believed they understood clearly. The reason for this is that *violence* is a primitive concept; that is, we all know it when we see it, but it is nearly impossible to write down a good definition. Another example of a primitive term is *red*. You cannot write a definitional rule for what is red and what is not, but you have high confidence that you know what it is and can spot it when it occurs.

We deal with many primitive concepts in our everyday life—love, chair, freedom, sex. We all "know" what these mean, even though it is very difficult to specify an adequate definition for any of them. But examining our definitions is an important task. For us to understand our world better and how we assess the meaning of it, we need to analyze the definitions we have for things. This helps us understand those things better; it also helps us understand ourselves better. So let's continue on this definitional task by looking at the questions in Table 19.3. Answer each of the eight questions. Then, when you are finished, compare your definition to your answers to each of the eight questions. Do you want to make any changes to your definition? After you have completed these tasks, try doing Exercise 19.1.

SUMMARY

The public continually complains that there is too much violence in the media, especially television. The public, however, underperceives the degree of violence because its perceptions are limited to violent acts that are graphic and therefore offensive to them. The implication of the public criticism is that the violence should be sanitized by making it less graphic. Sanitizing media violence, however, would increase the probability that viewers would become desensitized to the violence, and this is a negative effect.

The public also has a narrow perspective on the harm of exposure to media violence. Most people believe that continued exposure to media violence primarily harms unstable people who will behave aggressively or commit crimes. There are many, many negative

---

TABLE 19.3   Key Elements in Definitions of Violence

1. Does the act have to be directed toward a person? Gang members swing baseball bats at a car and totally destroy it. Is this violence?

2. Does the act have to be committed by a person? A mudslide levels a town and kills 20 people. Do acts of nature count? Remember that nature does not write the scripts or produce the programming.

3. Does the act have to be intentional? A bank robber drives a fast car in a getaway chase. As he speeds around a corner, he hits a pedestrian (or destroys a mailbox). Do accidents count?

4. Does the act result in harm? Tom shoots a gun at Jerry, but the bullet misses. Is this violence? Or what if Tom and Jerry are cartoon characters and Tom drops an anvil on Jerry, who is momentarily flattened like a pancake. A second later, Jerry pops back to his original shape and appears fine.

5. What about violence we don't see? If a bad guy fires a gun at a character off-screen and we hear a scream and a body fall, is this violence, even though we do not see it?

6. Does the act have to be physical (such as assaults), or can it be verbal (such as insults)? What if Tom viciously insults Jerry, who is shown through the rest of the program experiencing deep psychological and emotional pain as a result? What if Tom embarrasses Jerry, who then runs from the room, trips, and breaks his arm?

7. What about fantasy? If 100 fighting men "morph" into a giant creature the size of a 10-story building, which then stomps out their enemies, does this count as violence?

8. What about humorous portrayals? When the Three Stooges hit each other with hammers, is this violence?

effects, however, that result from exposure to media violence. These effects are not limited to behaviors but also include cognitive effects, attitudinal effects, emotional effects, and physiological effects.

Becoming more media literate with the issue of media violence requires that you think more broadly about the effects and understand the full range of risk to yourself and other people. Also, you need to change your criticism either to push for the reduction of violent acts or to increase (not decrease) the graphicness of the portrayals. If media programmers keep increasing the number of violent acts and keep sanitizing those portrayals to avoid public criticism, this exacerbates the situation where the public is increasing its risk of many negative effects of which people are largely unaware.

Chapter Resources: To test your knowledge and learn more about the topics discussed in this chapter, visit the Student Study Site at www.sagepub.com/potter6e.

FURTHER READING

Bushman, B. J., Huesmann, L. R., & Whitaker, J. L. (2009). Violent media effects. In R. L. Nabi & M. B. Oliver (Eds.), *Media processes and effects* (pp. 361–376). Thousand Oaks, CA: Sage.

This chapter presents a relatively current review of the empirical literature on the effects of exposure to violence in the media. The authors focus on studies that take a strong psychological perspective and use the methods of experiment and survey.

Cantor, J. (2009). Fright reactions to mass media. In J. Bryant & M. B. Oliver (Eds.), *Media effects: Advances in theory and research* (3rd ed., pp. 287–303). New York: Routledge.

This chapter reviews the literature on how violence and related media content have been found to trigger fear reactions in audiences, especially children.

National Television Violence Study. (1996). *Scientific report*. Thousand Oaks, CA: Sage. (568 pages with index)

The National Cable Television Association funded this $3.3 million project to examine the prevalence and context of violence on American television, the effects of warnings and advisories placed before violent programs, and the effect of public service announcements advocating the avoidance of violence. Some of the chapters are very technical and contain many statistics. But the overall report is the most comprehensive analysis of the issue of violence on television to date.

Potter, W. J. (1999). *On media violence.* Thousand Oaks, CA: Sage. (304 pages with index)

In this book, I take a narrow focus by looking at only one form of media content—violence. But I try to provide an in-depth analysis of the effects of exposure to this one type of content.

Potter, W. J. (2003). *The 11 myths of media violence.* Thousand Oaks, CA: Sage. (259 pages with index)

This book begins with a chapter illuminating the current state of public debate over media violence and ends with a chapter reflecting on the prognosis for change. In between are 11 chapters, each dealing with a faulty belief about media violence. Taken together, these myths lock people (the general public, people in the media industries, media regulators, and media researchers) into a maze of unproductive thinking. These myths include the following faulty beliefs: There is too much violence on television, the media are only responding to market desires, and reducing the amount of violence in the media will solve the problem.

Sparks, G. G., Sparks, C. W., & Sparks, E. A. (2009). Media violence. In J. Bryant & M. B. Oliver (Eds.), *Media effects: Advances in theory and research* (3rd ed., pp. 269–286). New York: Routledge.

This chapter presents a brief history of the media violence controversy, then moves on to review the research and theoretical work that tries to explain the phenomenon of violence in the media and how it affects audiences.

EXERCISE 19.1

Analyze Media Content for Violence

1. Watch a television show that has a reputation for presenting a lot of violence. Use your definition and see how many actions fit your definition. Count them.

   a. How many acts would you have counted using a definition that was based on a "no" answer to all eight questions in Table 19.3?

   b. How many acts would you have counted using a definition that was based on a "yes" answer to all eight questions in Table 19.3?

2. Watch another program with violence; this time, pay attention to how the violence is portrayed.

   a. How much of the violence is committed by bad characters and how much by the "good guys"?

   b. How many of the violent acts are punished in the scene, that is, where the perpetrator is stopped in his or her actions or sanctioned in some way?

   c. How many of the violent acts show realistic harm to the victims?

   d. How many of the violent acts are portrayed as being justified?

   e. What does this pattern of context tell you about whether committing violence is good or bad? That is, what are the producers of this program teaching you about whether using violence is good or bad?

3. Watch a situation comedy and count the number of acts of verbal violence—that is, verbal put-downs, slurs, insults, and comments designed to embarrass another character.

   a. What kinds of characters commit the most verbal violence? Are they the main characters? Are they attractive?

   b. What happens to characters who commit acts of verbal violence? Are they punished or rewarded (by laughter) or neither?

   c. Are the victims of the verbal violence shown as being harmed? If so, what kind of harm, and how long does the harm last?

   d. What does this pattern of verbal violence and its context tell you about whether committing verbal violence is good or bad?

EXERCISE 19.2

Can You Identify the Negative Effects?

1. Do you or your children feel like wrestling after watching several hours of cartoons or the *World Wrestling Federation?*

2. After watching a horror movie late at night by yourself, do you have a difficult time relaxing and falling asleep? Or do you lie awake in bed thinking that you should get up and check the locks once again or perhaps leave a light on in the hall?

3. You have seen a violent movie that took place in an inner-city ghetto. African American teenagers were dealing drugs and killing rivals with guns. You shake your head and think, "Inner cities are such war zones. I'm glad I don't have to travel through one of them!"

4. You're thumbing through the newspaper and notice that a new Quentin Tarantino action/adventure film has just been released. You feel excitement and can't wait until you get to see it.

5. You are watching the evening news and you hear about two brutal murders that took place last night in your town. You think back and remember previous newscasts about murders in your town over the past year. You conclude that the murder rate is sharply increasing.

6. You see a teenage boy slip on a puddle in a supermarket and fall down. You do not go over to help him, thinking, "Silly boy. It's his own fault for not looking where he was going. Besides, he is not really hurt." You walk away and do not give it another thought.

Interpreting Your Answers to Exercise 19.2

I have titled this section "Interpreting Your Answers to Exercise 19.2" because these are possible interpretations, not definitive psychoanalysis. There may be a lot of reasons for each of your answers. What I am doing in this exercise is suggesting a media violence explanation so as to increase your awareness of possible influences.

1. This is the standard imitation effect. In this situation, it is harmless, unless you get really carried away! But what is happening is that the viewing is getting

(Continued)

(Continued)

you involved in the mayhem. Your heart rate and blood pressure increase. You are moving into a fight-or-flight mode. When you see your partner in a similar condition, you agree that wrestling would be a fun thing to do.

2. This is a temporary fear reaction. The movie has planted strong images in your mind and a strong feeling of fear in your heart. Although your bedroom and surroundings are familiar, on this particular night, there is "something else in the room." That something else is not really a monster in the flesh but an apparition in your mind. This apparition can make your palms sweat and your heart pound— not very conducive to sleep!

3. This is likely a reinforcement of attitude effect. Most of the images the movie presented are probably not new to you. Although you have never seen a gang war in an inner city, you have these images through previous media exposures. And you have already held the attitude that inner cities and African American teenage males are highly dangerous. These are both stereotypes, of course. And the stronger the stereotypes, the less likely you will seek out real-world information to see if your attitude is distorted.

4. This is an attraction effect. You have a history of arousing and pleasurable experiences with past action/adventure films, especially those directed by Quentin Tarantino.

5. This is a cognitive effect of generalizing patterns. Your recollection of several stories about local murders has led you to see a pattern. You can't recall many murders 5 years ago or when you were a child, so you see a trend to the pattern—there is an increase in the murder rate in your town. What may be happening is that the actual murder rate in your town is down (the murder rate in the United States as a whole has been declining the past decade), but the local news is getting better at presenting gruesome images that stay in your mind longer.

6. This may be a desensitization effect. From watching so many acts of violence in the media, a simple fall is nothing. Also, because the victims of the serious acts of violence in the media rarely show any pain or harm, you think, "How can a silly slip hurt a young boy?"

Sports

CHAPTER 20

Key Idea: The money cycle drives sports. Some people think the money cycle is destroying sports, while other people think that it is improving sports.

Sports have changed dramatically over the past four decades. The reason is money—big money. The controversy concerning sports is whether big money has ruined sports or has made sports better. As you read this chapter, you will be presented with many facts about how the money cycle has changed sports. You must decide for yourself whether the money is now too much (i.e., the salaries of athletes are too high, the profits to team owners and leagues are too rich, and the cost to the average fan is beyond affordability) or whether the money has made the games and the athletes better than ever.

Sports in the United States now generate more than $414 billion annually in revenue (Plunkett Research, 2010). Not only have the revenues been increasing each year, but those revenues also have been increasing at an accelerating rate. The key to making sense of these increases as well as the nature of sports today is to understand the money cycle.

THE MONEY CYCLE

The mass media have been an integral part of making the money cycle possible. The media provide the means for advertisers to inject mammoth amounts of money into the cycle. Also, the media provide so much continual exposure for professional as well as college sporting events that millions of people have made sports an essential ritual in their lives. And the media have transformed hundreds of athletes into celebrities who can themselves command huge payments—both for playing their games and for endorsing the products of commercial advertisers.

This money cycle has the following five components:

1. *Athletic talent* demands higher salaries plus bonuses each year. Because athletic talent is in short supply, talented athletes will find a team willing to pay a high salary and bonuses.

2. *Owners of teams* are in the business of attracting fans to their games as well as fans to telecasts of their games, so they must field a competitive team to make the games exciting. Also, the fan base grows in size and is more loyal when teams are winning, so the owners must buy players and coaches who are better than the players on the teams they compete with; this requires them to bid high for the limited amount of athletic talent.

3. *Television networks* are in the business of creating audiences for their telecasts and renting out those audiences to advertisers. Network programmers know that sporting events can attract large numbers of fans, so they bid high for the rights to telecast sporting contests. Network programmers know that when they own the

rights to telecast sports, their network generates higher revenues and the network gets stronger; in contrast, a network gets weaker when it lets a competing network outbid it for the telecasting rights.

4. *Advertisers* of certain products find sports fans an especially desirable audience. They pay sports telecasting networks a premium to get their persuasive messages to those audiences. They also use sports magazines, sports websites, and the sports sections of newspapers to reach their audiences.

5. *We, the public,* receive a lot of satisfaction in following our favorite sports teams, so we follow the games on television, tolerate the commercial interruptions, and buy the advertised products. Also, we find certain sport events to be highly entertaining (*Monday Night Football,* Super Bowl, playoffs), so we watch them even when we do not have a favorite team in the contests.

When the five segments of the cycle cooperate and work well together, the cycle attracts more money. The public watches more games and buys more advertised products, especially those products endorsed by athletes. With higher viewership for sports shows, television networks charge advertisers more for access to the viewers. The television networks make more money and can afford to pay the sporting leagues higher fees for the rights to televise the games. The leagues and owners make more money and can afford to pay more to attract the best players and thereby play more games, which attracts more fans.

The cycle keeps going around and around, each time at a higher level of salaries for players, which requires more income for owners and leagues, which demand bigger contracts from television networks, which must charge more for commercial time to advertisers, who want larger audiences, who want more exciting games, which requires better players, who want more money . . . and the cycle continues.

Let's take a closer look at each of these segments of the money cycle. I make a distinction between the more *active* agents and the more *responding* agents in the cycle. The more active agents—the owners and players—have the most power in negotiating for money. The remaining agents—television networks, advertisers, and the public—are still essential to the money cycle, but their actions are largely in response to another agent; rarely do they initiate change.

Players

Salaries for players in all professional sports have been escalating in the past few decades. To illustrate this trend, let's begin by turning the clock back to 1959, when Ted Williams, a future hall of fame player for the Boston Red Sox baseball team, was offered a contract for $125,000. Williams returned his contract unsigned to management; he was rejecting their offer. His reason for rejecting the contract was that it was for *too much money.* Williams argued that he was not worth that much money because he was coming off a year in which he hit "only" .259, which was a bad year for Williams, although it would be a better than average year for almost everyone who ever played professional baseball. Williams asked for a pay cut of 25%, which was the maximum pay cut possible.

Over the past 30 years, salaries for Major League Baseball (MLB) players have been increasing rapidly. For example, in 2011, the highest paid pitcher was C. C. Sabathia, who was paid a salary of $23 million by the New York Yankees; this works out to about $100,000 per inning pitched. The New York Yankees paid Alex Rodriguez $32 million, which works out to about $200,000 per game or $64,000 per each at bat. Thus, in 2011, Alex Rodriguez was paid more to play five innings than Ted Williams was paid for playing an entire season.

As for the National Basketball Association (NBA), Michael Jordan was earning $4 million during the 1995–1996 season, when he led the Chicago Bulls to their fourth championship in professional basketball in 6 years. He was named the most valuable player of the year, and many basketball fans regard Jordan as the best basketball player of all time. A year later, he was a free agent and signed a new contract for $18 million, making him the highest paid player in the league—temporarily (Rhodes & Reibstein, 1996). A dozen years later, there were 12 players being paid more than $18 million per year in the NBA, and if you wanted to be the highest paid player, you needed to beat out Kevin Garnett at $25 million ("NBA Salaries," 2010).

Salaries for players in the National Football League (NFL) have also escalated dramatically. For example, the median earnings of the 2,000 NFL players in the 1999 season were $430,000, and a decade later, it had increased to $770,000. In 1999, if you earned $6.2 million, you would be in the elite top five of players, but by 2009, if you were paid $19 million, you would be the 15th highest player (Badenhausen, 2010; "National Football League," 2000). So while salaries of all NFL players increased over that decade, the really big increases came at the top end of the pay scale.

Athletes can also command large fees for endorsing products. Companies are willing to spend huge fees on athletes who endorse their products because such endorsements work to increase sales. For example, in 1983, $25 million was spent on endorsements; by 1988, it had doubled to $50 million. By the time he retired as a basketball player in 1999, Michael Jordan was making more than $40 million per year in product endorsements. Several top paid athletes can still earn more from endorsements than from their high salaries for playing their sport (see Table 20.1).

TABLE 20.1	Top Earning Athletes in 2010	2008 Income in Millions of U.S. Dollars		
Name	Sport	From Sport	From Endorsements	Total
Tiger Woods	Golf	2.3	60	62.3
Phil Mickelson	Golf	4.2	57	61.2
LeBron James	Basketball	14.5	30	44.5
Peyton Manning	Football	23.1	15	38.1
Alex Rodriguez	Baseball	32	4	36.0
Kobe Bryant	Basketball	24.8	10	34.8
Kevin Garnett	Basketball	18.8	14	32.8
Matt Ryan	Football	23.1	15	38.1
Tom Brady	Football	20	10	30.0
Dwight Howard	Basketball	16.6	12	28.6
Dale Earnhardt, Jr.	Auto racing	4.6	22	26.6
C. C. Sabathia	Baseball	23	0.8	23.8

SOURCE: Figures from Freedman (2011).

Until several decades ago, the owners and leagues were much more in control of players' contracts and salaries. Whitson (1998) explains that sport was commercialized early in the 20th century in the United States, where sports developed "labor markets of athletic talent, in which wealthy teams offered 'traveling players' financial inducements to come and play for them. It was this, of course, that created the phenomenon of the professional athlete, even though labor market mobility (and hence salaries) would quickly be contained by the emergence of cartels in all the major sports" (p. 60). These cartels controlled player salaries and player movement, but this arrangement broke down as a result of labor challenges in the 1970s, and now there is a great deal of player movement and escalation of salaries.

To help control the rise of salaries and to try to create parity among teams, several professional sports have established salary caps for teams in their leagues. However, many owners have routinely ignored the caps for years. For example, in the 1995 NFL season, the salary cap was $37.1 million per NFL team, and 26 of the 30 teams in the league went over that maximum. The Dallas Cowboys spent the most at $62.2 million; owner Jerry Jones spent almost $40.5 million in signing bonuses, including $13 million to Deion Sanders ("NFL Teams," 1996). By the 2009–2010 season, the salary cap had been increased so high (to $127 million) that only one team (New York Giants at $138.4) was over the spending cap. In that year, the median salary expenditure for teams was $106.5 million, with a range of $81.8 million for the most frugal team to $138.4 million at the top end (Sports City, n.d.).

Also, in the 1990s, the NBA instituted a salary cap per team. The 1996–1997 salary cap for the Chicago Bulls was $24.3 million, but the Bulls were able to pay Jordan $18 million that was not counted against the salary cap because the salary cap did not apply to the resigning of a team's existing players (Rhodes & Reibstein, 1996). All salary caps have loopholes. Owners and players' agents who are determined to make a deal can find a way around any limits on salaries and bonuses.

Why do owners continue to escalate salaries? The answer is that a star player at any price is a great investment. Not only can star players help their teams to win, but more important, they also bring fans out to the stadiums and, even more important, attract television viewers for their games. This greatly increases the value of the franchise. For example, the Chicago Bulls franchise was valued at $17.5 million in 1985—Jordan's rookie year. In 1996, after the Bulls won their fourth NBA title, the franchise was valued at $178 million. The owner had a huge yearly income from broadcast rights, merchandising, and ticket sales. The Bulls play at the United Center, where there are 216 suites each renting for $175,000 per year. In 1996, all games were sold out, and there was a waiting list of more than 17,000 fans for season tickets (Rhodes & Reibstein, 1996). Now the Bulls have been valued at more than $500 million (Badenhausen, Ozanian, & Settimi, 2011).

Owners and Leagues

The major professional sports leagues are all very profitable, although there are times when they claim to be losing money. For example, in the summer of 2011, when the NBA players' contract had expired and the league was negotiating a new deal with the players' union, the NBA claimed that during the previous season, 22 of its 30 teams were unprofitable and that the league lost about $300 million. This despite a record $4.3 billion in revenue from television contracts and record attendance at the games (Pugmire, 2011). The NBA argued that although it generated a huge revenue, its expenses were too high, especially players' salaries, and it was asking players to take a pay cut.

However, when we look at the big picture, it appears that all the major sports leagues in the United States are doing well (see Table 20.2). Notice that the NFL is the strongest of the four leagues in terms of team value. Notice also that the NFL has the smallest difference in salaries paid by the richest team and the poorest team. This is because the NFL controls all television rights to its games and distributes that money equally among all teams, so that teams in the smaller television markets can afford to be competitive. This serves to preserve parity among all teams, regardless of the size of their local television market. By sharing television revenue equally among its 32 teams, the NFL is able to keep the Green Bay Packers as a viable franchise. Green Bay, Wisconsin, is a town of well under 100,000 in population and is an outlying part of the Milwaukee television market, which is a relatively small media market. If the Green Bay Packers relied primarily on local television revenue, there is no way it could generate income anywhere near the revenue of teams in New York City, Chicago, or San Francisco, each with about 10 million viewers in their local markets. In 2011, the Green Bay Packers won the Super Bowl. If the Packers had had to rely solely on the team's income at the stadium and local television revenue, it could not have paid players enough to put together a playoff quality team, much less a Super Bowl champion.

TABLE 20.2 The Big Four American Professional Sports Leagues

	NFL	MLB	NBA	NHL
Number of teams	32	30	30	30
Games per season	16	162	82	82
Attendance per game	67,519	30,314	17,149	17,070
Average value per team	$1.0 billion	$419 million	$367 million	$223 million
Annual revenue per league	$7.8 billion	$6.8 billion	$4.0 billion	$3.0 billion
Salary paid by teams (millions)				
Highest team salary	$138.4	$202.7	116.9	70.1
Lowest team salary	81.8	36.1	32.2	29.7
Median team salary	106.5	87.0	76.2	56.0

SOURCE: Adapted from Plunkett Research (2010) and USAToday salaries databases (2011).

In contrast to the NFL, the other professional sports leagues allow teams to negotiate their own television contracts and keep the money. The NBA allows its teams to negotiate their own regional TV deals like the Lakers' recent 20-year deal with Time Warner Cable that is valued at $3 billion (Pugmire, 2011). MLB also allows its owners to negotiate their own local television contracts and keep that money. This has resulted in a very wide disparity of television revenue across local markets. This is the major reason why the New York Yankees is the most valuable professional sports franchise, even though baseball is a much weaker sport financially than football or basketball. In 2011, the New York Yankees had a payroll $30 million higher (15%) than the team with the second highest payroll (Philadelphia Phillies), and the Yankees payroll was larger than the payrolls of the Cleveland Indians, San Diego Padres, Pittsburgh Pirates, Tampa Bay Rays, and the Kansas City Royals combined!

TV money, while huge, is not enough for owners of professional sports franchises. These owners have also been aggressive in cultivating additional revenue streams, such as luxury skyboxes at stadiums and apparel merchandising. The owners frequently raise the prices of tickets, concessions, parking, apparel, and other souvenirs. The NFL also has other revenue streams, such as more than $4 billion per year in gross licensed merchandise sales.

Naming rights to major league sports stadiums range from a low of $620,000 per year for Altell Stadium, home of the Jacksonville Jaguars football team, to a high of $20 million a year for Citigroup, home of the New York Mets baseball team (ESPN.com, n.d.).

College sports have become huge businesses of mass entertainment. Colleges own their teams and make a huge profit on marquee sports such as football and men's basketball. These sports are subsidized by students, who are regarded as amateur athletes and therefore cannot be paid to play, although many are given scholarships. Even private colleges with high tuition can field a team for about $2 million, and most state schools have scholarship expenses one third of that figure; compare that figure to the annual payrolls of NFL teams at about $106 million. While NBA teams now have salary expenses of $76 million a year, colleges can put together a basketball team with about half a million in scholarship money. Colleges share in TV money and also have revenue for tickets, parking, and concessions. While colleges do not play as many games per season as do pro teams, they have another source of revenue that pro teams do not have—donors who as athletic program boosters get to write off their donations as tax deductions. Colleges are looking for even more sources of revenue. College football is now selling naming rights to particular regular season games. SBC Communication, the number two local telephone provider in the United States, bought the rights for the Ohio State–Michigan football game for 2 years for $1.06 million ("Big Game in Big Ten," 2005).

College sports can generate huge revenues at major universities, but their expenses are very high because universities support a wide range of sports programs (such as golf, tennis, track, volleyball, cross-country, etc.) that generate almost no income yet have considerable expenses. The National Collegiate Athletic Association (NCAA) estimates that the median athletic expense per college student athlete is $90,000. As a result of these high expenses for NCAA sports, only 22 out of 120 Division I college athletic programs make a profit, and the median loss for the remaining 98 program is $11.3 million. That difference must be made up by the university. In football and men's basketball, about half of the programs are at least self-sufficient (Bennett, 2011b). None of the women's programs cover their expenses, not even a single women's basketball program (Bennett, 2011a).

Television Networks

The biggest increase in sports revenue is from television. Without a television contract, no sports league could survive. The American Football League got started in the early 1960s with a TV deal of $1.7 million. Although this does not seem like much money today, it made the difference in whether the league survived in the early 1960s. In 1965, CBS paid $14.1 million to broadcast NFL games. By the mid-1990s, the NFL was charging $500 million per year for broadcasting rights, and this sum was so large that it had to be shared by five networks: ABC, NBC, ESPN, Fox, and TNT. Now in 2011, the NFL is able to command such huge sums for the rights to televised their games that the cost is shared across four television networks: ESPN ($1.1 billion), FOX ($720 million), NBC ($603 million), and CBS ($620 million) (Coller, 2011). The NFL also gets an additional $1 billion from DirecTV Corp. for its Sunday Ticket package, and its own cable channel, NFL Network, generates another $400 million a year (Flint, 2009a). The telecasting of the NFL games is so valuable that the NFL is asking for double the cost in its next round of contract negotiations. For example, ESPN is getting ready to sign a 10-year extension worth $2 billion per year to televise some NFL games and the NFL draft (Coller, 2011).

The television networks know they cannot depend on teams winning to keep increasing their viewership. With the four major professional sports (football, basketball, baseball, and hockey), each contest has only two teams, which means the number of losers is always the same as the number of winners. There is no way to increase the number of wins relative to the number of losses. Therefore, winning a competition is not enough to market sports successfully. The television networks have had to develop other means to increase the size of the sports audience. The way they have done this is to shift the focus from sports to an entertainment formula. This means that the announcers must be good storytellers. The announcers must fill in the history of the teams and tell compelling stories about "there is a tradition of bad blood between the teams" or some other subplot to keep people watching the games, especially when the score is lopsided. Announcers must tell human interest stories about the struggles of individual players both on and off the field. And they must turn certain players into larger-than-life heroes, who can take over a game at any instant with their courage or superhuman abilities.

Certain players are pushed into the spotlight each season, and those who perform well there become legends—players such as Babe Ruth, Wayne Gretsky, Magic Johnson, and Michael Jordan. Even non–sports fans know who these people are, and those reputations have attracted a lot of new fans to the games.

The television networks have branded their own sports shows, such as the *NBA on NBC* and *ABC's Monday Night Football* (Bellamy, 1998). They have done this to generate viewers loyal to shows and not just teams. If the game is bad, which it often is, the networks have to hold on to their audiences so that they can guarantee to advertisers that the audiences will be large.

With television and advertisers putting so much money into these sports, they demand that the leagues make their sports even more exciting and more amenable to advertising. The leagues have complied. For example, the coverage of a football game is more than 3 hours long, although the game itself takes 60 minutes, and there is less than 10 minutes of action on the field during those 60 minutes that the clock is running. So the announcers must provide lots of anecdotes, statistics, and color commentary. The director must provide lots of replays, slow motions, shots of the crowd and cheerleaders, and so on. The NFL changed the extra point rule so that teams could go for 2 extra points, thus helping the team behind to catch up faster and make the game more interesting. Rules were changed to provide more protection for the most valuable offensive player—the quarterback—who needed more time to engage in the game's most exciting play, which is the long pass. Basketball now has a shot clock that requires players to shoot the ball at least every 24 seconds. Basketball also instituted the 3-point play, which is much riskier and hence more exciting.

To accommodate advertisers, the NFL instituted the 2-minute warning in the mid-1960s to guarantee a break for commercial messages at a time when viewership is usually high. Also, the NFL and the NBA have frequent television time-outs. Uniforms are more colorful. All of these changes to the games were instituted to increase viewer interest and thereby provide advertisers with the largest possible audiences.

Advertisers

Advertisers pay huge fees to television networks to get their messages to their target audiences. During the first Super Bowl in 1967, broadcasting a 30-second ad cost advertisers $42,000; by 1995, the cost had increased to more than $1 million. Then in 2001, the cost broke through $2 million, and in 2011, the cost was more than $3 million for a single 30-second ad (BallHyped News, 2011).

Advertisers have also turned stadiums into advertising vehicles with the naming of the stadiums and by putting ads on scoreboards, walls, ticket stubs, concession stand product

packaging, and so on. Some basketball courts have ads painted on them; hockey has ads in the ice and around the rink's walls. Some football teams have ads on their jerseys (Nike swoosh), and in car racing, the drivers' uniforms as well as the cars are covered with ads.

In the spring of 2004, Major League Baseball even tried putting ads on the bases, but criticism flared up, and it has backed off, for now. One critic said that this "undermines the character of America's pastime at every level." This criticism makes one wonder whether the critic has seen a baseball game in the past two decades, with all the advertising that is already at the stadium. It is interesting to consider what another critic said as a way of thinking about what might be coming in the future: "How low will baseball sink? Next year, will they replace the bats with long Coke bottles, and the bases with big hamburger buns?" (Penner, 2004, pp. D1, D8).

Businesses are happy to contribute large sums of money to sports—as long as those businesses get high visibility for themselves in return. For example, Frito-Lay gave $15 million to the Fiesta Bowl and in return received 3 years of sponsorship rights to that college football game. This means that the name of the game was changed to the Tostitos Fiesta Bowl, and this name had to appear on all the signage and be mentioned by all announcers referring to the game.

Public

The public has always been interested in sports. But for the money cycle to grow, the number of fans has to grow each year. Also, the commitment of those fans needs to grow each year

so that those fans spend even more time watching the games, going to the stadiums, buying the team merchandise, and supporting all the advertisers. And most important, the general public in each locale must identify and support its local teams. All of these things have happened and continue to happen.

People spend a great deal of time watching sports on television. Almost a decade ago, two researchers counted more than 8,000 sporting events televised that year, and there are times when there are 10 events televised at the same time (Kinkema & Harris, 1998). That number is likely to be much higher today.

The most popular televised sport is the NFL, with an average rating of 16; MLB is second, with a rating of 11.1. The cost of a 30-second ad is about $130,000 and $80,000 for football and baseball, respectively. Golf and tennis are the least popular sports, but they still have a loyal following and generate average ratings of about 4.5 and 3.8, respectively. Also, these sports deliver a high-quality audience, that is, one that is very affluent and hence very attractive to companies that advertise luxury products.

Not only does the money cycle depend on continued support from fans, but it requires support from nonfans also. This is most clearly seen in the building of new sports stadiums across the country. The major sports leagues have been successful in getting local municipalities to finance a large part of these stadiums through public financing and taxes. For example, the NFL has been a very successful negotiator in getting cities to build new stadiums, parking facilities, and so forth to hold onto or to attract new football franchises. In the 5-year period from the summer of 1998 to the summer of 2003, 12 new NFL football stadiums were opened—many in cities with existing football stadiums. Each of these new stadiums had between 82 (Seattle) and 208 (Washington, D.C.) premium skyboxes that the owners of the NFL teams could rent out to wealthy clients and businesses. But the sweetest part of most of these deals was that the NFL got the cities to pay for most of the construction costs. Only one owner (Daniel Snyder, owner of the Washington Redskins) paid for at least half of the construction costs, and with three of the stadiums (Raymond James stadium in Tampa, Florida; Reliant Stadium in Houston, Texas; and the Coliseum in Nashville, Tennessee), the NFL saw to it that the cities paid the entire cost of the stadiums. Therefore, if you rent a car or rent a hotel room in a city with an NFL team (or a major league baseball team or NBA team), you are likely paying a tax that helps that city finance its stadiums (Metropolitan Sports Facilities Commission, n.d.).

Most cities feel that it is important to have major sports teams. Cities with such teams are willing to spend a great deal of public money to keep them, and those cities without such a team are willing to spend a great deal of public money to attract such a team away from another city. In the mid-1990s, four teams left their home NFL city to get a better deal. For example, the Los Angeles Rams went to St. Louis when St. Louis offered a brand-new stadium, plus guaranteed $16 million per year in gross ticket sales along with other financial considerations (Bellamy, 1998). After Los Angeles went several years without a football team, the NFL was getting pressure from advertisers that there was no team in the nation's second largest media market. In 1999, the NFL put pressure on Los Angeles to build a stadium and other facilities (parking lots, training areas, etc.) so the NFL could put a team back in that city. A Los Angeles billionaire put together an ownership group, and the city put in $150 million in state revenue bonds to build parking structures around an existing facility—the Los Angeles Coliseum. But the NFL commissioner, Paul Tagliabue, objected to the deal, saying that the municipality was not putting in enough taxpayer money, and because of this, the team would not be profitable for its owners—projecting an annual profit of only $25 to $28 million per year. The city of Houston offered $200 million in public money for a new stadium plus private investment in an adjacent football museum. When the city of Los Angeles would not put more taxpayer money into its offer, the NFL awarded the franchise to Houston, which is also a very important media market (Flanigan, 1999). Since that time, the NFL has been pressuring Los Angeles to invest hundreds of millions of dollars of taxpayers' money to build a state-of-the-art stadium so that it can award an NFL franchise to the country's second largest media market.

The costs of building professional sports stadiums are going up dramatically, and it is costing taxpayers a lot of money to have a team. For example, let's look at what happened in Houston, Texas. The city built the Astrodome at a cost of $35 million and opened it in 1965. It was the home of both football and baseball teams. Then, in 2000, Houston opened Minute Maid Park, which cost $250 million to build and was designed for baseball only. Then 2 years later, Houston opened the brand-new Reliant Stadium for football only, at a cost of $449 million. The Houston Rockets, the NBA team, began playing in the Compaq Center, which cost $27 million and opened in 1975. This was replaced by the Toyota Center in 2003, which was built at a cost of $175 million (Reinken, 2003).

NASCAR is a very expensive sport that could not survive without an extreme amount of advertising. It is estimated that it costs a minimum of $10 million a year (and can be twice that) to fund a competitive team in the 36-race stock car racing season. Winning some of these races pays only about $200,000, and winning all 36 races would bring in only about $9 million. So teams must sell advertising on every part of the car, as well as the driver's jumpsuit (Glick, 2004).

OLYMPICS

The ancient Olympics were a venue for amateur athletes to compete every 4 years. Of course, at the time, there were no professional sports. The ancient Olympics continued for more than 1,200 years, died out, and then were revived in 1896 as the "modern" Olympics. For a long time, the modern Olympics preserved its focus on amateur athletes and banned any professional athlete of any kind from participating.

Cities competed to host the Olympic Games every 4 years. By 1932, the cost of hosting the games had increased to a point where cities could not make back all the money they spent, so it was a sacrifice to host the games. Still, many cities competed because it was prestigious to be the host city. It also provided a great public relations opportunity to show off the host city to the world.

Eventually, with the rise of television, networks were willing to pay the International Olympic Committee fees for the rights to broadcast the games, and this helped host cities defray the costs of building all the venues and the cost of running the Olympics (see Table 20.3). In 1964, NBC paid $1.5 million to the International Olympic Committee for the rights to broadcast the Tokyo Summer Olympics. By 1980, the cost had skyrocketed to $85 million when NBC acquired rights to the Moscow Summer Olympics, despite the fact that the Soviets wanted $210 million plus $50 million in production equipment to be left behind. The broadcast was never made, though, due to the boycott of the 1980 games by the American government. ABC paid $225 million for the Los Angeles summer games in 1984 and $91 million for the winter games in Sarajevo. Despite losing money on the winter games, ABC came back with an even higher bid of $309 million for the 1988 winter games in Calgary. NBC got the 1988 summer games in Seoul, Korea, for $300 million. NBC paid $456 million for the 1996 Atlanta games, and CBS bid $375 million to broadcast the 1998 Nagano games in the Winter Olympics. NBC broke its record by bidding $705 million for exclusive U.S. rights to broadcast the 2000 summer games in Sydney, Australia, and another $545 million for the 2002 winter games in Salt Lake City. The total NBC package is worth about $1.3 billion—none of the other U.S. networks entered a bid (Nelson, 1995). NBC secured the rights to three Olympic Games (2014 winter games in Russia, the 2016 summer games in Rio de Janeiro, and the 2018 winter games and 2020 summer games) for $4.38 billion. The network has a history of losing money on these broadcasts. In broadcasting the 2010 winter games, NBC lost $233 million (Flint, 2011a).

Where does this money go? It is paid to the International Olympic Committee (IOC), which also sells rights to broadcast the games to media in other countries. When ABC paid $309 million for the 1988 winter games, the European Broadcast Union (EBU, which represents 32 countries and a population of several hundred million) paid $5.7 million, and the Soviet Union (along with it Eastern European allies), North Korea, and Cuba paid a combined total of $1.2 million. Thus, it is clear that the United States (or, rather, advertisers on U.S. television) really supports the games—without U.S. support, the Olympics would be very different.

The IOC also sells to advertisers the rights to sponsor the games or show their products during the games. Real (1998) explains that American TV has increasingly borne the cost of hosting the Olympic Games. In 1960, American TV money contributed about 0.3% of the cost of the games; in 1980, American money supported 6% of the cost; and in 1984, it contributed 50%. Now American TV totally supports the cost and allows the host city to make a big profit.

The Olympics have become a major venue for advertising. The modern Olympics have always accepted advertising. In 1896, there were ads for Kodak. Coke began its association with the games in 1928. But as the games got more expensive, planners needed more advertising revenue. The 1976 games in Montreal experienced a $1 billion deficit.

In 1984, when the Olympics were held in Los Angeles, the games not only covered their enormous costs but also made a huge profit of $215 million (Manning, 1987). They did this by selling corporate sponsorships of various events and locales. VISA alone spent $25 million on the rights and on promotions, and 146 corporations were official sponsors of various events. By the 1996 games in Atlanta, the IOC had signed up 180 companies and brands that used the Olympics for promotions (Grimm, 1996). The top 10 of these official sponsors (such

TABLE 20.3	Television Broadcast Contracts for Summer Olympic Games	
Year	Host City	Fee in Millions of U.S. Dollars
1960	Rome	0.6
1964	Tokyo	1.6
1968	Mexico City	4.5
1972	Munich	12.5
1976	Montreal	25.0
1980	Moscow	95.5
1984	Los Angeles	225.0
1988	Seoul	305.0
1992	Barcelona	401.0
1996	Atlanta	456.0
2000	Sydney	705.0
2004	Athens	793.0
2008	Beijing	894.0

SOURCE: Adapted from Real (1998, p. 19).

as Coke and IBM) paid a total of $2.1 billion (J. Jensen & Ross, 1996). This more than offset the total cost of $1.7 billion for holding the 1996 Atlanta games (Boswell, 1996). Now, almost all athletes have corporate logos on their clothing. Sponsorships are sold for each event and for the games in general. Companies use the event as an opportunity for global marketing.

Ever since the Los Angeles games in 1984, the Olympics have been highly commercial and highly profitable for the host city. Now, competition among cities to host the event is very strong.

The Olympics are less profitable for the television network that outbids its competitors and is awarded the rights to broadcast the games. This huge expense for the broadcast rights is only the beginning. Production is another big expense. In the 1984 Los Angeles Summer Olympics, the United States sent 500 athletes to compete; ABC sent 3,500 people (1,400 engineers, 1,800 support personnel, and 300 network production and management people). To produce 188 hours of coverage, they used 205 cameras, 660 miles of camera cables, 4 helicopters, 3 houseboats, 26 mobile units, 35 office trailers, and 404 hardwired commentary positions. There were microphones on basketball backboards, underwater in the diving pool, in boxing ring posts, and on equestrian saddles. The cost of covering the games was $100 million. This is why the television networks must sell a great deal of advertising. For the 1996 games in Atlanta, NBC sold a total of $675 million of ad time to 50 advertisers. More airtime was devoted to commercials than to the actual sports action (Farhi & Shapiro, 1996).

Ratings for the Olympic Games have been dropping over the past four decades from an average rating of over 20 down to an average rating of about 7 (Nielsenwire, 2008). Given the ratings drop and costs accelerating upward, television networks typically lose money televising the Olympic Games, but they continue to bid up the price for future telecasting rights. They reason that the Olympic telecasts attract large audiences that they can target their promotions for new entertainment shows. Thus, if those promotions can generate larger audiences for the shows premiering after the Olympics, the networks will more than earn enough to cancel out the loss of telecasting the Olympics and generate a larger overall yearly profit for the network.

Because of the highly commercial nature of the Olympic Games, the IOC was unable to maintain the prohibition against professional athletes. Now the Olympics are very different than they were even 25 years ago. They are a showcase for the best athletes— professional as well as amateur—in the world. But even more important, they are a showcase for international companies that want to develop markets worldwide for their products and services.

THE BIG PICTURE

This chapter has presented many figures illustrating how the money cycle has increased expenditures on sports over the years until now more than $414 billion is spent on sports annually in the United States. Most of those figures have focused on the high-profile spectator sports, especially from the big four of American professional sports—football, baseball, basketball, and hockey. But if you look at Table 20.2, you will see that the total revenues of those four powerful sports leagues total $21.6 billion, which is a huge sum of money but only about 5.2% of the total revenue generated by sports in the United States each year. What generates the other 94.8%? Other spectator sports generate an additional $15 billion. This includes racing (especially horses and cars), golf, tennis, volleyball, and all other sports. Also, this figure includes all sports spectatorship at levels below professional, such as college and high school. So when we add up all money for what we pay to watch sports, it accounts for about 8.9% of all money spent on sports each year in the United States. The other 90.1% is money we spend on participating in sports, such as buying sporting goods, joining recreational centers and leagues, fees to play golf, and so on.

The big picture, then, is that sports are extremely important to Americans, but 9 out of every 10 dollars we spend on sports are for participation. The money cycle drives the high-profile professional leagues, which provide better athletes, games, stadiums, and spectator experiences each year. And these high-profile professional leagues stimulate spectators to watch sporting contests at nonprofessional levels as well as expand our interest in watching other sports. And all this viewership stimulates us to participate in all sorts of amateur sports leagues and individual contests ourselves. Thus, the money cycle that is most apparent with the big four professional leagues and the Olympic Games has an influence far beyond those particular contests.

When you take a big picture view on sports, you need to think beyond the mega-salaries paid to star athletes and think about how those athletes might be inspiring you to participate in sports yourself or to simply exercise. And as you expand your thinking, consider how those high-profile sporting contests may be teaching you lessons about preparing for challenges, setting goals, working hard, and excelling in the many various contests we face in our everyday lives.

SUMMARY

Sports have become more exciting and entertaining to the general viewer over the past several decades. The public is showing increased interest in sporting events and personalities of all kinds. But the price for this continues to climb. As a fan, you support your teams by buying tickets, parking, refreshments, and souvenirs at the games. If you do not go to the stadium, you can still support your teams by watching them on television and buying products advertised on those telecasts. And even if you do not go to the games or watch the local teams on television, you are still supporting those teams financially through local taxes and paying the interest on revenue bonds your city council has sold to build the fancy new stadiums that will keep owners from moving their teams elsewhere.

There are three key concerns you should ponder with the issue of media and sports. First, think about limits—that is, how far can the money cycle go in changing professional sports? Is there a limit to what players can earn? Is there a limit to what we are willing to pay for tickets, concessions, parking, and clothing with the logos of our favorite teams? Is there a limit to what municipalities will add to the local tax burden to hold onto a local team? Is there a limit to how many commercial breaks we will tolerate when watching professional sports on television?

A second thing for you to ponder is a larger concern with all sports. How far have the changes in professional sports filtered down to college sports, high school sports, and recreational sports? Do the changes in professional sports change the expectations of those who play little league baseball; that is, is the pressure too high to win? Does it take the fun away from watching intramural sports or a community league game?

Third, the ultimate concern is with the value of these changes to us. How can we avoid experiencing potentially negative impacts on our own lives? How can we benefit more from the advantages offered to us by the positive changes?

Chapter Resources: To test your knowledge and learn more about the topics discussed in this chapter, visit the Student Study Site at www.sagepub.com/potter6e.

FURTHER READING

Raney, A. A. (2009). The effects of viewing televised sports. In R. L. Nabi & M. B. Oliver (Eds.), *Media processes and effects* (pp. 439–453). Thousand Oaks, CA: Sage.

This chapter presents a relatively current review of the empirical literature on the effects of exposure to sports in the media.

Raney, A. A., & Bryant, J. (Eds.). (2006). *Handbook of sports and media*. Mahwah, NJ: Lawrence Erlbaum.

This edited volume contains many chapters written by experts on sports in the media. It is organized into four sections of the development of sports media, the coverage and business of sports media, sports media audiences, and critical perspectives on sports media.

Wenner, L. A. (Ed.). (1998). *MediaSport*. New York: Routledge. (336 pages with index)

This edited book contains 17 chapters in four parts: playing field, institutions, texts, and audiences. Although this book is now a bit dated, with most of its research coming from the early to mid-1990s, it still presents valuable insights into how sports have developed primarily in the United States to become such a powerful economic and social force.

KEEPING UP TO DATE

ESPN (http://espn.go.com)

The television cable network devoted to sports has a website that presents a great deal of current information about players, teams, and contests.

Plunkett Research, Ltd. (http://www.plunkettresearch.com/Industries/Sports/SportsStatistics/tabid/273/Default. aspx)

This is the website of a company that conducts and reports research on a wide variety of topics. It is a valuable resource for information on sports statistics, such as players' salaries, value of different sports franchises, attendance at games, and so on.

USAToday Salaries Databases (http://content.usatoday.com/sportsdata)

This website presents a lot of detail about the salaries of professional athletes and teams in America's major sports.

EXERCISE 20.1

Extending Knowledge

In this chapter, I have presented you with some facts to illustrate the money cycle with sports. Use this information as a jumping-off point and see what research you can do to update and expand on the points in this chapter by considering the following questions.

1. *Extend your knowledge:* Pick one of the main points in this chapter, and do your own research to expand your knowledge and update the information. Some topics are the following:

   a. Product endorsements by professional athletes

   b. Cost of sports stadiums and how they are financed

   c. Comparison of player salaries across sports

   d. Track advertising expenditures by sport

   e. Find the demographic profiles of fans in different sports

   f. How have the games changed to make them more attractive to viewers?

   g. Who are the owners of the sports teams, and how did they make enough money to be able to buy a sports franchise?

2. *Analyze advertising content:* Watch several broadcasts of a particular sport. But instead of paying most attention to the game, pay attention to the advertisements. Keep track of all ads. Then answer the following questions:

   a. Which companies advertise the most on particular sports?

   b. Which product categories are most often advertised by sports?

   c. Given your answers to the above two questions, who do you think the target audiences are for those big advertisers?

   d. What kinds of appeals are used in those ads; that is, what are the advertisers telling you about their products and why you should use them?

3. *Project trends:* Pick one sport and see if you can find salary information for what the average salary was and what the highest paid players made in each decade.

   a. Project that information into the future for one, two, and three decades. How much will the average player be making when you are 30, 40, and 50?

b. Break those salary figures down by game; that is, what will the average player and the highest paid player make per game in the future?

c. What do you think your salary will be when you are 30, 40, and 50? How long will it take a pro player to earn what you make in a year?

4. *Get a historical perspective on these issues:* Talk to your father (or mother) and grandfather (or grandmother) about sports behaviors 40 to 50 years ago. Ask them the following questions:

a. Did they attend sporting events in person?

b. Did they follow sports through the media? Is so, which sports and which media?

c. Are they aware of any changes in their favorite sports over the past few decades? If so, what is their reaction to those changes?

d. What is their reaction to the salaries paid to athletes today?

e. What is their reaction to the amount of advertising at the games and during media coverage?

5. *Develop an informed opinion* about the amount of money spent on professional athletes.

a. Think about the pros and cons. Try to list all the positive reasons for the accelerating salary increases, and then list all the negative reasons.

b. Think of the ramifications on things beyond sports, such as the following:
Local taxes
Traffic patterns and congestion
Teaching your kids to play sports
Taking your family to sporting events
The cost of advertised products
The overall economy
Our sports as perceived by the rest of the world

c. On balance, what is your informed opinion?

d. What, if anything, should the following types of people do?
Elected leaders
Television networks
Future athletes
Advertisers

EXERCISE 20.2

Personal Inventory

This exercise is designed to guide you through a cost-benefit analysis of sports. Some of the questions in this cost-benefit analysis will require you to do some research on the Internet.

Begin by thinking about how many sports you follow. The big four are football, basketball, hockey, and baseball. But also think about golf, tennis, track, horseracing, car racing, volleyball, and so on. Think beyond professional sports and include college level and high school level. Also, think about city leagues, YMCA leagues, children's leagues, and so forth.

Step 1: Estimate your direct costs:

Think about how much time and money you spend following sports and estimate your answers to the following questions:

1. For each sport, estimate how much time you spend going to games.

   a. What is the cost of tickets?

   b. What is the cost of transportation to the games?

   c. What is the cost of parking at the games?

   d. How much do you spend on food and drink at the games?

   e. How much do you spend on souvenirs—programs, pennants, and so forth?

2. How much do you spend on items with team logos?

   a. Clothing (hats, shirts, jackets, etc.)

   b. Items for your car (flags, license plates, bumper stickers, etc.)

   c. Items for your desk (cups, pens, calendars, etc.)

   d. Sports gifts for others

3. How much money do you spend watching games on television?

   a. Cost for special cable or pay TV sports services?

   b. Cost of parties for friends who watch the games with you?

   c. Cost of food and drink at sports bars while watching games?

4. How much time do you spend in all the above activities?

5. How much time do you spend doing the following:

   a. Talking about sports teams, players, and scores of games?

   b. Reminiscing about past good times?

   c. Complaining about bad games, plays, and players?

   d. Projecting into the future of your team, players' careers, or games?

Step 2: Estimate your indirect costs:

1. How much money do you spend buying products advertised on sporting events? (To answer this completely, you need to analyze all the products advertising on all sports programs you watch and then find out what percentage of the purchase price of each of those products was spent on advertising of sports. To estimate your answer, think of the major sponsors of the teams you follow and add up all the money you spend each year on those products.)

2. How much money has your city spent to support the local sports teams? (Think of the cost of building the stadiums, parking lots, and access roads to the professional, college, and high school sports. Try to estimate how much of your taxes go into supporting all these sports.)

Step 3: Estimate your direct benefits:

1. How much satisfaction did you derive last season from the performance of the sports teams you followed? If you are a rabid fan and your teams all won championships, your satisfaction level should be extremely high. But think about the satisfaction you obtained from experiencing individual games and the performances of individual players.

2. How much satisfaction did you derive from displaying your teams' logos on your clothing, car, desk, and so on? Is it important to you that other people know which teams you support? If so, why? Do you identify so closely with a team that you, as a fan, feel partially responsible when they lose and that you have earned a celebration when they win?

(Continued)

(Continued)

Step 4: Estimate your indirect benefits:

1. How important are your teams to their home cities?

   a. What economic benefits do the cities get by having those teams?

   b. What public relations benefits do the home cities get from supporting their teams?

   c. Do the teams need to win for the city to achieve these benefits?

2. Now considering what the cities experience as benefits, how much of that passes down to individuals such as yourself?

Step 5: Compare costs to benefits:

Now that you have thought about the questions raised in the above four areas, make a comparison of the costs to the benefits. Do you feel that the benefits you derive (of all kinds) are more than enough to pay you back for all the time and money you put into your fan-ship?

- If yes, what is your most valuable benefit? Why do you value that so highly?
- If no, how can you bring this cost-benefit comparison more in line with the value you expect? Is there some way to reduce your costs while still getting the same benefits? Is there some way to increase the benefits without increasing your costs?

Finally, think about where you might be 5 years from now given the money cycle. The monetary costs to you are likely to be much higher than they are today. Do you think the media will be able to grow the benefits proportionally so that you still feel that your money and time spent with sports are worthwhile?

Part 7

The Springboard

As the final part of this textbook, the following chapters serve as a springboard for you to take certain ideas away from the readings and bring them into your everyday lives. Chapter 21 summarizes what you can do to help yourself maintain a high level of media literacy. Chapter 22 presents you with some ideas that you can use to help others.

As you finish this textbook and your college course, you need to confront the question: Is my interest in being media literate now ending or just beginning? It will be increasingly impossible for you to live a single day without considerable exposure to media messages. You have little ability to avoid media exposures or their influences, indirect as well as direct. But you have a good deal of potential to shape the influence of those messages on yourself and on people important to you.

CHAPTER 21

Key Idea: Only you have the power to increase your own level of media literacy.

Personal Strategy for Increasing Media Literacy

Congratulations for having worked on your knowledge structures in the previous chapters. By now you should have a fairly good awareness about what it means to be media literate. You should now be asking yourself, How can I preserve the skills and knowledge structures I already have? How can I improve?

The answers to these questions require you to think about developing a consistent strategy. In this chapter, I can help get you started and direct your thinking, but I cannot give you *The Strategy*. You must develop that for yourself in response to your particular needs. Think about what I say in this chapter as a platform—a jumping-off point for you to take greater control of the trajectory of your thinking as you glide through the rich atmosphere of media messages throughout the course of your life.

The purpose of developing a personal media literacy strategy is to gain control over the process of influence that the media currently dominate. This is not to say that you forsake all automatic processing of information. That is an unrealistic goal. Instead, the strategy should be one where you gradually improve your awareness of the process of influence and gradually exercise more and more control over it. This chapter begins with 12 guidelines to remind you what is most important to think about as you develop your own personal media literacy strategy. Then I will present some illustrations of milestones that mark the development of media literacy.

TWELVE GUIDELINES

1. Strengthen Your Personal Locus

Remember that your locus is a combination of an awareness of your goals along with the drive energy to search out information and experiences to attain those goals. Therefore, you need to analyze your goals. What really makes you happy? What do you really want to achieve in life? Are the answers to these questions things that have been programmed by the media? Think about where those answers came from and how comfortable you are with those answers.

Also, you need to increase your willingness to expend mental effort. We all have expectations about the appropriate amount of mental effort that is necessary to read a book, listen to a lecture on an iPod, play a video game, or watch a television program. Each medium requires a different amount of mental effort; each medium also requires a different kind of cognitive engagement. When a message meets our expectation, we typically continue our exposure but do so in an automatic state. However, when a message requires more effort than we expect, we might stop our exposure to that message and look for another message that requires less mental effort. This is a natural reaction, but sometimes it is helpful to stay with challenging messages and try to figure out why the message is so challenging. The greater the mental effort expended, the higher the comprehension, learning, and eventual recall.

2. Focus on Usefulness as a Goal

There are different reasons for media exposure. All can be valid and highly useful. But uses vary. We need to be clear about what our goals really are during each exposure session. We should remember that we are placing ourselves at risk for unwanted effects if we expose ourselves without an awareness of our goals. Make it a practice to ask yourself, Am I planning my media exposures to serve my own purposes, or am I just exposing myself to whatever comes along? If you are engaging in habitual exposure patterns with no personal goals, then you are clearly a tool of the mass media.

3. Develop an Accurate Awareness of Your Exposure

Periodically (maybe once a year), keep a diary of media usage for a week. By repeating this exercise, you can monitor your changing interests in media, vehicles, and messages. As you monitor changes, ask yourself the following types of questions:

- Am I broadening my exposure to different media, or am I staying primarily with only one or two?
- Am I broadening my exposure to different vehicles? (If you used to watch mainly sports and action/adventure on television, are you now spreading your viewing around to a wider range of genres?)

Explore a wider range of websites, new musical artists, new kinds of television shows, and different magazines. You don't have to like all these exposures; in fact, you are likely to hate many of them. But by trying new vehicles, you are giving yourself opportunities to find even better messages than those delivered through your habitual exposures. And you are likely to discover new messages that you might like even better than the messages you usually get in your habitual patterns of exposure. If you do not occasionally explore the range of media messages, you will likely default to a narrower and narrower focus over time.

4. Acquire a Broad Base of Useful Knowledge

The key to knowledge is that it is useful; acquiring knowledge that is not useful does not help you. This means we must be continually aware of our needs for knowledge, then focus on satisfying those needs.

There is always a gap between the knowledge we already have and the knowledge we need to understand the world better. We can close the knowledge gap for ourselves. But we must do this on a topic-by-topic basis. The means for closing the knowledge gap on a topic is under our control because the knowledge gap is influenced more by our interest in a topic than by our general level of education (Chew & Palmer, 1994). If we have high interest on a topic, we will search out information from many different media and many different sources. But when we have low interest on a topic, we allow the media to determine for us how much information we get.

5. Think About the Reality-Fantasy Continuum

Continually ask yourself the degree to which something is real or fantasy; this is a continuum. Some programs will be easy to spot as fantasy, such as *Looney Toons*. But other programs may not be so obvious. Some have a realistic setting and some realistic situations but are still fantasy, such as *Desperate Housewives* or *Two and a Half Men*. Others may have a fantasy setting but deal with situations in a realistic manner, such as *Star Trek*. Distinguishing reality from fantasy in the media is often a difficult task that requires you to think about the many different characteristics of a message. So you must think analytically and break a message down into its component parts, then assess which parts are realistic. Do not try to categorize messages as simply being either real or fantasy; media messages always have elements of both.

Being aware of the fantasy-reality continuum is especially important now, when there are so many so-called reality programs on television. Although all of these programs have reality elements, they also contain many fantasy elements. And some of these "reality" shows may have a mix of elements that make them less real than some fictional programs. The distinction between shows labeled reality and those labeled fiction is not a sharp, clear line. Be careful of accepting the simple labels for messages. The important thing is to know when you are being exposed to fantasy so that you can process those messages differently. If you aren't sufficiently analytical, many messages with embedded fantasy might appear realistic.

Do not go on a quest to avoid fantasy merely because fantasy elements are dangerous to use in real-world expectations. There is a place for fantasy in the enjoyment of the media. Fantasy messages can be very entertaining because of their imaginative or humorous appeal. They can stimulate our thinking creatively; however, we must realize that fantasy is a tool to stimulate our imagination—it is not a model to imitate.

6. Examine Your Mental Codes

As you engage in your habits of media exposures, periodically ask yourself why your habits are the way they are. To what extent have you programmed your habits to serve your needs? And to what extent have the mass media programmed your habits to meet their needs? After you consider answers to these questions, rethink your mental code and then reprogram your code to satisfy your own needs better. After this reprogramming, you can return to your routine exposures in a state of automaticity, but this time the code will be delivering on your goals rather than the media's goals.

7. Examine Your Opinions

Ask yourself the following: Are my opinions well reasoned?

Although people criticize television in general, their opinions are inconsistent. For example, The Roper Organization, under the sponsorship of NBC in the early 1980s, had respondents in a national survey express their reactions to 17 particular TV shows—16 of which had been the targets of complaints about sex and violence from religious organizations. Only 13% of respondents said there was too much violence on the *Dukes of Hazard,* and 10% said there was too much sex on *Dallas*—these were the most negatively rated shows! But when asked about television in general, 50% of the respondents said that there was too much sex and violence on TV (The Roper Organization, 1981). While this study was conducted before you were born, are the findings still valid for you? Do you systematically gather valid information before constructing your opinions? Then do you back up your opinions with behavior?

8. Change Behaviors

To what extent do your behaviors correspond with your beliefs? For example, if you think society is too materialistic, do you avoid buying many material goods? If you do keep your consumption of material goods at a minimum, then there is a match between your behaviors and your beliefs. But there are people who continually complain about waste in our materialistic society, then go out and buy lots of new things they don't need. In a recent survey, 82% of Americans agreed that most of us buy and consume far more than we need. And 67% agreed that Americans cause many of the world's environmental problems because we consume more resources and produce more waste than anyone else in the world. And yet we in the United States continue to consume nearly 30% of the planet's resources and services each year, although we account for less than 5% of the world's population. We can choose from more than 40,000 supermarket items, including 200 kinds of cereal. Do we really need all these material products?

Another example of a disconnect between beliefs and behavior is with pollution and cleaning up the environment. The media have put the issue of pollution on the public agenda as the prominence and length of these stories increased dramatically from the 1970s to the 1990s (Ader, 1995). During that same period, air pollution went down about a third, but solid waste went up about 25%. This shows us that as Americans become more concerned about pollution, they have put pressure on the government to clean up the air by regulating manufacturing plants and requiring emission controls on cars. But solid waste, which is under the control of individual citizens through voluntary recycling programs, has not been so successful. This means that individuals are not cutting back on their waste through lower consumption or recycling. Again, many people are looking to the government or someone else to solve their problems.

Changing your behavior to correspond with your beliefs demonstrates commitment to a moral responsibility of following through on your beliefs rather than simply blaming someone else and doing nothing, which has become a popular strategy for many of society's problems. The first step in behavioral change is a realistic assessment of the match between your beliefs and existing behaviors.

You could boycott advertisers, cancel subscriptions, and write letters when you see something you don't like in the media. This action, of course, will have almost no effect on the media themselves, unless large numbers of other people feel as you and do the same things. However, that is not a reason to stop yourself from doing these things. By taking action, you give yourself a sense of gaining control over the media, and this new sense of power will make a difference in your personal life.

9. Make Cross-Channel Comparisons

Although media literacy is a generic concept that spans across all media, there are some special challenges presented by different channels. For example, reading a magazine article requires some skills not required when watching a situation comedy on television. This point, of course, is obvious. But the nature of the differences themselves is not so obvious. To illustrate this, read about a news story on an Internet site, then look for that story in your local newspaper or local TV newscast. Analyze those similarities and differences—are they important?

These differences are especially clear when we consider the interactive media, such as social networking websites and video games. The obvious difference is that with interactive sites, you are not just the receiver of a message but also actively engaged in creating the messages. But there are also other more subtle differences. The more you engage with these sites while you are in the self-reflexive state, the more you will appreciate these differences and even begin to use them better to enhance your media experiences.

10. Become More Skilled at Designing Messages

Many media now not only offer you the chance to create your own messages but require it. The best example of this is when you create a Facebook account, you must design your own pages and you are expected to update them continually. How does your Facebook page compare to those of your friends? How well designed is it aesthetically? Do you have photos and graphics with your text? Would people want to visit your page just to see how well designed it is?

How well designed is your Facebook page from a personal information point of view? What have you decided to reveal about yourself? How will the information on your page affect your friends? Your parents? Future employers?

11. Do Not Take Privacy for Granted

In past generations, an individual's use of the media was a relatively private thing. However, today your media exposures are tracked in meticulous detail, and that information is sold to advertisers or to anyone else interested in your media use habits. When you post a message on your own Web page, write a blog, or send a tweet, you initially have some control over who will see your message. But you soon lose that control when the Web page server, Web browser, blog owner, or Internet service provider can make copies of your messages, repackage them, and sell them to other users of the Internet. Once your message is sent in digital form, it can be endlessly copied, stored, and distributed to anyone. Therefore, before you digitize a message and put it out on the Internet, think about all potential audiences who could read that message—marketers, potential employers, friends, future spouse, children, parents, government officials, and on and on. What impression are you likely to create among all those audiences?

12. Take Personal Responsibility

This may be the hardest to do. We as Americans are fond of placing blame on others, because it allows us to feel that the problem lies elsewhere and therefore it is someone else's problem to fix. For example, let's consider the problem of overeating. The American Medical Association tells us that one third of Americans are obese and another one third are overweight. This would seem to be a personal problem, but most people continue to eat too much and exercise too little. They wait for a government to impose some solution. In spring of 2002, the California legislature was considering the California Childhood Obesity Prevention Act. This act would have essentially banned the sale of carbonated beverages in public schools (Bartholomew, 2002). By summer of 2002, there were already eight states restricting junk food sales in some form, and another dozen states were considering their own legislation. Furthermore, people were filing lawsuits against fast-food chains (Tyre, 2002). Are people really that weak willed that they need the government to ban something before they will stop consuming something harmful? Many people are that weak. Are you one of them?

ILLUSTRATIONS OF MILESTONES

To help make you aware of differences in media literacy development, let's look at some examples of how people can react to different types of media content. Those reactions are best understood when compared to positions on the learning ladders of cognitive, emotional, moral, and aesthetic appreciation.

Learning Ladders

The learning ladders remind us that we can improve our degree of media literacy in four areas: cognitions, emotions, morality, and aesthetics. Progress up each of these ladders is accomplished by mastering the key skills of analysis, evaluation, grouping, induction, deduction, synthesis, and abstracting.

Cognitive Ladder

The first step is awareness, which is the ability to perceive information elements in media messages. This requires the use of analysis. The next step is understanding. This is the ability to perceive the relevant components in any messages and then group them to see how those elements are related to each other. The next step is evaluation, which requires a good deal of contextual information to have templates with which to compare current messages. To do this well, a person needs a great deal of context in the form of elaborate knowledge structures. At the highest step, people are able to appreciate a message by comparing it to their understanding of the constraints and resources of the people who produced the message. The more elaborate a person's knowledge structure is about the media industries, the more the person will be able to appreciate the valuable elements in those messages and discount the other elements.

Emotional Ladder

At low levels of emotional development, people's emotions control them. They get aroused and angry without being able to control those reactions. They experience fear so strongly they cannot shake it. Or they cry at a movie and cannot stop even though they are very embarrassed. Or they are unable to feel any emotions even though they long to do so.

At higher levels of emotional development, people can use the media to shape and control their emotions. For example, we have known for some time that stressed women watch more game and variety shows as well as more television in total, whereas stressed men watch more action and violent programming (D. R. Anderson, Collins, Schmitt, & Jacobvitz, 1996). Depressed people especially use television to escape unpleasant feelings and real-world stimuli that could exacerbate those feelings (Potts & Sanchez, 1994).

If people are aware of what they are doing and then use media to manage moods, this is a sign of high levels of media literacy; that is, people are consciously using the media as a tool to satisfy a particular need. If, in contrast, people are depressed and don't know what to do, they may watch television by default until they are tired enough to fall asleep. This is not an example of people controlling their exposure, so this is evidence of a low level of media literacy.

Moral Ladder

This requires the development of opinions about the ethical nature of media messages. Typically, we infer themes from shows by comparing elements in the portrayals against our personal values.

At the lowest level on this ladder, you construct your moral judgment of a message based purely on intuition or because someone else, whom you respect, gives you the judgment. You see the elements in the show as an undifferentiated mass or blur. You make quick intuitive reactions about whether the show feels right or not, according to your values. If there is a fit, you are happy; if there is no fit, you have a negative reaction. You really can't articulate your reaction very well because it is primarily emotional. For example, if a respected friend tells you that *American Idol* is a morally reprehensible program that belittles people and crushes their dreams, you may simply accept this opinion without watching the show. If you accidentally find yourself exposed to it, you immediately have a negative reaction and turn it off.

At the middle levels of this ladder, you make a distinction among characters on their values and find yourself identifying with those characters who have the same values as you do. If those characters are portrayed positively (rewarded, successful, attractive, etc.), then you are happy.

At the higher levels, you think past individual characters to focus your meaning making at the overall narrative level. You separate characters from their actions so that you might not like a particular character, but you still like his or her actions in terms of fitting in with (or reinforcing) your values. You do not tie your viewing into one character's point of view but try to empathize with many characters so you can vicariously experience the various consequences of actions through the course of the narrative. During a narrative, you are able to assume different moral perspectives to more fully appreciate the action from all participants' points of view.

Aesthetic Appreciation Ladder

This development is oriented toward the cultivation of enhanced enjoyment, understanding, and appreciation of media content. At lower levels on this aesthetic ladder, people have a very simple categorical opinion that the show is either good or bad. Not much reasoning goes into the intuitive decision, so viewers are not able to explain why they like something.

At the middle levels, people are able to distinguish acting from writing and directing. Viewers have the ability to perceive that one of these might be good while another is bad. Also, people are able to compare an artist's performance within this message with past performances and infer a trend in the work.

At higher levels, there is an awareness of media content as a "text" that provides insight into our contemporary culture and ourselves. An awareness of artistry and visual manipulation is also needed. This is an awareness about the processes by which meaning is created through the visual media. What is expected of sophisticated viewers is some degree of self-consciousness about their role as interpreters. This includes the ability to detect artifice (in staged behavior and editing) and to spot authorial presence (style of the producer/director).

Learning about visual conventions is not a prerequisite for interpreting visual messages. However, learning these conventions can help heighten our appreciation of artistry; it also provides viewers with the ability to see through the manipulative uses and ideological implications of visual images. This helps enhance critical viewing.

Can you make a quick assessment of your position on each of these four ladders? If you can, then your awareness is fairly high. But if you are unclear how to position yourself, then think about these ladders as you watch television or read a newspaper. As you reflect on your media exposures as they are happening, you will develop more insights about the levels at which you normally operate. Remember, you will move your positions on the ladders depending on the type of message and your mood. If you are simply looking for fantasy to help you relax, you are likely operating at lower levels. But you may be capable of operating at higher levels at other times. As you are exposed to media messages over a long period of time, develop a sense of where your "home position" is, that is, at what level you usually operate.

Now let's use these learning ladders as templates to examine some examples. This analysis will highlight the important differences across levels of media literacy.

Examples of Levels of Literacy

There are many different reasons why people expose themselves to different kinds of content, and there are many different benefits people can get out of any particular message. Because of this, it is not possible to analyze a message and assume that all those who are exposed will extract the same meaning or have the same experience from it. Below, we explore several examples to illustrate this point.

Reality Series on Television

Reality series as a genre can appeal to viewers of all levels of media literacy. At a low level of literacy, people feel that the characters are real and that the situations actually happened as presented. They cannot explain why they like the characters or the show. Because they don't analyze it, they just let it be.

At a bit higher level of development, people will watch reality series because they feel a personal identity with the characters and enjoy their parasocial interactions with those characters in their world, which is more exciting than their own barren existence. This leads to a strong emotional reaction. Other people will watch reality shows because they want to learn how attractive characters dress and act; this leads to some cognitive processing and evaluation of how characters look and act.

At a higher level, some people view reality series in groups so they can discuss the action as it unfolds. Or they will call their friends later and use the action as an important topic of conversation. These people use the viewing to maintain a community of friends that they would not have without the reality series. This requires a considerable amount of cognitive processing and emotional attachment.

At a higher level still, the viewing takes on an in-depth analysis of the aesthetic and moral elements displayed there. Viewers marvel at the editing that focuses their attention on the most exciting parts of the participants' lives and overdramatizes their mundane problems by blowing them up into huge moral dilemmas.

Facebook Page

At a low level of media literacy, creating a Facebook page entails uploading snapshots a person thinks are cool. The person adds elements and sends messages to maximize the list of friends. Then the person spends a lot of time monitoring the growing list of friends and sending them all short, superficial messages to maintain contact.

At a higher level, users try to improve the artistic quality of their images and sounds so as to impress visitors to their page. They take pride in the increases in hits and friends that are attracted by their updates.

At the highest levels of media literacy, users are very strategic in using Facebook as a tool to create and maintain a personal image to satisfy specific goals, such as reinforcing a few key friendships, attracting a specific kind of romantic partner, or showing off Web skills to a prospective employer. They are very conscious of what they reveal about themselves and make sure those revelations contribute substantially to constructing a positive image over the long term.

Remember that it is not the type of messages you watch or create that make you media literate. Instead, literacy is keyed to what you think and how you feel while you are engaging with the media. The more active and aware you are during those engagements, the more you will get out of the media and the more those experiences will help you achieve your personal goals.

SUMMARY

Media literacy is a perspective. To achieve this perspective, you need to increase your awareness and control. The exercises in this chapter are designed to help you make an assessment (and continue this practice over time) of your awareness about your own knowledge structures, about how your mind works, and about your ability to apply knowledge of the key elements in the effects process.

Media literacy is most clearly diagnosed when we compare people's patterns of thoughts and feelings to the positions on the learning ladders. Keep these ladders in mind during your exposures.

Chapter Resources: To test your knowledge and learn more about the topics discussed in this chapter, visit the Student Study Site at www.sagepub.com/potter6e.

KEEPING UP TO DATE

A good deal of information about media literacy is made available by various groups on their websites. While some of this information is offered for sale in the form of books, reports, CDs, and DVDs for a nominal price, a lot of this material is available for free. I recommend the following websites for media literacy organizations:

Center for Media Education

Center for Media Literacy

Children Now

Citizens for Media Literacy

Media Education Lab

Media Watch

National Association for Family and Community Education

National Association for Media Literacy Education

Parents' Choice

There are also groups providing information about advertising (Adbusters and Children's Advertising Review Unit), news (Fairness and Accuracy in Reporting), and movie and television ratings (Motion Picture Association of America, Inc. and TV Parental Guidelines). For contact information addresses, phone numbers, and Internet addresses for all of these organizations, please see Appendix C.

EXERCISE 21.1

Awareness of Your Knowledge Structures

Below is a list of chapters in this book. Each one presents a knowledge structure on its topic.

1. For each chapter in the book, try to recall the structure of the content.

   a. Can you remember the key idea of that chapter? Can you remember major ideas or sections of the chapter?

   b. Then go back to the first page of that chapter and check your recall. If you remembered the key idea, give yourself 1 point, and give yourself another point for your recall of *each* major idea (the major points in the outline). Thus, your score should be somewhere between 0 and 5 for that chapter.

   c. Enter your score in the left column, which is labeled "Book."

   d. Do the same procedure for each of the chapters listed below.

Book		Add. Exp.
Part 1: Introduction		
		Chapter 1. Living in the Message-Saturated World
		Chapter 2. Media Literacy Approach
Part 2: Audience		
		Chapter 3. Individual Perspective
		Chapter 4. Industry Perspective on Audience
		Chapter 5. Children as a Special Audience
Part 3: Industry		
		Chapter 6. Development of the Mass Media Industries
		Chapter 7. The Economic Game
		Chapter 8. The Current Picture
Part 4: Content		
		Chapter 9. Mass Media Content and Reality
		Chapter 10. News
		Chapter 11. Entertainment
		Chapter 12. Advertising
		Chapter 13. Interactive Media
Part 5: Effects		
		Chapter 14. Proactive Perspective on Media Effects
		Chapter 15. Broadening Our Perspective on Media Effects
Part 6: Confronting the Issues		
		Chapter 16. Who Owns and Controls the Media?
		Chapter 17. Privacy
		Chapter 18. Piracy
		Chapter 19. Violence
		Chapter 20. Sports

(Continued)

(Continued)

2. Next, think about additional reading you undertook after studying each chapter.

   a. For each book or article you read from the "Further Reading" list or from the reference list, give yourself 2 points.

   b. For each additional book you have read relevant to the topic since studying the chapter, give yourself 1 point.

   c. For each significant experience you have had concerning that topic since studying the chapter, give yourself 1 point. (A significant experience is an extended conversation you had with someone on the topic of the chapter, consciously trying to apply the principles in that chapter, etc.)

   d. Record your point totals for each chapter in the column labeled "Add. Exp." for Additional Experiences.

3. Look at the pattern of numbers across the chapters. What does this tell you about the state of your current knowledge structures?

   a. Look down the "Book" column. If you have mostly 4s and 5s, you have a very strong set of knowledge structures. If you have mostly 3s, you have a good beginning set of knowledge structures. If you have some zeros, you need to go back and reorient yourself to the structure of information in those chapters.

   Remember that having strong knowledge structures does not necessarily mean you have a great deal of knowledge on that topic, but it does mean that you are aware of the main ideas, and this will help you acquire additional knowledge much more efficiently.

   b. Look down the "Add. Exp." column. If you have 3s or above, you are showing a strong commitment to extending your knowledge and elaborating your knowledge structures. Look where you have zeros and ask yourself why you were not willing or able to extend your knowledge.

   c. Look at the total pattern of numbers. Were you stronger on certain chapters than others? It is understandable that you may have more interest in particular topics than others. But remember that balance is important. Be proud of your accomplishments—now build on them to overcome your weaknesses.

CHAPTER 22

Key Idea: You have the power to develop media literacy strategies to influence society and other individuals.

Helping Others Increase Media Literacy

In the previous chapter, the focus was on helping yourself increase your level of media literacy. This chapter shifts the focus to helping others increase their levels. The first section of this chapter helps you think about interpersonal settings—relatively small-scale opportunities to help others. Then the second section helps you think about institutional settings—the larger social structures of the educational system and the media industries. Whether you undertake the challenge of working with people one-on-one or on a large scale, it is essential that you first have developed your own media literacy to a relatively high level so that you have something worthwhile to offer other people.

INTERPERSONAL TECHNIQUES

Interpersonal techniques orient you toward helping other individuals with their media literacy. You begin by identifying individuals who might be at risk for negative effects from the media and work with them.

Many people target children. Recall from Chapter 5 that children are a special group because they are still at a low level of development and require more care to shape their media habits and their awareness of potential effects. But remember that everyone could use help in becoming more media literate. Although much of the research I cite in this chapter (as well as the previous chapter) focuses on children, many of those findings are generalizable to people of all ages. Even if you are not a parent concerned about the media literacy of your child, you can still use the principles from these chapters to help your friends, parents, grandparents, and all kinds of other people. So while it might seem that I am only talking to parents in many parts of this chapter, I am really trying to present suggestions that will be useful for anyone concerned about helping others become more media literate.

What the Research Says

After reviewing the literature on media literacy techniques that parents use with their children, Nathanson (2001a) concluded that some of these techniques work, whereas others do not; some work with certain kinds of parents or certain kinds of children; and the effects are varied, ranging from cognitions (learning about television messages), attitudes (developing skepticism for ads and news), perceptions (of television reality), and behaviors (including aggression, viewing habits, and response to advertising). For example, Nathanson (2001b) found that parental attitudes were a strong predictor of what techniques parents used and the effect those techniques would have on their children. Parents with negative attitudes concerning violence on television used active and restrictive mediation, whereas parents with positive attitudes used coviewing. From the child's perspective, restrictive mediation signaled parental disapproval of the content, and coviewing signaled approval of the content; interestingly, children interpreted active mediation as parental approval of the content (Nathanson, 2001b).

Rules

There is a difference of opinion about the effectiveness of restrictive mediation. Desmond, Singer, Singer, Calam, and Colimore (1985) argue that it has been found to be a useful technique. In contrast, Nathanson (2002) found that restrictive mediation was related to less positive attitudes toward parents, more positive attitudes toward the content, and more viewing of the content with friends. This appears to be the opposite of what parents intend as an outcome of using this technique. Nathanson says, "Unfortunately, parents' good intentions in using restrictive mediation may actually contribute to the harmful outcomes parents wished to prevent in the first place" (p. 221).

Coviewing

Coviewing, like restrictive mediation, has had mixed results in the research literature. Coviewing has also been associated with negative outcomes such as coming to believe that television characters are like real-world people (Messaris & Kerr, 1984) and learning aggression from violent television (Nathanson, 1999). Also, Nathanson (2002) found that coviewing was related to more positive attitudes toward viewing of television violence and sex. These were interpreted as unintended effects. Nathanson concludes that "parents' consistent pattern of coviewing objectionable television with their adolescents encourages the youngsters to develop similar media habits" (p. 223).

Coviewing has been shown to have positive outcomes, such as increasing the learning of educational content (Salomon, 1977). Children who coview with their parents say they enjoy the programs more (Nathanson, 2001b). However, even when positive effects are found, they are usually fairly weak. For example, Austin and Pinkleton (2001) found that although coviewing had a positive effect on political socialization, other factors, such as skepticism and negative mediation, had more impact.

Peers are also influential during the adolescent years. Nathanson (2001c) found that peer mediation is more influential than parental mediation during adolescence. Specifically, she found that peer mediation promotes more of an orientation toward antisocial behavior, which then leads to aggression. Thus, the positive influence of parental mediation serves to reduce aggressive behavior, but the negative influence of peer mediation serves to increase it.

Active Mediation

Active mediation techniques have been found useful in helping children reduce unwanted effects from viewing television (Austin, 1993; Nathanson & Cantor, 2000; Nathanson & Yang, 2003). Active mediation seems to work better than more punitive techniques. Parents who try to reason with their children while disciplining them are more effective in reducing the harmful effects of exposure to violence than those parents who use physical punishment (Singer, Singer, & Rapaczynski, 1984).

Children who experience active mediation in general are less vulnerable to negative effects of all kinds—cognitive, attitudinal, emotional, and behavioral. As for cognitive effects, active mediation has been found to be successful in teaching children to be more skeptical toward television news (Austin, 1993) and creating better understanding of television plots (Desmond et al., 1985). With children, parental involvement in media exposure serves to influence learning. Children increase their understanding and recall of both central and incidental program content when adults provide comments to guide their children's attention and understanding during viewing. When parents actively mediate during television viewing, they can influence their children's interpretations (Austin, 1993). Parents can make viewing active for their children by continually asking questions about meaning and structure, such as, "Who did what to whom?" and "Why?" This gets them practicing making connections.

As for attitudes, active mediation has been found to reduce perceptions of the reality of television messages (Messaris & Kerr, 1984), even with television news (Austin, 1993), and reduce negative cultivation effects (Rothschild & Morgan, 1987). Nathanson and Botta (2003) reported the results of a survey of adolescents and their parents which found that when parents commented on body images of characters on television, adolescents were more likely to process the images more and experience negative emotions more. These negative emotions had an impact on behaviors in the form of unhealthy eating or eating disorders.

Active mediation has been helpful in shaping emotional responses to media. Cantor and Wilson (1984) found that negative emotional responses to frightening films could be allayed with active mediation, at least with older children (older than 9 years old). Cantor (2001) provides some good advice for parents of children who are experiencing negative emotional effects from the media, especially horror content. Also, Hoffner (1997) says that prior knowledge of a happy outcome can reduce fear for some children.

These techniques can move beyond cognitive aspects and can also include emotional and behavioral aspects. Children who experience emotional media messages when they are among peers or adults will exhibit a reduced likelihood and intensity of immediate emotional effects, especially fear effects from scary movies. Also, the probability of a child behaving aggressively when watching violence can be reduced if adults verbalize comments and interpretations while observing with the child—such as pointing out unrealistic and inappropriate behavior in programs.

Children are likely to model their behavior after attractive characters they see in the media. This modeling can be shaped by interpersonal techniques. For example, Austin and Meili (1995) found that children use their emotion and logic to develop expectations about alcohol use in the real world when they see alcohol used by characters on television. When children rely on both real life and televised sources of information, children are more likely to develop skepticism about television portrayals of alcohol use when they rely on parents as primary sources of information and behavioral modeling.

As for behavior, active mediation has been found to lower levels of aggression (Corder-Bolz, 1980; Grusec, 1973; Hicks, 1968; Nathanson, 1999; Nathanson & Cantor, 2000; Singer et al., 1984) and reduce the influence of advertising (Reid, 1979).

Nathanson (2001c) found that peer mediation was more effective than parental mediation. She found that peer mediation led to more positive orientations toward antisocial television, which in turn led to greater aggression. Of course, the intention of parental mediation is to inhibit negative media effects, but peer mediation facilitates harmful outcomes.

The success of mediation techniques is also tied to the type of person who is the target. For example, Nathanson and Yang (2003) demonstrated that certain techniques worked well with younger children (ages 5–8). These techniques focused on emphasizing the factually inaccurate nature of a show as well as emphasizing how socially unrealistic the portrayals were. But these techniques were not found to work well with older children (ages 9–12). The authors speculated that perhaps the older children already understood those lessons and did not want to hear a lecture, feeling that such advice was pedantic or condescending.

Also, some techniques work better with one gender. For example, Nathanson and Cantor (2000) tested a mediation technique of getting children to become involved with victims of violence in cartoons rather than the aggressors. This worked with boys but not girls—that is, it was successful in preventing boys from increasing their aggressive behavior subsequent to viewing the violence in the cartoon.

Mediation works better when parents are more active during television viewing (Austin, 1993). Parents need to ask questions continually and engage their children in discussions about the meaning of actions. Parents need to explain the meaning of words, pictures, narratives, and so on.

Emotional reactions of children can be controlled through the use of both cognitive as well as noncognitive techniques. For example, Cantor (2001), who is an expert on children's fright reactions to horror shows in the media, explains that, in general, preschool children

benefit more from noncognitive than cognitive techniques. Among elementary school children, both types of techniques work well, but children prefer the cognitive techniques. Cognitive techniques rely on a person verbally casting the threat in a different light. "When dealing with fantasy depictions, the most typical cognitive strategy seems to be to provide an explanation focusing on the unreality of the situation" (p. 215). In contrast, noncognitive techniques "do not involve the processing of verbal information and appear to be relatively automatic" (p. 214). One noncognitive technique is visual desensitization, which involves showing a person repeated images that are sequenced to build from nonthreatening to very threatening depictions so the person is gradually desensitized. Also, Desmond (1997) provides some detailed suggestions about how parents can do things in their homes to increase the media literacy of their children, particularly to help them with their perceptions of reality, and to increase their knowledge about production techniques and the commercial nature of the media.

Role modeling has been found to be a successful technique. Oftentimes, children will select their own role models, but parents in active mediation can influence the models children choose and sensitize them to certain characteristics of those characters that make them good role models. Children are likely to model their behavior after attractive characters they see in the media. This modeling can be shaped by interpersonal techniques, especially from parents themselves as good role models (Austin & Meili, 1995; Hogan, 2001; M. D. Slater & Rouner, 2002). For example, Austin and Meili (1995) found that children use their emotion and logic to develop expectations about alcohol use in the real world when they see alcohol used by characters on television.

M. D. Slater and Rouner (2002) observe that social cognitive theory has been a useful explanation for the effectiveness of educational messages in entertainment programs because of the role modeling. However, they argue that the elaboration likelihood model is an additional explanation, especially for those people who do not have role models on shows; these people are likely to have low involvement, which makes them even more susceptible to the influence of such messages. Thus, if these people were highly involved and were likely to argue against the messages, their low involvement would defuse the counterarguments.

Boomerang

There are examples in the research literature where educators have designed interventions designed to increase the media literacy of the study's participants (usually children), and when they analyze their results, they find that the level of media literacy has declined rather than improved. This is known as a boomerang effect. An example of this effect was found by Byrne (2009), who ran an experiment on children in the fourth and fifth grades in an attempt to test how well her intervention could help children avoid behaving aggressively after being exposed to violence in the media. She had two interventions and a control group. One intervention consisted of an instructional lesson about not behaving aggressively. A second intervention was the same as the first but also included a cognitive activity. Children who experienced only the instructional lesson actually increased their willingness to use aggressive behavior, and this effect lasted over time—thus this treatment boomeranged. But the treatment with the lesson and the cognitive activity resulted in a reduction of willingness to use aggression, so it was successful. The lesson here is that people who are sincerely motivated to help others increase their media literacy may end up doing more harm than good.

What Can You Do?

There seem to be three keys to helping others become more media literate. The first key is to be positive and constructive. If you want to be successful in helping others, you must show them that you have their best interests in mind and that you are not trying to help for some ulterior motive, like exercising power over them.

A second key is to be balanced. You should exhibit an attitude about the media that balances criticism with appreciation. There are some people who drive around town with a bumper sticker that says "Kill Your TV." It is hard to take those people seriously because they do not seem to realize the enormous positive influence that television has exercised on our culture. Trying to make people more media literate by only criticizing the media is like trying to make people healthy by only forcing bad-tasting medicine on them. Media exposures can be fun, so help people have more fun and increase the ways they can appreciate media messages. Then help people be more analytical about media messages so they can identify the elements that warrant criticism. When parents have only a negative, critical attitude about the media, rules become restrictive and are regarded as arbitrary by children. Many children fail to understand why certain kinds of content are bad for them when that content is fun and fulfills their needs. These children are likely to subvert their parents' restrictions by continuing with exposures they find enjoyable.

A third key is to involve your children's cognitive processes and help them get better at thinking for themselves, especially as children grow older. If you want children to learn that certain content is harmful to them, you need to avoid simply telling them that. Instead, you need to help them analyze the content and see for themselves the silliness, the manipulation, or the harm.

When you become a parent, you will need to be especially careful in monitoring your children's experience with two types of messages. One type of message is the advertisement for food. A great deal of advertising of unhealthy foods to children in the United States (R. Page & Brewster, 2007) and other countries (M. Roberts & Pettigrew, 2007) uses very sophisticated appeals that exaggerate health claims and imply that the advertised foods have the ability to enhance popularity, performance, and mood. These ads can have a detrimental influence on children who are not media literate enough to analyze their claims and find many of them to be silly or false. Studies have found that along with genetics and reduced rates of physical activity, the flood of advertising for high-calorie, low-nutrition foods leads to unhealthy eating and weight gain. In 2005, after criticism of the U.S. food industry for advertising's role in childhood obesity, national advertisers announced new policies to reduce children's exposure to ads for unhealthy foods. However, a content analysis conducted on television food advertisements aired just before and one year after these announcements found very few changes in food advertising seen by children (Warren, Wicks, & Wicks, 2007). And it is not likely that this type of advertising will become more responsible or will be reduced, especially since there is such a huge market for these foods. So the spiral will continue with more unhealthy foods being advertised, leading to more consumption of unhealthy foods, which leads food companies to produce more of this type of product to satisfy the growing market. The best hope you have to break this spiral is to teach your children to take responsibility for their own actions and not to blame others, such as the government for lack of regulation, the food providers for providing what the market demands, or advertisers. When you blame others, the best that you can hope for is that those other people will change their practices. When you take responsibility for your own actions, you can move toward a more healthy lifestyle immediately. When we realize that the percentage of overweight and obese children in the United States has more than tripled over the past 30 years (Warren et al., 2007), we can see that we need more children to view themselves less as victims of outside forces and more as people in control of their own lives.

A second type of special concern for parents should be with Internet messages. The Internet provides easy access for children to encounter all kinds of messages that are

potentially harmful to them; I will focus your attention on three types in particular. One type of harmful message is that which contains material such as sexual matter and hate speech. Children's cognitive, emotional, and moral reasoning abilities are not developed well enough for them to process these messages in a way that protects them from harm. A second type of potentially harmful message includes communications from strangers who are trying to develop inappropriate relationships. The third type of message from which your children needs protection is from advertisers and others who solicit private information from your child.

Therefore, parents need to be careful in monitoring what sites their children visit. Parents need to tell their children never to give out any identifying information, such as an address, phone number, school name, and so forth, and never allow a child to arrange a face-to-face meeting with someone online. Parents who find information that may be illegal (such as child pornography or hate speech) should report it to authorities. Parents should build skepticism in their children because people on the Internet may not be who they claim to be; people can make up a persona in terms of gender, age, background, and so on. Parents should set time rules of access; too much contact can lead to addiction. And finally, surfing the Internet can be a fun activity for all family members to do together.

PUBLIC EDUCATION

This section shifts our attention to a more macro level. First, I briefly show the fragmentary nature of media literacy curricula in this country, then examine the barriers that prevent a more unified approach to media education. This section then concludes with a critique of curriculum concerns and recommendations.

Current Situation

Critics have observed that the United States lags behind many other countries in developing media literacy courses and curricula in public schools (J. A. Brown, 1991, 1998, 2001; Considine, 1997; Davies, 1997; Kubey, 1997; Piette & Giroux, 1997; Sizer, 1995). They point to a long list of countries that are far ahead of the United States with media literacy curricula. These countries include Australia, Canada, Great Britain, South Africa, Scandinavia, Russia, and Israel, as well as many other countries in Europe, South America, and Asia (J. A. Brown, 1991; Piette & Giroux, 1997). For example, Australia has had mandated media education from kindergarten to 12th grade since the mid-1990s. This curriculum stresses aesthetics and semiotics, with a liberal humanist approach to the popular arts (J. A. Brown, 1998).

In the United Kingdom and some Latin American countries, empowerment of media consumers is paramount, often focusing on industry control through corporate and governmental hegemony. Media education there stresses "representational" and oppositional ideologies, power, and politics and ways to participate in mainstream media or construct alternative media outlets (J. A. Brown, 1998, p. 45). This gap is getting smaller as many U.S. states have been enacting guidelines for media literacy (see Frank Baker's website listed in the Keeping Up to Date section at the end of this chapter).

Critics point out that the relative lack of attention to media education in the United States is a serious problem because the United States is the most media-saturated country in the world. More time and money are spent on media consumption in this country than any other country in the world, yet our educational system virtually ignores media education (Sizer, 1995). This is not to say that there are no media literacy efforts in America's schools; however, their existence is rare and largely unsupported by the institution of education. For example, J. A. Brown (2001) characterizes the teaching of media literacy in this country as "isolated teachers introduced mass media topics into their classrooms, usually within the context of traditional content such as English or history social studies" (p. 683). He continued, "Schedules already crowded with curricular mandates had no time for yet another addition, so whatever media study could be introduced was typically integrated into already existing courses" (p. 683).

Some states have been discussing media literacy and trying to get initiatives going. Kubey (1998) reports that there have been "significant statewide initiatives" in New Mexico and North Carolina, with "noteworthy developments" in Wisconsin and Minnesota. A few years ago, Hobbs (1998) reported that media literacy concepts were included in the curriculum frameworks in more than 15 states. And this is growing as "ongoing efforts are in place in many U.S. school districts. Interest in media education is even growing among mainstream education organizations and health professionals, including the National Association of Secondary School Principals and the American Academy of Pediatrics" (Hobbs, 1998, p. 24). Initiatives are growing, but we need to monitor whether this talk about the importance of media literacy and its inclusion in mission statements translates into meaningful implementation.

Barriers

Why is there so little sustained effort at developing and implementing media literacy curricula in the United States while there are many good efforts in other countries? There appear to be many obstacles for further development of media literacy (for a more complete treatment, see J. A. Brown, 2001; Considine, 1997; Davies, 1997; Kubey, 1997).

Arguably, the most critical obstacle is the lack of centralized decision making concerning education in the United States. J. A. Brown (1998) points out that curriculum decisions are spread out over 15,000 school districts, each with its own school board and administrators. Kubey (1990) elaborates on this argument by pointing out that the United States is a huge country with a highly diversified population and no central governmental policy on media literacy to pull things together. Also, only 4% of educational expenditures in the United States come from the federal government (Kubey, 1998). Thus, in this country, the power for curriculum decisions lies at the state and especially local levels. Each of these decision-making bodies has its mix of personalities, needs, and political agendas.

Not paying attention to the special circumstances in each school's culture has been credited in large part for the failure of media literacy efforts that were tried in the 1970s (J. A. Anderson, 1983). Hobbs (1998) extends this point by saying, "Media literacy initiatives have been most successful in school communities where teachers, parents and students have a shared, common vision about their love-hate relationship with media culture" (p. 23). J. A. Brown (1998) says, "If media literacy studies are to survive and grow, administrators in school systems and at individual schools must endorse and support them. They should not be left wholly dependent on the initiative and energy of isolated teachers" (p. 52). Brown calls for a more holistic and continuing approach. "To succeed, a curricular program of media literacy must be developed through collaboration among teachers, administrators, specialists, and parents, who together must build it into the systematic education process. Media study should not be a mere appendage of a random elective course, nor should media technology be used merely as a tool or aid to teach other subjects. That means developing studies geared to the participants' successive levels of cognitive development based on educational and behavioral research findings. It also means continuing and integrating studies into successive grade levels through the school years" (p. 52).

But all this comes with a high cost. Other curricula must be replaced with the media literacy one. Teachers need significant training, and this will require reduced teaching loads. Parents will need to become much more involved. It also requires a sustained commitment that includes substantial training of media literacy teachers. Hobbs (1998) says, "The most successful efforts to include media literacy in schools have taken 2 or more years of staff development to build a clearly defined understanding of the concept as it relates to classroom practice among a substantial number of teachers and school leaders within a school district" (pp. 23–24).

Then once trained, the teachers need to be supported continually by the institution rather than left on their own. Hobbs (1998) explains that a study of teacher performance in Great Britain yielded depressing results. Among the teachers who completed training in media literacy education, about 40% ended up doing nothing, 25% did something moderately well, 10% did something creatively exceptional, and the remaining 25% did something embarrassing, dangerous, or just a waste of time.

Unless resources are provided, there are significant barriers to implementation. For example, one recent study reports that although most high school teachers believe the study of media is important, 40% did not teach it at all because of constraints on time and curriculum space (cited in J. A. Brown, 2001). The same pattern was found in Maryland with language arts teachers; once again, the teachers regarded media literacy as important to teach, but the lack of training, materials, and time prevented many from teaching it (Koziol, 1989). J. A. Brown (2001) observed that few teachers receive training to deal with the challenge of teaching media literacy either in their college degree programs or in workshops for teacher certification. Most teachers, however, do feel that they are qualified to teach media literacy, even though only about one third had any training.

Curriculum designers often look to media literacy scholars for guidance. However, there is the lack of agreement among scholars about what media literacy is and what its goals should be (see Chapter 2). Two of the more pressing definitional issues when it comes to curriculum design are tone and texts. Regarding tone, J. A. Brown (1991) complains that "many media workshops and curricula are protectionist and defensive. They seek to inoculate consumers against blandishments of images and messages of media entertainment, news, and advertising" (p. 45). As for texts, Hobbs (1998) observes that although media texts have always been essential in education, rarely are those texts "considered beyond their function as conveyers of information" (p. 25). They need to be the objects of inquiry (Kress, 1992). Students need to analyze the people and corporations who produce and disseminate those texts and understand their motives. Also, the texts themselves need to be analyzed for what they leave out, how they are structured, and their basis for claims from both an aesthetic and a moral perspective.

This diversity of opinion gets magnified as we move out to consumer activists, teachers, and school administrators. There is also a wide variety of opinion concerning the composition of a media literacy curriculum, what should be taught, how it should be taught, and how the effect of the teaching should be assessed. The good thing about this diversity is that it provides a wide range of ideas for instruction and a variety of curriculum models to the many different school systems in the United States. If most of the school systems were entrepreneurial and willing to search out the techniques that would fit the special culture in their district, then this variety would pay big dividends. But most school districts are very conservative about change. The teachers and administrators already feel they are asked to cover too many topics, so they cannot add another one without a great deal of debate.

The diversity of ideas among scholars appears more as an academic debate than as a convincing argument to shift resources. For scholars to present a convincing argument, they must present a perspective that integrates the best thinking into a clear set of principles that can guide their decision making in three key issues: curriculum design, teaching, and assessment.

What You Can Do

When you become a parent, you can insist that your school district provide some sort of media education. You might have to begin small by volunteering in your child's classroom. Develop some mini-instructional units based on your own knowledge about media literacy. Typically, children will really like these sessions because such sessions involve them in something they use every day. If your mini-units work well, students will talk about them, and other students will create a demand for similar instruction. By beginning small, you can grow a demand locally in your child's school.

SOCIETAL TECHNIQUES

With societal techniques, the focus is on exerting pressure on a particular part of the industry, the government, or some institution to increase public awareness about a problem or to bring about some particular change. To do this successfully, you will first need a strategy supported by a great deal of commitment. Your strategy will require many years of effort to effect a change. Also, it requires money. Often, people will start a PAC (political action committee) or a consulting firm that will then apply for grants to support its work.

Contacts are also extremely important. By linking up with other powerful people and groups, you could become part of something that could potentially have enough power to get the attention of the large media companies. Look at the list of citizen action groups in Appendix C. Contact those that are of most interest to you and ask them to send you information.

Changing media industry practices or content is very difficult. Remember that the industries have grown and developed in response to demands from the public. If an industry or a vehicle does not respond well to the demand, it loses money. Successful CEOs have confidence that their decisions will result in greater profits. So don't expect change when you ask them to ignore their experience and to change their practices when they might risk losing millions of dollars by making those changes you suggest. This is why the public concern about television violence has resulted in so little change over the past 50 years. In explaining this nonaction, Stuart Fishoff (1988), a psychologist who writes for television and movies, said,

> Let's suppose the results, the conclusions were incontrovertible—TV and film modeling of aggression and other anti-social values has significant effects on the viewing audience. Would it really make any difference to the gate keepers of media fare in Hollywood and New York? I submit the answer is not on your life! (p. 3)

He cites an important principle in psychology for his conclusion,

> The more far-reaching and costly the consequences of accepting a message, the more facts needed before an audience will be persuaded as to the accuracy of the message—and the more energy will be expended in denigrating both the message and the messenger in order to maintain existing belief. (p. 3)

Therefore, the media industries have been very slow in acknowledging the value of any of the research on negative media effects while using the research on positive effects to show that they are acting responsibly. This attitude has outraged many media critics and stimulated many average citizens to want to do something to remedy the problem.

Another example of a societal technique is the concern over protecting very young children from the effects of television advertising. In the early 1970s, some consumer groups were formed to protect children from what was being seen as abuses by broadcasters. Prominent among these groups was Action for Children's Television, which found examples of children's programs that contained as many as 16 minutes of ads per hour—far above the industry's self-imposed limit of 9.5 minutes. And the products advertised were largely nonnutritious snacks and deceptively presented toys. Many products were being pitched by characters from the programs, thus making the distinction between the show and the ad indecipherable, especially for young children.

This pressure influenced the Federal Trade Commission (FTC) to hold hearings throughout the 1970s. The FTC considered banning certain types of ads. But in the end, the FTC concluded that although there was evidence that television advertising created risks for children, no practical effective remedies were open to federal policy making. The primary problems were determining who is a child; that is, at what age is a person no longer a child? Also, there was the fear that regulating advertising on children's television might cause broadcasters to stop programming for children.

Another example of a societal strategy took place in the fall of 1995, when some well-known political figures began a campaign to clean up talk shows on television. Headed by former Education Secretary William Bennett, Senator Joseph Lieberman (D-Conn.), and Senator Sam Nunn (D-Ga.), the campaign did not seek regulation of television content. Instead, it sought to influence public opinion and to shame certain television producers by characterizing the content of daytime talk shows as "lethal." These critics acknowledged that some of the 20 nationally syndicated talk shows dealt with serious issues of domestic abuse, drug abuse, and racism in a constructive way that enlightens viewers. But they pointed out that some shows had a circus atmosphere that included shouting matches, fistfights, foul language, and audience members yelling out unqualified advice. As an example of sleaze, they cited examples from the *Sally Jesse Raphael* show that featured girls who were sexually active at the age of 10 and from *Jerry Springer*, including a show about a 17-year-old who had four children with her 71-year-old husband, whom she called "Dad" (Hancock, 1995).

There are many other examples of people and groups who have tried to influence public awareness of problems with media content and to bring about change in the media industries. These efforts have been more successful in raising public consciousness about these problems than they have been in bringing about changes in programming. This leaves us with the following question: Should we continue to try? The answer, of course, is yes.

With societal techniques, we should have modest expectations for what it means to have a successful societal strategy. And we need to have a long timeframe. Societal change of this type moves at glacial speed—it takes decades to see change. But remember that a glacier is exerting constant pressure, and change is happening constantly—but we can't see it happening because it is happening very slowly. The same is true with societal campaigns. If we exert constant pressure, we will eventually be able to perceive changes. If you are impatient and want to see change happen more quickly, then try some interpersonal and personal techniques.

SUMMARY

This book is now ending. What kind of an effect have you let it have on you? Did you read it critically by analyzing the information and arguments? Did you compare and contrast the points made here with your existing knowledge structures? Did you evaluate my arguments and positions, agreeing with some and disagreeing with others? Did you synthesize the information you found most useful into your own perspective on media literacy and your own set of techniques to achieve that perspective? If you answered yes to these questions, then you have reacted well cognitively to the book. The key to a high-quality cognitive reaction is not whether you agree with me and accept all this information. Instead, the key is that your mind was continually active as you read the book.

Did you have some strong emotional reactions while reading the book? For example, did you get upset with some of the information or arguments? Do you feel challenged and motivated to become more media literate? If you answered yes to these questions, then you have reacted well emotionally to the book. The key to a high-quality emotional reaction is not whether you have positive feelings about me or about the book. Instead, the key is that you were able to let your emotions become engaged by hating parts of the book and loving others.

Did you take moral positions throughout the book? For example, did you develop a sense of what is right with our culture (and what is wrong) because of the media? Did you make a strong commitment to yourself to do certain things to help yourself and others? If you answered yes to these questions, then you have reacted well morally to the book. The key to a high-quality moral reaction is not whether you agree with my positions. Instead, the key is that you are able to perceive a sense of right and wrong about certain conditions and to take a stand for yourself.

Finally, were you aware of aesthetic reactions to the book? Were there times when you appreciated the way I structured a chapter or the way I illuminated an important point? Did you find certain examples useful and creative? Did you feel that certain sections could have been written better? If you were able to answer these questions, then you were sensitive to the aesthetic features of the book. I, of course, hope that your aesthetic reactions were favorable. But whether favorable or not, the more aesthetic reactions you had and the more aesthetic awareness you exercised, the better for your media literacy development.

Most important, I hope you can see that you have achieved a significant degree of media literacy. You have many useful knowledge structures and many useful skills. As you continue developing these knowledge structures and skills, remember to be aware of what you are doing and stay in control of your progress. And make it fun!

Chapter Resources: To test your knowledge and learn more about the topics discussed in this chapter, visit the Student Study Site at www.sagepub.com/potter6e.

KEEPING UP TO DATE

http://www.frankwbaker.com/state_lit.htm

This website offers a comprehensive list of educational standards that relate to elements of media literacy for all 50 states in the United States.

EXERCISE 22.1

Fantasizing About Your Societal Strategy

Let's say that next year, you win $10 million in the lottery. After you pay your taxes, pay off all of your current debts, and splurge on all sorts of luxuries, you still have $3 million left over. So you decide to do something more worthwhile with your money and your life—you decide to set up a citizen action group that will help people become more media literate and change some of the things in society. Think about techniques as you address the following issues.

1. *Goals:* What would the goals be for your organization?

   a. List some interpersonal goals you would want to achieve.

   b. List some societal goals you would like to achieve.

2. *Targets*

   a. To reach those goals set above, which groups would you target for change (see Appendix C)? List those targets.

   b. For each target, what specifically would you want them to change?

3. *Techniques:* How would you stimulate that change?

   a. What things would you do to get the people in your targets to understand your point of view?

   b. What things would you do to get the people in your targets to change their behaviors?

4. *Barriers:* What do you think would be the key barriers that might prevent you from achieving your goals?

Appendix A

Profiles of the Mass Media Industries

This appendix presents a profile of each of the nine mass media industries illuminated in Part 4 of the book. Each profile begins with key indicators showing how that mass media industry has developed according to the life cycle metaphor. Notice that some of those industries have not gone through all five stages. The industries are treated in the following order, which roughly corresponds to their ages:

1. Book
2. Newspaper
3. Magazine
4. Film
5. Recording
6. Radio
7. Broadcast television
8. Cable television
9. Computers/Internet

Before we get started on these profiles, I need to clarify the distinction between a vehicle and a company. For example, *Time* magazine is one such vehicle. *Time* publishes 52 weekly issues each year, but the issues are not the same as the vehicle. Also, we need to make a distinction between the company that publishes the vehicle and the vehicle itself. Time Warner is the company that publishes *Time* magazine, but Time Warner also publishes many other magazine vehicles such as *Money, Discover,* and *Fortune.* So when we talk about magazines, we must be clear about whether we are referring to the media channel (of all magazines), a vehicle (which is a title of a single magazine), an issue (which is the set of stapled pages laying on your coffee table), or the company (which usually owns and publishes several vehicles).

1. BOOK INDUSTRY

Innovation Stage

- The key technological innovation for book publishing—as well as all of the print media—was the invention of moveable type by Gutenberg in the mid-1400s.
- Book publishing was already well developed when the United States was first colonized. However, until the 19th century, books were not a mass medium because they were purchased and read by only the educated and the affluent.
- During the late 1800s, some entrepreneurs recognized that the reading literacy rate was relatively high, given the effects of compulsory education. They began selling paperback books that were affordable to the masses.
- Books really started developing into a mass medium about 1860, when the Beadle brothers (Irwin and Erastus) began publishing dime novels. Within 5 years of startup, they had sold more than 4 million volumes. In the 1930s, paperback books were introduced and now account for more than 1 million volumes sold per day.

Penetration Stage

- By 1900, public schools were widespread, and reading literacy was commonplace.
- Large publishing houses were being established, so many more books were being published and marketed, thus bringing the unit price down so that books were affordable to more of the general population.

Peak Stage

- The book publishing industry has never reached a peak; that is, it has yet to achieve dominance among the mass media.

Adaptation Stage

- The book industry has adapted to competition from other mass media by becoming niche oriented. Many publishers sell books to only one niche, such as college-level science texts, library reference books, religious books, children's mystery novels, and so on.
- There has been a strong trend toward concentration in the bookstore segment of the industry. In 1958, companies that owned more than one bookstore (chains) accounted for only 28% of all sales, and there were no chains with more than 50 stores. Now there are chains such as Barnes & Noble, which owns more than 1,000 bookstores. Chain-owned bookstores now generate more than two thirds of all the revenue in the book industry.
- Consolidation has been taking place in book publishing, although the deals are not as big as with mergers of film and television companies. For example, in the mid-1990s, The Penguin Group acquired a U.S. subsidiary of MCA for

$336 million. The Penguin Group publishes primarily classics and reference-type books (Lyall, 1996). The Putnam Berkley Group is known for its successful best sellers from authors such as Tom Clancy, Dick Francis, Patricia Cornwell, and Amy Tan. The merged company accounted for about 12% of all book sales in the United States.

Current Profile

- *Size:* There has been a growth in book publishers from about 20,000 in the later 1990s to more than 78,000 in the world today. Almost all of these book publishers are small—putting out only one to four titles a year (Teague, 2004).
  - The industry is now producing about 300,000 new books and editions per year. The number of titles published each year grew steadily from about 11,000 titles published in 1950 to 68,000 in 1996 and has increased dramatically each year since.
  - There are about 20,000 bookstores in the United States, but this number has been decreasing as small independent bookstores go out of business with competition from the large chains (like Barnes & Noble and Books-A-Million) and from Internet book sellers like Amazon.com. Online bookstores account for about 8% of all book sales annually. Also, there are 175 book clubs.
  - There are about 220,000 jobs in book publishing, book selling, and related fields (Mogel, 2000).
- *Revenue:* The book industry now has an annual revenue of about $30 billion on sales of about 2 billion books each year.
  - The market is segmented, with only about 24% of sales going to trade

books (hardbound and paperback books aimed at general readers such as books on hobbies, travel, self-help, cooking, and fiction). Another 18% is professional (to particular occupational groups), and elementary/high school textbooks and college texts each account for 14%. Mass-market paperbacks account for about 6% of sales.

○ Most of the books are sold through retail bookstores. Most of the sales in this segment are in the very large chains such as Barnes & Noble.

- *Expenses:* Many elements go into the expense of book publishing. Let's take a typical example of a hardbound trade book that lists for $19.95 in a retail bookstore. When this sells, the store keeps about 48% for its own expenses and profit and sends the remaining $10.37 to the publisher. It costs the publisher about $2.00 to manufacture the physical copy of the book (composition, typesetting, jacket design, paper, ink, printing, binding, etc.). Another $3.00 is for overhead, which includes the expense of editors, office staff, marketing, and so on. The author gets about $2.00 in royalties. The remaining $3.37 is profit unless the stores return the unsold copies—a common practice—and wipe out the potential profit.

- *Risk:* Only one book in five is successful, meaning it makes money for the publisher after all the expenses and returns are subtracted from sales. The small number of successful books, in essence, subsidizes the industry and makes it possible for publishers to take chances on all sorts of "risky" books and new authors. Out of the 68,000 new book titles published each year, well under 1% make it onto any

best-seller list. For example, in 1997, only 88 fiction titles made the lists; 85% of these books were written by authors who had been on the list before (Gulbransen, 1998a). Because of the high risk, publishers aggressively use the marketing concept; that is, they search for books they think the public wants instead of books they think are the best from a writing or education point of view. Publishers believe the public likes books on scandal, celebrities, cooking, self-help, and dieting; this is why there are so many books published on these topics each year.

- *Concentration:* Out of the 2,700 book publishers in the United States, 1,200 do not publish as many as five books a year. The top eight companies typically generate half the revenues (Albarran, 2002). Book publishing is a segmented field, with different sets of publishers specializing in certain submarkets. But even within these submarkets, there is a trend toward concentration. For example, in mass-market paperback publishing, the top seven firms account for more than 80% of all sales. As for the best-seller list, six major publishers (Random, Simon & Schuster, Penguin Putnam, Bantam Doubleday and Dell, HarperCollins, Time Warner) typically account for about 85% of the hardcover slots and 83% of the paperback slots. If you add in the titles of six other smaller houses, you account for 98% of all best sellers (Gulbransen, 1998a, 1998b).

- *Recent adaptations:* Book publishers have been looking for shorter and shorter books because the reading public has had its attention span reduced by years of TV viewing

(A. Beam, 2002). It used to be that the typical book was 75,000 words, which made about 300 printed pages, but now best sellers are much shorter. For example, *Who Moved My Cheese?* by Ken Blanchard and Spencer Johnson was only 77 pages.

The Internet is changing the way books are published and distributed. Now, when a publisher comes out with a new book, it is frequently offered in both paper and electronic form. Called e-books, these electronic books are handheld, battery-powered devices where the words appear on a screen rather than a paper page. Introduced in 1998, fewer than 10,000 books were sold that first year. By the following year, there were more than 1,500 fiction and nonfiction titles available (Stroh, 1999). By 2011, Amazon.com was selling more e-books than paperbacks, and it was projected that by 2014, e-books would be outselling print books of all kinds (B. Page, 2011).

Bookstores are going online on the Web. Amazon.com began in July 1995 and reached $15 million in sales the next year; however, its costs were $20 million that year. In May 1997, Barnes & Noble went online to add another revenue stream to its successful **brick-and-mortar stores.** By 2010, Barnes & Noble was closing its brick-and-mortar stores and moving all its marketing onto the Internet.

Self-Publishing

For a relatively small price, an individual can publish his or her own book with desktop software, then market it through an Internet website. Books that are published initially or exclusively online are called e-books. Some of these books are never printed by the publisher but instead are sold in electronic form to be downloaded by the buyer; these are called d-books.

2. NEWSPAPER INDUSTRY

Innovation Stage

- The innovation stage of newspapers dates back to before the United States was formed. Some key technological developments took place in Europe beginning in the 1400s. Also, in the 1600s, entrepreneurs set up newspaper publishing businesses and home delivery distribution systems.
- In the American colonies, publishers typically started newspapers not to make money but to shape political opinion. These early newspapers were more like propaganda leaflets, and each had a very small circulation. By 1776, there were already 30 weekly newspapers in the colonies, and these newspapers went into a total of 40,000 homes. These newspapers were run by political parties, which dictated their content. The parties used their own newspapers to present their own special version of the news.

Penetration Stage

- By the 1830s, a big shift in the purpose of newspapers took place. Newspaper publishers shifted away from trying to influence the political opinions of their small subscriber bases; instead, publishers changed their content to appeal to the greatest number of people as possible so that they could maximize their circulation and thereby maximize the rates they could charge advertisers. This change served to orient newspapers much more to a business model, and newspapers evolved into a mass medium by the 1870s.

- Technological developments made it possible for newspapers to create a better product and to distribute that product more widely and faster. For example, newer printing presses were invented, and these newer presses made the printing of the papers faster and cheaper. The telegraph allowed reporters in locations away from the newspaper office to wire their stories to the newspaper. By 1900, improved transportation allowed distribution to a larger territory.
- Newspapers were being run in a more business-like fashion. They used economies of scale to lower their unit costs. And even though they were selling copies for a penny apiece, their profits were increasing dramatically, because their volume was growing so fast.
- With the decline of political partisanship, more and more readers found a broad range of newspapers interesting and useful. Advertisers also found the medium very useful.
- Between 1880 and 1900, the number of newspaper businesses in America more than doubled from 850 to 1,967. In 1870, about 2.6 million copies were circulated daily to the 7.6 million households in America (1 out of every 3). By 1900, 93% of all households were subscribing.

Peak Stage

- In 1919, newspapers reached a peak of penetration as the average household was receiving an average of 1.4 newspapers per day.
- The number of daily newspaper organizations was at a peak at almost 2,500 firms.

Decline Stage

- Newspapers began to decline as the most important mass medium in the 1930s and 1940s as radio, then television, took away newspapers' functions of providing information and entertainment.
- Even more devastating was that the newer media eroded the base of advertising, especially among the national advertisers.
- The number of daily newspapers declined to about 1,750 in 1945.

Adaptation Stage

- Since the 1950s, newspapers have redefined their role as a local medium for audiences and advertisers.
- Newspapers have changed their content to compete with other media. Now content is more sensationalized and entertainment oriented. There are shorter stories and more graphics and color.
- To appeal to advertisers, newspapers have sectionalized their issues. Most newspapers now have clearly distinguished sections for sports, finances, home, cars, health, food, and lifestyles—each of which is designed to appeal to a different kind of reader and a different kind of advertiser.
- Although the newspaper industry has experienced overall growth, most of that growth has not been in big cities; the circulation of city newspapers has remained static. Most of the growth in circulation has been in the daily and weekly newspapers of smaller communities.

Current Profile

- *Size:* There are about 9,800 newspapers—15% are dailies, 77%

weeklies, and the remaining semiweeklies. Dailies have a combined circulation of 56 million, and weeklies have a combined circulation of 70 million. The newspaper with the largest daily circulation is the *Wall Street Journal* at 2.1 million.

- *Revenue* is now about $47.5 billion a year. Newspapers now have many major streams of revenue that include advertising, home delivery subscriptions, newsstand sales, Internet subscriptions, contract printing, licensing rights of content, distributions of inserts, graphic design services, and sales of mailing lists.

  o Newspapers' share of ad revenue has been shrinking from 27% in the 1980s down to about 18% today.

- *Expenses:* The biggest expense of newspapers is personnel costs, which account for about 60% of all expenditures. Although this cost goes up each year, it has been doing so at a slow rate of about 3% to 4% a year.

- *Profit:* The average profit margin for a newspaper company is about 17%, which is more than triple the median profit margin for companies in *Fortune* 500. Lacy and Blanchard (2003) analyzed 77 daily newspapers and found that publicly held daily newspapers produced higher profit margins than did privately held dailies. Public ownership and higher profits were associated with smaller newsroom staffs. The public dailies also had higher starting salaries.

  o Chain-owned newspapers are even more profitable. The primary purpose of a chain-owned newspaper is to maximize the profits of the parent company. Therefore, chain-owned newspapers have a strong incentive to increase revenues (eliminating competition) and reduce expenses (by using economies of scale). Of course, non-chain-owned newspapers also have a similar profit motive, but chains have more economic power. They use the following: (a) First-copy expenses are amortized over larger circulations, thus resulting in a lower per unit cost (first-copy costs are fixed, and these are very large in small-circulation newspapers—that is, as high as 40% of total revenue—so the more papers sold, the lower the per unit cost); (b) reproduction costs decline as circulation goes up (additional pages do not cost as much as the first few pages); and (c) the distribution process is more efficient with a denser circulation pattern, and this works against multiple deliverers of multiple papers.

- *Localism:* Almost all of the 1,500 daily newspapers printed in the United States have a local orientation; that is, they circulate to readers in their home city and the immediate surrounding suburbs. Only a small number of newspapers (such as *USA Today, Wall Street Journal, Christian Science Monitor*) truly have a national circulation and national editorial focus. In this way, America is unique in newspaper localism compared to other industrialized countries of the world. In most foreign countries, newspaper circulation emanates from a few large cities and spreads out across the entire country. For example, Tokyo has 11% of Japan's population, but daily newspapers from there account for 70% of the total newspaper circulation in that country. London, with 14% of England's population, accounts for 70% of circulation. In America, New York City and Washington, D.C., combined have 7% of population but account for only 10% of the country's daily newspaper circulation. Clearly, in this country, newspaper publishing is done at the local level.

- *Concentration:* Although publication takes place at the local level, ownership of the newspapers is becoming more and more concentrated; that is, there are fewer people controlling more and more newspapers. The trend toward greater concentration is evidenced in two ways: reduction in competition among newspapers and an increase in ownership by chains.

  ○ Competition among newspapers has been greatly reduced. For example, the number of cities with competing daily newspapers is decreasing. In 1900, more than 65% of all U.S. cities had competing newspapers, but now less than 1% do. Two reasons have been cited for the decline of newspaper competition. First, political parties do not support newspapers anymore as they once did, and there has been a decline in the partisanship in the U.S. press. Second, advertisers are demanding large circulations without duplicate readership. As a result, the larger newspaper in a two-newspaper town gets the advertising and continues to grow. The smaller circulation newspaper loses advertising and eventually goes out of business.
  ○ Chains have increased in size and number. In 1909, there were only 13 chains, and they owned only 2% of all newspapers. Chains grew slowly until 1970, when the majority of newspapers were owned or controlled by small private groups—often a single family. By the 1990s, three quarters of all newspapers were chain owned (Picard, 1993).
  ○ The top 13 chains now control more than half of daily circulation. Gannett is the nation's largest chain, with more than 100 daily newspapers and 500 non-dailies.
  ○ With concentration of newspaper control, access by individuals becomes harder. In 1900, there was one newspaper for every 36,000 people in the United States, but now there is only one newspaper for about every 170,000 people. Access to get one's voice heard is much more difficult.
- *Recent adaptations:* Print newspapers have lost readership and advertisers over the past decade. Most of these print newspapers have created websites in addition to their print versions to win back those readers and advertisers. However, the newspaper industry has not yet become successful in reversing these losses. As of the summer of 2011, only 6 of the top 20 Internet sites used by the public to get information were affiliated with newspapers, and 6 were Internet-only sites (Google news, Cnet news, Yahoo, Drudge Report, Huffington Post, and Bing).

3. MAGAZINE INDUSTRY

Innovation Stage

- The same technological innovations that made the book and newspaper industries possible were essential to the beginning of the magazine industry.

- The magazine industry began in the United States in the 1740s, but until 1800, no American magazine lasted more than 14 months. Advertising support was hard to find, so magazines struggled to stay in business.
- Circulations were very small, with the average circulation for a magazine being about 500 copies and large-circulation magazines selling between 2,000 and 3,000 copies.

Penetration Stage

- Magazines became a mass medium in the 1820s with the appearance of the *Saturday Evening Post* and others that were started to create a national audience that could be rented to advertisers. By the end of this decade, there were more than 100 such magazines. By the middle of the century, there were more than 700 such magazines, and by 1900, there were more than 3,000.
- Throughout the late 1800s, the magazine industry continued to grow because of several factors that benefitted all of the print media: Literacy rates increased, household incomes grew so people had more money for discretionary spending, and people had more leisure time. Also, another factor that was especially helpful to the growth of the magazine industry was that in 1879, the U.S. Postal Service made low-cost mailing available.
- Nearing the end of the 19th century, the magazine industry experienced a boom. By 1885, there were about 3,300 magazines, and by 1990, about 50 of those magazines had become well-known national magazines, each with a circulation of more than 100,000.

- In the 1890s, magazines cut their prices to below production costs to increase circulation. Thus, advertising revenue became essential to the survival of magazine companies.

Peak Stage

- Magazines have never reached a "peak" in the sense that they became the dominant mass medium.
- Magazines, however, exhibited some peak-like characteristics in the first few decades of the 1900s. They were the only mass medium with truly national circulation. Unlike newspapers, which had their circulations limited to small geographical areas in and around their home cities, magazines were mailed to subscribers all across the country. Advertisers who wanted to reach a national audience flocked to magazines.

Decline Stage

- From 1930 to 1960, the magazine industry declined primarily because of heavy competition from radio, then television, for advertising revenue.
- National magazines had the hardest time surviving not only because of the loss of advertising revenue but also because of steep rises in postal rates. In 1950, there were 40 magazines with a circulation of more than 1 million; within 25 years, all but 10 had gone out of business.

Adaptation Stage

- To survive, magazines became more specialized. They changed from trying to construct very large audiences with content that had mass appeal and instead targeted narrow, specialized audiences. Some magazines focused on news only, some focused on young women, some focused on particular hobbies, and so forth.

- There has been a generally steady growth in sales for more than 50 years. During that time, the price of subscriptions and newsstand sales has increased. Subscriptions, which average $30.50 a year, are increasing in popularity because they are more convenient and more economical for consumers than buying individual issues at the store.

Current Profile

- *Size:* There are currently 6,248 periodical establishments. They publish more than 22,000 magazines, most of which (17,000) are general interest consumer magazines, but 800 produce three quarters of all magazine revenue. Ten new magazines are launched every week (Magazine Publishers of America, 2004).

  - To be in the top 10, a magazine needs a circulation of only 4 million. The biggest circulation magazine is *AARP The Magazine* at 22.7 million. Fewer than 90 have a circulation of 1 million or more.
  - There are about 240,000 people working on 10,000 magazines in the United States (Mogel, 2000).

- *Revenue:* The magazine industry now generates about $21.5 billion in revenue per year.

  - Subscription revenue has become much more important. In 1950, single-copy sales of magazines were 43% compared to subscriptions at 57%. Now subscriptions account for

85%, an indication of an industry wanting habitual exposure.

- *Expenses:* As with newspapers, the biggest expense of a magazine is personnel, but this has not been climbing very fast. In contrast, expenses for paper and mailing have been increasing rapidly over the past few decades.

- *Competition:* The magazines that exist today do not really compete with each other for readers or advertisers. For example, *Boy's Life* does not compete with *Forbes,* and *Newsweek* does not compete with *Cosmopolitan.* Instead, each magazine tries to create a distinct audience base that it can rent to its own special set of advertisers. Magazines are niche oriented as they aim less at *quantity* of circulation and more for a *quality* audience. Within a niche, there are usually a small number of magazines that do compete against one another. For example, *Newsweek* competes against *Time* and *U.S. News & World Report* for essentially the same readers and same national advertisers.

  - The magazine industry is subdivided into niches. The big niches are consumer magazines (such as *Reader's Digest, TV Guide*), news (*Time, Newsweek*), sports (*Sports Illustrated, Runner's World*), opinion (*National Review, New Republic*), intellectual (*Commentary, American Scholar*), men's interest (*Esquire, Gentleman's Quarterly*), women's interest (*Cosmopolitan, Better Homes and Gardens*), humor (*National Lampoon, Mad*), sex (*Playboy, Playgirl*), and business (*Forbes, Money*). Within each of these niche markets, the magazine vehicles compete with one another for readers and for advertisers, but typically, a small handful of magazines account for most of the circulation and ad dollars within a niche.

- *Concentration:* The large media conglomerates publish magazine vehicles in several of these niches. For example, Time Warner publishes *Time, Sports Illustrated,* and *Money.* The magazine industry is very concentrated. Of all firms that publish magazines, the top four account for 77% of all magazine revenue each year (Albarran, 2002), and the top 160 firms account for 85% of the industry's total revenues (Daly, Henry, & Ryder, 2000).
- *Recent adaptations:* Many magazines have websites to support their paper copies. Also, there are now webzines such as Slate (www.slate.com) and the Onion (www.theonion.com) that are magazines that only appear online.

4. FILM INDUSTRY

Innovation Stage

- The film camera and projector were invented in the 1880s by Thomas Edison, who owned the early patents and therefore had a monopoly.
- By 1900, there were three companies marketing film equipment. These three companies also provided films and sold them outright to users as a way to encourage the sale of equipment.
- Theaters began to be an alternative to live entertainment, especially the popular vaudeville shows.

Penetration Stage

- In 1902, film exchanges were established so theaters could share films. Small producers consolidated their resources and formed studios for production and distribution. By 1905, there were more than 100 film exchanges, and the producer-wholesaler-retailer chain in the film industry became institutionalized. Five years later, there were 10,000 small theaters, each run by entrepreneurs who parlayed small investments into quick profits.
- By 1912, producers were making full-length feature films. During this time, audiences began to regard movies less as a novelty and more as a habit.
- The Hollywood star system was devised as a way to lure people to the movies by attaching identifiable names to an otherwise unknown film and by merchandising the star as an important part of the distribution process. These stars were chosen not on their acting skill but on their ability to attract audiences.

Peak Stage

- The peak of the film industry was reached in the 1920s and lasted into the late 1940s. In 1927, an average of 60 million people attended motion pictures *every week.* By 1929, this figure was more than 110 million people.
- Sound movies were introduced in 1927, and color was introduced in the late 1930s.
- The number of commercial films released to theaters grew to a peak of 497 films in 1941.
- The number of theaters in the 1940s was about 20,000. The number of movie seats, including car spaces at drive-ins, reached a peak of 11.1 million in 1935.

Decline Stage

- Starting in the late 1940s, the industry went into a decline because of competition from television. The number of commercial films released to theaters decreased steadily from a peak of 497 films in 1941 to a low of 203 films released in 1963. Costs skyrocketed. Massive advertising and marketing campaigns were necessary to build audience interest for each picture.
- The federal government regarded some of the very large film companies as monopolies and forced them to sell parts of their operations. For example, it became illegal for a single film company to produce, distribute, and exhibit films. So the large film studios sold off their theaters. After divestiture, film production companies lost some of their incentive because they no longer owned their own theaters. Production of films dropped.

Adaptation Stage

- Film studios adapted first by reducing their workforces and selling off their property.
- In 1965, film studios began making films primarily for television showing and have experienced steady growth since then.
- Not until 1970 did the production-distribution sector turn around financially. For example, the exhibition sector adapted by creating multiscreen theater complexes.
- Production costs skyrocketed through the 1980s but stabilized by the mid-1990s at about $50 million per Hollywood picture; at the same time, box office receipts went from about $1.2 billion in 1980 to $7.5 billion in 1999 (Albarran, 2002).

Current Profile

- The motion picture industry is now considered the motion picture and video industry because so much of its production is done for television, and much of its distribution is on video.
- *Size:* The film industry is divided into three distinct sectors: production, distribution, and exhibition. It has almost 20,000 establishments, with the production sector accounting for well over half of those establishments. Distribution is the smallest sector, accounting for fewer than 3% of the establishments, but it is the most central and visible because it is controlled by the Hollywood studios. The exhibition sector is composed of the theaters, with their total of about 39,000 screens in 6,000 theaters. The film industry now releases about 530 films per year. About 200 of these are considered major films, and these cost about $70 million to produce and another $40 million to promote. Most do poorly at the box office and disappear from theaters within days of release (Noam, 2010).
- *Revenue:* Film studios have several major revenue streams: domestic movie rentals to theaters, foreign rentals, sales of videos, and the licensing of films to television outlets. The United States is the world's largest film market and, for more than 50 years, has been the world's largest exporter of filmed entertainment to other countries. Home video revenues were projected to be $26 billion by 2004; international distribution to the world's 6 billion people is very profitable, but loss of revenues due to piracy is estimated to be $2 billion annually (Albarran, 2002). A new and growing revenue stream for

Hollywood studios is selling product placements in their films. Commercial advertisers now spend about $360 million annually to get their products used in Hollywood movies (James, 2003b). Another revenue stream is sponsorship of movie premiers. For example, Coors is now the sponsor of all Miramax Films premieres. The $300 million deal includes Coors products in 15 films during a 3-year period, along with placing the Coors logo on red carpets at openings and serving beer at Miramax parties ("Coors Scores Big," 2002). Perhaps the newest revenue stream is providing movie rentals from the Internet. Five major Hollywood studios joined to provide a service called Movielink, which, in November 2002, allowed consumers to download movies and play them for 30 days. This would compete directly with Blockbuster and other movie rental services (Healey, 2004).

- As for the revenue in the exhibition sector of the film industry, theaters now generate about $10.5 million at the box office annually. While the number of tickets sold per year has declined since a high in 2002, the cost of tickets has increased so much that the overall revenues at the box office have continued to increase ("Yearly Box Office," 2011). About 70% of this revenue is sent to the film distributor. Movie theaters have two revenue streams: (a) the portion of the ticket sales they get to keep and (b) high-margin concessions, such as popcorn, soda, and candy, which account for about 30% of their revenue.

- *Expenses* for film production broke through the $100 million level in the early 2000s and have remained that high ever since. The most dramatic increase in the cost of making films can be traced to the rising fees of stars—even lesser known stars. In 1929, the highest paid silent film star was John Gilbert, who made $520,000 a year or about $8 million in 1997 dollars. At his peak, Clark Gable was making $208,000 the year he made *Gone With the Wind* and *Mutiny on the Bounty.* Jean Harlowe made $78,000 at her peak. When Garbo was the highest paid actress in the 1930s, she made $250,000 a picture, and in the 1940s, Barbara Stanwyck was the highest paid at $225,000 a picture (LaSalle, 1996). The current box office mega-stars are Daniel Radcliffe and Robert Pattinson, who were each paid $25 million to star in their recent films of *Harry Potter and the Deathly Hallows* and *The Twilight Saga: Breaking Dawn,* respectively. Also, known actors can make a quick comeback with a successful film or two. John Travolta was down to $150,000 for *Pulp Fiction,* then bounced up to $10 million. Big-name directors also command high fees (usually about $3 million) but not as high as big-name actors. Scale salary for the members of the Screen Actors Guild (SAG) is $522 *a day,* which is much better than the U.S. average for salaried workers at $500 *per week* (Weinraub, 1995). However, a very small percentage of the 95,000 members of SAG work during any given day. Hollywood studios spend a total of about $100 million annually to test their movies and to run promotional campaigns (Dutka, 2003). Oscar awards are not always a purely aesthetic decision. There is a great deal of campaigning going on to woo the Academy's voters; it is a popularity contest, and some studios have been known to spend as much as $20 million on just one movie (Horn, 2003). That money is regarded as an investment. Films that win Academy Awards get people's attention, and people are more likely to go see them, thus increasing the studio's revenue for that film. With costs of films rising, studios have been appointing heads who are more adept at business than art (Eller & Bates, 1999).

- *Risk:* The production sector is the most risky for several reasons: First, a Hollywood feature film takes about 18 to 24 months between the inception of the idea and the actual theatrical release. In television, it is 3 months. Therefore, there is a danger that a film might miss the changing tastes of audiences. Second, the cost of making a feature film is very high, and it continues to escalate. The average cost of films, including their marketing, has doubled in the past 5 years. The average film now costs $50 million to make and another $50 million to market. This means that a film must gross more than $100 million at the box office to begin making money for the studio. However, the average movie makes only about $33 million.

- *Concentration:* Each of film industry's sectors (producers, distributors, and exhibitors) is very concentrated. Although there are many small independent producers, distributors, and exhibitors, power is concentrated in the hands of a few huge conglomerates that have diversified holdings beyond the film industry.

  o The film industry is dominated by seven major film studios. These seven account for 75% of all distribution.

Typically, the top 10 films each year account for one third to one half of the industry's total annual receipts. About one third of national admissions comes from nine major metropolitan areas. The 17 weeks of summer, Christmas, and Easter provide 40% to 50% of theater receipts. The four largest film exhibition companies account for about 20% of all receipts among the nation's 26,000 movie screens. The largest exhibition chain, Carmike Cinema, controls 2,401 of these screens.

- *Recent adaptations:* The biggest challenge to the traditional model of film distribution is the Internet, where people can download movies. For example, Netflix allows a user to download as many movies as he or she wants for a flat fee of $7.99 per month, which is the average cost of a ticket at a theater for one person to watch one movie. Also, Hollywood movies are experiencing severe competition for audience time by sites such as YouTube and Hulu that offer users hundreds of thousands of videos of all lengths and topics for free.

Now with deregulation and a more complex business environment, distributors are getting back into exhibition. For example, MCA, Inc., which owns Universal Films, also owns 40% of Cineplex Odeon, a large chain of theaters. Viacom, which owns Paramount Pictures, also owns Cinamerica. In total, major movie studios now have ownership stakes in about 2,300 screens nationwide (Standard & Poor's, 1996, p. L19).

The film industry has always struggled to balance art and commerce, but recently, the trend is much more toward business. For example, recent appointments of studio heads show that businesspeople rather than people with creative credentials are being selected. For example, Warner Brothers appointed Barry Meyer, a lawyer, as chairman; Universal Pictures appointed Brian Mulligan, a CPA, as co-chairman; and MGM appointed Chris McGurk, who had been a senior financial analyst at PepsiCo (Eller & Bates, 1999).

5. THE RECORDING INDUSTRY

Innovation Stage

- Thomas Edison invented the original technology for recordings and playback of sound in the 1880s.

Penetration Stage

- Technological advances have kept the industry growing and viable by continually improving the quality of the recordings and making playback more convenient. In 1925, Joseph Maxwell invented the jukebox, which allowed recordings to compete with radio music. In 1947, the long-playing record was marketed. Then, in the early 1950s, the sound quality of recordings was dramatically improved with high fidelity. In 1960, 34 million units were sold, and this climbed to almost 59 million in 1970.

Peak Stage

- Like the book and magazine industries, the recording industry never became a dominant mass medium.

Adaptation

- The delivery technology keeps changing for recordings; this requires consumers to buy new hardware.

Records were replaced by tapes (first eight tracks, then cassettes), then with CDs (compact disks). Advances in recording techniques (digital) and playback (boom boxes, car stereos, Walkmans, MP3 players, etc.) keep people buying new equipment. And the fast turnover in music styles and recording artists keeps people buying new recordings.

Current Profile

- *Size:* Now there are more than 5,000 U.S. record companies annually selling 1.2 billion tapes and disks of recorded music.
  - There are also thousands of independent record producers. These producers find talent, rent a recording studio to produce a recording, and get copies manufactured. Then they persuade one of the major six recording companies to distribute and market the recording. This is a high-risk endeavor because independent producers account for a very small percentage of all hit recordings (Albarran, 2002).
- *Revenue* from prerecorded music sales declined dramatically from $14.6 billion in 1999 to $6.3 billion in 2009 (Goldman, 2010).
  - A recording that sells 500,000 is regarded as gold, but it must sell 10 million copies to be considered a huge success; however, only one or two recordings per year reach this milestone.
  - Retailers who can't sell all the tapes and CDs return them to the recording company. The returns are then offered to club members at deep discounts. As a group, the clubs account for about 11% of all sales.

- *Expenses:* In the recording industry, the cost of manufacturing CDs is coming down, whereas the cost of signing artists is going up. In the early 1980s, it cost $3 to $4 to manufacture one CD, but now the cost has been reduced to less than 75 cents, including its jewel box container. The big costs are for the artists and for promotion. It now costs about $500,000 to sign a name band. When the retail price of a CD is about $16.98, the cost to the manufacturer is about $7.54, which is itemized as follows: recording expense, $0.65; manufacturing expense, $1.25; packaging, $1.30; advertising and promotion, $2.00; artists' royalty, $1.60; freight, $0.09; and payment to musicians' trust fund, $0.65. This leaves the manufacturer with a profit of $2.94. The distributor then has expenses and a profit of $1.50, and the retailer's expenses and profit are about $5.00 (Dominick, 1999). Producers must sell at least 300,000 to 500,000 copies of a CD before covering their costs. About 80% of all recordings lose money.
- *Concentration:* The record and tape industry is very concentrated, with its powerful distributors on one end and the chains of retail music stores on the other end.
  - Distribution is dominated by four major companies: Sony BMG (labels include Columbia, Epic, RCA, and Arista), Warner Music Group (Atlantic, Electra, and Warner Brothers), Universal Music Group (MCA), and EMI Records (BMI, Capitol, and Def Jam Records). These six control 90% of recording sales each year.
  - About one third of all recorded music worldwide is bought by Americans. Globally, annual sales are about $35 billion.

- *Recent adaptations:* The biggest challenge facing this industry is piracy of music that has been made very easy with the digitization of their recordings, compression of that information, and the fairly easy downloading to personal devices (computers and smartphones) from the Internet.
  - Transmission devices have changed from vinyl records to cassettes to CDs and now to digital downloads played back on MP3 players, smartphones, and computers.
  - In the 1970s, recordings shifted from analog to digital. Sound used to be preserved as waves in analogy recordings, and thus the movement of the needle in a groove in vinyl recordings read movements in terms of waves in the record's groove. With digital recording, musical information was translated into a binary computer code of 0 or 1. Digital recordings had three major advantages. First, it was a cleaner sound. Analog recordings usually played back with an audible hiss, but this hiss could be removed in the digital process. Second, the computer binary code could also be used with text and video, thus making translation of materials across these formats seamless. And third, binary code could be compressed for more efficient transmission and requiring smaller storage units.
  - In 1987, a German engineer developed a way to compress audio files to less than a tenth of their original size, thus allowing files to be sent more easily over the existing phone lines that connected users on the Internet. This technology was named MP3 (for MPEG-1 Audio Layer 3).
- Record companies and groups rely on radio stations to play their songs.

Between the recording companies and the radio stations are brokers called independent record promoters or "indies." Recording companies pay hundreds of millions of dollars each year to these indies, who try to get their recording companies whose recordings they represent airtime. Indies align themselves with certain radio stations and promise to provide promotional money. It's not payola strictly speaking, but it is close, and it's perfectly legal. Recording companies focus on the top 1,000 radio stations out of the 10,000 that broadcast in this country. These are the stations in the largest markets and have the largest audiences; therefore, these stations are the ones that recording companies rely on to create hits and sell their recordings. Each of those stations adds about three new recordings to its playlist each week. Indies get paid when a station adds a recording company's record to its playlist. Indies make about $3 million per week (Boehlert, 2001).

○ Payola is illegal but it continues. Sony BMG got caught in 2002 and had to make a $10 million settlement as punishment for paying radio station employees gifts and money to play their songs (Duhigg & Hamilton, 2005).

○ Up-and-coming musical groups used to have to get a record label to sign them in order for their career to take off. Now bands build audiences directly on websites. For example, CD Baby features the work of more than 155,000 artists who earn a combined $35 million a year. CD Baby takes $4 per album sold and turns the rest over to the artists, thus giving them a much bigger share of the sale than record companies do. Record companies are treating e-labels as farm clubs—that is, if a band can build a following on the Web, the record company knows there is a market and will try to sign the band (Semuels, 2006).

○ A musical group that signs a contract gets an advance against royalties. If their CD goes gold (sells 500,000 or more copies), then the artist's royalties will be close to $1 million. But by the time the group pays the record company back for the advance, travel expenses, managers, attorney fees, and so on, there may be nothing left. Thus, to be successful financially, musical groups must hit a string of gold CDs, and then they can negotiate better contracts with higher royalties.

6. RADIO

Innovation Stage

- Radio broadcasting began in 1920, when it combined a new technology with old content forms from vaudeville and the dramatic stage.
- In 1921, there were only five AM radio stations, and only about 1% of all the households in the United States had a receiver.

Penetration Stage

- Almost overnight, hundreds of radio stations sprang up. By 1923, there were more than 500 stations; almost half were owned by manufacturers of radio receivers who initiated the stations as a way of stimulating sales of receivers to the general public. Then, radio stations were started by other kinds of organizations, such as private businesses, local municipalities, and educational institutions.

- Radio had evolved from a novelty into a business as it developed the concepts of station, sponsorship through commercial advertising, and network.
- When radio began broadcasting, it received its income through the sale of home receivers. This continued to be a source of revenue to radio stations until the mid-1930s. Throughout the 1920s, stations realized that the sale of receivers would not bring in enough revenue to support the growing industry, so stations began selling advertising. Advertising was first introduced in 1922 as a way of supporting an increasingly expensive industry. Initially, advertising was of an institutional nature, with price not being mentioned and the hard sell being avoided. More obtrusive types of advertising were not fully accepted until the late 1920s, when advertising moved toward dominance. In 1927, 20% of radio network time was sponsored, and by 1940, more than half was.
- In the 1920s, the federal government favored localism when it awarded radio licenses to local owners. The local stations were mandated to serve the needs of the communities in which they were going to broadcast. But almost from the beginning, radio broadcasters began moving away from their mandate and instead made decisions that have primarily helped their businesses to function more profitably. They have done this mostly through network affiliation and group ownership.
- Instead of generating local programming, most broadcasters have chosen to affiliate with one of the large

commercial networks. These affiliates get their programming from these networks, and this programming is national in content. Network affiliation began in 1927, when 6% of available radio stations became affiliated with one of the four radio networks: ABC, CBS, MBS, and NBC. The peak period of affiliation was reached in 1947, when 97% of the country's 1,062 radio stations were affiliated with one of the four national radio networks.

Peak Stage

- Radio reached its peak in the 1930s and 1940s. By 1936, there was an average of one receiver per household, and in 10 years, this had doubled.
- People were spending more time with radio than any other medium.
- Radio had a national orientation for both entertainment and advertising. The radio networks played a crucial role in creating and maintaining this national orientation.

Decline Stage

- Revenues increased each year until television began taking away advertisers in the late 1940s and early 1950s. Radio hit bottom in 1955, when revenues dropped to $554 million with only 2,669 stations broadcasting.
- Radio ceased being a general national medium around 1950, when national advertisers began shifting their business to television.

Adaptation Stage

- To survive, radio replaced its full-service, mass-oriented, family-type general entertainment format with specialized music formats designed to appeal to unique target audiences.

- Radio stations replaced their national advertising revenue with local ad revenue. Now, 80% of a station's revenue comes from local advertising. Thus, radio stations compete primarily in local markets with newspapers for advertisers.
- Also, to survive the competition with television, radio became more mobile. With car radios and portable radios, people could listen to music and news anywhere—especially where they could not take a television set. Between 1950 and 1970, radio set production almost doubled, whereas the U.S. population only increased by one third.
- AM radio had a rough time in the 1970s and 1980s, when it lost a lot of its audience. But it has adapted by airing a host of syndicated talk shows beginning in the 1990s (Howard Stern, Rush Limbaugh, Dr. Laura Schlesinger, Don Imus, G. Gordon Liddy, etc.). FM continues to hold its audience with a variety of music formats targeted to specific audiences.
- By the early 1960s, more than 4,000 stations were broadcasting, and revenues were up to $700 million per year. By 1980, total revenues had climbed to $3.2 billion (U.S. Bureau of the Census, 2000).

Current Profile

- *Size:* The number of radio stations has grown dramatically from about 2,000 stations in 1948 to about 14,500 broadcast radio stations today.
  - ○ In an average week, 94% of the U.S. population will listen to radio at least once.

- *Revenue:* It now generates annual revenues of about $20 billion, almost all from advertising. Thirty-second spot ads range in cost from about $1,500 in large markets to a few dollars in small markets. Three quarters of this revenue comes from local sales.
- *Concentration:* Because of the profitability of well-run radio stations and the limited number of stations available, large companies want to buy radio stations. There has been a steady increase in group ownership of radio stations. In 1929, only about 3% of the country's 600 existing radio stations were group owned. By the late 1960s, the figure had climbed to about one third of all stations. The Telecommunications Act of 1996 significantly relaxed rules on radio ownership, touching off a buying spree so that now huge conglomerates own hundreds of stations (four companies own more than 100 stations each, and Clear Channel owns more than 1,000 stations). In 2000 alone, 133 AM radio stations were sold for an average station price of about $3 million, up from about $500,000 in 1995; in the same year, 192 FM stations were sold at an average station price of $8.6 million, up from $2.2 million in 1995 (Albarran, 2002). Radio is highly concentrated and is getting more so as Congress deregulates the industry in terms of the restrictions on the number of stations a single business can own. In 2004, Clear Channel Communications owned 39 TV and 1,238 radio stations.

  - ○ Now, radio stations are not likely to affiliate with national networks, or if they do affiliate, they usually only get news and features from the network.

However, this does not mean that radio stations now exhibit a wide variety of programming that reflects the local needs of their communities. Instead, radio stations are likely to affiliate with a certain type of programming such as top 40, golden oldies, album-oriented rock, country and western, all news/talk, and so on. For example, most radio markets have a top 40 station, and these stations sound the same all over the country, regardless of the locale in which they broadcast.

  o They all play the same songs on the same rotation, play the same lead-ins and lead-outs for the news, cover the same types of news stories with the same kinds of formulas, and have the same kinds of contests and promotions.

- *Recent adaptations:* Now in addition to broadcast radio, there is satellite radio as of 2002, when XM and Sirius entered the market. These are positioned as commercial-free stations that provide multiple formats to subscribers. Subscribers to satellite radio buy a special receiver and then pay a monthly subscription to receive the signal. Both services struggled and had to merge to survive in 2008.

7. BROADCAST TELEVISION

Innovation Stage

- By the 1930s, the technology had been developed to make the transmission and reception of television signals possible. The first television stations went on the air in 1941. These were commercial stations on the VHF (Very High Frequency) band.

- The first receivers were marketed in the New York City area, where the first broadcast signals were available. As stations began broadcasting in other metropolitan areas of the country, receivers were marketed in those additional areas.
- By 1948, almost 3% of all households already owned a TV receiver.
- Television broadcasting has followed the same pattern of development as radio.
- The Federal Communications Commission (FCC) attempted to reaffirm its perspective of localism as its guiding principle on licensing when it awarded television broadcasting licenses in the 1940s and 1950s. This decision led to the establishment of hundreds of local stations, and the FCC had to find new spectrum space to provide these stations with their own broadcasting frequencies. As a result, the UHF band (Channels 14–83) was set aside for television use in addition to the already used VHF band (Channels 2–13).
- Commercial broadcast stations were licensed to provide service to local communities. But over the years, the FCC has done very little to ensure that the stations do, in fact, provide responsible service to their communities. Television stations have been permitted to affiliate with national networks and to buy syndicated services, both of which feature national programming.
- From the beginning, local stations affiliated with national television networks. In 1954, network affiliates were already getting 50% of their total programming from networks. Within two decades, local stations were

producing only about 10% of their own programming. There are strong economic incentives for networking. Affiliates are able to share the production costs as well as the risks of a program. If something is to be produced locally, it must be inexpensive and very popular compared to the alternative program from the network. Therefore, the affiliates air most of the network programming, which is aimed at a national, not local, audience.

Penetration Stage

- By 1950, there were 107 television stations; all of these early stations were on the VHF band, and by 1953, the first UHF stations went on the air. The number of stations grew to more than 500 by 1960.
- By 1953, 50% penetration was reached; that is, half of all the households in the country had a television set that could receive a signal. Television was catching on, even though few homes had much of a choice in viewing alternatives. Only one third of television households could receive as many as four channels.

Peak Stage

- By the early 1950s, television was reaching a peak. It quickly became *the* entertainment medium, thus reducing movie attendances and radio listenership. Over time, it also became a primary source of information, thus reducing readership of newspapers and magazines. The public accepted this medium so quickly because television was seen as fulfilling the audience needs for entertainment as well as information better than any other medium.
- Advertisers, especially national advertisers, realized this shifting media preference among audiences, and they too shifted their support to television. This resulted in severe reductions in national advertising support for magazines, newspapers, and radio.
- By 1960, the average household owned at least one set; it could receive about seven channels. Television sets were turned on more than 5 hours per day in the average household. By 1980, 99.5% of all households had at least one television set, more than 90% had color sets, and over 50% had two or more sets. These household ownership rates are higher for television sets than for telephones or indoor plumbing.
- Revenue for broadcast television came primarily through one stream: advertising. So television stations and networks had to attract large audiences if they wanted a large amount of revenue. A single rating point over the course of a television series season could account for as much as $90 million.
- To maintain its peak, television had to generate the most revenue and attract the largest general audience, especially in primetime, which was from 7 to 11 p.m. each night. Unless a primetime program could generate an audience of at least 20 million viewers every week, it was canceled. To reach the widest audience possible, programmers adopted a policy of LOP (least objectionable programming). They need to avoid the risk of offending anyone, which would result in loss of audience or threat of governmental intervention. To determine what is least objectionable, television relied on proven

formulas. This is why programming became less diversified and more limited. When a particular program becomes very popular, programmers will try to develop similar shows in an effort to share the popularity. Because a popular show generates a great deal more revenue than an unpopular one, programmers are unwilling to take a chance on new types of shows for fear that they would be held responsible for losing money for the station or the network.

- Television networks do not produce much of their own programming; instead, they license broadcast rights from the producers. The fee to broadcast a program is not large enough to cover the producer's costs. These deficits are usually between $50,000 and $300,000 per episode. Producers hope that the series will run long enough so that they can make about 100 episodes and then sell it through syndication. A successful show like the *Cosby Show* was able to get $4 million per episode in licensing fees to television stations (Standard & Poor's, 1996, p. L30).

- Concentration in station ownership was initially limited by the FCC regulations, which restricted ownership to 7 television stations, but this limit was raised to 12 stations in the 1980s and now has been raised even more. By 1995, 75% of all TV stations in the top 100 markets were licensed to multiple owners. About one quarter of these were owned by publishers of newspapers, but it is rare for a newspaper and TV station in the same market to be owned by the same company. In total, 210 groups own more than 1 TV station. Twelve of these groups own 10 or more stations each (Howard, 1995).

- In the 1990s, broadcast television was in the latter days of its peak. It still had a higher reach than any other medium: TV was 88%; radio, 71%; newspapers, 56%; and magazines, 34%. There were about 1,600 broadcast television stations, and they generated revenue of more than $21 billion each year.

Decline

- Broadcast television is now in decline.
- The networks and stations are losing viewership. Until the late 1970s, more than half of all households watched television during primetime, and the three big television networks commanded a combined share of 95— that is, 95% of the television viewing audience at any given time was tuned into one of the three broadcast networks. By 2011, the combined share of the then four major networks (ABC, CBS, NBC, and Fox) dropped to about 22 (Fitzgerald, 2011). The reason for the drop is not because people are watching less TV; in fact, they are watching more than ever. The reason is because now people have so many alternatives to network TV—hundreds of cable stations as well as all kinds of video-on-demand programming.
- The survival of a program depends on reaching a large audience, which used to mean a rating of 10. Now even the highest rated television shows do not earn ratings as large as 10.
- Network costs for proven shows have been escalating dramatically. When *Seinfeld* retired, NBC feared losing *ER,* so it agreed to pay $13 million per episode for *ER,* up from $2 million an episode previously (Bauder, 1998). Therefore, the producers of *ER* increased their season's income (22 episodes) from $44 million to $286 million.

Current Profile

- *Size:* There are 1,937 broadcast television stations.
- *Revenue:* Broadcast TV brings in about $67 billion a year in advertising. A 30-second spot costs $100,000 on average and can cost up to $500,000 on a top-rated primetime show.

  - Product placement is another form of advertising that has the advantage of occurring during the program rather than during program interruptions (James, 2003b).

- *Expenses:* TV shows are getting more expensive while audience sizes are dwindling. In the fall of 2006, the price tag for a full season of a 1-hour dramatic series had increased to $62 million—up from $45 million in 2004. One of the increases is with high-priced talent—the stars of series who are paid more than $100,000 per episode. Also, advertisers are starting to shy away from the big increases for network primetime shows and putting their money more into the Internet (James, 2006).

  - Above-the-line costs are about 60% of a TV program's budget.

- *Risk:* Developing programs is highly risky. National TV networks look at about 4,000 proposals a year for new television series; of these, only about 100 get filmed as pilots; of those, only about 25 will make it onto the air; of these, only about a dozen will last a full broadcast season.

  - Independent producers make the shows and then lease them to the networks—but at a loss. A typical episode of a half-hour sitcom costs about $800,000 to produce, and the producer gets only about $600,000 per episode for two airings (premiere and rerun), so the producer losses $200,000 per episode. After 2 years of production (44 episodes), the producer is about $8 million in debt. Producers of 1-hour drama series are in about $14 million debt. The film studios finance this debt as well as providing production facilities in a package deal. But if the show is successful and goes into rerun syndication, the producers and film studios get their money back and then some. When the *Cosby Show* went into syndication in 1988, the producers made more than $800 million, and since the episodes were already produced, this was almost clear profit. Newsmagazines and reality shows cost much less to produce but are not attractive to program syndicators.

  - Because of the expense and the risk, there are fewer independent television production studios. As of the fall of 2003, there was only one—Carsey-Werner-Mandabach, which had deep pockets from successes with the *Cosby Show* and *Roseanne.* Up until 1995, broadcasters were prevented from owning their own shows; instead, they had to buy the rights from producers. Since 1995, they have been developing and producing their own programs. Typically, a 30-minute sitcom costs $1 million an episode to produce, and an hourlong drama costs $2.2 million per episode. In the fall of 2003, 77% of all primetime shows were owned by the six major television networks (James, 2003a).

- *Concentration:* The advertising on commercial television is concentrated in the hands of a few very large advertisers who can afford to buy great amounts of time each year. For example, 20 companies account for more than half of all advertising on broadcast television.

- *Recent adaptations:* Because audiences for broadcast programming have been shrinking steadily over the past few decades, broadcasters have had to abandon their strategy of trying to attract a large, heterogeneous audience and focus instead on attracting smaller niche audiences. No longer do mass audiences stay in front of their sets for appointment TV viewing. Now viewership is growing during the daylight hours due to video streaming to portable devices like iPods and cell phones along with office computers and laptops. This also has implications for programming principles because the audience is fragmenting by time. The TV networks will have to go to cheaper programs such as reality and game shows because no one can afford 3 hours of expensive programming every night (J. L. Roberts, 2006b).

In response to current challenges, broadcast television networks and stations have moved into HDTV quality picture and have also made much of its programming available on websites so as to increase viewership of their programs. They also continue to bid high fees to get the rights to broadcast programs that appeal to larger audiences—such as certain sporting events, awards shows, and the like.

8. CABLE TELEVISION

Innovation Stage

- Cable television began in 1948 as a retransmission service, that is, as a means of delivering television signals to areas unable to receive broadcast signals because of distance or interference.
- Until the 1950s, cable systems were quite small; each had a few hundred homes as subscribers and carried only three to four broadcast signals from the closest stations. They were generally confined to mountainous areas, where people living in valleys had little or no broadcast TV reception.
- The ownership of a cable system was typically a small local company often in some related primary line of business, such as selling TV receivers. They were marginally successful as businesses.
- By 1952, there were only 70 systems, and they served a combined total of 14,000 subscribers, which represented less than 0.1% of all television households at the time.
- Growth was slow. Not until late 1950s was 1% of television households reached by cable.

Penetration Stage

- By 1960, there were 640 systems with a total of 650,000 subscribers, which was 1.4% of all households for an average of 1,016 subscribers per system.
- By the mid-1960s, cable began expanding into areas that already received clear broadcasting signals without help, such as the urban areas of Los Angeles and New York City. Also, cable systems began adding channels to make their service more attractive to potential subscribers. In 1970, 3% of the systems offered more than 12 channels, and by 1976, 26% of the systems did. By the late 1960s, some

cable systems were even originating programming on their own.

- Cable systems are treated as natural monopolies—like utilities such as electricity and water companies. They are franchised on the local level and must therefore meet the requirements of the local community, such as time requirements for wiring the community, control of rates, and profit margins. Entry is controlled by economic cost, which requires capital-intensive construction and franchise requirements. However, once entry is achieved, the system typically has sole rights to the market for 10 to 15 years, and during that time, it is a monopoly.

- In the early years of cable, broadcasters welcomed cable systems as a means of extending their broadcast viewership into areas their signal could not reach. Cable systems then began using microwave relays to bring in more distant signals, such as broadcast stations from far-away markets and also signals from some superstations such as WTBS in Atlanta and WGN from Chicago. These new channels were in direct competition with local broadcasters, and the local broadcasters began resenting cable systems. Broadcasters began complaining that cable was receiving payment from subscribers but not giving any money to broadcasters who originated and paid for the production of the programs. Cable systems were no longer viewed by broadcasters as an expander of audiences but as direct competition. In 1962, the FCC began to regulate the selection of programming on cable systems. The FCC decided to allow cable systems to continue to use microwave relays and bring in distant

signals. But if a cable system did this, it would also have to carry all the local signals; that is, it could not ignore a local broadcast affiliate and instead bring in a station in another market in its place. During the next decade, many other regulations were added until 1972, when a period of deregulation began.

- By 1985, there were 6,600 systems serving a total of 32 million subscribers, which represented 37.7% of all television households. The 50% penetration mark was reached in early 1988.

Peak Stage

- It looks like cable television has entered the peak stage. By 1992, cable revenue had surpassed broadcast TV for the first time, with total revenues of more than $21 billion from a combination of subscriber fees and advertising. Subscription revenues are now about $25 billion per year, and ad revenues bring in another $4 billion. Then in 2001, the cable TV share of the viewing audience exceeded that of broadcast TV for the first time.

- The number of multiple-system operators (MSOs) is growing, and some of the larger ones rival the commercial television networks in terms of the size of the audience controlled through programming.

- The cable industry is taking steps to secure its position as the peak mass medium by heading off future challenges by computers. The cable TV industry has linked some computer technology with its existing services to offer what is called Smart TV. Smart TV is a collection of three types of services. First, there is

Interactive TV, which allows viewers to interact with the shows they are watching. Second, there is Internet TV, which lets viewers use their sets to access the Internet. Third, there is Personalized TV, which acts like a VCR.

Current Profile

- It is now referred to as the cable and satellite TV industry; this distinguishes it from broadcast TV.
- *Size:* About 47% of American homes now subscribe to cable TV services; of these homes, 75% get digital services (National Cable & Television Association, 2010).
  - ○ There are 565 cable networks, such as ESPN, BET, Bravo, MTV, SciFi, TBS, USA Network, and Family Channel (G. Fabrikant, 2004a).
  - ○ The industry includes 1,162 companies and employs 131,000 people in its production, distribution, and exhibition sectors.
- *Revenue:* The total revenue is now about $94 billion a year, of which $27 billion comes from advertising and the rest from subscriptions and fees (National Cable & Television Association, 2010).
- *Expenses:* From 1998 to 2003, cable television expenses increased 40%. This large increase was traced to a combination of escalating programming costs and the industry's investments in new technology (Hofmeister, 2003).
  - ○ Cable operators have to buy their programming. Costs range from about 5 cents per subscriber per month for low-demand channels such as C-Span to a high of about $2.60 for high-demand channels such as ESPN.

- *Concentration:* There are no ownership limits on MSO size. In the past 30 years, the major MSOs have continued to consolidate so as to build efficient clusters. The top five MSOs control 73% of all American cable households, up from a 38% share just since 1993.
- *Recent adaptations:* Cable TV's biggest competitor is DBS (Direct Broadcast Satellite), which now takes about one quarter of the multichannel video distribution market with cable TV taking the other three quarters. Also, websites that provide many cable programs are also creating serious competition for audiences.

9. COMPUTERS/INTERNET

Innovation

- The key innovations that are responsible for the computer becoming a mass medium are the affordable personal computer, the digitization of information, easy-to-use software, and the Internet.
- The computer as we know it was invented in the 1940s. ENIAC (Electronic Numerical Integrator and Calculator) weighed 30 tons and was several hundreds of times less powerful than the typical desktop computer of today. The first computers were very large, slow, and expensive. They were also energy hogs. Only the government and large businesses could afford to buy and use one until the 1980s, when relatively low-cost desktop personal computers began to be marketed.
- Another important innovation was the digitization of information; that is, all bits of information were reduced to a

binary code. This digitization allowed for fast computations, and it also led to seamless sharing of information of all forms (data, words, sound, pictures, video, etc.) across all media.

- The Internet is a network of computer networks designed to move information around among users. It has no centralized controlling body or mechanism. It was originally set up by the Pentagon in 1969 in such a decentralized structure so as to make it resistant to breakdown by attack. A bit of information sent across the country has many alternative paths it can take, so if one path is blocked (or down), the information can take one of the other many alternatives and arrive just as quickly. The Pentagon originated the system by linking up government computers with those at universities across the country. Since that time, many other networks from all over the world have attached themselves to the Internet. Since 1975, its cost has been supported by the National Science Foundation, but now that responsibility is being turned over to businesses that want to use the Internet to advertise their products and services. Anyone with a PC, a modem, and some accessing software can get onto the Internet. Once on the Internet, people can cruise around the different parts, send e-mail to specific people, post messages on bulletin boards, enter chat rooms where interactive conversations take place on a particular topic, play games, and download information, images, or software that others have made available. These services have become very popular and are attracting new audience members constantly.

- The computer is a fundamentally different type of medium from everything that came before. All media up to this point were channels to deliver uniform, intact messages from senders. Now, with a computer, each of us can customize messages by cutting and pasting from a wide range of sources and media, then send them out for display to a particular friend, e-mail them to a great number of people simultaneously, or simply make them available on the World Wide Web, where millions of people can come and visit your messages and even download them to their own computers, where they can undertake further manipulation.

Penetration

- Computers are well into the penetration stage, as this industry has been growing rapidly at 30% per year.
- By the mid-1990s, there were 40 million personal computers in homes, and half of all home computers had a CD player (Maney, 1995). Every minute, 40 novices were logging on to the Internet for the first time. Every year, the number of users was doubling and had climbed to 40 million users worldwide by the mid-1990s. About 26% of adults in the United States (or 51 million people) had access to the Internet (Bimber, 1996). A new corporate or academic network was being added every 10 minutes. There were already 100,000 networks linked (Simons, 1996). More than 97% of U.S. schools had computers—one for every 11 students, which is up from one computer for every 63 students just 10 years earlier (Intelligence Infocorp,

1996). The World Wide Web became a popular part of the Internet. Any user can create his or her own "Web page," which is usually a billboard with graphics. Many businesses created Web pages to display their services. The Internet became a really commercial medium. In 1995, only about $50 million was spent for online advertising in the United States out of a total of $120 billion spent on all advertising across all media. In 2004, it was projected to be $24 billion. Also, in the United States, e-commerce was about $500 billion in 2000 and was projected to be seven times that by 2004 (Albarran, 2002). This includes business to business (B2B), business to consumers (B2C), and consumer to consumer (C2C).

- This new industry was taking people and money away from other media. A 1998 survey reports that only 38% of young people had read the newspaper the day before, whereas 69% of seniors had. Those younger than age 30 were the heaviest users of Internet news sources (Pew Research Center, 1998). Newspapers had been losing readership, so they have been adapting to the Internet. An early adapter was the *San Jose Mercury News,* which began providing news summaries on America Online in 1994. It then created its own website and provided the full-text copy of its editions there, at first free and then for a fee (Dizard, 2000). Satisfaction with TV was declining among children. In 1970, 38% of sixth graders said they learned a lot most of the time when they watched TV; by 1999, the figure had dropped to 29%. Furthermore, when asked which one medium they would prefer to have if

they could have only one, only 13% of children said TV, whereas 33% picked computers (Rideout et al., 1999). Some bookstores created a strong presence on the Internet to capture a slice of the $3 billion annual market in college textbooks. Some sites advertised discounts of up to 40%. However, those who conducted systematic comparisons concluded that college bookstores offer prices just as low—if not lower, on average—than the prices offered by e-bookstores (Terrell, 1999). By 1997, the Knight Ridder news service had 32 websites but was losing money. The cost of the websites was $27 million, whereas the revenue from them was only $11 million. However, the company saw this as an investment that would pay off in the long run when more consumers log on to its sites to get their news (Dizard, 2000). Lin and Jeffres (2001) found that each medium (newspaper, radio station, and television station) had a relatively distinctive content emphasis in their websites, reflecting their strength of the primary medium. Radio stations were using the Web to complement their programming and promote their stations (R. F. Potter, 2002).

- By the year 2000, 49% of America's households had a computer, and 89% of those computer households had a modem. Overall, 32% of America's households were considered frequent Internet users (Dizard, 2000). The primary reasons for going online were to get news/information and to use e-mail.

- Three components were establishing themselves in the computer media industry. Each created its own stream of revenue. First, there was the hardware component of PCs and peripherals. This accounted for about $100 billion per year. Second, there was software, which had sales of $86 billion in 1995. Then there was online services, which accounted for about $1 billion per year and were growing at an annual rate of 27% (Standard & Poor's, 1996, p. C102). Profit margins were running about 20% to 25% annually on software and about 10% to 15% on hardware (Standard & Poor's, 1996, p. C127). In 1999, the computer hardware sector of the industry accounted for $229.2 billion in revenue, and the software sector accounted for an additional $199.3 billion (U.S. Bureau of the Census, 2000).

- There have been many Internet service providers (ISPs), with AOL as the largest, with a 32.5% market share (or about 22.7 million subscribers) in 2001; the next largest is MSN, with a market share of 7.2% (Albarran, 2002).

Current Profile

- Clearly, the computer medium is well through the penetration stage. Whether computers grow to a peak and replace cable television as the dominant medium remains to be seen.
- *Size:* The size of the World Wide Web has grown to about 50-billion indexed Web pages (WorldWideWebSize.com, 2011). Worldwide, there are now 2 billion regular users of the Internet ("The New Tech Bubble," 2011).
- *Revenue:* U.S. advertising revenue climbed to a record $26 billion in 2010. The most popular ad format was search, which represented 46%, or $12 billion, of the year's total revenue. Display-related ads accounted for 38%, or $9.9 billion, of 2010 ad revenue. That category includes banner ads, digital video ads, and sponsorships. The third largest Internet ad category is classifieds, which accounted for $2.6 billion, or 10%, of 2010 revenue (Ortutay, 2011).

- *Expenses:* Lots of money had to be spent to provide the infrastructure to make this new medium financially successful. Fiber-optic cable was needed as the conduit of information into American households. Fiber-optic cable is able to carry a tremendous amount of information. Old phone lines can transmit a few pages of text per second, but a single hair-thin fiber-optic line can transmit about 5,000 pages per second. Local phone companies were spending about $100 billion to build networks to connect all homes and buildings with fiber-optic cable— a job that was expected to be completed by 2010 (Maney, 1995).
- *Concentration:* The computer industry is very new, and there is great flux in the way companies grow quickly, get bought by larger firms, or go out of business. However, some trends reveal evidence of concentration in this new medium. For example, 80% of all pop-up ads were generated by just 63 companies ("E-commerce," 2002). About 77% of all Internet browsing activity is on two browsers—Explorer and Firefox. As for search engines, Google claims 72% of all search activity, with Yahoo! in second place at about 14% ("Top Ten Search Engines," 2010).
- *Recent adaptations:* Convergence (technological, marketing, and psychological) has shaped the development of this medium.

o Technological: Digitization of messages, along with new forms of transmission that allow for interactivity, has shaped the current nature of this industry. As recently as 1980, households were linked with copper wires that could carry less than a page of information per second. By 2006, most of the country had been linked by optical fiber that can carry the equivalent of over 90,000 volumes of an encyclopedia through strands of glass the thickness of a human hair.

o There is a convergence of media driven by computers and digitization. With the newer technologies, especially digitalization, companies are becoming more defined by their content products than by channels of distribution. For example, television networks are defining themselves much less in terms of television and more in terms of entertainment and news.

o Marketing: E-commerce is growing dramatically. In 1997, e-commerce accounted for only about $2 billion in online retail sales; this had climbed to $680 billion by 2010. Along with the increase in sales comes an increase in ads on the Web. The number of ad messages sent in 2002 was about 200 billion, and this climbed to more than 600 billion by 2006.

o Psychological: People are asking for a wider range of services and products from this industry as people coalesce into small-niche audiences around particular needs. People see themselves as not just consumers of message but also creators and shapers of messages through interactive platforms.

Appendix B

Examples of Mass Media Effects

Immediate Effects	Long-Term Effects
Cognitive effects	
Short-term learning	Learning agendas
Extensive learning	Hypermnesia
Intensive learning	• Generalization
	• Exposing secrets
	• Continuous partial attention
	• Blurring line reality/fantasy
	• Altering cognitive activity
Attitudinal effects	
Opinion creation	Sleeper effect
Opinion change	Sleeper curve
Contrast effect	Long-term reinforcement
Inoculation	Cultivation
Immediate reinforcement	Socialization
Emotional effects	
Temporary reaction	Stunting emotional development
Mood management	Desensitization
Physiological effects	
Temporary fight/flight arousal	Increasing tolerance
Temporary sexual arousal	Altering brain functioning
Behavioral effects	
Attraction	Displacement
Imitation	Narcoticization
Activation	Internet addiction disorder
Boomerang	• Learned helplessness
	• Disinhibition
	• Social cocooning

Macro-Level Effects

On society	On politics	On religion

IMMEDIATE EFFECTS

Cognitive Effects

Short-Term Learning. This is the acquiring of information and retaining that information in either short-term or long-term memory. If the information is retained only in short-term memory, it will be gone and unavailable for recall within several hours. When the information is rehearsed (thinking about it repeatedly) or consciously cataloged into an existing knowledge structure, it will be retained for a far longer time. When we encode information into our long-term memories, that learning can be intensive or extensive. These are immediate effects of the media because the encoding is done either during the exposure or shortly after. For example, people who watch late-night comedy shows learn political knowledge, but primarily on simpler ideas and mainly among the inattentive citizens (Baek & Wojcieszak, 2009).

Intensive Learning. Intensive learning adds information to a person's existing knowledge structure; that is, people acquire another example of the same information they already have. To illustrate, imagine that a person is following a political campaign and has built a knowledge structure about the candidates as well as their positions. The person reads a political blog on the Internet and learns that one of the candidates has changed her position on an important issue. The person adds this information to his or her existing knowledge structure. This is intensive learning. For example, media messages have been found to alter people's existing knowledge structures about advertised products (Lowrey, 2006; Yang, Roskos-Ewoldsen, Dinu, & Arpan, 2006) and political knowledge (Cho & McLeod, 2007).

Extensive Learning. In contrast to intensive learning, **extensive learning** refers to the acquisition of information on a new topic. If this information is related to an existing knowledge structure, the person can "add on" to the existing knowledge structure, thus making it broader than before. If this new information is not related to any existing knowledge structure but is still important, the person will create a new knowledge structure. For example, a person opens the newspaper and finds out that there is going to be an election on a proposition to institute a curfew on all students on campus. The person never heard of this issue before but now has some important information on a new topic.

Attitudinal Effects

Opinion Creation. The media provide information and images that can create a new opinion. This is most likely to happen the first time you hear a new song. You immediately develop an attitude about whether it is good or bad. You also immediately develop attitudes when you see a new character in a story (Mastro, Lapinski, Kopacz, & Behm-Morawitz, 2009), see an avatar in a video game (Chandler, Konrath, & Schwarz, 2009), or try out a new search engine (Kalyanaraman & Ivory, 2009). The media also trigger the formation of attitudes on controversial issues such as women's rights (Holbert, Shah, & Kwak, 2003), support for the death penalty (Slater, Rouner, & Long, 2006), racial policy and equality (Richardson, 2005), immigration (Igartua & Cheng, 2009), and homosexuality (Calzo & Ward, 2009).

Opinion Change. Media can change a person's attitudes about something by presenting information that challenges an existing attitude in a way that an alteration of attitude is motivated. For example, after watching a teenager insult her parents and be rewarded for this by the admiration of other characters, a child could change his or her attitude that it is okay (and even desirable) to insult one's parents. Or people who watch a political debate might not just acquire new information on an issue but might also change their opinion of one of the debaters. For example, media messages have been found to change people's attitudes about body image (Aubrey, 2006), expectations for relationships (Eggermont, 2004), and support for political leaders (Cho, 2005).

Contrast Effect. A contrast effect occurs when we see a portrayal of a very attractive character in the media and then judge our own romantic partner, friends, and self as less attractive (Myers, 2000; Weaver, Masland, & Zillmann, 1984).

Inoculation. Medical doctors inoculate people against disease by exposing them to a mild form of the disease so that their bodies can build immunity. Later, when those people are exposed to that disease, they are not susceptible and do not get sick. The effect of inoculation is sought by designers of media messages who want to make their audience's attitudes resistant to change. For example, advertisers will try to inoculate their target audiences to an upcoming claim about to be made by their competitors. In this case, advertisers will design a message to belittle the upcoming claim, so that the target audience will think the claim to be false or silly when they hear that claim later.

Immediate Reinforcement. The media can reinforce already existing attitudes and thus make them more resistant to change. This is an especially desired effect for advertisers. It has been estimated that up to 80% of all advertising is designed *not* to change the attitudes or behaviors of consumers but to reinforce already existing brand loyalties and purchasing habits. When people see an ad for a product they usually buy, they immediately feel good, and this helps to solidify their positive attitude toward the product. Researchers have found the reinforcement effect to be especially strong with solidifying existing partisan political attitudes (Holbert, 2005).

Emotional Effects

Temporary Reaction. When we are exposed to a story in the media, the events and characters trigger emotions in us that typically last only a few minutes. Storytellers know they must evoke our emotions to attract and hold our attention. Writers who want to tell an adventure story need to make us feel suspense, mystery, and fear. Writers of drama need to make us feel jealousy, anger, sadness, love, and happiness. Writers of comedies need to make us feel silly. The better the story, the more strongly our emotions are evoked. When the media arouse some emotions, usually those emotions dissipate shortly after the story is over. Fictional stories are especially good at triggering emotional connections with characters (Chory-Assad & Yanen, 2005; Eyal & Cohen, 2006). Also, researchers have found that certain kinds of avatars create a heightened feeling of social presence when playing Internet games (Skalski & Tamborini, 2007). This increased feeling is important because it leads to other types of effects, such as on attitudes and behaviors.

Mood Management. People use the media, especially music, to manage their moods (Knobloch, 2003). People who are stressed can calm themselves down with slow music. Conversely, people who are in a lethargic mood can pep themselves up with louder, more active music. For example, Knobloch and Zillmann (2002), in a study of university students, found that the choice of music is an emotional one. People who were in a bad mood elected to listen to highly energetic, joyful music more than did people in a good mood. The energetic music distracted them from their bad mood. Also, Knobloch (2003) reports that people who are preparing for a task requiring concentration are likely to choose to listen to "smoother tunes" rather than upbeat music.

Physiological Effects

Temporary Fight/Flight Arousal. We have certain physiological reactions hardwired into our brains. One of these is the fight/flight reaction when we are presented with danger. If we see a predator coming after us, the survival instinct is triggered. We must fight off the predator or run away. Our bodies get us ready for this by releasing adrenaline into our bloodstream, which increases our heart rate and blood pressure. The media frequently present us with situations where we identify with a character who is then put in danger. Vicariously, we experience the need for survival. Our bodies automatically release adrenaline into our bloodstreams. If we stop and think about what is happening, we know that the danger is not happening to us. But still our bodies are primed for fight or flight.

Temporary Sexual Arousal. Sexual arousal is also hardwired into our brains. When we see someone who is physically attractive to us, we become sexually aroused. This arousal ensures the propagation of the human race. The person who arouses us need not be a real person. The attraction may be to a character on a television screen or an image in a magazine.

Behavioral Effects

Attraction. The media present images that attract and hold our attention. We alter our behavior to follow what attracts us. For example, we may be flipping through the channels on our television set until we see something that attracts and holds our interest. At this point, our behavior changes; that is, we stop pushing the search button on our remote control device and keep our eyes on the screen.

Perhaps we even lean forward, turn up the volume, and stop talking to other people in the room. All of these are behavioral manifestations of attraction to a message on the television screen.

Imitation. Children as young as 2 have been found to imitate behaviors they see in the media (Comstock et al., 1978). In a survey of young children, 60% said they frequently copied behaviors they had seen on television (Liebert, Neale, & Davidson, 1973). The copying need not be identical to the action seen on the screen—it can be generalized to similar actions. For example, children may watch Superman jump off a building and fly across town to rescue someone. Children will imitate this by jumping up and down with their arms outstretched as they run across the backyard. If they watch two kickboxers beat each other to death, they will imitate this by spin-jumping around, kicking, chopping their arms at each other, shouting, and grunting. Seldom will they actually hit each other. By fantasizing, the "hitting" is in their minds as they imagine they are inside the kickboxing world that they saw on television. Usually, these imitations during play are harmless. But because so much of it is triggered by violent messages, the potential for actual physical harm is there. And once in a while, when a real weapon is available, the resulting physical harm can be very great. Positive examples of imitative behavior include performing physical exercises (Fox & Bailenson, 2009), signing up for organ donation (Morgan, Movius, & Cody, 2009), and voting (Kiousis & McDevitt, 2008).

Activation. The media can exert a triggering effect on our behavior. For example, when watching an ad, we might jump out of our chair and rush to the store to buy the product. Activation is different than imitation. With imitation, viewers take it upon themselves to emulate a specific behavior seen in the media.

In contrast, with activation, viewers are reacting to a suggestion to do something, such as go to the store to buy an advertised product. Viewers do not see the literal behavior portrayed, so there is no pattern to imitate.

Boomerang. There are times when people concerned about media literacy will try to help targets (especially children) to increase their media literacy and thereby avoid potentially negative effects from media exposure, but instead of helping their targets, their efforts will backfire and actually increase the negative effect. This is known as the boomerang effect. For example, Byrne (2009) conducted a series of experiments to determine the value of media literacy interventions in reducing the negative effects of exposure to media violence. She found that an intervention can have either a negative or positive effect depending on how it is designed. Positive effects were found when the intervention was followed by a cognitive activity such as writing an essay that reinforced the message of the intervention.

LONG-TERM EFFECTS

Cognitive Effects

Learning Agendas. With learning agendas, the media, by choosing certain images and themes, focus our attention on particular things while telling us to ignore other things. Called agenda setting, this effect was first observed in the political arena where the media were found to be very influential in telling us what to think *about* (McCombs & Shaw, 1972). For example, the media, through a continual stream of stories about social welfare programs, are effective at telling people that this is something worth thinking about, but the media are not effective in convincing people that they should support or reject social welfare programs. The agenda-setting function of the mass media is quite powerful, especially when there is an overlap in coverage among the various media.

This agenda-setting effect is not limited to telling us what to think about politics and current events. It is much broader. It tells us what kind of music we should listen to; what kinds of people we should regard as beautiful, smart, or successful; and what kinds of events are important. By bringing certain kinds of people to our attention, the media create celebrities. The media confer status on certain people, and we continue to hear what these people have to say even when they don't have anything important to say. The noncelebrities have not been given status, so we do not hear what they have to say, even if it is something potentially important. This is the agenda-setting effect.

In a recent test, Coleman and McCombs (2007) still found evidence of an agenda-setting effect even though the media now provide many more sources of news, those sources are more diverse in their perspectives, and today's youth are more likely to get their news from alternative media than mainstream sources of news, such as network television news and major daily newspapers. They reported that although the youngest generation used traditional media such as newspapers and television significantly less frequently than older generations and used the Internet significantly more often, this differential media use did not eliminate the agenda-setting influence.

Hypermnesia. This effect appears to be the opposite of forgetting. Instead of a person being *less* able to recall information from a message as time goes by, there are situations when people become *more* able to recall that information (Wicks, 1992). For example, a person reads a story in a magazine about forest fires and is not able to recall many of the facts after the reading. But during the next few weeks, the television presents stories about several big forest fires in his area, and he begins to recall more of the facts from the magazine story. This is hypermnesia.

How is hypermnesia possible? The key to understanding **hypermnesia** is to recognize that when we are exposed to information, the facts are recorded somewhere in our brains. On topics where we already have a good deal of knowledge, the recording of new facts is done in a highly organized manner by cataloging them quickly and accurately in the knowledge structure that we have previously developed on that topic. When we are asked about that information, we have no trouble retrieving it. But with a topic that is new to us, we don't have a knowledge structure on that topic. The new facts may be stored haphazardly inside other knowledge structures, and this makes those facts very difficult to retrieve. As we begin to learn more about the new topic, we construct a new knowledge structure on that topic and sort through our older knowledge structures to bring all the facts on that topic together in one place. During periods of rest (such as sleep), our minds sort out the facts and move them around to where they can be more efficiently cataloged. Once all the facts on the new topic are assembled into a new knowledge structure, they are then easier to recall.

Generalization. Generalization is the process of observing a few occurrences of something, perceiving a pattern that ties together those occurrences, and then inferring that the pattern reflects something more general than those specific occurrences. That "something more general" can be a claim about how all people behave or how things work. For example, a person watches a local news program and hears a story about a house that was vandalized in an area near his apartment. Then he hears a story on radio that a local bank was robbed. Next he reads the newspaper and sees that there was an assault in his town last night.

He has learned three facts—one from each message. But later that night, he might generalize from these three facts and draw a conclusion that crime has become a real problem in his town. This conclusion was not given to him in the media, but the media provided him with some facts that could set up his jump to this conclusion. Let's consider another example. A person watches a situation comedy where several teenagers are very witty and joke their way out of trouble. She then watches a stand-up comedian who wins the admiration of his audience. Then she watches a romantic comedy where the characters are attracted to each other because of their shared sense of humor. She has learned facts about how these televised characters behave and the consequences of their behaviors, then generalizes to a conclusion that humor is a very useful tool that can get her whatever she wants.

Exposing Secrets. For many people, the media, especially television, serve to expose secrets about how the world works. The media do this by restructuring social arenas, according to Joshua Meyrowitz (1985), in a fascinating book titled *No Sense of Place.* Meyrowitz argues that the media affect us not through their content per se but by changing the "situational geography" of social life. Meyrowitz says that we all change the way we act depending on whether we are in public or private. When we are in public, we perform on stage in front of others, such as colleagues at work. In contrast, we have "backstage" or private behaviors that we reserve for intimates, such as very good friends or spouses. The media expose important social secrets by taking viewers into the backstage, and this is often a negative effect. For example, Meyrowitz points out that adults used to be able to retreat to their private backstage area, which was hidden from children. While in the backstage, adults could talk about adult things (child-rearing practices, anxieties, sex, death, etc.) with each other without children being exposed. Parents could keep their shortcomings and anxieties in the backstage and thus hide from their children. Then, once parents had discussed how to handle their children, they could come onstage and take on the role of confident authority figures. The media, especially television, expose these adult secrets to children. When children watch situation comedies on television and see parents as buffoons and when they watch talk shows and see all the problems that some adults have, children lose the belief that adults have superior wisdom and experience. It is much harder, then, for parents to establish a sense of authority over their children.

Continuous Partial Attention (CPA). Continuous partial attention is the chronic fading in and out of attention while conducting multiple activities at the same time. It comes from our desire to be a live node on the network and is enhanced by so many new media distractions of laptops (e-mail, Web surfing, online bill paying, blogging, and chatting online), BlackBerry devices, mobile phones, and pagers. When your "bubble of connectedness" is large, your options are many and you are continually looking around for something better to occupy your attention (Levy, 2006a). Famed author Norman Mailer also criticized TV for constantly interrupting our attention and thus making it hard to concentrate on one idea for more than a few minutes. He claimed this reduces a child's ability and desire to read and hence a child's ability to learn (Mailer, 2005).

Blurring Line Between Reality and Fantasy. Playing video games, especially what are called MMORPGs (massively multiplayer online role-playing games), blurs players' perception of where this line is as well as breaking down the line itself between the real world and the cyberworld. For example, *WOW* (*World of Warcraft*) has guilds that function like mini-societies with their own websites, online

forums, and private lore. When one guild member died in real life, his guild members held a funeral for him in the game. People meet in the game and form lasting friendships, even get married. Some go into business with each other in the real world.

Altering Cognitive Activity. For decades, critics have warned that exposure to certain types of media messages leads to negative effects. For example, Marcuse (1964) argued that the mass media in America hammer the population into having a one-dimensional mind—that is, people's minds become paralyzed so that they are incapable of independent thought; they cannot criticize or oppose the messages in which they become immersed. More recently, Winn (2002), in her book *The Plug-In Drug: Television, Computers, and Family Life,* cautioned that television hooks children into entertainment, keeps their brains functioning at a low level, and makes them passive acceptors of the media messages as presented. With new methods of measuring brain activity, researchers have found evidence that exposure to media messages can alter that activity, but those alterations can be positive as well as negative. For example, Carr (2010) points out, "Dozens of studies by psychologists, neuro-biologists, and educators" using magnetic resonance imaging scanning has found that the brain activity of experienced Internet surfers is far more extensive than that of novice surfers when they are exposed to the Internet. Experienced surfers show much more activity in the prefrontal cortex, which is associated with problem solving and decision making. When the novices were measured about a week later, their brains were found to act like veteran surfers. Thus, Internet activity can rewire a person's brain by developing distinct neural pathways that have positive effects of increasing "hand-eye coordination, reflex response, and the processing of visual cues" (p. 118). It also strengthens brain functions related to fast-paced problem solving, particularly when it requires spotting patterns in a mass of data. The more we practice surfing and scanning, the more adept our brain becomes at those tasks. However, the brain alterations that help people become more skilled at navigating the Internet also come with a negative characteristic of turning them into shallower thinkers because Internet surfing promotes cursory reading, hurried and distracted thinking, and superficial learning. The navigating among linked documents requires skills that are extraneous to the process of reading because it disrupts concentration and that weakens comprehension. Thus, the Internet is an interruption system that attracts our attention only to scramble it.

Attitudinal Effects

Sleeper Effect. The sleeper effect takes a relatively long time to occur. During an exposure to a message, a person discounts the message because of a dislike for the source. But then over time, the person forgets the source, and the negative feeling about the information goes away and is replaced by a positive feeling. To illustrate, let's say you listen to a political pundit deliver an analysis of the problem of illegal immigration in which he expresses a certain opinion. You do not like or respect the political commentator, so you do not agree with his opinion while you are viewing the show. Several weeks later, you are in an argument about illegal immigration, and you start citing many of the facts that you learned from the commentator. You also express the same opinion as the commentator did. But you have now forgotten about the commentator, who made you feel bad. All you remember is the opinion and the supporting facts, which make you feel good.

Sleeper Curve. In his book *Everything Bad Is Good for You,* Steven Johnson (2006) argues that the popular opinion that the media are harmful

to us is wrong. Instead, he says that exposure to media, especially television and video games, produces more net good than harm. He calls this the sleeper curve after Woody Allen's movie *Sleeper,* where the characters in the future view our beliefs about what is harmful as silly. He says, "The most debased forms of mass diversion—video games and violent television dramas and juvenile sitcoms—turn out to be nutritional after all. For decades, we've worked under the assumption that mass culture follows a steadily declining path toward lowest-common-denominator standards, presumably because the 'masses' want dumb, simple pleasures and big media companies want to give the masses what they want. But in fact, the exact opposite is happening: the culture is getting more intellectually demanding, not less" (p. 9).

Long-Term Reinforcement. Although reinforcement can occur during exposure, the much stronger reinforcement effect is that which builds over time. With each additional message that is the same as or similar to all previous messages, a person's existing attitude gains greater and greater weight. Thus, over a long period, the attitude has gained so much weight that it is impossible to change it, no matter how powerful the arguments you use. The attitude has been reinforced so much that it is impervious to change even with reason, logic, and powerful counterarguments. For example, people have been found to use media to reinforce their existing political attitudes (Knobloch-Westerwick & Meng, 2009).

Cultivation. There are certain messages embedded in the way stories are presented, that is, the way plots develop and the way characters are portrayed over and over. After exposure to these constant themes over the long term, people are cultivated to believe certain things. For example, people have been cultivated to believe that the world is a mean and violent place after watching years of television, with its focus on crime in the news and on many programs. Also, after many years of exposure to ads, people have become more materialistic (Kwak, Zinkhan, & Dominick, 2002), hold more idealistic expectations about marriage (Segrin & Nabi, 2002), are more likely to distrust people in general (Shrum, 1999), and develop a "thin ideal" for body image in their characters and sports figures (Bissell & Zhou, 2004).

Some of these cultivation effects have been found to lead to behavioral changes. For example, women who have been cultivated to hold a thin body image are more likely to develop eating disorders (Bissell & Zhou, 2004). Also, a study conducted by Dartmouth University Media School reported that youngsters who watch movies in which actors smoke a lot are three times more likely to take up the habit than those exposed to less smoking on screen. It was found that 52% of adolescents who smoked said they started smoking because of seeing movie stars smoke on screen (Ross, 2003).

Socialization. This is a lifelong process whereby people acquire certain attitudes and beliefs by taking from the media certain lessons and themes about society. Throughout this long-term exposure to all kinds of messages (news, ads, movies, cartoons, talk shows, etc.), we infer patterns across the individual facts, events, and character portrayals. These inferences become our beliefs about how the world is constructed. This effect is similar to the cognitive effect of generalization. Both of these reflect the process of inference, whereby people are exposed to a few instances of something and infer general patterns from these few instances. With generalization, the inferences are about factual patterns concerning our society, such as the rate of crime, the proportion of women who work, the proportion of people who are on welfare, and so on. In contrast, socialization reflects inferences about how people should interact with one another and with their social world.

Emotional Effects

Stunting Emotional Development. Some critics have made the argument that watching a great deal of television stunts a child's emotional development. They point out that by the time a child reaches age 5, he or she has been exposed to about 6,000 hours of television. The high levels of exposure to television, coupled with the extreme level of stimulation presented by television, leave viewers with no time for reflection. On television, the pace is extremely fast, with new images replacing old ones every 3.5 seconds on average and with new shows replacing old shows every few weeks. There are sound effects, music, laugh tracks, and constant interruptions. This short-circuits the natural, emotional development people need to become healthy human beings; it strangles the development of children's own voices and denies them their imaginative powers.

Desensitization. Some things within the media are presented so often that we can no longer treat them with wonder or awe. Our tolerance has been increased so that those things that used to trigger emotional responses no longer do. This is especially important with the issue of violence where people can become desensitized to violence and the suffering of its victims (Liebert et al., 1973; Linz, Donnerstein, & Penrod, 1984, 1988; Thomas, 1982) as well as one's pleasure from sexual activity (Peter & Valkenburg, 2009). This desensitization can have positive effects in a therapeutic setting. People who fear something (such as dogs, heights, flying in airplanes, etc.) can be gradually desensitized (Dorr, 1981; Foa & Kozak, 1986; Goranson, 1970).

Physiological Effects

Increasing Tolerance. Your body builds a resistance—or tolerance—to certain experiences. Over time, your body requires greater and greater stimulation to trigger the same physiological response in you. For example, the first time you see a horror film, your body responds with a fight-or-flight reaction by substantially increasing your heart rate and blood pressure. As you continue to view horror films over the years, your body's reaction to these stimuli is not as strong. Your heart rate and blood pressure still increase but not as much. You are building a higher tolerance to this type of message physiologically. In the extreme case, with massive exposure to this type of message, you might even extinguish all physiological reactions to horror.

Altering Brain Functioning. Healy (1990), in her book *Endangered Minds,* argues that children's brains are being altered because of exposure to the visual media, especially computer games. Recent studies suggest that intensive game play actually redraws the brain's neural maps. And children who play a lot have cognitive strategies that are parallel—not sequential. This could make it more difficult for children who must learn sequential tasks such as reading or mathematical reasoning—both of which are very linear and analytical. She says that children who enter elementary school are smarter each year in some ways but are less able to handle school and its requirements.

Behavioral Effects

Displacement. Through **displacement**, the media have changed the way we spend our time. The media consume us by consuming our time. Almost 70% of the average person's day includes some form of media use (Ransford, 2005). The A. C. Nielsen company reports that the average amount of time that U.S. households had a TV set on each day during the yearlong 2005–2006 TV season increased 3 minutes from the previous year to a record of 8 hours and 14 minutes. As for individuals, the amount was up 3 minutes to a

record 4 hours and 35 minutes per day. Increases were seen in all age categories (Getlin, 2006).

There is also a concern that exposure to the media—especially with escapist fare—will prevent people from using their time more productively. This is especially an issue with children and their schoolwork. Although the media have been found useful in stimulating interest in some topics (Schramm et al., 1961), they have not been generally found to be either a positive or a negative factor—it depends on what is exposed. Also, there is a concern that for very young children with the television viewing habit, playtime is preempted (Singer & Singer, 1981). When TV structures a child's life, the child spends less time creatively making up his or her own games and situations.

Narcoticizing. The media can be like a powerful drug. The first exposure to a new magazine, CD, TV show, and so forth can bring a rush of excitement. So we go back to it to get the same feelings again. It is habit forming. When we build a tolerance to the effect, we want more. Each time we go back, we require more from the media to get the same rush. With entertainment, we want a more outrageous storyline, more attractive characters, and more visual effects. But if the media can give us only the same kinds of messages, we do not feel the rush. Over time, our expectations become very high, and we find ourselves flipping through 100 channels and saying, "There is nothing on!" What we mean by this, of course, is that TV is no longer able to exceed my expectations and to significantly arouse me in a surprising way. But we keep exposing ourselves to the TV anyway because, for many of us, it is better than not watching. People begin to withdraw from real life and become passive (Sayre & King, 2003).

Internet Addiction Disorder is a term coined in the mid-1990s by a psychiatrist who was seeing more and more patients who were unable to control their use of the Internet. These people typically forego sleeping, eating, and other activities to spend more time on the Internet. This disorder shows up as obsessions with chat rooms, games, pornography, gambling, and shopping. Some married people have extramarital affairs online; day traders get hooked on the stock market. Almost from the start, therapists began developing 12-step plans to help these people (Vranizan, 1995). A debate has been raging among health care professionals about whether to classify this as an addiction and include it as such in the Diagnostic and Statistical Manual of Mental Disorders, known as the DSM by the American Psychiatric Association. In 2007, the American Journal of Psychiatry called Internet addiction a common disorder and supported its recognition. But the American Psychiatric Association decided not to include it in its new DSM, which came out in 2010. In other countries, it is recognized as a mental disease; in South Korea, where the average high school student plays video games for 23 hours each week, the government estimated that more than 200,000 adolescents needed treatment for Internet addiction, and the government opened more than 100 clinics to help people with Internet addiction ("Addicted?" 2011). In China, the number of Internet users has climbed from less than 1 million in 1999 to more than 340 million in 2010. There is a growing epidemic of people who are addicted to the Internet, especially young people. The problem got so large that in 2004, that the government closed 16,000 Internet cafes and also created a center for the treatment of Internet addiction that treated more than 1,000 people a year (C. Stewart, 2010). A Harris poll surveyed a randomly selected sample of 1,178 American youth ages 8 to 18 and found that 8% of video game players were addicted to video game playing (Gentile, 2009).

Learned Helplessness. Television causes a decrease in persistence because viewers are learning to be helpless. This learned helplessness comes not from watching any one show or type of programming; it comes from the act of watching television itself.

Disinhibition. In the process of disinhibition, you gradually wear down your inhibitions, which prevent you from behaving in certain ways. For example, you may not like to dance in front of others, but after several months of watching dance programs, your resistance wears down, and you find yourself dancing in a club. Also, most of us have been raised to solve our problems in nonaggressive and nonviolent ways. However, after years of exposure to violent portrayals in the movies and on television, where attractive characters use violence successfully to get what they want, our aversion to using violence gradually wears down. One day, when someone steals the parking place we want, we find ourselves screaming and pounding the offender's car; our inhibitions that prevent us from behaving violently have been worn down and cannot prevent us from behaving violently.

Social Cocooning is an effect first identified by sociologist Raymond Williams in 1974 as mobile privatization: to describe the phenomenon of people forming technological bubbles around themselves. This is enabled by devices such as Sony's Walkman in 1979 and Apple's iPod in 2001 (Levy, 2006e, pp. 72, 74). New media allow us to be more individual. Now couples can cuddle while one person listens to music on her iPod while the other watches a sports contest on his cell phone—now that we have television on the go (Roberts, 2006a).

MACRO-LEVEL EFFECTS

Society

The overall level of happiness in society is generally down, and some critics are characterizing this as a media effect. Myers (2000) points out that from 1960 to 2000 in the United States, the divorce rate doubled, teen suicide rate tripled, violent crime quadrupled, and prison population quintupled. Lane (2000) points out that the rate of serious clinical depression has more than tripled over the past two generations. B. Schwartz (2004) says that the number of people who say they are very happy has been declining despite the fact that the GDP (gross domestic product, which is the primary indicator of economic prosperity) has more than doubled in the past three decades. Depression in 2000 was 10 times as likely as it was in 1900. He cites a UNICEF study that shows that suicide rates among adolescents and young adults have increased dramatically worldwide in the past several decades, especially in developed countries such as France (where it has tripled), Norway and Australia (where it has doubled), and Canada, England, and the United States (where it has increased 50%).

Fragmenting Society. Donnelly (1986) describes this fragmentation of society when he says that we are currently living in an Autonomy Generation that will soon change to a Confetti Generation. The Autonomy Generation people believe that each individual is the center of all relevant values. We are responsible only to ourselves, and we alone can decide which activities and ways of behaving have meaning for us and which do not. We live subjectively according to our own feelings with little need for outside reference. . . . We interpret life in terms of what's in it for us, seek authenticity by transcending society and external value systems, and insist on being ruled only by the laws of our character. . . . We live in the present, responding to momentary perceptions, relationships, and encounters. To us, what is most important is how outside events are perceived and understood by the individual" (p. 178). He says we experience

what Durkheim called *anomie,* the peculiar pain derived from individuals' inability to identify and experience their community.

Donnelly (1986) says that the new electronic media have five characteristics that will affect society: quantity (in terms of availability and use), speed (delivery and satisfaction), weightlessness of images (no context), remoteness (bring faraway information close), and choice (explosion of alternatives). Because the present generation does not possess the cultural tools to absorb such an explosion of information, we will become the Confetti Generation. The Confetti person is inundated by experience but ungrounded in any cultural discipline for arriving at any reality but the self.

Changing Social Interactions. The Internet serves to bring people together in cyber communities organized around common interests. This makes for a much more open and accessible social world (Weinberger, 2002). The Internet also reduces the time people spend with real individuals in real space (Nie & Erbring, 2002) and alters patterns of civic participation (Hampton, Livio, & Sessions-Goulet, 2010; Kang & Gearhart, 2010).

Changes to Worldwide Economy. Computers and the Internet have made the widespread use of credit cards possible. Visa has issued more than one billion cards worldwide and is used in 21 million locations in 300 countries and territories; Visa has 60% of the credit card market, so there are likely 1.7 billion credit cards in use in the world. This makes credit cards a universal currency. People don't need to deal with the currencies of individual countries (Hunter, 2002).

Creation of New Economies. Some MMORPGs have created cyber-economies that are now influencing real-world economies. For example, *WOW (World of Warcraft)* has created its own economy where players work to produce cyber-goods (such as gold pieces, exotic armor, and weaponry) that increase their power and prestige in the game. However, these cybergoods can also be exchanged in the real world for actual currencies. For example, some people in China work an 8-hour shift in the game to earn about 100 game gold pieces that they sell in a real-world market for $30 to newer players who want to advance fast in the game without having the time required to play themselves (Levy, 2006d).

Politics

Political campaigns have changed in many ways with the rise of the mass media. Campaign staffs now rely much more on media consultants. Campaigns must raise a great deal of money for paid advertising, especially on television. Candidates create pseudo-events so they can attract the press and get free coverage of their campaigns.

The way political parties choose their candidates has changed from selection by party bosses to primary elections and caucuses.

The newer media technologies have created a kind of e-democracy (Chadwick, 2006).

Religion

Religious bodies can use the media to attract more believers, reinforce their belief, and minister to their needs. About 25 million people per week watch religious services on television. The Catholic Church, with 2,000 years of history, is slow to change, but some changes relate to the mass media. Pope John Paul II used a laptop and was flooded with e-mails (Wilkinson, 2006). Also, the Catholic Church launched an Italian language website to allow people to ask questions about their religion and get answers. Questions are funneled out to 800 priests.

Appendix C

Contacts

Center for Media Education
2120 L Street, NW, Suite 200
Washington, DC 20037
Phone: (202) 331-7833
Website: http://www.densondesign
.com/CME.html

Center for Media Literacy
22631 Pacific Coast Highway, #472
Malibu, CA 90265
Phone: (310) 456-1225
Fax: (310) 456-0020
Website: http://www.medialit.com

Children Now
1212 Broadway, Suite 530
Oakland, CA 94612
Phone: (510) 763-2444
Website: www.childrennow.org

Citizens for Media Literacy
34 Wall Street, Suite 407
Asheville, NC 28801
Phone: (828) 255-0182
Website: http://main.nc.us/cml/

Media Education Lab
Temple University, School of Communications and
     Theater
2020 N. 13th Street, 1A Annenberg Hall
Philadelphia, PA 19122
Phone: (215) 204-3255
Fax: (215) 204-5081
Website: http://www.mediaeducationlab.com

Media Watch
P.O. Box 618
Santa Cruz, CA 95061
Phone: (831) 423-6355
E-mail: mwatch@cruzio.com
Website: www.mediawatch.com

National Association for Family and Community
     Education
Children's Television Project
73 Cavalier Blvd., Suite 106
Florence, KY 41042
Phone: (877) 712-4477 (toll free)
Fax: (859) 525-6496
Website: www.nafce.org

National Association for Media Literacy Education
Laurel Hill Drive
Cherry Hill, NJ 08003
Phone: (888) 775-2652
Website: http://namle.net/

Parents' Choice
201 West Padonia Road, Suite 303
Timonium, MD 21093
Phone: (410) 308-3858
Fax: 410-308-3877
Website: www.parents-choice.org

Consumer Groups Primarily Concerned With Advertising

Adbusters
1243 West Seventh Avenue
Vancouver, British Columbia
V6H 1B7, Canada
Phone: (604) 736-9401
Fax: (604) 737-6021
Website: www.adbusters.org/home/

Children's Advertising Review Unit
Council of Better Business Bureaus
70 West 36th Street, 12th Floor
New York, NY 10018
Phone: (866) 334-6272
Website: www.caru.org

Consumer Group Primarily Concerned With News

FAIR (Fairness and Accuracy in Reporting)
104 W. 27th Street, Suite 10B
New York, NY 10001
Phone: (212) 633-6700
Fax: (212) 727-7668
E-mail: fair@fair.org
Twitter: @FAIRmediawatch
Website: www.fair.org

Consumer Groups Primarily Concerned With TV and Movie Ratings

Classification and Rating Administration
Motion Picture Association of America, Inc.
15301 Ventura Blvd., Building E
Sherman Oaks, CA 91403
Phone: (818) 995-6600
Fax: (818) 285-4403
Website: www.mpaa.org

TV Parental Guidelines
Monitoring Board
P.O. Box 14097
Washington, DC 20004
Phone: (202) 879-9364
Website: www.tvguidelines.org

National Television Networks

ABC, Inc.
2040 Avenue of the Stars
Los Angeles, CA 90067
Phone: (310) 557-6655
Website: http://abc.go.com/

CBS Entertainment
7800 Beverly Boulevard
Los Angeles, CA 90036
Phone: (213) 460-3000
Fax: (213) 653-8266
Website: http://www.cbs.com/

Fox Broadcasting Company
P.O. Box 900
Beverly Hills, CA 90213
Phone: (310) 369-1000
Website: http://www.fox.com/home.htm

NBC Entertainment
3000 West Alameda
Burbank, CA 91523
Phone: (818) 840-4404
Website: www.nbc.com

Public Broadcasting Service
2100 Crystal Drive
Arlington, VA 22202
Phone: (703) 739-5040
Fax: (703) 739-5295
Website: www.pbs.org

U.S. Governmental Agencies

Federal Communications Commission
445 12th Street SW
Washington, DC 20554
Phone: (888) CALL-FCC (888-225-5322)
Fax: (866) 418-0232
E-mail: fccinfo@fcc.gov
Website: www.fcc.gov/vchip

Federal Trade Commission
Attention: Marketing Practices
Room 238
6th Street and Pennsylvania Avenue, NW
Washington, D.C. 20580
Fax: (202) 326-2222
Website: http://www.ftc.gov/bcp/consumer.shtm

United States House of Representatives
Subcommittee on Telecommunications and Finance
2125 Rayburn Building
Washington, D.C. 20515
Phone: (202) 225-2927
Website: http://www.house.gov/Welcome.shtml

United States Senate
Subcommittee on Communications, Technology, and
    the Internet
227 Hart Senate Office Building
Washington, D.C. 20510
Phone: (202) 224-5115
Website: www.senate.gov/ ~ commerce/

Glossary

Above-the-line employees: creative people who need talent in addition to hard work to do well in the media industries.

Abstracting: the skill of creating a brief, clear, and accurate description capturing the essence of a message in a smaller number of words than the message itself.

Activation: immediate behavioral effect where a media message triggers behavior suggested (but not actually depicted) in that message.

Active mediation: a media literacy technique that parents use with children that focuses on parents talking to their children during media exposures to help their children understand media messages better and to help them avoid negative effects.

Adaptation stage: fifth and last phase in the life cycle pattern of development of a mass medium where the medium redefines itself in the media marketplace and provides different messages or services not provided by the other media.

Analog coding: the recording, storage, and retrieval of information that relies on the physical properties of a medium; thus a sound is recorded, stored, and retrieved in a different manner than is a photographic image.

Analysis: the skill of breaking down a message into meaningful elements.

Attention: exposure to a media message that takes place in the attentional state; conscious awareness of the media message.

Attentional exposure state: the experience of being exposed to a media message, being aware of it, and actively interacting with the elements in the message.

Attitudinal-type effect: the media-influenced effect is manifested as the acquisition of an attitude, opinion, or belief or as the triggering, alteration, or reinforcement of existing attitudes, opinions, and beliefs.

Attraction: immediate behavioral effect where a media message attracts our exposure so we access a website, turn on the television, buy a book, and so on.

Audience conditioning: a strategy used by media organizations to make their existing audience members want to continually expose themselves to your messages.

Automatic exposure state: the experience of being exposed to a media message without being aware of the message.

Automaticity: an exposure state where we put our minds on "automatic pilot" and filter out almost all message options.

Automatic routines: sequences of behaviors or thoughts that we learn from experience and then apply again and again with little effort. Think of these as computer programs that run in the back of our minds without us consciously paying attention to them.

Baseline: a way of thinking about a person's typical probability of manifesting an effect.

Baseline effects: a form of process effect that alters a person's baseline by moving it up gradually to the manifestation level, moving it down away from the manifestation level, or reinforcing its position, thus making it more difficult to move in the future.

Behavioral-type effect: the media-influenced effect is manifested as the triggering of actions in a person or over time of altering or reinforcing patterns of action.

Below-the-line employees: typically the crafts and clerical people who need various skills to be able to perform their jobs well; these skills can be learned and improved with practice.

Blog: short for Web log; Internet sites set up by individuals, business, and news organizations that are designed to attract the attention of as many visitors as possible with text, audio, and video.

Boomerang effect: when researchers find that the interventions they have designed to improve media literacy have had the opposite effect, that is, actually resulted in decreasing media literacy.

Bootlegging: a form of media message piracy that refers to the unauthorized recording of a live delivery of a message and then the subsequent distribution of that recording.

Botnet: a network of infected computers (bots) that is remotely controlled by hackers.

Bot network activity: a technique used by spammers and hackers to hijack your computer so they can use your IP address and not their own so their activities cannot be traced back to them.

Brick-and-mortar stores: stores that people can physically (compared to virtually) visit to browse, touch the products (such as books, recordings, and DVDs), talk to live salespeople, buy the products, and leave the store with the physical product.

Cognitive development: the maturation of the human mind throughout childhood and throughout life; as the mind matures, it increases in its abilities for perception and reasoning.

Cognitive-type effect: the media-influenced effect is manifested as the acquisition of information (factual or social) as well as the

triggering, alteration, or reinforcement of a mental process.

Commercial mining: the ways businesses monitor your Internet activity and then sell that information to all kinds of other companies.

Company: a business that creates and markets media messages; not to be confused with the vehicles it markets, such as Google, which is a name that refers both to a company and to its vehicle.

Competencies: the ability to accomplish a task successfully, such as match the meaning of a media message element; in contrast to skills, competencies are categorical—that is, either you can perform the task successfully or you cannot.

Complex interdependence: the relationship among the five players in the economic game as they negotiate exchanges of resources.

Conceptual differentiation: the ability to classify objects into a large number of mutually exclusive categories.

Conglomerate merger: one company buys other companies that can be in the same industry (same type of business or a company's suppliers and distributors) as well as being in other industries.

Conglomerates: very large companies that own many different types of businesses.

Content analysis: a social scientific research method that focuses on certain characteristics of media messages (such as the demographics of characters or the portrayals of violence) and counts how frequently those characteristics occur.

Continuous partial attention: a long-term cognitive effect where the media reinforce a pattern of continually fading in and out of attention for media messages as we conduct multiple activities at the same time so that we lose the ability to devote full attention to any one thing.

Contrast effect: immediate attitudinal effect where people judge things in their real life as unfavorable (such as the attractiveness of their romantic partner) because their standards have been set unrealistically high by media messages.

Convergence: the moving together over time of things that were separated into a common group. This is a powerful force on the mass media that has three manifestations: techno-logical, business, and psychological.

Constraints: factors that put limitations on news stories; the major constraints are deadlines, resource limitations, and geographic focus.

Convergence: see *psychological convergence* and *technological convergence.*

Cookies: tiny computer files that are planted on your hard drive when you access many websites; these files store information about your browsing history and preferences and are activated next time you access the website that created the cookie.

Copyleft: the removing of restrictions so that media messages are free and all users have the right to distribute copies and modified versions of a work; based on the values of openness and common ownership.

Copyright: the legal establishment of owner-ship of a media message.

Counterfeiting: a form of media message piracy that refers to the duplication of a copy-righted message along with its packaging and selling it as the real product.

Coviewing: a media literacy technique that parents use with children that focuses on watching television with their children; it is believed that this has a positive effect because when parents coview, their children do not

watch undesirable programming or exhibit undesirable behaviors.

Creative commons: the sharing of resources for the common good such that everyone is allowed open access to the work of others and given the freedom to change that work and build on it for the common good.

Cross-media promotion: advertising your media message in another medium so as to attract people in that medium to try exposing themselves to your message.

Cross-vehicle promotion: advertising your media message in another vehicle so as to attract people in that medium to try exposing themselves to your message.

Crystalline intelligence: the ability to memorize facts as well as the facility to absorb the images, definitions, opinions, and agendas of others.

Cultivation: long-term attitudinal effect where, after exposure to many media messages, we come to believe the real world is like the world depicted in the media.

Decline stage: fourth phase in the life cycle pattern of development of a mass medium where the medium loses audience members and revenue due to competition from a newer medium that provides better messages or the same messages in a better way.

Deduction: the skill of using general principles to explain particulars.

Default strategy: when audience members do not think about their media exposures and do not make active decisions as they negotiate their resources of time and money; instead, they continue with their automatic habits that follow a goal of maintaining a minimal level of uninterrupted satisfaction.

Demographic segmentation: identifying a niche audience by their enduring characteristics, such as gender, ethnicity, and so on.

Denoted meanings: standard meanings for symbols that are shared by all people; these are the dictionary-type meanings we memorize for words and symbols when we are in elementary school.

Desensitization: long-term emotional effect where continual exposure to media messages that trigger emotional reactions is reduced; the most visible example of this is when repeated exposures to acts of aggression lead us to reduce our sympathy for victims of aggression.

Digital coding: the recording, storage, and retrieval of information that uses a sequence of symbols or bytes (usually numbers) that are not dependent on the physical characteristics of any one medium.

Direct support of media: consumers make payments directly to media companies in exchange for access to their messages.

Disinhibition: long-term behavioral effect where exposure to violent messages over time reduces the socialized inhibitions that prevent us from behaving in a violent or aggressive manner.

Displacement: long-term behavioral effect where the media gradually change how we spend our time by shifting our behaviors into media usage and away from other activities.

Economies of scale: the high costs of making the first copy of a media message are spread out over many copies; as additional copies are produced, the high cost of making the initial copy is averaged over a greater number of copies.

Economies of scope: the high costs of making a media message spread out over different messages; when an original message is translated into similar messages and distributed through different media.

Efficiency value: the belief that power in the government and the economy should be concentrated in the hands of a few people or businesses so that decisions can be made more quickly and enacted more smoothly.

Electromagnetic spectrum: a range of energy frequencies that are used for broadcasting messages without wires; in the United States, the Federal Communications Commission (FCC) is in charge of assigning frequencies to individuals and businesses for transmission of radio, television, and cell phone signals.

Electronic game: games that use an electronic format (compared to board games) and are delivered on several platforms: video, computer, console, and handheld device.

Emotional development: the maturation of one's abilities to recognize and understand the emotions in oneself and in others as well as the ability to control one's own emotional reactions.

Emotional intelligence: the ability to understand and control our emotions.

Emotional-type effect: the media-influenced effect is manifested as the triggering of an emotional reaction or the altering of emotional patterns over time.

Evaluation: the skill of judging the value of an element; the judgment is made by comparing a message element to some standard.

Exposure: the condition of being in proximity (place and time) to a message, having the message occur within our perceptual abilities, and leaving some impression (however slight) in our minds. Thus, there are three hurdles for exposure: physical, perceptual, and psychological.

Exposure states: four qualitatively distinct psychological states people can be in when experiencing a media message. These four states are automatic, attentional, transported, and self-reflexive.

Extensive learning: immediate cognitive effect of acquiring information that expands one's knowledge structure.

Factual information: discrete bits of information that can be confirmed by objective sources. Examples include names (of people, places, characters, etc.), dates, titles, definitions of terms, formulas, lists, and the like.

Federal Communications Commission (FCC): agency established by the U.S. Congress in the 1920s to regulate the new broadcasting industry and later the developing telecommunication industry; focuses primarily on establishing national standards for developing information technologies as well as regulating ownership of broadcasting and telecommunication businesses.

Field independency: a natural ability to distinguish between the signal and the noise in any message where the noise is the chaos of symbols and images, while the signal is the information that emerges from the chaos.

Fight/flight reaction: immediate physiological effect where a media message depicts a threat to a character in a story, and this triggers an automatic bodily response in audience members that prepares them to stand and fight off the threat or to flee from it to safety.

Filtering: the information-processing task where we continually make decisions about filtering out media messages (ignore them) or filter them in (pay attention to them).

Flow: when playing video games, the experience of being so focused on playing the game and achieving one's goals that the player loses track of time and place.

Fluctuation effects: a form of process effect where there is a temporary deviation off a person's baseline.

Fluid intelligence: the ability to be creative, make leaps of insight, and perceive things in a fresh and novel manner.

General entertainment story formula: all entertainment-type stories begin with a conflict or a problem; the conflict is heightened throughout the story, and the main characters try to solve the problem; the story is resolved in a climactic scene.

Generalization: a long-term cognitive effect that involves a process of observing a few occurrences of something in media messages, perceiving a pattern that ties together those occurrences, and then inferring that the pattern reflects something more general than those specific occurrences.

Genre: refers to a kind of message and suggests that there are categories within which media messages can be organized; the most general genres of media messages are entertainment, news/information, and persuasive messages (such as commercial messages and public service announcements [PSAs]).

Geodemographic segmentation: identifying a niche audience by a combination of where they live and their demographic characteristics.

Geographic segmentation: identifying a niche audience by where its members live and shop.

Grouping: the skill of determining which elements are alike in some way; determining how a group of elements are different from other groups of elements.

HDTV: high-definition television; video that has substantially higher (five times) resolution than standard television.

Hierarchy of needs: an organization of human needs as conceptualized by psychologist Abraham Maslow; human needs are arranged by five levels: survival, safety, social, self-esteem, and self-actualization. When the needs at a lower level are met, we focus on the needs at a higher level, so that we are always striving to satisfy some kind of need.

Hijacking: when hackers use your computer without your permission and often without your knowledge.

History stealing: a form of commercial mining where an Internet vendor records your activity on its site as it is allowed to do but then also allows other vendors to record this information.

Horizontal merger: one company buys another company of the same type so as to increase the number of outlets for the same products/services.

Hyperlocalism: the specialization of news vehicles in response to the fragmenting audience.

Hypermnesia: a long-term cognitive effect that is the opposite of forgetting information over time; instead, people seem to be able to recall more information over time without additional exposures to that information because their minds organize previously exposed information in ways that make it easier to recall.

Identity theft: thieves access enough personal information about you and then use your identity to get credit cards and buy products in your name.

Imitation: immediate behavioral effect where a media message triggers behavior that matches the behavior depicted in the media message.

Indirect support of media: consumers pay extra for advertised goods and services, and this extra amount goes to the media from advertisers.

Induction: the skill of inferring a pattern across a small set of elements, then generalizing the pattern to all elements in the set.

Information-processing tasks: a sequence of tasks of filtering media messages, then matching meaning and meaning construction.

Innovation stage: first phase in the life cycle pattern of development of a mass medium; it is characterized by technological and marketing innovations.

Inoculation: immediate attitudinal effect where designers of persuasive messages expose audiences to a preview of a message counter to their position so as to immunize those audience members against being influenced by the countermessage later.

Intensive learning: immediate cognitive effect of acquiring information that adds additional examples to a person's existing knowledge structure.

Interactive media: media platforms allow—and typically require—their audiences to create the content by themselves, in interaction with other audience members, or in interaction with employees of mass media organizations. Audience members are not paid for creating any of this content; to the contrary, audience members not only create the content for free but often pay the interactive mass media companies for access to the content either through subscription fees (as with many games) or by agreeing to be exposed to advertising.

Internet addiction disorder: long-term behavioral effect where people become addicted to accessing the Internet and lose control over their behavior.

Knowledge structures: sets of organized information stored in a person's memory. The crucial sets for media literacy are information about the media, their messages, their audiences, and their effects.

Learned helplessness: long-term behavioral effect where the media, especially television, has conditioned our behaviors to such a degree that we are helpless to change our behavior.

Learning agendas: long-term cognitive effect where we infer a pattern across many media messages that tells us what is important, that is, what should be on our agenda of things to pay attention to.

Life cycle pattern: a sequence of five stages of development typically followed by all mass media; the five stages are innovation, penetration, peak, decline, and adaptation.

Localism value: the belief that power in the government and the economy should be spread out over as many people as possible so that everyone has a voice that is heard as well as an influence on every decision.

Long tail marketing: a strategy of identifying smaller niche audiences that have been ignored by other media companies; the "long tail" refers to the extreme ends on the bell curve and ignoring the fat middle where the majority is represented.

Lowest common denominator: a programming principle where a media company (especially television) is seeking the largest audience possible so it creates messages that will not offend or challenge anyone, so the messages are highly formulaic and bland.

Macro-type effect: the media-influenced effect is manifested as the gradual altering or reinforcing of processes in aggregates of individuals such as organizations, institutions, and society.

Magic window: a perspective that regards media messages as a window on the world that presents the actual occurrences from the real world in an undistorted manner.

Manifested effects: media-influenced effects that can be observed and easily attributed to media influence.

Marketing concept: a practice among marketers that begins with research to identify audience needs, and then messages are developed to satisfy those special needs and thus attract a particular kind of audience.

Marketing convergence: because of technological convergence and digitization of media messages, media businesses have changed their focus away from channels of distribution to messages and now construct strategies to market a message to their target audience across as many platforms as possible.

Marketing innovations: a characteristic of the innovation states in the development of a mass medium where marketers attract new users to its medium and convince them that the new medium is a superior way for them to access media messages.

Marketing perspective: this is a news-framing influence where news workers pay careful attention to what kinds of stories and presentation formats generate the largest audience.

Mass audience: old conceptualization of the media audience as being very large, composed of all kinds of people who are anonymous and interchangeable; within the audience there is no social organization or interaction among audience members.

Mass communication: one-way communication from media organizations to members of a mass audience.

Maturation: the development of one's natural abilities physically, cognitively, emotionally, and morally.

Meaning construction: the information-processing task where we engage in a process of creating our own meaning for a media message. This process is usually engaged when we have no denoted meaning already residing in our memory or when the denoted meaning does not satisfy our current needs.

Meaning matching: the information-processing task where we engage in a process of recognizing elements (referents) in a media message and then automatically access our memory to find the meanings we have memorized for those elements.

Media literacy: a set of perspectives that we actively use to expose ourselves to the mass media to interpret the meaning of the messages we encounter. Media literacy is multidimensional, consisting of cognitive, emotional, aesthetic, and moral dimensions. And media literacy is a continuum, not a category.

Mental codes: rules for decision making that we have learned through exposure to media messages. These are stored in our memory and automatically activated when we engage in information-processing tasks of filtering and meaning matching.

Messages: the instruments that deliver information to us from the media.

Metered paywall: a device used by websites where visitors are allowed to access a certain number of pages, then their continued access is denied until they pay the subscription fee to give them further access.

Money cycle: the continual and accelerating flow of money in sports from the public to advertisers, to television networks, to leagues and owners, and to players.

Monopolistic competition: the economic condition within most media industries where a few powerful companies control the majority of resources that compete aggressively among themselves.

Moral development: the maturation of one's ability to reason about the value of the motives and consequences of the decisions of others and oneself.

Net loser: when engaging in exchanges of resources, people and organizations are net losers when the value of the resources they take is less than the value of the resources they give.

Net winner: when engaging in exchanges of resources, people and organizations are net winners when the value of the resources they take is greater than the value of the resources they give.

News-framing influences: constructions of journalists to help them do their jobs more easily and to fulfill the goals of the businesses that employ them; the major news-framing influences are commercialism, the marketing perspective, organizational structures, ownership, use of sources, branding, values, hyperlocalism, and story formula.

News perspective: a view of what is news that is developed on-the-job by journalists as they learn to work within all the news constraints and story formulas.

Next-step reality: the idea that media messages must be based on real-world elements (recognizable characters, situations, etc.) so that audiences can relate to them, but then the messages must also take a step away from pure reality by adding fantasy elements to capture and hold the audience's attention.

Niche audience: a relatively small audience that is defined by a shared interest or need among audience members.

Nonimpulsiveness: the willingness to avoid rushing into decisions for the sake of efficiency and instead analyze messages carefully to ensure greater accuracy.

Payola: an illegal practice where record companies pay radio disk jockeys to play their records on the air.

Paywall: a device used by websites where visitors are allowed to access some content while most of the content is walled off from them until they pay the subscription fee for access.

Peak stage: third phase in the life cycle pattern of development of a mass medium where the medium commands the most attention from the public and generates the most revenue compared to other media.

Penetration stage: second phase in the life cycle pattern of development of a mass medium where it attracts larger numbers of audience members of all kinds.

Perceptual exposure: the message falls within humans' bandwidth of visual and/or auditory perception.

Personal locus: a person's plan for building knowledge structures about the media along with the psychic energy needed to execute the plan.

Phishing: a technique used to acquire sensitive information from innocent users by seemingly trustworthy message senders; victims receive an e-mail message that typically directs them to a fake website whose look and feel are almost identical to the legitimate one (like a bank or insurance company) and the victim is asked to sign in and divulge private information.

Physical exposure: the message and the person occupy the same physical space for some period of time.

Physiological-type effect: the media-influenced effect is manifested as the triggering of an automatic body function, such as increasing blood pressure and heart rate.

Piracy: the unauthorized use of copyrighted material; with media messages, it typically takes three forms: bootlegging, counterfeiting, and sharing copyrighted messages without paying for access.

Primetime: a television viewing term that refers to the hours of the day when the audience is largest for television, so networks and stations present their strongest programming then and charge their highest advertising rates; those hours are 8 p.m. to 11 p.m. every day except Sunday, when primetime begins at 7 p.m. Also in the central time zone, primetime begins and ends 1 hour earlier than in the other time zones.

Privacy: the secluding of personal information by individuals about themselves.

Process effects: media-influenced effects that are continually occurring without being easily observed.

Profit: the positive difference between a company's revenue and expenses; often used mistakenly as a synonym for revenue.

Psychographic segmentation: identifying a niche audience by their psychological and lifestyle characteristics.

Psychological convergence: perception among audience members that they can easily access all kinds of media messages and transform them to fit their own needs in an interactive manner with other audience members; the breaking down of barriers between audiences and mass media organizations as well as the barriers separating audience members from one another due to geography or other social constraints.

Psychological exposure: the message creates a trace element in a person's mind.

Puffery: a technique used by advertisers to use words in a way that it appears they are making claims for the superiority of their products when in fact they are making claims that cannot be tested.

Quality audience goal: attempting to attract a particular kind of audience; the word *quality* refers to kind of audience, not to an elite audience.

Quantity audience goal: attempting to attract as large an audience as possible.

Restrictive mediation: a media literacy technique that parents use with children that focuses on setting and enforcing rules about media exposure, particularly television.

Revenue streams: sources of income for a business.

ROA: return on assets; the comparison of a business' annual profit compared to the size of its asset base expressed as a percentage.

ROR: return on revenue; the comparison of a business' annual profit compared to its annual revenues expressed as a percentage.

Sanitized violence: media portrayals typically clean up the way violence is portrayed so as not to offend viewers with graphicness and the suffering of victims.

Search engine: a service provided usually free to Internet users that allows them to type in a key term and the service provides them with a list of Internet sites relevant to that term; these sites are usually rank ordered by popularity but are often influenced by advertising support, where advertisers pay the search engine company a fee to have their website move up in the rankings of popularity.

Self-actualization: the highest level of need in Maslow's hierarchy of human needs; the needs at this level focus on fulfilling one's self through creativity and morality.

Self-reflexive exposure state: the experience of being exposed to a media message with a high degree of awareness of the media message as well as a high awareness of standing apart from the message while analyzing it.

Skills: tools we use to build strong knowledge structures. There are seven generic skills necessary with media literacy: analysis, evaluation, grouping, induction, deduction, abstraction, and synthesis. In contrast to competencies, skills are continuous in the sense that there are relative degrees of ability on the performance of skills.

Sleeper curve: long-term attitudinal effect where we develop the attitude that media messages are harmful.

Sleeper effect: long-term attitudinal effect where a person creates a negative attitude about a particular message during an exposure to a message because of a dislike for the source, but then over time, the attitude changes to a positive one because the person forgets about the source while remembering the message.

Social class segmentation: identifying a niche audience by the level of their social class, such as lower class, middle class, and upper class.

Social cocooning: long-term behavioral effect where people form technological bubbles around themselves to separate them from their real surrounding.

Social information: composed of accepted beliefs that cannot be verified by authorities in the same way factual information can be. People learn social information by observing how people behave in social interactions and the consequences of those behaviors.

Socialization: long-term effect where we use media messages to form our beliefs about how society works in the real world.

Social networking: a need among humans to experience contact with other humans by forming groups both formal and informal.

Spamming: using the media to invade your privacy with unsolicited and unwanted messages.

Spyware: a small program that is inadvertently downloaded by computer users when they access certain websites; the program installs itself on that person's computer and then collects information about users without their knowledge.

Story formulas: the guidelines that producers of media messages use to attract audiences, hold their attention throughout the message, and condition them for repeat exposures.

Subliminal advertising: a belief among conspiracy theorists that advertisers use subliminal techniques to manipulate audiences of their advertising unfairly. This is a false belief because subliminal means that the message elements are outside the ability of humans to perceive them.

Synthesis: the skill of assembling elements into a new structure.

Talent: an economic resource of above-the-line media employees that refers to their ability to attract and condition audiences for repeat exposures.

Technological convergence: the breaking down of barriers that separated the different media channels of communication (such as print media, broadcast TV, film, computers, etc.) primarily due to the digitization of information so that a message could move seamlessly across all media channels of communication.

Technological innovations: a characteristic of the innovation states in the development of a mass medium where inventors develop a new form of transmitting information.

Telescoping: the way electronic game players must keep the big picture of the overall game in mind while focusing on the immediate objectives that face them at any one point in the game.

Timing of effects: focuses on when a media-influenced effect is manifested; it has two values of immediate (where the manifestation occurs during the media exposure or shortly after) and long term (where the manifestation does not occur until the person has experienced many exposures to media messages).

Tolerance for ambiguity: the willingness to follow situations into unfamiliar territory that go beyond our preconceptions and take us out of our comfort zone.

Transported exposure state: the experience of being exposed to a media message and swept away by it into a different place and time such that the people lose sense of their current physical surroundings and current point in time.

Trolling: posting of willfully inflammatory, off-topic, or simply stupid remarks on the blogs of others.

Type of effect: refers to the form of the manifestation of the effect in individuals (cognitive, attitudinal, emotional, physiological, or behavioral) and in larger aggregates (macro-type effect).

Valence of effects: refers to whether an effect is positive or negative.

Vehicle: the means by which a media company sends its messages to audiences; for example, with television, the vehicles are the programs, and with Google, the vehicle is its Internet browser.

Vertical merger: one company buys suppliers and/or distributors to create integration in the production and distribution of products/services.

Viral spiral: the Internet provides for an upward spiral of innovation because of its open networking structure. By giving all people free access to ideas, the creators of those ideas can easily disseminate them widely and allow others to build on those ideas and extend them in creative ways.

Virus: a hidden element of computer code that lurks unobserved in the computer until it is activated, at which point it begins destroying some of the code in your computer and renders some programs and often your entire computer nonfunctional; it is highly contagious and is copied from computer to computer through e-mails and downloaded files.

Web 1.0: category of older Internet companies (such as Yahoo, AOL, and Netscape) that provided services that were proprietary—that is, their source code was kept secret so competitors could not use it.

Web 2.0: a perspective about the Internet that fosters a social dynamic where people have the freedom to share their work through all sorts of open websites. People are free to access all these sites, use what they want, create their own messages, and make their messages available to anyone.

References

Abelman, R. (1999). Preaching to the choir: Profiling TV advisory ratings users. *Journal of Broadcasting & Electronic Media, 43,* 529–550.

Addicted? Really? (2011, March 12). *The Economist,* pp. 9–10.

Ader, D. R. (1995). A longitudinal study of agenda setting for the issue of environmental pollution. *Journalism & Mass Communication Quarterly, 72,* 300–311.

Albarran, A. B. (2002). *Media economics: Understanding markets, industries and concepts* (2nd ed.). Ames: Iowa State Press.

Albarran, A. B., & Chan-Olmsted, S. M. (1998). The United States of America. In A. B. Albarran & S. M. Chan-Olmsted (Eds.), *Global media economics: Commercialization, concentration and integration of world media markets* (pp. 19–32). Ames: Iowa State University Press.

Altheide, D. L. (1976). *Creating reality: How TV news distorts events.* Beverly Hills, CA: Sage.

American advertising in the media. (2011, June 24). Retrieved June 24, 2011, from http://answers.google.com/answers/threadview?id=56750

American Obesity Association. (2004, June 24). *AOA factsheets.* Retrieved July 9, 2004, from http://obesity.org/subs/fastfacts/obesity_what2.shtml

Ammons, L., Dimmick, J., & Pilotta, J. (1982). Crime news reporting in a Black weekly. *Journalism Quarterly, 59,* 310–313.

Anderson, D. R., Collins, P. A., Schmitt, K. L., & Jacobvitz, R. S. (1996). Stressful life events and television viewing. *Communication Research, 23,* 243–260.

Anderson, J. A. (1983). Television literacy and the critical viewer. In J. Bryant & D. R. Anderson (Eds.), *Children's understanding of television: Research on attention and comprehension* (pp. 297–327). New York: Academic Press.

Angwin, J. (2009). *Stealing MySpace: The battle to control the most popular website in America.* New York: Random House.

Anonymous no more. (2011, March 12). *The Economist,* p. 8.

AOL is sued over privacy breach. (2006, September 26). *Los Angeles Times,* p. C2.

AP Online. (2000, March 13). *Timeline of major media mergers.* Financial Section.

Arens, W. F. (1999). *Contemporary advertising* (7th ed.). Boston: Irwin McGraw-Hill.

Arndorfer, J. B. (1998, December 21). A-B looking for women via daytime TV programs. *Advertising Age, 69*(51), 8.

Arnold, E. K. (2011, May 16). Another day, another gigantic media merger—Microsoft's $8.5 billion purchase of Skype. Retrieved July 25, 2011, from http://www.alternet.org/newsandviews/article/589431/another_day,_another_gigantic_media_merger_--_microsoft%27s_$8.5_billion_purchase_of_skype/

An audacious merger with a poor reception. (2011, March 26). *The Economist,* pp. 71–72.

Aubrey, J. S. (2006). Effects of sexually objectifying media on self-objectification and body surveillance in undergraduates: Results of a 2-year panel study. *Journal of Communication, 56,* 366–386.

Austin, E. W. (1993). Exploring the effects of active parental mediation of television content. *Journal of Broadcasting & Electronic Media, 37,* 147–158.

Austin, E. W., Bolls, P., Fujioka, Y., & Engelbertson, J. (1999). How and why parents take on the tube. *Journal of Broadcasting & Electronic Media, 43,* 175–192.

Austin, E. W., & Meili, H. K. (1995). Effects of interpretations of television alcohol portrayals on children's alcohol beliefs. *Journal of Broadcasting & Electronic Media, 39,* 417–435.

Austin, E. W., & Pinkleton, B. E. (2001). The role of parental mediation in the political socialization process. *Journal of Broadcasting & Electronic Media, 45,* 221–240.

Aversa, J. (1999, May 5). Government employees get no respect on TV. *Tallahassee Democrat,* p. 3A.

Badenhausen, K. (2010, September 9). The NFL's highest paid players. *Forbes.* Retrieved June 22, 2011, from http://blogs.forbes.com/kurtbadenhausen/2010/09/09/the-nfls-highest-paid-players/

Badenhausen, K., Ozanian, M. K., & Settimi, C. (Eds.). (2011, January 26). The NBA's most valuable teams. *Forbes.* Retrieved June 22, 2011, from http://www.forbes.com/lists/2011/32/basketball-valuations-11_land.html

Baek, Y. M., & Wojcieszak, M. E. (2009). Don't expect too much! Learning from late-night comedy and knowledge item difficulty. *Communication Research, 36,* 783–809.

Bagdikian, B. (1983). *The media monopoly.* Boston: Beacon.

Bagdikian, B. (1992). *The media monopoly* (4th ed.). Boston: Beacon.

Bagdikian, B. (2000). *The media monopoly* (6th ed.). Boston: Beacon.

Baker, C. (2003, August). Cracking the box office genome. *Wired,* p. 52.

BallHyped News. (2011, January 24). 2011 Super Bowl ad rates. Retrieved June 23, 2011, from http://news.ball hyped.com/2011/01/24/2011-super-bowl-ad-rates/

Bandura, A. (1986). *Social foundations of thought and action: A social cognitive theory.* Englewood Cliffs, NJ: Prentice Hall.

Bandura, A. (1994). Social cognitive theory of mass communication. In J. Bryant & D. Zillmann (Eds.), *Media effects* (pp. 61–90). Hillsdale, NJ: Lawrence Erlbaum.

Barber, B. R. (1995). *Jihad vs. McWorld.* New York: New York Times Books.

Barner, M. R. (1999). Sex-role stereotyping in FCC-mandated children's educational television. *Journal of Broadcasting & Electronic Media, 43,* 551.

Bartholomew, D. (2002, May 4). Bill would outlaw soda sales at schools. *Santa Barbara News-Press,* p. A3.

Bash, A. (1997, June 10). Most parents don't use ratings to guide viewing. *USA Today,* p. 3D.

The basics of selling on eBay: Student guide. (2007). San Jose, CA: eBay.

Battles, K., & Hilton-Morrow, W. (2002). Gay characters in conventional spaces: *Will and Grace* and the situation comedy genre. *Critical Studies in Media Communication, 19,* 87–106.

Bauder, D. (1998, January 15). NBC pays record price to keep *ER. Santa Barbara News-Press,* p. C3.

Bauder, D. (2000a, February 26). Fox network swears off spectacle TV—again. *Tallahassee Democrat,* p. 3E.

Bauder, D. (2000b, March 14). CBS to air two reality TV shows. *Tallahassee Democrat,* p. B1.

Bauer, R. A., & Bauer, A. (1960). America, mass society and mass media. *Journal of Social Issues, 10*(3), 3–66.

Beam, A. (2002, January 10). Attack of the teeny books. *Boston Globe,* p. D1.

Beam, R. A. (2003). Content difference between daily newspapers with strong and weak market orientations. *Journalism & Mass Communication Quarterly, 80,* 368–390.

Becker, L. B., Kosicki, G. M., & Jones, F. (1992). Racial differences in evaluation of the mass media. *Journalism Quarterly, 69,* 124–134.

Bellamy, R. V., Jr. (1998). The evolving television sports marketplace. In L. A. Wenner (Ed.), *MediaSport* (pp. 73–87). New York: Routledge.

Bennett, D. (2011a, April 5). There isn't a single women's college basketball program that makes money. *Business Insider.* Retrieved June 22, 2011, from http://www.businessinsider.com/womens-college-basketball-lose-money-2011-4

Bennett, D. (2011b, June 15). Only 22 of 120 Division I athletic programs made money last year. *Business Insider.* Retrieved June 22, 2011, from http://www.businessinsider.com/ncaa-revenue-expense-report-2011-6

Bennett, W. L. (2003). *News: The politics of illusion* (5th ed.). New York: Longman.

Bettig, R. V., & Hall, J. L. (2003). *Big media, big money: Cultural texts and political economies.* Lanham, MD: Rowman & Littlefield.

Bielby, D., & Bielby, W. T. (2001). Audience segmentation and age stratification among television writers. *Journal of Broadcasting & Electronic Media, 45,* 391.

Bielby, D., & Bielby, W. (2002). Hollywood dreams, harsh realities: Writing for film and television. *Context, 1*(4), 21–27.

Big game in Big Ten gets a title sponsor. (2005, October 27). *Los Angeles Times,* p. D3.

Bimber, B. (1996, December 3). Study: 51 million Americans have Internet access. *93106 Newspaper,* p. 3.

Bissell, K. L., & Zhou, P. (2004). Must-see TV or ESPN: Entertainment and sports media exposure and body-image distortion in college women. *Journal of Communication, 54*(1), 5–21.

Blumer, H. (1946). Collective behavior. In A. M. Lee (Ed.), *Principles of sociology* (pp. 185–186). New York: Barnes & Noble.

Boehlert, E. (2001, March 14). Pay for play. *Salon.com Magazine.* http://archive.salon.com/21st/feature/1998/02/cov_11feature.html

Bollier, D. (2008). *Viral spiral: How the commoners built a digital republic of their own.* New York: The New Press.

Boswell, T. (1996, July 20). Between the commercials, waiting for the real show. *Washington Post,* p. G9.

Brand Channel. (2011, June 24). Brandcameo: Films. Retrieved June 24, 2011, from http://www.brand channel.com/brandcameo_films.asp?movie_year=2011#movie_list

British Broadcasting Corporation. (1972). *Violence on television: Programme content and viewer perceptions.* London: Author.

Brown, J. A. (1991). *Television "critical viewing skills" education: Major media literacy projects in the United States and selected countries.* Hillsdale, NJ: Lawrence Erlbaum.

Brown, J. A. (1998). Media literacy perspectives. *Journal of Communication, 48*(1), 44–57.

Brown, J. A. (2001). Media literacy and critical television viewing in education. In D. G. Singer & J. L. Singer (Eds.), *Handbook of children and the media* (pp. 681–697). Thousand Oaks, CA: Sage.

Brown, J. D., Childers, K. W., Bauman, K. E., & Koch, G. G. (1990). The influence of new media and family structure on young adolescents' television and radio use. *Communication Research, 17,* 65–82.

Brownfield, P. (1999, July 21). As minorities' TV presence dims, gay roles proliferate. *Los Angeles Times,* p. A1.

Bruner, J. S., Goodnow, J., & Austin, G. A. (1956). *A study of thinking.* New York: John Wiley.

Bucy, E. P., & Newhagen, J. E. (1999). The emotional appropriateness heuristic: Processing televised presidential reactions to the news. *Journal of Communication, 49*(4), 59–79.

Buerkel-Rothfuss, N. L. (1993). Background: What prior research shows. In B. S. Greenberg, J. D. Brown, & N. Buerkel-Rothfuss (Eds.), *Media, sex and the adolescent* (pp. 5–18). Cresskill, NJ: Hampton.

Building with big data. (2011, May 28). *The Economist,* p. 74.

Bunting, G. F. (2007, April 15). $78 million of red ink? *Los Angeles Times,* pp. A1, A24–A25.

Bureau of Labor Statistics. (2011). *Occupational outlook handbook, 2010–11 edition.* Retrieved July 22, 2011, from http://www.bls.gov/oco/ocos320.htm#emply

Busselle, R., & Crandall, H. (2002). Television viewing and perceptions about race differences in socioeconomic success. *Journal of Broadcasting & Electronic Media, 46,* 265–283.

Byrne, S. (2009). Media literacy interventions: What makes them boom or boomerang? *Communication Education, 58,* 1–14.

Calzo, J. P., & Ward, L. M. (2009). Media exposure and viewers' attitudes toward homosexuality: Evidence for mainstreaming or resonance? *Journal of Broadcasting & Electronic Media, 53,* 280–299.

"Can Spam." (2004, January 5). *Providence Journal,* p. A8.

Cantor, J. (2001). The media and children's fears, anxieties, and perceptions of danger. In D. G. Singer & J. L. Singer (Eds.), *Handbook of children and the media* (pp. 207–221). Thousand Oaks, CA: Sage.

Cantor, J., & Wilson, B. J. (1984). Modifying fear responses to mass media in preschool and elementary school children. *Journal of Broadcasting, 28,* 431–443.

Cantril, H. (1947). The invasion from Mars. In T. Newcomb & E. Hartley (Eds.), *Readings in social psychology* (pp. 619–628). New York: Holt.

Caplan, J. (2008, December 15). De-cluttering your mailbox. *Time,* p. 58.

Carr, N. (2010, June). Chaos theory. *Wired,* pp. 112–118.

Cassata, M., & Skill, T. (1983). *Life on daytime television.* Norwood, NJ: Ablex.

Castronova, E. (2001, December). *Virtual worlds: A firsthand account of market and society on the cyberian frontier* (CESifo Working Paper No. 618). Munich, Germany: Center for Economic Studies and Ifo Institute for Economic Research.

Castronova, E. (2005). *Synthetic worlds.* Chicago: University of Chicago Press.

CBS Corporation. (n.d.). Retrieved Aug 30, 2009, from http://en.wikipedia.org/wiki/CBS_Corporation

CBS headquarters, name taken over by Westinghouse. (1997, December 2). *Santa Barbara News-Press,* p. A6.

Chadwick, A. (2006). Internet politics: States, citizens, and new communication technologies. Oxford, UK: Oxford University Press.

Chandler, J., Konrath, S., & Schwarz, N. (2009). Online and on my mind: Temporary and chronic accessibility moderate the influence of media figures. *Media Psychology, 12,* 210–226.

Chew, F., & Palmer, S. (1994). Interest, the knowledge gap, and television programming. *Journal of Broadcasting & Electronic Media, 38,* 271–287.

Chmielewski, D. C. (2011a, May 31). Bringing order to YouTube's chaos. *Los Angeles Times,* pp. B1, B3.

Chmielewski, D. C. (2011b, June 29). Two final bidders vie for MySpace. *Los Angeles Times,* p. B3.

Chmielewski, D. C., & Fritz, B. (2009, September 1). Marvel makes for mightier mouse. *Los Angeles Times,* pp. A1, A7.

Chmielewski, D. C., & Guynn, J. (2011, June 30). MySpace fetches $35 million in a fall as swift as its rise. *Los Angeles Times,* pp. A1, A16.

Chmielewski, D. C., & Semuels, A. (2006, September 23). In a high-tech world, I spy, you spy, we spy. *Los Angeles Times,* pp. C1, C3.

Cho, J. (2005). Media, interpersonal discussion, and electoral choice. *Communication Research, 32,* 295–322.

Cho, J., & McLeod, D. M. (2007). Structural antecedents to knowledge and participation: Extending the knowledge gap concept to participation. *Journal of Communication, 57,* 205–228.

Cho, S. (2007). TV news coverage of plastic surgery, 1972–2004. *Journalism and Mass Communication Quarterly, 84,* 75–89.

Chory-Assad, R. M., & Yanen, A. (2005). Hopelessness and loneliness as predictors of older adults' involvement with favorite television performers. *Journal of Broadcasting & Electronic Media, 49,* 182–201.

Christianson, P. G., & Roberts, D. F. (1998). *It's not only rock & roll: Popular music in the lives of adolescents.* Cresskill, NJ: Hampton.

Coleman, R., & McCombs, M. (2007). The young and agenda-less? Exploring age-related differences in agenda setting on the youngest generation, baby boomers, and the civic generation. *Journalism and Mass Communication Quarterly, 84,* 495–508.

Coller, M. (2011, January 6). ESPN and NFL on verge of extending TV contract. Retrieved June 23, 2011, from http://www.bizoffootball.com/index.php?option com_content&view = article&id = 743:espn-and-nfl-on-verge-of-extending-tv-contract&catid = 34:nfl-news&Itemid = 53

Coltrane, S., & Messineo, M. (2000, March). The perpetuation of subtle prejudice: Race and gender imagery in 1990s television advertising. *Sex Roles: A Journal of Research,* p. 363.

Columbia Broadcasting System. (1980). *Network prime time violence tabulations for 1978–1979 season.* New York: Author.

Combs, B., & Slovic, P. (1979). Newspaper coverage of causes of death. *Journalism Quarterly, 56,* 837–843, 849.

Comcast. (n.d.). Retrieved August 30, 2009, from http://en.wikipedia.org/wiki/Comcast

Common Cause. (n.d.). Media mega mergers: A timeline. Retrieved July 25, 2011, from http://www.commoncause.org/site/pp.asp?c = dkLNK1MQIwG&b = 4923181

Comstock, G. A. (1980). *Television in America.* Beverly Hills, CA: Sage.

Comstock, G. A. (1989). *The evolution of American television.* Newbury Park, CA: Sage.

Comstock, G. A., Chaffee, S., Katzman, N., McCombs, M., & Roberts, D. (1978). *Television and human behavior.* New York: Columbia University Press.

Considine, D. M. (1997). Media literacy: A compelling component of school reform and restructuring. In R. Kubey (Ed.), *Media literacy in the information age* (pp. 243–262). New Brunswick, NJ: Transaction Publishers.

Cooper, C. A. (1996). *Violence on television: Congressional inquiry, public criticism and industry response.* New York: University Press of America.

Cooper, R. (1993). An expanded, integrated model for determining audience exposure to television. *Journal of Broadcasting & Electronic Media, 38,* 401–418.

Coors scores big placement deal. (2002, August 13). *Santa Barbara News-Press,* p. D5.

Corder-Bolz, C. R. (1980). Mediation: The role of significant others. *Journal of Communication, 30*(3), 106–118.

Critser, G. (2004, January 25). Truth: A bitter pill for drug makers. *Los Angeles Times,* pp. M1, M2.

Croteau, D., & Hoynes, W. (2001). *The business of media: Corporate media and the public interest.* Thousand Oaks, CA: Pine Forge Press.

Csikszentmihalyi, M. (1988). The flow experience and its significance for human psychology. In M. Csikszentmihalyi & I. S. Csikszentmihalyi (Eds.), *Optimal experience: Psychological studies of flow in consciousness* (pp. 15–35). New York: Cambridge University Press.

D'Alessio, D., & Allen, M. (2000). Media bias in presidential elections: A meta-analysis. *Journal of Communication, 50,* 133–156.

Daly, C., Henry, P., & Ryder, E. (2000). The structure of the magazine industry. In A. N. Greco (Ed.), *The media and entertainment industries* (pp. 26–45). Boston: Allyn & Bacon.

Davenport, T. H., & Beck, J. C. (2001). *The attention economy: Understanding the new currency of business.* Boston: Harvard Business School Press.

Davie, W. R., & Lee, J.-S. (1993). Television news technology: Do more sources mean less diversity? *Journal of Broadcasting & Electronic Media, 39,* 453–464.

Davie, W. R., & Lee, J.-S. (1995). Sex, violence, and consonance/differentiation: An analysis of local TV news values. *Journalism & Mass Communication Quarterly, 72,* 128–138.

Davies, M. M. (1997). Making media literate: Educating future media workers at the undergraduate level. In R. Kubey (Ed.), *Media literacy in the information age* (pp. 263–284). New Brunswick, NJ: Transaction Publishers.

Davis, B. (1990). Media hoaxes. *Wilson Library Bulletin, 64*(10), 139–140.

Dennis, E. E. (1993, April 15). *Fighting media illiteracy: What every American needs to know and why.* Paper presented at the Roy W. Howard Public Lecture in Journalism and Mass Communication, Number 4, School of Journalism, Indiana University, Bloomington.

Desmond, R. (1997). Media literacy in the home: Acquisition versus deficit models. In R. Kubey (Ed.), *Media literacy in the information age* (pp. 323–343). New Brunswick, NJ: Transaction Publishers.

Desmond, R. J., Singer, J. L., Singer, D. G., Calam, R., & Colimore, K. (1985). Family mediation patterns and television viewing: Young children's use and grasp of the medium. *Human Communication Research, 11,* 461–480.

Diamant, A. (1994, October). Media violence. *Parents Magazine, 69*(10), 40.

Dickerson, J. (2005, March 8). Advertisers: Their skin is available. *Los Angeles Times,* p. E10.

Diefenbach, D. L., & West, M. D. (2007). Television and attitudes toward mental health issues: Cultivation analysis and the third-person effect. *Journal of Community Psychology, 35,* 181–195.

Diener, E., & De Four, D. (1978). Does television violence enhance programme popularity? *Journal of Personality and Social Psychology, 36,* 333–341.

Diener, E., & Woody, L. W. (1981). TV violence and viewer liking. *Communication Research, 8,* 281–306.

Dizard, W., Jr. (2000). *Old media new media* (3rd ed.).New York: Longman.

Dominick, J. R. (1999). *The dynamics of mass communication* (6th ed.). Boston: McGraw-Hill.

Donnelly, W. J. (1986). *The confetti generation: How the new communications technology is fragmenting America.* New York: Holt.

Dorr, A. (1981). Television and affective development and functioning: Maybe this decade. *Journal of Broadcasting, 25,* 335–345.

Dorr, A. (1986). *Television and children: A special medium for a special audience.* Beverly Hills, CA: Sage.

Dorr, A., Kovaric, P., & Doubleday, C. (1989). Parent-child coviewing of television. *Journal of Broadcasting & Electronic Media, 33,* 35–51.

Douglas, W., & Olson, B. M. (1995). Beyond family structure: The family in domestic comedy. *Journal of Broadcasting & Electronic Media, 39,* 236–261.

Douglas, W., & Olson, B. M. (1996). Subversion of the American family? An examination of children and parents in television families. *Communication Research, 23,* 73–99.

Dow, B. J. (2001). Ellen, television, and the politics of gay and lesbian visibility. *Critical Studies in Media Communication, 18,* 123–132.

Doyle, G. (2002). *Understanding media economics.* London: Sage.

Duhigg, C., Gaither, C., & Chmielewski, D. C. (2006, September 28). Creator of Morpheus is found liable. *Los Angeles Times,* pp. C1, C6.

Duhigg, C., & Hamilton, W. (2005, July 26). Paying a price. *Los Angeles Times,* pp. A1, A14.

Dutka, E. (2003, August 31). Audience tests: Plot thickens. *Los Angeles Times,* p. E8.

Easley, J. (2010, September 29). Fox News viewership plunges 21% while MSNBC grows. Retrieved July 27, 2011, from http://www.politicusa.com/en/fox-msnbc-ratings

eBay. (n.d.). Retrieved August 30, 2009, from http://en.wikipedia.org/wiki/EBay

E-commerce: The road ahead. (2002, September 30). *Newsweek,* p. 38V.

Eggermont, S. (2004). Television viewing, perceived similarity, and adolescents' expectations of a romantic partner. *Journal of Broadcasting & Electronic Media, 48,* 244–265.

Einstein, M. (2004). *Media diversity: Economics, ownership, and the FCC.* Mahwah, NJ: Lawrence Erlbaum.

Elasmar, M., Hasegawa, K., & Brain, M. (1999). The portrayals of women in U.S. prime time television. *Journal of Broadcasting & Electronic Media, 43,* 20–34.

Eller, C. (1999, July 9). Literary manager built career by not following script. *Los Angeles Times,* pp. C1, C5.

Eller, C., & Bates, J. (1999, August 13). In Hollywood, more business than show. *Los Angeles Times,* pp. A1, A23.

eMarketer. (2011a). US advertising spending. Retrieved July 15, 2011, from http://www.emarketer.com/Report.aspx?code = emarketer_2000442

eMarketer. (2011b, July 7). US online ad spending: The floodgates are open. Retrieved July 7, 2011, from http://www.emarketer.com/Reports/All/Emarketer_2000787.aspx

Entman, R. M., & Rojecki, A. (2001). The Black image in the White mind: Media and race in America. *CHOICE: Current Reviews for Academic Libraries, 38,* 1074.

Eron, L. D., Huesmann, L. R., Lefkowitz, M. M., & Walder, L. O. (1972). Does television violence cause aggression? *American Psychologist, 27,* 253–263.

ESPN.com. (n.d.). Retrieved September 1, 2009, from http://espn.go.com/sportsbusiness/s/stadium-names.html

Eyal, K., & Cohen, J. (2006). When good friends say goodbye: A parasocial breakup study. *Journal of Broadcasting & Electronic Media, 50,* 502–523.

Fabrikant, A. S. (1995, August 1). Disney to buy ABC for $19-billion. *Santa Barbara News-Press,* pp. A1, A2.

Fabrikant, G. (2004a, May 31). Need ESPN but not MTV? Some push for that option. *New York Times.* nytimes.com/2004/05/31/business/media/31cable.html

Fabrikant, G. (2004b, September 23). CBS fined $550,000 for Super Bowl. *Santa Barbara News Press,* p. B1.

Facebook. (n.d.). Retrieved August 30, 2009, from http://en.wikipedia.org/wiki/Facebook

Farhi, P., & Shapiro, L. (1996, July 27). Sports as an afterthought on NBC. *The Washington Post,* pp. A1, A14.

Farley, J. E. (1998). *Sociology.* Upper Saddle River, NJ: Prentice Hall.

FCC finds no indecency in the airing of "Private Ryan." (2005, March 1). *Los Angeles Times,* p. E12.

Fedler, F., & Jordan, D. (1982). How emphasis on people affects coverage of crime. *Journalism Quarterly, 59,* 474–478.

Ferguson, D. A. (1992). Channel repertoire in the presence of remote control devices, VCRs, and cable television. *Journal of Broadcasting & Electronic Media, 36,* 83–91.

Fernandez-Collado, C., Greenberg, B., Korzenny, F., & Atkin, C. (1978). Sexual intimacy and drug use in TV series. *Journal of Communication, 28*(3), 30–37.

Fico, F., & Soffin, S. (1995). Fairness and balance of selected newspaper coverage of controversial national, state, and local issues. *Journalism & Mass Communication Quarterly, 72,* 621–633.

Fiore, F. (2011, May). How many books were published last year? Retrieved May 4, 2011, from http://frankfiore.wordpress.com/2009/07/22/how-many-books-were-published-last-year/

Fisch, S. M. (2000). A capacity model of children's comprehension of educational content on television. *Media Psychology, 2,* 63–91.

Fisher, D. A., Hill, D. L., Grube, J. W., & Gruber, E. L. (2007). Gay, lesbian, and bisexual content on television: A quantitative analysis across two seasons. *Journal of Homosexuality, 52,* 167–188.

Fishman, J. M., & Marvin, C. (2003). Portrayals of violence and group difference in newspaper photographs: Nationalism and media. *Journal of Communication, 53,* 32–44.

Fishoff, S. (1988, August). *Psychological research and a black hole called Hollywood.* Paper presented at the annual meeting of the American Psychological Association, Atlanta, GA.

Fitzgerald, T. (2011, March 23). Broadcast ratings are down 11 percent. *Media Life Magazine.* Retrieved 2011, July 29, from http://www.medialifemagazine.com/artman2/publish/Broadcastrecap_64/Broadcast-ratings-are-down-11-precent.asp

Flanigan, J. (1999, July 30). There's no defense for NFL expecting more L.A. funds. *Los Angeles Times,* pp. C1, C2.

Flanigan, J. (2003, September 7). GE's broad vision may transform media. *Los Angeles Times,* pp. C1, C4.

Flint, J. (2009a, August 20). NFL makes big bet in aligning dates of 4 major TV deals. *Los Angeles Times,* p. B3.

Flint, J. (2009b, August 29). Appeals court sides with Comcast in market-share battle with FCC. *Los Angeles Times,* p. B2.

Flint, J. (2011a, June 8). NBC secures the Olympics through 2020. *Los Angeles Times,* pp. D1, D16.

Flint, J. (2011b, July 8). Coalition forms to crack down on Internet piracy. *Los Angeles Times,* p. B3.

Foa, E. B., & Kozak, M. J. (1986). Emotional processing of fear: Exposure to corrective information. *Psychological Bulletin, 99,* 20–35.

Foehr, U. G., Rideout, V., & Miller, C. (2000). Parents and the TV ratings system: A national study. In B. S. Greenberg, L. Rampoldi-Hnilo, & D. Mastro (Eds.), *The alphabet soup of television program ratings* (pp. 195–215). Cresskill, NJ: Hampton.

Foreman, J. (2009, June 6). Drug labels, ads at center of battle. *Los Angeles Times,* pp. E1, E5.

Forgas, J. P., Brown, L. B., & Menyhart, J. (1980). Dimensions of aggression: The perception of aggressive episodes. *British Journal of Social and Clinical Psychology, 19,* 215–227.

Fox, J., & Bailenson, J. N. (2009). Virtual self-modeling: The effects of vicarious reinforcement and identification on exercise behaviors. *Media Psychology, 12,* 1–25.

Freedman, J. (2011). The 50 highest-earning American athletes. *Sports Illustrated.* Retrieved June 21, 2011, from http://sportsillustrated.cnn.com/specials/fortunate50-2011/index.html

Friedman, T. (1995). Making sense of software: Computer games and interactive textuality. In S. G. Jones (Ed.), *CyberSociety: Computer mediated communication and community* (pp. 73–89). Thousand Oaks, CA: Sage.

Friedson, E. (1953). The relation of the social situation of contact to the media in mass communication. *Public Opinion Quarterly, 17,* 230–238.

Fritz, B. (2009, September 9). Friends in fantasy and reality. *Los Angeles Times,* pp. A1, A8.

Fritz, B., & Pham, A. (2011, February 9). Free online games moving up a level. *Los Angeles Times,* pp. B1, B5.

Frosch, D. L., Krueger, P. M., Hornik, R. C., Cronholm, P. F., & Barg, F. K. (2007, March–April). Creating demand for prescription drugs: A content analysis of television direct-to-consumer advertising. *Annals of Family Medicine, 5,* 179.

Gaither, C. (2004a, May 23). Can spam be canned? *Los Angeles Times,* pp. C1, C4.

Gaither, C. (2004b, June 24). Insider arrested in spam scheme. *Los Angeles Times,* pp. C1, C9.

Galician, M. L. (1986). Perceptions of good news and bad news on television. *Journalism Quarterly, 63,* 611–616.

Galloway, S. (1993, July 27). U.S. rating system: Sex before violence. *The Hollywood Reporter.*

Gardiner, B. (2010, July). Sony's wins and losses. *Wired,* p. 18.

Gardner, R.W. (1968). *Personality development at preadolescence.* Seattle: University of Washington Press.

Gellene, D. (1996, September 24). Seagram plans more TV ads for whiskey. *Los Angeles Times,* p. D2.

Gentile, D. (2009). Pathological video-game use among youth ages 8 to 18: A national study. *Psychological Science, 20,* 594–602.

Gerbner, G., Gross, L., Morgan, M., & Signorielli, N. (1980). The "mainstreaming" of America: Violence profile no. 11. *Journal of Communication, 30*(3), 10–29.

Getlin, J. (2006, September 22). Time spent watching television increases. *Los Angeles Times,* p. C3.

Giddings, S., & Kennedy, H. W. (2006). Digital games as new media. In J. Rutter & J. Bryce (Eds.). *Understanding digital games* (pp. 129–147). London: Sage.

Gilligan, C. (1993). *In a different voice.* Cambridge, MA: Harvard University Press.

Glascock, J. (2001). Gender roles on prime-time network television: Demographics and behaviors. *Journal of Broadcasting & Electronic Media, 45,* 656–669.

Gleick, J. (2011). *The information: A history, a theory, a flood.* New York: Pantheon.

Glick, S. (2004, September 1). Tracking the cash. *Los Angeles Times,* pp. D1, D8.

Goldman, D. (2010, February 3). Music's lost decade: Sales cut in half. Retrieved July 29, 2011, from http://money.cnn.com/2010/02/02/news/compa nies/napster_music_industry/

Goldstein, D. (1999, September 25). Biggest-grossing movies gross in other ways. *Tallahassee Democrat,* p. B1.

Goleman, D. (1995). *Emotional intelligence.* New York: Bantam.

Good news is no news. (2011, June 4). *The Economist,* p. 36.

Goranson, R. E. (1970). Media violence and aggressive behavior: A review of experimental research. In L. Berkowitz (Ed.), *Advances in experimental social psychology* (Vol. 5, pp. 1–31). New York: Academic Press.

Graber, D. A. (1994). *Processing the news: How people tame the information tide* (3rd ed.). New York: Longman.

Greenberg, B. S., Edison, N., Korzenny, F., Fernandez-Collado, C., & Atkin, C. K. (1980). Antisocial and prosocial behaviors on television. In B. S. Greenberg (Ed.), *Life on television: Content analysis of U.S. TV drama* (pp. 99–128). Norwood, NJ: Ablex.

Greenberg, B. S., & Rampoldi-Hnilo, L. (2001). Children and parent responses to the age-based and content-based television ratings. In D. G. Singer & J. L. Singer (Eds.), *Handbook of children and the media* (pp. 621–634). Thousand Oaks, CA: Sage.

Greenberg, B. S., Rampoldi-Hnilo, L., & Hofschire, L. (2000). Young people's responses to the age based ratings. In B. S. Greenberg, L. Rampoldi-Hnilo, & D. Mastro (Eds.), *The alphabet soup of television program ratings* (pp. 83–115). Cresskill, NJ: Hampton.

Greenberg, B. S., Stanley, C., Siemicki, M., Heeter, C., Soderman, A., & Linsangan, R. (1993). Sex content on soaps and prime-time television series most viewed by adolescents. In B. S. Greenberg, J. D. Brown, & N. Buerkel-Rothfuss (Eds.), *Media, sex and the adolescent* (pp. 29–44). Cresskill, NJ: Hampton.

Greenberg, D. (2006, July 24). The hand that feeds HBO. *Forbes,* p. 62.

Greimel, H. (2000, February 5). Mannesmann agrees to buyout. *Tallahassee Democrat,* p. E1.

Grimm, M. (1996, June 10). Olympic grab bag. *Brandweek,* pp. 26–28, 30, 32.

Gross, L. (2001). *Up from invisibility: Lesbians, gay men and the media in America.* New York: Columbia University Press.

Grusec, J. E. (1973). Effects of co-observer evaluations on imitation: A developmental study. *Developmental Psychology, 8,* 141.

Gulbransen, S. M. (1998a, February 15). Best seller lists are numbers, power, money. *Santa Barbara News-Press,* p. D7.

Gulbransen, S. M. (1998b, March 8). The wane of the paperback revolution. *Santa Barbara News-Press,* p. D7.

Gunter, B. (1985). *Dimensions of television violence.* Aldershot, UK: Gower.

Gunter, B., Furnham, A., & Griffiths, S. (2000). Children's memory for news: A comparison of three presentation media. *Media Psychology, 2,* 93–118.

Guynn, J. (2011a, March 10). Google's search fix sinks some websites. *Los Angeles Times,* pp. B1, B4.

Guynn, J. (2011b, June 12). Heading off Facebook's facial-recognition feature. *Los Angeles Times,* p. B1.

Haberkorn, J. T. (2009). A poverty of information: Public health and the local television news (Doctoral dissertation University of Delaware, 2009). *Dissertation Abstracts International: Section B: The Sciences and Engineering, 69*(9-B), 5346.

Hagel, J., Brown, J. S., Kulasooriya, D., & Elbert, D. (2010). Measuring the forces of long-term change: The 2010 Shift Index. Retrieved July 15, 2011, from http://www.edgeperspectives.com/ShiftIndex2010.pdf

Hall, A. (2003). Reading realism: Audiences' evaluations of the reality of media texts. *Journal of Communication, 53,* 624–641.

Hampton, K. N., Livio, O., & Sessions-Goulet, L. (2010). The social life of wireless urban spaces: Internet use, social networks, and the public realm. *Journal of Communication, 60,* 701–722.

Hancock, E. (1995, October 27). Culture cops take on sleazy TV talk shows. *Santa Barbara News-Press,* p. A1.

Harrington, C. L. (2003). Homosexuality on *All My Children:* Transforming the daytime landscape. *Journal of Broadcasting & Electronic Media, 47,* 216–235.

Hartman, T. (1999, March 22). Movie characters aren't reaping what they sow. *Tallahassee Democrat,* p. A1.

Hawkins, R. P. (1977). The dimensional structure of children's perceptions of television reality. *Communication Research, 7,* 193–226.

Hawkins, R. P., & Pingree, S. (1982). Television's influence on social reality. In D. Pearl, L. Bouthilet, & J. Lazar (Eds.), *Television and behavior: Ten years of scientific progress and implications for the eighties: Vol. II. Technical reviews* (pp. 224–247). Rockville, MD: U.S. Department of Health and Human Services.

Heads in the cloud. (2011, April 2). *The Economist,* p. 63.

Healey, J. (2003, October 25). Pair ordered to pay $2-million fine for spam. *Los Angeles Times,* pp. C1, C2.

Healey, J. (2004, March 7). Piracy fears limit film downloads. *Los Angeles Times,* pp. C1, C5.

Healy, J. M. (1990). *Endangered minds: Why children don't think and what we can do about it.* New York: Simon & Schuster.

Hetsroni, A. (2007). Three decades of sexual content on prime-time network programming: A longitudinal meta-analytic review. *Journal of Communication, 57,* 318–348.

Hicks, D. J. (1968). Effects of co-observer's sanctions and adult presence on imitative aggression. *Child Development, 39,* 303–309.

Himes, S. M., & Thompson, J. K. (2007). Fat stigmatization in television shows and movies: A content analysis. *Obesity, 15,* 712–718.

Himmelweit, H. (1966). Television and the child. In B. Berelson & M. Janowitz (Eds.), *Reader in public opinion and communication* (2nd ed., pp. 67–106). New York: Free Press.

Himmelweit, H., Oppenheim, A., & Vince, P. (1958). *Television and the child.* Oxford, UK: Oxford University Press.

HIPAA-HiTech Security and Privacy. (2009, May 7). Hackers want $10-million in ransom. Retrieved August 31, 2009, from http://www.hipaasecurityandprivacy.com/2009/05/health-care-hackers-want-10-million-in.html

Hobbs, R. (1998). The seven great debates in the media literacy movement. *Journal of Communication, 48*(1), 16–32.

Hoffner, C. (1997). Children's emotional reactions to a scary film: The role of prior outcome information and coping style. *Human Communication Research, 23,* 323–341.

Hoffner, C., & Cantor, J. (1991). Perceiving and responding to mass media characters. In J. Bryant & D. Zillmann (Eds.), *Responding to the screen* (pp. 63–101). Hillsdale, NJ: Lawrence Erlbaum.

Hofmeister, S. (1997a, February 19). $2.7-billion deal would create no. 2 radio group in U.S. *Los Angeles Times,* p. D1.

Hofmeister, S. (1997b, February 19). Seagram to buy USA Networks for $1.7-billion. *Los Angeles Times,* p. D1.

Hofmeister, S. (2003, October 25). Cable investments, sports blamed for high rates. *Los Angeles Times,* pp. C1, C2.

Hofmeister, S. (2005, September 8). Study ties indecency to consolidation of media. *Los Angeles Times,* pp. C1, C11.

Hogan, M. J. (2001). Parents and other adults: Models and monitors of healthy media habits. In D. G. Singer & J. L. Singer (Eds.), *Handbook of children and the media* (pp. 663–680). Thousand Oaks, CA: Sage.

Holbert, R. L. (2005). Debate viewing as mediator and partisan reinforcement in the relationship between news use and vote choice. *Journal of Communication, 55,* 85–102.

Holbert, R. L., Shah, D. V., & Kwak, N. (2003). Political implications of prime-time drama and sitcom use:

Genres of representation and opinions concerning women's rights. *Journal of Communication, 53,* 45–60.

Holland, J. (1998, January 15). Internal records show tobacco firm targeted teen-agers. *Santa Barbara News-Press,* p. A2.

Hollenbeck, A., & Slaby, R. (1979). Infant visual and vocal responses to television. *Child Development, 50,* 41–45.

Holstein, W. J. (1999, September 20). MTV, meet *60 Minutes. U.S. News & World Report,* pp. 44–46.

Horn, J. (2003, November 16). Oscar gold diggers. *Los Angeles Times,* pp. A1, A20.

Horowitz, D. (1996, June 24). Nowhere to hide from advertisers. *Santa Barbara News-Press,* p. B7.

Howard, H. H. (1995). TV station group and cross-media ownership: A 1995 update. *Journalism & Mass Communication Quarterly, 72,* 390–401.

Hudson, T. J. (1992). Consonance in depiction of violent material in television news. *Journal of Broadcasting & Electronic Media, 36,* 411–425.

Hunter, R. (2002). *World without secrets: Business, crime, and privacy in the age of ubiquitous computing.* New York: Gartner Press.

Huston, A., Wright, J. C., Rice, M. L., Kerkman, D., Seigle, J., & Bremer, M. (1983, June). *Family environment and television use by preschool children.* Paper presented at the Biennial Meeting of the Society for Research on Child Development, Detroit, MI. (ERIC Document No. ED230293)

Identity Theft Center. (2002). Facts and statistics. Retrieved May 9, 2004, from http://www.idtheft center.org/facts.shtml

Igartua, J.-J., & Cheng, L. (2009). Moderating effect of group cue while processing news on immigration: Is the framing effect a heuristic process? *Journal of Communication, 59,* 726–749.

Intelligence Infocorp. (1996, May 22). *Nando.net release.* La Jolla, CA: Author.

Internet Advertising Bureau. (2011, May 26). Internet advertising revenues hit $7.3 billion in Q1 '11: Highest first-quarter revenue level on record according to IAB and PwC. Retrieved June 26, 2011, from http://www.iab.net/about_the_iab/recent_press_releases/press_release_archive/press_release/pr-052611

Ito, M., Horst, H., Bittanti, M., boyd, d., Herr-Stephenson, B., Lange, P. G., et al. (2009). *Living and learning with new media: Summary of findings from the Digital Youth Project.* Cambridge, MA: The MIT Press.

James, M. (2003a, October 19). Indie TV studio still goes in alone. *Los Angeles Times,* pp. C1, C6.

James, M. (2003b, December 5). GE, Nielsen to follow popularity of product placement on primetime television. *Los Angeles Times,* pp. C1, C11.

James, M. (2006, October 2). TV: More bang for more bucks. *Los Angeles Times,* pp. C1, C3.

James, M. (2011, May 29). Redstone & Co. stand out. *Los Angeles Times,* pp. B1, B10–B11.

Jamieson, K. H., & Campbell, K. K. (1988). *The interplay of influence* (2nd ed.). Belmont, CA: Wadsworth.

Jamieson, K. H., & Waldman, P. (2003). *The press effect: Politicians, journalists, and the stories that shape the political world.* New York: Oxford University Press.

Jeffres, L. W. (1994). *Mass media processes* (2nd ed.). Prospect Heights, IL: Waveland.

Jenkins, H. (2006). *Convergence culture: Where old and new media collide.* New York: New York University Press.

Jensen, C. (1995). *Censored: The news that didn't make the news—and why.* New York: Four Walls Eight Windows.

Jensen, C. (1997). *20 years of censored news.* New York: Seven Stories Press.

Jensen, J., & Ross, C. (1996, July 15). Centennial Olympics open as $5 bil event of century. *Advertising Age, 67*(29), 1–2.

Jerome, R., & Bane, V. (2004, May 3). Spam I am. *Money,* pp. 125–126.

Johnson, S. (2006). *Everything bad is good for you.* New York: Riverhead Books.

Jones, C. (2005). *News media trends: Winning with the news media* (8th ed.). www.rtnda.org/resources/intnews/artmedia.htm

Jones, J. P. (2004). *Fables, fashions, and facts about advertising: A study of 28 enduring myths.* Thousand Oaks, CA: Sage.

Jones, T. Y. (2006, June 17). If this were a term paper, you might have seen it on the Web. *Los Angeles Times,* pp. A1, A12.

Jordan, A. B. (2001). Public policy and private practice: Government regulations and parental control over children's television use in the home. In D. G. Singer & J. L. Singer (Eds.), *Handbook of children and the media* (pp. 651–662). Thousand Oaks, CA: Sage.

Kagan, J., Rosman, D., Day, D., Albert, J., & Phillips, W. (1964). Information processing in the child: Significance of analytic and reflective attitudes. *Psychological Monographs, 78,* 1.

Kaiser Family Foundation. (1999). *Parents and the V-chip.* Menlo Park, CA: Author.

Kaiser Family Foundation. (2002, Fall). *Key facts: Children and video games.* Menlo Park, CA: Author.

Kaiser Family Foundation. (2003). *Sex on TV 3.* Menlo Park, CA: Author.

Kaiser Family Foundation. (2005, March). Key findings from new research on children's media use. Retrieved August 23, 2009, from http://www.kaiser network.org/health_cast/hcast_index.cfm? display = detail&hc = 1377

Kaiser Family Foundation. (2010). Daily media use among children and teens up dramatically from five years ago. Retrieved June 24, 2011, from http:// www.kff.org/entmedia/entmedia012010nr.cfm

Kalyanaraman, S., & Ivory, J. D. (2009). Enhanced information scent, selective discounting, or consummate breakdown: The psychological effects of web-based search results. *Media Psychology, 12,* 295–319.

Kang, S., & Gearhart, S. (2010). E-Government and civic engagement: How is citizens' use of city web sites related with civic involvement and political behaviors? *Journal of Broadcasting & Electronic Media, 54,* 443–462.

Kaniss, P. (1996, December 19). Bad news: How electronic media muddle the message. *Philadelphia Inquirer,* p. A35.

Kantrowitz, B. (2006, October 30). Brush with perfection. *Newsweek,* p. 54.

Kava, B. (2003, September 4). With goal of $10 CDs, record giant cuts price. *San Jose Mercury News.* bayarea.com/mld/mercurynews/business/ 6688650.htm

Kaye, B. K., & Sapolsky, B. S. (2001). Offensive language in prime time television: Before and after content ratings. *Journal of Broadcasting & Electronic Media, 45,* 303.

Kerr, A. (2006a). *The business and culture of digital games: Gamework/gameplay.* London: Sage.

Kerr, A. (2006b). The business of making digital games. In J. Rutter & J. Bryce (Eds.), *Understanding digital games* (pp. 36–57). London: Sage.

Khouri, A. (2011, July 27). Remodel is set for MySpace. *Los Angeles Times,* pp. B1, B4.

Kim, K., & Barnett, G. A. (1996). The determinants of international news flow: A network analysis. *Communication Research, 23,* 323–352.

King, C. M. (2000). Effects of humorous heroes and villains in violent action films. *Journal of Communication, 50*(1), 5–25.

King, P. M. (1986). Formal reasoning in adults: A review and critique. In R. A. Milnes & K. S. Kitchenor (Eds.), *Adult cognitive development: Methods and models* (pp. 1–21). New York: Praeger.

Kinkema, K. M., & Harris, J. C. (1998). MediaSport studies: Key research and emerging issues. In L. A. Wenner (Ed.), *MediaSport* (pp. 27–54). New York: Routledge.

Kiousis, S., & McDevitt, M. (2008). Agenda setting in civic development: Effects of curricula and issue importance on youth voter turnout. *Communication Research, 35,* 481–502.

Kirriemuir, J. (2006). A history of digital games. In J. Rutter & J. Bryce (Eds.), *Understanding digital games* (pp. 21–35). London: Sage.

Knobloch, S. (2003). Mood adjustment via mass communication. *Journal of Communication, 53,* 233–250.

Knobloch, S., & Zillmann, D. (2002). Mood management via the digital jukebox. *Journal of Communication, 52,* 351–366.

Knobloch-Westerwick, S., & Meng, J. (2009). Looking the other way: Selective exposure to attitude-consistent and counterattitudinal political information. *Communication Research, 36,* 426–448.

Koenenn, C. (1997, May 14). Let's get simple. *Los Angeles Times,* p. E1.

Kohlberg, L. (1966). Moral education in the schools: A developmental view. *School Review, 74,* 1–30.

Kohlberg, L. (1981). *The philosophy of moral development: Moral stages and the idea of justice.* New York: Harper & Row.

Koziol, R. (1989, August). *English language arts teachers' views on mass media consumption education in Maryland high schools.* Paper presented at the annual conference of the Association of Education in Journalism and Mass Communication, Washington, DC.

Krcmar, M., & Cantor, J. (1996, May). *Discussing violent television: Parents, children, and TV viewing choices.* Paper presented at the annual conference of the International Communication Association, Montreal, Canada.

Krcmar, M., & Greene, K. (1999). Predicting exposure to and uses of television violence. *Journal of Communication, 49*(3), 24–45.

Kress, G. (1992). Media literacy as cultural technology in the age of transcultural media. In C. Bazalgette, E. Bevort, & J. Savino (Eds.), *New directions: Media education worldwide* (pp. 190–202). London: British Film Institute.

Kubey, R. (1990). Television and family harmony among children, adolescents, and adults: Results from the experience of sampling method. In J. Bryant (Ed.), *Television and the American family* (pp. 73–88). Hillsdale, NJ: Lawrence Erlbaum.

Kubey, R. (1997). A rationale for media education. In R. Kubey (Ed.), *Media literacy in the information age* (pp. 15–68). New Brunswick, NJ: Transaction Publishers.

Kubey, R. (1998). Obstacles to the development of media education in the United States. *Journal of Communication, 48*(1), 58–69.

Kubey, R., Shifflet, M., Weerakkody, N., & Ukeiley, S. (1996). Demographic diversity on cable: Have the new cable channels made a difference in the representation of gender, race, and age? *Journal of Broadcasting & Electronic Media, 39,* 459–471.

Kunkel, D., Eyal, K., & Donnerstein, E. (2007). Sexual socialization messages on entertainment television: Comparing content trends 1997–2002. *Media Psychology, 9,* 595–622.

Kunkel, D., Farinola, W. J. M., Farrar, K., Donnerstein, E., Bielby, E., & Zwarun, L. (2002). Deciphering the V-chip: An examination of the television industry's program rating judgments. *Journal of Communication, 52*(1), 112–138.

Kunkel, D., & Wilcox, B. (2001). Children and media policy. In D. G. Singer & J. L. Singer (Eds.), *Handbook of children and the media* (pp. 589–620). Thousand Oaks, CA: Sage.

Kwak, H., Zinkhan, G. M., & Dominick, J. R. (2002). The moderating role of gender and compulsive buying tendencies in the cultivation effects of TV shows and TV advertising: A cross cultural study between the United States and South Korea. *Media Psychology, 4,* 77–111.

Lacayo, R. (1995, June 12). Are music and movies killing America's soul? *Time,* pp. 24–30.

Lacy, S., & Blanchard, A. (2003). The impact of public ownership, profits, and competition on number of newsroom employees and starting salaries in mid-sized daily newspapers. *Journalism & Mass Communication Quarterly, 80,* 949–968.

Lacy, S., & Riffe, D. (1994). The impact of competition and group ownership on radio news. *Journalism & Mass Communication Quarterly, 71,* 583–593.

Lane, R. E. (2000). *The loss of happiness in market democracies.* New Haven, CT: Yale University Press.

Lang, A., Potter, R. F., & Bolls, P. D. (1999). Something for nothing: Is visual encoding automatic? *Media Psychology, 1,* 145–163.

Larson, J. (1983). *Television's window on the world.* Norwood, NJ: Ablex.

LaSalle, M. (1996, July 7). Why overpaid stars aren't worth it. *Santa Barbara News-Press,* p. D9.

L.A. Times publisher errs, apologizes. (1999, October 31). *Tallahassee Democrat,* p. 5B.

Law, C., & Labre, M. P. (2002). Cultural standards of attractiveness: A thirty-year look at changes in male images in magazines. *Journalism & Mass Communication Quarterly, 79,* 697–711.

Lawrence, F., & Wozniak, P. (1989).Children's television viewing with family members. *Psychological Reports, 65*(2), 395–400.

Lawrence, S. (2004, September 24). Governor signs bills on vaccine, "spyware." *Los Angeles Times,* p. A6.

Lazarus, D. (2009, Sept. 23). Spammers adapt in anti-spam climate. *Los Angeles Times,* pp. B1, B4.

Lazarus, D. (2011, June 10). When hackers steal our data, tell us details. *Los Angeles Times,* pp. B1, B4.

The leaky corporation. (2011, February 26). *The Economist,* pp. 75–77.

Lee, K., & Light, J. (2003). Law and regulation, part I: Individual interests. In L. Shyles (Ed.), *Deciphering cyberspace: Making the most of digital communication technology* (pp. 293–322). Thousand Oaks, CA: Sage.

Lee, M., & Solomon, N. (1990). *Unreliable sources: A guide to detecting bias in news media.* New York: Carol.

Leo, J. (1999, September 27). And now . . . smut-see TV. *U.S. News & World Report,* p. 15.

Levy, S. (2006a, March 27). (Some) attention must be paid! *Newsweek,* p. 16.

Levy, S. (2006b, June 12). An identity heist the size of Texas. *Newsweek,* p. 18.

Levy, S. (2006c, September 11). Will you let them store your dreams? *Newsweek,* p. 12.

Levy, S. (2006d, September 18). Living a virtual life. *Newsweek,* pp. 48–50.

Levy, S. (2006e, October 23). The power of iPod. *Newsweek,* pp. 72, 74.

Levy, S. (2006f, December 11). Smile! You're an unwitting net star. *Newsweek,* p. 17.

Lewin, J. (2008, June 16). Average teen's iPod has $800 of pirated music. New Media Update. Retrieved September 11, 2009, from http://www.podcasting news.com/2008/06/16/average-teens-ipod-has-800-of-pirated-music/

Li, S. (2011, May 18). Maybe mister right is right over there. *Los Angeles Times,* pp. A1, A11.

Lichtarowicz, A. (2002, March 29). Virtual kingdom richer than Bulgaria. Retrieved September 21,

2005, from http://news.bbc.co.uk/1/hi/sci/tech/1899420.stm

Lichter, L. S., & Lichter, S. R. (1983). *Prime time crime.* Washington, DC: The Media Institute.

Liebert, R. M., Neale, J. M., & Davidson, E. S. (1973). *The early window: Effects of television on children and youth.* New York: Pergamon.

Lih, A. (2009). *The Wikipedia revolution: How a bunch of nobodies created the world's greatest encyclopedia.* New York: Hyperion.

Lin, C. A., & Jeffres, L.W. (2001). Comparing distinctions and similarities across websites of newspapers, radio stations, and television stations. *Journalism & Mass Communication Quarterly, 78,* 555–573.

Linthicum, D. S. (2010). *Cloud computing and SOA convergence in your enterprise: A step by step guide.* Upper Saddle River, NJ: Addison-Wesley.

Linz, D., Donnerstein, E., & Penrod, S. (1984). The effects of multiple exposures to filmed violence against women. *Journal of Communication, 34*(3), 130–147.

Linz, D., Donnerstein, E., & Penrod, S. (1988). Effects of long-term exposure to violent and sexually degrading depictions of women. *Journal of Personality and Social Psychology, 55*(5), 758–768.

Lippmann, W. (1922). *Public opinion.* New York: Harcourt, Brace.

Lorimer, R. (1994). *Mass communications: A comparative introduction.* Manchester, UK: Manchester University Press.

Lowrey, T. M. (2006). The relation between script complexity and commercial memorability. *Journal of Advertising, 35*(3), 7–15.

Lowry, B. (1997, September 21). TV on decline but few back U.S. regulation. *Los Angeles Times,* pp. A1, A40, A41.

Lowry, B., Jensen, E., & Braxton, G. (1999, July 20). Networks decide diversity doesn't pay. *Los Angeles Times,* p. A1.

Lowry, D. T., Nio, R. C. J., & Leitner, D. W. (2003). Setting the public fear agenda: A longitudinal analysis of network TV crime reporting, public perceptions of crime, and FBI crime statistics. *Journal of Communication, 53,* 61–73.

Luntz, F. (2000, March). Public to press: Cool it. *Brill's Content,* pp. 74–79.

Lussier, G. (2011, February 11). 2011 will break the all time record for movie sequels. Retrieved July 15, 2011, from http://www.slashfilm.com/2011-break-time-record-movie-sequels/

Lyall, S. (1996, November 27). Penguin's deal to buy Putnam will create major publishing force. *Santa Barbara News-Press,* p. A6.

Mad men are watching you. (2011, May 7). *The Economist,* pp. 87–88.

Magazine Publishers of America. (2004). Resources. www.magazine.org/resources/fact_sheets/html

Mahoney, J. (2009, January 16). 95% of music videos are pirated. Retrieved June 21, 2011, from http://gizmodo.com/5133065/95-of-music-downloads-are-pirated

Mailer, N. (2005, January 23). One idea. *Parade,* pp. 4–6.

Malamuth, N. M., & Check, J. V. P. (1980). Penile tumescence and perceptual responses to rape as a function of victim's perceived reactions. *Journal of Applied Social Psychology, 10,* 528–547.

Malcolm, J. G. (2005). Internet gambling is a serious problem. In J. D. Torr (Ed.), *The Internet: Opposing viewpoints* (pp. 61–66). New York: Greenhaven.

Maney, K. (1995). *Megamedia shakeout: The inside story of the leaders and the losers in the exploding communications industry.* New York: John Wiley.

Manning, R. (1987, December 28). The selling of the Olympics. *Newsweek,* pp. 40–41.

Marcuse, H. (1964). *One-dimensional man: Studies in the ideology of advanced industrial society.* Boston: Beacon.

Mashable. (2011). Outskirtspress. Retrieved May 4, 2011, from http://mashable.com/2010/08/06/number-of-books-in-the-world/

Mastro, D., Lapinski, M. K., Kopacz, M. A., & Behm-Morawitz, E. (2009). The influence of exposure to depictions of race and crime in TV news on viewer's social judgments. *Journal of Broadcasting & Electronic Media, 53,* 615–635.

Mastro, D. E., & Greenberg, B. S. (2000). The portrayal of racial minorities on prime-time television. *Journal of Broadcasting & Electronic Media, 44,* 690.

Mastro, D. E., & Stern, S. R. (2003). Representations of race in television commercials: A content analysis of prime-time advertising. *Journal of Broadcasting & Electronic Media, 47,* 638–647.

MC Marketing Charts. (2009, June 12). Primetime TV hour includes 41% commercials. Retrieved June 26, 2011, from http://www.marketingcharts.com/television/rimetime-tv-hour-includes-41-commercials-9434/

McCombs, M. E., & Shaw, D. (1972). The agenda setting function of the mass media. *Public Opinion Quarterly, 36,* 176–187.

McDonald, M. (2000, March 27). L.A. is their kind of town. *U.S. News & World Report,* p. 45.

McLeod, J. M., Fitzpatrick, M. A., Glynn, C. J., & Fallis, S. F. (1982). Television and social relations: Family influences and consequences for interpersonal behavior. In D. Pearl, L. Bouthilet, & J. Lazar (Eds.), *Television and behavior: Ten years of scientific progress and implications for the eighties: Vol. II. Technical reviews* (pp. 272–286). Rockville, MD: U.S. Department of Health and Human Services.

Meadowcroft, J., & Reeves, B. (1989). Influence of story schema development on children's attention to television. *Communication Research, 16,* 353–374.

Medich, R. (2002, October 18). Flashes. *Entertainment,* p. 16.

Medrich, E. A., Roizen, J. A., Rubin, V., & Buckley, S. (1982). *The serious business of growing up: A study of children's lives outside school.* Berkeley: University of California Press.

Meehan, M. (2004, January 20). The ratings game: System has its flaws, one of which is lax oversight. *Knight Ridder Tribune News Service,* p. 1.

Menn, J. (2007, April 17). Google plan raises privacy issue. *Los Angeles Times,* p. C1.

Messaris, P. (1994). *Visual "literacy": Image, mind, and reality.* Boulder, CO: Westview.

Messaris, P., & Kerr, D. (1984). TV-related mother-child interaction and children's perceptions of TV characters. *Journalism Quarterly, 61,* 662–666.

Metallinos, N. (1996). *Television aesthetics: Perceptual, cognitive, and compositional bases.* Mahwah, NJ: Lawrence Erlbaum.

Metropolitan Sports Facilities Commission. (n.d.). Next generation of sports facilities. Retrieved May 7, 2004, from http://www.msfc.com/nextgen.cfm

Meyrowitz, J. (1985). *No sense of place: The impact of electronic media on social behavior.* New York: Oxford University Press.

Middle-aged blues. (2011, June 11). *The Economist,* p. 68.

Mifflin, L. (1997, February 22). Parents give TV ratings mixed reviews. *New York Times,* p. A6.

Mitchell, A. (1983). *Nine American lifestyles.* New York: Warner.

Mnookin, S. (2002, August 19). The tobacco sham. *Newsweek,* p. 33.

Mogel, L. (2000). *Careers in communications and entertainment.* New York: Simon & Schuster.

Mohr, P. J. (1979). Parental influence of children's viewing of evening television programs. *Journal of Broadcasting, 23,* 213–228.

Money? There's an app for that. (2011, May 28). *The Economist,* p. 79.

Moody, N. M. (2002, June 16). Record industry seeking alternatives. *Santa Barbara News-Press,* pp. F1, F2.

Morgan, S. E., Movius, L., & Cody, M. J. (2009). The power of narratives: The effect of entertainment television organ donation storylines on the attitudes, knowledge, and behaviors of donors and nondonors. *Journal of Communication, 59,* 135–151.

Munoz, L. (2006, December 2). Movie bootleg whiz gets 7 years. *Los Angeles Times,* pp. C1, C3.

Music Piracy and the Audio Home Recording Act. (2002, November 20). *Duke Law and Technology Review.* Retrieved June 29, 2002, from http://www.law.duke.edu/journals/dltr/articles/2002dltr0023.html

Myers, D. G. (2000). *The American paradox: Spiritual hunger in an age of plenty.* New Haven, CT: Yale University Press.

Nathanson, A. I. (1999). Identifying and explaining the relationship between parental mediation and children's aggression. *Communication Research, 26,* 124–143.

Nathanson, A. I. (2001a). Mediation of children's television viewing: Working toward conceptual clarity and common understanding. In W. B. Gudykunst (Ed.), *Communication yearbook 25* (pp. 115–151). Mahwah, NJ: Lawrence Erlbaum.

Nathanson, A. I. (2001b). Parent and child perspectives on the presence and meaning of parental television mediation. *Journal of Broadcasting & Electronic Media, 45,* 201–220.

Nathanson, A. I. (2001c). Parents versus peers: Exploring the significance of peer mediation of antisocial television. *Communication Research, 28,* 251–274.

Nathanson, A. I. (2002). The unintended effects of parental mediation of television on adolescents. *Media Psychology, 4,* 207–230.

Nathanson, A. I., & Botta, R. A. (2003). Shaping the effects of television on adolescents' body image disturbance: The role of parental mediation. *Communication Research, 30,* 304–331.

Nathanson, A. I., & Cantor, J. (2000). Reducing the aggression-promoting effect of violent cartoons by increasing children's fictional involvement with the victim: A study of active mediation. *Journal of Broadcasting & Electronic Media, 44,* 94–109.

Nathanson, A. I., Eveland, W. P., Park, H.-S., & Paul, B. (2002). Perceived media influence and efficacy as predictors of caregivers' protective behaviors. *Journal of Broadcasting & Electronic Media, 46,* 385–410.

Nathanson, A. I., & Yang, M.-S. (2003). The effects of mediation content and form on children's responses to violent television. *Human Communication Research, 29*(1), 111–134.

National Cable & Television Association. (2010, December). Industry data. Retrieved July 29, 2011, from http://www.ncta.com/Statistics.aspx

National Center for Education Statistics. (2003). *National assessment of adult literacy.* Washington, DC: U.S. Department of Education.

National Center for Education Statistics. (2009). *The condition of education: Special analysis 2009.* Retrieved August 26, 2009, from http://nces.ed.gov/programs/coe/2009/analysis/

National Football League 1999 salaries. (2000, May 23). *USA Today,* pp. 14C–15C.

National Television Violence Study (NTVS). (1996). *Scientific report.* Thousand Oaks, CA: Sage.

Navarro, J., & Riddle, K. (n.d.). Violent media effects. Retrieved January 23, 2007, from http://www.uweb.ucsb.edu/ ~ ker/public_opinion.htm#polls

NBA salaries. (2010). Retrieved June 22, 2011, from http://www.insidehoops.com/nbasalaries.shtml

NBC Universal. (n.d.). Retrieved August 30, 2009, from http://en.wikipedia.org/wiki/NBC_Universal

NCTV says violence on TV up 16%. (1983, March 22). *Broadcasting Magazine,* p. 63.

Negroponte, N. (1995). *Being digital.* New York: Knopf.

Nelson, J. (1995, August 8). NBC gets Olympic TV rights in coup. *Santa Barbara News-Press,* p. A12.

Neuman, W. R. (1991). *The future of the mass audience.* New York: Cambridge University Press.

News Corporation. (n.d.). Retrieved August 30, 2009, from http://en.wikipedia.org/wiki/News_Corporation

The new tech bubble. (2011, May 14). *The Economist,* p. 13.

Newscientist.com. (2004, March 4). Net music piracy "does not harm record sales." Retrieved June 29, 2004, from http://newscientist.com/news/news.jsp?id = ns99994831

NFL teams dodge salary cap. (1996, January 2). *Santa Barbara News-Press,* p. B5.

Nie, N. H., & Erbring, L. (2002). *Internet and society: A preliminary report.* Palo Alto, CA: Stanford Institute for the Quantitative Study of Society.

Nielsenwire. (2008, August 5). Historical TV ratings for past Olympics broadcasts. Retrieved June 23, 2011, from http://blog.nielsen.com/nielsenwire/media_entertainment/historical-tv-ratings-for-past-olympics/

Noam, E. (2010). Hollywood 2.0: How Internet distribution will affect the film industry. In W. R. Neuman (Ed.), *Media, technology, and society: Theories of media evolution* (pp. 59–68). Ann Arbor: University of Michigan Press.

Number of viruses. (2011, June 21). Retrieved June 21, 2011, from http://www.cknow.com/cms/vtutor/number-of-viruses.html

Official Identity Theft Statistics. (2011, June 20). Retrieved June 20, 2011, from http://www.spendonlife.com/guide/identity-theft-statistics

100 people identified in piracy raid. (2004, April 23). *Los Angeles Times,* p. C3.

1100100 and counting. (2011, June 11). *The Economist,* pp. 67–69.

Olivarez-Giles, N. (2011, June 14). Facebook's growth is slowing, study says. *Los Angeles Times,* p. B3.

Oliver, M. B. (1994). Portrayals of crime, race, and aggression in "reality based" police shows: A content analysis. *Journal of Broadcasting & Electronic Media, 38,* 179–192.

Oliver, M. B., & Kalyanaraman, S. (2002). Appropriate for all viewing audiences? An examination of violent and sexual portrayals in movie previews featured on video rentals. *Journal of Broadcasting & Electronic Media, 46,* 283–300.

Online reputations in the dirt. (2011, April 30). *The Economist,* p. 65.

Ortutay, B. (2011, April 13). U. S. Internet ad revenue hit record in 2010. Retrieved July 29, 2011, from http://www.huffingtonpost.com/2011/04/13/us-internet-ad-revenue-2010_n_848809.html

Ozanich, G. W., & Wirth, M. O. (1993). Media mergers and acquisitions: An overview. In A. Alexander, J. Owers, & R. Carveth (Eds.), *Media economics: Theory and practice* (pp. 115–133). Hillsdale, NJ: Lawrence Erlbaum.

Page, B. (2011, January 28). Ebook revolution accelerates in sales and status: Amazon is reporting Kindle edition sales outstripping paperbacks in the US, and the Booker prize jury is now reading on ebooks. Retrieved July 29, 2011, from http://www.guardian.co.uk/books/2011/jan/28/ebook-revolution-accelerates-sales

Page, R., & Brewster, A. (2007). Frequency of promotional strategies and attention elements in children's food commercials during children's programming blocks on US broadcast networks. *Young Consumers, 8,* 184–196.

Parenti, M. (1986). *Inventing reality: The politics of the mass media.* New York: St. Martin's.

Pariser, E. (2011). *The filter bubble: What the Internet is hiding from you.* New York: Penguin.

Pashler, H. E. (1998). *The psychology of attention.* Cambridge, MA: MIT Press.

Penner, M. (2004, May 7). Baseball cancels plans for movie ad on bases. *Los Angeles Times,* pp. D1, D8.

Peraino, V. (1999, August). The law of increasing returns. *Wired,* pp. 144–147.

Perkins, K. (1996, November 27). Statistics blur image of American family. *Santa Barbara News-Press,* pp. A1, A2.

Peter, J., & Valkenburg, P. M. (2009). Adolescents' exposure to sexually explicit Internet material and notions of women as sex objects: Assessing causality and underlying processes. *Journal of Communication, 59,* 407–433.

Petty, R. E., & Cacioppo, J. T. (1986). *Communication and persuasion: Central and peripheral routes to attitude change.* New York: Springer-Verlag.

Pew Internet & American Life Project. (2000, August 20). Trust and privacy online: Why Americans want to rewrite the rules. Retrieved May 9, 2004, from http://pewinternet.org/reports/reports.asp? Report = 19

Pew Research Center for the People and the Press. (1998). *Internet news takes off.* Washington, DC: Author.

Picard, R. G. (1989). *Media economics: Concepts and issues.* Newbury Park, CA: Sage.

Picard, R. G. (1993). Economics of the daily newspaper industry. In A. Alexander, J. Owers, & R. Carveth (Eds.), *Media economics: Theory and practice* (pp. 181–203). Hillsdale, NJ: Lawrence Erlbaum.

Picard, R. G., Winter, J. P., McCombs, M., & Lacy, S. (Eds.). (1988). *Press concentration and monopoly: New perspectives on newspaper ownership and operation.* Norwood, NJ: Ablex.

Piette, J., & Giroux, L. (1997). The theoretical foundations of media education programs. In R. Kubey (Ed.), *Media literacy in the information age: Current perspectives, information and behavior* (Vol. 6, pp. 89–134). New Brunswick, NJ: Transaction Publishers.

Pingdom. (2011, May 4). Internet 2010 in numbers. Retrieved May 4, 2011, from http://royal.pingdom.com/2011/01/12/internet-2010-in-numbers/

Pipher, M. (1996). *The shelter of each other.* New York: Putnam.

Plack, C. J. (2005). Auditory perception. In K. Lamberts & R. I. Goldstone (Eds.), *Handbook of cognition* (pp. 71–104). London: Sage.

Plunkett Research. (2010). *Sports industry overview.* Retrieved June 22, 2011, from http://www.plunkettresearch.com/Sports % 20recreation % 20leisure % 20market % 20research/industry % 20statistics

Police cars to add advertisements. (1995, July 13). *Santa Barbara News-Press,* p. A4.

Polman, D. (2003, June 1). FCC vote may prove a windfall for media giants. *Santa Barbara News-Press,* pp. B1, B2.

Popper, N. (2011, July 1). Poker firm to be sold. *Los Angeles Times,* p. B3.

Postman, N., & Powers, S. (1992). *How to watch TV news.* New York: Penguin.

Potter, R. F. (2002). Give the people what they want: A content analysis of FM radio station home pages. *Journal of Broadcasting & Electronic Media, 46,* 369–385.

Potter, W. J. (1986). Perceived reality in the cultivation hypothesis. *Journal of Broadcasting & Electronic Media, 30,* 159–174.

Potter, W. J. (1987a). Does television viewing hinder academic achievement among adolescents? *Human Communication Research, 14,* 27–46.

Potter, W. J. (1987b). News from three worlds in prestige U.S. newspapers. *Journalism Quarterly, 64,* 73–79.

Potter, W. J. (1991). Examining cultivation from a psychological perspective: Component subprocesses. *Communication Research, 18,* 77–102.

Potter, W. J. (1999). *On media violence.* Thousand Oaks, CA: Sage.

Potter, W. J. (2003). *The 11 myths of media violence.* Thousand Oaks, CA: Sage.

Potter, W. J., Pashupati, K., Pekurny, R. G., Hoffman, E., & Davis, K. (2002). Perceptions of television: A schema approach. *Media Psychology, 4,* 27–50.

Potter, W. J., & Smith, S. (2000). The context of graphic portrayals of television violence. *Journal of Broadcasting & Electronic Media, 44,* 301.

Potter, W. J., & Vaughan, M. (1997). Aggression in television entertainment: Profiles and trends. *Communication Research Reports, 14,* 116–124.

Potter, W. J., & Ware, W. (1987). An analysis of the contexts of antisocial acts on prime-time television. *Communication Research, 14,* 664–686.

Potts, R., & Sanchez, D. (1994). Television viewing and depression: No news is good news. *Journal of Broadcasting & Electronic Media, 38,* 79–90.

Poulin, R. (2011, June 7). ESA releases updated statistics about the gaming industry. Retrieved July 7, 2011, from http://www.emarketer.com/Reports/All/Emarketer_2000787.aspx

Powers, E. (2006, September 27). House panel tackles piracy. *Inside Higher Ed.* Retrieved October 30, 2006, from http://insidehighered.com/layout/set/print/news/2006/09/27/piracy

Pritchard, D. A. (1975). Leveling-sharpening revised. *Perceptual and Motor Skills, 40,* 111–117.

Project for Excellence in Journalism. (2006). Audience. In *The state of the news media 2006: An annual report on American journalism.* Retrieved October 30, 2006, from www.stateofthenewsmedia.org/2006/narrative_online_audience.asp?cat = 3&media = 4

Pugmire, L. (2011, July 1). Labor woes shut NBA down. *Los Angeles Times,* pp. C1, C8.

Pulaski, M. A. S. (1980). *Understanding Piaget: An introduction to children's cognitive development* (Rev. and expanded ed.). New York: Harper & Row.

Rainey, J. (2005, March 14). Study warns of junk-news diet. *Los Angeles Times,* p. A14.

Rainey, J. (2007, March 12). Media's focus narrowing, report warns. *Los Angeles Times,* p. A8.

Rampoldi-Hnilo, L., & Greenberg, B. S. (2000). A poll of Latina and Caucasian mothers with 6–10 year old children. In B. S.Greenberg, L.Rampoldi-Hnilo, & D. Mastro (Eds.), *The alphabet soup of television program ratings* (pp. 177–194). Cresskill, NJ: Hampton.

Ransford, M. (2005, September 23). Average person spends more time using media than anything else. Ball State University News Center. Retrieved October 30, 2006, from www.bsu.edu/up/article/ 0,1370,32363-2914-36658,00.html

Real, M. R. (1998). MediaSport: Technology and the commodification of postmodern sport. In L. A. Wenner (Ed.), *MediaSport* (pp. 14–26). New York: Routledge.

Reid, L. N. (1979). Viewing rules as mediating factors of children's responses to commercials. *Journal of Broadcasting, 23,* 15–26.

Reinken, T. (2003, August 19). Dome and other homes. *Los Angeles Times,* p. A10.

Rhodes, S., & Reibstein, L. (1996, July 1). Let him walk! *Newsweek,* pp. 44–45.

Richardson, J. D. (2005). Switching social identities: The influence of editorial framing on reader attitudes toward affirmative action and African Americans. *Communication Research, 32,* 503–528.

Rideout, V. J., Foehr, U. G., Roberts, D. F., & Brodie, M. (1999). *Kids & media @ the new millennium.* Menlo Park, CA: Kaiser Foundation.

Riggs, D. (1999, February 28). True love is alive and well, say romance book writers. *Tallahassee Democrat,* p. 3D.

Roberts, D. F., & Foehr, U. G. (2008). Trends in media use. *Children and Electronic Media, 18.* Retrieved May 4, 2011, from http://futureofchildren.org/ futureofchildren/publications/journals/article/ index.xml?journalid = 32&articleid = 55&sectionid = 233&submit

Roberts, J. L. (2006a, July 17). Watching the watchers. *Newsweek,* pp. 38–39.

Roberts, J. L. (2006b, October 30). Why prime time's now your time. *Newsweek,* p. 56.

Roberts, M., & Pettigrew, S. (2007). A thematic content analysis of children's food advertising. *International Journal of Advertising, 26,* 357–367.

Robertson, L. (2001, March). Ethically challenged. *American Journalism Review,* pp. 20–29.

Rodriguez, S., & Pierson, D. (2011, June 2). China hackers accessed accounts, Google says. *Los Angeles Times,* pp. AA1, AA4.

Romenesko, J. (2011, June 10). Huffington Post passes NYT in Web visitors. Retrieved June 24, 2011, from http:// www.poynter.org/latest-news/romenesko/135401/ huffington-post-tops-nyt-in-web-traffic-in-may/

Romer, D., Jamieson, K. H., & Aday, S. (2003). Television news and the cultivation of fear of crime. *Journal of Communication, 53,* 88–104.

The Roper Organization. (1981). *Sex, profanity and violence: An opinion survey about seventeen television programs.* New York: Information Office.

Roshier, B. (1981). The selection of crime news by the press. In S. Cohen & J. Young (Eds.), *The manufacture of news: Deviance, social problems and the mass media* (pp. 40–51). Beverly Hills, CA: Sage.

Ross, E. (2003, June 10). Study links movies, teen smoking. *Los Angeles Times,* pp. B1, B2.

Rothschild, N., & Morgan, M. (1987). Cohesion and control: Adolescents' relationships with parents as mediators of television. *Journal of Early Adolescence, 7,* 299–314.

Rubin, A. M., Perse, E. M., & Taylor, D. S. (1988). A methodological examination of cultivation. *Communication Research, 15,* 107–133.

Salomon, G. (1977). Effects of encouraging Israeli mothers to co-observe *Sesame Street* with their five-year-olds. *Child Development, 48,* 1146–1151.

Samuelson, R. J. (2005, July 25). The world is still round. *Newsweek,* p. 49.

Samuelson, R. J. (2006, October 30). The next capitalism. *Newsweek,* p. 45.

Sang, F., Schmitz, B., & Tasche, K. (1992). Individuation and television coviewing in the family: Development trends in the viewing behavior of adolescents. *Journal of Broadcasting & Electronic Media, 36,* 427–441.

Sapolsky, B., & Tabarlet, J. (1990). *Sex in prime time television: 1979 vs. 1989.* Unpublished manuscript, Department of Communication, Florida State University, Tallahassee.

Sapolsky, B. S., Molitor, F., & Luque, S. (2003). Sex and violence in slasher films: Re-examining the assumptions. *Journalism & Mass Communication Quarterly, 80,* 28–38.

Sarno, D. (2009a, February 17). For Facebook, privacy issues remain a factor. *Los Angeles Times,* p. C3.

Sarno, D. (2009b, August 16). It's getting hard to hide in cyberspace. *Los Angeles Times,* pp. B1, B4.

Sarno, D. (2011, July 17). How to safeguard your PC from hackers. *Los Angeles Times,* pp. B1, B7.

Sayre, S., & King, C. (2003). *Entertainment & society: Audiences, trends, and impacts.* Thousand Oaks, CA: Sage.

Scharrer, E. (2001). From wise to foolish: The portrayal of the sitcom father, 1950s–1990s. *Journal of Broadcasting & Electronic Media, 45,* 23.

Schmitt, K. (2000). *Public policy, family rules, and children's media use in the home.* Washington, DC: Annenberg Public Policy Center of the University of Pennsylvania.

Schrag, R. (1990). *Taming the wild tube: A family guide to television and video.* Chapel Hill: University of North Carolina Press.

Schramm, W., Lyle, J., & Parker, E. B. (1961). *Television in the lives of our children.* Stanford, CA: Stanford University Press.

Schudson, M. (2003). *The sociology of news.* New York: Norton.

Schumpeter, J. (2011, April 16). Fail often, fail well. *The Economist,* p. 74.

Schwalbe, C. B., Silcock, B. W., & Keith, S. (2008). Visual framing of the early weeks of the U.S.-led invasion of Iraq: Applying the master war narrative to electronic and print images. *Journal of Broadcasting & Electronic Media, 52,* 448–465.

Schwartz, B. (2004). *The paradox of choice: Why more is less.* New York: HarperCollins.

Schwartz, S. (1984, Winter). Send help before it's too late. *Parent's Choice,* p. 2.

Second Life. (n.d.). What is second life? Retrieved June 29, 2011, from http://secondlife.com/whatis/?lang = en-US

Segrin, C., & Nabi, R. (2002). Does television viewing cultivate unrealistic expectations about marriage? *Journal of Communication, 52,* 247–263.

Semuels, A. (2006, December 10). More bands finding venues on the web. *Los Angeles Times,* pp. C1, C15.

Shiver, J., Jr. (2004, October 22). Viacom, Disney fined by FCC over TV ads. *Los Angeles Times,* p. C2.

Shoemaker, P. J., Danielian, L. H., & Brendlinger, N. (1991). Deviant acts, risky business, and US interest: The newsworthiness of world events. *Journalism Quarterly, 68,* 781–795.

Shoemaker, P. J., & Reese, S. D. (1996). *Mediating the message: Theories of influences on mass media content* (2nd ed.). White Plains, NY: Longman.

Shrum, L. J. (1999). The relationship of television viewing with attitude strength and extremity: Implications for the cultivation effect. *Media Psychology, 1,* 3–25.

Signorielli, N. (1982). Marital status in television drama: A case of reduced options. *Journal of Broadcasting, 26,* 585–597.

Signorielli, N. (1990). Television's mean and dangerous world: A continuation of the cultural indicators perspective. In N. Signorielli & M. Morgan (Eds.), *Cultivation analysis: New directions in media effects research* (pp. 85–106). Newbury Park, CA: Sage.

Signorielli, N., & Bacue, A. (1999). Recognition and respect: A content analysis of prime-time television characters across three decades. *Sex Roles, 40,* 527–544.

Signorielli, N., & Kahlenberg, S. (2001). Television's world of work in the nineties. *Journal of Broadcasting & Electronic Media, 45,* 4–22.

Silverblatt, A. (2007). *Media literacy: Keys to interpreting media messages* (3rd edition). Westport, CT: Praeger.

Simons, J. (1996, December 30). Waiting to download. *U.S. News & World Report,* p. 60.

Singer, J. L., & Singer, D. G. (1981). *Television, imagination, and aggression: A study of preschoolers.* Hillsdale, NJ: Lawrence Erlbaum.

Singer, J. L., Singer, D. G., & Rapaczynski, W. S. (1984). Family patterns and television viewing as predictors of children's beliefs and aggression. *Journal of Communication, 34*(2), 73–89.

Sizer, T. R. (1995). Silences. *Daedelus, 124*(4), 77–83.

Slater, E. (2004, April 5). Technology feeds a diet of news bites. *Los Angeles Times,* p. A11.

Slater, M. D., Long, M., & Bettinghaus, E. P. (2008). News coverage of cancer in the United States: A national sample of newspapers, television, and magazines. *Journal of Health Communication, 13,* 523–537.

Slater, M. D., & Rouner, D. (2002). Entertainment-education and elaboration likelihood: Understanding the processing of narrative persuasion. *Communication Theory, 12,* 173–191.

Slater, M. D., Rouner, D., & Long, M. (2006). Television dramas and support for controversial public policies: Effects and mechanism. *Journal of Communication, 56,* 235–252.

Slattery, K. L., & Hakanen, E. A. (1994). Sensationalism versus public affairs content of local TV news:

Pennsylvania revisited. *Journal of Broadcasting & Electronic Media, 38,* 205–216.

Smiley, J. (2006, June 18). Selling between the lines. *Los Angeles Times,* p. M1.

Smith, P. K., & Cowie, H. (1988).*Understanding children's development.* Oxford, UK: Basil Blackwell.

Smith, S. L., & Wilson, B. J. (2002). Children's comprehension of and fear reactions to television news. *Media Psychology, 4,* 1–26.

Smythe, D.W. (1954). Reality as presented on television. *Public Opinion Quarterly, 18,* 143–156.

Sony Corporation. (n.d.). Retrieved Aug 30, 2009, from http://en.wikipedia.org/wiki/Sony

Spam clogging Amazon's kindle. (2011, June 17). *Los Angeles Times,* p. B4.

Sports City. (n.d.). NFL salaries. Retrieved October 24, 2011, from http://www.sportscity.com/NFL-Salaries/

Standage, T. (2011, July 9). Special report: The news industry. *The Economist,* pp. 3–16.

Standard & Poor's. (1996, July). *Index to surveys.* New York: Author.

Stanger, J. (1997). *Television in the home: The second annual survey of parents and children in the home* (Survey Series No. 2). Philadelphia: Annenberg Public Policy Center of the University of Pennsylvania.

Steele, J. E. (1995). Experts and the operational bias of television news: The case of the Persian Gulf War. *Journalism & Mass Communication Quarterly, 72,* 799–812.

Stern, L. (2002, April 8). Is Orwell your banker? *Newsweek,* p. 59.

Sternberg, R. J., & Berg, C. A. (1987). What are theories of adult intellectual development theories of? In C. Schooler & K.W. Schaie (Eds.), *Cognitive functioning and social structure over the life course* (pp. 3–23). Norwood, NJ: Ablex.

Stewart, C. (2010, February). The lost boy. *Wired,* pp. 68–73, 107.

Stewart, L. (2004, March 24). Study criticizes school over diversity, graduation rates. *Los Angeles Times,* p. D5.

Stone, B. (2006, November 2). Diller weaves a web. *Newsweek,* p. 50.

Strasburger, V. C., & Wilson, B. J. (2002).*Children, adolescents, & the media.* Thousand Oaks, CA: Sage.

Stroh, M. (1999, October 9). From pulp to pixel. *Tallahassee Democrat,* p. E1.

Study links teen smoking to popular ads. (1996, April 14). *Santa Barbara News-Press,* p. A2.

Sunstein, C. R. (2006). *Infotopia: How many minds produce knowledge.* New York: Oxford University Press.

Sykes, J. (2006). A player-centred approach to digital game design. In J. Rutter & J. Bryce (Eds.), *Understanding digital games* (pp. 75–92). London: Sage.

Taylor, S. E., & Howell, R. J. (1973). The ability of three-, four-, and five-year-old children to distinguish fantasy from reality. *Journal of Genetic Psychology, 122,* 315–318.

Teague, D. (2004). U. S. book production soars to 175,000 new titles in 2003; trade up, university presses down. www.bowker.com/press/2004_0527_bowker.htm

Terrell, K. (1999, September 20). Textbooks 101: Web offers few bargains. *U.S. News & World Report,* p. 74.

Teslik, L. H. (2006, August 14). Branded with a brand. *Newsweek,* p. 8.

The test of time. (2011, June 11). *The Economist,* p. 20.

Thomas, M. H. (1982). Physiological arousal, exposure to a relatively lengthy aggressive film, and aggression behavior. *Journal of Research in Personality, 16,* 72–81.

Thompson, C. (2009, September). The new literacy. *Wired,* p. 48.

Time Warner. (n.d.). Retrieved August 30, 2009, from http://en.wikipedia.org/wiki/AOL_Time_Warner

Too much information. (2011, July 2). *The Economist,* p. 59.

Top ten search engines. (2010, August 28). Retrieved July 29, 2011, from http://www.seoconsultants.com/search-engines/

Trolling for your soul. (2011, April 2). *The Economist,* p. 58.

Trounson, R. (2006, December 12). Major breach of UCLA's computer files. *Los Angeles Times,* pp. A1, A26.

Tunes & 'tudes: Annual teen music survey. (2002, May 3–5). *USA Weekend,* pp. 8, 11.

Turow, J. (1992). *Media systems in society.* New York: Longman.

Turow, J. (2010). *Media today* (3rd ed.). New York: Routledge.

2 convicted in junk e-mail case. (2004, November 4). *Los Angeles Times,* p. C3.

Tyre, P. (2002, August 5). Fighting "big fat." *Newsweek,* pp. 38, 40.

Unkind unwind. (2011, March 19). *The Economist,* pp. 76–78.

USAToday salaries databases. (2011). *USA Today.* Retrieved June 22, 2011, from http://content.usato day.com/sportsdata

U.S. Bureau of the Census. (2000). *Statistical abstract of the United States: 1999.* Washington, DC: Department of Commerce.

U.S. Bureau of the Census. (2009). *The 2009 statistical abstract: The national data book.* Washington, DC: Department of Commerce.

U.S. Bureau of the Census. (2011). *Statistical abstract of the United States: 2010.* Washington, DC: Department of Commerce.

U.S. is No. 1 source of hacking, firm says. (2007, March 19). *Los Angeles Times,* p. C2.

Valkenburg, P. M., Krcmar, M., Peeters, A. L., & Marseille, N. M. (1999). "Instructive mediation," "restrictive mediation," and "social coviewing." *Journal of Broadcasting & Electronic Media, 43,* 52–66.

van der Voort, T. H. A. (1986). *Television violence: A child's-eye view.* Amsterdam: North-Holland.

Vande Berg, L. R., & Streckfuss, D. (1992). Prime-time television's portrayal of women and the world of work: A demographic profile. *Journal of Broadcasting & Electronic Media, 36,* 195–208.

Verrier, R. (2005, October 12). Hollywood writers still lack diversity. *Los Angeles Times,* p. C2.

Verrier, R., & James, M. (2003, October 9). GE, Vivendi finalize NBC Universal deal. *Los Angeles Times,* pp. C1, C11.

Viacom. (n.d.). Retrieved August 30, 2009, from http://en.wikipedia.org/wiki/Viacom

Vranizan, M. (1995, June 5). On-line junkie hooked on his screen. *Santa Barbara News-Press,* p. A11.

Wallace, B. (2011, February 7). The geek kings of smut. *New York Magazine,* pp. 27–31, 87–88.

Walsh, D. (1994). *Selling out America's children.* Minneapolis, MN: Fairview.

The Walt Disney Company. (n.d.). Retrieved August 30, 2009, from http://en.wikipedia.org/wiki/Disney

Wartella, E. (1981). The child as viewer. In M. E. Ploghoft & J. A. Anderson (Eds.), *Education for the television age* (pp. 28–17). Springfield, IL: Charles C Thomas.

Warren, R., Wicks, J. L., & Wicks, R. H. (2007). Food and beverage advertising to children on U.S. television: Did national food advertisers respond? *Journalism and Mass Communication Quarterly, 84,* 795–810.

Weaver, J. B., Masland, J. L., & Zillmann, D. (1984). Effect of erotica on young men's aesthetic perception of their female partners. *Perceptual and Motor Skills, 58,* 929–930.

Webpronews. (2011). Social media accounts for 22% of time spent online. Retrieved May 4, 2011 from http://www.webpronews.com/social-networks-blogs-account-for-22-of-time-spent-online- 2010-06

Weinberger, D. (2002). *Small pieces loosely joined.* Cambridge, MA: Basic Books.

Weinraub, B. (1995, September 18). Stars' salaries skyrocketing; pressure to produce heats up demand for top talent. *New York Times,* p. C1.

Whitman, D. (1996, December 16). I'm OK, you're not. *U.S. News & World Report,* pp. 24–30.

Whitman, D., & Loftus, M. (1996, December 16). Things are getting better? Who knew? *U.S. News & World Report,* pp. 30, 32.

Whitson, D. (1998). Circuits of promotion: Media, marketing and the globalization of sport. In L. A. Wenner (Ed.), *MediaSport* (pp. 57–72). New York: Routledge.

Wicks, R. H. (1992). Improvement over time in recall of media information: An exploratory study. *Journal of Broadcasting and Electronic Media, 36,* 287–302.

Wilkinson, T. (2006, September 24). Catholics embrace online priests. *Los Angeles Times,* p. A15.

Williams, T. M., Zabrack, M. L., & Joy, L. A. (1982). The portrayal of aggression on North American television. *Journal of Applied Social Psychology, 12,* 360–380.

Wilson, B. J., & Weiss, A. J. (1992). Developmental differences in children's reactions to a toy advertisement linked to a toy-based cartoon. *Journal of Broadcasting & Electronic Media, 36,* 371–394.

Windhauser, J. W., Seiter, J., & Winfree, L. T. (1990). Crime news in the Louisiana Press, 1980 vs. 1985. *Journalism Quarterly, 67,* 72–78.

Winik, L. W. (2004, March 14). How safe is your computer? *Parade,* p. 10.

Winn, M. (2002). *The plug-in drug: Television, computers, and family life.* New York: Penguin.

Witkin, H. A., & Goodenough, D. R. (1977). Field dependence and interpersonal behavior. *Psychological Bulletin, 84,* 661–689.

Wolff, M. (2003, May 26). Troubled times. *New York Magazine,* pp. 18–21.

Wolk, D. (2009, August). There's no such thing as too many friends. *Wired,* p. 95.

World's most powerful celebrities. (2011, May 16). *Forbes.* Retrieved July 15, 2011, from http://www.forbes.com/wealth/celebrities#p_7_s_arank_

WorldWideWebSize.com. (2011, May 4). The size of the World Wide Web (the Internet). Retrieved May 4, 2011, from http://www.worldwidewebsize.com/

Wright, J. C., Huston, A. C., Reitz, A. L., & Piemyat, S. (1994). Young children's perceptions of television reality: Determinants and developmental differences. *Developmental Psychology, 30,* 229–239.

Wulff, S. (1997). Media literacy. In W. G. Christ (Ed.), *Media education assessment handbook* (pp. 123–142). Mahwah, NJ: Lawrence Erlbaum.

Yang, M., Roskos-Ewoldsen, D. R., Dinu, L., & Arpan, L. M. (2006). The effectiveness of "in-game" advertising: Comparing college students' explicit and implicit memory for brand names. *Journal of Advertising, 35*(4), 143–152.

Yearly box office. (2011). Retrieved July 28, 2011, from http://boxofficemojo.com/yearly/

Yee, N. (2002, October). Ariadne: Understanding MMORPG addiction. http://www.nickyee.com/hub/addiction/home.html

YouTube. (n.d.). Retrieved August 30, 2009, from http://en.wikipedia.org/wiki/YouTube

Zillmann, D. (1991). Television viewing and physiological arousal. In J. Bryant & D. Zillmann (Eds.), *Responding to the screen: Reception and reaction processes* (pp. 103–133). Hillsdale, NJ: Lawrence Erlbaum.

Index

About the Author

W. James Potter, Professor at the University of California at Santa Barbara, holds one PhD in Communication Studies and another in Instructional Technology. He has been teaching media courses for more than two decades in the areas of effects on individuals and society, content narratives, structure and economics of media industries, advertising, journalism, programming, and production. He has served as editor of the *Journal of Broadcasting & Electronic Media* and is the author of many journal articles and books, including the following: *Media Effects, On Media Violence, Theory of Media Literacy: A Cognitive Approach, The 11 Myths of Media Violence, Becoming a Strategic Thinker: Developing Skills for Success,* and *How to Publish Your Communication Research* (with Alison Alexander).

SAGE research methods online

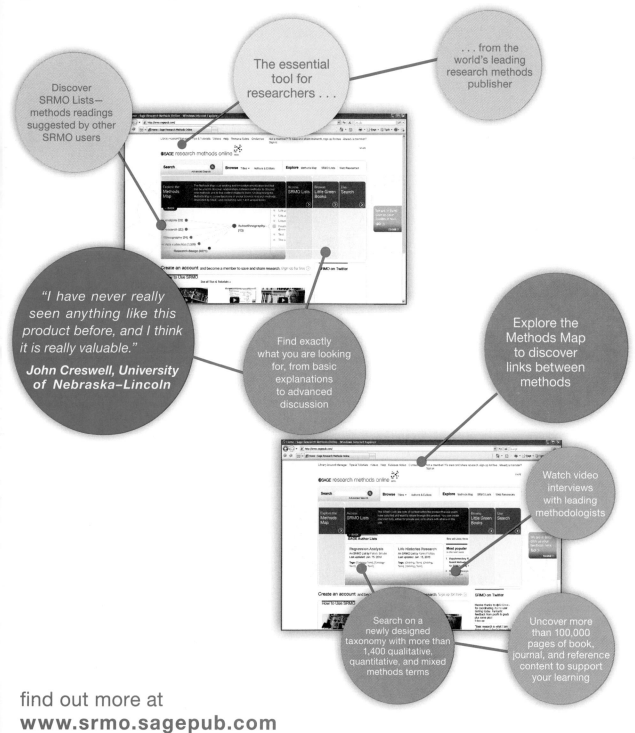

Discover SRMO Lists— methods readings suggested by other SRMO users

The essential tool for researchers . . .

. . . from the world's leading research methods publisher

"I have never really seen anything like this product before, and I think it is really valuable."

John Creswell, University of Nebraska–Lincoln

Find exactly what you are looking for, from basic explanations to advanced discussion

Explore the Methods Map to discover links between methods

Watch video interviews with leading methodologists

Search on a newly designed taxonomy with more than 1,400 qualitative, quantitative, and mixed methods terms

Uncover more than 100,000 pages of book, journal, and reference content to support your learning

find out more at

www.srmo.sagepub.com